INTERNATIONAL HANDBOOK ON PUBLIC–PRIVATE PARTNERSHIPS

International Handbook on Public–Private Partnerships

Edited by

Graeme A. Hodge

Director, Monash Centre for Regulatory Studies, Faculty of Law, Monash University, Australia

Carsten Greve

Professor, International Centre for Business and Politics, Copenhagen Business School, Denmark

and

Anthony E. Boardman

Van Dusen Professor of Business Administration, University of British Columbia, Canada

Edward Elgar
Cheltenham, UK • Northampton, MA, USA

Published by
Edward Elgar Publishing Limited
The Lypiatts
15 Lansdown Road
Cheltenham
Glos GL50 2JA
UK

Edward Elgar Publishing, Inc.
William Pratt House
9 Dewey Court
Northampton
Massachusetts 01060
USA

A catalogue record for this book
is available from the British Library

Library of Congress Control Number: 2010925942

Typeset by Servis Filmsetting Ltd, Stockport, Cheshire

ISBN 978-0-85793-248-8

Printed and bound by CPI Group (UK) Ltd, Croydon, CR0 4YY

Contents

List of contributors   viii
Acknowledgements   xvi
Abbreviations   xvii

PART I   CONCEPTUAL FRAMEWORKS

  1 Introduction: the PPP phenomenon and its evaluation   3
     Graeme A. Hodge, Carsten Greve and Anthony E. Boardman
  2 Mixes and partnerships through time   17
     Roger Wettenhall
  3 A brief intellectual history of the public–private partnership
     movement   43
     Tony Bovaird
  4 Public–private partnerships: deciphering meaning, message and
     phenomenon   68
     Erik-Hans Klijn
  5 Reviewing public–private partnerships: some thoughts on
     evaluation   81
     Graeme A. Hodge

PART II   DISCIPLINARY THEMES IN PUBLIC–
            PRIVATE PARTNERSHIPS

  6 Splintered logic and political debate   115
     Matthew Flinders
  7 The economics of public–private partnerships: some theoretical
     contributions   132
     Jean-Etienne de Bettignies and Thomas W. Ross
  8 Assessing the economic worth of public–private partnerships   159
     Anthony E. Boardman and Aidan R. Vining
  9 Different delivery models   187
     Colin F. Duffield
 10 Law and regulatory aspects of public–private partnerships:
     contract law and public procurement law   216
     Christina D. Tvarnø

11   Accounting for PPPs in a converging world   237
     David Heald and George Georgiou
12   Risk management   262
     Rui Sousa Monteiro
13   Governing partnerships   292
     Chris Skelcher

PART III   EMPIRICAL EXPERIENCE IN PUBLIC–
           PRIVATE PARTNERSHIPS

14   The UK's Private Finance Initiative: history, evaluation,
     prospects   307
     Mark Hellowell
15   Empirical PPP experiences in Europe: national variations of a
     global concept   333
     Gerhard Hammerschmid and Tamyko Ysa
16   P3s in North America: renting the money (in Canada), selling
     the roads (in the USA)   354
     Anthony E. Boardman and Aidan R. Vining
17   The Australian PPP experience: observations and reflections   399
     Graeme A. Hodge and Colin F. Duffield
18   Public–private partnerships: the Scandinavian experience   439
     Carsten Greve and Ulrika Mörth
19   Empirical evidence of infrastructure public–private
     partnerships: lessons from the World Bank experience   456
     Paul Noumba-Um
20   Public–private partnerships: the United Nations experience   479
     Benedicte Bull

PART IV   CRUCIAL ISSUES FOR THE FUTURE

21   The global public–private partnership industry   499
     Carsten Greve
22   Towards a process perspective on public–private
     partnerships   510
     Guðrið Weihe
23   PPPs in developed and developing economies: what lessons can
     be learned?   526
     David Parker and Catarina Figueira
24   A review of transport public–private partnerships in the UK   548
     Jean Shaoul

25 Reviewing public–private partnership performance in
developing economies 568
Argentino Pessoa
26 Conclusions: public–private partnerships – international
experiences and future challenges 594
Graeme A. Hodge, Carsten Greve and Anthony E. Boardman

Index 611

Contributors

Anthony E. Boardman is the Van Dusen Professor of Business Administration in the Strategy and Business Economics Division at the University of British Columbia. He studied for his BA at the University of Kent at Canterbury, UK and obtained his PhD from Carnegie-Mellon University, Pittsburgh, PA. His research interests include the analysis of the effects of ownership on performance, privatization, public–private partnerships, cost–benefit analysis, and strategic management in for-profit and non-profit organizations. He has published extensively in many leading academic journals and is co-author of *Cost–Benefit Analysis: Concepts and Practice* (Prentice-Hall, 2005). Currently he serves on the Patented Medicine Prices Review Board and is on the editorial board of the *Journal of Comparative Policy Analysis* and *Strategic Outsourcing*.

Tony Bovaird is Professor of Public Management and Policy, Institute of Local Government Studies and Third Sector Research Centre, University of Birmingham, UK. He worked in the UK Civil Service and several universities before returning to the Institute in 2006. He directed the evaluation of Local Government Modernisation Agenda 2002–07 for the UK government and is a member of Communities and Local Government Expert Panel on Local Governance. He is also on the strategy board of the UK Local Authorities Research Council Initiative and on the advisory panel of National Endowment for Science, Technology and the Arts / New Economics Foundation research programme on co-production of public services. He directed the evaluation of UK Civil Service Reform Programme for the Cabinet Office and is a member of OECD e-Governance Task Force and a member of Advisory Board of German Research Institute for Public Administration (FÖV) and Executive of Transatlantic Policy Consortium, as well as co-editor of *Public Management and Governance* (Routledge, 2003).

Benedicte Bull holds a political science PhD from the University of Oslo, Norway, and is Associate Professor at the Centre for Development and the Environment at the same university. She is the author of several books and articles on development and public–private relations in Latin America and the multilateral system, including *Aid, Power and Privatization* (Edward Elgar, 2005) and *Development Issues in Global Governance: public–private partnerships and market multilateralism* (co-authored with Desmond McNeill, Routledge, 2007).

Colin F. Duffield is an Associate Professor at the University of Melbourne and Academic Co-ordinator for postgraduate Engineering Project Management courses within the Department of Civil and Environmental Engineering. He practised as an engineer and then as a project manager for 15 years before joining the university as an academic in 1991. His research into efficient procurement of major projects includes the use of public–private partnerships where the long-term sustainability of service outcomes is governed by the interaction between policy, technical matters, risk management, financing and contractual arrangements. He is a Fellow of Engineers Australia and a member of their National Committee for Construction Engineering, a member of the Australian Institute of Project Managers and a registered building practitioner.

Jean-Etienne de Bettignies is Associate Professor and Commerce '64 Fellow of Managerial Economics at Queen's School of Business, Kingston, Canada. His research examines applications of contract theory to industrial economics, entrepreneurship and public policy, and is published in leading academic journals including *Management Science, Journal of Industrial Economics, International Journal of Industrial Organization* and *Canadian Journal for Economics.* Jean received his PhD and his MBA from the Booth School of Business at the University of Chicago in 2001. He also holds a BSc in Economics from the London School of Economics and an MA in Economics from the Université Catholique de Louvain. Before joining Queen's in 2007, Jean was Assistant Professor at the University of British Columbia, where he was nominated (2006) for the MBA Teaching Award.

Catarina Figueira is a senior lecturer in Applied Economics and Director of the Executive MBA at Cranfield School of Management, UK. She was previously a Robert Schuman Scholar at the Scientific and Technological Options Assessment Division at the European Parliament. Her research interests lie in the areas of financial modelling and economic development, particularly related to efficiency and regulatory issues in both developed and developing economies. Catarina has advised the OECD and the European Commission on regulation, and has advised a number of financial institutions on the UK housing market. She has published in leading international journals and is a frequent contributor to a wide range of international conferences. Catarina is also the editor of the Research Paper Series of Cranfield School of Management.

Matthew Flinders is Professor of Parliamentary Government and Governance in the Department of Politics at the University of Sheffield, UK. He is a recipient of the Harrison Prize (2002), Richard Rose Prize (2004) and the W.J. Mackenzie Prize (2009). His publications include

Delegated Governance and the British State (Oxford University Press, 2008), *Democratic Drift* (Oxford University Press, 2009) and the *Oxford Handbook of British Politics* (Oxford University Press, 2009).

George Georgiou is Senior Lecturer in Accountancy at the Business School of Birmingham University, UK. He undertook his undergraduate and postgraduate studies (Masters in Accountancy) in the USA and he is a US certified public accountant. He continued his studies in the UK and he holds a PhD in Accountancy from the University of Aberdeen. His doctoral thesis is a study of corporate lobbying behaviour in the context of the UK accounting standard-setting process. His specialist interests include regulation of financial reporting and public sector accounting reform. He has published in journals such as *Abacus, Accounting and Business Research, European Accounting Review, Public Administration, Public Money & Management* and *The British Accounting Review*.

Carsten Greve is Professor of Public Management and Governance at the International Centre for Business and Politics, Copenhagen Business School. His research concentrates on public management reform and market-based governance, including privatization, contracting out and public–private partnerships. His recent works include *The Challenge of Public–Private Partnerships: Learning from International Experience* (co-editor Graeme Hodge, Edward Elgar, 2005) and *Contracting for Public Services* (Routledge, 2008).

Gerhard Hammerschmid is Professor of Public and Financial Management at the Hertie School of Governance and serves as scientific head at the Institut für den öffentlichen Sektor e.V. in Berlin. He studied business administration at the University of St Gallen, Switzerland, and has been Assistant Professor at the Institute for Public Management at the Wirtschattsuniversitäth WU Wien for six years. He is co-author of several books on public management reforms, has published in various international journals such as *Public Administration, American Behavioral Scientist, Public Policy and Administration, Organization Studies* and *International Journal of Public Sector Management* among others, and has a solid record of public management expertise in an international context. He has served as an expert for the European Public Administration Network, the World Bank and PHARE (Poland and Hungary Assistance for Restructuring their Economies) Twinning.

David Heald is Professor of Accountancy at the University of Aberdeen, Scotland. He holds a visiting chair at the University of Sheffield Management School, UK where he was Professor of Financial Management (2003–07) and Associate Dean (2005–07). His research interests focus on public sector accounting reform, public expenditure management and control, and financing devolved governments. He has also written on the relevance of transparency to public policy, co-editing (with Christopher Hood) *Transparency: The Key to Better Governance?* (Oxford University Press for the British Academy, 2006). He has extensive public policy involvement, including being specialist adviser on government accounting and public expenditure to the Treasury Committee of the House of Commons (1989–2010) and member of the Financial Reporting Advisory Board (2004–09).

Mark Hellowell is a Fellow at the University of Edinburgh's School of Social and Political Science, Scotland. His background is in public policy, public management and political economy, and he has a specific research interest in the use of private sector finance and delivery in public services. Before becoming an academic, he was a journalist and has written for a number of publications including *The Guardian*, *The Times* and *Public Finance*, for all of which he continues to write. He was also editor of the specialist project finance journal, *Public–Private Finance*.

Graeme A. Hodge is Professor of Law and Director of the Monash Centre for Regulatory Studies, Faculty of Law at Monash University, Australia. A leading international analyst on privatization, outsourcing, technology regulation and public–private partnerships, he has served as a Special Adviser to several Parliamentary Committees and Inquiries. He has published in management, social and economic policy, public administration, law and regulation. His most recent publication was *International Handbook on Regulating Nanotechnologies* (Edward Elgar, 2010). He has acted as a consultant to the OECD, the European Commission, the Asian Development Bank, the Australian Government and the United Nations on a range of governance matters in Australasia, Europe, Indonesia, the Philippines and China.

Erik-Hans Klijn is Professor at the Department of Public Administration at Erasmus University, Rotterdam and Visiting Professor at the School of Public Policy at the University of Birmingham, UK. His research and teaching activities focus on complex decision-making and management in networks, institutional design and public–private partnerships mainly in the area of infrastructure and urban restructuring. He has published extensively in international journals such as *Journal of Public Administration Research and Theory* (2003, 2006), *Administration and Society* (1996, 2001, 2007), *Public Administration* (1995, 2000, 2007), *Public Administration Review* (2002) and *Public Management Review* (2000, 2003, 2006). Recently he wrote *Managing Uncertainties in Networks* (together with Joop Koppenjan, Routledge, 2004).

Rui Sousa Monteiro is a senior economist at Parpublica SA, the government firm that reviews and appraises PPPs on behalf of the Finance Minister of Portugal. He joined Parpublica SA in 2000, having intervened in the design of several major rail, tram, highway and health PPP contracts and public tenders. As a researcher and a practitioner, he is currently a member of the Tender Boards for the high-speed rail project, including the new road–rail Tagus bridge in Lisbon, and for several PPP hospital contracts, some of them including the provision of clinical services, currently being procured. As an economist, he puts strong emphasis on the use of incentive contracts and competitive schemes. Before joining Parpublica SA he lectured in Development Economics at Universidade Nova de Lisboa (UNL) and did applied research on fiscal matters and on large public projects (urban renewal, public infrastructure). He graduated in Economics (UNL, 1986) and is currently researching for a PhD in Economics at ISEG (Institute Superior de Economia e Gestão) in Lisbon.

Ulrika Mörth is a professor in the Department of Political Science at Stockholm University. Mörth is Chairman of the Department and of the Board at SCORE (Stockholm Centre for Organizational Research). She has published widely on European governance and EU policy-making in international journals: *European Journal of Public Policy, Journal of Common Market Studies* and *Governance*. In 2003 she published the monograph *Organizing European Cooperation* (Rowman & Littlefield) and in 2004 she was editor of the volume *Soft Law in Governance and Regulation* (Edward Elgar). Her recent publications are the monograph *European Public–Private Collaboration* (Edward Elgar, 2008) and a co-edited volume, *Democracy and Public–Private Partnerships in Global Governance* (Palgrave, Macmillan, fothcoming, 2010).

Paul Noumba-Um is an economist and PPP specialist member of the World Bank PPP Global Experts Team. He is currently a Lead Economist in the office of the Director of the Sustainable Development Department in the Middle East and North Africa Vice-Presidency of the World Bank. He leads country-specific and regional programmes on public–private partnerships and infrastructure regulation and finance. Paul managed the Public–Private Partnership in Infrastructure programme of the World Bank Institute and was also an infrastructure economist with the World Bank Group who contributed extensively to the successful implementation of telecommunications reform in developing countries from 1998 to 2004. He has taught infrastructure economics and regulation in the USA, France, South Africa, Côte d'Ivoire, Burkina Faso, Morocco, Jordan, Cameroon and Thailand, and has published articles and books in these areas. He holds a PhD in Economics from the University of Rennes 1 and a Masters Degree in Engineering from a French Grande Ecole.

David Parker is Emeritus Professor in Privatization and Regulation at the Cranfield School of Management, Cranfield University, UK and a member of the UK Government's Regulatory Policy Committee. He has written extensively on public–private issues and has acted as a consultant and adviser to numerous governments around the world. From 2000 to 2006 he was Co-Director of the Regulation Research Programme at the Centre on Regulation and Competition in the Institute for Policy Development and Management at the University of Manchester, UK. In September 2004 he was appointed the UK government's Official Historian on Privatisation. Volume 1 of the *Official History*, covering the years down to 1987, was published in February 2009, by Routledge.

Argentino Pessoa has a PhD in Economics (2003) from the University of Porto and a Masters in Teaching Economics (1996) from the Faculty of Economics of Porto, Portugal. Currently, he is Professor at the Faculty of Economics of Porto, where he teaches Economic Growth, and Knowledge and Innovation Economics in the undergraduate programme of Economics. He also teaches Innovation Policy in the Master Degree of Economics and Management of Innovation, and Economics and Policy of Development in the Doctoral Programme of African Studies of the University of Porto. He has published articles in several recognized Portuguese and international journals, such as the *Portuguese Economic Journal*, the *Journal of International Development* and *Applied Economics Letters*.

Thomas W. Ross is the Senior Associate Dean (Faculty and Research) and the UPS Foundation Professor of Regulation and Competition Policy in the Sauder School of Business at the University of British Columbia (UBC). He is also the Co-Director of the UBC P3 Project. An economist, he earned his undergraduate degree at the University of Western Ontario, his doctorate at the University of Pennsylvania, and he worked at the University of Chicago and Carleton University before moving to the University of British Columbia. His research in the areas of competition policy, industrial organization, public–private partnerships and experimental economics has been published in a number of scholarly journals. He has also served as a consultant to a number of public and private sector organizations.

Jean Shaoul is Professor of Public Accountability at Manchester Business School, UK, where she focuses on public accountability and social distributional issues in the context of business and public policy. She has written widely in both academic and more popular forums on privatization, particularly water and rail; the use of private finance in public infrastructure under the UK government's Private Finance Initiative and public–private partnerships, particularly in transport, hospitals and the London Underground; the use of private finance in roads in the UK, Spain and internationally; international regulatory reform, for example, the World Trade Organization's General Agreement on Trade in Services; and public expenditure. She is a regular contributor to the World Socialist website (www.wsws.org).

Chris Skelcher is Professor of Public Governance at the Institute of Local Government Studies in the School of Government and Society, and Director of Research and Knowledge Transfer for the College of Social Sciences, at the University of Birmingham, UK. His research examines the democratic implications of third-party government, with a particular focus on methodological development for the analysis of these varied institutions. His recent ESRC study, with colleagues in Birmingham, Denmark and the Netherlands, examined the evolution of network governance for migrant integration and urban regeneration.

Christina D. Tvarnø is Associate Professor at the Law Department, Copenhagen Business School (CBS). She has an MSc in Business Administration and Law from CBS and a PhD in EU internal market law and economics, also from CBS. Her research field consists of partnering, PPP, EU public procurement law, Danish contract law, legal theory, and law and economics. She is the Study Program Manager at the Master of Science Program in Business Administration and Law at CBS. She has published a number of articles in regard to PPP in academic books and journals. She is an active member of several PPP networks in Denmark, and holds both international and Danish lectures and presentations with regard to PPP and partnering.

Aidan R. Vining is the Centre for North American Business Studies Professor of Business and Government Relations in the Segal Graduate School of Business, Simon Fraser University, Vancouver, Canada. He obtained his PhD from the University of California and also holds an LLB (King's College, London), an MBA and an MPP. He teaches and researches in the areas of public policy, policy analysis and business strategy. Much of his recent research has focused on privatization, corporatization, contracting out and PPP. Recent articles have appeared in the *Journal of Public Administration Research and Theory*, *Canadian Public Administration* and the *Journal of Policy Analysis and Management*, among others. He is a co-author of *Policy Analysis: Concepts and Practice* (Pearson Prentice-Hall, 2005) and *Cost–Benefit Analysis: Concepts and*

Practice (Pearson Prentice-Hall, 2006), and recently co-edited *Investing in the Disadvantaged* (Georgetown University Press, 2009). He has served as a consultant to the government of British Columbia (Ministry of the Environment) and to other governments and related institutions.

Guðrið Weihe is a PPP specialist at the international consultancy COWI A/S, working in the Danish headquarters' Organization and Management team. She is also a research associate with the International Center for Business and Politics, Copenhagen Business School. She earned her undergraduate degree in Political Science at Copenhagen University, and her doctorate on public–private partnerships from the Copenhagen Business School. Her research and consultancy work primarily concerns public–private partnerships, green business models and public sector reforms, and, more broadly, management. Her research on public–private partnerships has been published in highly ranked international peer-reviewed public management journals. She was one of the co-founders of the Danish Public Management Forum (Forum Forvaltning), which, on a regular basis, addresses contemporary public management issues and concerns.

Roger Wettenhall is Professor of Public Administration Emeritus and Visiting Professor in the Australia and New Zealand School of Government Institute of Governance in the Faculty of Business and Government at the University of Canberra, Australia. He was Project Director and then Co-Chairman/Chairman of the Working Group on Public Enterprise Management and the Public–Private Mix of the International Association of Schools and Institutes of Administration from 1983 to 2001, editor of the *Australian Journal of Public Administration* from 1989 to 1995, and now chairs the management committee of the Institute of Public Administration Australia/University of Canberra Public Administration Research Trust Fund. His major research interests are non-departmental public bodies, public enterprise management, privatization and public–private mixing.

Tamyko Ysa is Assistant Professor at the Department of Business Policy and the Institute of Public Governance and Management at the Escuela Superior de Administración y Dirección de Empresas Business School, Spain. Her areas of interest are the management of partnerships and their impact on the creation of public value; the design, implementation and evaluation of public policies; and the relations between companies and governments. She is also the Principal Researcher in the Research Group for Leadership and Innovation in Public Management.

Acknowledgements

The editors would like to thank all the authors for their contributions, engagement and encouragement throughout this project; Ms Ally Cheah at the Monash Centre for Regulatory Studies (Monash University) for her editorial assistance; our multiple helpful proofreaders and all the staff at Edward Elgar. The editors would also like to acknowledge the important support of their institutions: Monash University, Australia; Copenhagen Business School, Denmark; and the University of British Columbia, Canada. The editors thank Translink for granting permission to use the image of the Golden Ears Bridge on the cover.

Abbreviations

AAC	annual affordability ceiling
AASB	Australian Accounting Standards Board
ACCC	Australian Competition and Consumer Commission
AMC	Advance Market Commitment (GAVI)
ASB	Accounting Standards Board (UK)
ATC	air traffic controller
AWA	Amalgamated Wireless Australasia Ltd
BOOT	build, own, operate, transfer
BOT	build, operate, transfer
BP	British Petroleum
BR	British Rail
BRE	Building Research Establishment (UK)
CAA	Comprehensive Area Assessment (UK)
CAMF	capital asset management framework
CAPEX	capital expenditure
CAPM	capital asset pricing model
COAG	Council of Australian Governments
COR	Commonwealth Oil Refineries Ltd (Australia)
CPA	Comprehensive Performance Assessment (UK)
CSD	Commission for Sustainable Development (UN)
CSR	corporate social responsibility
CUPE	Canadian Union of Public Employees
DBFO	design, build, finance, operate
DfT	Department for Transport (UK)
DOT	Department of Transportation (USA)
ECI	early contractor involvement
ECOSOC	Economic and Social Council (UN)
EIB	European Investment Bank
EU	European Union
FASAB	Federal Accounting Standards Advisory Board (USA)
FASB	Financial Accounting Standards Board (USA)
FDBOMT	finance, design, build, operate, maintain, transfer
FDBOOM	finance, design, build, own, operate, maintain
FDI	foreign direct investment
FfDI	Financing for Development Initiative (UN)
FHWA	Federal Highway Administration (USA)

FOSS	free and open source software
FRAB	Financial Reporting Advisory Board (UK)
GAAP	Generally Accepted Accounting Practice
GAO	General Accounting Office (USA); after 2008 General Accountability Office
GASB	Government Accounting Standards Board (USA)
GAVI	Global Alliance for Vaccines and Immunization
GDP	gross domestic product
GPA	Government Procurement Agreement (WTO)
HoTARAC	Heads of Treasuries Accounting and Reporting Advisory Committee (Australia)
IAP	Infrastructure Action Plan (World Bank)
IASB	International Accounting Standards Board
IBRD	International Bank for Reconstruction and Development
ICSID	International Centre for Settlement of Investment Disputes (World Bank)
ICT	information and communications technology
IDA	International Development Association (World Bank)
IFAD	International Fund for Agricultural Development
IFC	International Finance Corporation (World Bank)
IFI	international financial institution
IFRIC	International Financial Reporting Interpretations Committee
IFRS	International Financial Reporting Standards
ILO	International Labor Organization
IMF	International Monetary Fund
INFRA	Infrastructure Recovery and Assets (World Bank)
IO	Infrastructure Ontario (Canada)
IPPP	institutionalized public–private partnership
IPPR	Institute for Public Policy Research (UK)
IPSASB	International Public Sector Accounting Standards Board
IRR	internal rate of return
ISTC	Independent Sector Treatment Centre (UK)
IT	information technology
LIBOR	London inter-bank overnight rate
LIFT	Local Improvement Finance Trust (UK)
LSP	local strategic partnership (UK)
LTIC	long-term infrastructure contract
ME	mixed enterprise
MIGA	Multilateral Investment Guarantee Agency (World Bank)
MLG	multi-level governance
MoU	memorandum of understanding

NAO	National Audit Office (UK)
NATS	National Air Traffic Services (UK)
NBFI	non-bank financial institution
NCSL	National Conference of State Legislatures (USA)
NDP	New Democratic Party (Canada)
NGO	non-governmental organization
NHS	National Health Service (UK)
NPM	new public management
NPV	net present value
O&M	operations and maintenance
ODA	official development aid
OECD	Organisation for Economic Co-operation and Development
OIPP	Oregon Innovative Partnerships Program
ONS	Office for National Statistics (UK)
P3	public–private partnership
PAB	private activity bonds (USA)
PBC	Partnerships British Columbia (Canada)
PBI	performance-based infrastructure (USA)
PCM	perfect capital market
PFI	Private Finance Initiative (UK)
PPI	public–private initiative
PPP	public–private partnership
PSA	public sector alternative
PSBR	public sector borrowing requirement
PSC	public sector comparator
PSIRU	Public Services International Research Unit (UK)
PSND	public sector net debt
PUK	Partnerships UK
PV	present value
PwC	PricewaterhouseCoopers
R&D	research and development
RFEI	Request for Expression of Interest
RFP	request for proposals
RFQ	request for qualifications
RIBA	Royal Institute of British Architects
ROI	return on investment
SDR	social discount rate
SEM	société économie mixte (France)
SIAP	Sustainable Infrastructure Action Plan (World Bank)
SME	small to medium-sized enterprise
SNA	System of National Accounts

SNP	Scottish National Party
SOE	state-owned enterprise
SPC	shadow price of capital
SPV	special purpose vehicle
TARP	Troubled Asset Relief Program (USA)
TfL	Transport for London
TIFIA	Transportation Infrastructure Finance and Innovation Act (USA)
TIFU	Treasury Infrastructure Finance Unit (UK)
TNC	transnational corporation
TOC	train operating company
TSC	total social cost
UDAG	Urban Development Action Grant (USA)
UNCED	United Nations Conference on Environment and Development (Earth Summit)
UNCITRAL	United Nations Commission on International Trade Law
UNCSD	United Nations Commission for Sustainable Development
UNCTAD	United Nations Conference on Trade and Development
UNCTC	United Nations Center for Transnational Corporations
UNDP	United Nations Development Program
UNECE	United Nations Economic Commission for Europe
UNESCO	United Nations Educational, Scientific and Cultural Organization
UNF	United Nations Foundation
UNFIP	United Nations Fund for International Partnerships
UNICEF	United Nations International Children's Fund
UNIDO	United Nations Industrial Development Organization
UNITAR	United Nations Institute for Training and Research
URC	urban regeneration company (Netherlands)
VfM	value for money
WAA	wrap-around addition
WACC	weighted average cost of capital
WBCSD	World Business Council for Sustainable Development
WBG	World Bank Group
WHO	World Health Organization
WPC	Washington Policy Center
WTO	World Trade Organization

PART I

CONCEPTUAL FRAMEWORKS

1 Introduction: the PPP phenomenon and its evaluation

Graeme A. Hodge, Carsten Greve and Anthony E. Boardman

Introduction

There has been much debate about public–private partnerships (PPPs) over the past few decades. Indeed, the whole partnership movement has become increasingly professionalized, technical and rational. But beneath the veneer, a paradox remains. Despite its popularity and its iconic status as a visible pillar of contemporary public management practices, the PPP phenomenon remains an enigma. We still debate its definition, its historical origins and the degree to which it constitutes a genuinely new policy delivery solution to the provision of public infrastructure. We still debate why, if it is simply a modest evolution from traditional delivery techniques, some jurisdictions have taken on PPPs with enthusiasm while others have not. And we still debate the degree to which the real challenges faced by PPPs are not the technical complexity first evident, but the accusations of 'illegitimacy' that remain,[1] as well as concerns about the crucial governance challenges current governments are now placing on future generations through long-term contracts. In other words, despite the popularity of the partnership talk, we have yet to agree on just what PPPs actually are, and whether they are really a 'revolution' in thinking or just another fashionable business idea sold to us from the 'smartest guys in the room'.[2]

In thinking through this paradox, it is essential to work out just exactly what is new. With public infrastructure provision, for example, most governments around the world have for years made decisions about large-scale public infrastructure projects with long lives, have dealt with complex policy matters, and have worked with the private sector to build and develop infrastructure. So the challenge of infrastructure development has always, in a sense, been a central part of the democratic governance project. And as a consequence, it has by definition attracted political controversy. Indeed, many of the concerns voiced about modern PPP infrastructure projects are not new at all. What does appear to be new in these modern PPPs, however, is the preference often to use private finance arrangements, the highly complex contractualization of 'bundled' infrastructure arrangements, and altered governance and accountability assumptions.[3]

There is none the less little doubt that PPPs are an important part of government in the modern age. That is the justification for this international handbook. But to understand them, we need to retrace a few steps. First, there is a need to establish some modest definitions and boundaries. We need to characterize the PPP phenomenon as the multidisciplinary animal it is and to note some of the useful cross-disciplinary lenses that might help our investigations. Second, we then need to propose some important conceptual frameworks that will both assist in the successful delivery of PPPs as well as help our evaluation of the degree to which PPPs meet the objectives sought for them. This initial chapter aims to fulfil both these needs.

This initial handbook chapter adopts a 'sober reflection' philosophy similar to David Parker's earlier paper contemplating the UK's privatization experience (Parker, 2004). This handbook looks overall at the global experience of one particular form of partnership arrangement – that of long-term infrastructure contracts. As a consequence, this chapter first defines the PPP phenomenon and notes that infrastructure provision is one member of several PPP 'families'. It then outlines the multiple stakeholders and disciplines interested in PPPs and acknowledges a range of evaluation challenges this brings. Next, the chapter puts one eye to the future and articulates some of the crucial agenda items likely for partnerships. Finally, we set out the structure of this book and outline the contributions made by our team of international authors.

The PPP phenomenon
In some ways, neither the global spread of PPPs nor their popularity in government are a surprise. PPPs are a classic public policy issue. They are simultaneously a form of governance, a public policy delivery tool and a language-game involving multiple grammars.[4] So they are a political tool, a technical phenomenon and a rhetorical framing device for governments. But, more importantly, they remain slippery and defy repeated attempts to characterize and explain them simply.

Thinking further about these definitional issues, PPPs are loosely defined as cooperative[5] institutional arrangements between public and private sector actors. But this of course covers a wealth of possibilities. Governments have long had some degree of public sector and private sector cooperation over the centuries (Wettenhall, 2003, 2005). And in any event, history also brings with it both the good news of economic growth and the bad. On the one hand it is true, for example, that privateer shipping underpinned the historical growth and dominance of the British

Arena 2: security services, domestic and international

In the era leading up to Tilly's tight nation-state formation, there were elements of security provision (as well as elements of plunder) in the activities of mercenary armies, privateer shipping fleets and those medieval orders noted briefly in the last section. Tilly makes this point quite explicitly: 'From the fifteenth to seventeenth centuries – the critical period for European state formation – armies deployed through much of Europe consisted largely of mercenaries recruited by great lords and military entrepreneurs'. And the '[r]ented armies . . . lived chiefly on payments made or authorized by agents of the crowns they served'. So did the 'leased navies' (Tilly, 1990, pp. 81, 82).[8]

The Swiss were great suppliers of mercenary soldiers throughout this period. But the practice of using mercenaries began much earlier. In their monumental survey of military history through the ages, the Dupuys (1970, pp. 10, 21–2, 302, 421) note that, in the millennium before the birth of Christ, the Assyrians were using them in their military campaigns, Greek mercenaries were serving in Persian armies, and so on. Later, Norse mercenaries were manning Byzantine fleets, in England Henry Tudor was served by around 3000 French mercenaries in the Wars of the Roses – the list goes on.

In Europe the practice peaked in the seventeenth century and began to recede in the eighteenth. The mercenary forces were frequently troublesome and unreliable. Rulers such as Prussia's Friedrich Wilhelm pioneered in establishing durable domestic armies, aided by more cohesive territories, the growth of national sentiment, and the development of stable taxation systems. In a variety of ways, reported Tilly (1990, pp. 84, 106), this 'military reorganization entered a wedge for expansion of state activity into what had previously been local and private spheres'. Thus, as the nation states were taking control of their own agendas, the security function gradually became concentrated in national armies and navies – and public police forces.

For policing – and bridging this strong state period and the one that has followed it – I draw from the brief introduction to a recently published book exploring new challenges for police forces in 'Anglo-Saxon democracies'. There was a time not so long ago, this introduction explains, when such policing was 'very different from what it is today', being undertaken almost exclusively by career public employees who joined young, received both formal and on-the-job training, and mostly had a job for life in a reasonably well-resourced service under the command of a commissioner (or similar) with near quasi-judicial power (Ayling et al., 2009, p. 1).

It is likely that many of the older folk among us will still mostly think of policing in this post-eighteenth-century way. Are we wrong to do so? What has happened? Somewhat analogous to the military and naval experience, policing was long 'done by volunteers, or by commercial organisations', and the 'police as we know them did not exist before the creation of the London Metropolitan Police in 1829'. That decisive step had significant model value throughout the English-speaking countries and perhaps beyond. And thereafter, for more than a century but not so much more, such public policing had a virtual monopoly of the security business. But then:

> [the] 'mixed economy' of policing . . . enjoyed a renaissance after World War II, and became very noticeable by about 1980. The growth of the private security sector has continued unabated since it first began to attract attention a quarter-century ago. (Ayling et al., 2009, p. 2)

Now, whether or not most of us think seriously through what has been happening, we acquiesce in the massive employment of private security guards through commercial and industrial precincts that once would have depended on public police patrols. Our public police even engage private security guards to protect their own premises; they sell their own services to private organizers of big events and their technical advice to film and television producers; they enter into co-production schemes with citizen groups such as Neighbourhood Watch and speak of 'the police extended family'; and so on.

There is no longer a state–public monopoly of the policing function, and private actors are now firmly entrenched in the domestic side of this security industry. Often the effect is even clearer when we consider the international operations of individual states, and the extreme public–private messiness that occurs in and around states where the very legitimacy of government is in doubt.

When Krumholz drew attention to the massive use of contracting by US government agencies, he noted the use of US marines to protect the foreign investments of large private corporations. But so often the contracting system worked in reverse, and by the end of the twentieth century Guttman (2000, 2003) was noting that the US government, pushed in part by strict civil service personnel ceilings, had contracted out so much of its business that it had deprived itself of the expertise needed to monitor the contracting system – more contracting out had to take place to get a modicum of such monitoring! Of course this applied over most fields of government activity, but in the international security industry the effects were especially pernicious. It is now notorious that, in the US case, the war in Iraq 'spurred contracting to record-breaking heights' and that 'functions that were once the responsibility of military personnel [were] essentially in private hands' (Wedel, 2007).[9]

It is not the purpose of this chapter to undertake a critical analysis of such developments, but simply to point to the breadth of public–private mixing over the centuries, and contracting of this sort related to the military activities of governments furnishes another dramatic example of such mixing. So too does the extensive modern use of mercenary armies in weak and failing states as instruments of one or other of the civil war sides or of private firms, in the actual fighting and in much else besides. In recent times they have been particularly active in Africa, though by no means limited to that continent. Some, like South Africa's Executive Outcomes, have become effective commercial corporations, even entering into joint-venture partnerships with government leaders to undertake mining, construction and civil engineering projects as well as to provide training for the regular military forces. In documenting these developments, Muthien and Taylor suggest that 'in the contemporary era security is no longer a service by the state for all its citizens, but has become a market good', and that 'the concept of security has shifted . . . from the state providing security for individuals to individuals providing their own security', with 'non-state initiatives . . . rapidly filling the vacuum' (Muthien and Taylor, 2002, pp. 185–6, 189, 192; also Shearer, 1998; Pech, 1999).

For other analysts of these shifts, 'the erosion of a government's administrative capacity brings in its train the de-legitimization of public authority, a precursor to its confiscation by private actors' (Bayart et al., 1999, p. 96). Tilly's thesis is again relevant. The 'monopolization of the means of coercion' was an essential component, along with the 'differentiation of the instruments of government', in the rise of the modern nation state. Clearly both components have been in retreat for several decades. Muthien and Taylor (2002, p. 195) see the privatization of security in Africa as 'perhaps the most extreme manifestation of a global trend turning towards sources of private authority'. The evidence of the trend has been all around us for several decades. It is not that the recent developments have led to disappearance of the state as a significant governance force, but rather that it now has to share the governance stage with the non-state forces of the market and civil society.

Within this broad field, there has of course been a whole spectrum of types of relationships. A difference between coordinative and collaborative arrangements has already been noted. At this point of my exploration, it would be fair to say that the examples given have pushed the spectrum out towards openly conflicting or merely condescending relationships. It would be a huge research enterprise to seek to discover with precision where actual 'partnership' begins in this vast array of interactions, and I do not attempt that here. I move instead to consider one much more conceptually compact area in which functioning public–private organizations might arguably provide the organizational conditions in which such a partnership might flower.

Arena 3: mixed public–private enterprises
It is inevitable that observers contemplating the governance effects of the great economic meltdown of 2008–09 should have speculated about how related events would affect the universe of public–private relations. That state action was so obviously necessary to arrest the decline of numerous private financial and industrial corporations provided the answer to all those who have seriously speculated that we might have governance without government.[10] Political leaders who are far from socialist in their leanings reluctantly accepted that some degree of 'nationalization' was inevitable in their rescue agendas. However, while there have been some outright takeovers, for the most part the interventions involved governments making loans or grants to, or injecting funds through the purchase of equity in, existing commercial corporations. Wherever this happened, we were witnessing the reinvigoration of the public–private interface, not in any sense its decline. In the process, there has been a resurrection of the older idea of 'mixed enterprise' (ME), involving a sharing of public and private effort in the development and operation of an industry or service.

The term 'mixed enterprise' developed as a variant of 'public enterprise' as public sectors generally built up through the earlier twentieth century and through the big nationalizing period of the post-World War II years. Unlike the fully state-owned enterprises, in these mixes there was both public equity and private equity, the balance often, though not invariably, conferring a bare majority of shares on the state. The company format was a necessity, for it provided for divisible shareholdings.[11]

In the 1970s, senior UK Labour figures were becoming disenchanted with the public corporations running the nationalized industries and seeing virtue in the Italian Industrial Reconstruction Institute (IRI) shareholding arrangement. Established as part of a vast state rescue operation in the early 1930s depression, IRI and a few other large state corporations held shares along with private partners in a mass of financial, transport, communications, electricity and production companies (Holland, 1972). The UK National Enterprise Board, formed in 1975, involved in the rescue of Rolls-Royce and British Leyland, owed quite a bit to this Italian model (Prosser, 1986, ch. 3). Later, under Thatcher, more mixes appeared, but they were mostly halfway houses as the nationalized industry corporations were converted to companies and the shares sold off in tranches (Steel, 1984). Indian 'disinvestments' had similar organizational effects, with the government seeking to raise revenue and improve performance by selling part but not all of the equity in particular enterprises (Maheshwari, 2001, pp. 206–9). Vietnamese 'equitization' followed suit (Van Tiem and Van Thanh, 1996, p. 6). With Singapore Airlines, the aim was to provide performance incentives for staff and attract capital for new aircraft purchases, but not significantly to weaken state control (Thynne and Ariff, 1987).[12]

The classic UK case is that of the Anglo-Persian Oil Co., which became Anglo-Iranian and then British Petroleum (or BP). In this case the government signed a 'convention' with the infant Anglo-Persian Oil Co. in 1914 in order to secure a regular supply of oil for the Royal Navy. Government subscribed capital, acquired shares granting just over 50 per cent of ownership, and gained the right to appoint two directors to the board with power to veto any resolution, subject to appeal to the government (Davies, 1938, pp. 422–43). The deal also secured large ongoing contributions to Treasury revenue through dividends earned and shared with the private partner on the basis of shareholding ratios. The arrangement ended when, as part of her privatizing mission, Thatcher sold off the UK government shareholding.[13]

Anglo-Persian/Anglo-Iranian/BP had a significant precursor: the Suez Canal Co., in which the then British government bought the shareholding of the Khedive of Egypt in 1875 in order to obtain a strong voice in maintaining communications within the empire. In 1938 this was the UK government's largest shareholding in an ME, amounting to 39 per cent of the company, entitling the appointment of three directors, and contributing revenue to the Treasury of £2 812 500 in 1937–38 (at 1937–8 values!). That arrangement survived until Egyptian President Nasser 'expropriated' (or nationalized) the canal in 1956 (Davies, 1938, pp. 421–2; Samuels, 1968, p. 299).

Another early British case involved the Manchester Ship Canal, which was a joint venture between local government, as co-investor and seen as representative of the users, and a private company (Goodman, 1951, p. 30). The most notable Australian cases are probably those of Commonwealth Oil Refineries Ltd (COR) and Amalgamated Wireless Australasia Ltd (AWA), both of which played important national roles in the middle decades of the twentieth century. COR was created by an agreement between the Commonwealth government and the then Anglo-Persian Oil Co. – itself, as noted, a UK ME – ratified by statute in 1920, with the aim of establishing an Australian oil refining industry. AWA began life in 1909 as Australasian Wireless Ltd to serve as an agent of a pioneering overseas manufacturer of wireless equipment, and after a legal challenge expanded as Amalgamated Wireless (Australasia) Ltd to undertake a range of tasks necessary for the development of a local wireless industry closely connected with the expanding international communications network. In

1922 the Commonwealth government commissioned it to establish a direct radio link with the UK, in the process expanding the company's capital and becoming its majority shareholder. The formal agreement signed in 1924 followed the COR model.

Because these bodies have boards on which both contributing parties are represented more or less in proportion to their investments and take collective decisions about the development and management of the involved enterprise, and because there is a sharing of profits, losses and risks, they come much closer to partnership conditions than most of the cases of public–private mixing so familiar through this long history of such mixing. An expectation may therefore be that, given the apparent strength of the common interests that have led to their establishment, the relationship between the partners will exhibit trust, equality and reciprocity to a much higher degree than is apparent in market-style contracting arrangements or in all those other sorts of mixing that arise through changing policy agendas, cycles of economic activity and so on.

The subject attracted significant Canadian research in the 1980s. An early study suggested that the 'obvious advantage of joint ownership over total government ownership is the increased pressure for financial or commercial viability' (Eckel and Vining, 1982, p. 211). After careful study, however, it seemed that the advantages were not so clear-cut. Anthony Boardman and his colleagues explored the extent of mixed enterprise around the world, calling it a 'pervasive phenomenon' but noting also that it was often not sufficiently distinguished from mainline public enterprise (Boardman et al., 1986, p. 221). A comparison of the performance of fully state-owned, mixed and fully private enterprises led to the conclusion that some performance differences favourable to the mixed enterprises may be detected in competitive environments, but also that this is essentially a 'problematic' form, with '[s]ome patterns of joint ownership appear[ing] to generate conflict between public and private shareholders, leading to a high degree of managerial "cognitive dissonance"'. The speculation was that managerial autonomy is compromised in the mixed enterprise form (ibid., pp. 235–41; Boardman and Vining, 1989, p. 26).

In the Anglo-Persian/Anglo-Iranian/BP case, there is evidence that the commercial interests of the private partner sometimes conflicted seriously with the foreign policy interests of the public partner (Bailey, 1979; Yergin, 1991, pp. 622–4). In the two Australian cases, current research suggests that serious relationship problems emerged as, with the original construction-type objectives achieved successfully, the interests of the public and private partners diverged. Few tears were shed when the partnerships were dissolved in the early 1950s.[14]

Developments in this third arena may not fit so well the central thesis of this chapter – about the rise of the nation state and then the diversification of governance power, and the effects of both on public–private mixing – but they do highlight the need for the serious study of mixing arrangements generally. Notably, when governments poured public funds on a massive scale into failing financial and industrial corporations in their effort to assist the cause of recovery from the Great Financial Crisis of 2008–09, many more MEs of this sort were established. But the crisis was so sudden and severe that there was little opportunity for serious planning to take place based on knowledge of how such MEs had fared in the past. What conditions were conducive to successful operation? What arrangements facilitated joint decision-making, trust, reciprocity and an alliance spirit among the partners?

Research challenges
Here and elsewhere through the whole world of public–private mixing arrangements, more serious research is needed both to enhance general understanding of partnership working and to assist policy-makers facing the need to build and monitor new sharing arrangements.

In demonstrating the long history and broad scope of public–private mixing arrangements, this chapter has challenged certain assumptions running through much of the burgeoning literature on so-called PPPs. It has argued that, while many treatments in the literature begin by recognizing the length and breadth of this experience, they mostly give no more than lip-service to it. They then focus particularly on that special group of mixing arrangements following PFI (Public Finance Initiative) lines and relating mostly to infrastructure provision. Following the semantic conversion of the Blair government in the UK, these became *the* PPPs, even though much serious research suggests that there is little about them to warrant application of the term 'partnership'. More mixes certainly, but often not genuine partnerships.

In an effort to revive interest in mixing beyond PFI-style infrastructure schemes, this chapter looks particularly at three 'arenas' that abundantly illustrate these mixing processes in operation. Historical time-lines in two of these arenas connect with Charles Tilly's important work on the formation of nation states in Western Europe, work that proposes that this development matured when 'the instruments of government' became clearly differentiated from other sorts of organizations and when governments came to monopolize 'the forms of coercion' (Tilly, 1975, pp. 27, 40). As the chapter has shown, in the global economic development and international security theatres, in each case with some domestic manifestations thrown in, the shrinking of private sector involvement matched the emergence of strong nation states. It is equally clear that, as governments in the recent period have had to chart new courses in the tripartite (state–market–civil society) governance system that has evolved, there has been a massive resurrection of private sector involvement. So the ubiquity of the public–private interface is again apparent. Public–private mixing is again vigorously alive, with questions remaining about the extent to which it should be regarded as 'partnering'. Research that helps to answer these questions is to be welcomed.

The third arena reinforces this sense of challenge. The further heavy mixing that came with the economic meltdown of 2008–09 adds immediacy and piquancy to these questions. When governments invest so heavily in what have been mostly private firms and so produce a new breed of 'mixed enterprises', are they establishing good partnerships? What operating conditions are needed to ensure that both public and private interests are adequately considered and catered for? We need more good research on past and present cases, both to enhance general understanding in this important and now massive area of public–private mixing, and to aid those with practical responsibility for the development of relevant policies and the design of institutions to serve those policies.

Notes

1. I am grateful to an anonymous referee for the word 'chatter', which fits my argument very well.
2. There may have been other rises and falls. Thus Ghobadian and her colleagues (2004, p. 1) saw the early public–private mixing practice disappearing during the fifth century and reappearing during the Middle Ages.
3. In what is effectively a precursor volume to this handbook, Hodge and Greve offer an excellent summary discussion of these definitional issues in the Introduction to their earlier Edward Elgar volume (Hodge and Greve, 2005, pp. 4–8).
4. For this emphasis and this progression, see for example Fosler and Berger (1982); Boyer (1983); Brooks et al. (1984); Davis (1986); Barnekov et al. (1989); Squires (1989); Stephenson (1991); Pierre (1998); Walzer and Jacobs (1998); Ruane (2002); Corry (2004); Coulson (2005). See next section for further relevant references. See also Bovaird (2004) for a close study of the US urban development experience, along with a survey of mixing experience in EU countries.
5. For a decade or more, this network held annual conferences and published conference books and its own journal, the *International Journal of Public–Private Partnerships*.
6. As with so much else, the scheme was not as new or original as its proponents now proclaimed. For the UK, the Channel Tunnel served as a conspicuous earlier example. In the Australian states, broadly similar arrangements had become familiar over the previous decade under the general description of 'private infrastructure involvement'. Variations of the essential contract generated several acronyms revolving around the words 'build', 'own', 'operate', 'transfer': hence BOOT-type schemes. Sometimes the letter D (for 'design') is also invoked.
7. The coordination mechanism is very clearly at work in another area of mixing that has hitherto received little notice in the PPP literature: the provision of shipping services to transport emigrants generally, and convicts in particular, from source countries in Europe to countries of the 'new world' in the seventeenth, eighteenth and nineteenth centuries. Governments contracted variously with a mass of private interests – notably recruiting agents, ship owners and operators, victuallers – with sometimes scandalous

results, leading to a significant nineteenth-century search for an effective regulatory system. Consistent with the Tilly thesis, in 1832 the British Admiralty assumed direct responsibility for the provision of transports to take convicts to Australia, although much subsidiary contracting was still involved (Bateson, 2004, p. 16). First published in 1959, Bateson's book should be essential reading for those concerned with contracting out. See also MacDonagh (1961).

8. For more on the privateer shipping fleets, see Wettenhall (2005, p. 24–6).
9. In the critical literature spawned by these developments, one of the largest of the contracted US firms, heavily involved in the Iraq hostilities, was itself described as a 'mercenary army' (Scahill, 2007: sub-title).
10. It is likely that, in several of the explorations that flag this notion in their titles (e.g. Peters and Pierre, 1998; Rhodes, 1996; Rosenau and Czempiel, 1992), the intention of the authors has been to provide a conceptual demonstration of the full range of possibilities inherent in the notion of 'governance' as a three-way mix between state, market and civil society, rather than to express any strong conviction that one of those elements might be totally displaced.
11. The other dominant organizational form for public enterprise, the public or statutory corporation, did not do that: see Thynne and Wettenhall (2003) for a general discussion of organizations in public management. For more specialized treatments of mixed enterprise, see Daintith (1970), Musolf (1972); Eckel and Vining (1982) (in which the term 'joint enterprise' is preferred); Boardman et al. (1986); and Boardman and Vining (1989). There is also recent Italian experience (as well as the older IRI experience), as mixed public–private enterprise emerges as one of the forms of 'externalization' being used in the reform of the Italian local government system: see for example Argento et al. (2010).
12. There were some fairly mechanistic constructs as in Taiwan, where any enterprise with more than 50 per cent state shareholding (even 50.1 per cent) was legally defined as public, and any below 50 per cent (even 49.9 per cent) as private (Pu, 2005, p. 167).
13. She was, however, frustrated to discover that she was unable to prevent other *governments* from acquiring some of those shares. In a story that is too complicated to be spelt out here, the investment arm of the *Kuwaiti* government now became a significant shareholder. On cross-country public sector investments and activities, involving another kind of mix, see Wettenhall (1993).
14. I acknowledge the assistance of Sue Berger in this research. For another Australian case, that of the ActewAGL multi-utility in the Australian Capital Territory, established as an awkward compromise when the defenders of state ownership and the advocates of privatization produced a hung legislature, see Wettenhall (2007). In this case it does seem that a genuine public–private enterprise is operating successfully with a high degree of collegiality, trust and sharing among the partners.

References

Adam Smith Institute (2002), 'Contract management of water systems', in 'Around the world in 80 ideas', available online at www.adamsmith.org/80ideas/idea/51htm.

Argento, Daniela, Guiseppi Grossi, Torbjörn Tagesson and Sven Olof Collin (2010), 'The "externalisation" of local public service delivery: experience in Italy and Sweden', *International Journal of Public Policy*, 5 (1), 41–56.

Ayling, Julie, Peter Grabosky and Clifford Shearing (2009), *Lengthening the Arm of the Law: Enhancing Police Resources in the Twenty-First Century*, Cambridge: Cambridge University Press.

Bailey, Martin (1979), *Oilgate: The Sanctions Scandal*, London: Coronet.

Barnekov, Timothy, Robin Boyle and Daniel Rich (1989), *Privatism and Urban Policy in Britain and the United States*, Oxford: Oxford University Press.

Bartlett, D.L. and J.B. Steele (1998), 'Special report: corporate welfare', *Time*, 9 November.

Bateson, Charles (2004), *The Convict Ships 1787–1868*, Sydney: Library of Australian History (first published by Brown, Son and Ferguson, Glasgow, 1959).

Bayart, J.-F., F. Ellis and B. Hibou (1999), *The Criminalization of the State in Africa*, Oxford: James Currey.

Blanc, Hermann (1940), 'A great state enterprise of olden times: the Geneva Corn Chamber, 1628–1798', *Annals of Collective Economy* (now *Annals of Public and Cooperative Economics*), **16** (1), 136–91.

Boardman, Anthony E. and Adrian R. Vining (1989), 'Ownership and performance in competitive environments: a comparison of the performance of private, mixed, and state-owned enterprises', *Journal of Law and Economics*, **32** (1), 1–33.

Boardman, Anthony, Catherine Eckel and Adrian Vining (1986), 'The advantages and disadvantages of mixed enterprises', in Anant R. Negandhi, Howard Thomas and L.K. Rao (eds), *Multinational Corporations and State-Owned Enterprises: A New Challenge in International Relations*, Greenwich, CT: JAI Press, pp. 221–44.

Bovaird, Tony (2004), 'Public–private partnerships in Western Europe and the US: new growths from old roots', in Abby Ghobadian, David Gallear, Nicholas O'Regan and Howard Viney (eds), *Public–Private Partnerships: Policy and Experience*, Basingstoke: Palgrave Macmillan, pp. 221–50.

Boyer, Christine M. (1983), *Dreaming the Rational City: The Myth of American City Planning*, Cambridge, MA: MIT Press.

Broadbent, Jane and Richard Laughlin (1999), 'The private finance initiative: clarification of a future research agenda', *Financial Accountability and Management*, **15** (2), 95–114.

Brooks, Harvey, Lance Liebman and Corinne S. Schelling (eds) (1984), *Public–Private Partnership: New Opportunities for Meeting Social Needs*, Cambridge, MA: Ballinger.

Caiden, Naomi (1989), 'A new perspective on budgetary reform', *Australian Journal of Public Administration*, **48** (1), 53–60.

CoEC (Commission of the European Communities) (2004), *Green Paper on Public–Private Partnerships and Community Law on Public–Contracts and Concessions*, available online at europa.eu.int/.

Corry, Dan (2004), 'New Labour and PPPs', in Abby Ghobadian, David Gallear, Nicholas O'Regan and Howard Viney (eds), *Public–Private Partnerships: Policy and Experience*, Basingstoke: Palgrave Macmillan, pp. 24–36.

Coulson, Andrew (2005), 'A plague on all your partnerships: theory and practice in regeneration', *International Journal of Public Sector Management*, **18** (2), 151–63.

Daintith, T.C. (1970), 'The mixed enterprise in the United Kingdom', in W. Friedmann and J.F. Garner (eds), *Government Enterprise: A Comparative Survey*, London: Stephens, pp. 53–78.

Davies, Ernest (1938), 'Government directors of public companies', *Political Quarterly*, **9** (3), 421–30.

Davis, Perry (ed.) (1986), 'Public–private partnerships improving urban life', *Proceedings of the Academy of Political Science*, **36** (2), 1–161.

Dilke, Sir Charles (1890), *Problems of Greater Britain*, London: Macmillan.

Dupuy, Ernest R. and Trevor N. Dupuy (1970), *The Encyclopedia of Military History from 3500BC to the Present*, London: Macdonald.

Eckel, Catherine and Aidan Vining (1982), 'Towards a positive theory of joint enterprise', in W.T. Stanbury and Fred Thompson (eds), *Managing Public Enterprise*, New York: Praeger, pp. 209–22.

EIU (Economist Intelligence Unit) (2002), *Public v. Private*, London: The Economist Newspaper Group.

English, Linda M. and Matthew Skillern (2005), 'Public–private partnerships and public sector management reform: a comparative perspective', *International Journal of Public Policy*, **1** (1/2), 1–21.

Farazmand, Ali (2001), 'Privatization and public enterprise reform in post-revolutionary Iran', in Ali Farazmand (ed.), *Privatization or Public Enterprise Reform?*, Westport, CT: Greenwood Press, pp. 175–200.

Flinders, Matthew (2005), 'The politics of public–private partnerships', *British Journal of Politics and International Relations*, **7** (2), 215–39.

Fosler, Scott R. and Renee A. Berger (eds) (1982), *Public–Private Partnerships in American Cities*, Lexington, MA: Heath.

Friend, John (2006), 'Partnership meets politics: managing within the maze', *International Journal of Public Sector Management*, **19** (3), 261–77.

Ghobadian, Abby, David Gallear, Nicholas O'Regan and Howard Viney (2004), 'PPP: the instrument for transforming the public services', in Abby Ghobadian, David Gallear, Nicholas O'Regan and Howard Viney (eds), *Public–Private Partnerships: Policy and Experience*, Basingstoke: Palgrave Macmillan, pp. 1–12.

Ghuman, B.S. and Roger Wettenhall (eds) (2001), 'Symposium: from public enterprise and privatisation towards sectoral mixes', *Asian Journal of Public Administration*, **23** (2), 143–272.

Goldsmith, Stephen and William D. Eggers (2004), *Governing by Network: The New Shape of the Public Sector*, Washington, DC: Brookings Institution Press.

Goodman, Edward (1951), *Forms of Public Ownership and Control*, London: Christophers.

Greve, Carsten (2006), 'Public–private partnerships: a public policy perspective', in Graeme Hodge (ed.), *Privatization and Market Development: Global Movements in Public Policy Ideas*, Cheltenham, UK and Northampton, MA, USA: Edward Elgar, pp. 63–77.

Guttman, Daniel (2000), 'Public purpose and private service: the twentieth century culture of contracting out and the evolving law of diffused sovereignty', *Administrative Law Review*, **52** (3), 861–926.

Guttman, Daniel (2003), 'Contracting United States government work: organizational and constitutional models', *Public Organization Review*, **3** (3), 281–99.

Hall, David, Robin de la Motte and Steve Davies (2003), *Terminology of Public–Private Partnerships (PPPs)*, Public Services International Research Unit, London: University of Greenwich.

Hall, Rodney Bruce and Thomas J. Biersteker (2002), 'The emergence of private authority in the regulatory system', in Rodney Bruce Hall and Thomas J. Biersteker (eds), *The Emergence of Private Authority in Global Governance*, Cambridge: Cambridge University Press, pp. 3–22.

Hammerschmid, Gerhard and Renate Meyer (2006), 'Public–private partnerships in a Continental European context: current experiences from the City of Vienna', Paper for 10th International Research Symposium on Public Management, Glasgow, 10–12 April.

HM Treasury (2000), *Public–Private Partnerships: The Government's Approach*, London: HMSO.

Hodge, Graeme (2007), 'The PPP debate: taking stock of the issues', paper for International Workshop on Public–Private Partnerships: Promises, Politics and Pitfalls, City University of Hong Kong, 25–27 October.

Hodge, Graeme and Carsten Greve (eds) (2005), *The Challenge of Public–Private Partnerships: Learning from International Experience*, Cheltenham, UK and Northampton, MA, USA: Edward Elgar.

Holland, Robert C. (1984), 'The new era of public–private partnerships', in Paul R. Porter and David C. Sweet (eds), *Rebuilding America's Cities: Roads to Recovery*, New Brunswick, NJ: Center for Urban Policy Research, Rutgers University, pp. 209–11.

Holland, Stuart (ed.) (1972), *The State as Entrepreneur – New Directions for Public Enterprise: The IRI State Shareholding Formula*, London: Weidenfeld and Nicolson.

Jose, Jim (2007), 'Reframing the "governance" story', *Australian Journal of Political Science*, **42** (3), 455–70.

Kettl, Donald F. (1993), *Sharing Power: Public Governance and Private Markets*, Washington DC: Brookings Institution.

Klijn, Erik-Hans and Geert R. Teisman (2005), 'Public–private partnerships as the management of co-production: strategic and institutional obstacles in a difficult marriage', in Graeme Hodge and Carsten Greve (eds), *The Challenge of Public–Private Partnerships: Learning from International Experience*, Cheltenham, UK and Northampton, MA, USA: Edward Elgar, pp. 95–116.

Koppenjan, J.F.M. (2005), 'The formation of public–private partnerships: lessons from nine transport infrastructure projects in the Netherlands', *Public Administration*, **83** (1), 135–57.

Krumholz, Norman (1984), 'Recovery of cities: an alternate view', in Paul Porter and David Sweet (eds), *Rebuilding America's Cities: Roads to Recovery*, New Brunswick, NJ: Center for Urban Policy Research, Rutgers University, pp. 173–90.

Laffin, Martin and Joyce Liddle (2006), 'New perspectives on partnership', *International Journal of Public Sector Management*, **19** (3), editorial.

Linder, Stephen H. (1999), 'Coming to terms with the public–private partnership: a grammar of multiple meanings', *American Behavioral Scientist*, **43** (1), 35–51.

Lipschutz, Ronnie D. and Cathleen Fogel (2002), 'Regulation for the rest of us? Global civil society and the privatization of transnational regulation', in Rodney Bruce Hall and Thomas J. Biersteker (eds), *The Emergence of Private Authority in Global Governance*, Cambridge: Cambridge University Press, pp. 115–40.

MacDonagh, Oliver (1961), *Patterns of Government Growth 1800–1860: The Passenger Acts and Their Enforcement*, London: MacGibbon & Kee.

Maheshwari, S.R. (2001), 'Privatization and public enterprise reform in India', in Ali Farazmand (ed.), *Privatization or Public Enterprise Reform?* Westport, CT: Greenwood Press, pp. 201–15.

Musolf, Lloyd D. (1972), *Mixed Enterprise: A Developmental Perspective*, Lexington, MA: Heath.

Muthien, Bernedett and Ian Taylor (2002), 'The return of the dogs of war? The privatization of security in Africa', in Rodney Bruce Hall and Thomas J. Biersteker (eds), *The Emergence of Private Authority in Global Governance*, Cambridge: Cambridge University Press, pp. 183–99.

Pech, K. (1999), 'Executive Outcomes: a corporate quest', in J. Cilliers and P. Mason (eds), *Peace, Profit or Plunder? The Privatization of Security in War-Torn African Societies*, Pretoria: Institute for Security Studies, pp. 81–110.

Peters, B.G. and J. Pierre (1998), 'Governance without government? Rethinking public administration', *Journal of Public Administration Research and Theory*, **8** (2), 223–43.

Pierre, Jon (ed.) (1998), *Partnerships in Urban Governance: European and American Experience*, Basingstoke: Macmillan.

Pirotta, Godfrey (1996), *The Maltese Public Service 1800–1940: The Administrative Politics of a Micro-State*, Msida, Malta: Mireva Publications.

Porter, Paul R. and David C. Sweet (1984), 'Goals, processes, and leadership', in Paul R. Porter and David C. Sweet (eds) (1984), *Rebuilding America's Cities: Roads to Recovery*, New Brunswick, NJ: Center for Urban Policy Research, Rutgers University, pp. 212–29.

Powell, Martin and Caroline Glendinning (2002), 'Introduction', in Carolyn Glendenning, Martin Powell and Kirstein Rumney (eds), *Partnerships, New Labour and the Governance of Welfare*, Bristol: Policy Press, pp. 1–14.

Prosser, Tony (1986), *Nationalised Industries and Public Control: Legal, Constitutional and Political Issues*, London: Gerald Duckworth.

Pu, Cheng-Chiu (2005), 'Ownership and management issues in Taiwanese public enterprises', *Asia Pacific Journal of Public Administration*, **27** (2), 163–80.

Rhodes, R.A.W. (1996), 'The new governance: governing without government', *Political Studies*, **44** (4), 652–67.

Rhodes, R.A.W. (1997), *Understanding Governance: Policy Networks, Governance, Refllexivity and Accountability*, Buckingham: Open University Press.

Rosenau, J.N. and E.-O. Czempiel (1992), *Governance without Government: Order and Change in World Politics*, Cambridge: Cambridge University Press.

Ruane, Sally (2002), 'Public–private partnerships: the case of PFI', in Carolyn Glendenning, Martin Powell and Kirstein Rumney (eds), *Partnerships, New Labour and the Governance of Welfare*, Bristol: Policy Press, pp. 199–211.

Salamon, Lester M. (1989), *Beyond Privatization: The Tools of Government Action*, Washington, DC: Urban Institute Press.

Salamon, Lester M. (2002), 'The new governance and the tools of public action', in Lester M. Salamon (ed.), *The Tools of Government: A Guide to the New Governance*, Oxford: Oxford University Press, pp. 1–47.

Samuels, Alec (1968), 'Government participation in private industry', *Journal of Business Law*, October, 296–302.

Scahill, Jeremy (2007), *Blackwater: The Rise of the World's Most Powerful Mercenary Army*, London: Profile Books.

Scott, Colin (2003), 'Organizational variety in regulatory governance', *Public Organization Review*, **3** (3), 301–16.

Shearer, D. (1998), *Private Armies and Military Intervention*, New York: Oxford University Press.

Squires, Gregory D. (1989), 'Public–private partnerships: who gets what and why', in Gregory D. Squires (ed.), *Unequal Partnerships: The Political Economy of Urban Development in Postwar America*, New Brunswick, NJ: Rutgers University Press.

Steel, David (1984), 'Government and the new hybrids', in David Steel and David Heald (eds), *Privatizing Public Enterprises*, London: RIPA, pp. 101–12.

Stephenson, M.O. (1991), 'Whither the public–private partnership: a critical review', *Urban Affairs Quarterly*, **27** (1), 109–27.

Thynne, Ian (ed.) (1995), *Corporatization, Divestment and the Public–Private Mix*, Hong Kong: AJPA in collaboration with IASIA.

Thynne, Ian (2008), 'Institutional perspectives, issues and challenges', *Public Administration and Development*, **28** (5), 327–39.

Thynne, Ian and Mohamed Ariff (1987), 'Singapore Airlines: a study in the management of privatisation', in Colm O Nuallain and Roger Wettenhall (eds), *Public Enterprise: The Management Challenge*, Brussels: IIAS, pp. 111–29.

Thynne, Ian and Roger Wettenhall (eds) (2003), 'Symposium on organizations in public management', *Public Organization Review*, **3** (3), 215–332.

Tilly, Charles (1975), 'Reflections on the history of European state-making', in Charles Tilly (ed.), *The Formation of Nation States in Western Europe*, Princeton, NJ: Princeton University Press, pp. 3–82.

Tilly, Charles (1990), *Coercion, Capital, and European States, AD 990–1990*, Oxford: Basil Blackwell.

van der Wel, Paul (2004), Privatisation by stealth: the global use and abuse of the term 'public–private partnership', Working Paper Series No. 394, The Hague: Institute of Social Studies.

Van Tiem, Phan and Nguyen Van Thanh (1996), 'Problems and prospects of state-enterprise reform, 1996–2000', in Ng Chee Yuen, Nick J. Freeman and Frank H. Huynh (eds), *State-Owned Enterprise Reform in Vietnam: Lessons from Asia*, Singapore: Institute of Southeast Asian Studies, pp. 3–18.

Walzer, Norman and Brian D. Jacobs (eds) (1998), *Public–Private Partnerships for Local Economic Development*, Westport, CT: Praeger.

Wedel, Janine R. (2007), 'The shadow army', *Boston Globe*, 30 September.

Weihe, Guðrið (2006), 'Public–private partnerships: addressing a nebulous concept', paper for 10th International Research Symposium on Public Management, Glasgow, 10–12 April.

Wettenhall, Roger (1993), 'The globalization of public enterprises', *International Review of Administrative Sciences*, **59** (3), 387–408.

Wettenhall, Roger (2001), 'The Templars and Australia: crusading orders and a statutory authority', *Australian Studies*, **16** (2), 131–50.

Wettenhall, Roger (2005), 'The public–private interface: surveying the history', in Graeme Hodge and Carsten Greve (eds), *The Challenge of Public–Private Partnerships: Learning from International Experience*, Cheltenham, UK and Northampton, MA, USA: Edward Elgar, pp. 22–43.

Wettenhall, Roger (2007), 'ActewAGL: a genuine public–private partnership', *International Journal of Public Sector Management*, **20** (5), 392–414.

Wettenhall, Roger (2008a), 'Public–private mixes and partnerships: a search for understanding', *Asia Pacific Journal of Public Administration*, **30** (2), 119–38.

Wettenhall, Roger (2008b), '"Economic meltdown" and the resurrection of mixed enterprise', *Public Administration Today* (a journal of the Institute of Public Administration Australia), issue 16, 30–35.

Yergin, Daniel (1991), *The Prize: The Epic Quest for Oil, Money and Power*, New York: Simon and Schuster.

3 A brief intellectual history of the public–private partnership movement
Tony Bovaird

Introduction

The public–private partnership (PPP) phenomenon has been with us for a long time. The phrase first became used by a specialist audience in the 1970s, and books were being written about such partnerships even in the 1980s (e.g. Rose, 1986), although it was the 1990s before it was widely recognized, when the Private Finance Initiative was launched by the John Major administration in the UK, and the acronym 'PPP' became common currency. However, the actual phenomenon goes much further back into history.

This chapter explores the intellectual history of the PPP movement, both before and after it became a widely used acronym. It demonstrates that the intellectual provenance of PPPs is very varied, with major contributions from across the social sciences. This has contributed to the richness of our understanding of PPPs, but it has also made it difficult for critical comment to develop a constructive perspective from which to evaluate PPPs and suggest options for their change. In consequence, while there has been considerable criticism of specific manifestations of PPPs (like PFI), there is still considerable interest in and optimism about the potential of PPPs in general.

The intellectual foundations of PPPs

From the social science disciplines, there has been a wide range of rationales for PPPs and analyses of their consequences. In Table 3.1 we set out the range of theories we consider in this chapter (adapted and extended from Sullivan and Skelcher, 2002).

A stylized history of conceptual standpoints for rationalizing the role of PPPs

The way in which PPPs have been conceptualized and their potential rationalized has varied greatly over time. In this section, we pick out some of the key conceptual standpoints that have been used to provide an overall explanation for why PPPs can be useful. This territory has been increasingly contested – none of the old conceptual frameworks has been

43

Table 3.1   Social science theories influencing thinking on PPPs

Questions	Optimist	Pessimist	Realist
Why collaboration happened	Achieving shared vision *Collaborative empowerment theory* *Regime theory* *Collaborative advantage theory* *Welfare economics* Resource maximization *Exchange theory* Access to unique resources *Resource-based view of strategy* Cost minimization *Transaction cost economics*	Maintaining or enhancing position *Resource dependency theory* *Principal–agent theory* *Public accounting theory* *Conspiracy theories* Legitimation of dominant power coalitions *Marxist theories*	Responding to new environments *Complex adaptive systems theory* *Evolutionary theory*
What form of collaboration developed and why?	Multiple relationships *Collaborative empowerment theory* Power-sharing coalitions *Regime theory* Learning networks *Network theory* Knowledge- and information-sharing partnerships *Resource-based view of strategy*	Inter-organizational network *Resource dependency theory* Power-capturing coalitions *Urban growth coalition theory*	Organizational, promotional and systemic networks *Evolutionary theory* Policy networks as meso-level governance instruments *Policy network theories*

Table 3.1 (continued)

Questions	Optimist	Pessimist	Realist
Which factors affect collaboration?	Individual factors: reticulist skills and abilities, trust *Collaborative empowerment theory* Leadership *Regime theory*	Organizational factors: culture, bureaucracy, professionalization *Resource dependency theory* *Historical institutional theory*	Institutional factors: mediation of individual and organizational factors *New institutional theory* Initial conditions *Complex adaptive systems theory*
Unintended consequences	Opening up public services to wider stakeholder influences *Stakeholder theory*	Capture of public and social value by private interests *Radical public accounting theory* *Growth coalition theory* *Marxist theory* Undermining democratic decision-making *Marxist theory* *Postmodern theory*	Emergent hybrid organizational forms *Evolutionary theory* *Complex adaptive systems theory* New forms of democratic decision-making *Postmodern theory*

entirely superseded as new approaches have taken the stage. The various meta-theories rationalizing the role of PPPs have included the following:

- government regulation of business (dominant conceptual framework up to the 1970s);
- regional and urban dynamics (1950s onwards);
- new public management – NPM (from the 1980s);
- critique of PFI from public sector accounting perspective (from the 1990s);
- strategic management approach: collaborative advantage (from the 1990s);

- public governance (from 1990s);
- postmodernist theories (from 1990s).

Figure 3.1 presents these conceptual standpoints.

In reality, of course, these theories did not appear quite as neatly and as separately as Figure 3.1 indicates. It must also be stressed that all these approaches were always accompanied by intense debate, contestation of conceptual frameworks and alternative readings of the evidence bases paraded to illustrate (and sometimes to test) the theories.

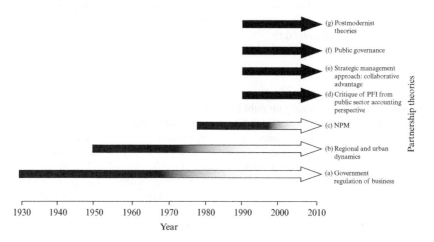

Figure 3.1   The succession of meta-theories rationalizing the role of PPPs

Government regulation of business

The analysis of the interrelationship between government and business was dominated throughout the early part of the twentieth century by the theoretical apparatus of welfare economics. This provided a rationale in relation to the need for, and the content of, state intervention in market behaviour, particularly to deal with market power, for example, arising from economies of scale. This was the approach used to consider the way in which US and UK utilities were regulated (largely private sector in the case of the USA, largely public sector in the case of the UK). The PPPs that were used in France over a long period for general public service provision and developed in the USA for regional and urban regeneration in the 1930s, and from the 1950s onwards in Germany, mainly for infrastructure services, were also largely analysed from this perspective. The main governance approaches were either through public sector regulatory bodies (although in the USA self-regulation was also partially used) or, mainly in Germany, ownership of a significant proportion of the shares, to ensure the ability to shape strategic decisions.

French utilities   Since the seventeenth century, many canals and bridges have been built in France through the government granting concessions to private firms (Cowie, 1996) and this continues for much transport infrastructure. Lorrain (1991, p. 89) notes that in France many more public services such as water, sewage, refuse collection and treatment, urban transport, mass housing, and facilities for culture, sports and social affairs have been operated by private companies since the nineteenth century. Famous examples include the water companies Compagnie Générale des Eaux (called Vivendi since 1998) and the Lyonnaise des Eaux (now called Suez). However, these companies were expected to operate within a public interest framework laid down in legislation. Since the 1980s they have led the international movement to privatize water services, within a public utilities regulatory framework. The most important institutional form of private involvement in public services in France has long been the société économie mixte (SEM), dating from the Poincaré decrees in 1926, when local authorities received a general power to run local services, either directly or through financial participation in firms (the first SEMs) (Burnham, 2001, p. 51). SEMs have the advantage of allowing the fragmented and small French communes to garner economies of scale in service provision, unlike in-house providers. The rationale here is clearly at least partly economic, but with a strong sense of maintaining political control over key local decisions, for which traditional outsourcing might be less effective. There has therefore been little sign in France of 'sharing partnerships' in any of this experience. The French are rather in the tradition of 'governmental regulation of business'. Indeed, Le Galès and Mawson (1994, p. 64) conclude that, in general, local authorities and ministries have only limited knowledge of how to engage, negotiate and take advantage of the skills and expertise of the private sector in urban regeneration. This is partly because, at the local level, mayors provide the main source of local leadership and do not wish to share it with private partners. It is also due to the 'global regulation system' (Lorrain, 1991, p. 106) by which many communes entirely delegate a service to a private company and forswear detailed monitoring unless users start to complain. Moreover, it is because PPPs have been institutionalized in France mainly through the SEMs over which the public sector has a significant degree of control and influence.

West (2005) has applied the 'thematization' conceptual framework, derived from Vincent-Jones (1994), in analysing the recent experience of France. West argues that while it has a long formal history of contracting in public services, contract has traditionally played only a minor role in ordering complex, long-term exchange relationships. Since the transaction costs associated with such detailed contract planning, monitoring and enforcement are minimized, it might be thought that the traditional French model has been an example of good contract governance. However, West argues that the role of contract is being reasserted because of decentralization, corruption scandals, more participatory democratic decision-making, EU competition rules and tougher environmental standards. She posits the emergence of a new thematization, lying nearer to the contractual end of Vincent-Jones's governance, whereby local government is urged to establish continuous contract monitoring and performance measurement regimes, establish common service standards and compare performance. West suggests that, if the traditional French model was an example of the most that could be wrung out of contract before hierarchy became the more 'efficient' mode of governance, its survival in the more risky context of active citizenship, strict accountability, competition and transparency looks uncertain. So, while the old model may once have demonstrated transaction-cost-economizing properties, it is now increasingly seen as inefficient and uncompetitive. However, the indiscriminate contractual thematization of exchange relationships, while meeting public expectations about appropriate conduct in the public domain, may also turn out to be inefficient in at least some respects.

Public ownership of private industry in Germany   Since 1945 a long tradition has developed in Germany of 'state partnership' with the private sector – evidenced, for example, by large-scale state shareholding in major industrial enterprises such as Volkswagen, Lufthansa, VEBA, VIAG at the national level, and RWE at the regional level. Some of these shareholdings still remain, while others have now been liquidated. (Although the German examples are perhaps the best known, state holding companies are also common in other European countries such as Italy and France, while in Austria the major nationalized banks serve as state holding companies for private firms – see Li and Akintoye, 2003, p. 13). However, in none of these cases is the relationship between public and private sector one of genuine 'sharing partners' – they have mainly been maintained to give the state a greater degree of control over strategic decisions affecting these industries, which are regarded as particularly important for the future of the overall economy.

US regional and urban development through PPPs from the 1930s   A key element in the story of PPPs in the modern era starts in the USA. Blakely (1994, p. 153) recounts how, in 1938, the federal government launched a set of housing assistance programmes by chartering the Federal National Mortgage Association to create a secondary market for home mortgages. (Survivors of the 2008–09 recession in the USA and elsewhere in the world may recognize parallels here!) This programme created a partnership between the public sector and the private market to produce housing in urban areas that was judged at the time to be highly effective. This can be seen as a relatively straightforward attempt to deal with financial market failure by reducing the impact of the market's overestimate of the degree of risk attached to particular financial transactions.

A decade later, a series of federal housing and development programmes, beginning with the Housing and Urban Renewal Act 1949, relied primarily on private developers to rebuild the inner cities, using public subsidies to stimulate private development (Fainstain, 1994, p. 115). Fainstain suggests that 'within the US, public–private cooperation has always formed the touchstone for urban redevelopment policy. Elite, business-dominated groups like Pittsburgh's Allegheny Conference, Boston's "Vault", and San Francisco's SPUR had long acted as quasi-official planning agencies for their municipalities' (ibid., 1994, p. 115). The Allegheny Conference on Community Development (ACCD) was a private-sector-led partnership that emerged from a conference on post-World War II planning organized in 1943 (Jacobs, 2000). It was incorporated in 1944 and was involved in subsequent decades in working with a wide range of partners in a myriad of partnerships. While this resulted in problems of fragmentation, Jacobs concludes that PPPs brought groups together to deal with complex problems that organizations working by themselves could not have overcome. Again, this approach can be seen as deriving from a straightforward welfare economics approach, where externalities between activities are internalized by bringing them all within the same decision-making entity, the PPP.

Regional and urban dynamics
From the 1950s onwards, the emerging PPPs being used for regional and urban regeneration were analysed from a more dynamic perspective than was available in welfare economics. In economics, this dynamic approach originally drew upon earlier 'growth pole' theories and later on theories of urban and regional agglomeration, driven by innovation and economies of scope. Here the key role of the public sector was seen to be pump-priming investment, sometimes with pay-offs through share-owning, but the PPPs that were set up were often dominated by private sector interests.

This phenomenon became the subject of intense interest in urban political science and sociology, leading to the formulation of theories of urban growth coalitions and regime theory.

The US urban development experience of PPPs from the 1960s onwards   In the 1960s and 1970s further PPPs were launched in the field of US urban regeneration (Fosler and Berger, 1982; Harding, 1994; Rose, 1986), for example, through such mechanisms as the Model Cities Programme and the Urban Development Action Grant (UDAG). Such PPP mechanisms were used by most US large cities to redevelop large parts of their down-town areas, including ports and harbours, and were supported through federal government transfers and loan guarantees. Partly to replace dis-appearing manufacturing jobs, projects frequently developed exhibition sites, convention and conference centres, and science and technology parks. Inner-city dereliction was usually seen by this time as caused by a variety of market failures. These included:

- prolonged disequilibrium (as developers reacted irrationally through unjustified speculation, often caused by the value-creation opportu-nities available if rezoning could be achieved);
- neighbourhood externalities (which gave rise to vicious circles of decline when investment was absent, but also to virtuous circles of growth if it could just be initiated);
- innovation externalities (justifying the 'growth pole' approach to urban redevelopment); and
- overcautious reactions by investors to the degree of risk and uncer-tainty in the urban property market.

During the 1970s, however, as the US federal government reduced its financial support and withdrew from its oversight role, localities had to turn to the private sector for funding of major projects. They therefore became increasingly entrepreneurial in their attempts to attract private investment. Blakely (1994, p. 154) observes that 'city officials became dealmakers by the late 1970s. These deals included the provision of essential infrastructure at little or no cost with promise of a return on the city's investment through a soft loan or a proportion of the profits from the project . . . In essence, cities moved from their traditional role as regulator to co-investor.' Here we see a retraction from the public sector role of compensating for all market failures towards a role focused more narrowly on addressing financial market failures, where private financial markets either reacted over-cautiously to the risk and uncertainty in city development markets or where other groups in the city gained from the wider externalities created by the developments.

The growth of PPPs was favoured by some features of US cities. For example, US capital was geographically dispersed, with corporate head-quarters and financial institutions being found in most cities, unlike the case in the UK (Harding, 1994). Also, there was an acceptance by local capital that they could and should play a key role in 'local growth coalitions' (Logan and Molotch, 1987). Harding (1994, p. 20) also suggests that there was a greater awareness of, and interest in, local economic development in US cities, and more social networks linking business people. Harding suggests that local business was therefore more able to self-organize, for example when faced with the economic crises of the cities from the late 1970s onwards, particularly around creating visions for local city growth. Stone (1989) also showed how the 'urban regime' (based on a coalition between public and private leaders) pushed through radical policies, including a moderation in race relations, in response to rapid social changes facing the city. Moreover, as the regime gathered momentum, it acquired a learning capacity and 'social intelligence' that allowed policy-makers to deal more successfully with complex problems. Here the rationalization of PPPs began to make a clear departure from the previous economics literature. While there was still attention to aspects of market failure, the key rationale for PPPs was located in stakeholder coalitions, conceptualized from the perspective of regime theory. In addition, this approach began to adopt some of the 'emergent strategy' and 'co-evolutionary' learning approaches associated with complex adaptive systems theory.

Brooks et al. (1984) played an important role in bringing wider attention to the ways in which PPPs were emerging as key instruments of urban development, at a time when Reaganomics was actively trying to discourage government intervention, at least at the federal level. Freed from the vetting processes in federal grant programmes designed to test the 'authenticity' of partnership working, many city governments became the driving forces in these partnerships. However, this also inevitably meant greater political sensitivity to local economic conditions (Harding, 1994, p. 21). As Harding points out, there was an element of instability in such arrangements, as partnerships could stand to lose much of their legitimacy and influence in those cities where control swung to populist mayors not backed by political elites (such as Cleveland and Atlanta), although in many other cities the two sides were able to align their interests with each other (Jezierski, 1988). This analysis borrows from the economic theory of unstable cartels to show how urban growth regimes are themselves constantly in flux.

Close working between public and private sectors was integral to these redevelopment partnerships. Fainstain (1994, pp. 108–9) explores the bargaining around public and private benefits, which she suggests constituted the principal vehicles by which the urban redevelopment process proceeded in New York and London during the 1980s. The arrangements took many different forms, depending on the area, but they often included trading of planning permission in return for construction of affordable housing; the collaboration of public agencies with community organizations in low-income neighbourhoods to form local development corporations; and the granting of tax holidays to private investors within enterprise zones in the hope of employment expansion (ibid., p. 109). Fainstain's conceptual position is implicitly based on a radical reading of urban economics, with borrowings from institutionalism – although, more recently, in the second edition of her book, she appears to accept that economic institutionalism has a stronger explanatory power than political institutionalism.

However, there was often tension in the USA between these urban PPPs and the local neighbourhoods in which they operated (albeit mainly downtown areas where there was already a low and declining population). While Harding (1994) suggests that the economic fortunes of the areas in which these PPPs operated were often transformed, and that public–private cooperation helped to smooth the process, he expresses doubt about the precise contribution of partnerships and as to whether the benefits have accrued to groups other than the local and non-local business community and middle- to high-income groups (ibid., p. 24). This argument, of course, is another rerunning of the early debate on 'trickle-down' or 'spread effects' versus 'polarization' or 'backwash' effects, identified with Myrdal (1957) and Hirschman (1958).

In a famous critique of the 'urban growth coalitions' behind these PPPs, Logan and Molotch (1987, p. 62) suggest that 'The people who use their time and money to participate in local affairs are the ones who – in vast disproportion to their representation in the population – have the most to gain or lose in land use decisions.' The analysis of the 'urban growth machine' by Logan and Molotch has been influential in the US urban economic development literature but is now generally subsumed as just one (corporatist) strand in urban regime theory. However, Davies (2003), in analysing urban regeneration partnerships in the UK, argues that regime theory neither describes nor explains the contrasting forms of collaboration in the UK. Unlike the US situation, in the UK the development of urban regeneration partnerships has been driven by the development of an ideological perception within local government elites that urban regeneration depends on market-led growth, and a series of central government regeneration initiatives that have encouraged, and sometimes coerced, local authorities into partnership arrangements with local business elites. He shows how these PPPs, while symbolically important, have been highly bureaucratized and business involvement has typically been marginal, so that US-style regimes are not likely to be found in the UK context.

David Harvey (1989, p. 8), from an explicitly Marxist perspective, perceives 'public private partnership' as an overall mechanism for coordinating the capitalist economy (rather than any explicit organization or organizational form), which provides a new way of generating surplus in the process of capital accumulation. Harvey is prepared to celebrate some aspects of this PPP:

> there is something positive also going on here . . . The idea of the city as a collective corporation, within which democratic decision-making can operate, has a long history in the pantheon of progressive doctrines and practices . . . it is also useful to recognize that many of the problems of collective corporatist action originate not with the fact of some kind of civic boosterism, or even by virtue of who, in particular, dominates the urban class alliances that form or what projects they devise.

He suggests that it is rather

> the generality of inter-urban competition within an overall framework of uneven capitalist geographical development which seems so to constrain the options that 'bad' projects drive out 'good' and well-intended and benevolent coalitions of class forces find themselves . . . playing to the rules of capitalist accumulation rather than to the goals of meeting local needs or maximizing social welfare.

Harvey suggests, too, that a critical perspective should focus on some of the dangerous macroeconomic consequences of public–private partnership in urban regeneration, in the context of inter-urban competition, including regressive impacts on the distribution of income, volatility within the urban network and the ephemerality of the benefits that many projects bring.

Similarly from a Marxist perspective, Derek Kerr (1998) argues that PFI is a mode of governance through which the state attempts to restructure itself and, indirectly, class relations, by transforming the social relations of service and infrastructure provision and subordinating them to the discipline of the market. However, he identifies that resistance to this transformation has come from both the state bureaucracy and also from the market itself, due to the difficulties inherent in subjecting labour to new modes of exploitation, which then perpetuates the tendencies to crisis within capitalism and undermines the state's ability to steer the capitalist economy.

The most influential writer on PPPs from the regulationist branch of neo-Marxism (taking an approach he labels 'strategic relational') has been Bob Jessop. Jessop and Sum (undated), drawing on experience of PPPs in Hong Kong (including comparisons with other global cities), consider how entrepreneurial cities can acquire coherence as collective social forces.

They emphasize the role played by a complex array of private–public part-nerships and networks cooperating under the leadership of the world city to promote the overall competitiveness of an emerging multi-centred city-region, not only in economic terms but also in cultural and community matters. They argue that the solidity of these great urban projects depends on their interpersonal, inter-organizational and institutional embedded-ness, so that networks of partnerships, both horizontal and vertical, are important, and also on their feasibility in the light of existing structural constraints and opportunities. As with Harvey, the concept of PPP here has expanded to describe both a specific organizational form but also a key building block in a meta-narrative about how the forces of capitalist development are coordinated. However, it is interesting to note that while explicitly seeking to take a regulationist approach to city development, their framework has many elements in common with the resource-based view of city strategy set out in Carmeli and Kemmet (2006).

New public management (NPM)
From the 1980s, NPM provided a very different set of rationales for PPPs. In particular, it was deeply influenced by public choice theory, which sug-gested that there might be major potential gains from use of market and quasi-market competition mechanisms, in which the public sector should manage markets where a 'mixed economy of provision' would achieve sig-nificant service improvements, through both increasing quality and reduc-ing costs. Moreover, NPM led to an interest in unbundling services, so that the 'public interest' component of public services could be attended to by public bodies but the other components could be provided by external (private and third sector) organizations. However, as Wettenhall (2003) points out, so-called 'privatization' often resulted not in a complete and clear transfer of activity from the public to the private sector, but rather in the development of arrangements involving some sort of public–private mix. Moreover, Thynne (2000) distinguished five main roles involved in the management of public affairs: producer, owner, provider, regulator, facilitator, and suggested that, since each of them could be performed by either the state, the market or civil society, many different state/market/ civil society combinations are possible.

From this perspective, PPPs of the traditional sort were highly suspect, being associated with a 'corporatist' model of 'welfare state' intervention, rather than a minimalist conception of the role of the state. Some forms of PPP were nevertheless potentially valuable, especially where the private sector could bring the 'discipline of the market' to public services. Following this line, Christensen and Laegreid (2007) argue that PPPs can be seen both as a continuation of the NPM agenda and as a break with it. On the one hand, PPPs can be seen as a break with NPM because they allow a greater role to public sector organizations than is strictly necessary in a 'market-based' conception of publicly commissioned services. On the other hand, they can be seen as adding a more refined dimension than pure privatization to the ways that private firms can be used in public service delivery – a 'softer option', and one that is seen by citizens, governments and even by firms themselves as less confrontational, while 'luring the public sector into sharing some of its authority and expertise' (ibid., p. 181).

Interestingly, while principal–agent theory was invoked to justify PPPs within the NPM agenda, it was often used in a rather narrow and mechanistic way to justify breaking up public sector monopoly of service provision. Actually, principal–agent theory explores the generality of governance mechanisms to regulate the self-serving behaviour of agents (or principals) in conditions of uncertainty and information asymmetry. However, Child et al. (2005) point out that a partnership, too, has a problem when its managers are partly or wholly accountable to the partners, rather than solely to the partnership itself – and the problem is magnified where there are multiple partners and multiple agents. They draw the implication that principals would be well advised to put in place a combination of incentives and monitoring mechanisms to ensure achievement of the partnership's objectives, in such a way as to reduce suspicion between partners and agents and help the development of mutual trust through their working relationship. Talking mainly of the private sector, they naturally do not recommend the mechanism chosen by the UK government – extensive external inspection and audit regimes.

'Extending the discipline of the market', specifically in terms of applying competitive pressures to costs and service quality, was a core rationale of the Private Finance Initiative (PFI) in particular. It also informed the creation of vehicles for shared services, often around a 'hub' provided by a private sector partner but with contributions from the service departments of public sector partners. However, there are some inherent contradictions here. Klijn and Teisman (2005), for example, argue that it is highly debatable whether most PFI projects are PPPs at all, as they are highly contract-driven and have few elements of sharing. This is 'sham' partnering. This concern is reinforced by definitions of PPPs such as 'long term purchase of service contracts between the state and for-profit private sector bodies' (Flinders, 2006). Similarly, Hodge and Greve (2005) discern a family of five clusters within which PPPs may be viewed: public policy networks; civil society development initiatives; central business district or urban redevelopment activities; institutional cooperation; and long-term contracts for the provision of infrastructure or services. They suggest that in Australia PPPs are commonly seen as the last of these.

It is also interesting that the logic of 'extending the discipline of the market' led to an interest in the 'prime contractor' model, where a public sector agency appoints one single (private) organization to undertake all procurement and contracting of the service on its behalf. This model has been used quite often since the 1990s in major construction projects and in defence procurement. More recently, it has become the chosen model in the UK for the government's Flexible New Deal programme to tackle joblessness. However, it is clear that this model actually removes all competitive pressure upon the prime contractor itself, once the contract is let (although it remains in the interest of the prime contractor to ensure that it gets the best deals possible from all subcontractors in the supply chain).

Mitchell-Weaver and Manning (1991) discuss how in the 1980s this 'market discipline' conception of PPPs quickly became advocated in third world development by agencies that were strongly driven by the NPM paradigm at that time (for example, US Agency for International Development, the World Bank, and the International Monetary Fund), alongside the concepts of economic adjustment, privatization and deregulation.

Critique of PFI from public sector accounting perspective
Popular though the PFI model of PPPs has been with many governments around the world, it has been subjected to continual critique, particularly in the UK. Indeed, the critique of PFI has been one of the main avenues for researchers seeking to undermine the overall NPM approach to public management and governance. The critique of PFI from public sector accounting, from the late 1990s onwards, has directly attacked NPM assumptions of the inherent efficiency of market and quasi-market solutions.

Pollock et al. (2002), for example, have argued that PFI has brought no new capital investment into public services but rather has produced a debt that has to be serviced by future generations and that the government's case for using PFI rests on a VfM assessment skewed in favour of private finance; that the higher costs of PFI are due to financing costs that would not be incurred under public financing; that many hospital PFI schemes show VfM only after risk transfer, but the large risks said to be transferred are not justified; and that PFI more than doubles the cost of capital as a percentage of trusts' annual operating income.

The issue of risk transfer in PFI has been especially contentious. Broadbent et al. (2008) point out that, whilst the nature of the risks transferred to the private sector is estimated quantitatively, this is not the case with those risks and uncertainties that are shared or remain with the public sector, where they are often ignored or buried within PFI contracts that are 'commercially confidential' and therefore not available for public scrutiny.

They argue, too, that, because of the pervading power of 'accounting logic' aimed at finding ways to capture everything of importance through measurement technologies and marginalizing those that cannot, quantitative risk estimation is given a privileged – but unjustified – position in PFI decision-making processes. Similarly, Khadaroo (2008) found that the financial benefits of school PFI contracts in Northern Ireland, which were generally marginal or even negative, were dependent on the adjustments for risk transfer. The Inquiry into PPPs in New South Wales (Public Account Committee NSW Parliament, 2006, p. 4) reported cases where, despite the private sector accepting risks at the outset of the project, governments were later forced to step in and run the facility because of their obligation to continue public services – this illustrates the point made by Froud (2003) that, although some risks may in theory be transferred under PPPs, when service breakdown occurs it is the nature of the state to step back in, since it can never transfer the political risk of a contract not being delivered. Similar experiences have been noted in other parts of the world and have been used as evidence for 'conspiracy' theory approaches, suggesting that business interests have promoted PPPs in the full knowledge that they may be able to avoid some risks in practice, although the payment structure of the PPP is in their favour precisely because they are believed to be bearing these risks (Chen, 2009). Heald (2003) demonstrates that VfM analysis needs to pay attention to total risks, which may be sensitive to the choice of service delivery mechanism, whereas the rules for accounting treatment in PFI have focused attention upon risk transfer (that is, the sharing of risk).

The PFI treatment of non-quantifiable costs and benefits is also widely criticized. Khadaroo (2008) found that appraisal of school PFIs in Northern Ireland paid inadequate attention to the implications for the broader education estate, non-PFI schools, other parts of the public sector, and future generations of users and taxpayers. While the PFI and traditional public sector comparison included some assessment of non-financial criteria, the criteria and the weightings were subjective and arbitrary, and changes in the weightings could easily shift the balance in favour of the traditional public sector procurement option.

The treatment of options for appraisal, particularly the choice of and assumptions behind the 'public sector comparator' (PSC), has also been widely criticized. Heald (2003) highlights that the exclusion of certain alternatives from the options available has distorted the meaning of 'best VfM'. He argues that the public sector fragmentation associated with NPM has complicated the interpretation of VfM and that affordability to the client is not necessarily the same as VfM for the public sector as a whole. Shaoul (2005) found that, even after including risks, there are only marginal differences between PFI and conventional procurement, and that the appraisal methodology does not provide a robust criterion for distinguishing between them. Coulson (2008) suggests that the PFI appraisal process significantly underestimates the extent to which transaction costs are higher with PFI and overestimates the cost of conventional procurement approaches, for example, through the severe treatment of life-cycle and residual costs of assets managed traditionally by the public sector. These concerns are partially interrelated with research into hospital PFIs, which has found that 'risk transfer almost equals the amount required to bridge the gap between the PSC and the PFI option' (Pollock et al., 2002, p. 1208). Indeed, this research team found that small changes in either would significantly affect the ranking of different types of scheme.

More recently, Hellowell and Pollock (2009) find that there is a strong pattern of underfunding in PFI trusts compared with all other National Health Service (NHS) trusts, with the scale of underfunding showing a strong association with the size of the PFI scheme and therefore the size of the 'availability charge' under PFI arrangements. They suggest that this is one of the reasons underlying the deficit of many NHS trusts.

We should also note the widespread criticism that many PFI projects are not a 'real' partnership but rather a 'marriage for money', based on pressure from HM Treasury to get public sector borrowing for major capital projects 'off balance sheet'. This pressure is not a direct consequence of the NPM approach to PPPs, however, and is derived more from a (highly suspect) macroeconomic model that attaches especial significance to the negative effects of public sector borrowing, particularly on inflation. This pressure is not unique to the UK. Ball (2009, p. 7), for instance, suggests that one key reason for PPPs in Australia derives from public sector accounting practice: 'to obscure the real public debt position of governments. Australian interview responses assert very strongly that credit rating agencies factor all outstanding liabilities into their credit ratings and that PPPs offer no particular benefits in this direction. It is not clear, however, where this is fully understood and accepted in Government.'

Finally, Kogut (1991) develops the concept of joint ventures (although not of the PPP type) as 'real (call) options' on the future opportunity to invest in joint activities by paying a relatively small current price. Liu and Cheah (2009) modelled as real options the support and repayment features of a PPP for a wastewater treatment plant in Southern China to construct a 'negotiation band' incorporating these option values, so that the feasible bargaining range for both parties can be enlarged. Alonso-Conde et al. (2007) show, in relation to a large toll road project, the Melbourne CityLink, that the imposed conditions can be treated as real options, that these options affect the incentive to invest and how the public sector may

be transferring considerable value to the private sector through government guarantees.

The strategic management approach: collaborative advantage
The strategic management approach to PPPs derives from four separate
strands of theory: the economics of collaborative processes (based on an
understanding of economies of specialization and integration); theories of
organizational studies on collaborative behaviour (particularly in relation
to trust); the literature on innovation, learning and dynamic capabilities;
and concepts of relational contracting from transaction cost economics.
Taken together, these strands were developed in the 1990s by a number
of authors (Huxham, 1993; Kanter, 1994) into a theory of 'collaborative
advantage' to rival the theory of 'competitive advantage' that dominated
the 1980s.

The traditional economics of collaborative processes typically focused
on the opportunities afforded for specialization, particularly through
economies of scale and economies of task learning, as each partner can
specialize. These specialized organizations were then expected to trade in
the marketplace. Williamson (1975) pointed out how rarely this happened
in many of the huge hierarchically organized firms of the day, which preferred internal to market trading. In doing so, they avoided opportunistic
behaviour by market suppliers – but also lost many of the advantages that
specialization might bring. His analysis led to the conclusion that collaboration based on more reliable governance structures and processes – for
example, relational contracting, trust-based alliances – might well significantly improve the efficiency of the overall production system, as well as
that of individual organizations. It has spawned a large literature on how
these collaborative governance structures and processes are designed and
what effects they have (Lorange and Roos, 1992; Dussauge and Garrette,
1999; Child et al., 2005).

A particular difficulty with this literature has been that the empirical evidence base has been relatively weak, consisting largely of (often contested)
case studies of specific collaborations and partnerships. Key parts of the
theoretical foundations have been tested only sporadically and weakly –
for example, the key propositions of transactions cost economics in relation to collaborative behaviour (Carter and Hodgson, 2006). However,
there is a plausible line of argument which suggests that this weakness
may be very difficult to correct – namely, that all the elements making
up collaborative advantage share one characteristic that is problematic
for empirical investigation, namely that they all involve synergy, that is,
positive non-linearities in the ways in which inputs, processes, outputs
and outcomes relate to each other. These are very hard to identify and

calibrate statistically, so that we are still rather in the dark about even their existence, never mind their magnitude.

There is also another section of the strategic management toolkit that has so far been rarely deployed in relation to PPPs – the analysis of the dynamics of change, innovation and dynamic capabilities. While there is now some interesting research on the distinctive features of innovation in the public sector (Hartley, 2009) and the role that dynamic capabilities play in enhancing innovative capacity (Harvey et al., 2010), these critically important concepts in modern strategic management have still not been rigorously applied to PPPs, so that the triggers of dynamic change in services provided through PPP mechanisms are still only vaguely understood.

Public governance (from the 1990s)
NPM was the dominant paradigm in public administration for a decade from the mid-1980s (although always contested), but by the mid-1990s the public governance paradigm was emerging and provided a very different way of viewing relationships between actors in the public domain, including PPPs. In the UK, New Labour's 'third way' and 'stakeholder society' were strongly influenced by the research on governance summarized in Rhodes (1997) and Rhodes and Stoker (1999). This early literature focused particularly on the importance of multiple goals held by multiple stakeholders, within a negotiated framework of 'rules of the game', including dimensions such as transparency, stakeholder engagement, the equalities agenda and sustainability. Partnerships now became celebrated not simply because of their ability to deliver on the NPM agenda of efficiency and service effectiveness (although this agenda has naturally never gone away), but also because of their ability to deliver on these governance criteria in a more reliable way than could be assured by externalization through competitive tendering to an anonymous market of potential suppliers. Consequently, the evaluation of such partnerships started to take note of the achievement of governance principles, not simply the '3Es' (Bovaird and Löffler, 2003). This was evident in the way in which audit and inspection regimes in the UK (particularly in local government, first under 'Best Value', then under 'Comprehensive Performance Assessment' (CPA)) broadened their remit and metrics to take into account a much wider range of criteria than those simply related to service delivery. Ironically, this meant that contract letting had to pay attention to criteria that under the previous Compulsory Competitive Tendering regime would have been regarded as illegal (because 'anti-competitive'). Moreover, these governance criteria may be seen as especially important in relation to those PPPs that lock in public agencies to 15- to 25-year deals with private sector providers, since this is likely to significantly reduce the policy flexibility of future governments.

However, few of these tendencies found their way into the 'traditional' PFI model, although they played an important role (at least in theory) in the design of the investment-led PPPs that were being used to rebuild all UK secondary schools and many new NHS hospitals and clinics, in close negotiation with local public sector agencies. Similar agendas were evident internationally (Wettenhall and Thynne, 2000) – for example, UNECE (2009) provided guidance for the UN family of organizations on governance criteria in PPPs.

Quickly, public governance developed further themes, such as 'joined-up government' ('whole of government' in Australia) and 'outcomes-oriented commissioning'. Interestingly, central government departments tended not to develop 'joined-up' (i.e. multi-department) PPPs, tending to keeping life simple by entering into single-department arrangements with private suppliers. However, they encouraged local government and other local service providers (NHS, police, fire, etc.) to form multi-service partnerships at local level, from the strategic level of the 'local strategic partnerships' (LSPs) to thematic partnerships (such as 'community safety partnerships') and functional 'service delivery partnerships' (such as customer service PPPs to coordinate a large proportion of citizen and service user interfaces with public services in an area, usually through large-scale new ICT systems). As all PPPs at local level were subject to assessment through the CPA for local authorities (and later 'Comprehensive Area Assessment' (CAA), which was multi-agency), they found themselves needing to jump through 'governance' hoops that were rather more demanding than those at central government level (Audit Commission, 2009).

Internationally, these public governance developments had different implications – there were few equivalents of the UK LSPs – and none of the CPA or CAA – but there were strong pressures in many countries for PPPs to take into account more objectives and outcomes than those of the narrow service areas that the PPP regarded as its 'core business'. (However, as in the UK, this tended to be more true at local than central government level.)

The increasing outcomes orientation of public service commissioning was consistent with both NPM – 'funding outcomes, not inputs' (Osborne and Gaebler, 1992) – and the public governance model (emphasizing incorporation of citizens and users in decisions about what the public sector should be trying to achieve) (Friedman, 1997). However, in practice it has been much more evident since the public governance model became more widespread, partly, it seems, because service providers are still more comfortable talking about inputs, processes and outputs than about outcomes, which they see as high risk, since influenced by so many external factors out of the control of either providers or commissioners.

This outcomes orientation developed at different paces in different countries. While it was common in many OECD countries, few built it into mandatory commissioning models in the way done by UK government departments, and it was even rarer to find outcome-based contracting for public services, as has recently occurred in the UK programmes for dealing with joblessness and some children's services (such as fostering).

Flinders (2006) identifies a common pattern of PPP development, in which governments first experiment with construction or 'low-salience' services (roads, waste etc.) but then move incrementally to other areas (e.g. social care, education). Moreover, he identifies 'organizational drift' – whereby services often move from centrally controlled through arm's-length agencies to the 'periphery', for example, in PPPs (with few instances of the reverse direction) – and this movement, in turn, often leads to the establishment of independent bodies to regulate the relationship between the state commissioning body and the private partner or the PPP responsible for service delivery. He suggests that therefore many modern PPPs exist within 'emergent structures of MLG' (multi-level governance), which consist of 'complex matrices in which functions have been redistributed both vertically and horizontally' (ibid., p. 233). Naturally, this 'fragmentation' of state structures (Rosenau, 2000) is likely to require 'joining up', for which regulatory bodies may provide one mechanism.

Finally, some insights into the public governance approach, with its emphasis on connected networks and decentralized decision-making through multiple stakeholders, have come in recent years from the complex adaptive systems approach, and the similar but rather narrower approach of evolutionary theory (Alter and Hage, 1993). Aritua et al. (2008), for example, apply the complex adaptive systems perspective to modern project management, arguing that the multi-project management which is now common is neither an extension nor a scaled-up version of single-project management. Situations faced by multi-project managers are often messy, unpredictable and non-linear. Genuine multi-project environments exhibit the characteristics of complex adaptive systems, so that multi-project managers must seek a balance between trusting project managers and allowing them flexibility while seeking the necessary level of control and accountability. Increased information-sharing among project teams and organizations affecting the objectives of a multi-project environment will allow projects to self-organize to respond to changing business environments. Attempts to deliver projects in strictly controlled internal environments hamper the ability of multi-projects to adapt to or fit real-world requirements such as innovation, sustainability, safety and security issues that affect modern projects.

Postmodern theory (from the 1990s)

During the latest stage in the intellectual journey of PPPs, in a variety of postmodernist theorizations, they have generally been treated as more interesting for their symbolic meaning than as specific manifestations of public service delivery mechanisms. Skelcher and Mathur (2004) analyse multi-organizational partnerships through a discourse–institutions–meaning framework to explore the relationship between partnership governance arrangements and public service performance. They suggest the need to investigate the 'new' from the position of the 'old', and that being attentive to the emotion behind a response, as much as the words actually used, can reveal what has been lost and what has been gained. This problematizes the concepts regularly used in partnership working – 'partnership', 'public involvement' – which are shown to be discursively constructed and therefore needing critical evaluation in terms of their impact on democratic and organizational performance. As Hodge and Greve (2005, p. 335) suggest, the 'PPP language game' fits the modern public sector like a glove and has acquired higher political legitimacy than the culture of competition through contracting or coordination through bureaucratic arrangements. Hodge (2009) comments that 'PPP symbolizes positive business relationships, a new way of governing, sophistication, innovation, . . . and performance . . . It is deliciously ambiguous'.

Bang (2002) argues that authority is not only hierarchical and bureaucratic, but also communicative and negotiable. The challenge faced by hypermodern political systems is to enable more and more organizations, individuals and communities to engage in their rule, transforming or reforming their identities and conducts so that they become amenable to this rule – a phenomenon he calls culture governance. He suggests that political parties must be able to combine concerns for government and governance by recognizing the limitations of the kind of individualist-oriented 'hit-and-run' politics that characterizes engagement in public–private partnerships. In future, public projects involving civil society and citizens must therefore be connected with a 'politics of presence'. He suggests that, if political parties wish to activate some of the huge governing potential drifting around in society, they must take charge of the processes of culture governance, in their role as ethically and politically responsive representatives, going beyond constitutionalism and beyond partnerships in the locality.

A final word

Theories shouldn't go round in circles, but fashions do, including fashions in theory. Welfare economists who found that their interest and contribution to government–business relations in the 1950s and 1960s were of no interest to governments in the 1980s now find a new home for their theories in current debates on regulatory regimes. Historical institutionalists now find that the 'neo-institutionalist' approach offers them much scope to resurrect their previous explanations of how decisions and behaviour are structured by social, economic and political institutions, albeit under new headings. Marxists who had filed away their cuttings on the Miliband–Poulantzas diatribes of the early 1970s now find they need to dust them off to follow Jessop's latest version of regulationist theory.

We are currently in an apparently 'rich' intellectual period where almost all the social science perspectives that have been chronicled in this chapter are currently making vibrant and, it would seem, potentially valuable contributions to the debate on the nature, role, impact and future of PPPs. These single-disciplinary and interdisciplinary understandings of PPPs do not simply coexist but actively jostle and co-evolve with each other. However, this may be a temporary phenomenon. It smacks of explanatory breakdown – since none of the perspectives is particularly convincing, all can find a place in the intellectual marketplace. In other words, rather than 'richness', this may simply signal theoretical ineffectiveness. It may be that another dominant paradigm is about to break, which will overshadow all of these approaches for a generation or so, as welfare economics did in the 1950s and 1960s and NPM did in the 1980s. (Or, then again, perhaps not!)

In the meantime, the multifarious nature of our understanding of PPPs now makes it difficult for critical comment to develop a constructive perspective from which to evaluate PPPs and suggest options for their change. In consequence, while there has been considerable criticism of specific manifestations of PPPs (like PFI), there is still a considerable interest in and optimism about their potential in general.

References

Alonso-Conde, Ana Belen, Christine Brown and Javier Rojo-Suarez (2007), 'Public private partnerships: incentives, risk transfer and real options', *Review of Financial Economics*, **16** (4), 335–49.

Alter, C. and J. Hage (1993), *Organisations Working Together*, London: Sage.

Aritua, Bernard, Nigel J. Smith and Denise Bower (2008), 'Construction client multi-projects – a complex adaptive systems perspective', *International Journal of Project Management*, **27** (1), 72–9.

Audit Commission (2009), *Good Governance Standard Diagnostic*, London: Audit Commission.

Ball, R. (2009), 'Provision of public service infrastructure-PPPs in the UK and Australia – a comparative study', paper to IRSPM Conference, Copenhagen, April.

Bang, Henrik P. (2002), 'Opening up the bureaucracy through culture governance', paper to Conference on New Forms of Democracy? The Reform and Transformation of Democratic Institutions, 17–18 May, UC Berkeley Institute of European Studies.

Blakely, Edward (1994), *Planning Local Economic Development: Theory and Practice*, 2nd edn, Thousand Oaks, CA: Sage.

Bovaird, Tony and Elke Löeffler (2003), 'Evaluating the quality of public governance:

indicators, models and methodologies', *International Review of Administrative Sciences*, **69** (3), 313–28.

Broadbent, J., J. Gill and R. Laughlin (2008), 'Identifying and controlling risk: the problem of uncertainty in the private finance initiative in the UK's National Health Service', *Critical Perspectives on Accounting*, **19**, 40–78.

Brooks, Harvey, Lance Liebman and Corinne S. Schelling (eds) (1984), *Public–Private Partnership: New Opportunities for Meeting Social Needs*, Cambridge, MA: Ballinger.

Burnham, June (2001), 'Local public–private partnerships in France: rarely disputed, scarcely competitive, weakly regulated', *Public Policy and Administration*, **16** (4), 47–60.

Carmeli, Abraham and Lynndee Kemmet (2006), 'Exploring fit in public sector organizations', *Public Money & Management*, **26** (1), 73–80.

Carter, Richard and Geoffrey Hodgson (2006), 'The impact of empirical tests of transaction cost economics on the debate on the nature of the firm', *Strategic Management Journal*, **27**, 461–76.

Chen, Cheng (2009), *The Impacts of Governance Problems on Risk Allocation of Public Private Partnerships: Case Studies from Taiwan and China*, doctoral thesis, Birmingham: University of Birmingham.

Child, John, David Faulkner and Stephen Tallman (2005), *Cooperative Strategy: Managing Alliances, Networks, and Joint Ventures*, Oxford: Oxford University Press.

Christensen, Tom and Per Laegreid (2007), *Transcending New Public Management: The Transformation of Public Sector Reforms*, Aldershot: Ashgate.

Coulson, Andrew (2008), 'Value for money in PFI proposals: a commentary on the 2004 UK Treasury Guidelines for Public Sector Comparators', *Public Administration*, **86** (2), 483–98.

Cowie, H. (1996), *Private Partnerships and Public Networks in Europe*, London: Federal Trust.

Davies, Jonathan S. (2003), 'Partnerships versus regimes: why regime theory cannot explain urban coalitions in the UK', *Journal of Urban Affairs*, **25** (3), 253–70.

Dussauge, Pierre and Bernard Garrette (1999), *Cooperative Strategy: Competing Successfully through Strategic Alliances*, Chichester: John Wiley.

Fainstain, Susan S. (1994), *The City Builders: Property, Politics and Planning in London and New York*, Oxford: Basil Blackwell.

Fainstain, Susan S. (2001), *The City Builders: Property Development in London and New York*, Lawrence, KA: University of Kansas Press.

Flinders, Matthew (2006), 'Public/private: the boundaries of the state', in Colin Hay, Michael Lister and David Marsh (eds), *The State: Theories and Issues*, Basingstoke: Palgrave Macmillan, pp. 223–47.

Friedman, Mark (1997), *Organizing by Outcomes, A Different Organization Chart for State/ Local Partnerships*, Fiscal Policy Studies Institute.

Fosler, R. Scott and R.A. Berger (eds) (1982), *Public Private Partnership in American Cities: Seven Case Studies*, Lexington, MA: Lexington Press.

Froud, Julie (2003), 'The Private Finance Initiative: risk uncertainty and the state', *Accounting Organisation and Society*, **28** (6), 567–89.

Harding, Alan (1994), *Public Private Partnerships in Urban Regeneration*, Liverpool: Liverpool John Moores University.

Hartley, Jean (2009), 'The innovation landscape for public service organizations', in Jean Hartley, Cam Donaldson, Chris Skelcher and Mike Wallace (eds), *Managing to Improve Public Services*, Oxford: Oxford University Press, pp. 197–216.

Harvey, David (1989), 'From managerialism to entrepreneurialism: the transformation in urban governance in late capitalism', Geografiska Annaler, Series B, *Human Geography*, **71** (1), 3–17.

Harvey, Gill, Chris Skelcher, Eileen Spencer, Pauline Jas and Kieran Walshe (2010), 'Absorptive capacity in a non-market environment: a knowledge-based approach to analysing the performance of public sector organizations', *Public Management Review*, **12** (1), 77–97.

Heald, David (2003), 'Value for money tests and accounting treatment in PFI schemes', *Accounting, Auditing & Accountability Journal*, **16** (3), 342–71.

Hellowell, Mark and Allyson M. Pollock (2009), 'The private financing of NHS hospitals: politics, policy and practice', *Economic Affairs*, **29**, 13–19.

Hirschman, Albert (1958), *The Strategy of Economic Development*, New Haven, CT: Yale University Press.

Hodge, Graeme (2009), 'Public–private partnerships: the phenomenon, the brand and the future', paper to Civil Contractors Federation National Conference, 21–25 October, Perth.

Hodge, Graeme and Carsten Greve (2005), 'Public private partnerships: a policy for all seasons?', in Graeme Hodge and Carsten Greve (eds), *The Challenge of Public–Private Partnerships: Learning from International Experience*, Cheltenham, UK and Northampton, MA, USA: Edward Elgar, pp. 332–50.

Huxham, Chris (1993), 'Pursuing collaborative advantage', *Journal of the Operational Research Society*, **44** (6), 599–611.

Jacobs, Brian (2000), 'Partnership in Pittsburgh: the evaluation of complex local initiatives', in Stephen Osborne (ed.), *Public–Private Partnerships: Theory and Practice in International Perspective*, London: Routledge, pp. 219–34.

Jessop, Bob and Ngai-Ling Sum (no date), 'An entrepreneurial city in action: Hong Kong's emerging strategies in and for (inter-)urban competition', Department of Sociology, Lancaster University at www.comp.lancs.ac.uk/sociology/soc045rj.html.

Jezierski, L. (1988), 'Political limits to development in two declining cities: Cleveland and Pittsburgh', in J. Rothenberg and M. Wallace (eds), *Deindustrialisation and the Economic Restructuring of American Industry*, Vol. 3, Greenwich, CT: JAI Press, pp. 173–89.

Kanter, Rosabeth Moss (1994), 'Collaborative advantage: the art of alliances', *Harvard Business Review*, July–August, 96–108.

Kerr, Derek (1998), 'The Private Finance Initiative and the changing governance of the built environment', *Urban Studies*, **35** (12), 2277–301.

Khadaroo, Iqbal (2008), 'The actual evaluation of school PFI bids for value for money in the UK public sector', *Critical Perspectives on Accounting*, **19** (8), 1321–45.

Klijn, Erik-Hans and Geert Teisman (2005), 'Public–private partnerships as the management of co-production: strategic and institutional obstacles in a difficult marriage', in Graeme Hodge and Carsten Greve (eds), *The Challenge of Public–Private Partnerships: Learning from International Experience*, Cheltenham, UK and Northampton, MA, USA: Edward Elgar, pp. 95–116.

Kogut, B. (1991), 'Joint ventures and the option to expand and acquire', *Management Science*, **37**, 19–32.

Le Galès, Patrick and John Mawson (1994), *Management Innovations in Urban Policy: Lessons from France*, Luton: Local Government Management Board.

Li, Bing and Akintola Akintoye (2003), 'An overview of public–private partnership', in Akintola Akintoye, Matthias Beck and Cliff Hardcastle (eds), *Public–Private Partnerships: Managing Risks and Opportunities*, Oxford: Blackwell, pp. 3–30.

Liu, Jicai and Charles Y.J. Cheah (2009), 'Real option application in PPP/PFI project negotiation', *Construction Management and Economics*, **27** (4), 331–42.

Logan, J.R. and H.L. Molotch (1987), *Urban Fortunes: the Political Economy of Place*, Berkeley, CA: University of California Press.

Lorange, Peter and J. Roos (1992), *Strategic Alliances: Formation, Implementation and Evolution*, Oxford: Blackwell.

Lorrain, Dominque (1991), 'Public goods and private operators in France', in Richard Batley and Gerry Stoker (eds), *Local Government in Europe: Trends and Developments*, Basingstoke, UK: Macmillan, pp. 89–109.

Mitchell-Weaver, Clyde and Brenda Manning (1991), 'Public–private partnerships in third world development: a conceptual overiew', *Studies in Comparative International Development*, **26** (4), 45–67.

Myrdal, Gunnar (1957), *Economic Theory and Underdeveloped Regions*, New York: Harper and Row.

Osborne, David and Ted Gaebler (1992), *Reinventing Government*, New York: Perseus Books.

Pollock, Allyson M., Jean Shaoul and Neil Vickers (2002), 'Private finance and "value for money" in NHS hospitals: a policy in search of a rationale?', *British Medical Journal*, **324** (7347), 1205–9.

Public Account Committee NSW Parliament (2006), 'Inquiry into Public–Private Partnerships', Report No. 159, available at: www.parliament.nsw.gov.all/publicaccounts.

Rhodes, Rod (1997), *Understanding Governance: Policy Networks, Governance, Reflexivity and Accountability*, Buckingham: Open University Press.

Rhodes, Rod and Gerry Stoker (1999), *The New Management of British Local Governance*, Basingstoke: Palgrave Macmillan.

Rose, Edgar (ed.) (1986), *New Roles for Old Cities*, Aldershot: Gower.

Rosenau, Pauline Vaillancourt (ed.) (2000), *Public–Private Policy Partnerships*, Cambridge, MA: MIT Press.

Shaoul, J. (2005), 'A critical appraisal of the private finance initiative: selecting a financial method or allocating economic wealth?', *Critical Perspectives on Accounting*, **16** (4), 441–71.

Skelcher, Chris and Navdeep Mathur (2004), 'Governance arrangements and public service performance: reviewing and reformulating the research agenda', Working Paper, Bristol: Advanced Institute of Management Research.

Stone, Clarence (1989), *Regime Politics: Governing Atlanta, 1946–1988*, Lawrence, KA: University Press of Kansas.

Sullivan, Helen and Chris Skelcher (2002), *Working Across Boundaries: Collaboration in Public Services*, Basingstoke: Palgrave Macmillan.

Thynne, Ian (2000), 'Notes on understanding the public–private mix', paper to Working Group on Public Enterprise Management and the Public–Private Mix, IASIA Annual Conference, Beijing, July.

UNECE (2009), *Guidebook on Promoting Good Governance for Public Private Partnerships*, UNECE.

Vincent-Jones, Peter (1994), 'The limits of contractual order in public sector transacting', *Legal Studies*, **14**, 364–92.

West, Karen (2005), 'From bilateral to trilateral governance in local government contracting in France', *Public Administration*, **83** (2), 473–92.

Wettenhall, Roger (2003), 'The rhetoric and reality of public–private partnerships', *Public Organization Review: A Global Journal*, **3**, 77–107.

Wettenhall, Roger and Ian Thynne (2000), 'Emerging patterns of governance: synergy, partnerships and the public–private mix', *International Journal of Public–Private Partnerships*, **3** (1), 3–14.

Williamson, Oliver (1975), *Markets and Hierarchies: Analysis and Antitrust Implications*, New York: Free Press.

4 Public–private partnerships: deciphering meaning, message and phenomenon
Erik-Hans Klijn

Introduction: deciphering public–private partnerships

There is no doubt that public–private partnerships (PPPs) have been a dominant issue in governmental rhetoric but also in governmental practice. In many countries, governments have turned to the idea of PPPs, or partnerships in general, as a vehicle to realize better policy outcomes, or to enhance investments in fields like infrastructure, health or even social policy.

However, at the same time the idea of PPPs has been a contested concept (see Hodge and Greve, 2005; Weihe, 2008). Even if we roughly define a PPP as a 'more or less sustainable cooperation between public and private actors in which joint products and/or services are developed and in which risks, costs and profits are shared' (Klijn and Teisman, 2003, p. 137), we can still find many different forms under this heading.

PPPs have been given many meanings, been used in a number of ways and seen in many manifestations. Now this is all very normal for many ideas and terms used both in the world of practice and in the world of science, but in this case there seems to be more confusion than usual. In general we can find confusion in at least three areas, which are also connected:

- confusion about the *meaning* of PPPs: not only do we find many different definitions, but also many different appraisals and emotions;
- confusion about the *argumentations and rationality* of PPPs: there is much discussion on what precisely PPPs should or could achieve (better value for money, more investments, innovations etc.) and these argumentations often seem to be contradictory;
- confusion about what preferable or *best form* PPPs should take: in both the scientific literature and the many policy documents that aim to promote PPPs we can find a wide variety of forms that are seen as the best or the most workable in which to cast the cooperation (Skelcher, 2005).

In this chapter we shall elaborate on each of these confusions. We shall show that the confusion about meaning has to do with the fact that a PPP is a brand, and brands are necessarily vague. We shall see that the confusion about argumentation has to do in essence with the fact that a PPP is a hybrid idea. And we shall show that we see so many forms because we are faced with many different situations, but also that the discussion about form is probably not the point. After we have examined these confusions and thus deciphered the PPP discussion, we shall ask ourselves what really matters in the whole discussion. And we shall find that it is not the form of PPPs.

PPP as brand: motivating and binding force
If we judge the PPP concept by scientific measures, we are of course disappointed by its ambiguity. But that is probably the wrong way to look at the concept, certainly if we consider its use in policy documents, party programmes and political speeches. And this certainly should be done, since in the case of the PPP the concept is created just as much, probably even more, by the practical use (policy documents, reports from audit commissions and departments etc.) as by the scientific use. The UK version of PPP, coming from the Private Finance Initiative (PFI), for instance, has dominated the discussion in both practical and scientific terms (see also Weihe, 2008). In PFI, innovating contracting is the most important element and partnership is translated into a long-term contracting relation between a public and a private partner. It also creates added value because the private partner can bid on a more generalized set of requirements and can profit from the long-term contract and economize on construction and maintenance.

This idea has spread to other countries. The core documents of the PPP knowledge centre in the Ministry of Finance in The Netherlands, and the ideas on PPP that are being put forward there, have been taken directly from the UK PFI documents (Klijn, 2009; see Kenniscentrum, 1998, 1999, 2001, 2002).

Partnership as brand
Thus, in relation to PPP, it is clear that the content of the discussion is more strongly influenced by the practical language and day-to-day life than are most discussions (see also Lindner, 1999). But in policy documents and political speech, concepts have a quite different use than in scientific debates. Concepts are brands – images that evoke meaning and emotions, and attract supporters. In that sense PPP is not a scientific concept but a (political) brand. A brand is 'name, term, sign, symbol or design, or a combination of these, intended to identify the goods or services of one seller or group of sellers and to differentiate them from those of competitors' (Kotler et al., 1999, p. 571). The brand is not the product

itself but the meaning and identity it defines. Someone buying a Dior product is not only buying the perfume but also the connected identity and status. And this is the same with partnerships or PPPs. It is not the product (the cooperation, the form, the phenomenon) that is the most important from the brand's point of view, but the identity and emotions that it communicates. Thus in the UK the word 'partnership' was closely linked with Blair's New Labour story. Partnership is about doing things differently, tackling problems together with society and private actors instead of doing it alone or privatizing it to the market. It holds a promise of both joined-up government (Pollitt et al., 2004) and efficiency, and thus points the way forward and motivates local governments, citizens or non-profit organizations. It helped Blair to distinguish himself and his New Labour from others, mostly the Tories. And distinguishing is exactly what a brand must do! So the brand PPP evokes images and emotions that are much more important that the precise definition.

When establishing an urban renewal corporation, the Sandwell Borough in Birmingham uses this image to motivate other actors in its text:

> The Sandwell URC will be a highly focused, task-driven, independent vehicle for driving the large scale, physical economic transformation of the central core of the Arc of opportunity . . . The company will be run in a business-like way and will be unfettered by its affiliation to two public sector agencies . . . Fundamental to achieve the Company's aim will be to engage and work in a coordinated manner with other agencies and partnerships with an interest in the physical development of this area.[1]

Thus from a brand point of view it is the meaning and identity that matter, not so much the product itself, although of course there must be a link between the two. 'Partnership' and 'public–private partnership' will be used in quite different ways by different governments, in different countries and so forth, in an attempt to create the right image (and connected emotion) that will do the trick. This will of course increase the ambiguity and confusion of the concept, but that is a scientific, not a practical worry.

Ambiguity is essential!
Ambiguity is even necessary to motivate many different actors. The more you specify the partnership construction beforehand, the more likely it is that disagreement will arise. Involved actors will have different views on problem, profit, division of risks etc., that will provoke conflict and possible deadlocks. The concept of PPP must be able to absorb all these complexities, and thus a certain amount of ambiguity is useful. Ambiguity creates the possibility that different actors embrace the idea despite the

fact that they do not agree on several aspects. That is exactly one of the strong points and advantages of a brand: because of its ambiguity and its emotional value, it can bind actors and connect them, but it can never live up to a scientific expectation of clarity and rigour!

Why PPPs? PPP as a hybrid idea

We not only see many meanings of PPP but also many different reasons why they might be useful. In general, policy-makers and researchers assume that a more intensive cooperation between public and private parties will produce better and more efficient policy outcomes (the so-called added value) and policy products (Savas, 2000; Ghobadian et al., 2004; Hodge and Greve, 2005). The key 'partnership' mechanism involves private parties in the decision-making process earlier and more intensively than is the case with more traditional client–supplier or principal–agent relationships. But the way this should be done and the assumption that this improves interactions and outputs are shown to be quite different in the available literature. This is because the idea of PPPs is a hybrid idea. One can find assumptions from two major theoretical perspectives in public administration: new public management (NPM) and governance.

PPP as new public management arrangement

On the one hand, one can recognize ideas from NPM that have become dominant in public administration since the 1980s. According to these ideas, governments should focus on the formulation of public policy and leave the implementation to other bodies (private organizations or non-profit organizations) (Osborne and Gaebler, 1992). For that, a separation of policy implementation and policy formation should be encouraged by privatization, outsourcing, agentification and a stronger emphasis on the market mechanism and on involvement of private actors (Hood, 1991). Public actors should control the implementation by performance indicators or market mechanisms.

One can clearly trace a number of these ideas in the PPP debate where it stresses efficiency, and mentions tendering and outsourcing as possible forms of organizing PPPs (NAO, 2002; Greve, 2007). This is especially strong in the literature on the PFI in the UK, which has so dominated the discussion on PPP in the last 10 to 15 years. This form of PPP stresses the contractual character of the arrangement. The design, build, finance and commercial operation of an infrastructure project (such as a road, or a building like a school) are integrated into a contract (a DBFO contract). The added value lies in the lower costs of coordination between the various components (often expressed as 'efficiency' or 'value for money' (VfM) gains). Even though these efficiencies are necessary for a PPP concession, they would not be sufficient to attract private or public sector interest. Their interest arises from the opportunity to create substantive added value. For example, the PFI tendering system used in the UK for the road construction bundles – design, build, finance, operate (DBFO) – are contracted out to private consortia for a period of 30 years. The consortium can use more sustainable (expensive) building materials to save on future maintenance costs. The payment system rewards the 'availability' of roads (NAO, 2002; Office of the Deputy Prime Minister (ODPM), 2002, 2004a) rather than second-guessing the costs of constructing them. The opportunity for a long-term involvement in a project provides both the potential for devising new solutions to problems and protects against risk aversion to what is untested. Of course the essence of such a model is that the public actor can clearly specify the goals at the beginning.

These ideas about efficiency, risk allocation and so on are obviously inspired by the ideas of NPM. However, this can also be said about the suggestion that PPP should be given clear performance indicators and about the idea that we should organize PPPs into separate bodies, at arm's length, as it were (Pollitt et al., 2004). Arm's length means that separate bodies are created at some distance from political institutions. Distinctions are often made between disaggregation (the degree to which a body is separated from political and governmental institutions) and autonomization (the degree to which these bodies have discretionary power to make independent decisions) (see ibid.). Being at arm's length enables managerial principles to become more dominant in these bodies, which will enhance efficiency and effectiveness (ibid.). These 'arm's-length' bodies should be guided by performance criteria previously set by political bodies. 'Arm's-length' bodies and performance indicators can both be found in the contractual PFI form, but also in the idea of urban regeneration partnerships, mentioned in the previous section (Geddes, 2008). These partnerships are joint initiatives of public and private actors and are used to develop, but above all to implement, urban policies and to restructure specific areas. Or, as Lord Rogers, who led the Urban Task Force in the UK, stated,

> The pace of regeneration could be increased if responsibilities for delivering area programs was placed in the hands of 'arm's length' organizations, owned by local partnerships. Urban Regeneration Companies could not only oversee work to completion, but also raise private finance and undertake direct development where necessary. (Urban Task Force, 1999)

PPP as governance arrangement
However, one can also recognize ideas in the PPP literature that resemble more closely the arguments presented in the vast literature. That literature stresses the importance of horizontal coordination between public actors

and other actors, and the fact that it is difficult or impossible to revert to top-down steering in a network society in which independence has increased because of specialization and knowledge spread, and in which citizens emphasize voice rather than loyalty (see Frederickson, 2005; Sørensen and Torfing, 2007; Koppenjan and Klijn, 2004). Governance literature emphasizes the complex nature of decision-making and service delivery, the dependence of other actors and the need for horizontal coordination and active forms of network management that promote cooperation between public and private actors, the generation of new innovative solutions and the use of knowledge among the actors to reduce veto powers and obstruction (see Agranoff and McGuire, 2001; Koppenjan and Klijn, 2004; Sørenson and Torfing, 2007).

One can clearly also find some core elements of the discussion on governance in the ideas about PPP, for example the assumption that co-production between public and private actors results in exchanging more information and the use of each other's knowledge to generate more innovative and better products and policy outputs for complex societal problems. Although the governance literature does mention organizational structure and form (Mandell, 2001), it tends to stress institutional and especially managerial characteristics that are decisive for achieving good outcomes. These managerial efforts are often labelled network management (Gage and Mandell, 1990; Agranoff and McGuire, 2001; Meier and O'Toole, 2001; Koppenjan and Klijn, 2004). Without these managerial strategies, reaching desirable outcomes is assumed to be very difficult.

Form or managerial activity?
If we look at the various arguments about why PPPs result in better or more efficient outcomes, we see different groups of arguments coming from different theoretical and practical perspectives. This is also a source of confusion about PPPs, which can be summarized in a nutshell. The question is whether it is the form and monitoring of the partnerships that makes them work, the assumption implicit in the NPM types of arguments for PPPs, or whether PPPs are an opportunity to work more closely together and it is the managerial effort (i.e. the network management activities) that makes them work. Government documents tend to stress the form because it can be predetermined and fits a more central control-oriented perspective of central government. But is this the most plausible argument? We come back to this issue in the next section.

The organizational form: theoretical arguments and practical forms
A wide variety of forms in which PPP cooperation is used exists. The forms range from strongly contractual, like the PFI contracts in the UK, to more

informal, like project groups without any formal judicial status, and to tightly organized consortiums. The discussion on the choice of organizational form is fairly prominent in the partnership literature and even more so in the government texts (NAO, 2002; Kenniscentrum, 2002; 2004; Klijn, 2009). This is also the case for the discussion about urban regeneration partnerships (Urban Task Force, 1999; Kort and Klijn, 2009). However, one cannot find definitive statements about which organizational form is the best for partnerships. The literature on PFI suggests that good and tight contracts are best. The implicit assumption is that public actors have a clear idea about what they want to achieve and thus to contract out. The literature on URCs suggests that tight partnership forms at arm's length from the government are best (Urban Task Force, 1999, 2005; VROM, 2002).

A typology of public–private partnerships
The wide variety of literature shows that the discussion focuses on the form of organization on the one hand (whether the partnership is organized in a strongly formalized way, like a contract or a newly established organization or not) and whether the relation between the public and private actors is more an equal (principal to principal) relation or more closely resembles principal–agent relations (see Osborne, 2000; Hodge and Greve, 2005; Weihe, 2008). The combination of these two dimensions produces Table 4.1. Each cell presents an example of the type of partnership that evolves out of the dichotomy.

When the form is tight and the relation has a strong principal–agent relation, we find ourselves in the DBFO contracts of the PFI in the UK (cell 1 in Table 4.1). The classic example of this form is the Dartford

Table 4.1   A typology of forms of PPP

Organizational form	Type of relation	
	A principal–agent relation	Partnership relation (equal principal–principal relations)
Tight organizational form	1. Design, build, finance, operate contracts (PFI-like partnerships)	2. Consortium (like Urban Regeneration Companies)
Loosely coupled	3. Intensive general cooperation between public–private actors (in policy programmes for instance)	4. Network-like partnership (intensive over a long time but loosely coupled organizational relationship)

Crossing over the Thames, which is financed by user fees. If we have a more principal–principal relation, public and private actors jointly create and fund a separate organizational form, as in the urban regeneration partnerships discussed earlier (cell 2 in Table 4.1). When the form is loosely coupled and the relation is a principal–agent one, we are talking about more general relations where public actors involve private actors to provide services or policy outcomes that match the goals and aims of the public actors (cell 3 in Table 4.1). Examples mentioned here are the relation between private schools and public actors, where public actors support private schools and private schools provide services that fit public goals (see, e.g., Weihe, 2008). This could be loosely formed contracts or implementation actions of private actors that fit policy programmes. One could question whether this belongs to the PPP category, because it is hardly a concrete partnership, but there are authors who claim that it does (see the policy approach as discussed by Weihe, 2008). If we look at a principal–principal relation with a loosely coupled organization form, we see PPPs that have a network-like character where there is mostly fairly intense interaction but only contract or organizational form when it comes to implementation activities (cell 4 in Table 4.1). This type of partnership can be found in complex urban restructuring where public and private actors have intense interactions during a fairly long period of decision-making, and development and organizational form are installed only at the end.

Theoretical arguments for PPP forms

What theoretical arguments are used in the literature to determine the best organizational form of PPP? Looking at the two most prominent theoretical perspectives used in the PPP literature, the resource dependency perspective and the neo-institutional theory, one would say that the overall expectation is that more tightly organized forms should generate better results (Benson, 1982; Negandhi, 1975). The resource dependency perspective suggests that the more dependent partners are on each other, the larger the need for organization of the interactions (see Mulford and Rogers, 1982; Donaldson, 1995). Since partnerships are organized because partners hope to achieve added value, they make their achievement of goals dependent on the other partner. This creates stronger resource dependency and thus, in general, partnerships are characterized by high dependency.

The same can be said from a neo-institutional economic perspective, since partners invest in the relationship and make specific transaction costs that they cannot use for another relation (Williamson, 1996). This again makes dependency high and the risk of opportunistic behaviour problematic.

This will lead to tight organizational structures in which partners will try to minimize the possibility of the other partner walking away with a large share of the profits. Of course one could draw another argument from that same neo-institutional economic theory: extensive contracts or organizing structures are costly in terms of transaction costs and can diminish the partners' space to manoeuvre and reduce the necessary difference between actors to create innovation and new solutions (Nooteboom, 2002; Parker and Vaidya, 2001). This argument for innovation is also used against the neo-institutionalist argument that one should centralize decision-making with high uncertainty and strong interdependency, because that would obliterate the necessary difference between actors to create innovation.

However in general the assumption that tight forms (either by good contracts that specify bonds and penalties in case of non-delivery of service or policy outcomes, or by setting up joint organizations at arm's length) are the best way to organize PPPs dominates the discussion. But is this a correct assumption?

Organizational form and managerial activities: some preliminary answers
So far we have discussed some assumptions about the tightness of the organizational form, and in the previous section we discussed some assumptions in the literature about whether form (and especially the 'arm's-length' character) or managerial activity was more important.

But what argument has most credibility? To test this, Steijn et al. (2009) and Klijn et al. (2010) performed an analysis on respondents to a questionnaire about environmental projects in the Netherlands. They asked respondents to answer a set of questions for a specific project they were most involved in, about the outcomes/evaluation of the projects, about various managerial activities, about the organizational form of the relation between public and private actors[2] and about project characteristics (among other questions). The researchers found no relation between the organizational form of the project and the outcomes, but a strong relation between the number of managerial strategies used and the outcomes (Steijn et al., 2009). These findings were confirmed in other research into urban regeneration companies (URC) in the Netherlands (see Kort and Klijn, 2009), which used a different sample of respondents. In that research we also tested the idea that 'arm's-length' character would make a difference. Two aspects were measured at arm's length: if the URC was positioned at a distance (measured by the amount the organization had to report, whether there was a clear framework for the freedom of the organization etc.) and the discretionary power of the URC (measured by if the URC had the ability to decide on a number of activities themselves). Neither of these features proved to be related to perceived outcomes.

This seems to point to the interesting finding that it is the managerial effort that makes a PPP work, and not the organizational form. The researchers also found no relation between organizational form, and number and types of managerial strategies (Steijn et al., 2009). This seems logical, since whatever form you choose for the partnership you have to do all the hard managerial work anyway.

Conclusion: what really matters in PPPs?

In this chapter we have explored the confusion that emerges out of the PPP discussion. Many authors have complained that the concept of PPP has so many meanings, rationales and different organizational manifestations that it is hard to tell what it is all about. We have seen that this confusion is partly due to the fact that a PPP is a brand used in the policy and political practice of everyday life, and that brands are not about the precise definition of the phenomenon but about creating images and (emotional) meaning and attachment.

Not surprisingly, we see various different forms, which we have explored in previous sections. These various forms are used in quite different situations. The PFI-like contracts are mainly used in situations where there are clear goals and a relatively clear product (a school building, a road etc.). If we look at other PPPs in the UK we see a large number of schemes other than PFI (like local educational partnerships, strategic service partnerships) that are in organizational terms more complex than the PFI partnerships.

But confusion is further increased because in the argument for PPPs one can find two different lines of argument: one from a more NPM point of view and one coming from a more governance point of view. The NPM view tells us to use performance indicators, to organize the PPPs at arm's length and lays heavy emphasis on efficiency and market mechanisms. The main argument for PPPs is that they are separate organizations (i.e. at a distance from the confusing world of politics) that can go on implementing urban regeneration schemes, attracting private money and getting the job done. This holds the promise of efficient bodies run in a private managerial way, delivering good outcomes for less money.

In the world of the governance argument, PPPs are cooperative bodies where the best from public and private is used, creating innovative solutions by matching knowledge and expertise, using horizontal coordination mechanisms, that is, various kinds of network management strategies, to improve coordination and produce valuable outcomes.

The empirical material we referenced showed that managerial network management strategies seem to be more important than organizational form, and certainly need to be expanded to other countries for us to be certain that this is the definitive answer.

But one could argue from the same material that maybe the excessive attention to the form of partnerships blurs the discussion; that is, if you want PPPs to succeed, you simply need a great deal of effort and hard work. This is a conclusion we are familiar with, from the early work on strategic alliances (Borys and Jemison, 1989; Niederkofler, 1991).

All the discussion about the organizational form may then be more about power and control (who is in control of the partnership) or about governmental rhetoric to provide clear and simple answers to a complex managerial problem (if you have the right contract, everything will turn out fine) because the management story is much more difficult to communicate. And that brings us back to the beginning: the brand character of PPPs.

Notes

1. This quotation is borrowed from the case study performed by Michiel Kort for his PhD on URCs and their effectiveness.
2. They made a distinction between categories: no organizational form, project group, a project organization and a juridical entity. The categories show a movement from low organization to tight organization.

References

Agranoff, R. and M. McGuire (2001), 'Big questions in public network management research', *Journal of Public Administration Research and Theory*, **11** (3), 295–326.
Benson, J.K. (1982), 'A framework for policy analysis', in D.L. Rogers and D.A. Whetten (eds), *Interorganizational Coordination: Theory, Research and Implementation*, Ames, IA: Iowa State University Press, pp. 137–76.
Borys, B. and D. Jemison (1989), 'Hybrid arrangements as strategic alliances: theoretical issues in organizational combinations', *Academy of Management Review*, **14** (2), 234–49.
Donaldson, L. (1995), *Contingency Theory*, Aldershot: Dartmouth Publishing Company.
Frederickson, H.G. (2005), 'What happened to public administration? Governance, governance everywhere', in E. Ferlie, L. Lynn and C. Pollitt (eds), *The Oxford Handbook of Public Management*, Oxford: Oxford University Press, pp. 282–304.
Gage, R.W. and M.P. Mandell (eds) (1990), *Strategies for Managing Intergovernmental Policies and Networks*, New York/London: Praeger.
Geddes, M. (2008), 'Inter-organizational relations in local and regional development partnerships', in S. Cropper, M. Ebers, C. Huxham and P.S. Ring (eds), *The Oxford Handbook of Inter-organizational Relations*, Oxford: Oxford University Press, pp. 203–30.
Ghobadian, A., D. Gallear, N. O'Regan and H. Viney (eds) (2004), *Public Private Partnerships: Policy and Experience*, Basingstoke: Palgrave Macmillan.
Greve, C. (2007), 'Recent insights into the performance of public–private partnerships in an international perspective', *Tidskrifted Politik*, **10** (3), 73–82.
Hodge, G. and C. Greve (2005), *The Challenge of Public Private Partnerships*, Cheltenham, UK and Northampton, MA, USA: Edward Elgar.
Hood, C. (1991), 'A public management for all seasons', *Public Administration*, **69**, 3–19.
Kenniscentrum PPS [Knowledge Centre] (1998), Ministerie van Financiën, Projectbureau PPS (1998), *Eindrapport Meer Waarde door Samen Werken* [*Final report on Added Value through Cooperation*], The Hague.
Kenniscentrum PPS [Knowledge Centre] (1999), Ministerie van Financiën, *Kenniscentrum Publiek–Private Samenwerking, Voortgangsrapportage PPS*, [Ministry of Finance, Knowledge Centre Public–Private Partnership, *PPP Progress Report*], The Hague, April.

Kenniscentrum PPS [Knowledge Centre PPP] (2001), Ministerie van Financiën, *Voortgangsrapportage 2001* [Ministry of Finance, *Progress Report 2001*], The Hague.
Kenniscentrum PPS [Knowledge Centre PPP], (2002), *Ministerie van Financieen, Voortgangsrapportage 2002* [Ministry of Finance, *Progress Report 2002*], The Hague.
Kenniscentrum PPS [Knowledge Centre PPP] (2004), (Ministerie van Finianciën), *Voortgangsreportage 'van incidenteel naar structureel'*, November, The Hague.
Klijn, E.-H. (2009), 'Public private partnerships in the Netherlands: policy, projects and lessons', *Economic Affairs*, March, 26–32.
Klijn, E.-H. and G.R. Teisman (2003), 'Institutional and strategic barriers to public–private partnership: an analysis of Dutch cases', *Public Money and Management*, **23** (3), 137–46.
Klijn, E.-H., B. Steijn and J. Edelenbos (forthcoming 2010), 'The impact of network management strategies on outcomes in governance networks', *Public Administration*.
Koppenjan, J.F.M. and E.-H. Klijn (2004), *Managing Uncertainties in Networks: A Network Perspective on Problem Solving and Decision Making*, London: Routledge.
Kort, M. and E-H. Klijn (2009), 'Urban Regeneration Companies at work: does arm's length matter? Looking at the impact of organizational features and network management efforts of URC and their impacts', paper for the 13th IRSPM Conference, Panel Public Private Partnerships, Copenhagen Business School, Copenhagen, 6–8 April.
Kotler, P., G. Amstrong, J. Saunders and V. Wong (1999), *Principles of Marketing* (2nd edn), London: Prentice Hall.
Lindner, S. (1999), 'Coming to terms with public–private partnership: a grammar of multiple meanings', *American Behavioral Scientist*, **43**, 35–51.
Mandell, M.P. (ed.) (2001), *Getting Results through Collaboration; Networks and Network Structures for Public Policy and Management*, Westport, CT: Quorum Books.
Meier, K.J. and L.J. O'Toole (2001), 'Managerial strategies and behaviour in networks: a model with evidence from U.S. public education', *Journal of Public Administration and Theory*, **11** (3), 271–93.
Mulford, C.L. and D.L. Rogers (1982), 'Definitions and models', in D.L. Rogers and D.A. Whetten (eds), *Interorganizational Coordination: Theory, Research and Implementation*, Ames, IA: Iowa State University Press, pp. 9–31.
NAO (2002), *Managing the Relationship to Secure a Successful Partnership in PFI Projects*, London: NAO.
Negandhi, A.R. (ed.) (1975), *Interorganization Theory*, Kansas City, KA: Kansas University Press.
Niederkofler, M. (1991), 'The evolution of strategic alliances: opportunities for managerial influence', *Journal of Business Venturing*, **6** (4), 237–57.
Nooteboom, B. (2002), *Trust: Forms, Foundations, Functions, Failures and Figures*, Cheltenham, UK and Northampton, MA, USA: Edward Elgar.
ODPM (2002), 'Best value and performance improvement – circular 2002–03', London: Office of the Deputy Prime Minister.
ODPM (2004a), *Strategic Partnering Task Force – final report*, London: Office of the Deputy Prime Minister.
ODPM (2004b), *Urban Regeneration Companies – Guidance and Qualification Criteria*, London: Office of the Deputy Prime Minister.
Osborne, S.P. (ed.) (2000), *Public–Private Partnerships: Theory and Practice in International Perspective*, London: Routledge.
Osborne, D. and T. Gaebler (1992), *Re-inventing Government: How the Entrepreneurial Spirit is Transforming the Public Sector*, Reading, MA: Addison-Wesley.
Parker, D. and K. Vaidya (2001), 'An economic perspective on innovation networks', in O. Jones, S. Conway and F. Steward (eds), *Social Interaction and Organisational Change: Aston Perspectives on Innovation Networks*, London: Imperial College Press.
Pollitt, C., C. Talbot, J. Caulfield and A. Smullen (2004), *Agencies, How Governments Do Things Through Autonomous Organizations*, Basingstoke: Palgrave Macmillan.
Savas, E.S. (2000), *Privatization and Public–Private Partnerships*, New York: Seven Bridges Press.

Skelcher, C.K. (2005), 'Public private partnerships and hybridity', in E. Ferlie, L. Lynn and C. Pollitt (eds), *The Oxford Handbook of Public Management*, Oxford: Oxford University Press, pp. 347–70.

Sørenson, E. and J. Torfing (eds) (2007), *Theories of Democratic Network Governance*, Cheltenham, UK and Northampton, MA, USA: Edward Elgar.

Steijn, B., E-H. Klijn and J. Edelenbos (2009), 'Public Private Partnerships: added value by organizational form or management?', paper for the Partnership Conference, School of Social and Political Sciences, John Medley Building, University of Melbourne, Australia, 26 February.

Urban Task Force (1999), *Towards an Urban Renaissance*.

Urban Task Force (2005), *Towards a Strong Urban Renaissance*.

VROM (2002), *Ministerie van Volkshuisvesting Ruimtelijke Ordening en Milieu* [Letter of the Dutch Minister of Housing, Spatial Planning of urban regeneration and the selection of fifty priority urban areas], The Hague.

Weihe, G. (2008), 'Ordering disorder: on the perplexities of the partnership literature', *The Australian Journal of Public Administration*, **67** (4), 430–42.

Williamson, O.E. (1996), *The Mechanisms of Governance*, London: Oxford University Press.

5 Reviewing public–private partnerships: some thoughts on evaluation

Graeme A. Hodge

Introduction

The performance of PPPs has seen wide debate. It has been characterized, though, as much by colourful and provocative rhetoric as by informed evidence-based observations. But given the breadth of available evaluation techniques, what awaits us if we want to properly assess PPPs? And what exactly do we mean by 'evidence' in evaluations? It is on these issues that this chapter offers some thoughts.

It has already been noted that the PPP phenomenon covers a wealth of different meanings, including the taxonomy of five families[1] noted in Chapter 1. One family, the long-term infrastructure contract (LTIC) category itself also encompasses a wide variety of arrangements aiming to provide infrastructure through legal contracts with consortia. Such public infrastructure PPPs have, throughout history, had multiple stakeholders, whether those associated with the project under way, or those with a common interest in the public decisions being made. Also, such PPPs these days directly involve a range of professional disciplines: from law and finance, through to accounting, economics and project management. Moreover, there are also several disciplines interested in these PPPs given that they are matters of public interest, including public policy, political science, regulation and governance. The implication of these observations is that any attempt at evaluating PPPs as an infrastructure delivery mechanism is likely to be subjected to the usual policy evaluation difficulties and language-games at the same time as incorporating inherently technical aspects. Such evaluation discussions are certainly not likely to be limited to one single disciplinary group and will continue to be hotly contested – not only because conflicts of interest are present for many of the important stakeholders, but also because different disciplines inherently emphasize different assessment criteria and favour different evaluation methods.

Within this context, this chapter aims to articulate some of the tensions existing in the task of evaluating PPPs as an infrastructure delivery mechanism, and then to reconcile them. From a utilitarian perspective, we might begin by surmising that assessing PPP performance simply involves evaluating the degree to which the many promises of LTIC-type PPPs are

81

met. But the evaluation task in reality is probably broader than that. This chapter begins by outlining what is meant by the notion of evaluation, and what evaluation tasks are entailed. It then briefly contemplates what is expected from today's loud call for more 'evidence-based' approaches to public policy decision-making. The chapter then argues that PPPs present evaluators with six challenges ranging from the breadth of the PPP phenomenon, the multiplicity of inherent objectives and its multidisciplinarity, to the role of the evaluator, along with technical issues of assessment veracity and the need for care when reviewing multiple PPP evaluation studies. The chapter then draws some conclusions as to the strength of international PPP evaluations to date and the challenges and opportunities this presents to us.

The notion of evaluation

It is difficult to separate questions of evaluation from broader questions of research. Perhaps the truth of the matter is close to the single three-hour exam question set by University of Sydney academic Professor Fred May years ago. His challenge to the Italian-language students being examined at the time was simple: 'Think of a question. Answer it.' In this context, numerous evaluative questions are possible through many methods, and the opinions, values and skills of the writer all shine through. But while colourful and philosophical, this does not provide much assistance in terms of a more technical quest to locate evaluation. We could also begin to map evaluative discourses in terms of disciplines (e.g. from quantitative research methods such as statistical analysis, probability, mathematical modelling and welfare economics to qualitative traditions such as biography, phenomenology, grounded theory, ethnography and case studies (Cresswell, 1998)). Indeed, there are many learned texts today on evaluation and its relevant technical aspects.[2]

Starting from first principles, however, recourse to a dictionary explains that 'to evaluate' is 'to determine the amount, value or significance of something by careful appraisal and study'.[3] This definition clearly emphasizes the need for evaluation to be undertaken with careful appraisal and study. Looking further at the notion of the 'value' of something, this is further characterized in the dictionary in terms of 'the worth in money', or 'the relative worth, utility or importance'. What is crucial here is that evaluation clearly covers a broad domain in which we carefully study not only value in the economic or financial sense, but a wealth of other domains in which we might choose to judge its relative importance or societal worth.

More formal definitions of evaluation could also be pursued. Weiss (1998, p. 4), for example, suggests that 'evaluation is the systematic assessment of the operation and/or the outcomes of a program or policy, compared to a set of explicit or implicit standards, as a means of contributing to the improvement of the program or policy.' This definition emphasizes the crucial need for a systematic assessment of what has been achieved. An alternative definition is given by Bingham and Felbinger (2002, p. 3), who suggest that evaluation is 'the use of scientific methods to estimate the successful implementation and resultant outcomes of programs or policies for decision-making purposes . . .'. This alternative definition sees the use of scientific methods as more central to evaluation.

While this chapter is not the place to map the technical evaluation terrain[4] any further, there is still much to learn from our evaluative past. Parsons (1995, p. 567), for instance, cites Guba and Lincoln (1987) and suggests that in terms of the professional identity of evaluators, the discipline itself has gone through a series of personality changes. After World War I, the role of the evaluator was seen as essentially a technical one, but this had changed by the 1940s, when it was seen more as a descriptive role in which we discerned patterns, strengths and weaknesses. By the 1960s and 1970s, the evaluator's role had evolved further to become more that of a judge who would pronounce the degree to which 'success' had been achieved. More recent views have included responsive models of evaluation that have increasingly viewed the task of evaluation in terms of negotiating the claims, concerns and issues present among a multiplicity of constructions.[5] Over time, then, our desire for more rational assessments of what governments have been achieving through their policy initiatives appears to have resulted in the evaluation role gradually changing from being an essentially technical one, to one of learning and examining achievements against the complex expectations of multiple actors. Today's evaluation climate is characterized by loud calls for 'evidence-based' approaches to policy development and learning. But what exactly is meant by evidence? And how might we interpret such calls when evaluating PPPs?

The notion of evidence

There is little doubt that the language of 'evidence-based' policy approaches dominates today's governing environment. But such calls are clearly one part of a larger and longer-term appeal to rationality in policy-making. It is, as Sanderson (2002, p. 1) neatly put it, 'a reaffirmation of the "modernist" project, the enduring legacy of the Enlightenment, involving the improvement of the world through the application of reason'. It also builds on the simple proposition that 'scientific research evidence has an inherent value in the everyday politics of policy making' (Marston and Watts, 2003, p. 36).

There is little doubt as to the popularity and immediate appeal of calls for stronger use of evidence today. In Australia, former prime minister,

Kevin Rudd, announced that 'evidence-based' policy-making is at the heart of being a reformist government (Banks, 2009), and the former UK prime minister, Tony Blair, was fond of repeating the simple and pragmatic-sounding phrase 'what matters is what works'. Public policy scholars and others have traced back longstanding concerns as to the limited use of research evidence in policy-making; however, the recent offshoot has evolved from the concept of 'evidence-based medicine' and 'evidence-based practice'. The logic of evidence-based medicine has as its core the gold standard for evidence – that of the randomized control trial (Marston and Watts, 2003). Appeals for evidence-based approaches have, not surprisingly, also spread to other arenas.[6]

To most researchers, I suspect that there is something deeply appealing in the idea that government decision-making and evaluation ought to be 'evidence-based'. What works 'best' is clearly crucial. We all yearn for policy that is more 'rational' – and therefore 'evidence-based'. The appeal of the gold standard for evidence is also admirable. But what exactly is evidence? Whose evidence matters most? Works best for whom? And are we now assuming that science should be placed above politics? These questions are all legitimate.

The evidence-based policy notion has been the subject of considerable debate as to its meaning and its practice. While evidence clearly forms one basis for policy decisions, they are not solely deduced in a neutral and objective manner from empirical–analytical work. Walker (2007, p. 235) even observes that some 'intellectuals have a problem with the sheer messiness of politics', and that modern governance practices based on the need for independence from political processes are founded on the belief that 'politicians interfere while experts and a caste of disinterested grandees govern rationally and hence benignly'. He characterizes the evidence-based policy movement as one that assumes a privileged role for research-based evidence in public policy, and he accuses experts of essentially supporting an aristocracy that elevates the demand for technocratic evidence over the value-driven, and the bureaucratic over the political. Marston and Watts (2003, p. 44) put a similar salutary point, arguing that 'what is urgently needed in the debate are some critical reflections on the assumptions that are constituted and passed off as "evidence"'. They push this line further and remark that 'contrary to what many people think, the shift to evidence-based policy is no guarantee that either good research or good policy will automatically eventuate from embracing evidence-based policy'.[7] Policy-making to them is 'an irreducibly linguistic and political process'.[8]

So, what do we mean by evidence? There is much to explore here. Head (2008, p. 4), for instance, remarks that 'there are multiple forms of policy-relevant knowledge' and that as a consequence, 'there is not one evidence-base but several bases'. He observes that while some might see evidence as simply knowledge generated by applied research, political knowledge and practical implementation knowledge are both also just as relevant. Thus there are three lenses of 'knowledge' and 'evidence' for Head. What is also evident without too much contemplation here is that the role of values and how value conflicts are reconciled are both central to public policy-making and, by extension, to evaluation. Indeed, governments are by their very nature, as Van de Walle (2009, p. 45) says, 'constantly dangling in an uneasy equilibrium between competing values'. So it is crucial that such policy values are revealed and clear in PPP evaluation rather than buried under scientific methods.

Far from being 'self-evident', the meaning of just what constitutes an 'evidence-based' approach in evaluation is therefore contestable. It has always been important to make use of the best evidence available. But this evidence will most likely come from multiple sources, will include both soft and hard knowledge, and will involve multiple frontiers (from the scientific to the political and the practical). It appears that scientific knowledge will always have a place in this evidence base, but it will also not monopolize it.

PPP evaluation challenges
A multitude of challenges arise in contemplating an evaluation of PPPs. In this chapter we shall look only at a few in order to establish some conceptual foundations to assist PPP evaluations. We have highlighted six challenges:[9]

1. The challenge of defining the 'evaluand'
2. The challenge of multiple PPP objectives
3. The challenge of multiple discourses and disciplines
4. The challenge of the evaluator's role
5. The challenge of evaluative rigour for individual studies
6. The challenge in accurately reviewing multiple individual studies of PPPs.

We shall briefly elaborate on each.

1. The challenge of the 'evaluand'
The subject of an evaluation has been termed the 'evaluand' by the evaluation discipline. In the case of PPPs, the first question to ask is therefore what is being evaluated. Based on the international literature to date on PPPs, this simple-sounding question is not so simple to answer. What is at

the heart of the difficulty in defining the 'evaluand' is the existence of the PPP 'phenomenon'. Depending on how we view the PPP phenomenon, the evaluand at the centre of an evaluation could logically be construed as many things. These include:

(a)   a symbolic political movement
(b)   all infrastructure dealings between governments and business
(c)   a governance mechanism
(d)   a developmental approach
(e)   a policy
(f)   a programme of activities or projects
(g)   a group of mechanisms using particular rules to provide public infrastructure
(h)   the specific set of financial arrangements underpinning project provision
(i)   delivery of a particular PPP project (or the infrastructure itself).

To seasoned observers, a PPP is all of these things, and more. But an evaluation of any one of these items needs a degree of initial conceptual clarity on which to build a strong assessment.

2.   The challenge of multiple PPP objectives

Of central relevance to our assessment here are the objectives of PPP delivery. At the outset, different stakeholders clearly have differing objectives for the delivery of a PPP. Companies associated with delivering the project want primarily to make a profit. Users, on the other hand, want a new facility at minimum cost and fuss. Governments want to both lead and stay in power. But focusing currently just on the role played by government, what have been the broader policy promises made to citizens? Under John Major's UK government, the initial rationale was to get around restrictions on formal public sector debt levels. Private financing promised a way to provide infrastructure without increasing the public sector borrowing requirement (PSBR). This was followed by the promise that PPPs would reduce pressure on public sector budgets. Neither the availability of off-budget financing nor avoiding accountability for capital funding are particularly valid criteria on which to evaluate PPPs, however. A mechanism through which governments may turn a large, one-off capital expenditure into a series of smaller, annualized expenditures has simply been provided. And, like any domestic credit card or mortgage arrangement, this does not reduce pressure on the family budget, because all debts must be repaid in the end.[10] The third promise of PPPs was that this delivery mechanism provides better value for money (VfM) for taxpayers. This is a policy promise worthy of examination and one that has also formed the primary PPP rationale in countries such as the UK and Australia. Added to these three initial promises have been a dozen more – some explicit, such as reduced risk to government from projects, better accountability, better on-time and on-budget delivery, and greater innovation, and some implicit, such as encouraging a more innovative public sector, improved business confidence, improved palatability for user funding for infrastructure, provision for long-term infrastructure life-cycle costs, and boosted sales of professional PPP services abroad. To these 13 PPP objectives, we might nowadays also add two more objectives following recent credit market failures and stock market downturns. It may well be that two new implicit objectives for PPPs will be the desire for governments to broadly support businesses and preferentially adopt the PPP mechanism in difficult market circumstances (the objective of business assistance) or the broader societal objective of economic development. These various PPP objectives are summarized in Table 5.1.

Additional objectives are also possible. But the point here is clear. Many separate objectives have been set for PPPs, and beneath all of them, Western democratic governments, while of course always speaking within the rubric of 'the public interest', usually want fundamentally to get re-elected.

Table 5.1   Fifteen objectives of PPPs

	Objective / promise made by government
1	Enables provision of infrastructure without increased public sector borrowing
2	Reduces pressure on public sector budgets
3	Provides better VfM for taxpayers
4	Reduces risks to government from infrastructure projects
5	Improves accountability
6	Provides better on-time delivery
7	Allows better on-budget delivery
8	Allows greater infrastructure (project) innovation
9	Encourages a more innovative public sector
10	Improves business confidence
11	Improves political feasibility to impose user fees
12	Enables the full life-cycle costs of infrastructure to be provided
13	Boosts sales of professional PPP services abroad
14	Supports businesses in difficult global market conditions (business assistance/subsidy)
15	Provides a crucial tool to underpin the broad societal objective of economic development

The 15 objectives listed above range from, at the one end, broad efforts to better govern and pursue economic development, through to the other end, where narrower objectives cover project delivery in terms of VfM and timeliness. Furthermore, not only have these objectives covered a huge range, they have also altered over time and, today, remain slippery in the rough and tumble of government policy speak.

3.   *The challenge of multiple PPP discourses and disciplines*
Assessments of PPPs have to date most often used narrow traditional lenses, and cross-disciplinary learning has not been common.[11] It is little surprise that each of the disciplines places an emphasis on quite different questions. At the risk of overly stereotyping the players here, the accountants tend to emphasize matters of on-balance-sheet figures and the appropriate recording of transactions and commitments (Broadbent and Loughlin, 2002). The engineers and bureaucrats emphasize the desirability of infrastructure projects, improvements to contract specifications, the development of information databases, and financial incentives for early project completion (Fitzgerald and Duffield, 2006). The economists emphasize evaluations of relative managerial efficiency and allocative efficiency across different infrastructure delivery methods (Blanc-Brude et al., 2006; Boardman and Vining, 2010). The political scientists emphasize the degree to which PPPs have seen central advocacy in different jurisdictions; how traditional policy debates have been avoided (Coghill and Woodward, 2005), or how the debate arena has shifted elsewhere (Flinders, 2005). The policy and planning scholars emphasize the need to meet policy goals amidst negotiated knowledge, the need for both procedural as well as analytical rationality, the numerous conflicts of interest now buried inside government and the need for greater transparency rather than continued calls for contract information to remain confidential (de Bruin and Leijten, 2008; Hodge and Greve, 2007). And regulatory scholarship has made the observation that unlike other essential infrastructure such as private electricity supplies or telecommunications, it is the individual *ad hoc* contract-by-contract arrangement that 'governs' our future, not the newly elected government of the day or a robust independent regulator (Hodge, 2006).[12]

While the disciplines have not, strictly speaking, all been this narrow, the above discussion nevertheless reminds us that assessments from all disciplines matter. Inasmuch as PPPs are a multidisciplinary phenomenon with differing expectations from stakeholders, different criteria for success will clearly be relevant. The implication here is that disciplines need to learn more from each other and combine efforts. This ought to be an objective for evaluators. A further implication is that we need to be far more careful when we say that 'PPPs work'. Work for whom? And work in terms of whose eyes? Governments, business and citizens are three quite different sectors of actors and each has their own ideas as to what constitutes success in their own domain as well as the domains of others.

What multiple objectives and multiple discourses mean is that when making judgements about the success of PPPs, successful performance itself has a range of meanings (Jeffares et al., 2009). Disciplines all have their own preferences for measuring success. But there are also many alternative broader frameworks that could be adopted to marshal our observations as to performance and PPP effectiveness. We could assess the relative achievement of a range of political, economic and social goals across stakeholders from government, business and civil society, as we noted in Chapter 1. Alternatively we could adopt the Weimer and Vining (2004) framework of four goals of government: allocative efficiency; equity; budget impact; and politics. Furthermore, many other performance evaluation frameworks are possible. For instance, Jeffares et al. (2009, p. 7) acknowledge both the breadth of PPP performance conceptions among high expectations from multiple stakeholders as well as 'the politically loaded nature of PPPs as public policy instruments'. They assert that six performance domains are relevant to PPP evaluation: democracy; policy goal achievement; transformation (to produce new public sector behaviours); connectivity (to stimulate innovation); coordination (to achieve synergies); and coalition (to achieve sustainable partnership).[13] Each of these alternative frameworks is valuable. But each is also arbitrary and brings different values to light. The relative merit of each individual framework is therefore wholly contestable.

4. The challenge of the evaluator's role
Of course even if we have defined the 'evaluand', clearly articulated the PPP objectives we shall be investigating, and are aware of the multiple disciplines in the field, the role to be taken by the evaluator is contestable. At a simple level, we can view evaluation as the use of alternative techniques such as statistical assessment, performance audit, empirical measurement, case study or even institutional learning. But there are more fundamental philosophical issues at stake here. Building on the ideas noted earlier, we know that evaluation has enjoyed a long pedigree and nowadays the task may be viewed as including technical matters, description, issues of judgement and intelligently negotiating the various competing claims made about the evaluand. Today, many advocates for evaluation cast the task in terms of simply assessing outcomes or goals. But 'evaluation as such cannot be reduced to this one role and function' as Dahler-Larson (2005, p. 616) states.

So, just what is the evaluator's role? Are we as evaluators there to undertake a 'scientific approach' and discover knowledge through experimental analysis so that we may determine the degree to which explicit objectives are met, the reason for success or failure and how to improve our success? Alternatively, should we behave more as enlightened consumers or citizens, who may wish to judge the actual goals and objectives set by others without necessarily being constrained by them? As a third option, are we there more as the facilitator, whose role is to present information to others and enable them, not us, to make the judgement? These are three of the many possible philosophical approaches possible in evaluation (Stufflebeam and Shinkfield, 2007). Figure 5.1 illustrates this idea.

Scientific knowledge discovered through experiments

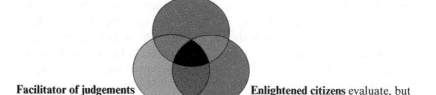

Facilitator of judgements   **Enlightened citizens** evaluate, but
to be made by others   are unconstrained by set objectives

Figure 5.1   Alternative roles of the PPP evaluator

Overall, then, what is being suggested here is that the philosophical stance we take on our evaluation role is itself important. Knowledge discovery through rigorous experimentation, as a citizen unconstrained by the policies or goals set by others, or else acting as a facilitator for others to then make judgements are all very different possibilities. And each comes with differing priorities as to emphasis, approach and values.

5.   The challenge of evaluation rigour for individual studies
We noted earlier that the PPP phenomenon has many layers, from governance and political symbolism at the highest level down to more technical matters of costs and logistics. Evaluations of PPPs need to acknowledge this. But disciplines not only have different perspectives as to what constitutes success, they also have differing ideas as to what constitutes a strong and rigorous evaluation. Indeed, the evaluation discipline itself has its own requirements for rigour. There is much potential to learn here.

On this note, the formal techniques available to evaluate PPPs as a 'policy' are numerous. Early work by Wholey (1979) suggested that a wide range of evaluation types was possible: from the costly but scientific (or 'intensive') evaluation at one extreme through 'performance monitoring' and 'rapid feedback' evaluation, to 'evaluability' (or quick and dirty) assessments at the other. A similar theme was emphasized again, over two decades later, by Bingham and Felbinger (2002). They saw a continuum of evaluation possibilities, from outcome evaluations (focused on the end results and impacts of policy initiatives, along with the causes of these changes) through to process evaluations (where the implementation of a policy or programme was assessed).[14]

Looking at the question of evaluation approaches from another perspective, Dahler-Larson (2005) suggests that three general approaches are possible to evaluation, each with a plethora of possibilities. These three approaches include the goal-centred approach (where the goals of a programme 'constitute the only legitimate source of criteria for judging the programme'); theory-based approaches (where a central challenge is to explain why activities at hand are likely to plausibly lead to outcomes); and responsive/participatory approaches (where the responsibility for the evaluation is shared with local stakeholders through dialogue).

Of course, this all still begs the question as to what makes a strong evaluation study. This issue has been the lifeblood of the evaluation debates for the past five decades and we shall not fan the flames further. We need simply to observe that evaluators aim to inform our judgements and 'enable conclusions to be made beyond reasonable doubt' (Stufflebeam and Shinkfield, 2007, p. 301). So in the case of PPP outcomes and impacts, the role of evaluators is to assist us to reach defensible conclusions about cause and effect. Libraries of evaluative methods exist, and what is defensible is, again, still an open question. Bingham and Felbinger (2002), for example, take a scientific frame to the issue of defensibility and suggest a continuum of four methods[15] of 'before-and-after' studies for evaluating outcomes:

1. One-group pre-test–post-test design: the most common but least powerful design, as the evaluator cannot know what caused the changes observed.
2. Simple time-series design: where actual observations are compared with a forward projection based on earlier activity, using, say, a statistical regression model. Again, the evaluator knows little of the causes behind observed changes, however.
3. Pre-test–post-test comparison group: where a comparison group closely resembling programme recipient groups is created and differences between actual observations and such comparison groups are measured. In this case, recipients are rarely chosen randomly, however.

4.   Pre-test–post-test control group: the most powerful programme design, where participants are assigned to treatment and control groups randomly.

In all cases, the evaluation consists of measuring real-world behaviour and comparing these measurements or observations against a counterfactual (or control scenario) that we assume would most likely have occurred had not the policy intervention taken place. Ensuring through statistical methods that any differences in observations could not simply have arisen by chance is also part of this assessment.

These remarks still beg the issue as to what constitutes 'evidence' for PPPs – and what data are actually used for analytical purposes – whether gleaned from the legal contract or based on historical case study outcomes. But aside from the obvious proviso that we would all prefer evidence to be historically accurate and based on case outcomes rather than be guesstimates or forward projections, such questions are again the lifeblood of those interested in evaluations in each of the disciplines. One particular challenge of PPP evaluations is the severe limitation of data usually available. A PPP is not usually a separate legal entity that publishes publicly available accounts or other data. And neither is the traditional delivery alternative a separate legal entity either. Even if some data are available as the basis for comparative purposes, they are not usually subject to standards such as those governing a firm's accounting reports. Their reliability is therefore somewhat contestable.

We are certainly interested in establishing the degree to which each of the 15 instrumental objectives identified above for PPPs are being met in reality thus far. But there are also questions as to non-instrumental values that can be important in evaluations. In the case of PPPs, these might include questions of clarity, flexibility and accountability, as well as the legitimacy of government activities. Moreover, the simple matter of evaluation timing is crucial with long-term PPPs. Evaluations may be undertaken before implementation, during implementation or after implementation. But with long-term contracts spanning over 30, 50 or even 100 years, many evaluation options may well leave the jury without any real capacity to make rigorous judgements regarding the worth of PPPs.

Overall, then, the question of evaluation rigour is crucial to our quest. Casual observations and commentary, while interesting, rank lowest on a strict scale of veracity. Formal evaluation implies a systematic approach. The use of statistical techniques, experimental designs including the use of control groups, econometrics and case studies explicitly including carefully chosen counterfactuals all rank higher. An additional characteristic crucial to rigorous evaluations is transparency. The studies held in highest regard are those that are not only careful, but present the data (or make them accessible), are balanced in their approach, are transparent and are peer contestable. Those evaluations that present their findings, but then hide the data, hide the methods and hide questions of funding, rank as least trustworthy.

6. The challenge of accurately reviewing multiple individual PPP studies
Academics have for years conducted literature reviews, and have largely assumed that this was an accurate way of establishing the 'truth of the matter' when synthesizing existing research on a topic. The advent of meta-analysis, however, challenged this. Literature reviews, it turns out, are difficult to undertake properly, and reliability cannot simply be assumed.

Integrating the findings of even a small number of studies is not necessarily straightforward.[16] In fact, different reviewers often see the same empirical results quite differently. The reasons for this are many-fold. Definitions may be inconsistent, differing performance dimensions can slant the conclusions, and the potential influence of the confounding variables all matter. But a more profound explanation concerns the research methodology adopted for the review process itself.

When reviewers attempt to integrate findings from multiple studies, they may simply provide dizzying lists of studies along with an overall qualitative impression of 'the truth'. Alternatively, they may base their conclusions on a smaller number of studies – usually deemed to be those of the best design or analysis. This is a common review technique, but Glass (1976, p. 4) explains that it is rather unreliable:

> a common method of integrating several studies with inconsistent findings is to carp on the design or analysis deficiencies of all but a few studies – those remaining frequently being one's own work or that of one's students or friends – and then advance the one or two acceptable studies as the truth of the matter . . .

So, the reviewer may indeed reject all but a few of the studies as being deficient in one way or another, and then take notice of those one or two studies deemed to be acceptable. This approach puts the evaluator in the position of knowledge gatekeeper and judge, and also fails to use much of the available information – perhaps even basing final conclusions on unrepresentative studies.

Another important aspect of the narrative review is the requirement of reviewers to describe to the reader the sampling, measurement, analytical methods and findings of each of the studies under review. Both Hunter and Schmidt (1990, p. 498) and Glass et al. (1981, p. 13) point out that published reviews often violate these reporting precepts. Both report Jackson's pivotal work in 1978 in which a random sample of 36 integrative reviews were drawn from the leading journals in education, psychology and sociology for analysis. Hunter and Schmidt reported that Jackson's (1978) analysis of 36 review articles in quality journals found that only four of the 36 reported major aspects of the search for relevant studies; only seven indicated whether or not the full set of located studies on the topic was analysed; just over half of the 36 reported the direction and magnitude of the findings of any of the primary studies; and only three cited the mean, range or another summary of the magnitude of the primary study's findings.

Without information on the degree to which a reviewer uses a systematic approach in their review, the reader cannot sensibly interpret or intelligently assess any conclusions made.

Meta-analysis aims to make sense of the vast number of accumulated study findings. In doing so, it seeks, as Glass et al. (1981) argued, 'clarity, explicitness, and openness' in the review. First coined by Gene Glass and his colleagues in 1976,[17] meta-analysis employs statistical techniques to summarize many primary evaluation study findings. It is based on the central desire to 'discipline research synthesis by the same methodological standards that apply to primary research'.[18] Over the past 40 years meta-analysis has been applied to fields such as education, psychology, medicine, law, business, commerce and public policy[19] (Hodge, 2000, p. 70). Overall, then, when reviews are undertaken of the multiple evaluation studies conducted to date, such reviews should also be subject to the ethos of strength and veracity that we expect of primary evaluation studies.

To decide whether we should trust a literature review of PPPs, then, there is much to contemplate. We might posit a few suggestions for a trustworthy review of published PPP evaluation studies. First, a review should present the evidence supporting and disputing claims and counter-claims fairly and accurately, and against a pragmatic rather than a perfect counterfactual. And second, a strong review would usually rely more on those evaluations with stronger statistical or case research designs. There are clearly many common traits. We might also expect that a strong evaluation review is undertaken by an evaluator with knowledge across many stakeholders, having a reputation for modest judgements and clearly independent of the evaluated transactions. Also necessary is the open presentation of the data on which it is based in a clear and accessible way, so that peer review and commentary of the review and its conclusions is possible and encouraged.

An overview of PPP VfM

If we were to gather up our evaluation kit bag and courageously present a quick overview of PPP evaluations focusing primarily on just one PPP objective, better VfM for taxpayers, what might we discern? For this purpose, we shall adopt as our evaluand the privately financed infrastructure project (PFI-type project) as pioneered in the UK.[20]

First, there have of course been numerous evaluation studies and reviews of PPPs. But much of this assessment has amounted to little more than blatant salesmanship on the one hand, to stinging, and just as blatant, criticism on the other. Like past privatization debates, learning has been limited as the terrain of competing values has been articulated. There are numerous more professional reports in the mix as well, including the reviews of international organizations such as OECD (2008) and the impressive-looking reports of PricewaterhouseCoopers (2005), Ernst & Young (2007) and Deloitte (2006). But empirical substantive performance measurements made to date have been limited, including legal outcomes of LTIC-type PPPs.[21] So, while there may well be a series of conditions under which we might expect privately financed infrastructure projects to deliver superior VfM than traditional projects (de Bettignies and Ross, Chapter 7 in this volume), the real VfM performance of PPPs remains empirically open. What then does the more rigorous evidence on the veracity of PPP performance say?

The second point here is that in terms of high-level rigorous statistical reviews of PPPs, there is little to go on. In contrast to earlier evaluations of privatization performance, for example, there have been no meta-analyses or statistical overviews summarizing multiple quantitative PPP performance results to date.[22] Notwithstanding this, there have been several narrative assessments that have attempted to go past polarized advocacy or criticism on partnerships, covering either more general ground[23] or focused on particular PPP concerns.[24] A full assessment and commentary on this range of works deserves book-length treatment. So we shall simply skirt around the edges of the VfM evaluation terrain here. Table 5.2 summarizes a range of evaluation studies and reviews from the international literature. Drawn from the past decade, it reflects only some of the pieces going to make up the overall LTIC-type PPP evaluation picture rather than anything more statistically careful.[25] We trust that it is more or less representative. It includes reviews varying from general philosophical guidance to detailed project analyses and statistical reviews. Looking then at the simple promise of PPPs to deliver better VfM for taxpayers, several additional observations could be made to assist our evaluation quest.

The third point is that statistically solid evidence on LTIC-type PPPs is weak if we look at individual evaluation studies using primary data. In other words, the evaluation evidence at the level of individual study is weak as well as being controversial. This contrasts with both the often-repeated assurance of PPP advocates as well as critics. Few analyses have employed

Table 5.2 Selected PPP evaluations over the past decade

Study	Sample/cases	Country	Type of publication	Better VfM?	Comments/conclusions
Bloomfield et al. (1998)	A Massachusetts correctional facility	USA	Case study	No	• 7.4% more expensive through PPP lease purchasing • 'inflated sales pitches' camouflaged real costs and risks to the public, and project was 'wasteful and risky'
Arthur Andersen and LSE Enterprise (2000)	29 business cases analysed	UK	Initial evaluation	Yes	• 17% cost savings estimated against the PSC • risk transfer accounted for 61% of forecast savings
Savas (2000, p. 240)	General observations	USA	Literature review	Yes	• '[the private sector through PPPs] build more quickly and more cost effectively than governments usually can . . .'
National Audit Office (2000)	7 business cases from NAO (2000)	UK	Business cases	Yes	• 10–20% cost savings estimated
Walker and Walker (2000, p. 204)	General observations of Australian cases	Australia	Literature review	–	• PPP infrastructure financing deals seen as 'misleading accounting trickery' with eroded accountability to Parliament and the public • Private project consortium real rates of return were up to ten times those returns expected for the public
Teisman and Klijn (2001)	General observations	4 EU countries	Review of strengths and weaknesses	–	• PPPs have strengths and weaknesses

Source	Sample	Country	Method		Findings
Department of Transport (2002)	250 London Underground projects	UK	Unknown	–	• Cost overruns averaging 20% were found (1997–2000)
Mott Macdonald (2002)	39 traditional projects and 11 PFI projects	UK	Multiple cases reviewed	Yes	• Traditional 'public' infrastructure provision arrangements were on time and on budget 30% and 27% of the time, but PFI-type partnerships were on time and on budget 76% and 78% of the time respectively
Pollock et al. (2002)	3 NHS hospitals and 8 trusts	UK	Review and re-analysis	No	• The PFI justification is a 'sleight of hand'
Pollitt (2002)	10 major PFI cases	UK	Review of NAO cases	Yes	• The best deal was probably obtained in every case, and good VfM was probably achieved in 8 of the 10 cases
Audit Commission (2003)	10 traditional and 8 PFI schools were compared	Scotland	Audit report	No	• 'We found no evidence that PFI projects delivered schools more quickly than projects funded in more conventional ways' • 'The public sector comparator has lost the confidence of many people . . .'
Greve (2003)	Case study of Farum Municipality	Denmark	Case analysis	No	• PPP assessed as 'the most spectacular scandal in the history of Danish Public Administration' • It resulted in raised taxes for the citizens of Farum, higher debt for citizens and a former mayor currently on trial in the courts

Table 5.2 (continued)

Study	Sample/cases	Country	Type of publication	Better VfM?	Comments/conclusions
Fitzgerald (2004)	8 PPP cases from Victoria	Australia	Report to government	uncertain	• The superiority of the economic partnership mode over traditional delivery mechanisms was dependent on the discount rate adopted in the analysis • Opposite conclusions were reached when using an 8.65% discount rate at one extreme (where the PPP mechanism was 9% cheaper than traditional delivery) compared to an evaluation adopting a 5.7% discount rate (where the PPP mechanism was 6% more expensive)
Edwards et al. (2004)	8 cases from roads and 13 hospitals case studies	UK	Case reviews and interviews	No	• Contracts reviewed 3 years in • 'PFI is an expensive way of financing and delivering public services . . .' • 'the chief beneficiaries are the providers of finance and some of . . . the private sector service providers . . .'
Ghobadian et al. (2004b, p. 300)	General observations	UK	Literature review	–	• 'we have no firm evidence that the current PFIs would deliver on their long-term objectives . . .'
Grimsey and Lewis (2004, pp. 81, 245)	Global observations across several sectors	Several countries	Literature review	Yes	• 'preliminary evidence does seem to indicate strongly that PPPs offer one solution to the public procurement problem . . .' • 'there is not one "model" of a PPP . . .'

Source	Cases	Country	Method	Positive assessment	Findings
Pollitt (2005)	General observations of UK cases plus 5 cases	UK	Literature review	Yes	• 'it seems difficult to avoid a positive overall assessment'
Shaoul (2005)	General observations of UK cases	UK	Literature review	No	• PFI has turned out to be very expensive with a lack of accountability • Suspects that PFI policies 'enrich the few at the expense of the majority and for which no democratic mandate can be secured'
Boardman et al. (2005, p. 186)	5 North American cases across several sectors	Canada and USA	Case reviews	No	• Unless contracts both compensate the private sector for risks and then ensure that they actually bear it, 'P3s will not improve allocative efficiency'
Hodge (2005, p. 327)	General observations of UK cases plus 3 cases	Australia	Literature review	Uncertain	• There have been no rigorous and transparent evaluations of all Australian PPPs • The few available assessments suggest mixed performance to date • Government has moved away from its traditional stewardship role to a louder policy advocacy role. It now faces multiple conflicts of interest (as advocate, developer, steward, elected leader, regulator, contract signatory and planner)
Auditor-General of New South Wales (2006)	Construction of 19 schools in New South Wales	Australia	Audit report	Yes	• Between 7 and 23% cheaper • Auditor saw as 'persuasive' the business case for these two PFI contracts

Table 5.2 (continued)

Study	Sample/cases	Country	Type of publication	Better VfM?	Comments/conclusions
Pollock et al. (2007)	Re-analysis of Mott Macdonald and other reports	UK	Academic paper	No	• 'there is no evidence to support the Treasury cost and time overrun claims of improved efficiency in PFI' [estimates being quoted are] 'not evidence based but biased to favor PFI' • 'only one study compares PFI procurement performance, and all claims based on [this] are misleading'
Allen Consulting Group (2007)	Sample of 21 PPPs and 33 traditional projects	Australia	Consulting report	Yes	• PPPs reported as being an 11% cheaper alternative to traditional projects • Research project funded by Australia's infrastructure suppliers
Blanc-Brude et al. (2006)	227 new road sections across 15 EU countries, of which 65 were PPPs	EU	31 regression analyses	Not tested	• *Ex ante* construction costs of PPPs were 24% higher than traditional procurement • This is a similar magnitude to the traditional cost overruns • Whether PPPs deliver lower overall life-cycle costs remains unknown
Leviakangas (2007, p. 211)	A Finnish toll-road case study	Finland	Financial models	No	• The hypothesis that private finance enabled welfare gains to be achieved was not confirmed

Vining and Boardman (2008)	10 cases across several sectors	Canada	Case studies	Uncertain	• In these 10 case studies, exactly half were judged as economic 'successes' while the other half were judged as 'not successful' • Those projects judged as not successful were generally bigger projects
Hellowell and Pollock (2009)	Financial viability of NHS organizations analysed	UK	Case study	No	• PFI funding of capital investment is highly problematic • It is associated with reduced capacity in England's healthcare system
Jupe (2009)	Rail transport in the UK	UK	Case study	–	• Nationalization and PPPs both represent imperfect solutions for transport • PPP risk transfer and VfM are difficult to achieve and cannot be left to the market discipline of bankruptcy

Source: Adapted from Hodge and Greve (2009).

any control groups in their 'before-and-after' time-series or cross-sectional comparisons. So, in the midst of many stories of PPP success and failure, our interpretation of the results from existing PPP evaluation reports should be treated with considerable caution from a strict statistical perspective.[26] This is a rather sobering conclusion on evaluations to date and is not just an issue of academic whining. Our early simple VfM evaluations of contracting out local government garbage collection to the private sector (such as Bennett and Johnston, 1979, and the work of Savas, 2000, for example) were initially just as confident as today's PPP assessments. Such contracting-out evaluations, however, were found to be statistically unreliable compared to the more careful later assessment of teams such as Domberger et al. (1986). This later assessment was careful to control for eight variables, and their results showed the overwhelming importance of controlling for the amount of work done as well as its quality before we proselytized over matters such as the sector undertaking the work.[27]

Fourth, the reality is that the counterfactual of 'traditional procurement' is both horribly vague and also largely unquantified in most assessments. As Ball et al. (2007) remind us, traditional projects may also adopt incentives such as fines or payments levied for project delays, so that analyses of, say, on-time or on-budget delivery measurements are again made less believable by omitting these confounding variables.[28]

Fifth, looking at the type of cost measurement taken, there is further reason for concern. Nearly all studies are business cases in which estimates are made before the contract is signed or at an early stage in the project life. Few studies existed where actual empirical cost measurements into the contract life were being made, the exceptions here including several works by Shaoul and her colleagues, see for example Edwards et al. (2004), Pollock et al. (2002) and Shaoul (2004, 2005), as well as Fitzgerald (2004), Allen Consulting Group (2007), Leviakangas (2007) and Blanc-Brude et al. (2006).

Sixth, an observation here is that there appear to be two separate academic areas of PPP literature: the political science/public policy/public administration literature (e.g. Hodge and Greve, 2007) and the economics/engineering literature (e.g. Grimsey and Lewis, 2004). These two separate literatures have not been acknowledged thus far, and few if any evaluation reviews to date seem to have covered both well.[29] As well as these academic literatures, there are numerous audit, government and consulting reports (Deloitte, 2006; PricewaterhouseCoopers, 2005; HM Treasury, 2008).

The seventh point concerns the VfM results themselves. On this matter, there is clearly an array of criteria on which VfM has been constructed and wide-ranging empirical findings. Individual evaluation findings range from the early analyses at one extreme of the UK Treasury Task Force reports

(Arthur Andersen and LSE Enterprise, 2000) and National Audit Office (2000) to later papers by Pollitt (2005). Mainly through the calculus of risk transfers, good VfM was reported as being achieved most of the time, with lower costs compared to traditional procurement by between 10 to 20 per cent. Supporting this conclusion were other Australian analyses reporting persuasive business cases and the industry-funded Allen Consulting Group (2007) study, which reported PPPs as being 11 per cent cheaper than traditional projects. Further support came from Mott Macdonald (2002) and National Audit Office (2003) in their early reporting of PPPs as being delivered on time more often (76 per cent compared to 30 per cent for traditional projects) and on budget (78 per cent compared to 27 per cent for traditional arrangements). Also, the stereotypical public works stories of over-budget and late projects did not help.

On the other side were studies saying the opposite. The most damning of this evidence came from Shaoul (2005), who presented a litany of failed PFI project examples, a VfM appraisal methodology biased in favour of policy expansion, and pitiful availability of information needed for project evaluation and scrutiny. Even the UK Public Accounts Committee of Parliament labelled the public sector comparator (PSC) process as clearly 'manipulation' in the midst of conspicuously unsuccessful IT projects and risk transfer arrangements where risks had not been transferred to the private sector at all but taken by the public. Ball et al. (2007, p. 301) noted the flimsy risk analyses and criticized these as 'almost entirely subjective'. Moreover, the Audit Commission (2003, p. 21) in the UK 'found no evidence that PFI schemes delivered schools more quickly than projects funded by more traditional ways'. Capping this criticism was the analysis of Pollock et al. (2007, p. 127) which reviewed the on-time and on-budget findings of Mott Macdonald (2002). Their review was unequivocal, stating simply 'there is thus no evidence to support the Treasury cost and time overrun claims of improved efficiency in PFI' and that 'all claims based on [this] are misleading'.[30] Later findings from Hellowell and Pollock (2009) also concluded that PFI projects were associated with reduced capacity in England's healthcare system.

In the middle were the evaluation study by Fitzgerald (2004), and the reviews of Hodge (2005) in Australia and Boardman et al. (2005) in North America. Fitzgerald's work concluded that the estimate made of costs savings was largely dependent on the discount rate used (with a lower discount rate suggesting a cost increase of 6 per cent rather than the 9 per cent cost saving estimated using the higher discount rate). Both of the reviews concluded independently that 'caveat emptor' was the most appropriate philosophy for governments taking on PPPs. And the fact that Treasuries had gradually abdicated their traditional role of stewardship in preference to a louder policy advocacy role matters. Governments now find themselves in the middle of multiple conflicts of interest, acting in the roles of policy advocate, economic developer, steward for public funds, elected representative for decision-making, regulator over the contract life, commercial signatory to the contract and planner. Added to these middleground observations were the review of ten Canadian PPPs by Vining and Boardman (2008), who judged only one half of these as economic successes, and the conclusion by Jupe (2009) that both nationalization and PPPs were 'imperfect solutions' for transport services in the UK. Also, the statistically careful work of Blanc-Brude et al. (2006) ought to be particularly acknowledged. Blanc-Brude et al. conducted multiple regression analyses of 227 new road sections across EU countries and revealed PPPs as 24 per cent more expensive than our expectations from traditional procurement. They did note, however, that in their view, this was also about the same magnitude of traditional project cost overruns.[31]

Overall, then, the veracity of the analytical studies underpinning VfM evaluations has generally been low, and analysts who have been apprehensive of the political promises made for LTIC-type PPPs using private finance appear to have been on the money. To put it diplomatically, the evaluation designs used for these studies have most often been weak, and the data mostly dirty. It is perhaps little wonder that evaluations thus far point to contradictory VfM results. Given their importance and continuing political popularity, however, the implication here is that far greater care is needed to strengthen future PPP evaluations. More care is also needed to conduct such assessments away from the policy cheerleaders. The other side of the coin here, though, is that PPPs as a governance tool may well be effective for reformist governments, and that more serious research is probably needed in order to better define the contributions made by PPPs in this way. Several PPP objectives relate to governance issues and deserve a better evidence base rather than the current anecdotal observations and assertions.

Conclusions

Multiple evaluation challenges are presented by the PPP phenomenon. We now need to get past the current debates over LTIC-type PPPs, which are characterized by language-games, and either loud criticism or gushing praise rather than evidence-based learning and synthesis. Evaluating the degree to which the many promises of LTIC-type PPPs are met, however, is not an easy task, and it demands a cross-disciplinary set of perspectives and skills. Six challenges face evaluators. First, the very subject of the evaluation is not simple given the fluidity of the PPP phenomenon across the globe and the breadth of different contractual and structural arrangements possible for PPPs. Second, PPPs clearly have multiple objectives. We counted 15, and these have changed over time. Third, there are many disciplines and discourses with an interest in PPPs, each with their own dominant views on what matters most and which methodologies count as strong evaluations. Improved conceptual frameworks are now needed in order to undertake comprehensive evaluations. Fourth, evaluators have a philosophical decision to make as to the role that they wish to play: whether one of scientifically searching for knowledge, testing how well policies look from the unconstrained perspective of citizens, or else presenting information that enables others to judge PPP performance. Fifth, while evaluators might simply wish to assist conclusions to be made beyond reasonable doubt, this is not so easy in practice. Even considering an assessment of one objective such as VfM, decades of evaluation experience in other disciplines reminds us that strong experimental designs are needed to enable defensible conclusions as to cause and effect to be reached. Looking at the international VfM evidence base to date, individual PPP evaluations are still widely contestable and have a long way to go before claiming a strong degree of rigour. And sixth, the challenge of accurately reviewing the multiple international studies conducted to date requires a discipline and transparency rarely seen in practice. All these challenges nevertheless present us with a real opportunity to reassess where we currently stand with PPPs, re-establish just what we know, and re-evaluate where we may wish to go next in our PPP research and practice.

Notes

1. See Hodge and Greve (2007).
2. See also for example, Bingham and Felbinger (2002), Black (1999), Dahler-Larson (2005), Fowler (1993), Hardy and Bryman (2004), Pawson and Tilley (1997), Spiegel and Stephens (1999), Stufflebeam and Shinkfield (2007), Weiss (1998), Wholey (1979), Yin (2002).
3. See Allen's Penguin English dictionary (2004).
4. Bingham and Felbinger (2002) also note that evaluations can be broadly categorized as being undertaken in two groups, and as either formative or summative. Formative evaluations tackle questions about process, and determine the answer to questions such as 'To what extent are contract obligations being met?', 'What activities are taking place?', and 'Are clients satisfied with the services?' Summative evaluations, on the other hand, are more concerned with outcomes and the impacts of programmes. Summative evaluations therefore ask questions such as 'What is the result of activities conducted?' or 'Has the problem (such as poverty or illiteracy) been reduced as a result of this programme?'. Evaluation texts also emphasize issues of validity, whether it is internal validity (i.e. the degree to which the impact measured is actually attributable to the treatment and no other factors), or external validity (i.e. how generalizabile the research findings from one particular study might be to other sites and other situations).
5. Another view of some of the dynamics behind evaluation is that given by Dahler-Larson (2005), who looked at several different alternative potential explanations for our current interest in evaluation. He argued that no single source properly explained the reasons for

our current interests in evaluation, and concluded that the evaluation wave had many sources. It was, to him, 'a composite rather than a monolithic phenomenon'.

6. After medicine, this approach has then moved into allied health, social work and human services, as well as broader social policy research, criminal justice and education (Nutley et al., 2003).

7. They cite the 1939 'problem' to the German state of racial hygiene and the genocidal solution as an extreme example of evidence-based policy.

8. A language-game is therefore being played when governments talk about 'better' policy outcomes or 'better regulation'. Van de Walle (2009) put it nicely when he observed that talking about 'better' outcomes (or better policies!) tends to drive out contradictions and 'pursues efficient solutions to messy social problems'.

9. Of course this is only one way of describing the challenges of evaluation. Dahler-Larson (2005), for example, suggests four dimensions. These include the knowledge dimension (with its aim of systematically producing knowledge), the values dimension, the utilization dimension (which encompasses the use to which an evaluation is to be put) and the evaluand (which itself requires clarity).

10. The one important exception to this is the case where a government enters an infrastructure deal requiring users or citizens to pay directly, such as tolls on a new road. Here, such an arrangement does reduce pressure on public sector budgets, because government has essentially purchased the infrastructure through the commitment of funds from future (private) road users rather than using its own resources.

11. Interestingly, this observation has not been widely acknowledged in the literature.

12. In other words, the regulatory scholars note that the private contract domain regulates (Saunders and Yam, 2004; Freiberg, 2006).

13. Jeffares et al. (2009) note the development of theory-based evaluation for complex public policy arenas, particularly in terms of well-known examples such as theories of change (Connell and Kubish, 1995) and realistic evaluation (Pawson and Tilley, 1997). Building on the work of Skelcher and Sullivan (2008), they nominate six theoretical bases for their six performance dimensions: democratic theory; network theory; institutional theory; innovation theory; exchange theory/power dependency theory and discourse theory.

14. Bingham and Felbinger (2002, p. 4) in fact indicate a continuum of possibilities ranging from process-based (formative) evaluations such as monitoring daily tasks and assessing programme activities through to outcome-based (summative) evaluations such as enumerating outcomes, measuring effectiveness, establishing costs and benefits and assessing impacts on the problem.

15. Note that authors such as Black (1999) add more types of experimental design to this: e.g. single group post-test only.

16. Some examples illustrate this. Glass et al. (1981, p. 19) cite Miller's classic work in 1977 in which the findings of five reviews of the efficacy of psychotherapy and drug therapy were reviewed. These five reviews integrated the findings from 14 studies and were completed within a period of about five years. Largely the same body of literature was available for review. The reviews came to conflicting resolutions, with some concluding that the combination of both psychotherapy and drug therapy together were quite clearly superior to drug therapy alone, while others concluded that no firm conclusions could be reached. Clearly, different reviewers see the same empirical results quite differently (Hodge, 2000, p. 60).

17. Cook et al. (1992).

18. Ibid., p. viii.

19. Johnson et al. (1995) report in their comparison of meta-analytic approaches over a decade ago that 'literally hundreds of meta-analyses have been published' in a wide range of disciplines.

20. This assessment draws on Hodge and Greve (2009).

21. See Hodge (2004), for example.

22. For earlier comprehensive evaluations of privatization see, e.g., Megginson et al.

(1994), Boubakri and Cosset (1998), D'Souza and Megginson (1999) and Hodge (2000) (statistical meta-analyses), or Martin and Parker (1997), Parker (2004) and Cook and Kirkpatrick (2003) (comprehensive review assessments of various types).

23. See, e.g., Hodge and Greve (2007), Berg et al. (2002), Bovaird (2004), Ghobadian et al. (2004a), Edwards et al. (2004), Grimsey and Lewis (2004), Osborne (2001), Perrot and Chatelus (2000), Pollitt (2005), Savas (2000), Shaoul (2005), Teisman and Klijn (2001), Vaillancourt Rosenau (2000) and Wettenhall (2003).

24. See Flinders (2005), Mott Macdonald (2002), National Audit Office (2000), Pollock et al. (2002) and Shaoul (2004) for examples of PPP reviews taking a more specific focus.

25. One of the notable absences from this table, for example, is the many audit reports for individual PFI projects in the UK.

26. The design strength of evaluation studies was noted earlier as covering four levels from the weakest design, a simple before/after comparison (level 1), time-series (level 2), comparison groups (level 3) to the strongest design, experimental-control group (level 4) where a random assignment occurs to treatment and control groups (Bingham and Felbinger, 2002). Nearly all of the above PPP VfM studies are rated level 1 ('weak').

27. The early assessment of contracting out garbage collection services undertaken by Bennett and Johnston (1979) analysed 29 private firms in the USA and announced that municipal provision (at $127 per year) was statistically more expensive than private firms (at $87 per year). But as the analysis did not control for distance from the dump, dispersal of households served, quality and frequency of service or other factors, the results were a good deal less convincing than asserted (Donahue, 1989, p. 60). A later analysis by Savas looked at 1378 US communities and after controlling for scale, organizational form and pick-up, found that contracted private firms were 9 per cent cheaper than municipal provision. Interestingly, however, he also found that competitive arrangements were one-third more expensive than the local government service. The importance of ensuring collection route contiguity in refuse collection was evident here. There have since been dozens of other studies of this issue over the years. One of central importance to us, though, was the seminal econometric analysis undertaken by Domberger et al. (1986) in the UK. Analysing 610 authorities through 1983–84 revealed cost differentials of 22 per cent when contracting was being undertaken with the private sector and 17 per cent when the service was tendered but retained in house. Importantly, controls for a wide range of variables were present. Domberger's cost equations to model production assumed that the cost was a function of the level of output, the frequency of pick-up, input wage costs, the method of collection, the density of housing, the distance to disposal, the proportion that was domestic, the extent of reclamation of paper and bottles, and whether, after tendering, the collection was undertaken by in-house or external private companies. The strength of Domberger's experimental design has enabled his findings to stand the test of time until the present day. There is much here of significance to an analysis of PPPs. A sophisticated analysis was needed to get reliable answers for a simple service – collecting the garbage. Some eight variables were controlled for before getting statistical data articulating the effectiveness of contracting and competitive arrangements. The same philosophical attitude is needed in evaluating PPPs. And analytically, the biggest statistical finding in Domberger's analysis of garbage collection was the clear and extremely strong relationship between the cost of collection and the number of units collected. In other words, 'the more work done, the higher the cost', as we might expect from common sense. The need to carefully control for the multiple dimensions of 'the work done' in any PPP analysis is therefore clear, as well as the many other variables such as contract types, incentives and source of finance, and so on.

28. Pollock et al. (2007) also note that public procurement practices have improved significantly over time, but that this effect generally goes unacknowledged.

29. Table 5.2 is principally drawn from the former domain, that is, the political science/public policy/public administration literature. It is worthwhile acknowledging that other literatures clearly also have an interest in PPP matters, such as the arena of megaprojects; Priemus et al. (2008).

30. Difficulties in extracting these research data from behind government claims of 'commercial-in-confidence' also amplified concerns that peer review scrutiny was not welcomed and that the well-publicized Mott Macdonald study lacked rigour.
31. This review, however, cautioned against making any further VfM conclusions, arguing that life-cycle costs over the longer term were still unknown.

References

Allen, R. (ed.) (2004), *The Penguin Dictionary*, Penguin Books.
Allen Consulting Group (2007), *Performance of PPPs and Traditional Procurement in Australia*, Final Report to Infrastructure Partnerships Australia, 30 November.
Arthur Andersen and LSE Enterprise (2000), *Value for Money Drivers in the Private Finance Initiative*, London: UK Treasury Task Force.
Audit Commission (2003), *PFI in Schools*, London: Audit Commission.
Auditor-General of New South Wales (2006), *The New Schools Privately Financed Project*, Auditor-General's Report Performance Audit, March, Sydney.
Ball, R., M. Heafey and D. King (2007), 'The Private Finance Initiative in the UK', *Public Management Review*, **9** (2), 289–310.
Banks, G. (2009), 'Evidence based policy making: What is it? How do we get it?', ANZSOG/ANU Public Lecture Series, 4 February, Canberra.
Bennett, J.T. and M.H. Johnston (1979), 'Public versus private provision of collective goods and services: garbage collection revisited', *Public Choice*, **34**, 55–63.
Berg, S., M. Pollitt and M. Tsuji (eds) (2002), *Private Initiatives in Infrastructure: Priorities, Incentives and Performance*, Cheltenham, UK and Northampton, MA, USA: Edward Elgar.
Bingham, R.D. and C.L. Felbinger (2002), *Evaluation in Practice: A Methodological Approach*, 2nd edn, New York: Chatham House.
Black, T.R. (1999), *Doing Quantitative Research in the Social Sciences: An Integrated Approach to Research Design, Measurement and Statistics*, London: Sage Publications.
Blanc-Brude, F., H. Goldsmith and T. Valila (2006), *Ex Ante Construction Costs in the European Road Sector: A Comparison of Public-Private Partnerships and Traditional Public Procurement*, Economic and Financial Report 2006/01, European Investment Bank.
Bloomfield, P., D. Westerling and R. Carey (1998), 'Innovation and risks in a public–private partnership: financing and construction of a capital project in Massachusetts', *Public Productivity and Review*, **21** (4), 460–71.
Boardman, A., F. Poschmann and A. Vining (2005), 'North American infrastructure P3s: examples and lessons learned', in Graeme Hodge and Carsten Greve (eds), *The Challenge of Public–Private Partnerships: Learning from International Experience*, Cheltenham, UK and Northampton, MA, USA: Edward Elgar, pp. 162–89.
Boardman, A. and A. Vining (2010), 'Assessing the economic worth of public–private partnership', in Graeme A. Hodge, Carsten Greve and Anthony Boardman (eds), *International Handbook on Public–Private Partnerships*, Cheltenham, UK and Northampton, MA, USA: Edward Elgar.
Boubakri, N. and J.C. Cosset (1998), 'The financial and operating performance of newly privatised firms: evidence from developing countries', *Journal of Finance*, **53** (3), 1081–110.
Bovaird, T. (2004), 'Public–private partnerships in Western Europe and the US: new growths from old roots', in Abby Ghobadian, David Gallear, Nicholas O'Regan and Howard Viney (eds), *Public–Private Partnerships: Policy and Experience*, Basingstoke: Palgrave Macmillan, pp. 221–50.
Broadbent, Jane and Richard Loughlin (2002), 'Accounting choices: technical and political trade offs and the UK's Private Finance Initiative', *Accounting, Auditing and Accountability Journal*, **15** (2), 622–54.
Coghill, K. and D. Woodward (2005), 'Political issues of public–private partnerships', in Graeme Hodge and Carsten Greve (eds), *The Challenge of Public–Private Partnerships:*

Learning from International Experience, Cheltenham, UK and Northampton, MA, USA: Edward Elgar, pp. 81–94.

Connell, J.P. and A.C. Kubish (1995), 'Applying a theory of change approach to the evaluation of comprehensive community initiatives: progress, prospects and problems', in K. Fulbright-Anderson (ed.), *New Approaches to Evaluating Community Initiatives: Volume 2 Theory, Measurement and Analysis*, Washington, DC: The Aspen Institute, pp. 15–44.

Cook, P. and C. Kirkpatrick (2003), 'Assessing the impact of privatisation in developing countries', in D. Parker and D. Saal (eds), *International Handbook on Privatization*, Cheltenham, UK and Northampton, MA, USA: Edward Elgar, pp. 209–19.

Cook, T.D., H. Cooper, D.S. Cordray, H. Hartmann, L.V. Hedges, R.J. Light, T.A. Louis and F. Mosteller (1992), *Meta-Analysis for Explanation: A Case Book*, New York: The Russell Sage Foundation.

Cresswell, J.W. (1998), *Qualitative Inquiry and Research Design: Choosing Among Five Traditions*, Thousand Oaks, CA: Sage Publications.

Dahler-Larson, P. (2005), 'Evaluation and public management', in Ewan Ferlie, Laurence E. Lynn, Jr and Christopher Pollitt (eds), *The Oxford Handbook of Public Management*, Oxford: Oxford University Press, pp. 615–39.

De Bruin, H. and M. Leijten (2008), 'Mega-projects and contested information', in Hugo Priemus, Bent Flyvbjerg and Bert van Wee (eds), *Decision-Making on Mega-Projects*, Cheltenham, UK and Northampton, MA, USA: Edward Elgar, pp. 23–39.

Deloitte (2006), *Closing the Infrastructure Gap: The Role of Public–Private Partnerships*, A Deloitte Research Study.

Department of Transport (2002), 'Public sector comparators factsheet', available at: www.railways.dtlr.gov.uk.

Domberger, A., S.A. Meadowcroft and D.J. Thomson (1986), 'Competitive tendering and efficiency: the case of refuse collection', *Fiscal Studies*, 7 (4), 69–87.

Donahue, J.D. (1989), *The Privatization Decision: Public Ends, Private Means*, New York: Basic Books, HarperCollins.

D'Souza, J. and W.J. Megginson (1999), 'The financial and operating performance of privatisation firms during the 1990s', *Journal of Finance*, 54 (4), 1397–438.

Edwards, P., J. Shaoul, A. Stafford and L. Arblaster (2004), *Evaluating the Operation of PFI in Roads and Hospitals*, London: Certified Accountants Education Trust.

Ernst & Young (2007), *The Road Ahead: Future of PPP in Australian Road Infrastructure*, Ernst & Young Australia.

Fitzgerald, J.P. and C.F. Duffield (2006), 'The performance of major Australian projects: a comparison of PPP projects versus more traditional procurement strategies', in M. El-Bady (ed.), *1st International Construction Specialty conference, 23–26 May*, Canadian Society for Civil Engineering, Calgary, Alberta, Canada, pp. 1–8.

Fitzgerald, P. (2004), *Review of Partnerships Victoria Provided Infrastructure*, Melbourne: Growth Solutions Group.

Flinders, M. (2005), 'The politics of public–private partnerships', *British Journal of Political and International Relations*, 7, 215–39.

Fowler, F.J. (1993), *Survey Research Methods*, 2nd edn, London: Sage Publications.

Freiberg, A. (2006), 'The tools of government', paper presented to the Australasian Compliance Institute, 26 April, unpublished.

Ghobadian, A., D. Gallear, N. O'Regan and H. Viney (eds) (2004a), *Public–Private Partnerships: Policy and Experience*, Basingstoke: Palgrave Macmillan.

Ghobadian, A., D. Gallear, H. Viney and D. O'Regan (2004b), 'The future of public–private partnership', in A. Ghohabian, D. Gallear, N. O'Regan and H. Viney (eds), *Public–Private Partnerships: Policy and Experience*, Basingstoke: Palgrave Macmillan, pp. 271–302.

Glass, G. (1976), 'Integrating findings: the meta-analysis of research', *Educational Researcher*, 5 (10), 3–8.

Glass, G.V., B. McGaw and M.L. Smith (1981), *Meta-Analysis in Social Research*, Beverly Hills, CA: Sage Publications.

Greve, C. (2003), 'When public–private partnerships fail: The extreme case of the

NPM-inspired local government of Farum in Denmark', paper for the EGPA conference, 3–6 September, Oeiras, Portugal.

Grimsey, D. and M. Lewis (2004), *Public–Private Partnerships: the Worldwide Revolution in Infrastructure Provision and Project Finance*, Cheltenham, UK and Northampton, MA, USA: Edward Elgar.

Guba, E.G. and Y.S. Lincoln (1987), 'The countenances of fourth-generation evaluation: description, judgement and negotiation', in D.J. Palumbo (ed.), *The Politics of Program Evaluation*, Newbury Park, CA: Sage, p. 127.

Hardy, M. and A. Bryman (2004), *Handbook of Data Analysis*, London: Sage Publications.

Head, B. (2008), 'Three lenses of evidence-based policy', *The Australian Journal of Public Administration*, **67** (1), 1–11.

Hellowell, M. and A.M. Pollock (2009), 'The private financing of NHS hospitals: politics, policy and practice', *Economic Affairs*, **29** (1), 13–19.

HM Treasury (2008), *Infrastructure Procurement. Delivering Long-term Value*, London: HMSO.

Hodge, G.A. (2000), *Privatisation: An International Review of Performance*, New York: Perseus Books, Westview Press.

Hodge, G.A. (2004), 'The risky business of public–private-partnerships', *Australian Journal of Public Administration*, **63** (4), 37–49.

Hodge, G.A. (2005), 'Public–private partnerships: the Australian experience with physical infrastructure', in Graeme Hodge and Carsten Greve (eds), *The Challenge of Public–Private Partnerships: Learning from International Experience*, Cheltenham, UK and Northampton, MA, USA: Edward Elgar, pp. 305–31.

Hodge, G.A. (2006), 'Public-private partnerships and legitimacy', *University of New South Wales Law Journal, Forum*, **29** (3), 318–27.

Hodge, G.A. and C. Greve (2007), 'Public–private partnerships: an international performance review', *Public Administration Review*, **67** (3), 545–58.

Hodge, G.A. and C. Greve (2009), 'PPPs: the passage of time permits a sober reflection', *Economic Affairs*, **29** (1), 33–9.

Hunter, J.E. and F.L. Schmidt (1990), *Methods of Meta-Analysis: Correcting Error and Bias in Research Findings*, Thousand Oaks, CA: Sage Publications.

Jackson, G.B. (1978), *Methods for Reviewing and Integrating Research in the Social Sciences*, Final Report to the National Science Foundation for Grant No. DIS 76-20309, April, Washington, DC: Social Research Group, George Washington University.

Jeffares, S., H. Sullivan and T. Bovaird (2009), 'Beyond the contract – the challenge of evaluating the performance of public–private partnerships', paper presented at the International Research Society for Public Management (IRSPM), 6–8 April, Copenhagen, Denmark.

Johnson, B.T., B. Mullen and E. Salas (1995), 'Comparison of three major meta-analytic approaches', *Journal of Applied Psychology*, **80** (1), 94–106.

Jupe, R. (2009), 'New Labour, public private partnerships and rail transport', *Economic Affairs*, **29** (1), 20–25.

Leviakangas, P. (2007), *Private Finance of Transport Infrastructure Projects: Value and Risk Analysis of a Finnish Shadow Toll Road Project*, ESPOO 2007, VTT Publications, p. 624.

Marston, G. and R. Watts (2003), '"Just the facts Ma'am": a critical appraisal of evidence-based policy', *Just Policy*, **30**, 32–46.

Martin, S. and D. Parker (1997), *The Impact of Privatisation: Ownership and Corporate Performance in the UK, Series on Industrial Economic Strategies for Europe*, London: Routledge.

Megginson, W.L., R. Nash and M. Van Randenborgh (1994), 'The financial and operating performance of newly privatized firms: an international empirical analysis', *The Journal of Finance*, **XLIX** (2), 403–52.

Mott Macdonald (2002), *Review of Large Public Procurement in the UK*, London: Mott Macdonald.

National Audit Office (2000), *Examining the Value for Money of Deals under the Private Finance Initiative*, London: The Stationery Office.

National Audit Office (2003), *PFI: Construction Performance*, London: The Stationery Office.

Nutley, S., H. Davies and I. Walter (2003), 'Evidence-based policy and practice: cross sector lessons from the UK', paper presented to the Social Policy Research and Evaluation Conference, Wellington, New Zealand.

OECD (2008), *Public–Private Partnerships: In Pursuit of Risk Sharing and Value for Money*, Paris: OECD.

Osborne, S. (ed.) (2001), *Public–Private Partnerships: Theory and Practice in International Perspective*, New York: Routledge.

Parker, D. (2004), *The UK's Privatisation Experiment: The Passage of Time Permits a Sober Assessment*, CESifo Working Paper 1126, Cranfield University.

Parsons, W. (1995), *Public Policy: An Introduction to the Theory and Practice of Policy Analysis*, Aldershot, UK and Brookfield, USA: Edward Elgar.

Pawson, R. and N. Tilley (1997), *Realistic Evaluation*, London: Sage.

Perrot, J.-Y. and G. Chatelus (eds) (2000), *Financing of Major Infrastructure and Public Service Projects: Public Private Partnerships, Lessons from French Experience Throughout the World*, Paris: Presses de l'ecole nationale des Ponts et Chaussees.

Pollitt, M. (2002), 'The declining role of the state in infrastructure investment in the UK', in Sanford V. Berg, Michael G. Pollitt and Masatsuga Tsuji (eds), *Private Initiatives in Infrastructure: Priorities, Incentives and Performance*, Cheltenham, UK and Northampton, MA, USA: Edward Elgar.

Pollitt, M. (2005), 'Learning from the UK Private Finance Initiative experience', in Graeme Hodge and Carsten Greve (eds), *The Challenge of Public–Private Partnerships: Learning from International Experience*, Cheltenham, UK and Northampton, MA, USA: Edward Elgar, pp. 207–30.

Pollock, A., J. Shaoul and N. Vickers (2002), 'Private finance and value for money in NHS hospitals: a policy in search of a rationale?', *British Medical Journal*, **324**, 1205–8.

Pollock, A., D. Price and S. Playe (2007), 'An examination of the UK Treasury's evidence base for cost and time overrun data in UK value-for-money policy and appraisal', *Public Money and Management*, April, 127–33.

PricewaterhouseCoopers (2005), *Delivering the PPP Promise. A Review of PPP Issues and Activities*, available at: www.pwc.com/, 26 November 2008.

Priemus, H., B. Flyvbjerg and B. van Wee (eds) (2008), *Decision-Making on Mega-Projects*, Cheltenham, UK and Northampton, MA, USA: Edward Elgar.

Sanderson, I. (2002), 'Evaluation, policy learning and evidence-based policy making', *Public Administration*, **80** (1), 1–22.

Saunders, C. and K.K.F. Yam (2004), 'Government regulation by contract: implications for the rule of law', *Public Law Review*, **15**, 51–70.

Savas, E.S. (2000), *Privatization and Public–Private Partnerships*, New York: Chatham House Publishers and Seven Bridges Press.

Shaoul, J. (2004), 'Railpolitik: the financial realities of operating Britain's national railways', *Public Money and Management*, **24** (1), 27–36.

Shaoul, J. (2005), 'The Private Finance Initiative or the public funding of private profit', in Graeme Hodge and Carsten Greve (eds), *The Challenge of Public–Private Partnerships: Learning from International Experience*, Cheltenham, UK and Northampton, MA, USA: Edward Elgar, pp. 190–206.

Skelcher, C. and H. Sullivan (2008), 'Theory driven approaches to analysing collaborative performance', *Public Management Review*, **10** (6), 751–7.

Spiegel, M.R. and L.J. Stephens (1999), *Statistics, Schaum's Outline Series*, New York: McGraw-Hill.

Stufflebeam, D.L. and A.J. Shinkfield (2007), *Evaluation Theory, Models, and Applications*, New York: John Wiley & Sons.

Teisman, G. and E.-H. Klijn (2001), 'Public–private partnerships in the European Union: official suspect, embraced in daily practice', in Stephen Osborne (ed.), *Public–Private Partnerships: Theory and Practice in International Perspective*, New York: Routledge, pp. 165–86.

Vaillancourt Rosenau, P. (ed.) (2000), *Public–Private Policy Partnerships*, Cambridge, MA: MIT Press.

Van de Walle, S. (2009), 'International comparisons of public sector performance: how to move ahead', *Public Management Review*, **11** (1), 39–56.

Vining, A.R. and A.E. Boardman (2008), 'Public–private partnerships in Canada: theory and evidence', *Canadian Public Administration*, **51** (1), 9–44.

Walker, B. and B.C. Walker (2000), *Privatisation: Sell Off or Sell Out? The Australian Experience*, Sydney: ABC Books.

Walker, D. (2007), 'Is evidence good for democracy?', *Public Money and Management*, September, 235–7.

Weimer, D.L. and Vining, A.R. (2004), *Policy Analysis: Concepts and Practice*, 4th edn, Upper Saddle River, NJ: Pearson Prentice Hall.

Weiss, C.H. (1998), *Evaluation: Methods for Studying Programs and Policies*, 2nd edn, Upper Saddle River, NJ: Prentice Hall.

Wettenhall, R. (2003), 'The rhetoric and reality of public–private partnerships', *Public Organisation Review: A Global Journal*, **3**, 77–107.

Wholey, J.S. (1979), *Evaluation: Promise and Performance*, Washington, DC: The Urban Institute.

Yin, R.K. (2002), *Case Study Research: Design and Methods*, 3rd edn, London: Sage Publications.

PART II

DISCIPLINARY THEMES IN PUBLIC–PRIVATE PARTNERSHIPS

6 Splintered logic and political debate
Matthew Flinders

In 1983 the American political scientist Graham Allison wrote a seminal article in which he posed the question: are public and private organizations fundamentally alike in all unimportant respects? In asking this question Allison sought to explicate and define the differences between the values, principles and motivations – the very underlying logic – of public and private organizations. A quarter of a century later Allison's question remains as salient, if not more so, than when it was first posed. More specifically, his conclusion that 'public and private management are at least as different as they are similar, and the differences are more important than the similarities' provides a canvas on which it is possible to explore emergent themes and tensions in relation to the role of public–private partnerships (PPPs) in the provision or supply of public goods in the twenty-first century. Exploring these themes, particularly those concerning sociopolitical relationships, is critical due to the fact that although a great deal has been written about the growth, role and technicalities of PPPs, very little has been written about the political implications of the global trend towards promoting a greater role for the private sector in the design and delivery of public services. More critically for the focus of this chapter, much of the literature on what might be termed 'the politics of PPPs' has exhibited a lazy style of thinking and little conscious theorizing – lazy in the sense that political debate has been couched in terms of broad polarizations that have sought to portray PPPs *in toto* as either 'good' or 'bad', 'unaccountable' or 'accountable', 'efficient' or 'inefficient', when in fact such crude conceptualizations are too blunt to fully understand the role of PPPs as a tool of governance in the twenty-first century. Even the most cursory analysis of parliamentary and auditor reports reveals that PPPs are more efficient than traditional (i.e. direct state funding and provision) procurement projects in *some* areas (like road building) but not others (like the provision of schools or hospitals in some cases). To seek to label PPPs as unaccountable also flounders against the uncomfortable fact that *some forms* of PPP, in *some policy areas*, in *some countries* clearly exist within a much tighter and more transparent accountability framework than similar institutions in the public sector. An example of this would be the privately designed, built and managed prisons in the UK. The basic point being made is that for too long the advocates and opponents of PPPs have tended to talk *at* each other and *past* each other but not *to* each other.

As a result, this chapter is not concerned with history, definitions, technical assessments, country profiles or statistical analysis – issues dealt with at length in other contributions within this volume – but will instead seek to tease apart and unravel some of the deeper political debates concerning PPPs in the context of much broader arguments concerning the role and structure of the state in the twenty-first century – debates that touch upon and develop many of the themes raised by Allison in his influential analysis of organizational forms. In this sense the approach of this chapter is likely to be slightly broader than that of some of the other contributions in this collection because it seeks to set out the political backcloth on which debates and controversies surrounding PPPs tend to be located. As a result it focuses on the broader process of 'marketization', referring to the process of taking goods and services that were previously provided by the state and transferring them to a form of market-based arrangement (see Crouch, 2009), in addition to the specific position of PPPs within this debate.

Unlike the vast majority of documents on PPPs that currently exist, the normative position of this chapter is agnostic – in the sense that it does not seek to promote or disavow the role of PPPs but instead seeks to understand the roots of ongoing political tensions. It is exactly by exposing these roots and locating them within the sphere of public contestation that this chapter makes a distinctive and provocative contribution to the wider literature. At the heart of this contribution lies a focus on governing logic (i.e. the primary values and principles underlying reform processes). The central argument of this chapter is that political debates emanate from the existence of splintered logic – splintered in the sense that the values and principles on which PPPs are based and promoted are at odds with those traditionally found within the political and public sphere. While this disparity can be utilized as a resource through which politicians can seek to promote and compel institutional and cultural change within the public sector, it can also be interpreted as a political and democratic liability if the underlying logic of PPPs gradually erodes and eviscerates longstanding sociopolitical relationships concerning the logic of collective action.

The simple argument of this chapter is therefore that PPPs are founded on a governing logic that does not sit comfortably with the values and principles on which modern state systems were established during the nineteenth century, and developed during the twentieth century. The baseline logic of PPPs involves: (1) accepting the supremacy of market-like relationships in all transaction situations; and (2) focusing on *economic* efficiency and outputs as the primary indicator of performance. Participants in the debate concerning PPPs need to be honest about this basic fact. It is for this reason difficult to blend or interweave these central tenets with those that have for centuries underpinned public bureaucracies. The logic of the private sector and that of the public sector are antagonistic (they splinter rather than unite), and contemporary debates concerning PPPs provide a basic empirical manifestation of this fact.

In order to demonstrate the existence of this splintered logic and how it creates a number of seemingly intractable political debates, this chapter focuses on three specific topics: (1) the logic of contestability; (2) the logic of the market; and (3) the logic of public expectations. It then seeks to locate the specific issue of PPPs within the contours of much broader debates concerning political disengagement, falling levels of trust in politicians and 'disaffected democracies'.

The logic of contestability

The logic of contestability simply asserts that public services can be provided by a range of organizations drawn from beyond the public sector. In this sense the logic of contestability seeks to sever the assumption that public services should be provided by public bodies. It also views the existence of choice and competition between potential service providers as a positive development that should, in theory, drive down prices while increasing performance. The logic of contestability is therefore a normative political standpoint. Drilling down still further allows us to locate the roots of this normative position, as Hay (2004; see also Green, 1996) has shown, within public-choice theoretic assumptions regarding the perceived innate inefficiencies of the public sector. The critical element of public choice theory, cloaked frequently beneath the veil of seemingly neutral 'new public management' (see Dunleavy and Hood, 1994), was that it sought to challenge dominant understandings concerning the respective roles of the public and private sectors. For much of the twentieth century numerous functions had been explicitly located within the margins of state projects due to a concern that the market, notably the profit motive, could not (or should not) play a role in the equitable distribution of primary resources (water, gas etc.) or collective public goods (education, healthcare, incarceration, policing etc.).

The final quarter of the twentieth century was, however, marked by the emergence of a powerful epistemic community that sought to challenge and dispel dominant assumptions regarding the respective strengths and weaknesses of public and private sectors. This community was to some extent crystallized around a global 'reinventing government' (Osborne and Gaebler, 1992) narrative within which the private sector, in general, and the profit motive, in particular, was viewed from this position not as a threat to the state but as a potential partner of the state with the capacity to reduce inefficiencies and increase performance while also injecting much-needed dynamism and cultural change within the public sector. The logic of contestability therefore seeks to open up the provision of public services to a wider range of delivery bodies and, as Pierre (2000) illustrates, views the role of the state increasingly in terms of 'steering' (i.e. contracting with a range of delivery bodies to provide agreed services) rather than 'rowing' (i.e. the direct delivery of services). Political science as a discipline has couched this transition within a shift from 'government' to 'governance' (see Rhodes, 1997).

The splintered logic in this area arises from the fact that the logic of contestability is primarily driven by economic rationality. In this sense it gauges performance and efficiency through a fairly crude fiscal calculation based upon inputs (i.e. invested resources) and outputs (i.e. units delivered). 'Public sector comparisons', the technical concept through which PPP tenders are assessed, tend to be derived and compared in terms of, for example, prisoner cost per day or medical procedures per staff member, when it could be argued that this approach overlooks the subtle yet critical qualitative elements of social provision. This point flows into three interrelated issues concerning (1) quantification and contestability; (2) the public service ethos and contestability; and (3) the myth of contestability.

The processes of contracting and tendering demand the quantification of public services. This has resulted in an 'audit explosion' and similar 'rituals of verification' (Power, 1999) whereby internal audits, external audits, teaching audits, quality-compliance audits, risk audits, social audits, value for money audits etc. now form core elements of any public sector manager's role. This is problematic for at least two reasons. First, many aspects of roles within the public sector, particularly in relation to 'street-level bureaucrats' (i.e. those at the actual interface with service users) are simply not amenable to simple quantification. Put slightly differently, the fact that Police Officer X arrests more people than Police Officer Y does not automatically make the former a 'better' police officer; indeed, the opposite may be true. The danger of viewing the public sector as little more than a political marketplace in which goods can be bought and sold risks promoting a focus on out*puts* (i.e. goods and services provided by the contract) rather than out*comes* (i.e. the effect on society arising from services). We would not want to focus solely on the number of arrests when the outcome we ultimately seek is a safer and more just society in which to live.

For auditors and public servants an orientation on outcomes is harder to achieve due to complexity, time lags and other influences that make ascribing direct causation difficult. And yet focusing on quantifiable price-per-unit outputs risks creating unintended externalities, as would be the case, for example, with a prison that achieved extremely high performance efficiencies by keeping all inmates locked in their cells. The downside in terms of societal outcomes is that evidence of such efficiency savings are counterproductive in the long term as the reduction in more expensive educational and therapeutic prisoner services is likely to lead to a higher incidence not only in recidivism but also in relation to secondary social problems, notably drug abuse and mental health conditions (the costs of which will fall to other public agencies). Although this focus on auditing and performance measurement may at first glance appear somewhat dry and technical, it actually feeds into a major element of this chapter's focus on splintered logics by introducing the contested nature of the public service ethos.

So far this section has argued that public services cannot simply be viewed as synonymous with those transactions that occur within the private sphere and are generally couched in financial terms. Many qualitative elements of public service roles are not amenable to ready quantification and therefore might be overlooked in a myopic focus on inputs and outputs. At a much broader level it has been argued that the logic of contestability fails to recognize the existence, importance and role of the public service ethos among public sector employees (see Denhardt and Denhardt, 2007). The public service ethos is generally accepted to involve a combination of high ethical standards (trust, propriety etc.) and a degree of altruism in which individuals commit to working within the public sector due to a sense of personal commitment and loyalty to collective action, and for which they will be rewarded with a secure job, a moderate income, and even the possibility of a public honour or distinction for senior or outstanding public officials. Phrased in this way, the public service ethos can be interpreted as a form of cultural resource that promotes a high-trust, high-commitment workforce – 'knights' instead of 'knaves', to use Le Grand's (2003) influential distinction. The public service ethos is directly related to broader criticisms, made by scholars including Marquand (2004), Freedland (2001) and Crouch (2002), regarding the marketization of the public domain and how this damages under-acknowledged societal values.

As such, the logic of the public service ethos is frequently interpreted as being incompatible with the logic of the market, and particularly with the profit motive. Private sector business methods and working relationships such as, for example, performance-related pay, may lead to the construction of a quite different public service bargain in which distinctive and traditional values become replaced with an individually focused incentives and structures framework that cannot easily be regained (see HC 263, 2002; Hood and Lodge, 2006). The point being made is simple – the use of PPPs imports a new set of quite different motivational assumptions and values into the public sector and a debate exists regarding whether this is a positive or negative development.

The final element of the logic of contestability focuses on the power and role of ideas, irrespective of whether those ideas are founded upon actual facts. This section therefore seeks to emphasize the social and political construction of dominant understandings, irrespective of truth, as a strategic mechanism of achieving change. This can be demonstrated at a number of levels. At the level of institutional competition, for example, one of the clear features of research on PPPs is that the actual level of contestability for contracts tends to be low, not least because the front-loaded costs of preparing a bid effectively rule out small- and medium-sized businesses as well as third-sector bodies (Parker and Hartley, 2003). Furthermore, the larger (international) organizations (Group4, Capita etc.) with a history of winning contracts and providing a service tend rapidly to come to dominate certain areas of competitive tendering. Moreover, the removal of the possibility of changing providers – at least without massive financial costs – within the lifespan of a PPP contract arguably runs counter to the logic of the market (i.e. securing efficiency, flexibility, innovation etc.). As Bult-Spiering et al. (2006, p. 186) stress, 'One-off contestability at the beginning of a contract is unlikely to make up for a twenty-five to thirty-year period in which a single provider has an effective monopoly'. The logic of contestability can therefore mutate very quickly towards a monopolistic situation if not carefully managed.

And yet in many ways this does not matter. One of the most powerful elements of the logic of contestability exists within the realm of ideas rather than institutions and performance. Even if PPPs do not deliver increased performance at lower costs, as many scholars have argued, the logic of contestability provides politicians with an influential tool or mechanism with which to pressurize those elements of the public sector that are deemed, for whatever reason, to be under-performing. The efficiency benefits of PPPs may therefore, if this logic is accepted, accrue in the wider public sector through a reverberation effect as public servants seek to avoid being audited as either 'poor' or, worse still, 'failing' in performance audits and thereby remove the threat of having their service transferred to an alternative service provider – a point that shifts the analytical spotlight to the logic of the market.

The logic of the market
The central argument of this chapter is that political debates emanate from the existence of splintered logic – splintered in the sense that the values and principles on which PPPs are based and promoted are at odds with those

traditionally found within the political and public sphere. This section looks more squarely at the logic of the market and compares this with the historical logic of collective public action in order to identify and expose the origins of broader debates concerning PPPs. A valuable starting point for any discussion of the logic of the market compared to the logic of the public sector is Hirschman's (1970) *Exit, Voice and Loyalty*. The basic theory is simple: individuals have two options when faced with an organization that is providing a declining or unsatisfactory level of service – *exit* (withdraw from the relationship) or *voice* (attempt to rectify the situation by complaining to the organization). *Loyalty* (personal commitment to an organization) can affect decisions regarding exit or voice because personal and less instrumental variables may create an organizational allegiance.

Individual decisions regarding 'exit' and 'voice' clearly depend to a large degree on the availability of alternative choices. Within the private sphere, 'exit' is deemed the crucial option as customers are free, even encouraged, to take advantage of a competitive marketplace in order to achieve satisfaction. In this sense relationships are constantly formed and destroyed as consumers move between alternative service providers. Within the public sphere, 'voice' is generally accepted as the critical indicator of preferences because the level of choice is highly restricted. For the majority of citizens, private education or healthcare are not options. Voice mechanisms are therefore inherently political and frequently confrontational. As has already been discussed in relation to the logic of contestability (above), the whole thrust of marketization, of which the use of PPPs is a central element, has been based around an attempt to import the logic of the market into the public sector. Members of the public are interpreted and modelled as consumers or customers in a political marketplace rather than as citizens within a collective endeavour articulated through a state system. The clash between these logics (one individualized and modelled on the private sector and one collectivized and driven by public goods) is thrown into sharp relief when examined against the topic of accountability.

Public sector accountability operates through a relatively clear chain of delegation. The public elect politicians who, in turn, are responsible and accountable for the management and actions of public servants. The focus on 'voice' (rather than 'exit') within the public sector also creates an internal quality loop in that redress and grievance mechanisms can be utilized by the public in order to ensure that failures are rectified and standards improved. Accountability is not, however, solely about the distribution of culpability. Ministers and officials may also be held to account and rewarded for innovative and successful policy experiments or examples of 'best practice' that can then be transferred to other sections of the public sector. The latter element of what might be termed positive accountability is critical within any organizational context, but is frequently devalued by a positivity offset and negativity bias (i.e. an emphasis on focusing on problems and allocating blame) arising from a societal context that is often interpreted as low-trust high-blame. Being accountable within the public sector, as the work of Behn (2001), Koppell (2005) and Bovens (2006) has shown, rarely involves a balanced review of performance, but more commonly involves an exercise in problem amplification and blame allocation. The pressure for blame avoidance may well suffocate organizational creativity and lead to 'automacity', in which procedures are rigidly based around avoiding errors and minimizing risk at all costs, or even the termination of services to avoid liability (Anechiarico and Jacobs, 1996; Flinders, 2008).

And yet the attempt to draw upon the logic of the market by importing the notions of contestability and market-type mechanisms in order to reform the public sector falters due to two key factors. First, as discussed above in relation to the 'myth of contestability', the development of real choice, thus facilitating 'exit'-type accountability mechanisms, for service users remains limited. This also creates an issue for commissioners of services. In the UK, for example, a number of critical parliamentary reports have censured the government for failing to penalize PPP contractors for their failure to fulfil the terms of their contracts (see, e.g. HC 764, 2003). The government, however, is reluctant to enforce penalty clauses for fear of deterring private companies from entering an already limited pool of contractual candidates. There exists a more basic incompatibility in relation to the logic of public and private accountability mechanisms that takes us back to the issue of the public service ethos (discussed above).

The logic of the market is aggressive and insular. It is attached to the notions of competitive advantage and competition. The logic of the state, at least in relation to the state as it evolved in most liberal democracies during the second half of the twentieth century, harbours more open and cooperative values for the common good. How then can a market actor's need to protect and defend their competitive advantage be reconciled with the emphasis on sharing 'best practice' and 'beacon status', which form core tenets of recent public management reforms? This basic clash of values is well known in relation to debates concerning the role of PPPs within the public sector. Marketization was originally viewed as a tool through which new and innovative management procedures and techniques could be imported from the private sector, and through this process the public sector would be renewed and re-skilled. However, the incentive for private actors holding lucrative contracts with the state is not to share information that allows them to deliver effective services, but quite the opposite: to utilize the legal defence of 'commercial confidentiality' in order to sustain and maintain their competitive advantage.

PPPs, along with other forms of marketization, disrupt traditional accountability structures. More broadly, they insert another potential veto point into the chain of delegation and in so doing create greater political space for 'blame games' (Hood, 2002) in which ministers, officials and private actors seek to transfer and deflect blame on to each other. The aim of this section has not been to look into the empirical manifestation of these 'blame games' in practice, but to dig a little deeper and expose the splintered logic of attempting to unite the logic of the market within the public sector without accepting that both sectors operate on markedly different governing variables and values. The potential friction between those logics becomes even clearer when viewed through the lens of public expectations.

The logic of public expectations
To recap, the central argument of this chapter is that political debates concerning the role and value of PPPs, and their possible long-term consequences for the state, emanate from the existence of splintered logic – splintered in the sense that the values and principles on which the broad thrust of marketization is based, of which the creation of PPPs is a central aspect, are at odds with those traditionally found within the political and public sphere. This argument has so far been examined and demonstrated through a focus on what has been termed the logic of contestability and the logic of the market, and how they grate against the logic of the state. In order to take this line of analysis even further and contribute a distinctive variation on dominant themes, this section focuses on the logic of public expectations, or what might equally be termed 'the politics of public expectations' (see Flinders, 2009a), because this exposes with even greater clarity the potential conflict between governing logics and how this tension may manifest itself with public disillusionment with politics.

To understand the logic of public expectations, it is useful to return to Hirschman's work on exit, voice and loyalty. Market-based allocation mechanisms operate in the basis of *internalized* rationing systems (i.e. individuals make personal choices about where and when to spend their resources) because free exchange, in theory, is intended to match supply and demand in an efficient manner. State-based allocation mechanisms, as Przeworski (2003) has emphasized, operate on a fundamentally different basis. Democratic collective decision-making frameworks involve an *externalized* rationing system in which decisions concerning policies and services (and paying for them) are imposed and enforced by the state. This externalized rationing system may sometimes appear overly centralized, controlling and even unfair, but it has been established and sustained on the basis of a coherent logic based upon at least three tenets: (1) that externalized/imposed rationing is necessary to avoid what Hardin (1968) termed the 'tragedy of the commons' – the dilemma in which multiple individuals acting independently in their own self-interest can ultimately destroy a shared limited resource (e.g. fish stocks, fossil fuels, water pollution, a sense of social solidarity/public service ethos etc.) even where it is clear that it is not in anyone's long-term interest for this to happen; (2) externalized rationing is viewed as necessary in order to avoid inferior social outcomes and protect individual freedoms. Drivers are compelled to drive on one side of the road, abide by certain speed limits, and have their vehicle tested regularly. The outcome of these measures is a transport infrastructure in which individuals can drive (relatively) safely and enjoy a level of freedom that would not be possible if no rules existed. Finally, and possibly most importantly in relation to debates about PPPs and the increasing marketization of the state, (3) centralized decision-making and external rationing are viewed as vital because many individuals share certain values concerning the need to protect sections of society from the vagaries of a pure market. This generally involves the provision of a social safety net in terms of state benefits, an educational and healthcare system that does not discriminate on the basis of money, and a variety of public bodies concerned with supporting, protecting and retraining disadvantaged social groups.

In short, the logic of the state was intended to inculcate certain values that stand in direct opposition to the logic of the market. As such, the public's expectations about the behaviour and role of the state accepted that in a system based upon an externally imposed rationing system some people would take out more than they put in, and not everyone would receive the level of service provision they might wish for. The emphasis was therefore on collective goods and equality of access and service provision. The general process of marketization and the use of PPPs are frequently interpreted as a threat to the basic rational foundations of the state because they seek to alter the nature and emphasis of public expectations about the state (cf. Crouch, 2002; Freedland, 2001), while at the same time raising fundamental questions about the role and functions of the state (Flinders, 2009b).

How does marketization alter public expectations about the state and how, in turn, does this relate to increasing survey evidence of declining levels of public satisfaction with politics and the state? The implicit logic of marketization as the dominant paradigm of 'good governance' brings with it a clear tendency for politicians and their officials to compare public services with those provided by the private sector. As a result, the public are encouraged to expect the same standards of personalization, choice and control in their interactions with the state that they enjoy with organizations within the private sector, where the mode of exchange is purely financial. But the conception of citizens as consumers, reflected in the introduction of mechanisms such as 'public service guarantees' that provide an explicit statement of entitlements, or 'personalized budgets' through which members of the public effectively 'buy in' public services, risks inflaming rather than reshaping public expectations. As Stoker (2007, p. 181) emphasizes,

> the discourse and practice of collective decision-making sits very uncomfortably alongside the discourse and practice of individual choice, self-expression and market-based fulfilment of needs and wants. So it turns out that a propensity to disappoint is an inherent feature of governance even in democratic societies.

It is in this context that PPPs create high expectations about what will be delivered – but more than this, they also fit within a broader managerial thrust through which the public are encouraged to expect those levels of service provision that are found within the private sector. This is clearly reflected in two recent initiatives in the UK. First, the 'Policing Pledge' is a national initiative launched in September 2009 that sets out an explicit set of objectives (for the police) and expectations (for the public). This includes a commitment that police patrols will be visible and active wherever the public want them, that the police will visit members of the public and take statements at a time that is suitable for the user, that the police will take action in relation to *all* complaints and stay in regular contact with the complainant. The police will also organize monthly public meetings, distribute information about their performance, provide 'crime maps' in relation to specific offences and data on what happened to those brought to justice. Similar patterns of public expectation creation are evident within the health service, where the government's Choice Agenda is intended to ensure that all patients can see a doctor or consultant of their own choice, where they want and when they want (for a review see Appleby et al., 2003). And yet by indulging in this behaviour without massive increases in resources, politicians are arguably deluding the public about the capacity of the state and increasing the 'expectations gap' (i.e. the gap between what is promised and what is actually delivered), thereby fuelling public frustration with politics (see Flinders, 2009a). The Royal College of Nursing (2005, p. 2), for example, states 'there should be more honesty in the public debate about the limitations of choice. We have repeatedly pointed out that *unconstrained* choice in a *constrained* health and social care budget is undeliverable.' This point takes us back to the logic of the market: the Choice Agenda is driven by an econometric or consumerist conception of human behaviour and this is reflected in the overlaying of market-based mechanisms or frameworks within the public sector. The creation of a 'marketplace democracy' (Needham, 2003) based upon citizen consumers injects a very subtle yet critical change into a number of dimensions of the sociopolitical relationship that is mediated through the state.

Following on from this, how does the use of PPPs give rise to fundamental questions about the role and functions of the state? The answer links back to the previous point concerning the creation of unrealistic expectations. The public's demand for improved public services, while being resistant to tax increases, arguably places governments in an invidious position in which they have little choice but to fully explore the potential efficiency savings of PPPs. Indeed, if the state cannot deliver the standard of services demanded by the public with the available resources, there may have to be a review of the functions undertaken by the state. Glennerster and Hills (1998, pp. 327–8) note,

> This might mean that the state should retreat to its core concerns and concentrate on doing them really well . . . Deciding what is the core role of the state, and what is not is going to be the central task for politicians.

The diffusion of PPPs into policy fields that have traditionally been viewed as core parts of the public sector (e.g. clinical care, teaching children, managing prisons, probation services etc.) is likely to increase as PPPs become a mainstream governance tool rather than an instrument of last resort for failing services (see Institute for Public Policy Research (IPPR), 2002). The growth in the role of PPPs within a broader context of increasing public demands and expectations concerning the state has therefore ignited a debate regarding the residual core of the state and the limits of the private sector. As the UK's former prime minister, Gordon Brown (2003), has noted:

> we must have the strength to face up to fundamental questions that cannot be side-stepped about the role and limits of government and markets – questions in fact about the respective responsibilities of individuals, for markets and communities including the role of the state. As long as it can be alleged that there is no clarity as to where the market requires an enhanced role, where we should enable markets to work better by tackling market failure, and where markets have no role at all, an uncertain trumpet sounds and we risk giving the impression that the only kind of reform that is valuable is a form of privatization and we fail to advance – as we should – the case for renewal and a reformed public realm for the coming decades.

As the work of Hodge and Greve (2005) has illustrated, governments around the world in both developed and developing countries are experimenting with increasingly creative forms of PPP. Although it is arguably overstating the contemporary extent of PPPs to talk of a 'worldwide revolution', as some have (Grimsey and Lewis, 2007), the boundaries between the public and private sectors, between the state and the market, are certainly becoming increasingly blurred and yet there has been very little *political analysis* of this development. Critically, cooperative endeavours to draw in private market actors in the delivery of public services remain a particularly central element of the 'progressive governance' project that seeks to redefine modern social democratic thinking.[1] This 'progressive governance' project and the whole 'politics of public–private partnerships' debate has to a great degree been recast, or has at the very least taken on new emphasis, as a result of the global financial crisis from 2008 onwards. Assumptions regarding the dominance and superiority of the market that had become almost uncontested towards the end of the twentieth century are now receiving renewed attention, and this may have important ramifications for the future utilization of PPPs.

The recapitalization of politics and the market

The central argument of this chapter has been that political debates concerning marketization in general and PPPs in particular emanate from the existence of splintered logic – splintered in the sense that the values and principles on which marketization and the growth of PPPs is based and promoted are at odds with those traditionally found within the political and public sphere. While this disparity can be utilized as a resource through which politicians can seek to promote and compel institutional and cultural change within the public sector, it can also be interpreted as a political and democratic liability if the underlying logic of PPPs gradually erodes and eviscerates longstanding sociopolitical relationships concerning the logic of collective action. The role of this chapter has therefore been to set out the political backcloth on which debates concerning the use of PPPs are commonly set. The aim of this final section is to emphasize that the changed political context following the global financial crisis during the first decade of the twenty-first century poses acute questions for the future politics of PPPs, not least because long-established arguments and understandings regarding the respective qualities of the public and private sectors, and particularly the role of neoliberalism within accepted notions of good governance, have become highly contested as governments around the world have been forced to intervene in a variety of markets. If public trust is the lifeblood of political systems and the flow of money fulfils the same function for markets, then it seems that both sectors are in need of urgent recapitalization.

The global financial crisis is likely to affect PPPs in a number of ways because the broader ideational context in which debates concerning marketization take place has shifted and a public–private paradox has been created. This paradox resonates directly with the logic of contestability, the logic of the market and the logic of public expectations discussed above. The logic of contestability stems from the fact that the reduction in the amount of available financing, particularly at attractive rates, means that not only are there likely to be fewer bidders for PPPs contracts, but also that the cost of those bids is likely to increase (as a reflection of the higher loan costs, which is itself a reflection of the perceived existence of higher risks). This may well, as PricewaterhouseCoopers have emphasized (2008), make PPPs less attractive as a tool of governance when assessed against traditional procurement methods. Evidence and data from around the world underline this point (for an international review see Public Services International Research Unit (PSIRU), 2009). In the UK the government is likely to spend around £4 billion during 2009–10 simply to ensure that infrastructure projects that have already started do not collapse. Only 34 private finance investment contracts were signed in 2008, the smallest number since 1997. In Spain large PPP payment obligations are taking a larger and larger share of a decreasing revenue stream and as a result limiting the flexibility of the government to respond to the crisis. In Australia and New Zealand several concession-type PPPs (i.e. funded through service-user charges rather than regular government payments) have run into trouble due to a combination of over-optimistic forecasting and falling demand. In France the 'plan de relance' (the post-crisis economic recovery scheme) seeks to maintain a central role for PPPs through the creation of new tax allowances and the advance of large sums of money to private banks to effectively guarantee the scheme and pass on lower interest rates. However, as many commentators have stressed, the logic of the market is clearly corrupted, to a greater or lesser extent, by the increased role of the state *vis-à-vis* PPPs because the vaunted transfer of risk to the private sector is effectively nullified.

The logic of contestability is also relevant in relation to both individual and micropolitical decision-making. Individual members of the public will operate within a much more constrained fiscal environment, which may well remove certain choices in relation to purchasing services from the private sector, such as private healthcare or education. The paradox stems from the fact that this is likely to increase pressure on state systems that are already facing significant financial pressures but are now less able to rely on private sector involvement – PPPs are to a great extent 'buy now pay later schemes' – in order to vent that pressure. At the same time existing PPP contracts with private companies will have to be honoured, leaving the burden of cutbacks to fall disproportionately on other services.

In simple terms, the global economic crisis has made PPPs more expensive and banks less willing to lend over long periods. The logic of the market has become contested. The logic of public expectations will need to be reviewed. As a result, the debate regarding the politics of PPPs has shifted dramatically and in this context many of the debates outlined above, particularly those concerning the values and principles of the public sector in respect of the private sector, are likely to take on added emphasis during the opening decades of the twenty-first century.

This brings us back full circle to this chapter's focus on splintered logics and political debates. Much of the political discourse surrounding the creation of PPPs has been sustained on the basis of a need to avoid 'ideological preconceptions' (Blair and Schröder, 1999) regarding traditional political debates (left versus right, public versus private etc.). However, the emphasis on 'what matters is what works' (see Shaw, 2004), or what could be viewed as utilitarian politics, within 'progressive governance' or 'third way' prescriptions for state reform and the delivery of public policy was arguably never ideologically neutral or open. In fact it veiled an implicit acceptance of neoliberal values and then sought to impose them within the public sector. However, the global economic crisis may well have the unintended political consequence of forging a more balanced and evidence-based assessment of the respective roles of the public and private sectors. If this is the case, there will have to be a much broader acceptance of the divergent logics that underpin and activate those domains. Blending those logics and avoiding a further splintering is likely to form a key political challenge for the twenty-first century.

Note

1. See www.progressive-governance.net.

References

Allison, G.T. (1983), 'Public and private management: are they fundamentally alike in all unimportant respects?', in J.L. Perry and K.L. Kraemer (eds), *Public Management*, Palo Alto, CA: Mayfield, pp. 72–93.

Anechiarico, F. and J. Jacobs (1996), *The Pursuit of Absolute Integrity*, Chicago, IL: Chicago University Press.

Appleby, J., A. Harrison and N. Devlin (2003), *What is the Real Cost of Patient Choice?*, London: King's Fund.

Behn, R. (2001), *Rethinking Democratic Accountability*, Washington, DC: Brookings Institution.

Blair, Tony and Gerhard Schröder (1999), *The Way Forward for Europe's Social Democrats – A Proposal*, London: The Labour Party.

Bovens, M. (2006), *Analysing and Assessing Public Accountability. A Conceptual Framework*, European Governance Papers (EUROGOV) No. C-06-01.

Brown, G. (2003), 'A modern agenda for prosperity and social reform', speech to the Social Market Foundation at the Cass Business School, London, 3 February.

Bult-Spiering, M., G. Dewulf and A. Blanken (2006), *Strategic Issues in Public–Private Partnerships*, Oxford: Blackwell.

Crouch, C. (2002), *Commercialisation or Citizenship: Education Policy and the Future of Public Services*, London: The Fabian Society.

Crouch, C. (2009), 'Marketization', in Matthew Flinders, Colin Hay, Mike Kenny and Andrew Gamble (eds), *Oxford Handbook of British Politics*, Oxford: Oxford University Press, pp. 879–98.

Denhardt, J. and R. Denhardt (2007), *The New Public Service: Serving not Steering*, New York: Sharpe.

Dunleavy, P. and C. Hood (1994), 'From old public administration to new public management', *Public Money and Management*, **14** (3), 9–16.

Flinders, M. (2008), *Delegated Governance and the British State: Walking Without Order*, Oxford: Oxford University Press.

Flinders, M. (2009a), 'Bridging the gap: revitalising politics and the politics of public expectations', *Representation*, **45** (3), 339–48.

Flinders, M. (2009b), 'The future of the state', *Political Quarterly*, **79** (5), 19–40.

Freedland, M. (2001), 'The marketization of public services', in C. Crouch, K. Eder and D. Tambini (eds), *Citizenship, Markets and the State*, Oxford: Clarendon Press, pp. 90–110.

Glennerster, H. and J. Hills (1998), *The State of Welfare: The Economics of Social Spending*, Oxford: Oxford University Press.

Green, D. (1996), *Pathologies of Rational Choice Theory*, New Haven, CT: Yale University Press.

Grimsey, D. and M. Lewis (2007), *Public Private Partnerships: The Worldwide Revolution in Infrastructure Provision and Project Finance*, Cheltenham, UK and Northampton, MA, USA: Edward Elgar.

Hardin, G. (1968), 'The tragedy of the Commons', *Science*, **162** (Dec.), 1243–8.

Hay, C. (2004), 'Theory, stylised heuristic or self-fulfilling prophecy? The status of rational choice theory in public administration', *Public Administration*, **82**, 39–62.

HC 147 (2000), *The Private Finance Initiative*, Fourth Report of the Treasury Committee, Session 1999–2000, London: HMSO.

HC 263 (2002), *The Public Service Ethos*, Seventh Report from the Public Administration Select Committee, Session 2001–2002, available at: www.parliament.the-stationery-office. com/pa/cm200102/cmselect/cmpubadm/263/26302.htm.

HC 764 (2003), *Delivering Better Value for Money from the Private Finance Initiative*, 28th Report from the Public Accounts Committee, Session 2002–2003, London: HMSO.

Hirschman, A. (1970), *Exit, Voice and Loyalty*, Cambridge, MA: Harvard University Press.

Hodge, G. and C. Greve (2005), *The Challenge of Public–Private Partnerships*, Cheltenham, UK and Northampton, MA, USA: Edward Elgar.

Hood, C. (2002), 'The risk game and the blame game', *Government and Opposition*, **37** (1), 15–37.

Hood, C. and C. Lodge (2006), 'From Sir Humphrey to Sir Nigel: what future for the public service bargain after Blairworld?', *Political Quarterly*, **77**, 360–68.

IPPR (2002), *Building Better Partnerships*, London: Institute for Public Policy Research.

Koppell, J. (2005), 'Pathologies of accountability', *Public Administration Review*, **65**, 94–108.

Le Grand, J. (2003), *Motivation, Agency and Public Policy*, Oxford: Oxford University Press.

Marquand, D. (2004), *The Decline of the Public*, Cambridge: Polity.

Needham, C. (2003), *Citizen Consumers*, London: Catalyst.

Osborne, D. and T. Gaebler (1992), *Reinventing Government*, Reading, MA: Addison-Wesley.

Parker, D. and K. Hartley (2003), 'Transaction costs, relational contracting and public–private contracts', *Journal of Purchasing and Supply Management*, **9** (3), 97–108.

Pierre, J. (2000), *Debating Governance*, Oxford: Oxford University Press.

Power, M. (1999), *The Audit Society*, Oxford: Oxford University Press.

PricewaterhouseCoopers (2008), *Delivering the PPP Promise*, London: Pricewaterhouse-Coopers.

Przeworski, A. (2003), *States and Markets*, Cambridge: Cambridge University Press.
PSIRU (2009), *A Crisis for Public–Private Partnerships?*, London: Public Services International Research Unit.
Rhodes, R.A.W. (1997), *Understanding Governance*, Milton Keynes: Open University Press.
Royal College of Nursing (2005), *Real Choice in the Health Service*, London: RCN.
Shaw, E. (2004), 'What matters is what works', in S. Hale, W. Leggett and L. Martell (eds), *The Third Way and Beyond*, Manchester: Manchester University Press, pp. 64–82.
Stoker, G. (2007), 'Politics in mass democracies: destined to disappoint?', *Representation*, **42** (3), 181–94.

7 The economics of public–private partnerships: some theoretical contributions

Jean-Etienne de Bettignies and Thomas W. Ross

Introduction

As the very appearance of this volume suggests, public–private partnerships (PPPs) have hit 'prime time'. Governments around the world, in countries rich and developing, from the East and West, have been looking to alternative models for the procurement of public services. Their motives may be multiple, but one motive surely is to find better ways to deliver services to their citizens – services of the quality those citizens desire with the lowest burden possible on the public purse. Just as earlier movements towards privatization and contracting out provided examples of the potential for more efficient operations through private sector involvement, the hope has been that even the delivery of core 'public services' such as education, healthcare, roads and prisons will benefit from the competitive private sector's emphasis on efficiency and its comparative advantage in innovation.

In this chapter we do not wish to cover ground already familiar or material well covered by other chapters in this volume. We shall therefore not review definitions of PPPs, the history of PPPs or the geographic or industrial scope of PPPs. Our focus is on the economics of PPPs, and specifically on the important contributions made by economic theorists towards helping us understand where the PPP model will have its advantages and disadvantages relative to more traditional models of procurement.[1] We shall not review here the valuable empirical work and case studies done, by economists and others, to evaluate the actual success of various PPP projects.[2]

We would argue that, in this area as in others related to public policy, economic theory has much to contribute. We are pleased to report that some important contributions have already been made with respect to PPPs, although the literature is still quite young. Economic theory provides guidance as to the potential costs and benefits of alternative policy approaches. This guidance can then be used to assess the empirical significance of the data. Out of this process, it is hoped, will come better policy.[3]

The challenges posed by PPPs: getting task allocation right

The provision of public services involving a significant infrastructure component – a highway, bridge, school, prison or hospital, for example – requires the performance of a number of tasks. A basic list of these tasks would include:

1. Defining the need to be addressed by the project
2. Designing the infrastructure
3. Financing the project
4. Building the infrastructure
5. Maintaining the infrastructure
6. Operating the facilities to provide the service
7. Paying for the services provided

The allocation of these tasks between public and private sector players varies by project and by government, and in most places it has changed over time. Indeed, PPPs represent a relatively new approach to task assignment, one in which the private sector performs more tasks than it has typically performed in the past. In all true PPPs, the government continues to perform some of these tasks – if it does not, we have complete privatization and we are no longer dealing with the provision of a public service as such a service would normally be defined.

It is important to recognize from the start that, in market economies, the private sector is almost always involved in the provision of public services to some extent, even under so-called 'traditional procurement' methods. Quite obviously private firms will provide inputs used (bricks, lumber, gasoline, paper, pens etc.) to deliver public services, but they will typically also directly perform a number of the major tasks listed above relating to the creation of the infrastructure. Handing over the task of providing one of these services to a single private entity is often referred to as 'contracting out'. Most commonly, private parties (e.g. architectural and engineering firms) will be contracted to develop the designs, and the task of building the facility will be contracted out to a private sector construction firm. Traditional procurement of public services using significant infrastructure then commonly assigns tasks 1, 3, 5 and 6 to the public sector while putting a significant part of the burden of tasks 2 and 4 on private firms.

Task 7 – paying for the services – most often falls to the public sector as well, with services financed from taxation revenues or with borrowed money. In some cases, however, task 7 is taken up, at least in part, by users who are required to pay for the services they receive. This is most common in road and bridge projects, where tolls may be charged by either public or private sector operators, but versions also appear in other projects such as community or recreation centres, where users are required to pay small amounts (e.g. for access to the swimming pool or ice-skating time) to partially cover the costs of operating the facility.[4]

In other cases, some of the maintenance and operation of the facilities may be contracted out as well. For example, a publicly operated hospital may, even under a traditional procurement model, choose to contract out the laundry services, the food service operations and/or the landscaping of its grounds.

Viewed in this way, PPPs are really just an extension of contracting out, and the line between simple contracting out and PPPs is not very clear. However, in our view, a few key characteristics of modern PPPs distinguish them from traditional procurement, even when the latter involves some degree of contracting out.

1. Most obviously, modern PPPs make more extensive use of contracting out than do traditional procurement models. That is, more of the tasks are contracted out than would be normal under traditional methods. For example, in the famous 'FDBOOM' model, the private sector finances, designs, builds, owns, operates and maintains the facility.
2. Critically too, the tasks are typically contracted out as a bundle to a single contractor – usually a special-purpose corporation created by consortium members for the sole purpose of developing and operating the project. In contrast, standard contracting out would essentially allocate one task (or part of a task) per contract, and the various contractors would have no obvious or contractual connection to each other.
3. Modern PPPs typically allocate to the private sector certain tasks that were historically the preserve of the public sector. Specifically, financing and operation tasks are now frequently taken on by the private partners. In both cases this task allocation is somewhat controversial.

With respect to financing, the argument is frequently heard that, since governments can borrow more cheaply than private firms, governments should always do the financing. While this solution is superficially appealing, the question of who should finance projects is in fact rather complicated. Although we do not wish to go into detail here on this question, it is worth making a few points on this critical issue.[5] First, for many projects, the private sector consortia, made up of multinational blue-chip companies, have been able to secure financing at rates very close to the rates at which even solid governments can borrow. This is in part because the projects' revenues typically come from governments, and governments are just as reliable as clients as they are as debtors, making contracts with them strong assets with which to support debt.

Second, when governments do secure a lower rate for their borrowing, it is because the lenders expect the governments to repay the loans even if the projects turn bad.[6] Thus the government is on the hook to pay for the project, whether it is a success or a failure. If a private party finances the project and it fails, the private party (and its creditors) carry the loss, not taxpayers.[7] So while it might appear that having the private partner borrow will be more costly to the client (government and its citizens), this is because the client is also getting an option to 'put' the debt back to the bank if the project fails. Comparing private and public sector borrowing rates then is an 'apples to oranges' comparison – one loan includes a put option while the other does not.

Third, there will be cases in which significant government borrowing for large infrastructure programmes could push that government's debt over critical threshold ratios such that ratings agencies will downgrade the government's total debt. This could have an enormous impact on the cost of all the government's borrowing, an effect much larger than the higher rate a private sector borrower might have to pay.[8] Put another way, the marginal cost of the government's debt could be much larger than the average cost.

Finally, even if the private sector's cost of financing is higher, putting the financing burden on the private side may be a necessary mechanism for creating the right incentives for the private partners to complete projects as designed and on time. That is, private financing puts more risk on the private side, which may be necessary to drive efficiency.

Private operation has been controversial, in part because it is here that public sector (often unionized) workers find themselves losing jobs to private sector firms. As a result, public sector labour unions have been among the most organized and vocal of the opponents of PPPs. There are, however, also legitimate concerns that the very long contracts typical of PPP relationships may not adequately constrain private operators pursuing profits rather than social welfare. Certainly the task of crafting contracts to regulate partners' behaviour over several decades is a daunting one – and expensive for all the parties involved. Since such long contracts must inevitably be incomplete in some respects, we have reason to worry that the private sector operator may fail to provide services of the quality and quantity desired. Of course, it is also true that the private partners have reason to worry about the extent to which they can count on governments – which may change several times over the life of the contract – to continue to honour their obligations under the contract.

Confronted with all the tasks associated with the provision of public services, the government's real problem is to allocate tasks between public and private sector actors in such a way as to minimize the cost of providing those services at the quality, and in the quantity, desired. In some cases, the optimal allocation will involve allowing the private sector to do it all – i.e. privatization. In others, the government will perform all (or almost all) the tasks itself, giving us something closer to traditional procurement. Finally, there will most certainly be, in theory at least, conditions under which the optimal allocation of tasks will leave a few with the public sector while allocating several to the private sector, perhaps in a bundled fashion. This is a PPP solution. The challenge for economic theorists has been to determine which conditions are conducive to PPP-style solutions to the task allocation problem.

Economic issues arising in PPPs

Economic theorists did not come to the study of PPPs completely unarmed. Rather, a great deal of prior research on related issues has given PPP theorists much to build upon. While this chapter is not the place to review this related work, we can list some of the most important themes. An obvious place to start is with the long list of economic literature, theoretical and empirical, that argues for the efficiency benefits of competition.[9] Economists have long argued that competition promotes three kinds of efficiency, where they use efficiency to mean the ability of an economy to convert lower-valued inputs into the greatest amount of higher-valued outputs. 'Allocative efficiency' requires that the right quantity of goods and services be produced and that this quantity be allocated to the consumers who value them the most. Competitive markets, by driving prices toward cost levels and then using those prices to separate buyers from non-buyers, promote allocative efficiency. 'Productive efficiency' demands that outputs be produced at the lowest possible cost. Again, competitive markets promote productive efficiency by rewarding more efficient firms with higher profits and encouraging the exit of less efficient producers. Finally, 'dynamic efficiency' requires that optimal investments in new product development and process improvements be made so that firms can more efficiently address consumers' needs in the future. Again, the pressure on firms that is associated with competition in markets is believed to be a major contributor to dynamic efficiency in modern economies.[10]

To an important extent, the real point of considering PPPs to help provide public services is to try to harness the efficiency of private firms – pushed by competition – to deliver those services more economically. Traditional procurement models typically rely on provision of services by designated 'monopoly' government departments or agencies. As a consequence, the relative lack of competition inherent in the traditional approach compromises the achievement of all three kinds of efficiency.[11]

The problems posed by PPP design are a special version of problems economists have been studying for many years – problems associated with buying and selling of goods and services in an environment of imperfect information and incomplete contracts. As such, the PPP problem is a special case of the famous principal–agent problem – here, the principal wishes to procure public services on behalf of its citizens by using the services of multiple agents, some of whom may be profit-seeking private sector firms, while other agents may be public sector players with less clear motives.[12]

In fact, the PPP problem is potentially a many-layered principal–agent problem because of the many kinds of agency relationships that may exist. In what is perhaps the most obvious view, the government (as principal) contracts with the private consortium (as agent) to deliver services valued by the principal, where the government's interests are assumed to be consistent with the 'public interest' while the private consortium strives to maximize its own profits. Analysing this problem leads to a number of interesting hypotheses about PPP design. Another set of problems can be analysed when we view the government as the principal, and public sector workers as the agents to be controlled. For example, in such a world, PPPs might arise as ways to control the behaviour of public sector workers who might otherwise take advantage of their status as monopoly providers of public services.

Still another approach might consider the citizenry or electorate as the principal 'contracting' with the government, and its civil servants, as well as the private sector firms, as the agents. In such a world, governments may act strategically in ways that serve to preserve their popularity (before elections especially) without necessarily being socially efficient in the long run.

As should be clear from this short and incomplete list, principal–agent problems will arise in both PPP arrangements and with traditional procurement methods. In both cases we have agents (citizens or maybe, on their behalf, governments) working with others (public sector workers and/or private sector firms) to procure public services.

Past economics research in a few other areas – some related to agency issues as well – has clearly also provided economists working on PPPs with insights useful for their work. We are thinking specifically about past work on privatization, contracting out and transaction cost economics. Work on privatization and contracting out has shown conditions under which private production can be more efficient than public provision.[13] Work on transaction costs and incomplete contracting has analysed the challenges associated with crafting contracts in complex environments in which some parties need to protect substantial project-specific investments.[14]

Contributions of economic theory[15]

The theoretical economic literature that relates most closely to PPPs largely examines three key characteristics associated with these kinds of arrangements. In almost all this work, the focus of the analysis is on efficiency – that is, what arrangements will provide the most desired output for the least input?

First, PPPs involve a great deal of complex contracting – PPP contracts are typically very long and complicated. In such a situation contracts are likely to be found to be incomplete in important respects, and this leads to a variety of inefficiencies.[16] The literature reviewed in a later section discusses these inefficiencies and how organization structure (e.g. PPP or not PPP) may be altered to minimize them. The kinds of contracting problems reviewed in this section can arise in any complex contracting situation – including those between private firms. However, a second distinguishing feature of PPPs is that the government is on one side of all these contracts, and governments may have different objectives and may face different kinds of constraints than private firms. A later section then reviews the literature on performance issues surrounding contracts between public and private agents. The third distinguishing feature is that PPPs typically involve the bundling of multiple tasks in one large contractual agreement between the government and a private sector consortium. When it makes sense to bundle particular tasks together is the subject of the literature reviewed in a later section.

Finally, we return to consider the contracting out of one task, but go deeper by focusing on one particular task: financing. This is the single task that, when allocated to the private sector, most defines PPPs. Having the private sector provide financing is also the most controversial aspect of PPPs. There is an emerging literature that looks at whether the public or the private sector should provide the financing for PPPs, and this is reviewed in a later section.

Contracting out as the foundation of PPPs: theoretical background

In the last 20 years, dissatisfaction with the costs associated with government production has led many governments to consider expanded use of the private sector in the provision of certain public services. Often this has involved the contracting out of various services that had previously been provided by governments themselves. Of course, most governments have had experience with contracting out to some degree – some tasks have been contracted out for a very long time.

Construction is the task most often delegated to the private sector – in fact it is the norm in North America. While governments may maintain crews to maintain, repair and renovate physical facilities, seldom do they undertake large-scale construction projects. Whether the project involves the construction of a bridge, school, hospital or prison, the norm is that private contractors will do the work. It is worth remembering this, as it reminds us that the current wave of PPPs is not really so revolutionary – the private sector has always been engaged in many parts of the provision of public services, including architectural work and construction. What is newer is the larger number of tasks assigned to the private sector and the way they are bundled together. Contracting out remains the foundation of modern PPPs.

Much of the theory on contracting out has focused on the relationship between ownership structure, efficiency and incentives. Here we present the main directions of research on the topic in recent years. This literature has come to distinguish between problems of *ex post* inefficiencies – those inefficient decisions made because a contract is suboptimal – and *ex ante* inefficiencies, which involve the suboptimal contract design decisions that can arise because the parties know they cannot perfectly implement what would be in fact the truly optimal contract.

Ex post *inefficiencies*   Consider the design, construction and operation of a bridge, hospital or school. What do these projects have in common? One commonality is that once the provider (the government employee or private sector company) and the customer (the government or taxpayer) start to trade, i.e. start to work together towards the completion of, say, a bridge, they are better off completing the project together than terminating the relationship and starting to trade with other parties. The reason is that both the provider and the customer make relationship-specific investments that are more valuable if the project is brought to completion than if trade breaks down. The provider invests in building a bridge that corresponds specifically to that particular customer's request (in terms of location, design, equipment, timing etc.). If the negotiations between the provider and the customer break down, the provider may indeed have trouble finding another customer for that bridge.

The initial customer also makes relationship-specific investments (e.g. search effort, time, design effort) that are worth more with the current provider than with another designer/builder/operator for the bridge. The investment to find the provider, or to collaborate on the design, may be worth little if a new provider must be found, and that new provider may have completely different technological capabilities and require a very different design.

Thus the consequence of relationship-specific investments is the formation of a surplus from trade. Transaction costs arise because both the provider and the customer want to appropriate that surplus from trade, and the bargaining and opportunistic behaviour that is generated may in itself be costly.

One way to mitigate these so-called *ex post* inefficiencies is to limit opportunities for negotiations and bargaining by writing long-term contracts. We limit transaction costs by reducing the number of transactions. In our example, the government can mitigate transaction costs by writing a long-term contract with the (private) bridge operator, and by encouraging long-term contracts between the operator and other suppliers, such as the designer and/or the contractor, for example. This is the PPP scenario.

However, trade relationships are often very complex and uncertain. This level of complexity implies that (1) it is impossible to plan for every potential contingency, and (2) even if every contingency could be predicted, it would probably be difficult to write down these plans in a contract between the customer and the provider that is enforceable by law. In that case, long-term contracts such as the ones just described are less helpful because they cannot be made to bind in some circumstances: we say that the contracts are incomplete.[17] Coase (1937) was the first to recognize the economic consequences of contractual incompleteness, and his ideas, as well as those of Williamson (1975, 1979, 1985) and Klein et al. (1978), sparked a new literature on the subject. It was argued that because of their incomplete nature, contracts must constantly be revised and/or renegotiated as time goes on (long-term contracts are infeasible), and the problem of *ex post* inefficiency generated by relationship-specific investments cannot be easily mitigated.[18]

Hence, when contracts are highly incomplete, vertical integration, by avoiding renegotiation altogether, may offer the best alternative. In such cases it may be optimal to put the same party (the government) in charge of the different tasks, such as design, financing, construction and operation. This avoids the bargaining cost that would be generated if the tasks were allocated to different parties. This is the public provision scenario.

Crocker and Masten (1996) make this comparison between long-term contracts and vertical integration in the context of franchise bidding versus regulation. They summarize the choices very clearly in Figure 7.1, which we have adapted slightly to fit our PPP versus public provision context.

Without relationship-specific investments, transaction costs are low and spot market provision is the better solution: it allows more flexibility relative to long-term contracts and it permits the efficiencies associated with competition and private provision. A good example of this would be food stamps: the government provides a product (food) that requires no specific investment via the spot market (supermarkets).

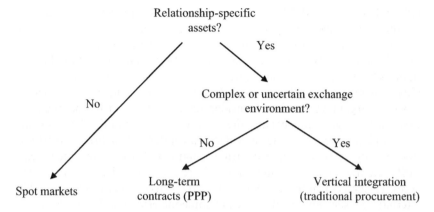

Figure 7.1   Optimal procurement of public services

When there are switching costs, two sub-possibilities arise: long-term contracts offer the best alternative when the relationships remain relatively simple (e.g. building a bridge), such that writing effective contracts is possible, but vertical integration is sometimes necessary when transactional complexities make *ex post* inefficiencies too large (e.g., perhaps, some types of healthcare).

Ex ante *inefficiencies*   Note that although the theory on *ex post* inefficiencies provides powerful insights into the advantages of long-term contracts relative to spot market exchange, and of integration relative to long-term contracts (the mitigation and/or elimination of *ex post* transaction costs), it remains vague as to their disadvantages (inflexibility, bureaucracy). The following discussion of *ex ante* inefficiencies should clarify these issues by formalizing the tradeoff between benefits and costs for each organizational structure.

Recall that with relationship-specific investments, a situation of bilateral monopoly arises in which a surplus from trade is created; and that when contracts are incomplete, the trading parties behave opportunistically in their attempt to appropriate that surplus. The ability to behave opportunistically depends greatly on *ex post* bargaining power, which itself depends on the party's outside alternative, i.e. that party's payoff should negotiations break down. When a party has an attractive outside alternative relative to her trading partner, she is in a better bargaining position because she suffers a smaller penalty for leaving the relationship than does the other party.

In the late 1980s Grossman and Hart (1986), and Hart and Moore

(1990), henceforth GHM, gave new impetus to the literature by underlining the importance of property rights. Property rights over an asset confer *ex post* bargaining power, because the owner of the asset keeps control over the asset, and can prevent the other party from using it, should negotiations break down. In other words, property rights increase one's outside alternative relative to that of one's trading partner, and that puts one in a better bargaining position. Consider again the relationship between the customer (the government) and the provider involved in the development of an office building. If the provider is an independent firm/consortium (the private sector) trading at arm's length with the government (e.g. PPP), she has some bargaining power in renegotiation because she keeps access to her assets if trade breaks down, and thus has an attractive outside alternative – she can rent the space to someone else, or sell it. In contrast, if the assets used by the provider are owned by the government, the public sector essentially builds the building (public provision), with the provider as government employee. In case of disagreement, the government can just fire her, and thus the provider's outside alternative in that case is much less attractive, and she is in a weaker bargaining position.

Bargaining power in renegotiation, and hence asset ownership, is important because it affects investment incentives. The more *ex post* bargaining power the provider anticipates, the less likely she is to be 'held up', the larger the fraction of the surplus created she will be able to appropriate, and the greater incentive she has to make relationship-specific investments in the first place. Of course, more bargaining power to the provider means less bargaining power to the government, and thus fewer incentives and less investment by the public sector customer. Thus, when the government chooses a PPP contract with a private provider for the design and/or construction of a bridge instead of public provision, it transfers property rights and bargaining power to the provider. This increases the provider's incentives to invest, but reduces its own incentives.

GHM's great insight is that property rights over an asset should be allocated to the agent whose marginal product of *ex ante* investment is the highest. The government should use a private sector provider for a particular task (e.g. design, financing, construction or service provision for a hospital) only if the marginal efficiency of the provider in this 'relationship' is higher than that of the customer (government), because the transfer leads to a net efficiency improvement.

Delivering public services: public versus private ownership of the underlying asset

In the description of the literature on incomplete contracts offered in the section above, we adapted the theory to the relationship between the government and the provider. These models, however, were originally developed to explain the boundaries of private firms. In the past few years, economists have started to apply incomplete contract theory more specifically to policy surrounding public versus private ownership.

Schmidt (1996)   Schmidt investigates the tradeoff between public and private ownership in an incomplete contracts framework. His model is based on the following assumptions: (1) the manager can exert an unobservable effort to reduce production costs; (2) the manager receives a private benefit from production; and (3) property rights confer access to information: the government knows about costs and profits in the case of public provision, but not in the case of private provision. These assumptions yield two interesting results.

First, with private provision, the associated lack of information enables the government to credibly commit to an incentive scheme for the manager. Based on a revelation game, this incentive scheme punishes the manager with low production when production cost is revealed to be high. In contrast, with public provision, the government cannot credibly commit not to renege on production decisions, and thus the manager has lower incentives and exerts lower effort. Public provision thus leads to lower productive efficiency.

Second, with private provision, the government's commitment to cut production when costs are high leads to too low a level of production compared to public provision. Public provision thus leads to higher allocative efficiency. Schmidt thus defines the tradeoff between public and private ownership as follows: although private provision generates higher productive efficiency, public provision generates greater allocative efficiency.

Hart et al. (1997)   Hart et al. focus on the much-debated tradeoff between lower cost and lowering quality of service provision. Indeed, they provide the formal foundation for the argument that private provision may lead to greater efficiency in reducing the cost of service provision relative to public provision, but this must be traded off against a lower quality of service.

Their key result hinges on two assumptions: incomplete contracts, and a positive relationship between cost of service provision and quality of service, i.e. lowering cost has a negative effect on the quality of the service provided. The incomplete contracts assumption makes ownership important: private provision implies that the provider owns its production technology and therefore has more bargaining power relative to government than if the service were provided by a government employee. Thus, if the service provider is the private sector, it will have a greater incentive to invest in cost reduction *ex ante*, and in equilibrium, service is provided at a lower cost by the private sector. On the other hand, the private sector fails to internalize the negative effect that cost reduction has on service quality, and therefore has too much incentive to reduce costs, to the detriment of service quality. In Hart et al. (1997), the private sector has better incentive to produce more efficiently, but so much so that it tries to 'cut corners', affecting quality. The choice between private and public provision depends on the importance of production efficiency relative to this 'corner-cutting'.

King and Pitchford (2008)   King and Pitchford also deal with optimal (public or private) ownership in a framework not unrelated to that of Hart et al. In its simplest form, their model can be understood as follows: a government must decide whether to allocate ownership of a project to a 'public' manager or to a 'private' manager.

The key difference between public and private ownership in this incomplete contracts setting is that while, under public ownership, the government can prevent – at some fixed monitoring cost – the manager from extracting any rents from the project, this is not feasible under private ownership. Under private ownership the manager extracts all project rents. Anticipating this outcome, the private manager exerts more effort than the public manager *ex ante*.

Now suppose that an external benefit is generated by the project, which can be either positively (positive externality) or negatively (negative externality) affected by the manager's effort. In this simple framework, the main result is that, when the externality is positive, private ownership is optimal; but when the externality is sufficiently negative, public ownership is the superior allocation of property rights.

Besley and Ghatak (2001)   Besley and Ghatak focus specifically on the provision of a public good.[19] They ask whether a public good should be provided by the public sector, or by a private entity such as a non-governmental organization (henceforth NGO), for example. The two parties invest in the production of the public good and negotiate over the surplus created. Recall that, in the simplest GHM framework, if negotiations break down, the owner gets some benefit while the other party gets nothing. Because of that, the owner of the asset has more bargaining power and higher incentives, and transferring ownership to the agent with highest marginal efficiency in investment maximizes the total surplus and is optimal.

When the good is public, however, both parties enjoy some benefit if negotiations break down. Even if trade breaks down between the NGO and the government and the NGO is no longer involved in the development of the public good, it still gets an 'alternative' benefit, due to the public nature of the good. For example, the NGO with an educational mandate may get a benefit from the creation of a new school even if it is not involved with its operation.

Besley and Ghatak's model has two key features. First, an increase in the alternative benefit (due to investment by one or both parties *ex ante*) raises one party's valuation of that alternative benefit more than the other party's valuation. The former is labelled the 'caring' party, while the latter is labelled the 'non-caring' party. The main consequence of this feature is that an increase in the alternative benefit improves the caring party's bargaining position and expected payoff, and conversely worsens the non-caring party's bargaining position and expected payoff.

The second key feature of the model is that giving ownership to a party maximizes her marginal product of investment on the alternative benefit, and minimizes the other party's marginal product of investment on the alternative benefit. Suppose that ownership is transferred from the non-caring party to the caring party. How does this affect the marginal impact of increased investment by each party on that party's payoff? For the caring party, after the ownership transfer, an increase in investment leads to a larger increase in alternative benefit (due to feature 2), which in turn leads to a larger increase in payoff (due to feature 1). As a result, such a transfer leads to increased investment by the caring party.

For the non-caring party, after the ownership transfer, an increase in investment leads to a smaller increase in alternative benefit, but this is beneficial for her, because increases in alternative benefits reduce her payoff anyway. As a result, for the non-caring party, transferring ownership away from her actually leads to an increase in investment on her part.

Indeed, transferring ownership from the non-caring party to the caring party leads to higher investment by both parties, and hence giving ownership to the most caring party is optimal: if the NGO values the school more than the government, it should be granted the ownership right to provide the service.

Bundling of PPP tasks

One of the aspects of PPPs most studied by economists relates to the optimal bundling of tasks. That is, what tasks (if any) should be bundled and given to one party, and once the bundles are defined, which should be allocated to the public partner and which to the private partner? Not surprisingly, perhaps, the results are very sensitive to the parties' abilities to write more or less complete contracts.

Bundling when contracts are well specified – under complete contracting
Bentz et al. (2002) consider the construction and service provision related

to a product such as a school. They analyse whether a government should opt for 'conventional delivery' – in which case it contracts with a builder, takes possession of the school, and then writes a separate contract with a service provider – or for a PPP, in which case there is a unique contract between the government and a 'consortium' that builds and manages the school.

Bentz et al. assume that the builder can exert effort to improve efficiency of service provision, and that this efficiency is observable only to the service provider but not to the government. With PPPs, there is a unique contract and the model simplifies to a standard adverse selection set-up in which the builder/service provider is induced to truthfully reveal whether service provision efficiency is high or low. The information rent given to the agent to induce truth-telling also generates incentives to exert effort at the building stage, thus providing incentives is relatively inexpensive with a PPP: it allows the government to 'kill two birds with one stone'. Conventional delivery does not have this advantage and therefore the payment made by the government to induce high effort is higher with conventional delivery.

On the other hand, compensation has to be paid less frequently with conventional delivery than with a PPP. Indeed, efficiency may be high due to the builder's effort, or simply due to the forces of nature. With conventional delivery, the agent/builder must be compensated only when she has exerted the effort, whereas with PPPs the payment from the government is made whenever efficiency is revealed to be high, which includes the case where high efficiency is the result of nature. Hence the tradeoff between conventional delivery and PPPs in this chapter: compensation to the agent is higher but less frequent in the former than in the latter.

Martimort and Pouyet (2008) consider the government's choice between bundling and unbundling of tasks in a public service project to be built and then operated. The builder can exert effort to increase project quality, and the operator can exert effort to lower the operating cost. The builder's effort may also reduce the operating cost (positive externality), or increase it (negative externality).[20] Neither type of effort is observable. Both quality and operating cost are verifiable (and hence contractible). Both builder and operator are risk-averse.

The builder receives a linear quality-contingent contract and the operator receives a linear cost-contingent contract as before. Under unbundling, in equilibrium, each agent exerts a strictly positive but second-best level of effort reflecting the usual tradeoff between incentives and insurance.

Under bundling, i.e. when the operator both builds and operates the project, she internalizes the impact of building effort on operating cost. Thus, in the case of a positive externality where building effort reduces operating cost, for a given power of incentives she exerts higher building effort under bundling than under unbundling. This increases the government's marginal return to an increase in incentive power, leading to higher-powered incentives and in turn to higher building effort and operating effort in equilibrium. Hence, when the externality is positive, both building and operating effort are strictly higher under bundling than under unbundling, leading to higher social welfare.

In contrast, under bundling with negative externality, for a given power of incentives, building effort falls (relative to unbundling). This leads to lower-powered incentives for both building and operating efforts, and to lower efforts in equilibrium. Indeed, bundling dominates unbundling from a social welfare point of view if, and only if, the externality is positive.

Iossa and Martimort (2008; Case 1) start from essentially the same framework as Martimort and Pouyet (2008): the government chooses whether or not to bundle the building and operation of a public service project, where the risk-averse builder (respectively operator) exerts unobservable effort to increase quality (respectively reduce operating cost). Again the builder's effort may reduce the operating cost (positive externality), or increase it (negative externality).

The key difference is that here project quality is not verifiable and cannot be contracted upon. The builder is now assumed to receive a fixed payment, while, as before, the operator receives a linear cost-contingent payoff. Under unbundling, the builder exerts zero effort (as a result of the fixed payment), while the operator exerts the usual second-best level of effort. For the same reasons as in Martimort and Pouyet (2008), under bundling with positive externality, the operator exerts higher building effort and higher operating effort than under unbundling. In the case of a negative externality, the operator exerts zero building effort and the same operating effort as under unbundling. Accordingly, bundling either yields the same outcome as unbundling (when the externality is negative), or a strictly superior outcome (when the externality is positive): in other words, bundling weakly dominates unbundling. Again, we see that it is valuable to bundle together at least those tasks that impose positive externalities on each other – as when better construction leads to lower operating and maintenance costs.

Bundling when contracts are not well specified – under incomplete contracting Hart (2003) adapted the Hart et al. (1997) model to analyse PPPs specifically. The government is concerned with the building and the operation of an asset, say a hospital or a prison. At the time of construction the builder can make two types of investment that affect the operation of the asset. The productive investment increases the benefit and reduces the cost of operation (e.g. an investment in building quality), while the unproductive investment reduces operating cost but also reduces the project's benefit [21] (e.g. this is an investment in 'corner-cutting', similar to that in Hart et al. (1997)). With 'conventional provision', the government contracts separately for the building and then for the operation of the prison. The builder is thus paid before the fruits of his two investments are realized. Anticipating this, the builder invests nothing in the first place. In contrast, with a PPP, the government contracts with the builder to both construct and operate the prison. The builder anticipates that he will be able to reap some benefits from investing – in terms of lower operating costs – and thus makes positive investments in both building quality and corner-cutting. Therefore, relative to PPPs, conventional provision leads to more underinvestment in productive effort to increase building quality, while PPPs lead to overinvestments in corner-cutting. Hart concludes that PPPs may be optimal when building quality cannot be well specified and 'corner-cutting' investments are relatively easy to monitor, because in that case both over-investment in corner-cutting and under-investment in building quality are relatively low.

Bennett and Iossa (2006) examine the decision whether or not to bundle building and operation in an incomplete contract environment in a fashion not unlike Hart et al., but propose a more general framework that focuses more explicitly on innovations at the building stage generating (positive or negative) externalities at the operation stage. They find that bundling, which leads to the internalization of the externality, reinforces incentives, and for that reason dominates unbundling, when the externality is positive. By the same logic, bundling may not be optimal when the externality is negative, due to depressed incentives.

Iossa and Martimort (2008; Case 2) is the same as in Iossa and Martimort Case 1, but for the introduction – at the end of the operating stage – of a residual asset value that is not contractible *ex ante* and must be bargained over at the end of the game. This residual asset value is positively affected by the builder's effort, but is higher if the asset is used by the government for public service provision than if it is used for private purposes. Accordingly, it is efficient for the government to be the owner of the project at the end of the game.

- *Public ownership.* If the government owns the project from the beginning of the game then no transfer of ownership is needed at the end of the game, and the outcome of the game is the same as in Case 1: under unbundling, the builder exerts no effort and the operator exerts a second-best level of effort. Under bundling with a positive externality, the operator exerts higher building effort and higher operating effort than under unbundling. In the case of a negative externality, the operator exerts zero building effort and the same operating effort as under unbundling.

- *Private ownership.* If the project is privately owned from the beginning of the game, transfer of the asset to the government through efficient Nash bargaining occurs at the end of the game. Under unbundling, the builder, anticipating that she will be able to extract some rents through bargaining at the end of the game, exerts a strictly positive effort, higher indeed than under public ownership (with unbundling). The operator exerts the same effort as under public ownership. Under bundling, the private consortium also anticipates extracting bargaining rents at the end of the game, and this has a positive marginal effect on incentives to exert effort. As a result, whether the externality is positive or negative, effort levels with bundling are higher under private ownership than under public ownership. Moreover, if, under a negative externality, the positive effect of rent extraction on building effort more than offsets the negative impact of the externality, leading to higher quality-enhancing effort, then private bundling dominates public unbundling, and in turn, more generally, private ownership dominates public ownership.

The tradeoff is then reduced to one between private bundling and private unbundling. The rent extraction effect on incentives is present in both cases and cancels out, leaving only the sign of the externality to determine when bundling is optimal: as expected, when the externality is positive, its internalization through bundling is optimal, while when it is negative, it is unbundling that is optimal.

Uncertainty and contract flexibility   Iossa and Martimort (2008; Case 3) is similar to Iossa and Martimort's Case 1, except that (a) the externality from building effort to operating cost is specifically assumed to be positive, and (b) the marginal product of the operator's effort is a random variable. If this marginal product were deterministic, then we would be back in a Case 1 situation where bundling would strictly dominate unbundling.

However, if this variable is random and unknown at the time of the initial bundling contract, then the contract cannot be made contingent on it, with adverse effects on incentives and welfare. In contrast, under unbundling the government can 'wait' for the value of the variable to be realized and make the operator's contract contingent on it, leading to more efficient incentives and possibly higher welfare. Indeed, unlike in Case 1, for a small enough positive externality, unbundling dominates bundling.

Privatizing the finance function

Engel et al. (2009)   Engel et al. formally examine the irrelevance of financing choice the result of which suggests that PPPs and the associated private financing of projects cannot be justified as a way to release public funds or save distortionary taxes. Indeed, 'resources saved by the government by not having to finance the upfront investment are offset one-for-one by ceding revenue flows to the private sector later on'.[22]

de Bettignies and Ross (2009)   The model in our 2009 paper considers a particular project, the construction and operation of a bridge, for example, which can be financed and developed by a private firm/consortium, or by a government agency. Either type of developer (public or private) can turn out to be 'good' or 'bad', with the result that the project can succeed or fail. Whoever undertakes the project, private or public developer, must secure the initial capital required from an investor. The paper draws from the incomplete contracts frameworks of Bolton and Scharfstein (1990, 1996), and Hart and Moore (1998) to determine the optimal (debt) contract between the developer and the investor; and derives several key results.

With private development, two issues arise. The first is related to contractual incompleteness: the possibility of strategic default by the developer caps the debt repayment that she can commit to make, and limits the amount a lender is willing to provide to the developer in the first place. Accordingly, contractual incompleteness under private development leads to fewer projects being financed relative to the first-best benchmark. The second issue results from the private developer maximizing profits rather than social surplus, and thus ignoring the impact of her decisions on consumer surplus. This has two consequences here: (1) the private developer might make profit-maximizing but socially inefficient decisions. This lowers the social surplus relative to the first-best benchmark. In turn, it has a negative impact on the debt repayments that can be made to the investor and on the number of projects that can be financed in the first place; and (2) of that social surplus generated, the private developer extracts profits, but does not internalize the consumer surplus, and this also lowers the size of the debt repayments she is willing to make and the number of projects financed. Thus contractual incompleteness and externalities both make private development *ex ante* inefficient in limiting the number of projects being financed. Externalities also yield an *ex post* inefficiency in reducing surplus generated by the projects that are indeed financed. However, government intervention is shown to help mitigate these concerns: through simple contract design and financial subsidies, the government can eliminate all externality-related inefficiencies.

With public development – when the government does the borrowing – the problem is different. To the extent that the electorate can use the public developer's observable actions to infer information about the government's underlying quality, the public developer may take actions that are socially inefficient, in an attempt to manipulate the electorate's beliefs about government quality, and improve re-election prospects. We show that these attempts also lead to both *ex post* and *ex ante* inefficiencies.

Comparing private and public financing from both *ex ante* and *ex post* standpoints, we find that – when both types of financing are available – private development may be preferred, as it gets around the belief manipulation problem faced by the public developer. On the other hand, private developers can commit only to smaller debt repayments, and hence can find lenders only for a subset of socially valuable projects. Indeed, some projects can be financed only by public developers, who do not have the same commitment problems.

Iossa and Martimort (2008; Case 4)   Iossa and Martimort compare 'public financing' to 'outside financing' in a simplified version of their Case 1, in which there is no builder effort. Under public financing, the government provides funds to cover initial capital outlay, and offers the same linear cost-contingent contract to the operator, yielding the same second-best level of effort as in Case 1.

Under outside financing, the operator obtains the required funds from a private financier. The particularity of the financier is that he has access to an informative signal about the operator's effort, and can make the contract contingent on that signal. In equilibrium, the operator's payoff depends on a combination of the realized cost and the informative signal, and this combination elicits a higher effort than the second-best level of effort exerted under public financing. Accordingly, private financing dominates public financing in that case.

Concluding remarks
This chapter reviews the contributions of economic theory towards a better understanding of the potential costs and benefits of the PPP form. Three key features of PPPs are examined here in particular: contracting out and asset ownership, the bundling of PPP tasks; and the privatization of the finance function. In all three cases, economic theory emphasizes the importance of two main factors: the contracting environment as it relates to the ability (or inability) to write well-specified contracts; and the incentives of the relevant players and how they relate to one another.

As a result of all this work, we now have a better idea of when particular PPP arrangements are likely to be problematic as a result of an inability to correctly align the parties' incentives. We also have a better idea of when tasks to be contracted out to the private sector are more efficiently bundled into a PPP rather than assigned on a one-task-per-contractor basis. Finally, we are beginning to learn of the conditions under which the task most controversially allocated to the private sector in PPPs – financing – might efficiently be assigned to private partners, even when it might seem that the private sector pays more for its borrowing than the public sector.

While economic theory has already contributed a great deal towards our understanding of PPPs, much remains to be done, and the theory needs to be tested. Given the huge sums involved in building public infrastructure in developed and developing countries, even a very small percentage improvement in the efficiency with which public services are produced and delivered to citizens will result in very substantial benefits to those citizens. This suggests that further research on PPPs could be of very significant social value.

We conclude, then, with a short list of research areas we see as fertile ground for more work of value to policy-makers. The list certainly reflects, to some extent at least, our personal interests, and is by no means intended to be exhaustive.

1. While work on the 'bundling' question has been quite extensive, much less attention has been paid to the question of how effectively governments can control aspects, particularly the quality, of the delivered services without destroying the private sector's ability to pursue efficiency. In particular, in designing long-term PPP contracts there would appear to be a tradeoff between providing flexibility for adaptation of the contract to meet changing circumstances and control of the private partner, which is, after the contract is awarded, effectively in a monopoly position.

2. In a related way, very little research has been done on the benefits and costs of building flexibility into the PPP contract: flexibility both for the private partner in how it chooses to deliver services and for the public sector in defining what services it wishes produced. The flexibility question is particularly important when we contemplate PPPs in dynamic industries such as healthcare, where the services we wish delivered by our hospitals in ten years' time (and the technology available to deliver them) might be very different from the services we wish delivered (and the way we deliver them) today.

3. It is very clear to those in the PPP industry that what economists refer to as 'commitment problems' loom large. We are referring to problems created when a party is not actually able to commit itself,

in a credible way, to follow through on its promises. For example, a private sector player might strategically underbid in order to win a PPP project only to plead poverty when it comes time to deliver (and all the other bidders have moved on) – hoping then to persuade an embarrassed government to 'top up' its payments to keep the project moving. Since private players can always declare bankruptcy and shut down, it is hard for them to truly commit to following through on their promises. Commitment problems can bite the other way too, as when governments – perhaps newly elected governments from other political parties – refuse to honour contractual promises. Most governments are powerful enough that they can, to some extent at least, renege on promises with limited penalties.[23] This creates 'political risk' that the private partners must include in their profitability calculations. It should be clear that commitment problems can hurt both sides of the exchange even if it is only one side that cannot commit. Faced with a party on the other side that cannot commit always to honour its promises, one may choose not to contract at all, or to do so only on better terms. Thus, as is made clear in the economic theory of commitments, the ability to commit is frequently a good thing for an economic actor even if it means that he or she will – in some cases – need later to honour promises that he/she would prefer to forget. Commitment problems have entered into some of the theoretical treatments of PPPs, but they have seldom played a central role. Some work in this direction would be welcome.[24]

4. It is well recognized that the PPP process is very costly to both the public and private sector players. Preparing bids for relatively unique, and very complex, large-scale projects is time-consuming and expensive, as is reviewing those bids. The problems here might be largely practical and not particularly amenable to solutions derived from economic theory but, at the very least, the tradeoff between more precise processes that more often select the 'right' winner at the lowest cost, and speedier or less costly processes, should be considered.

5. There will undoubtedly be better and worse ways for both the public and private sector players to organize their activities in the PPP world, and these undoubtedly merit study. For example, governments undertaking PPP projects may choose to create separate, specialized (and centralized) PPP agencies such as Partnerships UK in the UK or Partnerships BC in the Canadian province of British Columbia. Alternatively, they may choose to create PPP capability within existing departments – for example, the Ministry of Highways could have a PPP unit to lead on its highway PPPs, the Ministry of Health its own PPP unit to develop PPP hospitals, etc. There will undoubtedly be

costs and benefits of each approach.[25] Similarly, there are many ways to build a private sector consortium to bid on and deliver the public services. Which providers should be 'owners' of the consortium and what allocation of ownership shares provides the incentives that will maximize the value of the enterprise? What is the role of debt and of the institutions, often banks, providing debt capital?

6. Finally, there are unresolved challenges associated with how the public sector should evaluate the bids it has received for a PPP project. For example, the design and use of the public sector comparator has received little or no attention from economic theorists. Also, many of the comparisons of the private sector versus the traditional public sector alternatives for the delivery of public services turn importantly on the rate used to discount future costs and benefits. Traditional procurement typically involves large public expenditures in the early years of a project as the infrastructure is constructed, followed by low expenditure levels when the facility is in its operation phase. By contrast, in most PPP projects, the government pays nothing (or very little) until the project is operational and then makes a long series of payments to the private parties that must be high enough to cover operation and maintenance costs, and to recover the capital costs. Therefore, in a PPP project, more of the costs to the public are pushed into the future. If the future is discounted more heavily than it should be when traditional procurement versus PPP procurement decisions are made, this will bias decisions towards the PPP approach.[26] The challenge here – related to similar questions arising in the cost–benefit analysis of other public projects – is to determine just what is the 'right' discount rate for these purposes. Is it the same as the private sector's cost of capital and, if so, the cost of which capital – debt capital or equity capital? Is it a (lower) number closer to (or equal to) the government's cost of borrowing?[27]

In closing, we repeat our claim that the current interest in PPPs presents some terrific opportunities for economists of an applied theory bent to contribute in a meaningful way to the development of public policy. Arrangements such as PPPs pose a number of fascinating questions about efficient contracting in a complex environment and, given past work in related areas such as agency models, contracting out and privatization, economists have valuable and relevant tools. We have been pleased to report that considerable progress has been made on a number of fronts, in particular with respect to questions about which tasks should be bundled together and on some of the consequences of incomplete contracts, but much work remains to be done.

Acknowledgements

The authors wish to thank the many colleagues and friends who have contributed to their work on public–private partnerships over the years, including Neil Alexander, Larry Blain, Anthony Boardman, Nicholas Hann, Mark Hayllar, Graeme Hodge, Elisabetta Iossa, John Langford, Rui Sousa Monteiro, Maurice Rachwalski, Alan Russell and Aidan Vining. Financial support for much of this research came from funding provided by Infrastructure Canada through its Knowledge-Building, Outreach and Awareness programme to the UBC P3 Project. The very capable research assistance of Jennifer Ng is also gratefully acknowledged.

Notes

1. Parts of this chapter draw extensively from some of our previous work, specifically de Bettignies and Ross (2004 and 2009).
2. See, e.g., Vining and Boardman (2008) and Vining et al. (2005), as well as other chapters in this volume.
3. None of this is to deny the importance of other kinds of scholarship, for example, by organization theorists, political scientists, policy scholars and others, who will focus on other aspects of the problem.
4. In some cases, part of the costs of a project may be covered by voluntary contributions, as when charitable organizations partner with government and the private sector to have a new community centre built or when an international aid agency supports a hospital project in a developing country.
5. We offered some thoughts on this question in de Bettignies and Ross (2004), on which we rely here.
6. In some cases, governments might be seen to be less reliable debtors than the large companies that participate in the consortia, in which case the governments will pay higher rates of interest on their debt.
7. This assumes that the government does not bail out the private partners in order to keep the project moving forward – a not uncommon occurrence.
8. It is important to note that this last argument requires that the government auditors and the ratings agencies do not treat the long-term obligations under the PPP as debt. This is now not the case for many or even most PPPs.
9. For some background as to the thinking of economists regarding the efficiency benefits of competition, see any major microeconomics or industrial organization textbook, such as Kreps (2004, ch. 12).
10. As Kreps (2004, p. 310) notes, the case for competition in the promotion of dynamic efficiency is somewhat less clear-cut than that for allocative and productive efficiency. Nevertheless, there is in general fairly broad support among economists that, in most cases, higher levels of competition will be associated with higher rates of innovation. See also de Bettignies and Baggs (2007).
11. Naturally, some of the tasks described above may involve competition, even in the case of traditional procurement. The point here is that PPPs are more likely to promote competition and hence more likely to benefit from the efficiencies associated with competition, given that they generally involve the contracting out of more tasks.
12. Principal–agent problems have a long history in economic theory. A classic reference is the book by Laffont and Martimort (2002). Also related is the extensive literature related to the regulation of firms in cases of asymmetric information; Laffont and Tirole (1993) is a classic reference.
13. The theoretical and empirical work on privatization is voluminous. In particular, see the important work of Jones et al. (1990) and an important recent survey of empirical

work with good references to the larger literature by Netter and Megginson (2001). The literature on the economics of contracting out includes work by Domberger and Rimmer (1994), Domberger and Jensen (1997); Rimmer (1994) and Hodge (2000). There is a large, related, literature on the relative efficiency of public versus private production of goods and services. See, e.g., Vining and Boardman (1992).

14.   The classic economics references on transaction cost economics begin with Coase (1937) and Williamson (1985). The application of transaction cost economics to PPP issues is also considered by Boardman and Vining, Chapter 8 of this volume.

15.   Parts of this section – and the next two subsections in particular – borrow significantly from de Bettignies and Ross (2004). However, we supplement that analysis by adding discussions of a number of new papers that were not written at the time of our earlier work.

16.   That contracts will be incomplete seems a reasonable assumption in the context of PPPs. The difficulty in negotiating PPP contracts is, in part, due to the typical length of these agreements – 20 to 30 years is not uncommon when large facilities are involved – and in part it is due to a wide variety of risks that can have an impact on the value obtained in the partnership. These risks can include engineering risk, construction risk, regulatory risk, demand risk and environmental risk. Attempts to allocate these risks in the most efficient manner and to anticipate all important shocks over many years will undoubtedly leave gaps that can be exploited opportunistically.

17.   In contrast, if the rights and duties of the trading parties could be specified for every possible future state of the world, the contract would be complete. In that case there would be no gaps in the terms of the contract, and no scope for renegotiation.

18.   Work on the problem of designing economic arrangements between parties so as to mitigate the costs associated with contract design, monitoring and enforcement – transactions costs – while also taking advantages of other opportunities for the exploitation of economies of scale and scope, was originally part of work on the optimal boundaries of the firm. The ideas have been adapted to consider problems associated with contracting out by the public sector. For example Boardman and Hewitt (2004) and Hewitt and Boardman (2006) have noted a number of important ways in which models developed for private sector operations will need to be modified when it is the public sector that is doing the contracting out. Three key differences identified in Hewitt and Boardman (2006), for example, involve: (i) separating of a task so that it can be allocated to another party may be more difficult in a public sector environment; (ii) it may not be reasonable to expect that there can be a competitive market to provide services subject to contracting out in the public sector; and (iii) governments may not have the contract management skills necessary to negotiate and monitor complex contracts. See also Vining and Boardman (2008).

19.   Economists generally define public goods as having two key characteristics: (i) public goods are non-rival in consumption, meaning that everyone who wishes to can enjoy the same units of the good without diminishing the benefits received by other consumers (e.g. a television broadcast); and (ii) it is difficult to exclude people from consuming public goods even if they do not pay for their consumption.

20.   Much of the work on bundling focuses on these externalities. It is easy to see how positive externalities can arise, e.g. a more careful design and construction with more durable materials could lead to lower maintenance costs and a longer asset life. These are the kinds of externalities much discussed by PPP practitioners. It is harder to come up with pure examples of possible negative externalities. Something like negative externalities is possible in some circumstances, however – e.g. when a higher-quality school with more and larger windows leads to higher cleaning and window replacement cost. (This is not a pure example of a negative externality because adding windows does more than add to the cost of the building, it probably adds to the quality of services delivered using the school, so there is a bit more going on.)

21.   The parameters are chosen such that in the first-best the unproductive investment should be set to zero.

22. See also informal discussions on this issue in Grout (1997) and de Bettignies and Ross (2004), and in the section above.
23. Of course, reneging on promises is never costless to governments, as such behaviour has the effect of frightening away other partners and future investment.
24. A related commitment issue arises with respect to the difficulties many governments seem to have in committing themselves to maintain infrastructure after it is built. The belief seems to be that voters are more excited about money spent to build new projects than about money spent to maintain old projects. As a result, many governments have huge deferred maintenance problems. Here the PPP form would, in theory, help address this problem as maintenance costs are built into the contract from the start and the private operator is compelled to (and rewarded for) maintain the facility.
25. A start in this direction is provided by Rachwalski and Ross (2010).
26. Many opponents of PPPs argue that governments are making this mistake regularly.
27. There is some work emerging on this important question. See, e.g., Chapter 8 in this volume by Boardman and Vining, and Boardman et al. (2010).

References

Bennett, J. and E. Iossa (2006), 'Building and managing facilities for public services', *Journal of Public Economics*, **90** (10–11), 2143–60.
Bentz, A., P. Grout and M.L. Halonen (2002), 'Public–private partnerships: what should the state buy?', CMPO Working Paper No. 01/40, University of Bristol.
Besley, T. and M. Ghatak (2001), 'Government versus private ownership of public goods', *Quarterly Journal of Economics*, **116** (4), 1343–72.
Boardman, A. and E. Hewitt (2004), 'Problems with contracting out government services: lessons from orderly services at SCGH', *Industrial and Corporate Change*, **13** (6), 917–29.
Boardman, A.E., M.A. Moore and A.R. Vining (2010), 'The social discount rate for Canada based on future growth in consumption', *Canadian Public Policy*.
Bolton, P. and D. Scharfstein (1996), 'Optimal debt structure with multiple creditors', *Journal of Political Economy*, **104**, 1–25.
Bolton, P. and D.S. Scharfstein (1990), 'A theory of predation based on agency problems in financial contracting', *American Economic Review*, **80** (1), 93–106.
Coase, R.H. (1937), 'The nature of the firm', *Economica*, **4** (16), 386–405.
Crocker, K.J. and S.E. Masten (1996), 'Regulation and administered contracts revisited: lessons from transaction-cost economics for public utility regulation', *Journal of Regulatory Economics*, **9** (1), 5–39.
de Bettignies, J. and J. Baggs (2007), 'Product market competition and agency costs', *Journal of Industrial Economics*, **55** (2), 289–323.
de Bettignies, J. and T.W. Ross (2004), 'The economics of public–private partnerships', *Canadian Public Policy*, **30** (2), 135–54.
de Bettignies, J. and T.W. Ross (2009), 'Public–private partnerships and the privatization of financing: an incomplete contracts approach', *International Journal of Industrial Organization*, **27**, 358–68.
Domberger, S. and P. Jensen (1997), 'Contracting out by the public sector: theory, evidence, prospects', *Oxford Review of Economic Policy*, **13** (4), 67–78.
Domberger, S. and S. Rimmer (1994), 'Competitive tendering and contracting in the public sector: a survey', *International Journal of the Economics of Business*, **1**, 439–51.
Engel, E., R. Fischer and A. Galetovic (2009), 'Public–private partnerships: when and how', Centro de Economia Aplicada, Universidad de Chile, Documentos de Trabajo, 257.
Grossman, S.J. and O.D. Hart (1986), 'The costs and benefits of ownership: a theory of vertical and lateral integration', *Journal of Political Economy*, **94** (4), 691–719.
Grout, P.A. (1997), 'The economics of the Private Finance Initiative', *Oxford Review of Economic Policy*, **13** (4), 53–66.
Hart, O. (2003), 'Incomplete contracts and public ownership: remarks, and an application to public–private partnerships', *Economic Journal*, **113** (486), 69–76.

Hart, O. and J. Moore (1990), 'Property rights and the nature of the firm', *Journal of Political Economy*, **98** (6), 1119–58.

Hart, O. and J. Moore (1998), 'Default and renegotiation: a dynamic model of debt', *Quarterly Journal of Economics*, **113** (1), 1–41.

Hart, O., A. Shleifer and R.W. Vishny (1997), 'The proper scope of government: theory and an application to prisons', *Quarterly Journal of Economics*, **112** (4), 1127–61.

Hewitt, E. and A. Boardman (2006), 'Key questions to ask when contracting out government services: an application to orderly services', in Peter Barrar and Roxane Gervais (eds), *Global Outsourcing Strategies: An International Reference on Effective Outsourcing Relationships*, Aldershot, UK: Gower Publishing, pp. 285–301.

Hodge, G. (2000), *Privatisation: An International Review of Performance*, New York: Perseus Books Westview Press.

Iossa, E. and D. Martimort (2008), 'The simple micro-economics of public–private partnerships', Department of Economics, University of Bristol, UK, The Centre for Market and Public Organisation.

Jones, L.P., P. Tandon and I. Vogelsang (1990), *Selling Public Enterprises: A Cost–Benefit Methodology*, Cambridge, MA: MIT Press.

King, S. and R. Pitchford (2008), 'Private or public? Towards a taxonomy of optimal ownership and management regimes', *Economic Record*, **84** (266), 366–77.

Klein, B., R.G. Crawford and A.A. Alchian (1978), 'Vertical integration, appropriable rents, and the competitive contracting process', *The Journal of Law and Economics*, **21** (2), 297.

Kreps, D. (2004), *Microeconomics for Managers*, New York: W.W. Norton.

Laffont, J.J. and D. Martimort (2002), *The Theory of Incentives: The Principal–Agent Relationship*, Princeton, NJ: Princeton University Press.

Laffont, J.J. and J. Tirole (1993), *A Theory of Incentives in Procurement and Regulation*, Cambridge, MA: MIT Press.

Martimort, D. and J. Pouyet (2008), 'To build or not to build: Normative and positive theories of public–private partnerships', *International Journal of Industrial Organization*, **26** (2), 393–411.

Netter, J. and W. Megginson (2001), 'From state to market: a survey of empirical studies on privatization', *Journal of Economic Literature*, **39**, 321–89.

Rachwalski, M. and T.W. Ross (2010), 'Running a government's P3 program: special purpose agency or line departments?', *Journal of Comparative Policy Analysis*.

Rimmer, S. (1994), 'Competitive tendering and contracting: theory and research', *Australian Economic Review*, 3rd quarter, 79–85.

Schmidt, K.M. (1996), 'The costs and benefits of privatization: an incomplete contracts approach', *Journal of Law, Economics, and Organization*, **12** (1), 1–24.

Vining, A. and A. Boardman (1992), 'Ownership versus competition: efficiency in public enterprise', *Public Choice*, **73**, 205–39.

Vining, A. and A. Boardman (2008), 'Public–private partnerships in Canada: theory and evidence', *Canadian Public Administration*, **51** (1), 9–44.

Vining, A., A. Boardman and F. Poschmann (2005), 'Public–private partnerships in the U.S. and Canada: there are no free lunches', *Journal of Comparative Policy Analysis: Research and Practice*, **7** (3), 1–22.

Williamson, O.E. (1975), *Markets and Hierarchies, Analysis and Antitrust Implications: A Study in the Economics of Internal Organization*, New York: Free Press.

Williamson, O.E. (1979), 'Transaction-cost economics: the governance of contractual relations', *Journal of Law and Economics*, **22** (2), 233–61.

Williamson, O.E. (1985), *The Economic Institutions of Capitalism: Firms, Markets, Relational Contracting*, New York; London: Free Press, Collier Macmillan.

8 Assessing the economic worth of public–private partnerships
Anthony E. Boardman and Aidan R. Vining

Introduction

Many governments throughout the world are using public–private partnerships (P3s) to provide public goods, especially for infrastructure. The allure of P3s is obvious: they appear to offer the prospect of government control and ultimate ownership, while providing the benefits of private sector efficiency and private sector capital. For these and other reasons, they have been adopted in many areas, including highways, transit, hospitals and wastewater treatment plants. Billions of dollars of infrastructure spending have been incurred using variants of the P3 model. This trend may continue or even accelerate as governments try to stimulate their economies and face reduced tax revenues. Despite their importance and growing use, however, there has been little meaningful evaluation of P3s. For meaningful evaluation we must address the question: how should governments assess the economic worth of P3s? Or more familiarly: have governments spent taxpayers' money wisely?

In practice, the success of P3s has been measured in many different ways. The private sector mantra is that P3s come in 'on time and on budget'. Somewhat more rigorously, P3s have been evaluated in terms of their ability to deliver 'value for money' (VfM). However, from an economic perspective the appropriate measure of government projects' success is whether they increase economic (allocative) efficiency or, more broadly, aggregate social welfare. Thus far, no empirical study that we are aware of has attempted to measure allocative efficiency and to actually carry out a cost–benefit analysis (CBA) for a P3, whether *ex ante* or *ex post*. This chapter describes and discusses the different evaluation methods that have been used to evaluate P3s or have been proposed to evaluate P3s. The main focus, however, is to propose and describe how (social) cost–benefit analysis could and should be used to determine the economic efficiency of P3s.

The chapter is organized as follows. The second section discusses the normative and positive goals of P3s from government's perspective. It also provides some historical context and argues that the main normative and positive rationales for P3s are similar to those given for the privatization of state-owned enterprises (SOEs). Therefore we argue that it makes sense to evaluate P3s using basically the same criteria that have been used to evaluate privatizations, where possible. The third section discusses the most frequently used or proposed methods to evaluate P3s. This section includes an illustration and evaluation of the 'classic' VfM method. While VfM is a relatively simple concept in principle, in practice there are many variations. The fourth section describes how cost–benefit analysis can and should be used to evaluate P3s, drawing on Jones et al. (1990) and Boardman et al. (2006). The final section provides a brief conclusion.

The goals of P3s

Before discussing alternative methods to evaluate P3s, it is essential to first consider the goals of P3s and the alternatives to P3s. It goes without saying that private sector 'partners' in a P3 will attempt to maximize profits. The focus of this section is on the goals of government.

To many of those interested in the performance of P3s, the natural alternative to P3 provision is a provisioning mechanism, such as government provision or more traditional government contracting using the private sector. For simplicity, we label the best perceived alternative provision mechanism as the 'public sector alternative' (PSA). In the P3 literature, this alternative is more usually labelled the 'public sector comparator'. However, we prefer a label that explicitly clarifies that the comparison is to some notional alternative project provided by traditional (public sector based) methods. We assume initially that government has decided to proceed with a particular project and the decision issue is whether to use a P3 or the PSA.

It is important to recognize, however, that there is an important, conceptual, precursor question: should there be any provision? Or, more precisely, should the government be involved in any provision (whether P3 or PSA), or should the market provide the good or service? In well-functioning, competitive markets, there is no efficiency rationale for government intervention. Apart from those circumstances where provision on distributional (equity) grounds is justified, in order to have the government involved in the provision of some service, there should be some market failure; otherwise, the private sector will provide the service efficiently (Vining and Boardman, 2008c). We shall return to this issue later, but for now we assume that the infrastructure will be provided through some public mechanism and the issue is by which provision mechanism.

We can adopt, of course, either a normative or positive perspective in assessing P3 provision. In other words, we can assess the criteria the government *should* use in considering the use of a P3 (i.e. the normative perspective), or we can assess the criteria the government *do* use in deciding on the use of a P3 (i.e. the positive perspective). Of course, if governments and elected politicians always tried to act in society's best interests, there would be no divergence between these perspectives. The only issue would be whether governments were selecting the appropriate normative perspective. But, given that governments do sometimes act in their own interests rather than in ours, we should consider both.

The key relevant normative criteria for most government decision-making is social welfare, which can be thought of as consisting of economic (allocative) efficiency and equity. As equity is rarely relevant for P3s, the appropriate normative criteria for government projects, including P3s, should be allocative efficiency. Thus the key normative issue is whether a P3 is more allocatively efficient than the PSA. There are two main reasons for thinking that a P3 might be more efficient than the PSA.

First, the private sector may be more technically efficient than the public sector due to the greater preponderance of high-powered incentives. Property rights theory offers such an incentives story: private ownership and the market for corporate control generate superior (or at least more high-powered) incentives for efficiency. Put another way, the private sector will deliver projects that are less subject to X-inefficiency. Or, the private sector may deliver superior technical efficiency (lower costs) because of prior learning or the ability to benefit from superior economies of scale. While these arguments might justify private sector provision rather than government provision, they are not *per se* sufficient arguments for using P3s versus other forms of contracting with the private sector.

Second, the use of the P3 might allow those actually delivering the infrastructure to take advantage of economies of scope. An advantage of the P3 model is that, in theory, one firm (or consortium) can own and manage a project from project initiation until the asset is handed over to the public sector, possibly 30 or more years later. Put another way, activities are 'bundled' together. *Ceteris paribus*, the P3 consortium has an incentive to minimize the present value (PV) of the total costs of the project over its life cycle. Such a life-cycle orientation would provide the correct incentives to invest more money in the design or construction phases if this later led to sufficient operating or maintenance savings. Of course, one could argue that governments should themselves adopt a similar cost-minimizing life-cycle orientation.[1] In practice, however, there are stronger 'silos' among government branches and there is less incentive for a government design department, for example, to spend more of its resources on a better design in order to reduce operating costs many years later. Current governments are also likely to be more interested in minimizing their own costs rather than the joint costs of current and future governments combined.

In short, the main normative rationale for P3s is greater private sector efficiency (lower costs, holding quality constant) over the life cycle of the project. In practice, though, government may not always (or even often!) act as a welfare-maximizing 'angel'; rather it may act as a vote-maximizing politician. To understand what this means in practice requires a positive analysis of P3s.

There are several positive explanations as to why governments like P3s. First, P3s postpone government cash outlays. The nice thing about a P3 is that the government gets political credit for delivering a project now, but has to pay only a relatively small part of the cost up front and often little or nothing throughout the construction phase. Relative to the PSA, this improves short-run cash flow and minimizes or reduces the government deficit (i.e. current incremental borrowing), at least in the short run. In the UK in the early 1990s, a main motive for encouraging public finance initiatives (PFIs) was to reduce or minimize the budget deficit, which was then called the public sector borrowing requirement (PSBR). Similarly, sales of existing road concessions, such as the Chicago Skyway or the proposed (but aborted) sale of the Coquihalla Highway in British Columbia, replace future ongoing cash flows with a more substantial upfront, lump-sum cash infusion.

Of course, government does not avoid paying for the project by using a P3: it just pays later (and sometimes considerably more). But as politicians usually employ a high political discount rate, this is not accorded much weight. Even though government would probably pay less in total if it financed the infrastructure (e.g. via issuing a bond), Boardman and Vining (Chapter 16 in this volume) explain that governments prefer to 'rent the money'.

This brings us to the second reason that governments like P3s. In most PSAs the liabilities are recorded on the government budget books immediately, even if the assets are also shown (see Eisner, 1989 for details). However, even though the future cash flows that government must pay for a P3 are liabilities, governments did not and generally still do not reflect the full liability on their books. In effect, the cost of the P3 could be placed 'off budget' or, put another way, the government could 'have its cake and eat it too'. Over the last decade, the accounting profession, government auditors, regulatory accounting bodies and academics have increasingly emphasized that future P3 liabilities must be explicitly and clearly recognized in government accounts (e.g. Eurostat, 2004; Hemming et al., 2006). However, despite increasing pressure to reveal future liabilities, many governments are still reluctant to do so, and continue to underreport their liabilities. Edwards (2009), for example, notes that before the UK Treasury's Pre-Budget Report of November 2008, PFIs did not appear as part of the public sector net debt (PSND). Whether such liabilities will appear as part of the public sector debt in the future, as a result of the introduction of International Reporting Standards, depends on whether the transaction is recorded as a public sector finance lease and on other technical accounting details. Edwards (2009, p. 102) argues that 'considerably less than half of the debt of the PFI projects is reported to be included in the PSND'.

The third positive reason is really a variant of the first reason. The use of a P3 may actually improve government net cash flow (holding the cost of the project constant). This usually occurs where the P3 requires tolls or user charges. Government may calculate that users are willing to pay a toll, or at least a higher toll, to a private sector operator than to a government operator. Thus, in new road projects (e.g. the I-495 Capital Beltway HOT Lane project), the tolls might be higher with a P3 than under the PSA, and therefore government cash flow might be higher with a P3 than with a PSA. In effect, greater distance from stakeholder toll-payers may increase governments' willingness to charge tolls. Conceptually, one can think of this as being able to conduct a different project under a P3 (e.g. one with high tolls) than under the PSA (one with low or no tolls). Government may also use a P3 to increase cash flow by reducing maintenance costs. At the Kelowna General Hospital in British Columbia, maintenance staff were unionized and relatively expensive. Construction of a new tower and maintenance of the whole site (not just maintenance at the tower) will be delivered through a P3, thereby forcing out relatively more expensive, unionized staff. Again, this would not have been possible under a PSA.

Fourth, the government transfers risk to the private sector. The UK government has long argued that the various dimensions of risk transfer should be the primary goal of P3s (UKNAO, 1999; NHS, 1999; HM Treasury, 2000). Supposedly risk is transferred 'to the party most able to bear it'. One might think that this is a normative argument for P3s. However, this brings to mind the old adage 'you cannot get something for nothing'. One should certainly not expect profit-maximizing private sector firms to assume this risk without compensation, and indeed they do not. While risks may be transferred to the private sector, this is likely to be costly. More importantly, from a normative perspective, though, much of the risk transfer is indeed a transfer and is therefore irrelevant. Risk transfer is a zero-sum game: risk is transferred, not necessarily reduced. Thus risk transfer is a positive theory explanation of the use of P3s, not a normative rationale. It is only if the private sector efficiency is more efficient than there is a net social benefit. Finally, we might mention that financing risk may be higher for the private sector.

Fifth, political risk may be lower with a P3. It is worth clarifying that some risks are different to different participants. In a P3 the government transfers construction risk to the private sector but expects to pay more. From a financial perspective it may be indifferent in this tradeoff. However, it may actually be better off because, in addition, it has trans-ferred the political risk associated with construction cost overruns.[2] As mentioned above, greater distance from stakeholders tends to mollify the political risks.

These normative and positive rationales for P3s are very similar to those posited for privatization. The key normative rationale for privatization was greater private sector technical efficiency. The main positive explanations as to why governments actually embraced privatization were that it increased revenues (cash flow), reduced the government deficit and debt and, in addition, reduced the power of government unions. One can think of the P3 movement as an extension of a path that began with deregulation and privatization (starting in the mid-1980s), followed by the increasing focus on contracting out of government services (in the 1990s) and then the more recent use of P3s for the provision of infrastructure. (This is, of course, not to say that P3s were not used before privatization.) The common theme is that the private sector takes a larger role in the provision of goods and serv-ices that were previously provided by government. The key basic rationale is greater private sector efficiency. Given this, it is logical to suggest that the evaluation of P3s should be conducted along similar lines as the evaluation of privatization and contracting out of government services.

It is worth noting, however, that while governments do sometimes use the rationale of technical efficiency and reduced government cash flow, it is rare for them to discuss allocative efficiency. One might conclude that either consumers are ignored or, implicitly, the P3 and PSA are assumed to be equal from consumers' perspectives.

Current evaluation criteria for P3s
Independent studies on P3 performance do now exist.[3] However, there is still a dearth of research when compared to the evaluation of privatiza-tions. There are two obvious reasons for this. First, before/after com-parisons are not relevant if the issue is to compare the provision of new infrastructure via P3s or PSAs. Second, it is very difficult to get reliable data. P3 contracts are generally unavailable to the public unless there is a public inquiry. Also, P3 projects are heterogeneous and involve multiple private sector participants. Many of the private sector participants are private companies whose accounts are inaccessible to the public. Even if it were possible to access a particular company's corporate accounts, it would be impossible to determine the impact of a particular P3, as financial information for possibly multiple P3 projects and other projects are consolidated. Also, this would provide information from only one company's perspective for part of a P3 project. Quite simply, there are not

appropriate data to conduct any meaningful statistical analysis. Therefore the only feasible way to go is case studies.

One problem with generalizing from case studies is that a potential performance bias is introduced because the most extensive case study data usually emerge if there is some kind of fiasco. This is illustrated by the Metronet bankruptcy in the UK, where various parliamentary committees have held extensive hearings. Even then, public inquiries, commissions and legislative hearings tend to provide highly heterogeneous information. The informational value largely depends on the expertise of witnesses and staff.

In this section we review the two most commonly used criteria to evaluate P3s: 'on time and on budget' and 'value for money', or VfM. Other methods, such as benchmarking, have been used in some areas, for example, hospitals in Portugal, but it is not widely used. We also discuss the proposed criterion of total social costs.

'On time and on budget'

P3 advocates push the 'on time and on budget' criterion because P3s often perform well on it; see for example, HM Treasury (2003b). The issue is, of course: is the budget reasonable? A cynic will note that if the budget is padded enough, anyone can come in on time and on budget. Edwards et al. (2004), for example, conclude that in the UK, the Highways Agency paid a 25 per cent premium on construction cost on its first four road projects to ensure that they were built 'on time and to budget'. In general, they conclude that the Highways Agency in the UK paid inflated prices to ensure that they could show a record of being on time and on budget. Suspicions about budget padding would be less of an issue if the government's P3 advocacy agency weren't the agency deciding what the budget should be, but it often is.

A second problem with this criterion is that 'on time and on budget' almost inevitably focuses exclusively on the construction phase of a project. A key normative rationale for a P3 is that it might lower PV of total costs over the life cycle of the project. The 'on time and on budget' criterion does not get at this defining characteristic of P3s.

Value for money

Unfortunately, in almost all jurisdictions most VfM studies are conducted by the agency that is responsible for administering the P3, for promoting the use of P3s or by external consultants to such agencies, rather than by arm's-length analysts, whether internal or external to government. For example, in the UK, the UK Treasury is responsible for both promoting PFIs and regulating VfM analyses. In British Columbia, Partnerships BC is both a proponent of P3s but also often carries out the VfM analysis.

Perhaps not surprisingly, reviews from government agencies closely identified with a P3 (or their consultants) usually conclude that the P3 does
provide better VfM.

A number of scholars have criticized the accuracy, depth and objectiv-
ity of many of the available VfM studies (e.g. Heald, 2003; Shaoul, 2003;
Edwards et al., 2004; Shaffer, 2006). For example, Edwards et al. (2004)
provide a comprehensive review of these comparability problems in their
review of hospital and road P3s in the UK. However, it is worth noting that
in many other jurisdictions many VfM studies are simply unavailable.

In a typical VfM study, the cost to government of a P3 is compared to
the cost to government of a hypothetical counterfactual, the PSA. The
usual criterion used is the net cost to government, measured in PV terms.
When there are no revenues from tolls or taxes, this criterion selects the
project that has the smallest PV of the costs. Using terminology we introduced a few years ago, a VfM study is best described as a government
revenue–expenditure analysis (Boardman et al., 1993).

Table 8.1 summarizes the results of one VfM study: the Sea-to-Sky
Highway in British Columbia (Partnerships BC, 2005, p. 17). In this
example, the most significant costs are production costs, which include
construction costs, and operating and maintenance costs. Somewhat surprisingly, according to Partnerships BC, the P3 cost the government $46
million more than the PSA. There are, however, a number of issues that
arise in this type of study.

*Table 8.1   P3 – PSA cost comparison of Sea-to-Sky Highway Project by
Partnerships BC ($2005 millions, as of December 2005)*

	P3	Public sector alternative (PSA)
Payments to P3	578.5	–
Capital costs (MoT)	208.1	516.0
Operating and maintenance costs (MoT)	3.2	107.5
Rehabilitation costs (MoT)	–	36.3
Risk adjustment	–	42.9
Competitive neutrality adjustment	–	41.3
Total adjusted cost (2005 $ million, PV @ 7.5% disc. rate)	789.8	744.0

Note: MoT refers to the B.C. Ministry of Transportation.

Source: Adapted from Partnerships BC (2005), p. 17.

The first issue is: are the project alternatives directly comparable; that is, is the P3 project the same as the PSA project? In this Sea-to-Sky Highway example, the PV of the cost of the P3 was $46 million more than the PV of the cost of the PSA, but Partnerships BC argued that the P3 offered better VfM because it contained improvements that resulted in additional time savings and reduced accident risks that were estimated to be worth more than $46 million. However, it would have been more appropriate to have compared 'like with like' in the first place. Possibly it was a matter of timing – perhaps the PSA was evaluated according to the initial specifications, while the final specifications for the P3 were settled later. However, these studies are usually conducted *ex post*. Therefore it should have been possible to obtain the PSA cost of the actual project.

A second, related, issue is that in P3s risk is transferred to the private sector, but it is not free: government should expect to pay an uncertainty premium. Project budgets are partly a function of the particular institutional mechanism and the particular contract; in other words, they are endogenous. The more risk that is transferred, the more expensive it is likely to be. One way to account for the risk transfer in a P3 is to include a risk premium for the risk retained in the PSA. Indeed, Table 8.1 includes a 'risk adjustment' cost of $43 million. Estimating the monetary value of the risk transferred is itself highly uncertain.

Generally, the value of the risk transferred is often overestimated. Put simply, small risks can be transferred but big risks cannot be transferred, but are often assumed to be. In fact, if the P3 fails completely, the government will invariably bail it out. It has to for political reasons. Furthermore, this knowledge creates moral hazard problems and further increases the risk of P3 failure. This is particularly problematic for essential services, such as air traffic control, but also for infrastructure, such as Metronet. In general, then, the value of risk transfer is not as great as estimated or, equivalently, the amount of risk retained in the PSA is overestimated.

The third issue is the choice of the discount rate. Typically, PSAs require a government to incur expenditures earlier than it would in a P3. Indeed, in some P3s the government may pay virtually nothing until the construction phase is completed and the infrastructure is 'open'. Assuming that the same discount rate is applied to the P3 and the PSA cash flows, then the higher the discount rate, the more favourable the P3 will appear – in effect, future costs are discounted more, thereby reducing their present values. Given the long time frames for P3s, the choice of the discount rate is critical. In the above highway example, Partnerships BC discounted the annual cash flows of both projects using the weighted average cost of capital (WACC) of the P3, which was 7.5 per cent. This is considerably higher than the government borrowing rate, which was about 3.5 per cent.

Table 8.2 illustrates the effect of discounting at different rates.[4] Suppose that the PSA cost the government $100 per year now and each year for the first five years (the design and construction period), followed by $10 per year for 30 years (the operating and maintaining period).[5] Also suppose that the P3 cost $85.42 per year for the 30-year operating period. If these cash flows were discounted at a WACC-like discount rate of 10 per cent, the PVs of the PSA and P3 would be $538 and $500 respectively, which suggests that the P3 is the preferred alternative (see columns 2 and 4). However, if these cash flows were discounted at a government-borrowing-like discount rate of 3.5 per cent, the PVs of the PSA and P3 would be $706 and $1328 respectively, indicating a strong preference for the PSA (see columns 3 and 5). Thus the choice of discount rate is critical.

Table 8.2   Annual costs and the present value of a hypothetical PSA and P3 evaluation

Year	PSA at 10%	PSA at 5%	P3 at 5%	P3 at 10%	PSA financed by a bond
0	100	100	0	0	0
1	100	100	0	0	24.723
2	100	100	0	0	24.723
3	100	100	0	0	24.723
4	100	100	0	0	24.723
5	100	100	0	0	24.723
6–35	10	10	85.42	85.42	24.723
35	0	0	0	0	706.37
Discount rate (%)	10	3.50	10	3.50	10
PV	537.6	706.4	500	1322.8	489.8

In effect, the Partnerships BC approach ignored an obvious attractive alternative: rather than assuming that the government finances the project out of ongoing cash flows, assume that the government issues a bond at the beginning and then repays it over the same time span as the P3 alternative. Given that the interest rate on the government bond would be lower than the P3 WACC, then discounting these bond payments at the P3 WACC rate would lower the PV of the cost of the PSA. Continuing with this hypothetical example, the government could issue a bond of $706.4 at 3.5 per cent, which would be sufficient to finance the PSA cash flows (in columns 2 and 3). With the bond, however, the government's actual cash flows would be $24.723 per year for 35 years (interest at 3.5 per cent), plus

$706.37 at the end of the thirty-fifth year (repayment of the bond); see column 6 of Table 8.2. If these cash flows were discounted at 10 per cent, the PV would be $489, which is lower than that for the original PSA and for the P3 alternative.

Partnerships BC argued that the P3's WACC was higher due to the project's risk. However, the PSA costs already include a 'risk adjustment' of $43 million. Typically there are two ways to handle risk: one can include a risk premium in the cash flows and discount at a (low) risk-free rate, or one can not adjust the cash flows, but discount at a (higher) risk-adjusted rate.[6] One should not do what Partnerships BC did: include a risk premium *and* discount at a high risk-adjusted rate. In so far as the government actually pays either the PSA cash flows (columns 2 and 3, in our hypothetical example) or the P3 cash flows (columns 4 or 5), and would finance these flows by borrowing, it makes sense to discount at the government's borrowing rate. This will give the PV of the net cash flows to the government and is consistent with 'revenue–expenditure' analysis. The logic is simple: if the government has transferred the risk to the private sector (in exchange for usually higher expected costs), then it should discount at the 'after-one-has-transferred-the-risk' discount rate. Interestingly, the Province of Alberta in Canada discounts its P3 cash flows using the provincial borrowing rate (see Boardman and Vining, Chapter 16 in this volume).

Before leaving this topic, it is important to note that this discussion has been conducted in the context of presuming that the government wants to minimize its net cash outflow. We should emphasize that this is a positive theory rationale, or explanation, for the adoption of the P3 form. The more relevant normative question is whether the P3 makes sense from a social welfare perspective, in which case we might use a different discount rate. We return to this issue in the section on CBA.

Total social costs
Following work on government contracting out by Globerman and Vining (1996) and Boardman and Hewitt (2004), Vining and Boardman (2008a) propose that the most appropriate criterion for choosing between a P3 and a PSA government is to select the alternative with the lowest total social costs (TSC), recognizing that TSC includes not only production costs, but also transaction costs and externality costs (e.g. quality). While production costs are routinely included in the VfM studies of P3 procurement agencies, the other two costs are usually not.

Williamson (1975) emphasized the importance of transaction costs in choosing among alternative provision mechanisms, focusing on the choice between hierarchies and markets. He emphasized that market contracts will necessarily not be complete, and that parties may behave opportunistically (strategically) to benefit themselves. The transaction costs associated with negotiating, monitoring and, if necessary, renegotiating contracts, both *ex ante* (before the award of a contract) and *ex post* (after the contract has been let) can be considerable and can 'drive' the total costs and, therefore, the choice. This applies to government contracting as well as private sector contracting.

In a number of articles, Vining and Boardman have examined the transaction costs of a fairly large number of P3s. They argue that government transaction costs depend crucially on the level of *ex ante* competition, asset specificity, complexity/uncertainty and government contract management skills. They also depend on the level of risk transfer. The authors find that in many P3s, asset specificity and complexity are high. Indeed, one can think of a P3 as a complex form of contracting out. Also, government contract management skills are often low. Primarily for these reasons, the transaction costs of P3s are often high and usually exceed the transaction costs of the PSA; see, for example, Vining and Boardman (2008a).

In most choices between government provision (e.g. in-house provision or PSA) and private sector provision (e.g. contracting out or P3), there is an implicit assumption that the alternatives are equal from the perspective of users or third parties (the citizenry in general). However, this is often not the case. There may be important quality differences. Such effects, although 'external' to the government and public sector contractor, should be accounted for in assessing TSC. Interestingly, Partnerships BC, for example, does sometimes take such effects into consideration. Indeed, they argued that the Sea-to-Sky P3 offered better VfM because it resulted in additional time savings and reduced accident risks that were worth more than $46 million. Similarly, some of the VfM studies conducted in Portugal have included some consumer impacts.

Proposed P3 evaluation method: cost–benefit analysis

From an economist's perspective, the most appropriate way to evaluate P3s is to determine whether they increase allocative efficiency. This criterion is applicable whether the purpose is to decide whether or not government should engage in a project at all, or whether it should utilize a P3 or a PSA.

Following Jones et al. (1990), the total welfare gain from a P3 relative to the status quo can be written:

$$W_{P3} = \lambda_c CS_{P3} + \lambda_p PS_{P3} + \lambda_e ES_{P3} + \lambda_g GS_{P3} \qquad (8.1)$$

The total welfare gain from a PSA relative to the status quo can be written:

$$W_{PSA} = \lambda_c CS_{PSA} + \lambda_p PS_{PSA} + \lambda_e ES_{PSA} + \lambda_g GS_{PSA} \qquad (8.2)$$

And the total welfare gain from a P3 relative to a PSA can be written:

$$\Delta W_{P3-PSA} = \lambda_c \Delta CS_{P3-PSA} + \lambda_p \Delta PS_{P3-PSA} + \lambda_e \Delta ES_{P3-PSA} + \lambda_g \Delta GS_{P3-PSA}$$
$$(8.3)$$

where W is social welfare, CS is consumer surplus, PS is producer surplus to firms (firms' profits), ES is employee surplus, that is, producer surplus (Ricardian rents) to employees,[7] and GS is government surplus (government net cash flow or net revenue), all measured in present values.[8] The *P3* subscript implies that comparison is made between the surplus under a P3 project and the surplus under the status quo, the *PSA* subscript implies that comparison is made between the surplus under the PSA option and the status quo, and the *P3 − PSA* subscript implies that comparison is made between the surpluses under the P3 option relative to the PSA option. The Δ emphasizes that these surpluses reflect differences, for example:

$$\Delta W_{P3-PSA} = W_{P3} - W_{PSA} \qquad (8.4)$$

The parameters λ_c, λ_p, λ_e and λ_g are distributional weights (sometimes called welfare weights). These weights may reflect allocative efficiency or distributional considerations, that is, the view that some groups in society should be weighted more than other groups. In practice, analysts who are concerned only with allocative efficiency often set the λs equal to unity. We believe that this is incorrect. Even if one is interested only in allocative efficiency, net government revenue should be adjusted to take account of the deadweight loss of taxation, and producer surplus should be adjusted to reflect the fact that returns in the private sector are higher than the return to displaced consumption (the social marginal rate of time preference). Thus, on the basis of allocative efficiency considerations, one should set $\lambda_c = \lambda_e = 1$, λ_p equal to the shadow price of capital and $\lambda_g = 1 + \text{METB}$, where METB = marginal excess tax burden.[9] We shall discuss these parameters in more detail later. The P3 is preferable to the PSA if $\Delta W_{P3-PSA} > 0$.

To illustrate how these formulae would work, consider the example in Table 8.3. Here we presume that an *ex ante* decision is being made for a hypothetical road improvement project with no tolls: the choices are between a P3 project, a PSA project or the status quo (no project). The top part of the table compares the P3 to the status quo as in equation (8.1), the middle part compares the PSA to the status quo as in equation (8.2) and the bottom part compares the P3 to the PSA as in equation (8.3).

To begin, note that the construction cost and incremental operating

Table 8.3   A hypothetical CBA evaluation of a highway project

	Benefits	Costs	Net benefits	λ	Weighted surplus
P3 versus status quo					
Consumers	1000	100	900	1.0	900
Producers	680	620	60	1.1	66
Employees	200	200	0	1.0	0
Government		750	−750	1.4	−1050
			210		−84
PSA versus status quo					
Consumers	1000	80	920	1.0	920
Producers	750	700	50	1.1	55
Employees	250	205	45	1.0	45
Government		800	−800	1.4	−1120
			215		−100
P3 versus PSA					
Consumers	0	20	−20	1.0	−20
Producers	−70	−80	10	1.1	11
Employees	−50	−5	−45	1.0	−45
Government		−50	50	1.4	70
			−5		16

cost of the P3 relative to the status quo ($620) is less than the construction and incremental operating cost of the PSA ($700). This reflects greater P3 efficiency and higher PSA wages; the latter are $200 for the P3 and $250 for the PSA.[10] The opportunity cost of the workers is slightly higher in the PSA because there are slightly more employees. However, they are paid considerably more and therefore they enjoy employee surplus of $45 in the PSA, versus no surplus in the P3.

Government would pay for the highway improvement and its maintenance. The cost of the PSA ($750) is slightly higher than the cost of the P3 ($700), reflecting some willingness on the part of the P3 to pass on some of the benefits of their greater efficiency and the fact that the PSA costs a bit more because it minimizes the negative impact on the environment. Note, however, that the private sector does not pass on its entire cost savings to the government. While the private sector may be more technically efficient than the public sector, the first-order outcome of great private sector efficiency is generally higher private sector profits, not lower government costs. However, these profits ($60 in the case of the P3 and $50 in the case of the PSA) are a benefit to society as a whole and are included in the CBA. For both alternatives the cost to the government is higher than the amount the producers receive due to government transaction costs. The government transaction costs are $70 ($750–$680) for the P3 and are $50 ($800–$750) for the PSA. In this example the P3 transaction costs are higher than the PSA transaction costs, as one might expect in most applications.[11]

Corporate taxes reduce firms' producer surplus (profits) and increase government surplus. Implicitly, they are included in this example. Thus firm producer surplus (profits) referred to above are profits after tax. With all λs equal to unity, the tax payments are a transfer and cancel out. However, if the λs differ, then these payments might be important.

Consumers' benefits reflect the value of time saved, lives saved, vehicle operating cost savings and other benefits that accrue to highway users. Consumers' costs reflect negative externalities, such as increases in pollution, or negative scenic impacts that are borne by third parties. Congestion externalities are reflected in user benefits. In this example, we assume that the user benefits are the same for the P3 and the PSA alternative. However, the negative externalities of the PSA alternative are slightly smaller than those for the P3 because it causes less damage to the environment.

Which project should the government choose, if any? Assume, to begin with, that the welfare weights equal unity. The net social benefits (NSB) of the P3, which is denoted as W_{P3} in equation (8.1), equals $215. This positive number indicates that the P3 is superior to the status quo in terms of allocative efficiency. The NSB of the PSA, which is denoted as W_{PSA} in equation (8.2), equals $210. This positive number indicates that the PSA is superior to the status quo in terms of allocative efficiency. The PSA project alternative is slightly preferred to the P3 project alternative since its NSB is slightly lower: using equation (8.3), $\Delta W_{P3-PSA} = 5$.

The differences between the two projects are highlighted in the bottom part of the table. Consumers' surplus is higher in the PSA due to lower negative environmental impacts, producers' surplus is higher in the P3 primarily due to greater private sector efficiency and lower wages, employee surplus is higher in the PSA due to higher wages, and government surplus is higher in the P3 because the total cost (including transaction costs) is less.

However, when welfare weights are taken into account the

recommendations change completely. The P3 is now preferred to the PSA, but neither project is preferred to the status quo. This conclusion is 'driven' by the METB: the PSA is more expensive (has a more negative government cash flow) and therefore it requires higher taxes and results in a higher deadweight loss of taxation.

Most of the issues concerning the calculation of *CS*, *PS* and *GS* are relatively uncontroversial; see, for example, the textbook on CBA by Boardman et al. (2006). However, this brief discussion has skipped over some important issues. One is whether to include the producer surplus (profits or costs) accruing to firms outside the jurisdiction. For example, should all the profits that accrue to Kiewit Corporation, a US-based employee-owned firm, be included in a CBA of a road project in British Columbia, Canada? Or should the profits be weighted by the proportion of British Columbian or Canadian employee shareholders? Usually, the decision to include or exclude such impacts on firms depends on the perspective of the CBA evaluation – the question of 'standing'. If the analyst is taking a global perspective, then costs borne by all firms should be included. However, for many P3s, the appropriate level of analysis is at the province or state (i.e. sub-national) level. For these evaluations, the financial impacts on foreign firms should probably not be included.

Similar issues apply to corporate taxes. A sub-national government may pay for a project but the federal government might receive the tax revenue. If the analysis is conducted at the sub-national level, then tax revenues received by the federal government would not be treated as a benefit.

This example illustrates that the shadow multipliers (the shadow price of capital and the METB) can be very important. We also pointed out earlier that, due to the long lives of many infrastructure projects, the choice of the discount rate is absolutely critical. We discuss that issue next and then return to discuss the shadow multipliers.

The appropriate discount rate(s) to use to evaluate P3s[12]
This section discusses and derives the appropriate discount rate to use to evaluate P3s in Canada. The 'bottom line' is that for intragenerational projects (no impacts beyond 50 years), analysts and governments should use an annual discount rate of 3.5 per cent. In Moore et al. (2004) we argue that this rate should also be used in the USA. Coincidentally, the UK government has recently switched from using a 6 per cent real rate to a 3.5 per cent real rate (HM Treasury, 2003a). Thus we have some confidence that this rate is a reasonable one to use for the evaluation of government projects in most developed countries. However, many governments and many organizations that perform P3 evaluations use an incorrect rate. This section explains how we derived what we think is a reasonable rate to use.

Since 1976, the Treasury Board of Canada Secretariat has required that federal CBAs use a real annual social discount rate (SDR) of 10 per cent (Treasury Board Secretariat, 1976; Treasury Board Secretariat, 1998, ch. 5). Recent interim guidelines (Treasury Board Secretariat, 2007) now recommend a real discount rate of 8 per cent with sensitivity rates of 3 per cent and 10 per cent. These values are based on the weighted social opportunity cost of capital (WSOC) method. In our view, this is an inappropriate methodology and, even if it were not, the 8 per cent rate is too high.

Most academics now recommend deriving the SDR by basing it on the rate of future growth in per capita consumption (Ramsey, 1928). The basic idea is that policy-makers should choose the level of public investment to maximize the present value of the well-being of society, where well-being depends on social (public and private) per capita consumption. Ramsey (1928) suggested that the SDR, denoted o, should be computed as the sum of two elements:

$$o = d + ge \qquad (8.5)$$

The first term, d (the pure rate of time preference), measures the rate at which society discounts the utility of present versus future (per capita) consumption (due to impatience), holding constant economic growth. The second term assumes economic growth and reflects a preference for more equality in per capita consumption over time than would otherwise occur. It is the product of the growth rate of social per capita consumption, g, and the rate at which the marginal value of per capita consumption decreases as per capita consumption increases, e.

The most plausible way to predict g is to estimate it based on historical per capita consumption growth rates. Boardman et al. (forthcoming) estimate that the average annual growth rate of per capita consumption in Canada was 1.7 per cent per annum for 1971–2006 with a standard error of 0.056 per cent, and recommend using this value as an estimate of g for Canada, with sensitivity analysis at 1.5 per cent and 2.0 per cent.

The parameter e reflects society's preference for reducing inequality in per capita consumption over time (across generations), given positive economic growth. It equals the absolute value of the elasticity of the social marginal utility of consumption with respect to per capita consumption. In principle, it could vary between zero and infinity. Setting the parameter equal to zero implies no discounting of future consumption: society treats each unit of consumption received in the future as identical to a unit of consumption in the present, implying an indifference to intergenerational inequality. In contrast, as e approaches infinity, society would completely discount each unit of consumption received in the (richer) future, signifying a dominating desire to equalize per capita consumption over time. When *e* equals 1 the relative weight of society's consumption in each time period equals the inverse of its relative per capita consumption.

Boardman et al. (forthcoming) suggest that the best method of choosing *e* is to prescribe it based on some plausible distributional perspective. Stern (2007) used an *e* value of 1, and Cline (1992) chose *e* equal to 1.5. Dasgupta (2007) has criticized Stern and points out that in simple growth models, such a low value for *e* implies that the current generation should save approximately 97.5 per cent of its income in order to increase the consumption of future, wealthier generations! Accordingly, Dasgupta argues that reasonable attitudes towards inequality of consumption imply that *e* would fall within the range of 2 to 4. With prescribed rates in the range of 0.5 to 4, and a recent empirical estimate for Canada equal to 1.3 (Policy Research Initiative, 2007), Boardman et al. (forthcoming) suggest that a central estimate of 1.5 is reasonable, with sensitivity analysis at 1 and 2.

There has been considerable debate about the value of *d* since Ramsey (1928, p. 543), who argued that it is 'ethically indefensible' to use a positive value, as this would devalue future generations' utility relative to the present generation. However, *d* may be interpreted as the probability of non-survival for either an individual or a society. On this interpretation, *d* would represent the fact that individuals prefer consumption now to consumption later, as they may not be around later. It can plausibly be estimated as the instantaneous probability of death, measured by the average population death rate. Thus Kula (1984) estimated *d* at 0.8 per cent per year. More recent data suggest that it is closer to 1 per cent (TBS, 2007). Some authors, including Stern (2007), suggest that *d* should be much smaller. However, Arrow (1995) demonstrates that setting *d* close to or equal to zero – essentially weighting all generations' welfare equally – results in very high rates of savings being required of the current (or even of every) generation. He shows that under reasonable parameter values the current generation would be required to save approximately two-thirds of its income. To avoid this result, a positive pure rate of time preference has to be employed. Arrow has proposed around 1 per cent for *d*, which we think is reasonable.

With an estimate of *g* = 1.7 per cent, *e* = 1.5 and *d* = 1 per cent, we obtain *o* approximately equal to 3.5 per cent. Sensitivity analysis with *e* ranging between 1 and 2, and with *g* varying between 1.5 per cent and 2.0 per cent, implies that *o* ranges between 2.5 per cent and 5.0 per cent. Thus Boardman et al. (forthcoming) recommend using a central estimate of *o* equal to 3.5 per cent, with sensitivity analysis at 2.0 per cent and 5.0 per cent.

Many P3 projects have impacts that stretch beyond 50 years (in other words, they are intergenerational). For example, the Vasco da Gama bridge in Portugal is designed to last 100 years. In such situations, Boardman et al. (forthcoming) recommend time-declining SDRs. Both Pearce et al. (2003) and Groom et al. (2005) have reviewed the rationales for the use of declining rates. The most plausible reason stems from the fact that the inherent uncertainty as to the future growth rate of the economy, the return on investment, and the SDR all increase as we look further into the future. Allowing for this increasing uncertainty means that lower discount rates over time should be used to discount consumption flows, essentially because one must average discount factors, not discount rates.[13] Recently, Hepburn et al. (2009) have applied the Newell and Pizer (2003) approach to data from four countries, including Canada. Based partially on this analysis, Boardman et al. (forthcoming) recommend a schedule of time-declining SDRs: 3.5 per cent from year 0 to year 50; 2.5 per cent from year 51 to year 100; 2.0 per cent from year 101 to year 200; and 1.5 per cent from year 201 on.

Weighting investment flows to the private sector by the shadow price of capital

In general, financial flows into the private sector earn a higher return than the rate individuals (or society as a whole) require for postponing present consumption in return for increased consumption in the future (Boardman et al., 2006). That is, the marginal return on private investment is higher than the marginal rate of time preference. For this reason, when applying equations (8.1) to (8.3), flows in or out of the private sector should be weighted by the shadow price of private sector funds, λ_p, also known as the shadow price of capital (SPC).

Lyon (1990) shows that an estimate of the SPC, which is denoted s, can be obtained using:

$$s = \frac{(i + f)(1 - a)}{o - ia + f(1 - a)} \tag{8.6}$$

where i is the net rate of return on capital after depreciation (the ROI), f is the depreciation rate of capital, a is the fraction of the gross return that is reinvested, and o is the SDR. An estimate of the SPC requires a measure of the marginal, pre-tax ROI, the depreciation rate of capital, and of the fraction of the gross return on capital that is reinvested. Boardman et al. (forthcoming) estimate these parameters and then estimate the SPC using equation (8.6). Their best estimates are as follows: the SDR, o, equals 3.5 per cent; the ROI, i, equals 5.2 per cent; depreciation, f, equals 13.5 per cent; and the reinvestment rate, a, equals 17 per cent, which yields a measure of the SPC, s, equal to 1.12, implying that one dollar of private sector investment would produce a stream of consumption benefits with an NPV equal to \$1.12. Given this, they recommend using $o = 3.5$ per cent with $s = 1.1$ as a best estimate. Based on Moore et al. (2004), we recommend using $o = 2.0$ per cent with $s = 1.2$, and $o = 5.0$ per cent with $s = 1.0$ for purposes of sensitivity analysis. Although Moore et al. (2004) found that the SPC is fairly sensitive to the parameters used in its estimation, the NPV of a project will not be very sensitive to the precise value of the SPC unless a substantial share of the project's benefits augment domestic investment or a large proportion of the costs displace domestic investment.

Earlier we suggested estimating allocative efficiency using equations (8.1) to (8.3) with $\lambda_c = \lambda_e = 1$, $\lambda_p = $ SPC and $\lambda_g = 1 +$ METB. That was partially for expositional convenience. It is correct under the assumption that all changes in consumer surplus reflect changes in consumption and all changes in firm producer surplus represent changes in private sector investment flows. However, it is possible that some elements in consumer surplus affect private sector investment flows and some producer surplus accruing to firms may be consumed and not reinvested. In such circumstances, flows of private sector investment (in or out) should be multiplied by the SPC and changes in consumption should not. Multiplying private sector investment flows by the SPC converts them to consumption equivalents. These flows and the 'pure' consumption flows are then discounted at the SDR. Moore et al. (2001) explain and illustrate this procedure in detail.

Weighting cash flows to government by 1 + METB
Taxes on goods or incomes generally result in a transfer from consumers to the government and a deadweight loss in consumer surplus or producer surplus. This particular deadweight loss is called the deadweight loss of taxation. Its magnitude depends on the type of tax and how individuals respond to the tax. The marginal excess tax burden equals the ratio of the deadweight loss to the amount of tax collected. Estimates by Galal et al. (1994) and Boardman et al. (2006) suggest that, on average, the deadweight loss of taxation is about 30 per cent or 40 per cent of the tax collected, implying that $\lambda_g = 1.3$ or 1.4. Put another way, there is a consumer surplus or producer surplus loss of about \$1.35 for each \$1 in tax raised by the government.

Many P3s involve tolls. From an allocative efficiency perspective, tolls can be wonderful things. Imposing a toll on a congested highway improves consumer surplus because it reduces congestion and saves users' time. Furthermore, each dollar of toll revenue going to the government (directly or indirectly) should be multiplied by $1 +$ METB to reflect the fact that the government does not have to raise taxes by a dollar. The P3 may actually collect and keep the tolls, but if this means that the government's cost is reduced by the amount of the tolls collected, then the benefit to society is still equal to the toll times 1 + METB.

VfM reconsidered

As mentioned and discussed above, VfM studies focus on the PV of the cash flows to government, adjusted for risk. Earlier we referred to this as government surplus, which is denoted *GS* in equations (8.1)–(8.3). How appropriate is it to use a VfM study (i.e. *GS*) as a measure of allocative efficiency? That is, can we measure allocative efficiency (or the difference in allocative efficiency) thus?

$$W_{P3} = GS_{P3} \qquad\qquad (8.7a)$$

$$W_{PSA} = GS_{PSA} \qquad\qquad (8.7b)$$

$$\Delta W_{P3-PSA} = \Delta GS_{P3-PSA} \qquad\qquad (8.7c)$$

In fact, these are often poor measures of allocative efficiency.

First, it is not appropriate to use equation (8.7a) to decide whether or not to use a P3. It implies that consumer surplus, producer surplus and employee surplus are zero, or that consumers, producers (firms) and employees have no weight ($\lambda_c = \lambda_p = \lambda_e = 0$). How about using equation (8.7c)? Most importantly, this equation tells us nothing about the allocative efficiency of either project. It cannot indicate whether either project is worth doing. However, it does provide information about which option to pursue, given that government has decided to proceed with *a* project. It provides a correct measure of the difference in allocative efficiency between the two projects if the *differences* in consumer surplus, producer surplus and employee surplus are zero between the alternative projects, or if consumers, firms and employees have no weight. Implicitly, VfM studies assume that the P3 and PSA projects are identical from the consumers' perspective. This assumption may or may not be valid, as we discussed above. To be fair, there are sometimes marginal adjustments. It is not at all clear what assumptions, if any, practitioners of VfM studies make about producer surplus or employee surplus. They may think that the difference in surplus is small (possibly in the case of employee surplus) or that the group should receive no weight (private sector firms, perhaps).

Second, government transaction costs should be included in the computation of GS, as we discussed above, but they are usually excluded from the VfM computation. They are likely to vary between a P3 and a PSA. Excluding them may bias the conclusions, even if one is interested only in government surplus.

Third, in terms of comparing a P3 to a PSA, VfM studies assume that there are no differences between the two alternatives in terms of consumer surplus, producer surplus and employee surplus. However, to be fair, there are sometimes marginal adjustments.

Fourth, VfM studies cannot actually be thought of as measuring GS properly if, as is often the case, they use a private sector discount rate rather than the SDR. This is particularly problematic for P3s that have long lives. Discounting at the wrong rate over a long period can have a huge impact on the estimated GS (or allocative efficiency).

In short, VfM studies are generally not a good way to evaluate P3s according to normative economic principles.

Conclusion

Governments are likely to perceive P3s as an attractive institutional mechanism for the delivery of infrastructure over the next decade or longer. This is especially likely to be the case in contexts where the demand for infrastructure investment is rising and governments face severe budget constraints. However, this chapter argues that as yet no government has performed normatively appropriate analyses of P3s. From a normative perspective, evaluation should estimate the change in allocative efficiency or equity. This chapter outlines how to conduct a social welfare analysis that reflects allocative efficiency and equity, but it focuses on allocative efficiency.

Here and elsewhere we have argued that the evaluation of P3s should be performed by arm's-length analysts, either inside or outside government; see 'Rule 2' in Vining and Boardman (2008b). Too many evaluations of P3s are conducted by organizations or consultants with a vested interest in their success. To put it another way, such organizations become 'captured' by the firms they are evaluating.

Most 'on time and on budget' analyses are naturally conducted *ex post*. VfM studies should obviously be conducted *ex ante* and they should be made public. Often, though, *ex ante* analyses are not done at all – P3s are presumed to be the best option. When VfM studies are conducted, whether *ex ante* or *ex post*, they are often hard to track down. Overall, there should be more analyses *ex ante* and *ex post*, and the studies should be readily available.

Thus far, two main criteria have been used to evaluate P3s *ex post*: 'on time and on budget' and VfM. 'On time and on budget' is obviously a weak criterion. VfM is more meaningful. To put it in context, it is really a positive criterion related to minimizing current government expenditures and keeping government debt as low as possible, again, in the short run. However, as we show, it does relate to government surplus, which is an important component of allocative efficiency.

In practice, the VfM criterion suffers from several problems. To begin, it cannot be used to determine whether or not to engage in a P3 or PSA project because it ignores consumer surplus and other social impacts. For comparing between alternative provisioning mechanisms, it assumes that projects are equal on all dimensions except government cash flow. This is often inappropriate. Transaction costs are often ignored and they are likely to vary across alternatives. Also the quality of the projects may differ in important ways.

Most importantly, government-conducted VfM studies regularly use an inappropriate discount rate. Partnerships BC, for example, often discounts at the private sector weighted average cost of capital. The decision about whether or not to engage in a project or which provision alternative should be used, should be made by discounting future benefits and costs at the social discount rate. This chapter argues that the real social discount rate equals about 3.5 per cent with sensitivity analysis at 2 per cent and 5 per cent. For long-term (more than 50 years) projects, the discount rate should decline with time. In the special case where the government will borrow all of the funds, then it may be reasonable to use the government's borrowing rate, which is currently less than 3.5 per cent in real terms. One of the main consequences of P3 projects is that they shift the timing of the cash flows. More specifically, the (negative) cash flows of P3s relative to a PSA are shifted from the start of the project towards the end of a project. Using a high discount rate reduces the impact of cash flows far in the future and, therefore, biases the analysis in favour of the P3.

An important step in the right direction would be to compare the P3 with the PSA using total social costs. These costs equal production costs plus transaction costs plus externalities (reflecting quality and other third-party effects). Vining and Boardman have examined the transaction costs of quite a large number of P3s in a number of articles and conclude that transaction costs of P3s are often high and usually exceed the transaction costs of the PSA.

However, this criterion still does not go quite far enough. This chapter argues that the appropriate criterion for deciding on whether to undertake a project and whether to use a P3 or not should be based on allocative efficiency. We advocate the use of cost–benefit analysis to estimate the net social benefits of alternative projects and we explain how this might be done.

Some might argue that this is an ambitious goal to ask of government analysts. Indeed we are not aware of any CBAs. Thus we conclude that few, if any, studies have properly evaluated P3s. P3s are becoming a very important part of infrastructure development in both developed and developing countries, and require very significant budget outlays. It is time to conduct proper evaluations of them.

Acknowledgements
An earlier version of this chapter was presented at the UBC P3 Project Third Research Workshop, 4–5 December 2008. The authors would like to thank Mark Moore for his contributions to the section on the social discount rate. We would also like to thank Tom Ross for some helpful comments. Finally, we would also like to thank the UBC P3 Project and Infrastructure Canada for financial assistance.

Notes

1. Maskin and Tirole (2008, p. 413) point out that bundling may reduce operational efficiency because 'the best developer might not also be the best operator'. While this is likely to be correct, P3s usually consist of consortia in which different activities are performed by different firms, ideally with each activity performed by the firm best at that activity.
2. Interestingly, though, some risks can be higher to the government in a P3 as in the case of legal costs in the Canada Line in Vancouver, British Columbia (Boardman and Vining, Chapter 16 in this volume).
3. See, for example, for North America (Boardman et al., 2005; Vining et al., 2005; Ouyahia, 2006; Vining and Boardman, 2008a); for the UK (Pollock et al., 2000, Shaoul, 2003; Broadbent and Laughlin, 2004; Grout and Stevens, 2003; Pollitt, 2005; Shaoul et al., 2006; Vining and Boardman, 2008b), for Ireland (Reeves, 2003), for France (Chong et al., 2006), for the Netherlands (Klijn and Teisman, 2003; Koppenjan, 2005), for Denmark (Greve and Ejersbo, 2003); for Spain (Acerete et al., 2009) and for Australia (English, 2005; Hodge, 2005).
4. For more illustrations, see Parks and Terhart (2009).
5. Obviously it would be more realistic to show these numbers in millions of dollars, but that would not change the substantive conclusions.
6. Boardman et al. (2006) argue that in CBA it is better to convert the cash flows to certainty equivalents and discount at a risk-free social discount rate. Using the latter approach requires an estimate of the risk-free social discount rate (r). One way to estimate r is to use the capital asset pricing model, which is written: $r = r_f + \beta(r_m - r_f)$, where r_f is the risk-free rate (for example, government bond rate), r_m is the expected return to the market portfolio, and β, called beta, is a measure of systematic risk, which reflects the correlation between the return on the infrastructure project and the return on the market portfolio. In general, the beta for 'necessities', such as infrastructure projects that cater to commuters, would be relatively low (<1), while the beta for 'luxuries', such as a project that catered mainly to tourists, would be relatively high (>1).
7. We ignore Ricardian rents going to factors of production other than employees.
8. For applications of this criteria to privatization see Galal et al. (1994) and Boardman et al. (2009).
9. For more discussion of these concepts see Boardman et al. (2006).
10. It is often surmised that P3s cost less than PSAs because the private sector pays lower compensation, partly because of lower rates of unionization. On these differentials, see, for example, Disney and Gosling (1998), Donald et al. (2000), Bender et al. (2006), Lucifora (2006), and Peoples and Wang (2007).
11. This illustrative example excludes the costs incurred by unsuccessful bidders (e.g. the opportunity of employee time in preparing the bid). In practice, these costs should also be included.

12. This section is based on Boardman et al. (forthcoming).
13. To see why discount rates decline as they apply to flows that occur further out in time, consider a project that delivers a single benefit of $1 billion in 400 years. Also suppose there is a 50 per cent chance that the appropriate (constant) discount rate over this period will be 7 per cent and a 50 per cent chance that it will be 1 per cent. One might simply average these two rates to obtain an expected discount rate of 4 per cent and then use this average rate to compute the expected PV of the future benefit (assuming continuous compounding). If so, the PV would be $1 billion $* e^{-0.04*400}$, which is approximately $110. However, this would be incorrect. Assuming continuous compounding, the expected PV equals $\frac{1}{2} * 1 billion $* e^{-0.07*400} + \frac{1}{2}*1 billion $* e^{-0.07*400}$, which is approximately $9 157 800. It is the discount factors of $e^{-0.07*400}$ and $e^{-0.01*400}$ that should be averaged. This average equals approximately $e^{-4.69} = e^{-0.012*400}$, which is equivalent to using a single, certain discount rate of approximately 1.2 per cent. Note that this is much closer to 1 per cent than to 7 per cent. The larger discount rate almost completely discounts itself out of the average: $e^{-0.07*400} = 6.9 * 10^{-13}$. This effect grows over longer time horizons, thereby resulting in time-declining discount rates.

References

Acerete, B., J. Shaoul and A. Stafford (2009), 'Taking its toll: the private financing of roads in Spain', *Public Money & Management*, **29** (1), 185–94.

Arrow, K.J. (1995), 'Intergenerational equity and the rate of discount in long-term social investment', paper presented at the IEA World Congress, available at: www-econ.stanford.edu/faculty/workp/swp97005.pdf.

Bender, K., H. Mridha and J. Peoples (2006), 'Risk compensation for hospital workers: evidence from relative wages of janitors', *Industrial and Labor Relations Review*, **59** (2), 226–42.

Boardman, A.E. and E. Hewitt (2004), 'Problems with contracting out government services: lessons from orderly services at SCGH', *Industrial and Corporate Change*, **13** (6), 917–29.

Boardman, A.E., A.R. Vining and W.G. Waters, II (1993), 'Costs and benefits through bureaucratic lenses: example of a highway project', *Journal of Policy Analysis and Management*, **12** (3), 532–55.

Boardman, A.E., F. Poschmann and A.R. Vining (2005), 'North American infrastructure P3s: examples and lessons learned', in G. Hodge and C. Greve (eds), *The Challenge of Public–Private Partnerships: Learning from International Experience*, Cheltenham, UK and Northampton, MA, USA: Edward Elgar, pp. 162–89.

Boardman, A.E., M.A. Moore and A.R. Vining (2010), 'The social discount rate for Canada based on future growth in consumption', *Canadian Public Policy*, **36** (3), 325–43.

Boardman, A.E., D.H. Greenberg, A.R. Vining and D.L. Weimer (2006), *Cost–Benefit Analysis: Concepts and Practice*, 3rd edn, Upper Saddle River, NJ: Prentice Hall.

Boardman, A.E., C. Laurin, M.A. Moore and A.R. Vining (2009), 'A cost–benefit analysis of the privatization of Canadian National Railway', *Canadian Public Policy*, **35** (1), 59–83.

Broadbent, J. and R. Laughlin (2004), 'Perils of partnership', *Australian CPA*, **74** (4), 56–8.

Chong, E., F. Huet, S. Saussier and F. Steiner (2006), 'Public–private partnerships and prices: evidence from water distribution in France', *Review of Industrial Organization*, **29** (1/2), 149–69.

Cline, W.R. (1992), *The Economics of Global Warming*, Washington, DC: Institute for International Economics.

Dasgupta, P. (2007), 'Commentary: the Stern Review's economics of climate change', *National Institute Economic Review*, **199**, 4–7.

Disney, R. and A. Gosling (1998), 'Does it pay to work in the public sector?', *Fiscal Studies*, **19** (4), 347–73.

Donald, S.G., D.A. Green and H.J. Paarsch (2000), 'Differences in wage distributions between Canada and the United States: an application of a flexible estimator of distribution functions in the presence of covariates', *Review of Economic Studies*, **67**, 609–33.

184 Internationalhandbook on public–private partnerships

Edwards, C. (2009), 'Private gain and public loss: the Private Finance Initiative (PFI) and the Norfolk and Norwich University Hospital; a case study', available at: www.uea.ac.uk/polopoly_fs/1.116274!Private%20Gain%20and%20Public%20Loss%20-%20June%20 2009.pdf (accessed 5 November 2009).

Edwards, P., J. Shaoul, A. Stafford and L. Arblaster (2004), *Evaluating the Operation of PFI in Roads and Hospitals*, London: Certified Accountants Educational Trust.

Eisner, R. (1989), *The Total Incomes System of Accounts*, Chicago, IL: University of Chicago Press.

English, L. (2005), 'Using public–private partnerships to deliver social infrastructure: the Australian experience', in G. Hodge and C. Greve (eds), *The Challenge of Public–Private Partnerships: Learning from International Experience*, Cheltenham, UK and Northampton, MA, USA: Edward Elgar, pp. 290–304.

Eurostat (2004), 'News Release No. 18', 11 February, available at: europa.eu.int/comm/eurostat/Public/datashop/print-product/ EN?catalogue=Eurostat&product=2-11022004-EN-AP-EN&mode=download.

Galal, A., L. Jones, P. Tandon and I. Vogelsang (1994), *Welfare Consequences of Selling Public Enterprises: An Empirical Analysis*, Oxford: Oxford University Press.

Globerman, S. and A.R. Vining (1996), 'A framework for evaluating the government contracting-out decision with an application to information technology', *Public Administration Review*, **56** (6), 40–46.

Greve, C. and N. Ejersbo (2003), 'When public–private partnerships fail – the extreme case of the NPM-inspired local government of Farum in Denmark', paper for Nordisk Kommunalforskningskonference, Odense, Denmark, 29 November–1 December.

Groom, B., C. Hepburn, P. Koundouri and D. Pearce (2005), 'Declining discount rates: the long and short of it', *Environmental and Resource Economics*, **32**, 445–93.

Grout, P. and M. Stevens (2003), 'The assessment: financing and managing public services', *Oxford Review of Economic Policy*, **19** (2), 215–34.

Heald, D. (2003), 'Value for money tests and accounting treatment in PFI schemes', *Accounting, Auditing and Accountability Journal*, **16** (3), 342–71.

Hemming, R., M. Alier, B. Anderson, M. Cangiano and M. Petri (2006), *Public–Private Partnerships, Government Guarantees, and Fiscal Risk*, Washington, DC: International Monetary Fund.

Hepburn, C., P. Koundouri, E. Panopoulou and T. Pantelidis (2009), 'Social discounting under uncertainty: a cross-country comparison', *Journal of Environmental Economics and Management*, **57** (2), 140–50.

HM (Her Majesty's) Treasury (2000), *Public Private Partnerships – The Government's Approach*, London: HM Stationery Office.

HM (Her Majesty's) Treasury (2003a), *Appraisal and Evaluation in Central Government (The Green Book)*, London: HM Stationery Office.

HM (Her Majesty's) Treasury (2003b), *PFI: Meeting the Investment Challenge*, London: HM Stationery Office.

Hodge, G. (2005), 'Public–private partnerships: the Australasian experience with physical infrastructure', in G. Hodge and C. Greve (eds), *The Challenge of Public–Private Partnerships: Learning from International Experience*, Cheltenham, UK and Northampton, MA, USA: Edward Elgar, pp. 305–31.

Jones, L.P., P. Tandon and I. Vogelsang (1990), *Selling Public Enterprises: A Cost–Benefit Methodology*, Cambridge, MA MIT Press.

Klijn, E. and G. Teisman (2003), 'Institutional and strategic barriers to public-private partnerships: an analysis of Dutch cases', *Public Money and Management*, **23** (3), 137–46.

Koppenjan, J. (2005), 'The formation of public–private partnerships: lessons from nine transport infrastructure projects in the Netherlands', *Public Administration*, **83** (1), 135–57.

Kula, E. (1984), 'Derivation of the social time preference rates for the United States and Canada', *Quarterly Journal of Economics*, **99** (4), 873–82.

Lucifora, C. (2006), 'The public sector pay gap in France, Great Britain and Italy', *Review of Income and Wealth*, **52** (1), 43–59.

Lyon, R.M. (1990), 'Federal discount rate policy, the shadow price of capital, and challenges for reforms', *Journal of Environmental Economics and Management*, **18** (2), S29–S50.

Maskin, E. and J. Tirole (2008), 'Public–private partnerships and government spending limits', *International Journal of Industrial Organization*, **26**, 412–20.

Moore, M.A., A.E. Boardman and D.H. Greenberg (2001), 'The social discount rate in Canada', in A.R. Vining and J. Richards (eds), *Building the Future: Issues in Public Infrastructure in Canada*, Toronto: C.D. Howe, pp. 73–130.

Moore, M.A., A.E. Boardman, A.R. Vining, D. Weimer and D.H. Greenberg (2004), 'Just give me a number! Practical values for the social discount rate', *Journal of Policy Analysis and Management*, **23** (4), 789–812.

National Health Service (NHS) (1999), *Public Private Partnerships in National Health Service: The Private Financial Service: Good Practice*, London: Her Majesty's Stationery Office.

Newell, R.G. and W.A. Pizer (2003), 'Discounting the distant future: how much do uncertain rates increase valuations?', *Journal of Environmental Economics and Management*, **46** (1), 52–71.

Ouyahia, M. (2006), 'Public–private partnerships for funding municipal drinking water infrastructure: what are the challenges?', discussion paper, Ottawa: Policy Research Initiative (PRI), Government of Canada.

Parks, R. and R. Terhart (2009), *Evaluation of Public Private Partnerships: Costing and Evaluation Methodology*, Vancouver, BC: Blair, Mackay and Mynett Valuations Inc.

Partnerships BC (2005), 'Project report: achieving value for money – Sea-to-Sky Highway Improvement Project', December.

Pearce, D., B. Groom, C. Hepburn and P. Koundouri (2003), 'Valuing the future: recent advances in social discounting', *World Economics*, **4** (2), 121–41.

Peoples, J. and B. Wang (2007), 'Privatization and labor cost savings: evidence from health care services', *Atlantic Economic Journal*, **35**, 145–57.

Policy Research Initiative (2007), 'Social discount rates for Canada (draft)', PRI Project (May).

Pollitt, M. (2005), 'Learning from UK Private Finance Initiative experience', in G. Hodge and C. Greve (eds), *The Challenge of Public–Private Partnerships: Learning from International Experience*, Cheltenham, UK and Northampton, MA, USA: Edward Elgar, pp. 207–30.

Pollock, A., D. Price and M. Dunnigan (2000), *Deficits before Patients: A Report on the Worcestershire Royal Infirmary PFI and Worcestershire Hospital Configuration*, London: University College.

Ramsey, F.P. (1928), 'A mathematical theory of saving', *Economic Journal*, **38** (151), 543–59.

Reeves, E. (2003), 'Public–private partnerships in Ireland: policy and practice', *Public Money & Management*, **23** (3), 163–70.

Shaoul, J. (2003), 'A financial analysis of the national air traffic services PPP', *Public Money & Management*, **23** (3), 185–94.

Shaoul, J., A. Stafford and P. Stapleton (2006), 'Highway robbery? A financial analysis of design, build, finance and operate (DBFO) in UK roads', *Transport Reviews*, **26** (3), 257–74.

Shaffer, M. (2006), 'Value for money assessment of the Sea-to-Sky P3', working paper, SFU.

Stern, N. (2007), *The Economics of Climate Change: The Stern Review*, New York: Cambridge University Press.

Treasury Board of Canada Secretariat (TBS) (1976), 'Benefit–cost analysis guide', mimeo, Planning Branch, March.

Treasury Board of Canada Secretariat (TBS) (1998), 'Benefit–cost analysis guide (draft), available at: www.tbs-sct.gc.ca/fin/sigs/Revolving_Funds/bcag/BCA2_e.asp (modified 16 December 2002, accessed 11 February 2008).

Treasury Board of Canada Secretariat (TBS) (2007), 'Canadian cost–benefit analysis guide: regulatory proposals (interim)', Ottawa, Ontario: Treasury Board Secretariat, available at: www.regulation.gc.ca/documents/gl-ld/analys/analystb-eng.asp, accessed 7 January 2009.

UK National Audit Office (UKNAO) (1999), *Examining the Value for Money of Deals Under the Private Finance Initiative*, London: National Audit Office.

Vining, A.R. and A.E. Boardman (2008a), 'Public–private partnerships in Canada: theory and evidence', *Canadian Public Administration*, **51** (1), 9–44.

Vining, A.R. and A.E. Boardman (2008b), 'Public–private partnerships: eight rules for governments', *Public Works Management and Policy*, **13** (2), 149–61.

Vining, A.R. and A.E. Boardman (2008c), 'The potential role of public–private partnerships in the upgrade of port infrastructure: normative and positive considerations', *Maritime Policy and Management*, **35** (6), 551–69.

Vining, A.R., A.E. Boardman and F. Poschmann (2005), 'Public–private partnerships in the U.S. and Canada: "There are no free lunches"', *Journal of Comparative Policy Analysis*, **7** (3), 199–220.

Williamson, O. (1975), *Markets and Hierarchies: Analysis and Antitrust Implications*, New York: The Free Press.

9 Different delivery models
Colin F. Duffield

Introduction

Common definitions for PPPs range from concession-based financing arrangements where repayment is based solely on user charges, to institutional PPPs. Such institutional PPPs frequently comprise mixed ownership structures involving public and private joint ownership. Other models involve a 'special purpose vehicle' (SPV), straight project finance arrangements under long-term contractual arrangements between the public and private sectors to provide a service for the term of the contract. The definition adopted for PPPs in this chapter is that of a long-term contract based on service outputs where there is significant risk transfer to the private sector. Typically these long-term contract obligations involve design, major procurement, operation and/or maintenance along with the provision of significant private finance.

The transfer of responsibility for long-term service outcomes to the private sector is conceptually undertaken on the basis that bundling aspects of technical, commercial and financing activities (i.e. design, procurement, construction, operation and maintenance, business operations and project/facility financing) brings efficacy (or effectiveness), efficiency, sustainability and value for money. To understand if PPPs are likely to bring such value to a particular situation it is important to know the contextual situation and industry's appetite for risk, the commercial opportunity and the availability and cost of finance. It is also important to understand the myriad of alternative procurement strategies that may provide mechanisms to achieve high performance.

This chapter takes us through the range of 'counterfactuals' on the techniques to procure major public infrastructure, from simple public works, through competitive tendering, design and construct, and relationship-style contracts, to outline the wide range of possible alternatives to PFI (Private Finance Initiative)-type PPPs. It considers the theoretical advantages and disadvantages of the various contractual options and includes a discussion of the drivers that may warrant the inclusion of long-term commercial arrangements and private finance with a long-term contract. Having discussed the range of contractual mechanisms for procurement, we move on to consider the relationship between long-term contracts, ownership and finance, and their influence on governance. The chapter concludes with a range of thoughts as to when or when not to consider PPPs as a mechanism for value adding, and describes some issues and lessons learned worthy of consideration should a PPP approach be chosen.

Procurement strategies

Procurement of major public infrastructure invariably involves considerable debate, planning and justification to align the anticipated service outcome required by an agency with the engineering and construction activities necessary to bring a facility into operation. The procurement strategy is a key element in the relationship to be forged between public and private sectors, as it drives the commercial behaviour and helps to mould the resulting relationship between the parties to an agreement. Assuming the process of procurement is not done solely 'in house' by government, i.e. public works, the range of options by which to scope and engage with the private sector is wide and varied, and often the lexicon referring to this process is inconsistent and somewhat confusing. In this chapter procurement strategies are named on the basis of their structure and philosophy rather than on specific features within each strategy. Procurement features such as the terms of payment or risk allocation are discussed in the context of the strengths or weaknesses of specific procurement strategies, as many of these features may vary within a particular procurement strategy. Broad procurement strategies are listed below and are followed by a brief description of each strategy:

- Public–private partnership (PPP) / Private Finance Initiative (PFI)
- Relationship contracting; alliances are currently popular and are a specific form of relationship contracts
- Early contractor involvement (ECI)
- Managing contractor
- Project management
- Design and construct (also termed engineer, procure, construct or design–build)
- Document and construct
- Construction management
- Construct only (traditional)
- In house by government (public works)

Public–private partnership (PPP)/PFI

These are long-term contracts (typically in the order of 25 years) where the focus of an owner is on the purchase of a stream of services over the concession period rather than simply on the provision of an asset. In these projects a government contracts with one party, generally referred to as the special purpose vehicle (SPV), and payments are based either on direct payment from consumers (as in a toll road) or via a payment stream from government based on performance. The SPV takes responsibility for organization of components of a project's finance, design development, implementation and operation.

There is considerable debate and discussion as to what is, or is not, a PPP, and thus it is worthwhile to contextualize the definition of PPP contracts just provided. The World Bank (2009) states that PPP agreements range from management or service contracts to full privatization or divestiture (outright sale), with intermediate arrangements involving leases, concessions for long-term management of state-owned enterprises, or the provision of new infrastructure and components of service operation. The Asian Development Bank (2008) excludes privatizations, as do the UK, Australia, Canada and most other Western jurisdictions. The ADB (2008, p. 27) handbook provides clarity on the types of contracts considered basic PPPs; these are service contracts, management contracts, affermage or lease contracts, build–operate or transfer, concessions and joint ventures. The UK government uses a narrow definition in its guidance to HM Treasury (2007) to limit PFI contracts to arrangements which involve some development or a construction phase, followed by an operational phase during which the full service is provided; and the project is wholly or partly financed by limited recourse debt. This definition starts to concentrate on procurement, finance and service provision and it is this form of PPP that I concentrate on in this chapter.

It is the subtlety of what is included in the scope[1] of work for an SPV that starts to provide some insight into the different forms of PPPs. There are two broad groups of PPPs, the simplest of which may be termed a vertical partnership between the public partner and the SPV (Alfen, 2009) where the SPV is solely responsible for the service outcome and obtains a 'concession' from the public partner for this privilege. The second form involves a direct working relationship between the public and private sectors. The arrangements here may range from a contract detailing the services and obligations expected by either party to joint-venture arrangements. The terms 'core' and 'non-core' services are useful to describe the underlying intent of this form of PPP. Core services are those services that the public sector wishes to retain in its full control, and non-core services are those aspects of a project that a community is comfortable simply to have delivered by an external provider. The list of acronyms used to describe these two broad intents are manifold, and tend to describe the specific scope of work included in the contract rather than provide any guidance as to the obligations and responsibilities underpinning the

Table 9.1   A selection of PPP contract abbreviations

Abbreviation	Description
BLT	Build, lease and transfer
BLTM	Build, lease, transfer and maintain
BOL	Build, operate and lease
BOO*	Build, own and operate
BOOR	Build, own, operate and remove
BOOST	Build, own, operate, subsidize and transfer
BOOT*	Build, own, operate and transfer
BOT*	Build, operate and transfer
BRT	Build, rent and transfer
BTO	Build, transfer and operate
DBFM	Design, build, finance and maintain
DBFO	Design, build, finance and operate
DBFOM	Design, build, finance, operate and maintain
DBOM	Design, build, operate and maintain
DBOT	Design, build, operate and transfer
DCMF	Design, construct, manage and finance
DOD	Design, operate and deliver
FBOOT	Finance, build, own, operate and transfer
LROT	Lease, renovate, operate and transfer
ROT	Rehabilitate, operate and transfer

*Common forms of early concession contracts

agreement. Some of these acronyms are listed in Table 9.1 (compiled from Duffield, 2001 and Grimsey and Lewis, 2004).

In countries like Australia, Canada, South Africa and the UK, the relationship between government and the SPV is via a highly documented contract that details project and system risks and responsibilities (Grimsey and Lewis, 2004, p. 6). Countries like Japan have a greater reliance on relationship in the drafting of their agreements. Regardless of the legal details of the agreement, there is a very high degree of risk transfer to the SPV.

Relationship contracts (alliance)
A project alliance contract is an agreement between parties to work cooperatively to achieve agreed outcomes on the basis of sharing risks and rewards. Typically the projects are complex and have numerous unpredictable risks. These arrangements frequently involve multiple companies (e.g. design consultants and constructors) working collaboratively with an owner's resources to form an integrated group that works towards

achieving 'best for project' outcomes without the adversarial relationships common in more traditional contracts (Wood and Duffield, 2009, p. 6).

Alliances involve an integrated high-performance team, sharing all project risks and opportunities. They are selected on a 'best for project' basis and incentivized to achieve outstanding performance in pre-aligned project objectives with uncompromising commitments to trust, collaboration, innovation and mutual support in order to achieve breakthrough results (Gallagher, 2002; DTF, 2006). A key factor in an alliance is a 'no-blame' culture and thus no disputes as participants are, by definition, endeavouring to achieve 'best for project' outcomes.

An alliance can take considerable time and effort to establish, as an alignment of cultures is important for project success. High early-development costs are involved with this approach as project teams build a mutual project culture and then undertake an in-depth assessment of project risks. There appears to be less commercial tension in an alliance than traditional bidding and thus 'value for money' (VfM) on the basis of competitive pricing can be questioned; the counterargument to this is that the alignment of the parties and the desire for open communication makes it counterproductive to engage in competitive behaviour. The engagement process is frequently a two-stage process. The first stage typically involves selection of parties on the basis of their expertise and fit to the project requirements; the second stage involves commercial alignment of the parties and results in an agreed risk-adjusted target price. A client carries significant risk for project outcomes under this strategy.

Early constructor involvement (ECI) (Minter Ellison, 2008)
ECI involves engaging the constructor during the early phases of a project to assist in the evolution of the design and to promote a better understanding by the parties of a project and its potential risks.

ECI can be used with a variety of procurement forms and the ECI process involves the constructor working with the owner in the initial stages of a project to develop the design and to prepare a detailed project plan. In parallel, the parties also develop a 'risk-adjusted price' (RAP) for the delivery phase. Although similar to a design and construct model, ECI has the added benefit that the RAP is not agreed until all the risks can be assessed.

Managing contractor
A managing contractor arrangement involves an owner engaging a head contractor to act as its agent to administer, engage others and deliver the project. Ideally the managing contractor is brought into the project early to assist with project scope and choice of delivery strategy. In a sense, the

managing contractor becomes a specialist resource for the owner. The payment mechanisms used in this approach may vary depending on the risks allocated to the managing contractor. In this technique, the benefits gained from having specialist resources in the owner's team are traded off against uncertainty associated with the project's duration and budget until trade packages of work are detailed and arranged, and time and cost deliverables committed to.

Project management

Not unlike the managing contractor form, a project management form of delivery involves the engagement of consultant to act as agent of the owner to arrange, administer and engage others to be involved with a project. The key difference from the managing contractor model is that the engagement of an agent shifts the risk allocation back to the owner, whereas in the managing contractor model the risks associated with performance are generally allocated away from the owner.

Design and construct

The difference between 'design and construct' and 'construct only' contracts (traditional) is in the scope of work. The constructor takes responsibility for the detailed design, with the designer as a subcontractor. This brings potential efficiencies in terms of constructability. This technique, along with 'document and construct' and 'traditional', tends to be competitively bid with the market. Successful constructors using these techniques have historically been chosen through a strong bias towards lower cost and proven delivery performance.

Construction management

The approach taken for construction management is similar to that of the managing contractor except that the scope is limited to the construction phase.

In house – public works

Government takes full responsibility for all elements of project delivery using its own in-house design and construction resources.

In terms of trying to determine which procurement strategy adds the most value, it is important to acknowledge that there are different drivers for various projects. These drivers are discussed and analysed later; however, critical to the choice of procurement strategy is risk allocation and the desired relationship between the parties.

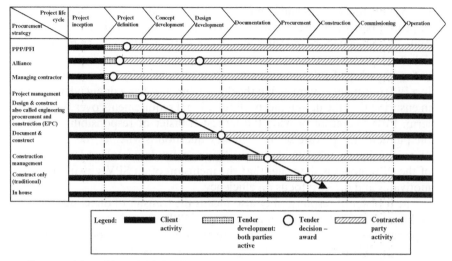

Source: Adapted from ACA (1999).

Figure 9.1 Procurement strategy versus project life cycle

Risk and relationships within procurement strategies

Each of the procurement strategies discussed above is presented in Figure 9.1 and has been plotted against the life cycle of a typical project. Superimposed on this figure is the responsibility for phases of the life cycle depending on the particular procurement strategy. The terms used in this life cycle are generally self-explanatory, with the exception of 'Procurement', which in the context of the figure refers to the act of purchasing goods, whereas 'Procurement strategy' refers to the overall approach being taken to decide what is required and who is responsible for achieving the required outcome. Responsibilities have been divided into: client activity for activities before going to market; tender development where both parties are involved; the tender decision by the client; and the work, which is the responsibility of the contractor. The arrow indicates that the responsibility of an owner increases as one progresses down the list of procurement strategies, given the order in which they have been presented. The figure also details who is responsible for long-term maintenance and operation of a facility.

The first thing to note from the comparison of procurement strategies detailed in Figure 9.1 is that the various procurement strategies encompass quite different responsibilities for the scope over the life cycle. For example, in 'construct only' procurement the owner is responsible for inception, definition, development, documentation, procurement arrangement and ongoing operation and maintenance, while the private party is responsible for delivery and commissioning. A fundamental underpinning of project performance is the notion that these changes in global responsibility drive behaviour, and this has a major bearing on the way a project is delivered. At one extreme, a 'construct only' contractor has little interest in functionality of a design as it is not their responsibility, whereas an SPV in a PPP is not only interested in the design, but also has a financial interest in ensuring that the design meets all functional requirements over the long term. PPPs therefore provide the largest transfer of responsibility from the public to the private sector. The key question is whether this transfer of responsibility constitutes value. Again, a fundamental underpinning of the PPP model is the belief that the inclusion of an SPV's own finance motivates and drives a focus on efficiency.

The transfer of responsibility also means the transfer of direct decision-making (or flexibility), and thus scoping of PPPs such that they meet the expectations of government, is far more onerous than, say, 'construct only' contracts; this is particularly true given the responsibility for part of the project definition and concept development phases in the life cycle. The result is that PPPs require detailed documentation of what an owner wants described by way of outcomes. Alliance and managing contractor arrangements overcome the complexity in scoping by leaving the scope flexible until later in a project. For alliances, finalization of scope and associated pricing are left until the project is well detailed and undertaken collaboratively. In PPPs it is done by both the owner (in setting the evaluation criteria, e.g. a public sector comparator) and by the SPV (which is what is delivered). For the managing contractor model the price and scope are typically open almost until the end of the work. In short, while PPPs, alliances and managing contracts appear to cover a similar delivery scope (i.e. the tasks of procuring goods, construction and commissioning), only PPPs lock down the commercial arrangements at the same time as responsibility passes to a contractor. Some clients refer to this as certainty of budget.

The scope of work passed to the private sector should ideally be done on the basis of where value can be added. Implicit in this is an expectation that each party has the appropriate level of skills for activities allocated to them, as each of these activities carries ultimate responsibility for risks associated with the task.

The responsibility for different components of the project life cycle depends on the procurement strategy, as in Figure 9.1, and these responsibilities flow through to the different tasks and risk allocations associated with each particular procurement strategy. This leads the discussion to the commercial dynamic established through the different forms of procurement. Critical to the ultimate success of a project are specific features, including:

- scope of work included in contract
- inclusion of finance
- responsibility for price, i.e. payment regime, e.g. cost plus, lump sum, schedule of rates, guaranteed maximum price
- resource implications, e.g. fully provided by contractor, shared resources, joint or shared responsibilities
- timelines, e.g. fixed, fast track
- appetite for risk
- service/outcome focus
- 'whole of life' responsibility
- relationship management
- responsibility for outcomes and motivation, e.g. incentives and/or abatements
- price-sensitive versus VfM drivers.

Another common difference between contract forms is the payment structure and it is here that PPPs differ significantly from other forms of procurement.

Figure 9.2 outlines a risk transfer continuum that provides guidance on where the risk lies with certain delivery mechanisms. This figure also details whether a price is fixed (i.e. risk with the private sector – termed SPV or contractor in the diagram) or based on actual cost (i.e. risk with the owner). This diagram similarly outlines who takes responsibility for major decisions in respect of particular tasks throughout a project life cycle. PPP is the only procurement strategy among those detailed where finance is provided by the private sector. It is also evident that PPPs have the highest level of price certainty, being fixed over the whole project life, and that the private sector has the highest influence, and responsibility, for decisions.

In terms of trying to evaluate which procurement strategy adds the most value, it is important to acknowledge that there are different drivers for various projects. To decide whether a PPP may be appropriate, it follows that selection factors appropriate for PPPs need to be fully understood.

Specific factors in the selection of a PPP delivery option
In addition to specific project-related drivers required to select the appropriate procurement strategy, specific contextual, cultural (political) and country variants also influence the choice and style of procurement.

Specific contextual variants are best described by provision of examples, and thus a brief potted history of situations that have encouraged the use of PPPs follows that covers project drivers such as poor economic conditions, a lack of infrastructure assets of appropriate quality, competition and risk transfer, and VfM.

High private sector risk

Risk continuum

High owner risk

Procurement strategy	Predominant payment method				Main decision-maker			
	Concept	Design	Construct	Maintain & operate	Concept	Design	Construct	Maintain & operate
PPP	Fixed	Fixed	Fixed	Fixed	SPV	SPV–contractor	SPV–contractor	SPV–operator
Design & construct	Actual	Fixed	Fixed	Actual	Owner	Contractor	Contractor	Owner
Early contractor involvement	Actual	Fixed	Fixed	Actual	Shared	Contractor	Contractor	Owner
Managing contractor	Actual	Fixed	Actual	Actual	Shared	Contractor	Contractor	Owner
Project management	Actual	Fixed	Fixed	Actual	Owner	Owner	Contractor	Owner
Construct only	Actual	Actual	Fixed	Actual	Owner	Owner	Contractor	Owner
Construction management	Actual	Actual	Actual	Actual	Owner	Contractor	Contractor	Owner
Relationship contract – alliance	Actual	Actual	Actual	Actual	Owner	Shared	Shared	Owner
Public works	Actual	Actual	Actual	Actual	Owner	Owner	Owner	Owner

Notes:
Fixed: Cost risk with contractor
Actual: Cost risk with owner
SPV: Special purpose vehicle management
SPV–contractor: SPV generally subcontracts this work as design and construct
SPV–operator: SPV generally subcontracts this work to an operator or facilities management firm

Figure 9.2   Risk transfer continuum

Poor economic conditions

The Thatcher era of UK leadership was a turbulent economic period in which the government lacked sufficient public funds to adequately improve public infrastructure.

> The economy was in recession, unemployment was high, as were interest rates and the Public Sector Borrowing Requirement (PSBR) had been on the increase to finance the public sector deficit. (AMA Research, 2003, p. 13)

Reduced access to funds and finance is not peculiar to the 1980s; the global financial crisis of 2008–09 has reminded both developing and developed nations that large expenditure on infrastructure can aid or hinder a nation's economic well-being.

Against this backdrop, the UK government sought to create innovative solutions to invest in public infrastructure without further increasing the PSBR (Heinecke, 2002).

November 1992 saw the formal launch of the 'Private Finance Initiative', and this policy relaxed the provisions of the Ryrie Rules that required private funding for infrastructure projects to be matched by an equivalent amount of public funding (Merna and Smith, 1994).

Critique of projects undertaken in the UK for these early PFI projects leads to questioning of the underlying premise that

> the government must take account of the benefits that tend to go with private finance such as improved efficiency, lower costs and reduction of the risks falling on to the taxpayer. (Secretary to the Treasury UK, 1989 in Merna and Smith, 1994, p. 7)

The outcomes from the projects undertaken during this period (1992–97) are well summarized by Heinecke (2002), who reported that a number of PFI projects were inefficient due to protracted negotiations, unrealistic risk allocations, restrictive documentation and insufficient administrative systems to finalize the tendering process. This position is also supported by the review conducted by Hodge and Greve (2007).

Without trying to generalize, it is evident that the process by which PFIs were being implemented had deficiencies, and it is suggested that selection of a PPP procurement strategy solely on the basis of economic pressure is fraught with difficulties. Indeed, some projects at this time did not meet government expectations (van Leeuwen, 1997).

Lack of appropriate assets

It has been firmly established (Duffield and Regan, 2004) that investment in economic infrastructure has both direct and indirect effects on the economy. The direct effects are significant and enduring, although there is evidence of a positive causal connection flowing from infrastructure investment to output and growth (Erenburg, 1994; Sanchez-Robles, 1998; Poot, 2000). The pressure to invest can be driven by functional need, as demonstrated by Geoffrey Robinson (Treasury Taskforce, 1999), where he linked the need for renewal with the pressure for money as follows:

> The success of PFI is vital for Britain. Our infrastructure is dangerously run down. Our schools and transport networks are seriously neglected and all too often our urban environment has been allowed to deteriorate. In an age of tight public spending, VfM public/private partnerships will be at the heart of a much needed renewal of our public services.

Competition and risk transfer

The premise that improved outcomes can be achieved for the public through the involvement of the private sector is reliant on willing

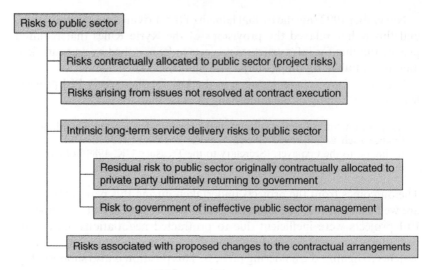

Source: Adapted from DTF (2003).

Figure 9.3   Risks retained by public sector

participation by the private sector. Willing participation is generally encouraged by the expectation of investment return and confidence that payments will be made in accordance with the deal over the long-term life of the agreement. The literature is clear that financial expectations of a bidder reduce with increasing numbers of bidders, thus making the buyer (in this case government) better off (McAfee and MacMillan, 1987). Hence, to get a good PPP outcome governments want strong competition for the opportunity. This infers a robust and competent market of multiple willing participants.

A lack of competition, a lack of technical innovation, poor transparency or inappropriate risk allocation may all lead to suboptimal outcomes. Many of the early PPP projects involved near full risk transfer to the private sector, a phenomenon unlikely to be repeated and one that has a high risk of ultimately being suboptimal.

In terms of the commercial and contractual obligations for risk within PPPs, it must be understood that the public sector must and will always be held responsible for the management of certain risks. These should not be inappropriately allocated to others. A good summary of such risks is provided in Figure 9.3.

If there is insufficient market appetite for a particular PPP, the project will require modification or abandonment.

Value for money

'Value for money' (VfM) is another widely used term, of which there are numerous interpretations. A sound definition from the perspective of the public is as follows:

> Value for money denotes, broadly, a balanced benefit measure covering quality levels, performance standards, risk exposure, other policy or special interest measures (for example, environmental impacts), as well as price [of inputs and outputs]. Generally, Value for Money is assessed on a 'whole of life' or 'total cost or ownership' basis, which includes the transitioning-in, contract period and transitioning-out phases of a contractual relationship. (DTF, 2009, p.2)

Post-1997, the UK government instigated the so-called 'Bates Review' of PFI projects. Major findings from this (the review for which stage two was completed in March 1999) led to greater clarity of which projects should be attempted as PPPs, improved management of major projects and revised tendering arrangements to minimize the bidding costs. Concurrent with these UK changes, the Victorian government in Australia refined its process to change the focus from full risk transfer to appropriate risk allocation to achieve value. The focus also changed from capital procurement to the delivery of a service. While building on the UK PFI experience, the Victorian government took the initiative to develop a broad suite of guidance material to support its Partnerships Victoria (PV) policy (DTF, 2000). Both the principles of this policy and associated guidelines were shared widely between governments, and features from these documents are now used widely throughout the world (ADB, 2008). Due to their wide use, the Victorian approach to PPPs forms a basis for much of the discussion in this chapter.

Using the PV style of PPP, it has been established that there is the potential to achieve excellent outcomes in the delivery of the CAPEX[2] component of projects using a PPP structure (Allen et al., 2007; Duffield, 2008). The mechanisms to consistently achieve these outcomes appear dependent on factors such as:

- strong leadership
- a detailed understanding of what service outcomes are required
- a mechanism to measure the service outcomes
- a focus on 'value for money' and optimal risk allocation
- confidence to participate in PPPs by the financial markets, i.e. market appetite
- strong governance and sovereign stability
- confidence in the ability to repay the loans raised as part of the PPP
- a legal system that provides confidence in the reliance on contracts

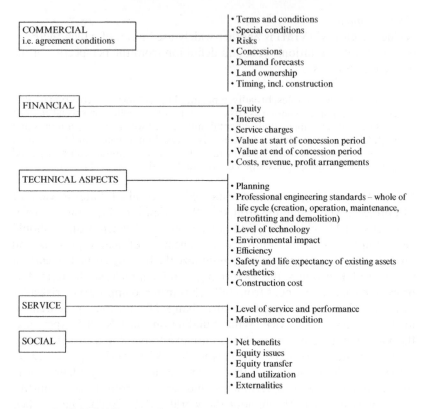

COMMERCIAL
i.e. agreement conditions
• Terms and conditions
• Special conditions
• Risks
• Concessions
• Demand forecasts
• Land ownership
• Timing, incl. construction

FINANCIAL
• Equity
• Interest
• Service charges
• Value at start of concession period
• Value at end of concession period
• Costs, revenue, profit arrangements

TECHNICAL ASPECTS
• Planning
• Professional engineering standards – whole of life cycle (creation, operation, maintenance, retrofitting and demolition)
• Level of technology
• Environmental impact
• Efficiency
• Safety and life expectancy of existing assets
• Aesthetics
• Construction cost

SERVICE
• Level of service and performance
• Maintenance condition

SOCIAL
• Net benefits
• Equity issues
• Equity transfer
• Land utilization
• Externalities

Source: Duffield (2001).

Figure 9.4   Issues for consideration in a PPP

The full range of issues to be considered as a part of sound governance of PPP projects is summarized in Figure 9.4. To compare PPP projects with other forms of procurement, it must be recognized that the scope of a PPP is broader than the alternative forms of capital delivery, as outlined previously.

Procurement strategies financed from the public sector generally seek value via consideration of commercial, technical and functional matters as detailed in Figure 9.4. Thus to ascertain whether PPP is the most appropriate form of procurement involves an area of further checking as finance and social factors are considered. There must also be the political and managerial acceptance of making a long-term contractual commitment. Discussion of the political realities of adopting PPPs is left to others in this book to explore.

Social factors are generally tested in PPPs identically to best practice through the conduct of environmental and social impact studies, as and if required. PPPs also have a specific public interest test that assesses factors including effectiveness, accountability and transparency, equity, public access, consumer rights, security, privacy, and rights of representation of affected individuals and communities.

Grimsey and Lewis (2004) emphasized that accountability and a regard for the public interest is most important as it assists in legitimizing and acceptance of the contractual arrangement.

The inclusion of finance into the structure of a procurement strategy brings with it complexity and vastly more stringent requirements for due diligence by management. This influences the corporate management, risk management and detailed review and testing of the business strategy underpinning the business proposition for the project. From a finance perspective, these parameters are given an even greater emphasis in PPPs than in many other business transactions because of the long-term nature of the contracts. Financiers effectively become another layer of management seeking to assist in meeting the provisions of the required service obligation as specified in the agreement. In a sense, to fulfil their fiduciary duties the providers of finance to the PPP need to confirm and test the investment case before becoming involved. Multiple financiers are involved, and thus multiple checks and tests are undertaken. This provides a significantly more robust process than when government makes the decision solely on the basis of its own commercial assessment and management of the business proposition.

The last major difference in PPPs is the use of an SPV, generally focused on one project, as this corporate structure brings the full accounting and reporting obligations of the corporate world to a project environment. This makes the performance of a PPP highly accountable and the reporting clear and transparent.

In assessing the potential for value from a PPP, it is worth considering the advantages and disadvantages of the alternative procurement strategies.

Choice of appropriate procurement strategy

There is a growing body of evidence that the procurement of major public infrastructure is not always as successful as anticipated when a project begins. Over recent years a number of major reviews of the construction industry have been conducted, including those by Latham (1994), Egan (1998), the Australian Constructors Association, ACA (1999), Bourn (2001), Hampson and Brandon (2004), ACA/Clayton Utz (2005), ACA/ Blake Dawson Waldron (2006). Overall, these reviews repeatedly describe an industry that was not delivering what it set out to achieve and suggest that a major contributor to these poor outcomes was the approach adopted for procurement (Allen et al., 2007). The prevailing culture assessed was one deeply entrenched in competitive tendering, selection of the lowest-priced bid and adversarial behaviour that frequently led to contractual disputes (Latham, 1994; Egan, 1998). A number of diverse procurement strategies have been introduced in an attempt to improve outcomes; these techniques range from heavy reliance on the private sector to a diversity of relationship and incentivized arrangements to 'better' manage risk.

The success of the strategy in developing a plethora of procurement strategies, many of which appear to be hybrids of each other, to improve project outcomes remains somewhat untested. There are examples where the increased reliance on enforcement of onerous contractual conditions, which often involve inequitable risk-sharing, has further exacerbated the problem (Gallagher, 2002). Even where the emphasis has been directed heavily to relationship management, issues have emerged in terms of scope and price creep, resulting in questions pertaining to the 'value for money' achieved. The additional effort then required to manage these contracts contributes to a lowering of profit and decreases in efficiency as these additional costs are not related to direct productive effort. These issues have encouraged the development of guidelines for the choice of procurement systems, for example, Infrastructure Australia (2008) and ISO (2008).

These guidelines do not specify exactly how to choose the 'best' procurement strategy, but instead offer general principles as to what may be most appropriate. A generic set of evaluation criteria has been proposed as detailed in Table 9.2. This set of criteria (with the addition of common project requirements of quality, performance and relationship) has been compared with the suggestions in the procurement options analysis section of Infrastructure Australia (2008), and the results are presented in Table 9.3.

In trying to evaluate which procurement strategy adds the most value, it is important to acknowledge that there are different drivers for various projects. It is also worth remembering that the particular procurement strategy selected is also a function of a client's risk profile and willingness to accept or mitigate exposure to risk; this may well be a political decision in the case of PPPs.

The choice of a particular style of project delivery system will nearly universally be made by the client bearing in mind:

- government's public accountability constraints
- ease of definition of user requirements
- need for a firm budget

Table 9.2   *Generic procurement evaluation criteria*

Procurement evaluation criteria	Description
Scope and design requirements	The confidence in delivering the required design outcome. This includes the degree to which the project can be scoped Projects vary from those that have clearly defined and straightforward specification to output specifications that cannot be clearly defined up front, and/or a high likelihood of scope changes during design and construction
Ongoing fitness for purpose	The ability for functional outcomes that enable ongoing fitness for purpose
Scope for innovation	The ability of the approach to enable innovation
Future flexibility	The ability to enable change and development associated with changing expectations or legislation over the long term
'Whole-of-life' consideration	The philosophy of balancing capital costs with whole-of-life outcomes
Value for money	Value should take the broad perspective of 'whole-of-life' costs, risk, service quality, tangible and intangible externalities
Risk management	Effective management of risks by seeking optimal risk allocation rather than simply maximum risk transfer Risk can be strongly influenced by the number of interfaces as well as their complexity, e.g. can the risks be clearly defined, costed and allocated, or are the risks numerous, complex and/or unpredictable?
Timeline	Confidence in achieving completion date. This is influenced by tightness of the timeframe
Budget certainty	Confidence in the final cost of the project. This is influenced by the clarity of the scope and cost pressures or cost targets
Resource availability	Capability available internally or externally that is fit for purpose
Market interest	The appetite of the market for the particular procurement strategy. This includes consideration of the level of competition. This also takes into account the economic state of the market, i.e. is it boom or bust?
Stakeholder issues	The level of potential stakeholder issues that range from straightforward through to complex matters. The scale of a project also influences the complexity of stakeholder issues
Public interest	Confidence that the procurement strategy will result in an outcome consistent with the public's interest

Table 9.3 Strengths of different procurement strategies

Procurement evaluation criteria	PPP	Alliance	Managing contractor	Design and construct	In-house
Scope and design requirements	Good integration. Difficult to specify	Developed collectively	Full control by owner. There is a tendency for over-specification and late changes	Needs to be well defined	Tendency for over-specification
Ongoing fitness for purpose	Long-term certainty	High level of control but dependent on future budgets	High level of control but dependent on future budgets	Depends on design and future budgets	High level of control but dependent on future budgets
Scope for innovation	Strong incentive for innovation	Incentives for savings	Innovation only at the direction of the owner	Little requirement for innovation	Little incentive
Future flexibility	Based on process rather than specification, i.e. negotiable but not overly flexible	Significant initial consideration but long-term based on future management	Based on future management	Based on future management. Assets fixed based on original construction	Lack of focus on whole of life
'Whole-of-life' consideration	Strong focus on 'whole-of-life' outcome	Strong focus on best for project. Not always whole of life unless specifically incentivized	Often limited consideration of long-term issues	Limited consideration of long-term issues	Often limited consideration of long-term issues

Value for money	Strong test and evaluation for VfM	Strong delivery performance once price is agreed	Final cost ill defined	Competitive provided no variations	Final cost ill defined
Risk management	Strong business risk transfer and management	Strong focus on management of delivery risk	Risk frequently resolved in a piecemeal manner and ultimate responsibility remains with the owner	For specified construction risks	Responsibility of owner. Frequently resolved if risks materialize
Timeline	Strong incentive for early delivery and start of service	Strong incentive to better target to receive incentivized bonus	No commercial driver for early completion	Ample time is required to document and deliver sensibly	Longer overall timeline – no hard imperative to finish early
Budget certainty	Purchase service for agreed fee	Once fully priced target cost is agreed, strong incentive to complete within this budget	No commercial driver for containment of cost	Purchase asset Requires high management Often adversarial Initial price generally fixed for agreed scope	Minimal opportunity for cost value Often adversarial
Resource availability	Low requirement for government resources	Team focus on meeting project targets	High flexibility in resources brought to the project	Range of quality of resources	Large pool of resources
Quality	Based on outputs and abatements	Culture and Key Result Area (KRA) driven	Owner-driven	Contract-driven	Owner-driven
Performance	Output target	Agreed target	Owner-driven	Specified	Owner-driven

Table 9.3 (continued)

Procurement evaluation criteria	PPP	Alliance	Managing contractor	Design and construct	In-house
Market interest	Driven by commercial reasoning and market demand	Driven by relationships	Risk with owner to obtain the required resources	Generally strong competition	Risk with owner to obtain the required resources
Stakeholder issues	Private control	Shared control	Government control	Shared control	Government control
Public interest	Checks and balances managed	Alliance-driven – shared	Government process	Government process	Government process
Relationship	Adversarial/partnership	Partnership	Owner-driven	Adversarial	Owner-driven

Note: The analysis of procurement options has drawn guidance from Infrastructure Australia (2008), ADB (2008), Grimsey and Lewis (2004).

- size of the project
- complexity of the project
- desire for design flexibility during construction
- overlap of design and construction
- change of requirements throughout the process
- attitudes to risk
- time at which the contractor is introduced into the process
- management of changes and variations through use of schedules
- specific clauses identifying and allocating risk
- organizational structures
- requirements for insurance, security, retention, performance bonds and guarantees
- availability of suitable builders/project managers, and balance sheets of such builders
- budget constraints versus performance of completed project
- long-term certainty.

Given that PPPs involve the greatest scope of work when compared to alternative procurement strategies (refer to Figures 9.1 and 9.2) for the capital procurement phase of a project, and that they also involve ongoing responsibility for operation of a facility, it is worth contrasting this with a more typical form of public infrastructure procurement. This reflection should assist in comparison of the strengths and weaknesses of each procurement strategy against the evaluation criteria detailed in Table 9.2, which are presented in Table 9.3. It should also be remembered from the discussion in the second section of this chapter that PPP is the only strategy to bring finance into the mix of capital procurement.

For design and construction projects (a typical form of government-led procurement), the client is responsible for all aspects of the project associated with inception, feasibility, qualification, project definition and concept development; see Figure 9.1. The constructor is solely responsible for the project from award of the contract until completion of commissioning.

The linking of design and construction tasks into one contact brings potential innovation and efficiency as the constructor then has overall control such that the design can be modified to suit their particular construction preferences. However, this approach does little to encourage the constructor to similarly optimize costs over the whole of life of the facility (i.e. including operation and maintenance). Even the linking of design and construction changes the dynamic of the contracting relationship and the associated risks taken by the parties to the contract. For this case it brings complexity to the clients as they seek to adequately describe what they want in a design brief [3] rather than via detailed drawings without the need for later changes. Should a client seek full control of a design, the 'construct only' or public works strategies may be appropriate.

Strategies involving multiple participants create numerous interface risks between each party's individual responsibility and the need of the overall project. Both alliances and PPPs have single point responsibility for overall coordination and this is a strong feature of these forms of delivery, particularly for large or complex projects.

Given all the factors detailed in Table 9.3, it is evident that the choice of an appropriate procurement option is complex. It is also evident that conditions that suit the use of a PPP are likely to be relevant to only a minority of large projects. For example, in Australia PPPs account for about 10 per cent by value of government-procured capital projects.

A summary of conditions that suit the use of PPPs follows.

Conditions that suit PPP procurement
The Australian industry appears to understand how to work sensibly with the benefits of PPPs. This has required integration and understanding of political, policy, financial, technical and legal aspects of projects by all senior governmental and private sector decision-makers. Conditions that facilitate successful PPP projects have been investigated by many (e.g. Arthur Andersen, 2000; Fitzgerald, 2004; Grimsey and Lewis, 2004; Jefferies et al., 2002; KPMG, 2000, and NAO, 2001 and 2004). A critique of these investigations led to the consolidation of a series of factors required for successful PPP, as follows:

- change in payment timing, potentially enabling more projects to begin
- significant risk transfer to the private sector
- development of business opportunities
- the potential for direct user pay arrangements
- leverage of underutilized land to achieve enhanced service outcomes
- innovation by way of a mix of commercial, financial and technical outcomes
- state-of-the-art functionality and operational outcomes
- improved management
- independent checking that a project is viable through robust commercial testing
- improved efficiency in capital procurement by way of early completion and price surety
- enhanced integration of design, procurement, maintenance and operational activities
- long-term commitment to appropriate asset management.

This level of maturity has required substantial development, cultural reform and upskilling of both public and private sectors. These changes have been brought about by government's increased awareness of commercial aspects associated with service delivery, a focus on outputs rather than inputs, and detailed consideration of 'whole of life' benefits.

In addition to this maturing of the market, government has also undertaken reform and enhancement of policy, legal and legislative matters, taxation and its own project organizational structures.

The experience in Australia does not appear materially different from the outcomes based on a questionnaire survey conducted in the UK by Li et al. (2005). Li proposed a three-level risk factor classification and checklist for risks associated with PPP projects in order to achieve VfM. VfM criteria and a qualitative risk allocation were analysed upon which models have been developed. It was found that in order to fully achieve VfM in construction PPP projects, project participants should adopt measures associated with 'project efficiency', 'sustainability', 'multi-benefit consideration' and 'effective procurement arrangement'. The specific factors identified by Li are outlined in Table 9.4 and an enhanced list of factors is detailed in Table 9.5.

To achieve good outcomes if a PPP is chosen as the procurement strategy, a number of issues and lessons learned warrant reflection.

Issues and lessons learned

Throughout the development of a mature PPP market, such as Australia, a number of issues have been identified that need to be addressed. These include:

- *Skills*: There was a steep learning curve for participants in PPP projects. Government needs to recognize that strong commercial skills are required if VfM is to be achieved. The private sector has also had to learn that long-term PPP projects are quite different from other forms of procurement; risks need to be priced and managed in accordance with the service being delivered.
- *Ownership*: There have been a number of early examples where the private proponent's consortium was led by financiers (e.g. Southern Cross Station – Duffield and Regan, 2004). There was a mismatch of objectives, as these financiers saw as their key focus achievement of the deal rather than the effective long-term management of the service delivery. It should be emphasized that the flexibility in the agreements, and goodwill from all stakeholders, has meant that there are no reported examples where the service standard delivered via the PPP fell below that detailed in the agreement due to

Table 9.4   Factors enhancing VfM in PPPs

Component	Variables
Project efficiency	Low project life-cycle cost
	Optimal use of asset/facility and project efficiency
	Improved and additional facilities to the public sector
	Private sector technical innovation
	Early project service delivery
	Private management skill
Sustainability	Reduction in disputes, claims and litigation
	Nature of financial innovation
	Long-term nature of contracts
	Output-based specification
	Off the public sector balance sheet treatment
Multi-benefit	Risk transfer
consideration	Environmental consideration
	Level of tangible and intangible benefits to the users
	Profitability to the private sector
Public effective	Competitive tender
procurement measures	Efficient risk allocation

Source: Adapted from Li et al. (2005).

ownership changes within the SPV. Also, these transactions within the SPV did not affect the terms of the original agreement with government.

- *Bidding costs*: The bid costs for many PPP projects are high. All stakeholders need to actively pursue mechanisms such as standardized commercial terms, improved communication and clarity, and shorter negotiation periods in an attempt to reduce these bidding costs. A consistent flow of deals is also sought by the private sector, thus creating an industry with depth.
- *Risk and risk management*: Improved understanding of project risks and clear risk allocation principles continue to develop.

Numerous lessons have been learned and implemented. Some of the more general lessons worthy as sharing are:

- *Contract management*: Contract management has been identified as such an important feature of successful service delivery from PPPs that concerted efforts have been made to develop and train practitioners in, for example, developing contract management plans,

Table 9.5 Factors contributing to successful PPPs

Issue	Factors
Preparation and project development	Clarify that use of PPPs is a strategic choice Articulate clear objectives through: • output-based specification • performance regime with sensible measurable indicators Clarify interfaces with other contracts and service requirements Establish flexible processes for long-term contracts, including: • customer needs and expectations • clearly defined social outcomes Careful preparation, including: • VfM • allocation of ownership rights • a clear business model • clear and manageable allocation risks
Accountability	Ensure accountability to the public via thorough testing of public interest and: • transparency • appropriate pricing Ensure accountability to the private consortium via: • incentives • governance
Competitive pricing	Facilitate high-quality competitive bids Actually transfer risks as allocated Confirm final deal makes sense
Ongoing contract management	Develop a culture of partnership Transfer knowledge throughout the contract

manuals and procedures to systematize the vast array of terms and conditions in the multiple agreements that document a PPP project. Similar effort has gone into development of skills to manage change and relationships, and to negotiate new arrangements in the spirit of the initial agreement.

- *Availability of finance*: Issues of capital raising are subject to the market and thus PPPs are open to the vagaries of the market.
- *Clarity and speed*: The industry clearly recognizes the need for speed and clarity as a mechanism to contain costs. Clarity and a firm commitment to proceed with the project in accordance with stated policy is an important criterion of all government procedures.

Reflecting on active PPP projects in Australia confirms that strong political leadership and unambiguous commitment to seek VfM for the community are clear drivers for the successful implementation of PPPs.

New issues continually emerge; currently solutions to the influence of the global financial crisis are critical. However, the cost of bidding for PPP projects, appropriate allocation (and pricing) of risk and the inherent difficulty in quantifying long-term VfM of infrastructure investment appear to be ongoing issues.

The long-term nature of PPPs is such that ongoing successful performance of the project over the full life of the agreement will require continuous management attention if the original intent and specified services are to be delivered appropriately.

Conclusion

This chapter has described a range of procurement strategies that may be adopted to meet the needs of society when seeking new or enhanced public infrastructure. These strategies have ranged from PPPs to in-house provision of the infrastructure, and it is evident that PPPs are significantly different from other procurement approaches. PPPs involve the private sector taking the greatest responsibility for service delivery over the life of the facility compared with the other contracting options considered. They also have the highest level of price certainty, but this comes at the cost of responsibility for day-to-day decisions relating to both assets and the way in which services will be delivered – the setting of service standards remains a governmental decision.

It has also been demonstrated that PPP policies and processes have undergone a series of refinements since the PFI style introduced in the UK in 1992, and that these refinements have resulted in a procurement strategy that has a good chance of achieving the benefits as outlined by the UK government:

the government must take account of the benefits that tend to go with private finance such as improved efficiency, lower costs and reduction of the risks falling on to the taxpayer. (Secretary to the Treasury UK, 1989 in Merna and Smith, 1994, p. 7)

This chapter argues that PPPs are a complex undertaking, and part of a broader set of procurement strategies possible for major infrastructure. Moreover, while they have strengths and weaknesses, they may well apply to only a minority of projects, given the decision to adopt a PPP or not is governed by whether the approach achieves value to the community over the life of the agreement. Here it is critical to consider not only the strategy to procure assets but also the specific contextual, cultural (political) and country variants that together influence the choice and style of procurement.

In summary, PPPs can work well in the right situation. However, they are complex and generally require a very large financial transaction, due caution and high levels of expertise.

Notes

1. 'Scope' – this is particular terminology from the Project Management lexicon that means 'the sum of products, services and results to be provided on a project', PMI (2008, p. 448).
2. CAPEX – capital expenditure.
3. Design Brief – a written document describing what is to be designed but to do so in such a way that it is not taken to be prescriptive.

References

Australian Constructors Association (ACA) (1999), *Relationship Contracting*, Sydney: Australian Constructors Association.

ACA/Blake Dawson Waldron (2006), *Scope for Improvement*, Blake Dawson Waldron Report, ISBN 0-646-45998-8.

ACA/Clayton Utz (2005), *Succeeding in a Fraught Construction Market*, Clayton Utz Special Report, June.

Alfen, H.W. (2009), *Public–Private Partnership in Infrastructure Development – Case Studies from Asia and Europe*, Bauhaus-Universität, Weimar.

Allen Consulting Group, C.F. Duffield and P. Raisbeck (2007), *Performance of PPPs and Traditional Procurement in Australia*, Melbourne, Infrastructure Partnerships Australia, 57.

AMA Research (2003), *The Private Finance Initiative Report UK 2003*, AMA Market Research Report AM 75073, March.

Arthur Andersen (2000), *Value for Money Drivers in the Private Finance Initiative*, Report commissioned by the Treasury Taskforce, 17 January, 5–6.

Asian Development Bank (ADB) (2008), *Public–Private Partnership Handbook*, Asian Development Bank, Manila, available at: www.adb.org/Documents/Handbooks/Public-Private-Partnership/default.asp (accessed December 2009).

Bourn, J. (2001), *Modernising Construction*, Report by the Comptroller and Auditor General, London: National Audit Office Press Office.

Department of Treasury and Finance (DTF) (2000), *Partnerships Victoria*, Department of Treasury and Finance, State of Victoria.

Department of Treasury and Finance (DTF) (2003), *Partnerships Victoria: Contract Management Guide*, Department of Treasury and Finance, State of Victoria.

Department of Treasury and Finance (DTF) (2006), *Project Alliancing Practitioners' Guide, State of Victoria*, available at: www.dtf.vic.gov.au/CA25713E0002EF43/pages/asset-management-project-support-project-alliancing (accessed 13 February 2009).

Department of Treasury and Finance (DTF) (2009), *Good Practice Guidelines: Strategic Procurement – General*, Department of Treasury and Finance, State of Victoria.

Duffield, C.F. (2001), *An Evaluation Framework for Privately Funded Infrastructure Projects in Australia*, PhD thesis, Department of Civil and Environmental Engineering, The University of Melbourne.

Duffield, C.F. (2008), *National PPP Forum – Benchmarking Study, Phase II: Report on the performance of PPP projects in Australia when compared with a representative sample of traditionally procured infrastructure projects*, Report to the PPP Forum by the Melbourne Engineering Research Institute, 15 November: 44, available at: repository.unimelb.edu.au/10187/3148.

Duffield, C.F. and M. Regan (2004), 'Public private partnership arrangement for the Spencer Street Station upgrade in Victoria, Australia', *Journal of Financial Management of Property and Construction*, **9** (3), 163–77.

Egan, M. (1998), *Rethinking Construction*: *The Report of the Construction Taskforce*, United Kingdom Department of Trade and Industry.

Erenburg, S.J. (1994), *Linking Public Capital to Economic Performance*, Public Policy Brief no. 14/1994, The Jerome Levy Economics Institute of Bard College, Annandale-on-Hudson, New York.

Fitzgerald, P. (2004), *Review of Partnerships Victoria Provided Infrastructure*, Final Report to the Treasurer, Growth Solutions Group.

Gallagher, J. (2002), 'Project alliancing – creating the possibilities', International Cost Engineering Council 3rd World Congress, Melbourne.

Grimsey, D. and M.K. Lewis (2004), *Public Private Partnerships: The Worldwide Revolution in Infrastructure Provision and Project Finance*, Cheltenham, UK and Northampton, MA, USA: Edward Elgar.

Hampson, K. and P. Brandon (2004), *Construction 2020*: *A Vision for Australia's Property and Construction Industry*, Cooperative Research Centre for Construction Innovation, Icon.Net Pty Ltd ISBN 0 9750977 25.

Heinecke, B. (2002), 'Involvement of small and medium sized enterprises in the private realisation of public buildings', Working Paper, Faculty of Business Administration, Technische Universität Bergakademie Freiberg.

HM Treasury (2007), *Standardisation of PFI Contracts: Version 4*, London: HM Treasury.

Hodge, G.A. and C. Greve (2007), 'Public–private partnerships: an international performance review', *Public Administration Review*, **67** (3), 545–58.

Infrastructure Australia (2008), *National PPP Guidelines Volume 1: Procurement Options Analysis*, Canberra: Commonwealth of Australia.

International Organization for Standardization (ISO) (2008), Draft International Standard ISO/DIS 10845-1: Construction procurement – Part 1: Processes, methods and procedures, Geneva: International Organization for Standardization.

Jefferies, M.C., R. Gameson and S. Rowlinson (2002), 'Critical success factors of the BOOT procurement system: reflections from the stadium Australia case study', *Engineering, Construction and Architectural Management*, **9** (4), 352–61.

KPMG (2000), *Review of Public Private Partnership Processes*, Province of Nova Scotia, Department of Finance.

Latham, M. (1994), *Constructing the Team, Joint Review of Procurement and Contractual Arrangements in the UK Construction Industry*, London: HMSO.

Li, B., A. Akintoye, P.J. Edwards and C. Hardcastle (2005), 'The allocation of risk in PPP/PFI construction projects in the UK', *International Journal of Project Management*, **23** (1), 25–35.

McAfee and MacMillan (1987), 'Auctions with stochastic number of bidders', *Journal of Economic Theory*, **43** (1), 1–19.

Merna, T. and N.J. Smith (1994), *Projects Procured by Privately Financed Concession Contracts*, Project Management Group, UMIST.

Minter Ellison (2008), A-C-Early+constructor+Involvement, available at: www.minterellison. com/public/connect/Internet/Home/Legal+Insights/Newsletters/Previous+Newsletters (accessed 6 November 2009).

National Audit Office (2001), *The Channel Tunnel Rail Link*, Report by the Comptroller and Auditor General, HC303, Session 2000–2001, 28 March.

National Audit Office (2004), *London Underground PPP: Are the Public Private Partnerships likely to work successfully?*, Report by the Comptroller and Auditor General, HC644, Session 2003–2004: 17 June.

PMI (2008), 'A Guide to the Project Management Book of Knowledge – Fourth Edition', Project Management Institute, Pennsylvania.

Poot, J. (2000), 'A synthesis of empirical research on the impact of the government on long-run growth', *Growth and Change*, **31** (4), 516–46.

Sanchez-Robles, B. (1998), 'Infrastructure, investment and growth: some empirical evidence', *Contemporary Economic Policy*, **1**, 98–109.

Treasury Taskforce (UK) (1999), Private finance treasury taskforce – Information – Guides to PFI, available at: www.treasury-projects-taskforce.gov.uk/series_1/pfp/into/intro.htm (accessed 5 November 1999).

van Leeuwen, H. (1997), 'Business hit by $200bn freeze', *The Australian Financial Review*, 8 September.

Wood, P. and C.F. Duffield (2009), *In Pursuit of Additional Value: A Benchmarking Study into Alliancing in the Australian Public Sector*, Department of Treasury and Finance Victoria, available at: www.dtf.vic.gov.au/CA25713E0002EF43/WebObj/InPursuitofAddi tionalValue/$File/InPursuitofAdditionalValue.pdf (accessed 15 December 2009).

World Bank (2009), 'Public–private infrastructure advisory facility – resources: what are public private partnerships?', available at: www.ppiaf.org/content/view/118/153/ (accessed December 2009).

10 Law and regulatory aspects of public–private partnerships: contract law and public procurement law
Christina D. Tvarnø

Introduction

The aim of this chapter is to present a number of rules and legal principles in regard to contractual[1] public–private partnerships (PPPs). Contractual PPPs are often used in infrastructure projects, for example, in sectors such as transport, public health, education and national security. There are several relevant legal aspects surrounding PPP projects. This chapter concerns PPPs in a contract law and public procurement law context, with special focus on the European Commission (EC) public procurement rules and an introduction to the legal PPP principles in the World Trade Organization (WTO) and United Nations Commission on International Trade Law (UNCITRAL). It is not the purpose of the analysis in this chapter to cover different national legal rules and regulations, but instead to analyse and describe some more general principles in regard to PPPs.

In a broad legal context, a PPP can be characterized[2] as a long-term contract arrangement between a public authority and a consortium of private parties based on cooperation, aiming to provide a mechanism for developing public service provision involving significant assets or services for a long period of time. The asset or service is entrusted to the private sector, and a part or all of the funding comes from the private sector. This means that the private party in a PPP holds all equity and handles the works, operation and maintenance of the project.[3] The PPP contract is, or at least should be, based on needs/functions instead of demands/concrete descriptions.

By basing the contract on the needs of, for example, a school project, the public authority focuses on learning strategy, teaching environment, the differences in the learning abilities of pupils and so on. This is different from a traditional contract between those kinds of parties. In a traditional procurement of a school building, the public party would instead focus on number of classrooms, number of square metres, types of furniture and facilities. In a PPP such reflections are left to the private parties.

The aim of a PPP contract is to reduce the cost and price, increase the quality, reduce the risks and failures, and improve the coordination and share responsibility and capacity. Those objectives result in a shift of content in the contract. Normally, a traditional public contract is based on demands and concrete descriptions. To fulfil the objectives, the PPP contract focuses on needs and functions, and it must be built on trust and transparency through open books and cooperation between the parties.[4] In the end all these factors can fulfil the main scope of a PPP agreement, which is to ensure joint utility between the parties, thereby guaranteeing the most efficient product at the lowest price.

The private party is responsible for the funding, design, completion, implementation, service and maintenance.[5] The incentive is to reduce the cost of service and maintenance in the long run. The PPP concept thereby provides the contractor with a compelling reason to create the cheapest building or infrastructure for a period of 20 to 30 years. In contrast to a traditional public contract, it is the contractor who has the obligation to provide service and operation. The PPP contract must run for a period equal to the time it takes for the private party to regain the investment. This is the main reason for the long duration of PPP projects.

The public procurement legal context is relevant because the relationship is between a public and a private party. In many countries this type of relationship normally falls under the scope of public procurement law. National legislation,[6] the European Union (EU) and the WTO do not have legal rules that specifically cover the PPP arrangement in regard to public contract rules.

The legal framework in regard to PPPs in the European Union
For almost 20 years the public sector in the EU and the UK has used PPPs as an alternative to traditional public contracts, in most cases with great advantage.[7] The use of PPPs is still increasing. With its 27 member states and 500 million citizens, the EU is a relevant international legal institution as regards public procurement law and the impact on PPPs. Most of the national procurement legislation in the member states derives from EU law, both in the EC Treaty and in the procurement directives.[8] The EC procurement law is based on the common market and the elimination of barriers to trade in goods between member states and barriers to movement in business, labour and capital. The political and economic reasoning behind the common market is based on the economic theory of comparative advantages (Krugmann and Obstfeld, 2003, part I).

The purpose of the EC procurement law is to ensure an opening up of the public procurement market (Arrowsmith, 2005, p. 121; 2000, p. 709; Burnett, 2008; Hjelmborg et al., 2006; Nielsen, 2005; Steinicke and Groesmeyer, 2008). The EC public procurement rules apply to purchases by public bodies that are above set monetary thresholds. They cover all EU member states and, as a result of international agreements, their benefits also extend to several other countries worldwide.[9] The EC procurement directives set out the legal framework for public procurement. The directives apply when public authorities and utilities seek to acquire goods, services, civil engineering or building works. The importance of this in regard to PPPs is that the principles in the EC Treaty and the procurement rules in the procurement directives set out rules and procedures that must be followed before awarding a contract when its value exceeds set thresholds, but the EC rules do not lay down any specific rules in regard only to PPPs.[10]

There are many positive elements in the EC procurement rules. One is the possibility of eliminating a corrupt governmental practice; another is that effective public procurement is essential for good public services and good government. The procurement rules ensure that the government applies the highest professional standards when it spends money on behalf of taxpayers. This procedure helps to ensure competition as the cornerstone of public sector procurement and to maintain market interest – particularly where a well-established and competitive market does not already exist. In markets with no or limited competition, the procurement rules can allow for market soundings, adaptation to the requirements to the capacity and capabilities of the marketplace, and advertising and marketing contracting opportunities as broadly as possible.

The objectives of the specific EC public procurement directives are to ensure fairness and equal treatment and better procurement practices, and to open up the competition and lower overall prices. The basic means to obtain these goals are transparency, non-discrimination, equal treatment, proportionality and competition.

The EC procurement law is not only used by the 27 EU member states. The EU public procurement rules also apply to a number of other countries because of an international agreement negotiated by the WTO entitled the Government Procurement Agreement (GPA).[11] In regard to PPPs, the legal situation in all member states is that a PPP is a public contract falling within the scope of the public procurement law.

No legal definition of PPPs in the EU

PPP arrangements are usually complex projects; in accordance with COM 2004/324 (EC, 2004), several member states have already indicated that there was a need for a common set of EU rules on PPPs. Even though PPP projects are complex, EU law does not legally define PPPs. In COM 2004/327 (EC, 2004b),[12] the Commission states that 'PPP is not defined at Community level'. The reason for this lack of definition is to be found in the legal tradition. If the Commission set up a legal definition of PPPs, it would open itself up to a long list of projects that would not be covered by this definition and the EC public procurement rules.

The European Commission has identified two types of PPP used in the member states: PPPs of a purely contractual nature[13] and PPPs of an institutional nature, in which the public and private parties establish a joint public limited company.[14]

Instead of a specific legal definition, the Commission explains PPPs in general as 'forms of cooperation between public authorities and the world of business which aim to ensure funding, construction, renovation, management or maintenance of an infrastructure or the provision of a service'. The Commission makes it clear in COM/2005/569 (EC, 2005a)[15] that PPPs in general qualify as a 'public Contract' under Directive 2004/18/EC.[16] The procedure for the award of the PPP must comply with the detailed provisions of the directive, while also abiding by the rules and principles of the EC Treaty: the free-movement rules and the principles of transparency, equal treatment, proportionality and mutual recognition.[17] By using this specific legal method, the Commission ensures the use of the EC procurement rules in a large number of PPPs.

The discussion in legal theory in regard to the lack of specific procurement rules started almost ten years ago.[18] In accordance with COM/2004/327 (EC, 2004), several member states indicated that there was a need for a common set of EU rules on PPPs. The European Commission has participated in the discussion, but does not agree that the lack of specific rules is a problem. The result of the *Green Paper*[19] did, however, show the need in the member states for clarification on the use of PPPs under the EC public procurement rules.[20] In COM/2005/569 (EC, 2005a) the Commission did not, however, consider this necessary, and has subsequently made several announcements regarding the interpretation of PPPs. Hence the Commission is not at this time planning to create any legislative PPP rules. The Commission stated in COM/2005/569 (EC, 2005a) that a non-binding initiative would provide the required guidance to address perceived uncertainties in regard to institutional public–private partnerships (IPPPs). The lack of legal definition of an IPPP at Community level was most recently stated in C/2007/6661 (EC, 2007) and Memo/08/95 of 18 February 2008.[21]

The EC's explanation of PPPs

In the *Green Paper* on PPPs,[22] the EC sets up some elements characterizing them. A PPP relationship has a relatively long duration, and involves cooperation between the public partner and the private partner on different aspects of a planned project. The project is funded, in part from the private sector, sometimes by means of complex arrangements between the various players. In some situations public funds can be added to the private funds. The economic operator, who participates at different stages in the project (design, completion, implementation, funding), has an important role. The public partner concentrates primarily on defining the objectives to be attained in terms of public interest, quality of services provided and pricing policy, and it takes responsibility for monitoring compliance with these objectives. The distribution of risk, generally borne by the public sector, is transferred between the public partner and the private partner.[23]

IPPPs in the EU

In regard to EC law, an IPPP is either a jointly held legal entity created by a public authority and a private party with the task of ensuring the delivery of a work or service for the benefit of the public, or is set up in situations where a private party takes control of some part of an existing public undertaking.[24] In both situations, the private party will own a part of the stocks and control in the legal entity.[25] Apart from the equity, the input of both the public and the private party is very active participation in the operation of the contracts awarded to the public–private entity and in the management of the joint company. The Commission explained in COM/2004/327 (EC, 2004)[26] that an IPPP 'involves the establishment of an entity held jointly by the public partner and the private partner'. By changing the investment structure concerning a work or service, the government can offer a work or service that perhaps would not otherwise be offered to the citizens. At the same time, an IPPP can ensure more efficient services and infrastructure projects based on public needs, public and private funding, risk, know-how and an efficient change in both parties' incentives.[27]

The EC rules apply when private partners are chosen for an IPPP. According to the Commission, it depends on the nature of the task (public contract or concession) to be attributed to the IPPP, whether the public procurement directives or the general EC Treaty principles apply to the selection procedure of the private partner.[28]

The public authorities must be applied together with the EC procurement rules when setting up and contracting with an IPPP as long as the task falls within the material scope of the procurement directives. The EC procurement rules and principles cannot be avoided by claiming that the IPPP task is in house. When the public authority holds part of the IPPP capital and one or more private parties also holds parts of the IPPP, the IPPP is defined as a company legally distinct from the public authority. The European Court of Justice (ECJ) concluded in the *Stadt Halle* case[29] that the directive must always be applied when a contracting authority intends to conclude a contract (relating to services within the material scope of the procurement directive)[30] with a company legally distinct from it, in which the public authority holds capital together with one or more private undertakings.[31] The ECJ is clearly specifying that private capital investment in an undertaking must follow considerations proper to private interests and pursue objectives of a different kind than considerations and requirements proper to the pursuit of objectives in the public interest.[32] If the award of a public contract to a semi-public company takes place without calling for tenders, this will, according to the ECJ, interfere with the objective of free and undistorted competition and the principle of equal treatment.[33] If the task is covered by the procurement directives and the IPPP is not procured in the correct legal way, the IPPP will have an advantage over its competitors, which would interfere with the objective of free and undistorted competition and the principle of equal treatment.[34]

The Commission has published an interpretative communication C/2007/6661 (EC, 2007)[35] that, according to the Commission, will clarify 'the rule of the game'. The Commission concludes that the aim of the interpretative communication is to enhance legal certainty and alleviate the concerns that procurement rules and EC law in general would make IPPPs unattractive or impossible to carry out (Williams, 2008). The question is whether this is the best solution and whether this approach will succeed. The reason for publishing the IPPP interpretation communication C/2007/6661 (EC, 2007) is the perceived lack of legal certainty in the member states in relation to the involvement of private partners and the risk of the IPPP's non-compliance with EC law.[36]

According to C/2007/6661 EC (2007), the Commission does not consider a double tendering procedure practical. The Commission interprets the EC law in such a way that one tendering procedure suffices, and the procedure applies when selecting the private partner concerning setting up an IPPP.[37] Either the public procurement directives or the general EC Treaty principles apply to the selection procedure of the private partner in the IPPP. Hence the IPPP must be set up by a fair and transparent procedure. The Commission recommends in EC (2007) that the invitation to tender should include information on the public contracts to be awarded to the future public–private entity, the statutes of association, the shareholder agreement, all elements governing the contractual relationship between the contracting entity and the private partner, and all future adjustments in concern of the task. Thus, when setting up an IPPP, it is not necessary to have one procedure for selecting the private partner to the IPPP and another tendering procedure for awarding public contracts to the IPPP after the establishment of the IPPP.[38]

The lack of a legal definition of the IPPP is a problem because EC law does not consider cooperation as the key instrument in a successful IPPP.

Both parties must have influence on the IPPP project. However, the public procurement rules require that the public party in the tender procedure set up all conditions and only minor matters can be changed after the award, otherwise a new procedure must be set up. These rules do not support the idea and key element of cooperation. The Commission believes that the existing public procurement rules can cover all new ideas and the creation of new types of cooperation between public and private parties as well as all situations created by the market. However, the Commission does not take into consideration that both PPPs and IPPPs have very specific characteristics with regard to cooperation and output that are not reflected in the EC public procurement rules. The lack of acknowledgement of the cooperation and the need for negotiation between the parties is troublesome. The main priority of the present legislation is equal treatment, transparency and free movement, all fundamental principles in the EU. But the citizens, the private parties and the public authorities must also be given the possibility to achieve the most efficient agreement and outcome of an IPPP.

PPPs and public procurement law in the EU
The public procurement law in the EU is based on the fundamental principle that public contracts over the EC public procurement thresholds must be exposed to competition.[39]

EU procurement thresholds
Thresholds applicable from 1 January 2008 are given in Table 10.1. Thresholds are net of VAT.[40]

Table 10.1   Applicable thresholds

Public contracts	Supplies (€)	Services (€)	Works (€)
Entities listed in Schedule 1[a]	133 000	133 000[b]	5 150 000
Other public sector contracting authorities	206 000	206 000	5 150 000

Notes:
[a]   Schedule 1 of the Public Contracts Regulations 2006 lists central government bodies subject to the WTO GPA. These thresholds will also apply to any successor bodies.
[b]   With the exception of some specific services.

Thus a public contract depends on respect for the procurement rules, respect for the fundamental principle of competition concerning equal access to the market, the ban on anti-competitive agreements, and the economic and financial equilibrium of the projects.

In February 2004 the Commission adopted two new directives in regard to public procurement.[41] The purpose of Directive 2004/18/EC[42] was to consolidate the existing directives on works, supply and services into one single directive.[43] At the same time, some important changes in regard to PPP were made with the introduction of the competitive dialogue.

The competitive dialogue and the need for negotiation in a PPP

To ensure the economic benefits from the PPP concept, PPPs require both negotiation and cooperation. This can pose serious problems with regard to community law. According to the 2004/18/EF Directive, Article 29, a public authority is allowed to use the 'competitive dialogue' procedure in regard to PPP arrangements.[44]

Earlier on, the award of public works contracts or public service contracts normally had to be subjected to either an open or a restricted procedure. With the 2004/18/EF Directive, the competitive dialogue procedure tries to set up a procedure that can handle the need for negotiation and cooperation. The competitive dialogue procedure can, pursuant to Article 29(1), be used when the open or restricted procedure will not allow the award of the contract,[45] particularly in cases concerning complex contracts where the contracting body is objectively unable to define the technical means that would best satisfy its needs and objectives, or in cases where it is objectively unable to define the legal and/or financial form of a project.[46] The competitive dialogue procedure can be used when the public party is awarding particularly complex contracts.

When awarding a PPP contract by means of competitive dialogue, the contract must be awarded on the sole basis of the award criterion for the most economically advantageous tender, pursuant to Article 29(1), and the public party must set up the needs and demands in the notice document, pursuant to Article 29(2). The public party opens a dialogue with the tenders after the selection in accordance with Articles 44–52. The aim of the dialogue is to identify and define the means best suited to satisfy the complex needs of the public party.[47] The public party may discuss all aspects of the contract during this dialogue as long as it can ensure equality of treatment among all tenders according to Article 29(3).[48] When the dialogue is concluded, the tenders submit their final tenders based on the solution specified during the dialogue; see Article 29(6). The public party then assesses the tenders on the basis of the most economically advantageous tender, pursuant to Article 29(7).

According to the Commission, the competitive dialogue will provide the necessary flexibility in the discussions with the tenders on all aspects of the PPP contract during the set-up phase. At the same time, this procedure will ensure that the dialogue is conducted in compliance with the principles of transparency and equality of treatment and the EC Treaty principles.[49] The member states still have a legal obligation to fulfil the requirements of EU procurement law by paying constant attention to the restraints following from the ban on negotiations in the EC procurement directives.

Perhaps the competitive dialogue is not enough to ensure the economic benefits from PPP. The central legal challenge in regard to PPPs in the EU is that in order to benefit fully from a PPP, and that the parties can include a high degree of negotiation and collaboration, a measure that to some extent is prohibited by the Public Service Directive 2004/18/EC and by the EC legal principle in regard to the ban on negotiation. However, the ECJ[50] has yet to address the degree of negotiation in a PPP project using competitive dialogue.

WTO's Agreement on Government Procurement (GPA)

In most countries the government, combined with the agencies controlled by it, is the biggest purchaser of goods of all kinds, ranging from basic commodities to high-technology equipment. At the same time, the political pressure to favour domestic suppliers over foreign competitors can be very strong. Traditionally, the focus of international trade agreements has been on market access. However, many developing countries have opposed the launch of negotiations to extend the principle of non-discrimination to procurement.[51]

WTO's Government Procurement Agreement (GPA)[52] is the only legally binding agreement in the WTO focusing on the subject of government procurement to date. Its present version was negotiated in parallel with the Uruguay Round in 1994, and it entered into force on 1 January 1996.[53] It is a pluri-lateral treaty administered by a committee on government procurement, which includes the WTO members that are parties to the GPA and thus have rights and obligations under the Agreement.[54] Apart from procurement rules, the GPA enforces rules guaranteeing fair and non-discriminatory conditions of international competition.[55]

Under WTO law there is no legal definition of PPPs[56] even though several WTO member states resort to PPPs in, for example, infrastructure projects.[57] The importance of legal instruments in regard to encouraging PPPs has been recognized in the WTO.[58] The GPA is based on transparency and non-discrimination principles.[59] All suppliers should have the opportunity to apply for, for example, a PPP or other types of public contracts. In accordance with the GPA, the government must ensure that public contracts are awarded in a non-arbitrary way.

Thus the GPA is based on similar rules and principles as the EU public procurement law presented above. Contrary to the EC Public Procurement Directive, however, the GPA does not consist of procurement procedure rules similar to the competitive dialogue. This means that the special need for cooperation in a PPP and some kind of negotiation between the parties when it comes to defining the needs of the public sector will not be possible within the scope of the GPA.[60]

The UNCITRAL 1994 Model Law on Procurement

The 1994 UNCITRAL Model Law on Procurement of Goods, Construction and Services, with Guide to Enactment, was adopted by UNCITRAL on 15 June 1994. The Model Law recognizes that certain aspects of the procurement of services are governed by different considerations from those applicable to the procurement of goods and construction.

The UNCITRAL model law is not a binding legal instrument but an instrument for national governments to use in regard to implementing public procurement legislation. Public procurement constitutes a large portion of public expenditure in most states, and PPPs will often fall under such legislation. Also, the UNCITRAL Model Law is a model for legislative provisions on procurement of goods, constructions and services, which are all parts of a PPP project.

The objective behind the UNCITRAL Model Law is to establish procedures designed to foster integrity, confidence, fairness and transparency in the procurement process, and also to promote efficiency and competition in procurement, and thus lead to increased economic development. The aim was that the establishment of model legislative provisions on procurement of services that are acceptable to the states with different legal, social and economic systems contributes to the development of harmonious international economic relations.[61]

The UNCITRAL Model Law does not contain any rules directly concerning PPPs. Also, it does not define PPPs. Thus it cannot be used as an international guide for PPPs.

The PPP contract

From a contractual point of view, it is a general rule in civil law and common law countries that the parties have contractual freedom. The reason behind freedom of contract is individual autonomy and public benefit. The contract is binding upon the parties and determines rights and liabilities (Flume, 1992, p. 7). The principle is a product of a liberalist belief that when the individual is free from historical constraints and authorities, he/she is capable of determining his/her acts and responsibilities, and thereby the person can decide whether or not to make a contract (Zweigert and Kötz, 1998, p. 324).

In regard to two private parties, this contractual freedom means that the parties can agree on what they want. To some extent the private law principle also covers public contracts. The legal regulation of public contracts usually adheres closely to the ordinary private law (Collins, 1999, p. 304). But when a public party contracts with private parties, the public procurement rules and principles must be followed when setting up the procurement procedure and choosing the private party. Pursuant to Article 1(2)(a) in the EC Directive 2004/18/EC, public contracts are contracts for pecuniary interest concluded in writing between one or more economic operators and one or more contracting authorities, and having as their object the execution of works,[62] supply[63] and provision of services[64] (Bovis, 2007, p. 157).

Thus, in accordance with the public procurement rules in the procurement directive or in the GPA, the public contracting authority in a PPP must choose the private contracting party by a tender procedure, and the contract must be concluded on the basis of the draft contract laid down in the tender documents without any scope for amendments and negotiations (Hjelmborg et al., 2006, p. 201).

On the one hand, public procurement law does not define the content of the contract, and the content of the PPP contract is not covered by the public procurement rules. But on the other hand, the parties cannot negotiate the terms of the contracts as freely as two private parties. The public procurement regulation and the tender procedures set restrictions to a negotiation similar to private contracts. These rules and principles mentioned above result in a contract situation where the public party must tender out the contract terms in such a way that all potential bidders can see the terms and bid on the same terms. This results in a situation where the public contract cannot take into account the evolution of a product or service over a longer duration period. By this restriction, public contracts tend to be incomplete by design in situations where the product is not typical or easy to define.[65]

Some economic consequences in regard to PPP contracts
Private partnership can be described as an effect of globalization and the types of private contracts that arose from these changes in market behaviour. Globalization increased the cost of competing in a global arena because the number of competitors increased, the cost of selling products on a global market increased, and the cost of the use of IT increased. Thus companies found new ways to compete by entering into joint ventures and strategic alliances, and the emergence of the concept of cooperation led to new types of business strategies. Companies could then ensure a higher product quality, reduce the cost of R&D, IT, sales and distribution, thereby increasing their competitive capacity. The motivation for making a strategic alliance was and still is to make a business arrangement that creates synergy, collaboration and mutual learning among the parties (Doz and Hamel, 1998, pp. 9, 15). The new business strategies created a

need for a new type of contract fulfilling the changes in business behaviour, the social contract and later on the partnering contract. Governments in the USA, the UK and other EU member states had the same problem as the private industries. Citizens in all the member states want higher quality and better service, but wish to pay less tax. The new economic challenges in the member states are similar to those faced by private businesses earlier on. Thus the PPP contract is a contractual arrangement between a public and a private party where the level of cooperation is high compared to a normal public contract.

PPP as an alternative to classic public contracts
The contractual part of the PPP can be defined as a combination of the *partnering* contract – used in the construction industry in connection with works contracts – and the *partnership* contract – used in services contracts (Tvarnø, 2005b, p. 183). Both contract types build on the classic public contract. The basis of all three types of contract is to create more value for money, and the PPP contract contains the contract elements shown in Table 10.2.

Table 10.2   Clauses in the PPP contract

Legally binding clauses	Process-based clauses
The parties share all information.	The parties optimize the transaction, which means they optimize joint utility and not their own utility.
They have open books and calculations.	
At the beginning of the relationship, the parties do not know the final product. Instead, the parties' demands are in focus.	The relationship is built on cooperation and trust.
	The process is more important than the product because the process facilitates the creation of the best and most efficient product.
The parties share the responsibility and cost of failures.	

Setting up the entire contract in a collaboration can be problematic for a public party in an EU member state, for example, because of the EC procurement rules and the principle of a ban on negotiation.[66] Nevertheless, the governments should try to set up these rules in the PPP contract because they can significantly affect incentives on a long-term basis, a shift of focus to needs instead of demands, improvement of coordination, a better use of core competencies, shared capacity with the private party, an increase in quality, a reduction of risks and failures, shared risks and a reduction in costs (Barlow et al., 1997; Doz and Hamel, 1998; Scheuing, 1995).

The aim is that both the public and the private party benefit from such a contractual relationship if the performance is based on needs instead of demands. Thus the contract should not state exactly what the private party must perform; rather, it should state which needs the end product must fulfil. This can be ensured if the public party defines the needs and objectives of public interest instead of the traditional definition of demands. Then it will be up to the private party to create the design, completion, implementation, services and funding, as these are all core competencies of a private party.[67]

From a contractual point of view, a PPP can be set up as one single contract running until the investment has been returned or as two separate contracts – one concerning the works agreement and one concerning the service, maintenance and operation agreement. In the long run the private party runs the building or infrastructure and the public party provides the typical public service – for example, the teaching and education services in a school in regard to the PPP project.[68]

Legal challenge in regard to PPPs
It should be acknowledged that one of the key elements in a PPP is cooperation between the private and public party. However, the procurement rules in general require that the public party in the tender procedure set up almost all conditions, and only minor matters can be changed after the award (Hjelmborg et al., 2006, p. 201). Since cooperation is such an important aim of the PPP, problems arise because the EU, the UN and the WTO procurement rules do not ensure this cooperation. Indeed, the principles of the procurement rules are to ensure competition, equal treatment and transparency, not cooperation. Instead, there is a general legal ban on negotiation.

Specific PPP regulation in respect of legal certainty
The aim of specific PPP rules must be to enhance legal certainty and alleviate concerns that traditional procurement rules might make PPPs unattractive or impossible to carry out. With regard to legal uncertainty, there are two approaches.

One approach is to acknowledge that existing public procurement rules and principles cover all PPPs, rendering a definition of PPP unnecessary. This is the natural legal solution. Under this approach, the view is that the existing rules cover all new ideas, the creation of new types of cooperation between public and private parties and all situations created by the market. However, this traditional legal solution does not take into consideration that a PPP has very specific characteristics with regard to cooperation and output needed to create an efficient PPP.

Another approach is to let the public authorities use the option of cooperating with private parties under conditions similar to market conditions. This solution is in conflict with the procurement procedure in general. A simple solution is to set up specific PPP rules in public procurement regulation – in the EU, WTO and UNCITRAL – and legally define exactly what a PPP is, how it must be set up, how to ensure fair and transparent competition when selecting the private parties, and how to run a PPP. When this is accomplished, the PPP can use a different set of procurement rules that acknowledge the special aim of the PPP, the public service can be operated on market conditions with the benefits related to the market, and cooperation can be prioritized.

Specific PPP rules in the EU

It should be emphasized that the aim and purpose of EU public procurement law are good, but not when there is a particular need or market for new types of cooperation between public and private parties. While also subject to special procedural rules, the PPP rules should allow special turnaround in the traditional incentive procurement structures necessary for PPPs. A PPP has the intention of achieving greater economic efficiency by changing the incentive structure of cooperation.

If and when the national interpretation of procurement rules creates uncertainty, and when EC public procurement law does not specify concrete PPP rules, it creates barriers to the use of PPPs in some member states.[69] At the same time, national interpretation creates barriers that increase the transaction costs in connection with procurement of PPP projects. This problem should be addressed by the European Commission. The member states should have equal opportunities to apply and implement PPP projects. PPPs can provide a significant economic advantage that can be removed by restrictive national interpretation of the EC procurement rules.[70] A more uniform interpretation and application of procurement rules in regard to PPP can perhaps ensure a more efficient use of PPP at the national level.[71]

The general development and more than ten years of knowledge concerning PPPs should make it possible now to introduce specific rules for PPP in the current EC public procurement directives. Specific PPP rules can help create a functioning PPP market with the economic benefits that a market can create. Such rules could contain a tight definition stating which PPP arrangements are covered by these rules. If a PPP project is excluded from the definition in the specific PPP rules, the project should instead be subject to general procurement rules and regulations.

Thus, if the PPP falls outside the scope of any definition of a PPP, the traditional public procurement rules will apply to the set-up. So, on the one hand, the Commission is correct in stating that the traditional procurement rules and principles can handle the founding of a PPP. On the other hand though, the Commission still ought to consider specific PPP rules at community level to allow the best and most effective outcome of the PPPs, including a precise definition of the PPP.[72]

Conclusions

This chapter has dealt with some general principles regarding PPPs in the EU, the WTO and UNCITRAL. National rules and regulations have not been analysed but will of course affect the use and structure of PPPs. The purpose of this chapter has been to analyse and describe some of the overall legal challenges that PPP projects will face.[73]

The first legal challenge in respect of the PPP is that PPPs will often fall under the public procurement rules and legislation, and that no unique rules cover PPP contracts. Instead, public procurement rules are made with a view to traditional public contracts, which are generally based on measures other than the PPP. The EC does not comment on the problem that a large part of the traditional EC procurement rules in the 2004/18/EC Directive[74] are made to cover the traditional procurement arrangement and not new cooperative arrangements between a public and private party.[75]

Another legal challenge is that the EU, the WTO and UNCITRAL do not recognize the need for special PPP rules and definitions for the purposes of reducing the transaction costs and increasing the level of legal information. For example, the EC Communication in EC (2005a) concludes[76] that there will be no new PPP rules or directives within the EU in the near future. Also, the Commission does not take into account that some EU member states have very limited experience of PPP and that the lack of transparency and definition of PPPs in general may result in fewer PPPs.

This lack of legal definition in regard to PPPs is a serious problem. Today, PPPs are used in many countries. In the near future other countries will also use them, but the award of a PPP in general takes place in many different ways, which may result in some nervousness in the public sector because of the lack of a uniform award procedure designed for public procurement of PPP projects. This creates uncertainty about how and when to use PPPs, along with a high risk of claims. In some situations it may be easier not to use PPPs because the uncertainty and the transaction costs are simply too high. This scenario could pose a future problem for the use of PPPs. Instead, the EU, the WTO and UNCITRAL should encourage the use of PPPs by insisting on transparency and uniformity in this highly regulated procurement area.

Notes

1. The chapter focuses primarily on contractual PPPs. The institutional public–private partnership (IPPP) is defined in a later subsection.
2. See EC (2004).
3. See Arrowsmith (2000, 2005). See also EC (2004).
4. Another legal constellation in regard to PPPs is the institutionalized public–private partnership (IPPP). This is outlined in a later section of this chapter. (See also note 21 below.)
5. See EC (2004).
6. A few countries have enacted specific national rules covering PPPs: Brazil enacted a PPP act in December 2004, designed to encourage investments for crucially needed infrastructure projects. See Law No. 11.078, D.O.U. 31 December 2004. See also Filho and Lee (2005).
7. In the UK, PPPs are often used in construction and infrastructure projects. Some of the first PPP projects in the UK were arranged in 1996 by the Public–Private Partnership Programme, the 4PS. The 4PS was initiated by the Local Authority Association in England and Wales and had all-party support. It was launched in April 1996 with the purpose of identifying and assisting in delivering 'pathfinder' projects in key sector areas, for example, education, social services, IT and so on, to be used as models by other local authorities. See also www.4ps.gov.uk.
8. In Denmark the only regulation in regard to PPP is a governmental notice and a guideline to this notice. The notice, *BEK nr. 1394 af 17/12/2004, Bekendtgørelse om anvendelse af offentlig-privat partnerskab (OPP), partnering og oplysninger svarende til nøgletal*, instructs the public authorities to evaluate whether a PPP is an efficient possibility in large projects, but it does not define PPPs in general. See the PPP guidelines at www.ebst.dk/file/1182/opp_vejledning. The Danish Competition Authority's interpretation of the duration of public contracts in general is shown in its *Guidelines to the Public Procurement Directives of 30th June 2006 section 8.6. (Konkurrencestyrelsens vejledning til udbudsdirektiverne, 30 June 2006).*
9. Where the regulations apply, contracts must be advertised in the *Official Journal of the European Union (OJEU)*, and other detailed rules must be followed. The rules are enforced through the courts, including the European Court of Justice (ECJ). Even when a tender process is not required under the directives, for example because the estimated value of a contract falls below the relevant threshold, EU Treaty-based principles of non-discrimination, equal treatment, transparency, mutual recognition and proportionality apply, and some degree of advertising, appropriate to the scale of the contract, is likely to be necessary to demonstrate transparency.
10. Bovis (2007), p. 52.
11. The countries are Aruba, Canada, Hong Kong, China, Iceland, Israel, Japan, Republic of Korea, Liechtenstein, Norway, Singapore, Switzerland and the USA.
12. See EC (2004).
13. In some situations a PPP has been, and probably will be, set up as a concession. If the PPP can be legally defined as a concession, there are only a few provisions of secondary legislation to coordinate this type of PPP. These provisions are Article 3(1) of Directive 93/37/EEC and Articles 56 to 59 in Directive 2004/18/EC. See also Bovis (2007), pp. 53–4.
14. See ibid., p. 52. In accordance with EC (2004), PPPs of a purely contractual nature are in general the most common PPP solution in most member states. See note 2.
15. See EC COM (2005a) and Concessions.
16. European Parliament (2004).
17. If EC procurement rules are an advantage for PPPs, then the Commission's decision not to provide a definition may be a good idea legally. Hence many PPPs will be governed by the procurement rules and principles in the EC Treaty, the procurement directives and the relevant case law. If, on the other hand, the procurement rules are a disadvantage for PPPs, the lack of definition may have negative implications resulting

in a reduced use of PPPs. One reason for a low rate of PPPs currently is too high trans-action costs caused by the high degree of uncertainty.

18. See Arrowsmith (2000), where the author argues that there are many difficulties in rela-tion to PPPs and the EC procurement rules.
19. EC (2004).
20. In addition, the European Parliament (2004) asked for some guidelines and relevant clarifications in connection with the award of IPPP.
21. A legal definition of IPPPs and specific rules concerning IPPPs are not to be found at Community level; see EC (2007), which is a consequence of EC (2005a), 569 final section 4.1. In this document the Commission stated that an Interpretative Communication would be the best way to encourage competition and to provide legal certainty. Specifically, the Commission stated in EC (2005a) 569 that a non-binding initiative would provide the required guidance to address perceived uncertainties in regard to IPPPs. The lack of legal definition of an IPPP at Community level is stated again in EC (2007) 6661 (see note 2 above), and Memo/08/95 of 18 February 2008. See also European Parliament (2006).
22. See EC (2004), p. 3.
23. The Commission notes that a PPP does not necessarily entail that the private partner assumes all the risks, or even the major share of the risks linked to the project. The precise distribution of risk is determined case by case, according to the respective ability of the parties concerned to assess, control and cope with this risk.
24. In its interpretative Communication, EC (2007), the Commission understands an IPPP as 'a co-operation between public and private parties involving the establishment of a mixed capital entity which performs public contracts or concessions'. Thus an IPPP can be set up in relation to a public task, either by creating a jointly held entity or in situa-tions where the private party takes control of an existing public undertaking.
25. An IPPP can also be described as a joint venture company as defined in Arrowsmith (2000), p. 720.
26. See note 2 above.
27. Considering the positive effects of setting up an IPPP, it is interesting that the number of IPPPs is very low in some member states.
28. Thus Community law is neutral as regards whether public authorities choose to provide an economic activity themselves or to entrust it to a third party. See also EC (2005a), section 1.
29. Case C-26/03, *Stadt Halle and RPL Lochau* (2005), E.C.R. I-00001. In the *Stadt Halle* case the ECJ concluded, in regard to the in-house situation, that the directive must always be applied when a contracting authority intends to conclude a contract for pecu-niary interest relating to services within the material scope of the procurement directive (the ECJ referred to the Directive 92/50 in the *Stadt Halle* case, but this also applies to the 2004/18 Directive) with a joint company, as, for example, an IPPP. This means that the IPPP can be awarded a public contract only if the joint company wins the contract in a competition under the procurement rules. See also Arrowsmith (2005), p. 392.
30. The ECJ referred to the Directive 92/50, but this must still be the case concerning Directive 2004/18/EC; see note 16 above.
31. This means that in this situation the public award procedures laid down by the directive must always be applied; see the *Stadt Halle* case, Paragraph 52; see note 29 above.
32. Ibid., Paragraph 50.
33. Ibid., Paragraph 51.
34. The only exemption to the main in-house rule in the *Stadt Halle* case is, according to the ECJ, if the public authority can perform the tasks conferred on it in the public interest by using its own administrative, technical and other resources without being obliged to call on outside entities. In an IPPP this situation will never be relevant, since the public authority will always call upon external entities, as this is the aim and purpose of setting up the IPPP.

The ECJ very clearly states, in the *Stadt Halle* case, Paragraph 49, that the exemption does not apply when the participation, even as a minority, of a private undertaking in the capital of a company in which the contracting authority in question is also a participant excludes in any event the possibility of that contracting authority exercising over that company a control similar to that which it exercises over its own departments.

Thus it follows from the *Stadt Halle* case that if the public authority itself performed the tasks in the public interest for which it is responsible by its own means, without calling upon external entities, the EC rules do not apply. The ECJ referred to *Parking Brixen*, Case C-458/03, (2005) E.C.R. I-8585, Paragraph 61, second part.

35.   See EC (2007).
36.   This legal uncertainty and risk can discourage both public authorities and private parties from entering into an IPPP at all. This risk constitutes a problem since public authorities at all levels are interested in types of cooperation with the private sector, and this interest is increasing in the member states. The interest in constructing IPPPs is increasing because of national needs for ensuring infrastructure and services; see EC (2008). The IPPP interpretation communication therefore sets out the Commission's understanding of how the Community provisions on most types of public procurement and concessions are to be applied to the funding and operation of an IPPP as a legal guidance to the member states. The interpretation communication does not create new rules concerning IPPPs; it only reflects the Commission's understanding of the rules in the procurement directive and the EC Treaty and the relevant case law by the ECJ.
37.   See EC (2008).
38.   The Commission defines in EC (2007) that simple capital injections made by private investors into publicly owned companies do not constitute an IPPP.
39.   European Parliament (2004).
40.   Council Regulation 1422/2007 (L317/34 5/12/07). Official Journal number C301/07 13/12/07.
41.   European Parliament (2004), and the Directive 2004/17/EF of the European Parliament and of the Council of March 321, 2004 on coordinating the procurement procedures of entities operating in the water, energy, transport and postal service sectors (2004) O.J. L134/1 (the new utilities Directive). The latter directive is not analysed in this chapter.
42.   European Parliament (2004).
43.   This chapter will not describe the public procurement rules in this directive. For this legal subject, see Arrowsmith (2005) and Bovis (2007).
44.   See European Parliament (2004) and EC (2004).
45.   Article 29(1): 'that where contracting authorities consider that the use of the open or restricted procedure will not allow the award of the contract, the latter may make use of the competitive dialogue in accordance with this Article'.
46.   See also EC (2004) 327, section 25.
47.   Ibid.
48.   Contracting authorities may not reveal to the other participants solutions proposed or other confidential information communicated by a candidate participating in the dialogue without his/her agreement, also according to Article 29(3).
49.   See also EC (2004) 327, section 25.
50.   Some countries in the EU, for example, Denmark, have a special administrative complaint board in regard to procurement. This institution is set up to review complaints about infringements of the procurement directive and Danish public procurement regulation. The cases decided by the Danish Procurement Complaints Board represent an important source of law in regard to the interpretation of public procurement in Denmark. See also Hjelmborg et al. (2006), p. 39.
51.   For further information, see WTO, *Introduction to the GPA*, at www.wto.org. See also Henrick Andersen (2010), in Christina D. Tvarnø (ed.), *Public Private Partnership – an International Analysis in a Legal and Economic Perspective*, available at: www.cbs.dk/staff/tvarno.
52.   At present the GPA is therefore the only international agreement on public procurement in force.

53. An agreement on government procurement was first negotiated during the Tokyo Round and entered into force on 1 January 1981. Its purpose was to open up as much of this business as possible to international competition. It was designed to make laws, regulations, procedures and practices regarding government procurement more transparent and to ensure that they do not protect domestic products or suppliers, or discriminate against foreign products or suppliers.

54. Government procurement is an important aspect of international trade, given the considerable size of the procurement market (often 10 per cent to 15 per cent of GDP) and the benefits for domestic and foreign stakeholders in terms of increased competition. Many WTO members use their purchasing decisions to achieve domestic policy goals, such as the promotion of specific local industry sectors or social groups. Open, transparent and non-discriminatory procurement is generally considered to be the best tool to achieve 'value for money', as it optimizes competition among suppliers.

55. For example, governments will be required to put in place domestic procedures by which aggrieved private bidders can challenge procurement decisions and obtain redress in the event such decisions were made inconsistently with the rules of the agreement.

56. See Andersen (2008).

57. See, for instance, Brazil, *Trade Policy Review*, WT/TPR/G/140 of 1 November 2004, point 102; India, *Trade Policy Review* (revised), WT/TPR/S/182/rev. 1 of 24 July 2007, point IV.5,58,132 and 179; Singapore, *Trade Policy Review*, WT/TPR/S/202 of 9 June 2008, IV.25.

58. See Report of the Working Group on Trade and Transfer of Technology to the General Council, WT/WGTTT/9, report of 12 December 2007, point 9.

59. Article III of the GPA.

60. See Andersen (2008).

61. See the notes to the preamble in The 1994 UNCITRAL Model Law on Procurement of Goods, Construction and Services, with Guide to Enactment as adopted by UNCITRAL on 15 June 1994.

62. Article 1(2)(b) in Directive 2004/18/EC.

63. Article 1(2)(c) in ibid.

64. Article 1(2)(d) in ibid.

65. See also Collins (1999), p. 308.

66. The public authority also will face a number of other challenges. See for this subject Burnett (2008), p. 116.

67. For further discussion and analysis of Danish PPP arrangements, see Tvarnø (2006, 2005a, 2005b).

68. The UK was the first EU member state to use partnering agreements. The UK government uses partnering agreements to build schools, roads, office buildings etc., and has done so for more than ten years. See for example www.4ps.gov.uk and www.ogc.gov.uk.

69. See Arrowsmith (2000), where the author argues that there are many difficulties in relation to PPP and the EC procurement rules.

70. See also the Advocate General's opinion in the *Acoset case* C-196/08, OJ C 197 of 2 February 2008, p. 9, paragraph 58, in which the Advocate General concludes, 'Integrated legislation would remove a number of difficulties and would provide guidance to public authorities and private entities, since the prevailing uncertainty frequently deters them from founding PPPs (as the Communication states), to the detriment of the financing of infrastructure and public services, in view of the likelihood that they would be incompatible with the system sought by the European Union.'

71. See also Tvarnø (2010).

72. In relation to the same concern, the Committee of the Regions states that given the lack of definition of PPPs, adequate legislation is not yet in place and the lack of experience in the member states, mostly the new member states, there is a need for an interpretative communication covering all forms of PPP agreements. Thus the Committee asks for a communication covering more that the aim of COM (2007) 6661 (EC, 2007), which only covers the IPPP.

73. In regard to, for example, national rules and regulations in the EC member states, see the EPEC home page, www.eib.org/epec/link/index.htm?action=changeFormat&format=PRINT. EPEC stands for the European PPP Expertise Centre (EPEC) and was launched by the European Investment Bank (EIB) and European Commission on 16 September 2008. EPEC is a collaboration between the EIB, European Union Member and Candidate States and the European Commission, which is designed to strengthen the organizational capacity of the public sector to engage in PPP transactions. EU member states and candidate countries can share experience and expertise, analysis and best practice relating to PPP transactions.
74. See European Parliament (2004).
75. See EC (2005a), section 2.3.
76. Based on the analysis in SEC (2005) 629 (EC 2005b), section 3.1.

References

Andersen, Henrik (2008), 'Global Telecommunication Services and WTO Law', available online at www.cbs.dk/law.

Arrowsmith, Sue (2000), 'Public private partnerships and the European procurement rules: EU policies in conflict?', *Common Market Law Review*, **37**, 709–37.

Arrowsmith, Sue (2005), *The Law of Public and Utilities Procurement*, 2nd edn, London: Sweet & Maxwell.

Barlow, James, Michael Cohen, Ashok Jasphapara and Yvonne Simpson (1997), *Towards Positive Partnering: Revealing the Realities in the Construction Industry*, Southampton: The Policy Press, reprinted 2002.

Bovis, Christopher H. (2007), *EU Public Procurement Law*, Elgar European Law, Cheltenham, UK and Northampton, MA, USA: Edward Elgar.

Burnett, Michael (2008), *Public-Private-Partnerships (PPP): A Decision Maker's Guide*, Maastricht: Institut Européen d'Administration Publique.

Collins, Hugh (1999), *Regulating Contracts*, Oxford: Oxford University Press.

Doz, Yves L. and Gary Hamel (1998), *Alliance Advantage, The Art of Creating Value through Partnering*, Boston, MA: Harvard Business School Press.

EC (2004), COM/2004/327 final, *Green Paper, on Public Private Partnerships and Community Law on Public Contracts and Concessions*, Brussels, 30 April 2004.

EC (2005a) COM/2005/569 final, *Communication from the Commission to the European Parliament, the Council, the European Economic and Social Committee and Committee of the Regions, on Public–Private Partnerships and Community Law on Public Procurement and Concessions*, Brussels, 15 November.

EC (2005b) SEC/2005/629, Commission Staff Working Paper, 'Report on the Public Consultation in the Green Paper on Public–Private Partnerships and Community Law in Public Contracts and Concessions', Brussels, 3 May.

EC (2007) C/20076661, The Commission Interpretative Communication on the Application of Community Law on Public Procurement and Concessions to Institutionalised Public Private Partnerships (IPPPs), Brussels, 5 February 2008.

EC (2008), *Public Procurement: Commission Issues Guidance on Setting up Institutional Public–Private Partnership*, Brussels, 18 February.

European Parliament (2004), Directive 2004/18/EC of the European Parliament and of the Council of 31 March 2004 on the Coordination of Procedures for the Award of Public Work Contracts, Public Supply Contracts and Public Service Contracts, *Official Journal* L 134, 30/04/2004, 0114–240.

European Parliament (2006), *Resolution on Public–Private Partnerships and Community Law on Public Procurement and Concessions* (2006/2043(INI)), 26 October.

Filho, C.V. and J.B. Lee (2005), 'Brazil's new public–private partnership law: one step forward, two steps back', *Journal of International Arbitration*, **22** (5), 419–26.

Flume, Werner (1992), 'Allgemeiner Teudes Bürgerlichen Rechts', Brand 2, *Das Rechtgeschäft*, Wyd. 4, Berlin: Springer.

Hjelmborg, Simon Everts, Peter Stig Jakobsen and Sune Troels Poulsen (2006), *Public Procurement Law: the EU Directive on Public Contracts*, Copenhagen: DJØF Publishing.
Krugmann, Paul and Maurice Obstfeld (2003), *International Economics, Theory and Policy*, 6th edn, Reading, MA: Addison-Wesley.
Nielsen, Ruth (2005), *Udbud af offentlige kontrakter*, Copenhagen: DJØF Publishing.
Scheuing, Eberhard E. (1995), *The Power of Strategic Partnering*, Portland, OR: Productivity Press.
Steinicke, Michael and Lise Groesmeyer (2008), *EU's udbudsdirektiver*, Copenhagen: DJØF Publishing.
Tvarnø, Christina D. (2005a), 'PPP and public service broadcasting', in Ruth Nielsen (ed.), *Julebog*, Copenhagen: DJØF Publishing, pp. 181–202.
Tvarnø, Christina D. (2005b), 'Public private partnership in the European Union', in Steen Treumer and Ruth Nielsen (eds), *The New EU Public Procurement Directives*, Copenhagen: DJØF Publishing, pp. 183–94.
Tvarnø, Christina D. (2006), 'Public–private partnerships from a Danish perspective', *Public Procurement Law Review*, **3**, 98 f.
Tvarnø, Christina D. (2010), 'Does the Danish interpretation of EC public procurement law prevent PPP?', *Public Procurement Law Review*, (2), 73–89.
Tvarnø, Christina D. (ed.) (2010), *Public Private Partnership – an International Analysis in a Legal and Economic Perspective*, available at: www.cbs.dk/ staff/tvarno.
Williams, Rhodri (2008), 'The Commission Interpretative Communication on the Application of Community Law on Public Procurement and Concessions to Institutionalised Public Private Partnerships (IPPs)', *Public Procurement Law Review*, **17** (4), 116.
Zweigert, Konrad and Hein Kötz (1998), *An Introduction to Comparative Law*, 3rd edn, Oxford: Oxford University Press.

11 Accounting for PPPs in a converging world[1]
David Heald and George Georgiou

Why does PPP accounting matter?

Accounting academics often focus on the tension between setting accounting standards on the basis of 'principles' (high-level statements and aspirations) and 'rules' (prescriptions about how to do it). Principles are difficult
to state in unambiguous language, whereas the precision of rules invites
sophisticated ploys to circumvent their intention. The best way to grasp
the essence of technical debates about PPP accounting is to recognize two
key points:

- Mapping economic reality, whether in terms of the financial reporting of entities or the compilation of national accounts, requires the
  drawing of lines (i.e. distinctions), the location of which may substantially affect reported data.
- There is a gulf between the high-mindedness that officially surrounds the promulgation of accounting standards and the incentives
  of various actors to game the standards, at both the formulation and
  implementation stages.

Whereas few people know the detail of financial reporting or national
accounts standards, far more understand the notions of seeking the
best deal available and of gaming the rules. 'Arbitrage' in financial
markets involves taking advantage of price differentials between markets,
thus improving market efficiency and liquidity. In contrast, the 2008
global financial crisis has highlighted the effects of non-market forms of
arbitrage:

> In the past, authorities around the world have tended to be tolerant of the
> proliferation of complex legal structures designed to maximise regulatory and
> tax arbitrage . . . Now we may have to demand clarity of legal structure. (Lord
> Adair Turner, Chairman of the UK Financial Services Authority, quoted by
> Giles et al. 2009)

'Venue shopping' is the term established by Mazey and Richardson
(2006) in relation to multi-venued and multi-tiered regulation within the

European Union (EU). Those involved take the battle to that venue/ jurisdiction (courts, regulatory system) where they have the best chance of winning. Arbitrage, when used in this broader sense, and venue shopping are almost synonyms, with wide applicability. For example, London has the reputation of being the divorce, bankruptcy and libel capital of the world, attracting litigants who have negligible connection with the UK.

PPP accounting is fundamentally important for a number of reasons:

- PPP accounting damages fiscal transparency when the assets that should have a counterpart in public debt are missing from the balance sheets of public sector clients. Various arguments are mounted in defence of such arrangements, ranging from denial that any public liability has been created to claims to be 'doing good by stealth' by securing assets for public service provision that would have been denied by 'irrational constraints'. Arguments about 'doing good by stealth', though tempting to those down the power chain, should always be regarded with suspicion as such devices erode accountability mechanisms.
- PPP accounting may generate hidden fiscal risks, as when the extent of government indebtedness is concealed. This would happen under cash accounting, as it would under accruals accounting whenever PPPs are artificially kept off the government's balance sheet. The IMF has frequently expressed concern about the fiscal risks associated with PPPs, particularly in relation to Eastern Europe and developing countries (Akitoby et al., 2007; Schwartz et al., 2008).
- PPP accounting can lead to distorted decision-making on public investment, at large resource cost, when the underlying criterion for project acceptance is balance-sheet treatment, not an assessment of best value for money (VfM). Not only might the project appraisal be manipulated, but also the project might be inefficiently designed so that a particular accounting treatment can be secured. Moreover, the widespread view that the accounting is manipulated will damage the credibility even of *bona fide* assessments of PPP versus the public sector comparator (PSC).[2]

Outside the scope of this chapter is whether PPPs offer better VfM than conventional procurement, a quite separate question from that of accounting treatment (Heald, 2003). These two issues are often run together, sometimes intentionally. It is important to emphasize that one can be critical of PPP accounting practice, yet be positive, neutral or negative on the VfM question.

The structure of this chapter is as follows. The second section notes that the term 'public–private partnerships' may be attached in different contexts and countries to substantively different economic relationships. The scope of this discussion is therefore specified. The third section considers the regulation of PPP accounting, both for purposes of financial reporting and for national accounts. It establishes that there has been inadequate enforcement of standards, in large part because of the availability of arbitrage opportunities. These have allowed the exercise of choice between accounting standards/guidance on the basis of which yielded the desired accounting treatment. This parallels venue shopping between the courts of different jurisdictions.

The fourth section discusses 'risks and rewards' as the criterion for determining the balance-sheet treatment, both for financial reporting and for national accounts. The accounting principles developed for lease accounting have been applied for financial reporting and for national accounts, though leading to markedly different treatments. Then the fifth section examines the adoption of the 'control' approach to PPP accounting, which has been propelled by the globalization of private sector financial reporting, with public sector financial reporting following. Although there is substantial convergence in financial reporting, both between public and private sectors and across countries, this introduces greater distance from national accounts, which will remain on the risks and rewards criterion. This creates new arbitrage opportunities, this time between financial reporting treatment and national accounts treatment; the latter is used for fiscal surveillance and for assessing country compliance with international obligations, such as those of EU countries under the Stability and Growth Pact.

Whereas the fourth and fifth sections focus on balance-sheet treatments, the sixth section examines the charges to the income statement in cases of both on- and off-balance-sheet treatment. Finally, the last section draws conclusions on PPP accounting, relevant to the concerns of public policy academics and PPP practitioners.

Service concession arrangements
Definitional matters are extremely important for two reasons. First, the terminology in which public policy initiatives are described can influence their reception. The emphasis can be placed on the 'public' (delivering public services), or on the 'private' (emphasizing the role of the private sector in public services which would not (yet) be privatized). 'Partnership' is an imprecise term, which in part accounts for its popularity. Second, the contracts that attract the label of PPP cover a wide range of commercial relationships. These include full privatization (i.e. complete transfer of the entity to the private sector), joint ventures and conventional

subcontracting. Such arrangements are outside the scope of this chapter, which focuses on commercial arrangements involving fixed assets used by the private sector in the supply of public services.

Although a wide range of specific arrangements can be devised, the principal arrangements can be illustrated by examples:

1.   A government entity leases a photocopier from a specialist supplier.
2.   A government entity leases its headquarters building from a property company.
3a. A government entity grants a service concession to a private sector operator to design, build and operate a prison and, at the end of the concession period, transfer the prison to the government entity.
3b. As in 3a, except that, at the end of the concession period, the prison remains the property of the operator.
4a. A government grants a service concession to a private sector operator to design, build and operate a bridge over a major river crossing, with all costs being covered by user tolls, and, at the end of the concession period, the bridge reverts to the government.
4b. As in 4a, except that, at the end of the concession period, the bridge remains the property of the concessionee.

These illustrative cases highlight the key characteristics relevant to accounting treatment:

(a) Is the commercial arrangement necessarily between a public sector client and a private sector operator?
(b) Does it necessarily involve the provision of 'infrastructure' or of a 'public service'?
(c) Does it necessarily involve the supply of services to the public or can it involve intermediate outputs (e.g. administrative offices or computing systems) that are part of the production process of public services?
(d) Are other services (e.g. facilities management) bundled with the supply of the services from the fixed assets?
(e) Do the costs of provision fall on the public budget or are these met by the operator having the conditional right to charge service users?
(f) Do the fixed assets revert to the public sector client at the end of the concession period and, if so, does this occur at a zero or positive price?

An important question is whether the PPP is a service concession or a lease, although there is not necessarily a clear dividing line. Bundling of other services, the supply of infrastructure or public services, and a contract life considerably shorter than the asset life, often indicate that this may be a service concession rather than a lease.

Regulation and enforcement of PPP accounting
The problems that have arisen with PPP accounting are not essentially technical ones, but relate to (a) contested regulatory space, and (b) weak enforcement of relevant standards. Nevertheless, some of the detail is intricate and what follows is condensed as far as is practicable.[3] The objective in this section is to provide an accessible overview, before considering the more technical material in the fourth to sixth sections.

Two systems of accounting
There are two parallel systems of accounting that must accommodate PPP schemes: financial reporting and national accounting. The former is largely the preserve of accountants belonging to recognized accountancy institutes. The latter is the preserve of a different epistemic community, that of economic statisticians who mostly work in national statistical institutes or in international/supranational agencies such as Eurostat, the IMF and the OECD. There is limited career overlap between these two communities.

Government financial reporting   Government financial reporting has traditionally been done on a cash basis, with detailed rules and procedures usually being the responsibility of finance ministries. Under cash accounting, government entities have no balance sheet, so that aspect of PPP treatment is irrelevant. The governance of financial reporting is likely to change when governments move from cash accounting to accruals, a conversion that may take many years to cover the whole of the public sector. Essentially, there are two options. The government could sign up to private sector standards, thereby giving leadership to the private sector accounting regulator. This has been the approach in Australia and New Zealand, where there has been strong commitment to sector-neutral accounting. The UK left primary responsibility with the Treasury, although the Financial Reporting Advisory Board (FRAB) has had an influential role and has been philosophically committed to minimizing adaptations from UK GAAP (Generally Accepted Accounting Practice) (2001–02 to 2008–09) and from IFRS (International Financial Reporting Standards) (2009–10 onwards). In contrast, the Government Accounting Standards Board (GASB) was established in 1984, with a remit restricted to US state and local governments. This has reinforced the separation of private sector accounting (Financial Accounting Standards Board

(FASB)) and public sector accounting (Federal Accounting Standards Advisory Board (FASAB) and GASB) in the USA.

The Accounting Standards Board (ASB), the UK private sector accounting regulator, and the Treasury clashed on how PPP schemes should be accounted for under UK GAAP (Broadbent and Laughlin, 2002; Hodges and Mellett, 2002). Heald and Georgiou (2009) demonstrated that there were huge variations across functional areas of UK government as to whether PPPs were on or off balance sheet under UK GAAP. They attributed this not to objective differences between PPPs but to the expenditure control and audit arrangements. Whereas the National Audit Office (the UK's supreme audit institution which audits central government) was insistent on implementation of ASB's (1998) FRS 5A, the appointed auditors of the Audit Commission (both direct employees and private subcontractors) were willing to accept recourse to Treasury Technical Note 1 (Revised) (TTN1R) (Treasury Taskforce, 1999a). This was supposedly an interpretation of FRS 5A but in practice acquired the influence of a competitor standard.

The exposition so far emphasizes the national jurisdiction. However, private sector accounting regulation has shifted dramatically to the global arena, with there now being only two first-tier regulators: the International Accounting Standards Board (IASB) and FASB. In principle there will be convergence on uniform global standards for the private sector, but that is a path strewn with difficulties outside the scope of this chapter. What is striking in terms of public sector accounting is the emerging influence of the International Public Sector Accounting Standards Board (IPSASB). Whereas at national level it is possible to conceptualize accounting regulation as a task delegated by the state to a private body, there is no world government to legitimize delegation at the global level.

The IPSASB was formerly the Public Sector Committee of the International Federation of Accountants, itself the international association of professional accountancy institutes that have increasingly been sidelined from accounting regulation in their own jurisdictions. The IPSASB has sought to derive legitimacy not only from due process in standards development but also from its engagement with the IMF and the World Bank. Its emergence creates potential difficulties for those countries that self-consciously see their own public sector accounting as being aligned to best private sector practice (now IFRS). Such countries may be uncomfortable with the intrusion of a separate standard-setter, which might develop standards diverging from best private sector practice, or whose adoption of IASB-derived standards lags adoption by the private sector. Moreover, government finances are always close to politics, and finance ministries may be reluctant to relinquish power to standard-setters of uncertain capacity, legitimacy and authority.

National accounts   In terms of national accounts, the key issue is whether there is a calculation of imputed debt when PPPs are used rather than conventional procurement. In this way, published deficit and debt figures are affected by how the national accounting is done. The key source is the System of National Accounts (SNA) 93 (United Nations Statistical Division, 1993), which is interpreted for EU countries by the European System of Accounts (ESA) 95 (Eurostat, 1995).[4]

ESA 95 adopts the risks and rewards approach towards determining the national accounts treatment of both leases and PPPs. Further guidance on PPPs was provided in Eurostat (2004). A sequence of events analogous to what happened to UK government financial reporting can be observed. Eurostat (2004) purported to be an interpretation of ESA 95, but substantively changed it. For an asset to be off the balance sheet of the public sector client, the following two conditions must be met:

1.   Construction risk has to be transferred to the private sector operator.
2.   *Either* availability risk (covering volume and quality of output) *or* demand risk has to be transferred to the private sector operator.

Most UK PPPs aim to transfer construction risk. Moreover, availability risk (e.g. the hospital facilities are not fully operational on a particular date) can generally be assumed to be lower than demand risk (i.e. demand for the facilities is lower than available capacity). Accordingly, the Eurostat criterion simplifies to the transfer of both construction risk and availability risk. There is insufficient evidence in the public domain to determine whether this weak test was knowingly designed to allow off-balance-sheet treatment or was an unintentional outcome.

On this basis, it can be argued that most UK PPPs should not be on the public sector balance sheet for national accounts purposes. However, this immediately raises the issue that, unlike financial reporting where the accounts of the client and operator have no formal connection, the accounts of sectors in the national accounts must articulate. In the financial statements of the operator, whether prepared under UK GAAP (contract debtor accounting) or under IFRS (IFRIC 12) (Austin, 2009), the PPP will not be on the balance sheet as property, plant and equipment. Moreover, the Office for National Statistics (ONS) is unlikely to have the information necessary to make appropriate adjustments to the account of the non-financial corporations sector to offset any exclusion of PPP assets from the account of general government.[5] For the foreseeable future – and cycles of national accounts revisions are long – the national accounts test will remain one of risks and rewards.

Lack of enforcement mechanisms
Setting standards does not mean that they are applied. A fundamental element of effective accounting regulation is enforcement. There is no point in having pristine standards if there is no implementation or enforcement capacity. In some developing countries the problem might well be a lack of accounting capacity, but elsewhere it is a regulatory issue.

The problem in the UK has been the lack of enforcement mechanisms with regard to financial reporting. Over the period 2001–02 to 2007–08, during which FRS 5A and TTN1R both existed, there was regulatory arbitrage, using the weak standard (TTN1R) to undermine the strong standard (FRS 5A).[6] The arbitrage opportunity was to follow TTN1R rather than FRS 5A, thereby securing off-balance-sheet treatment in a context where public expenditure controls would have prevented an on-balance-sheet project. Provided that the relevant auditors did not qualify the accounts of public sector bodies on the grounds of PPP accounting, there was no enforcement mechanism. There was nowhere to complain about 'orphan' (off–off) assets. Whatever the original circumstances that created this arbitrage opportunity, the Treasury could – if it had so wished – have closed it down by withdrawing TTN1R. In contrast, with regard to UK private sector accounts, the Financial Reporting Review Panel has the right to call in company accounts, irrespective of the audit opinion, if it considers that there has been a breach of accounting standards. An order to rectify can be made where deemed appropriate.

Enforcement with regard to national accounts takes place within a different institutional context. Savage's (2005) analysis of the role of Eurostat in the run-up to the launch of the euro depicted the highly political context within which it operates. Given the laxness of Eurostat (2004), vigorous enforcement would, in the case of the UK, paradoxically lead to ONS putting fewer assets and associated debt on the UK government balance sheet.

Risks and rewards as the criterion for PPP accounting
Risks and rewards is the criterion governing the treatment of leases, both for financial reporting and national accounts. Standard-setters require capitalization as an asset by the entity that bears substantially all of the risks and rewards associated with ownership, as captured by the estimated variability in profits attributable to that asset. The risks and rewards approach was extended to service concessions in the 1990s.

This analysis proceeds on the assumption that the context is accruals accounting in relevant government entities. Whether a lease or a service concession, the central accounting issue is whether the cost to the government of a PPP arrangement should be treated on an annual basis as a government outgoing (as it definitely would be under cash accounting), or whether the long-term nature of this relationship with the private sector requires accounting recognition because government assets and liabilities have been created. These issues are important because commercial arrangements of this type can substitute for traditional procurement of photocopiers, headquarters buildings, prisons and toll bridges. In terms of the rationale of accounting treatment, whether the commercial arrangement is a lease or a service concession must be determined. However, the substantive accounting treatment will not necessarily differ.[7]

Lease accounting has been a highly unsatisfactory part of national GAAPs. The UK standard SSAP 21 (ASC, 1984) and IFRS's IAS 17 (IASB, 2003b) both provide for a distinction between an operating lease (the photocopier payments should be expensed annually as payment is made) and a finance lease (the office building should be capitalized as a fixed asset, subject to meeting certain tests regarding the allocation of risks and rewards, with an offsetting liability on the balance sheet). The UK standard, but not IAS 17, contains quantitative tests, which have long been known to be manipulated to justify treatment as an operating lease.[8] The IASB aims to develop a new leasing standard and to remove the operating lease option (IASB, 2010).

Given that the efficiency drivers behind PPPs are widely believed to be located in the transfer of risk from the public sector client to the private sector operator, there is logic in aligning the accounting treatment with the efficiency-enhancing mechanism. The economic case developed to justify PPPs emphasized the decomposition of total project risks, on the basis that the PPP should not transfer all risks to the operator but assign risks to the party best able to manage that risk. Managing risk should be understood to mean (a) reducing the absolute amount of risk, and (b) reducing the cost of bearing unavoidable risk.

In analyses of which party bears the majority of the risks and rewards of ownership from service concessions, the following decomposition of risk has often been used: construction risk, demand risk, third-party revenue risk, design risk, penalties for underperformance, penalties for non-availability, potential changes in relevant costs, obsolescence risk, and residual value risk. The intellectual and business climate of the late 1990s played a role, in conferring confidence in the benefits of financial innovation in general and in its specific application to the management of risk in PPPs.

The ASB's FRS 5A regarded the retention of demand risk (e.g. pupil numbers) and residual value risk (e.g. valuation of the school at the end of the concession period) by the public sector client as generally decisive. The Treasury's TTN1R was worded in such a way that it allowed for a

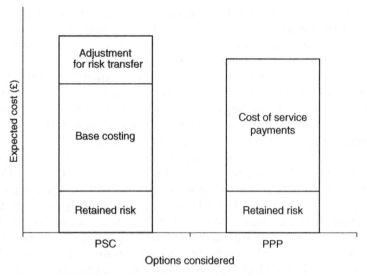

Figure 11.1   Bid evaluation and cost components

wider spectrum of risks to be brought into the assessment. This expansion made it easier to show that the majority of the risks and rewards were transferred to the private sector, and thus to justify off-balance-sheet treatment. Moreover, the PwC (PricewaterhouseCoopers) Method Statement (Treasury Taskforce, 1999b), supposedly an explanation of how to use TTNIR, encouraged quantification, including the use of Monte Carlo simulation methods (Heald, 2003). Quantification has the air of being more objective, although Power (2004) has highlighted the dangers inherent in the urge to quantify the unquantifiable. In the context of a physical asset with a life of perhaps 60 years, held in concession for 30 years, putting large weight on quantified analysis may generate too much confidence in the risk analysis.[9] It also enlarges the scope for consciously or subconsciously manipulating the quantitative analysis to support the desired decision.

Figure 11.1 illustrates how the quantified amount of risk assessed as transferred to the private sector operator will be decisive in terms of whether the project appraisal shows the PPP or the PSC as offering the best VfM. Irrespective of which is chosen, the cost of the risk retained by the public sector client is the same. The base costing of the PSC is shown as less than the PPP's service payments. However, the PPP transfers risks from the public sector client to the operator, and so the valuation placed on these risks is added to the PSC costing as the adjustment for risk transfer. In Figure 11.1, the PPP is shown as considerably cheaper than the PSC. There has been adverse comment with regard to UK PPPs that this adjustment for risk transfer has in many appraisals just been sufficient to make the PPP marginally better VfM than the hypothetical PSC for which public funding is not available.

Control as the criterion for PPP accounting

For those countries with a commitment to link public sector accounting directly to best private sector practice, the rapid adoption of IFRS by the non-US world had clear implications. Sooner or later there would have to be a change of anchor from national GAAP to IFRS.

Private sector accounting standard-setters attach little priority to the reporting needs of the public sector. One example is how the Joint FASB/ IASB Conceptual Framework project relegated consideration of the government and not-for-profit sector until the end of its programme of work. IFRS does not contain a standard on accounting for PPPs. Rather than develop such a standard, IASB referred the topic of operator accounting alone to the International Financial Reporting Interpretations Committee (IFRIC), its own interpretations committee. The result was IFRIC 12 (IASB, 2006), dealing with a more substantive matter than would normally be left to an interpretation. Possible explanations for this route were the workload pressures confronting IASB, the expectation that the IFRIC route would be quicker, and concerns that a standard that addressed only operator accounting would be subjected to criticism.

Control is the criterion adopted in IFRIC 12 for dealing with the private sector operator side of service concessions. This substitution for risks and rewards is, in part, a consequence of how widespread abuse of lease accounting in the private sector (i.e. disguising finance leases as operating leases, and thereby avoiding capitalization) has persuaded IASB to move away from risks and rewards to control in the protracted process of developing a new leasing standard.

The control tests in IFRIC 12 will normally show that the private sector operator does not control the 'infrastructure' subjected to the service concession. Accordingly, the private sector operator will not account for the PPP as property, plant and equipment, but as either an intangible asset or as a financial asset.[10] Given that public policy interest in PPP accounting largely focuses on accounting by the public sector client, this exposition will concentrate on what has become known as the 'mirror-image of IFRIC 12' rather than on IFRIC 12 itself.

The mirror-image of IFRIC 12 fills the gap in IFRS regarding public sector client accounting. Using the argument that, if an IFRIC 12 analysis determines that the PPP should not be on the operator's balance sheet as property, plant and equipment, then symmetry requires that the public sector client should record the PPP assets as property, plant and equipment. This stretching of IFRIC 12 has been accompanied by an elastic definition of what constitutes 'infrastructure', designed to make PPPs fall within the scope of IFRIC 12.

There have been uncertainties about what IPSASB will require, so the exposition will start with the UK requirements that are operational from 2009–10 (Treasury, 2008). Then attention will turn to developments at IPSASB, which are proceeding along a similar path, albeit slowly and with some differences. Subsequently, there will be a brief examination of developments in other jurisdictions.

Mirror-image of IFRIC 12 – the UK version
Figure 11.2 is a more pedagogic version of the flowchart developed by the UK Treasury to explain PPP accounting by UK departments and other public bodies that are subject to the IFRS version of its *Financial Reporting Manual* (Treasury, 2009c). It shows what should be put on the public sector client's balance sheet and what should be charged to its income statement, whether that is called an operating cost statement, an income and expenditure account or a profit and loss account. In the context of service concessions, the client is customarily called the 'grantor'.

The top two boxes of Column 1 contain the two principal questions that have to be answered:

(a)   Does the grantor control or regulate what services the operator must provide with the infrastructure, to whom it must provide them, and at what price?
(b)   Does the grantor control through ownership, beneficial entitlement or otherwise, any significant residual interest in the infrastructure at the end of the service arrangement?

If both these complex questions are answered in the affirmative, then this is a service concession within the scope of IFRIC 12.[11] The property will be reported by the grantor as an asset and related liability (IAS 16).

The dual test therefore depends on control of use and pricing and on control of significant residual interest. In (a), the verb 'control' is supplemented by the verb 'regulate', the implications of which will be discussed in the subsection on IPSASB. In (b), the adjective 'significant' qualifies the role that residual interest will play in the determination of accounting treatment. If residual interest is not significant, accounting treatment would depend on (a) alone.[12] The control approach uses the term 'residual interest' (e.g. who determines what happens to the asset at the end of the concession period), whereas the displaced risks and rewards approach considered 'residual value' (one of the categories of risks to be considered

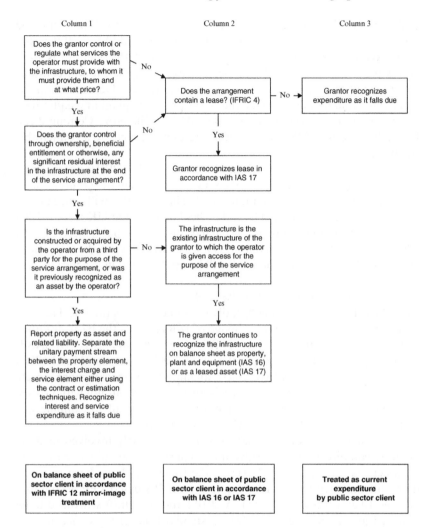

Column 1   Column 2   Column 3

Does the grantor control or regulate what services the operator must provide with the infrastructure, to whom it must provide them and at what price?

No → Does the arrangement contain a lease? (IFRIC 4) — No → Grantor recognizes expenditure as it falls due

Yes

Does the grantor control through ownership, beneficial entitlement or otherwise, any significant residual interest in the infrastructure at the end of the service arrangement?

No

Yes → Grantor recognizes lease in accordance with IAS 17

Yes

Is the infrastructure constructed or acquired by the operator from a third party for the purpose of the service arrangement, or was it previously recognized as an asset by the operator?

No → The infrastructure is the existing infrastructure of the grantor to which the operator is given access for the purpose of the service arrangement

Yes

Yes

Report property as asset and related liability. Separate the unitary payment stream between the property element, the interest charge and service element either using the contract or estimation techniques. Recognize interest and service expenditure as it falls due

The grantor continues to recognize the infrastructure on balance sheet as property, plant and equipment (IAS 16) or as a leased asset (IAS 17)

On balance sheet of public sector client in accordance with IFRIC 12 mirror-image treatment

On balance sheet of public sector client in accordance with IAS 16 or IAS 17

Treated as current expenditure by public sector client

Source: Adapted from Treasury (2008).

Figure 11.2   *UK Treasury flowchart for public sector PPP client under IFRIC 12*

when assessing which party enjoys the majority of risks and rewards of ownership).

Column 2 deals with those cases where the grantor does not control pricing or a significant residual interest (where such exists). This PPP is not a service concession. Using IFRIC 4, the arrangement must be tested to determine whether it contains a lease. If so, the asset will be accounted for in accordance with IASB's (2003b) leasing standard IAS 17. If the asset is the existing infrastructure of the grantor, to which the operator is given access for the purpose of the service arrangement, then it will continue to be recognized on the balance sheet of the grantor. Depending on the facts, this capitalization would either be as property, plant and equipment under IAS 16 or as leased assets under IAS 17. Therefore Column 2 can lead, albeit along a different channel of accounting logic, to a comparable treatment to Column 1.

Column 3 completes the analysis of Figure 11.2. If a PPP is not a service concession and moreover does not contain a lease, then the grantor recognizes the unitary payment as it falls due.[13] Therefore this will be treated as current public expenditure. The widely held belief in the UK is that IFRS will bring almost all PPPs on to the balance sheet of the public sector client, whether as a service concession or as a lease. In other words, Columns 1 and 2 will dominate and Column 3 will be rarely found in practice.

Mirror-image of IFRIC 12 – the IPSASB version
The IPSASB is moving along broadly the same track as the UK Treasury in terms of adopting the mirror-image of IFRIC 12 as the basis of public sector client accounting under IFRS. The February 2010 (IPSASB, 2010) Exposure Draft incorporates modifications to the March 2008 Consultation Paper (IPSASB, 2008), aligning its proposals more closely with IFRIC 12 and the UK Treasury's mirror-image, but not with GASB. Notwithstanding these changes of position, it is useful to examine key issues raised by the March 2008 Consultation Paper.

Given that there is an overlap of personnel closely involved in these matters, combined with the substantive considerations discussed above, alignment is unsurprising. However, the timetables have been substantially different, with the UK going live on IFRS-based PPP accounting in 2009–10 and IPSASB's February 2010 Exposure Draft scheduled to be followed at a later date by an IPSAS standard on service concessions.[14] Clearly the operating environment of IPSASB as a global accounting standard-setter is different from that facing the UK Treasury, in particular as FRAB was strongly supportive and opposition from some spending departments could therefore be brushed aside. It is difficult for those outside the IPSASB process, and that includes the present authors, to differentiate the effects of due process considerations, genuine technical difficulties and delaying tactics.

First, IPSASB's (2008) Consultation Paper on service concessions included flowcharts broadly consistent with Figure 11.2. The difference that attracted much criticism in the consultation responses was the dropping of 'significant' from 'significant residual interest' (the IFRIC 12 wording) in the second half of the dual test. If a residual interest controlled by the grantor exists but is not significant, then a PPP could be determined not to be a service concession on the basis of an irrelevant consideration.

Generally, the length of a concession is substantially less than the forecast economic life of an asset; figures such as 30 years and 60 years, respectively, are often used. Given the pace of change of modes of public service delivery, it is possible that the economic life of a facility (e.g. hospital, school or prison) might turn out to be substantially less than its physical life. Although this brings uncertainty as to residual value (risks and rewards), it does not directly affect control of residual interest. A possible loophole (i.e. structure the contract so that residual interest is not significant) has been closed by the Exposure Draft returning to the IFRIC 12 wording. Given the history of manipulation of PPP accounting under risks and rewards, allowing control of residual interest that is not significant to determine accounting treatment might have become a vulnerability of the control-based standard. A PPP judged, for this reason, not to be a service concession might then fail the leasing test – given the acknowledged weaknesses of the risks and rewards-based IAS 17 – and therefore be off the balance sheet of the public sector client.

Second, there are interconnected questions about the scope of service concessions:

(a)   Is a service concession necessarily public-to-private, thereby requiring specification of which entities are public?

(b)   Which economic activities are included within the definition of 'infrastructure' and 'public services', and does the definition of a service concession extend beyond tolled and untolled services to the public to include activities which support front-line service delivery?

(c)   In the first part of the dual test, does 'regulate' function as a synonym for control or does it extend the coverage of the mirror-image of IFRIC 12?

Many of the practical difficulties arise because of the patchwork nature of accounting standard-setting for service concessions. If IASB had developed a standard for service concessions, it would have been less likely that only operator accounting would have been addressed. If IFRIC had simultaneously addressed both client and operator accounting, it seems likely that this would have been developed on a sector-neutral basis.

Logically there is no reason why service concessions are necessarily public-to-private.[15] If either path had been followed, then questions (a) and (b) would have been answered. The traditional notion of infrastructure, in relation to the physical networks that underpin the functioning of an economy, would not have been stretched to include almost any asset – office blocks and tanks included – that contributes to the production of a public service. Given the exclusively private sector priorities of IASB, those responsible for public sector accounting standard-setting have to respond in messy ways, working on the basis that service concessions are necessarily public-to-private and having to stretch the concept of infrastructure beyond its credible limits.

Third, in relation to question (c), does the insertion of 'regulate' extend 'control' and therefore the coverage of a standard based on the mirror-image of IFRIC 12? 'Control' is a concept that has caused great difficulties for private sector accounting standard-setters, both in terms of defining it and devising criteria for establishing its existence.[16] These difficulties are greatly magnified in the public sector, in which context 'control' has many ambiguities. Given the ultimate authority of government, with its monopoly of legitimate violence, almost no activity or entity within its jurisdiction is outside the potential scope of government action.

'Control' is straightforwardly present in core government, but more subtle in public entities that have been deliberately distanced from core government (e.g. various forms of agency) or are subject to their own forms of democratic legitimacy (e.g. state and local governments). If accounting depends on the application of specified control indicators, other mechanisms can be substituted. There is a vast political science literature on the complexities and ambiguities of control in the public sector, of which a seminal collection is Kaufmann et al. (1986). Around the edges of the public sector, there are many bodies with private sector status, regarding which there can be disputes about whether control according to IAS 27 (IASB, 2003c) does exist.

If 'control' is a difficult term to operationalize, then the introduction of 'regulate' greatly increases those difficulties. With its remit restricted to the operator side, IFRIC did not follow through the implications for the public sector client of the 'control or regulate' wording. This poses less of a problem in the context of national regulation of government accounting, in which context there are shared understandings of institutional arrangements, than it does for IPSASB. 'Regulate' introduces ambiguity, not least because governments regulate almost everything, not just 'inside government' (Hood et al., 1998), but they also regulate the private sector in ways that go beyond the general regulation of the market economy. For example, through various mechanisms governments across the world have long intervened in the pricing policies of public utilities, whatever their ownership status. In the Exposure Draft, IPSASB (2010, para. AG 8) narrows the meaning of 'regulate' by stipulating that this refers specifically to regulation by contract and not by statute. Nevertheless, this seems likely to be an area of future problems, not least because this narrowing is not in IFRIC 12, as applied by the operator.

The GASB's proposed control-based standard

The GASB has responsibility for US state and local government, but not federal, accounting standards. It published an Exposure Draft on PPP accounting in June 2009 (GASB, 2009) which was revised in June 2010 (GASB, 2010). Although based on control, this differed from IPSASB in certain important ways. First, it explicitly covers public-to-public as well as public-to-private arrangements, considering the public 'transferor' (in US terminology) and the public operator. This extension reflects the institutional reality of US state and local governments; inter-jurisdictional collaboration is extensive and there is not the assumption that the operator will be private. The fact that private-to-private arrangements receive no mention is attributable to GASB's remit for state and local governments. Neither FASB, whose responsibilities cover private operator accounting, nor the Federal Accounting Standards Advisory Board, responsible for US federal government accounting, have pronounced on service concessions.

Second, GASB's (2010, para. 4) conception of a service concession arrangement is narrower than that of IPSASB, relating only to arrangements in which the operator is remunerated by third-party payers (e.g. toll bridges or roads). Much of what would be regarded internationally as service concession PPPs is therefore excluded: for example, prisons, untolled roads and schools. The GASB labels PPPs without user charges as 'service and management arrangements' and believes that existing guidance – presumably a reference to leasing standards – is sufficient.

Third, GASB is explicit that, for a PPP to be a service concession arrangement and therefore within the scope of the proposed standard, the transferor must retain a significant residual interest in the asset. In the absence of significant residual interest, GASB (2009) regards the arrangement as a 'privatization, potentially with regulatory oversight'. Moreover, GASB's explanation of paragraph 4(c) of the Exposure Draft states that 'Assessment of whether the residual value is significant should be made based on the service utility of the facility at the end of the arrangement rather than on a fair value notion' (2010, para. 39). This formulation blurs the distinction between residual interest and residual value, seemingly using them interchangeably. Moreover, the rejection of fair value and insistence on service utility seems to make it more likely that a significant residual interest will be identified.

Fourth, the accounting treatment of up-front payments from the operator to the transferor figures prominently in the GASB Exposure Draft.

The GASB (2009, para. 10) originally proposed that the transferor should report the up-front payment or present value of instalment payments as a liability. The revised proposal treats these as a 'deferred inflow of resources' (GASB, 2010, para. 48), to be recognized as revenue in a systematic and rational manner over the term of the arrangement.

Developments in other jurisdictions

It is impossible within the space constraints to be comprehensive, but interesting points of comparison can be drawn with developments in Australia, South Africa and France.

Australia, like New Zealand, pioneered the application of accruals accounting in government. Unlike New Zealand, where PPPs have not been promoted because they were not regarded as good VfM, Australia has made extensive use of PPPs. These are mostly at the state government level, particularly in New South Wales and Victoria: tolled 'hard' infrastructure, such as roads and tunnels, are prominent. The Australian Accounting Standards Board (AASB) is a government body that sets standards for both private and public sectors, on the basis of sector neutrality. On public sector accounting issues, the Heads of Treasuries Accounting and Reporting Advisory Committee (HoTARAC) plays a coordinating role, although formal responsibility and authority rests with the individual treasuries and accounts are audited by the respective auditors general. For example, the New South Wales Treasury (2006) published its version of HoTARAC guidance in June 2006. In the absence of AASB standards to cover all aspects of PPPs, this required compliance with the UK standard FRS 5A. It also provided guidance on topics not explicitly covered by FRS 5A, namely up-front contributions, the residual interest in the infrastructure, and associated leases of land.

Three points are worthy of note. The first is that the application of FRS 5A appears to have produced different results in Australia from those in the UK, though some of this may be attributable to the importance of tolled infrastructure in Australian PPPs. Because the majority of risks and rewards are assessed to fall on the operator, these schemes are generally not on the public sector balance sheet, which does, however, account for an 'emerging asset' (see next section). Second, the AASB has made IFRIC 12 optional for grantors, and the New South Wales Treasury has decided not to adopt ahead of a standard being published by IPSASB. Moreover, HoTARAC's (2008) response to the IPSASB consultation expressed a strong preference for continuing with risks and rewards. In contrast, writing about a prison PPP in Victoria, English and Walker (2004, p. 62) concluded that the 'experience suggests that it is inappropriate to choose accounting treatments on the basis of *ex ante* assessments of risk transfer and risk sharing'. Their criticism is directed at both FRS 5A and its Australian application, on the grounds of being too subjective and of risk profiles changing through the phases of a PPP. Third, it seems likely that Australia will adopt an IPSASB control-based standard when it comes into force, with the effect of bringing on balance sheet at least some of those tolled infrastructure PPPs that are currently off.

South Africa offers a contrast to Australia. In November 2008, the Accounting Standards Board of South Africa issued its guideline on PPP accounting: 'guidelines explain and expand on the principles in the Standards of [Generally Recognized Accounting Practice]. Guidelines do not, however, replace any of these principles' (ASBSA, 2008, p. 5), on the basis that PPPs are sufficiently covered by existing standards. Under the terms of the Public Finance Management Act 1999, these guidelines applied the mirror-image of IFRIC 12 to public sector clients. This move from risks and rewards under leasing standards has brought tolled concession roads on to the balance sheet of the National Roads Agency.

Another indication of the trend to international convergence is the use of IFRIC 12 in France, as required by EU-approved IFRS for listed companies that are concessionees. France has a long history of service concessions, in some cases public–public (as in the case of electricity before the partial privatization of Electricité de France) and in some cases public–private (as in the case of municipalities and privately owned water companies) (Heald, 1995). The development of concession accounting by the Concessions Commission of the Conseil National de la Compatabilité stalled in the mid-1990s, but the move of government accounting to accruals will highlight grantor accounting issues when the operator is using IFRIC 12.

The charge to the income statement
Earlier in the discussion, two key results of accounting treatment decisions were identified: treatment of the PPP in the public sector client's balance sheet (with implications for what is scored as borrowing and debt), and the amount and timing of the charge that goes through the public sector client's income statement (with implications for the time profile of the budget deficit). If the PPP is not a service concession and does not contain a lease, then the full amount of the unitary charge goes through the income statement in the year when that expenditure falls due.

Several complications arise when there is a service concession or a lease, although the discussion here will concentrate on the former. First, irrespective of whether the approach is risks and rewards or control, the unitary charge implicitly consists of (a) the property element, (b) the interest charge, and (c) service expenditure. An early issue in PPP accounting was the separability, or unbundling, of expenditure on non-property-related services that had been packaged into the PPP contract. The motivations for bundling included making the PPP contract more inviting to potential private sector bidders and making it easier to claim that there had been sufficient risk transfer to justify off-balance-sheet treatment for the property assets. Even when non-property services have been unbundled and accounted for separately on relevant standards, there will be property-related services falling in category (c).

Second, the public sector client does not necessarily know the actual capital cost of the property, as the 'special purpose vehicle' (SPV) may refuse to provide this information. Also, the construction member of the consortium may have incurred more or less cost than the price charged to the SPV. Accordingly, there may be estimation involved in the balance-sheet capital value and in the annual depreciation charge to the income statement.

Third, the decomposition of the unitary charge by the public sector client involves complications that can substantially affect the reported numbers. The interest rate to use in the computations is the rate implicit in the PPP contract, or as close to that as possible, because that represents the actual financing charge being paid out by the grantor. If the grantor does not know this rate, the estimated rate chosen should be as close as possible to the unknown implicit rate; otherwise, the financing costs that are disclosed would depart substantially from the unknown actual financing cost. If other rates, such as the grantor's cost of capital, are used, the reported decomposition of the unitary charge will be distorted. Moreover, the partitioning of the unitary charge is also sensitive to the indexation provisions in the contract, as these apply to the entire unitary charge, even though the construction costs have already been incurred and the financing costs will have been locked in at the beginning of the concession.

Fourth, part of the unitary charge is implicitly paying for the unexpired life of property, plant and equipment handed over, often without payment, to the public sector client at the end of the concession period. When the asset is off balance sheet to the client, the unitary charge should be abated in recognition of the building up of the reversionary interest ('emerging asset') as the life of the concession progresses. This involves estimating the residual value of the asset at the reversion date, and then building up this asset according to a predetermined time profile, while also testing for impairment.

Conclusion

This section concentrates on key issues that are important to academic and policy communities interested in PPPs. First, there is a quickening and irreversible shift in accounting regulation from the national to the global sphere. This brings issues of capacity, legitimacy and authority that are particularly difficult with regard to public sector accounting. There will be intensified competition for command of the regulatory space in which accounting standards are established and enforced. Unlike private sector accounting, where the tensions at the top tier are between the USA (FASB) and the rest of the world (IASB), the tensions in public sector accounting may be between IPSASB and national regulatory arrangements in some countries, and – more fundamentally – between financial reporting and national accounts. There will also be conflict between governments and accounting regulators because public finance numbers are always close to politics.

Second, regulatory arbitrage between financial reporting and national accounts may damage transparency about PPP assets and liabilities. In the national accounts, public sector net investment includes conventional procurement and those PPP projects that the national accounts treat as on balance sheet. The UK Treasury (2009a) announced in June 2009 that future spending plans and budgets will be prepared on a national accounts basis. This creates a divergence between spending plans and Estimates and Resource Accounts (both on IFRS and thus using the mirror-image of IFRIC 12), entirely at odds with the Treasury's (2009b) own Alignment project intended to improve comparability. This divergence exploits Eurostat's (2004) lax interpretation of risks and rewards, introducing a new form of arbitrage.[17]

With globalization and the growing importance of fiscal surveillance of countries by international organizations (for example, IMF, OECD and – for EU countries – the European Commission and the European Central Bank), there is emerging a greater interconnectedness between the technical substance of financial reporting and that of national accounting. Given the markedly different governance arrangements, and the hitherto limited contact between accountants and economic statisticians, the separate systems will generate different numbers. Ability to reconcile these different numbers will acquire more importance, especially in connection with sensitive topics such as PPP accounting.

Third, the issue is not just conceptual differences but also the mechanics of application of whichever criterion is in use. FRS 5A, TTN1R and Eurostat (2004) all use risks and rewards, yet generate dramatically different numbers. The lack of symmetry between operator and client accounting is disturbing in the context of financial reporting, even though there is not the formal articulation of sectors as in the national accounts. There is much to be said for the popular intuition that something is amiss when governments can make available new hospitals, prisons and schools without there being accounting recognition of either assets or associated debt. This intuition regarding PPP accounting aligns with the principle of 'substance over form': the accounting should penetrate behind the legal form to identify the economic substance of transactions. There is also a warning that, whereas accountants instinctively want to produce quantified 'objective' evidence, quantification in complex settings is vulnerable to back-working to generate desired answers.

Fourth, without a clearly specified and credible enforcement mechanism, the move to a control-based standard may not resolve the problem. A new generation of PPPs might be design-engineered around the control-based mirror-image of IFRIC 12: for example, writing contracts under which the assets do not revert to the public sector client even though they are integral to continuing public service delivery and the creation of alternative capacity is improbable. A harsh public spending environment in the aftermath of the global financial crisis makes this more likely. Unless these are genuine privatizations (e.g. roads, fully transferred to the private sector), there will be concerns about hidden fiscal risks, inferior VfM and inconsistencies in the national accounts.

Fifth, accounting for PPPs should attempt to convey the economic substance of transactions and relationships so that decisions about asset acquisition and procurement mechanisms are based as far as possible on the best available estimates of costs and benefits. VfM will be damaged if the project appraisal is manipulated to generate the desired accounting treatment, or if the asset is designed to secure a particular accounting treatment. Distorting the accounting so as to privilege off-balance-sheet procurement mechanisms breaches transparency and distorts consideration of intergenerational equity. Moreover, evidence of disreputable accounting practice will damage the image of PPPs and discourage even-handed assessments of their role as an instrument of public procurement.

Notes

1. The views expressed in this chapter are solely those of the authors and should not be attributed to organizations with which they have connections.
2. The PSC is best thought of as the alternative conventionally procured asset against which the PPP project is tested at the appraisal stage. However, it should be stressed that this comparison is often made in the context of knowledge that conventional funding is unavailable, making the PSC hypothetical. The effective choice might reduce to a PPP or no investment (Heald, 2003).
3. The interested reader is referred to the specialist writings of the authors, particularly Heald (2003) and Heald and Georgiou (2009).

4. ESA 95 is the only 'regional' version of the United Nations System of National Accounts (SNA 93) (United Nations Statistical Division, 1993). A revised SNA 2008 (United Nations Statistical Division, 2009) has now been published but not yet implemented, to be followed by a new ESA. At the time of writing, Eurostat (2004) remains the authoritative guidance for EU countries.

5. 'General government' includes central government, subnational governments and social security funds. Public corporations are part of the public sector but outside general government.

6. This explanation simplifies a more complex chain (Heald and Georgiou, 2009).

7. Classifying a contractual arrangement as a service concession rather than a finance lease does not necessarily lead to different accounting treatment, although the accounting logic differs. Under IFRS, IAS 16 (IASB, 2003a) and IFRIC 12 (based on control) apply to service concessions while IAS 17 and IFRIC 4 (IASB, 2004) (based on risks and rewards) apply to leases. IAS 17 (IASB, 2003b, para. 31) requires, *inter alia*, that lessees disclose in the notes the net carrying amount in the balance sheet for each class of asset.

8. According to SSAP 21 (ASC, 1984, para. 16) a lease is treated as a finance lease if the present value of the minimum lease payments (including any initial payment) amounts to 90 per cent of the fair value of the leased asset.

9. The Chicago economist Frank Knight (1885–1972) strongly emphasized the distinction between risk (quantifiable and reducible to a probability distribution) and uncertainty (not quantifiable and reducible) (Phelps, 2009).

10. Under IFRS as opposed to UK GAAP, there is no fixed asset option for the private sector operator. Under UK GAAP, there was a decisive move around 2001–02 away from this to contract debtor accounting for taxation and ability to distribute profit considerations. Under IFRS the private operator may use a financial asset, intangible asset or composite model. The financial asset model, similar to contract debtor accounting, is likely to be adopted. Moreover, PPP projects are delivered through 'special purpose vehicles' (SPVs), which have so far been able to stay on national GAAP, even when the parent companies are listed and required to adopt IFRIC 12 in their IFRS financial statements. For consolidation purposes, SPVs must prepare shadow IFRS accounts but these do not reach the public domain (Austin, 2009).

11. The third box in Column 1 refers to whether an asset is being constructed by or for the operator, or whether the asset was previously recognized by the grantor. In the context of a PPP, this condition is likely to be satisfied if the first two conditions are.

12. This collapsing of the dual condition into condition (a) only is consistent with IFRIC 12: 'Infrastructure used in a public-to-private service concession arrangement for its entire useful life (whole-of-life assets) is within the scope of this Interpretation if the conditions in paragraph 5(a) are met' (IASB, 2006, para. 6).

13. See, however, the discussion of the income statement charge in the next section.

14. The due process of accounting standard-setters normally follows this sequence: Discussion Paper (when the issues are articulated, and alternatives are voiced); Exposure Draft (where what is proposed as a forthcoming standard is declared); and then Standard (the definitive statement).

15. IFRIC 12 (IASB, 2006, para. 5) explicitly restricts itself to 'public-to-private service concession arrangements'. However, this contractual relationship could exist between (a) a retail chain and a property management company, and (b) a municipality and a publicly owned water utility. These arrangements would be outside the scope of IFRIC 12.

16. The current IASB proposals define control of another entity as 'the power to direct the activities of that other entity to generate returns for the reporting entity' (IASB, 2008, para. 10).

17. Whereas IASB seems likely in the medium term to revise IAS 17 on a 'right of use' (i.e. control) basis, the fact that the new SNA 2008 remains on a risks and rewards basis for leases and concessions means that an equivalent change will not be made to the national

accounts. Revision intervals are extremely long: the previous SNAs were in 1978 and 1993.

References

Akitoby, B., R. Hemming and G. Schwartz (2007), 'Public investment and public–private partnerships', *Economic Issues*, **40**, Washington DC: International Monetary Fund.

ASB (1998), *Amendment to FRS 5: Reporting the Substance of Transactions – Private Finance Initiative and Similar Contracts*, London: Accounting Standards Board.

ASBSA (2008), *Guideline on Accounting for Public–Private Partnerships*, Pretoria: Accounting Standards Board of South Africa.

ASC (1984), *SSAP 21: Accounting for Leases and Hire Purchase Contracts*, London: Accounting Standards Committee.

Austin, P. (2009), 'Accounting for PFI projects: impact of IFRS on UK PFI', presented at SMI Conference, 'IFRS – Impact on UK PFI', 26–27 January, mimeo, London: Mazars.

Broadbent, J. and R. Laughlin (2002), 'Accounting choices: technical and political trade-offs and the UK's Private Finance Initiative', *Accounting, Auditing and Accountability Journal*, **15** (5), 622–54.

English, L. and R.G. Walker (2004), 'Risk weighting and accounting choices in public–private partnerships: case study of a failed prison contract', *Australian Accounting Review*, **14** (2), 62–76.

Eurostat (1995), *European System of Accounts – ESA 95*, Luxembourg: Eurostat.

Eurostat (2004), *Long Term Contracts between Government Units and Non-government Partners (Public–Private Partnerships)*, Luxembourg: Eurostat.

GASB (2009), *Exposure Draft: Proposed Statement of the Governmental Accounting Standards Board – Accounting and Financial Reporting for Service Concession Arrangements*, Norwalk, CT: Governmental Accounting Standards Board.

GASB (2010), *Exposure Draft (Revised): Proposed Statement of the Governmental Accounting Standards Board – Accounting and Financial Reporting for Service Concession Arrangements*, Norwalk, CT: Governmental Accounting Standards Board.

Giles, C., G. Parker and P. Jenkins (2009), 'Living wills to be forced on banks', *Financial Times*, 15 September.

Heald, D.A. (1995), 'An evaluation of French concession accounting', *European Accounting Review*, **4** (2), 325–49.

Heald, D.A. (2003), 'Value for money tests and accounting treatment in PFI schemes', *Accounting, Auditing & Accountability Journal*, **16** (3), 342–71.

Heald, D.A. and G. Georgiou (2009), 'The substance of accounting for public–private partnerships', paper presented at the 12th Biennial Comparative Governmental Accounting Conference, 28–29 May, Modena and Reggio Emilia University, Italy (forthcoming, in a revised version, *Financial Accountability and Management*, 2011).

Hodges, R. and H. Mellett (2002), 'Investigating accounting standard setting: accounting for the United Kingdom's Private Finance Initiative', *Accounting Forum*, **26** (2), 126–51.

Hood, C., C. Scott, O. James, G. Jones and T. Travers (1998), *Regulation inside Government: Waste-watchers, Quality Police and Sleaze-busters*, Oxford: Oxford University Press.

HoTARAC (2008), *Comments Regarding ITC 16 Service Concession Arrangements*, mimeo, Hobart, Tasmania: Department of Treasury and Finance.

IASB (2003a), *IAS 16: Property, Plant and Equipment*, London: International Accounting Standards Board (updated).

IASB (2003b), *IAS 17: Leases*, London: International Accounting Standards Board (updated).

IASB (2003c), *IAS 27: Consolidated and Separate Financial Statements*, London: International Accounting Standards Board (updated).

IASB (2004), *IFRIC 4: Determining Whether an Arrangement Contains a Lease*, London: International Accounting Standards Board (updated).

IASB (2006), *IFRIC 12: Service Concession Arrangements*, London: International Accounting Standards Board (updated).

IASB (2008), *Exposure Draft: Leases*, London: International Accounting Standards Board.

IASB (2010), *Exposure Draft: Leases*, London: International Accounting Standards Board.

IPSASB (2008), *Proposed International Public Sector Accounting Standard – Service Concession Arrangements: Grantor, Exposure Draft 43*, New York: International Federation of Accountants.

IPSASB (2010), *Accounting and Financial Reporting for Service Concession Arrangements – Exposure Draft*, New York: International Federation of Accountants.

Kaufmann, F.X., G. Majone and V. Ostrom (eds) (1986), *Guidance, Control and Evaluation in the Public Sector*, Berlin: de Gruyter.

Mazey, S.P. and J. Richardson (2006), 'Interest groups and EU policy-making: organisational logic and venue shopping', in J. Richardson (ed.), *European Union Power and Policy-Making*, 3rd edn, London: Routledge, pp. 247–68.

New South Wales Treasury (2006), *Accounting Policy: Accounting for Privately Financed Projects*, Sydney, Office of Financial Management, Policy & Guidelines Paper TPP 06-8, mimeo.

Phelps, E. (2009), 'Uncertainty bedevils the best system', in *The Future of Capitalism – The Big Debate, Financial Times*, 12 May supplement.

Power, M. (2004), 'Counting, control and calculation: reflections on measuring and management', *Human Relations*, **57** (6), 765–83.

Savage, J.D. (2005), *Making the EMU: The Politics of Budgetary Surveillance and the Enforcement of Maastricht*, Oxford: Oxford University Press.

Schwartz, G., A. Corbacho and K. Funke (2008), *Public Investment and Public–Private Partnerships: Addressing Infrastructure Challenges and Managing Fiscal Risks*, Basingstoke: Palgrave Macmillan.

Treasury (2008), *Clarifying Text on Accounting for PPP Arrangements, including PFI, under IFRS*, Financial Reporting Advisory Board Paper, FRAB (94) 04, London: HM Treasury.

Treasury (2009a), *Consolidated Budgeting Guidance from 2009–10 (IFRS updated)*, London: HM Treasury.

Treasury (2009b), *Alignment (Clear Line of Sight) Project*, Cm 7567, London: Stationery Office.

Treasury (2009c), *Financial Reporting Manual 2009–10*, London: HM Treasury.

Treasury Taskforce (1999a), *How to Account for PFI Transactions*, Technical Note No. 1 (Revised), London: Office of Government Commerce.

Treasury Taskforce (1999b), *Method Statement for Implementing Technical Note No. 1 (Revised) 'How to Account for PFI Transactions'*, mimeo, London.

United Nations Statistical Division (1993), *System of National Accounts 93*, New York: United Nations.

United Nations Statistical Division (2009), *System of National Accounts 2008*, New York: United Nations.

12 Risk management
Rui Sousa Monteiro

The conventional approach to risk in PPPs, born of project finance, suffers from some naïvety, because it disregards two main characteristics of this kind of contractual relationship:

- PPPs present special characteristics due to their link to public service;
- the public partner has a much higher (almost infinite) ability to absorb risk, while the private partner has limited legal and financial responsibility.

In addition, the conventional approach disregards two important additional institutional aspects:

- risk assessment depends on agents' expectations regarding not only conventionally assessed risks, but also the capacity of the public partner to manage the contract, and the stability of the institutional environment of the project;
- risk perception changes with the increasing use of PPP contracts, changing the risks themselves.

The consequences of these factors for the efficiency and fiscal sustainability of PPP projects are wide-ranging. This will be the central argument put forward in this chapter. In pursuing this argument, the first section will review the conventional risk management for PPP projects. The next section presents a public-choice context that focuses on strategic moves by some players. The third section briefly studies the sources of uncertainty and risk in infrastructure projects. The fourth section discusses the role of risk transfer and risk creation in PPPs. The next section discusses the main risks in PPP projects, using a non-naïve approach. Finally, the last section addresses risk management in a non-naïve context and proposes some institutional mechanisms for addressing PPP risks, and for promoting efficiency and fiscal sustainability.

Conventional risk management in PPP projects

Infrastructure projects (and mainly public infrastructure projects) are often affected by significant risks, leading to large cost overruns and completion delays, as well as shortfalls in revenue (see Flyvbjerg, 2003; Flyvbjerg et al., 2004). Bundling design and construction (i.e. procuring design–build contracts) is no solution, as it creates incentives for 'cutting corners', reducing the quality of the infrastructure and its expected lifespan. Bundling construction and maintenance allows contractors to link defaults to design errors and so obtain compensation for increased costs. Bundling design, construction and maintenance (and often the operation of the infrastructure, or the delivery of several services using the infrastructure) creates powerful incentives for efficient delivery of infrastructure, linking payment to the performance of infrastructure or to the effective delivery of those services.

Risk is defined as uncertainty of outcome, whether positive opportunity or negative threat, of actions and events. In the project management approach, a risk is an event that may or may not occur and can lead to cost overruns, delays in project completion, or failure to satisfy some project requirements. In economics and in finance, risk has a slightly different meaning, being considered as having an upside and a downside: a party facing risk suffers from negative events, but may also benefit from positive events. In this way, the party will have higher incentives for putting effort into preventing negative outcomes.

Risk analysis

PPP risk analysis follows the model developed in the past 30 years for project finance schemes, initially developed for private projects and then adapted to PPPs. During the tender process, competitive pressure and systematic due diligence is supposed to induce a risk allocation not far from the theoretical optimum. In concept, risks are allocated to the party best able to manage them. The due diligence process itself – the set of reviews (financial, commercial, legal, even environmental) made on behalf of an investor or financing party, aiming at allowing him to deliver an informed decision – gives very strong rationality characteristics to project finance schemes.

PPPs, long term and risk transfer

In order to induce efficient delivery of infrastructural services, we do not procure the infrastructure directly, but the services (public service directly offered to the end-users, or the availability of infrastructure offered to the public administration) delivered by the infrastructure. PPPs are long-term contracts between a public entity and a private entity for the provision of services; usually they include the construction or acquisition of infrastructure or assets with a long economic life. (This PPP definition encompasses concession contracts and even some projects that are called privatization but, being related to public services, share many characteristics and risks of those formally called PPPs.)

Without long-life assets there is no rationale for a long-term contract. Without a long-term contract, public authorities would not be able to get an infrastructure built by a private entity if that infrastructure is specific (and so not easily adaptable to alternative uses).

The efficiency of a PPP contract depends on the effective transfer of some risks to the private partner. Private entities are efficient in the management of a project if they have money at stake, and if they face risks that they can manage. PPP efficiency implies committing private capital to the management of a public project. But private management efficiency will only arise if they face risks: a private manager protected from risks will only manage rents.

In general, PPPs are perceived as providing effectiveness in the provision of good-quality infrastructure and services. Projects tend to be completed on schedule and on budget. Compared to the track record of infrastructure projects, this outcome is welcome. But efficiency is much more than effectiveness: it implies an optimized allocation of production factors (allocative efficiency) and an optimized design and sizing of the project.

Risk transfer and whole-life costing
The private partner in a PPP long-term contract will be forced to design an infrastructure and manage a project using a whole-life costing approach. The efficient design of the infrastructure will depend on the credible expectation that the private partner will assume the long-term risks. PPP procurement now benefits from a large volume of recommendations and best practice, presented in several manuals (Partnerships Victoria, 2001; CBI, 2006; Treasury, 2006a, 2006b, 2007; and 4ps, 2007).

A public-choice approach to PPPs
Taking a public-choice perspective, we may understand the importance of PPPs in terms of the particular interests of several agents, not the public interest. A very special interest is the politicians' interest. Nordhaus (1975), for example, takes a political-cycle approach, assumes myopic voters, and sees politicians as having no long-term view and as anxious to maximize short term re-election prospects. The bureaucrat presents a utility that is a function of both the public interest and his own personal interest, and the weight of public interest in this utility function is dependent on the institutional incentives he faces.

The agents

Politicians, bureaucrats, entrepreneurs and consultants are the main agents. The politicians in charge of government may be opportunistic (looking for the benefits they can get from being in power) or individuals with a long-run view and willingness to work for the benefit of the population, but who, having no statesperson profile and not enough political culture, perceive voters as short-memory myopic people, and so cannot stop considering the coming elections (and not the future of the country) as the main goal. Immersed in a political culture that disregards the long term (even everything that will happen beyond the coming elections), they try to maximize what they can 'do' while they are in power.

The bureaucrats, the higher civil servants and public administrators, may face a career path in the public administration, half-dependent on the fulfilment of their public service mission, half-dependent on the goodwill of the politicians whom they are also supposed to serve; but they know that, having the appropriate technical ability, and mainly having no reputation of troublemakers among the entrepreneurs with whom they deal, they may have an alternative future in a private firm; they may have ethical concerns, or not (and then simply fulfil their managerial roles).

The entrepreneurs are profit-maximizers: they organize production factors in order to explore market (or non-market) opportunities and generate profits; they may also have ethical concerns, or not (and then simply fulfil their managerial roles).

The external consultants are experts, supposed to provide informed opinion to their clients, but are often invited (and gladly accept) to draw public policies and to implement them, receiving orders from the politicians in charge, or from the bureaucrats who serve the politicians; they may also have ethical concerns, or not (and then simply act as profit-maximizers).

The main 'problem'

The agents in charge of power – the politicians – know that the 'rules of the game' constrain their ability to 'show' work done, because they face budgetary constraints each year. In their anxiety to maximize the probability of winning the coming election, they want to launch all public projects that present benefits for the users, even without financial resources to do so. Deficit and debt constraints (being explicit or implicit, resulting from international commitments or as a consequence of past budgetary indiscipline) cap the public expenditure for each year.

Interministerial competition for scarce budgetary resources (coming from taxes or from additional debt) creates healthy incentives. Large projects need to be presented to the Finance Ministry and to Parliament, and in this process there is some assessment of costs and benefits. Therefore projects that do not present net benefits tend to be scrapped, and the surviving ones tend to be ordered, prioritized, with the best of them funded from the public budget.

From the individual viewpoint of a line minister, of each politician in power, even of the prime minister, the result is not satisfactory: they always want to deliver more projects.

The PPP 'solution'

PPP contracts may be presented (and quite often are actually presented) as a way to overcome budgetary constraints, delivering more projects with the same financial resources available in the long term. The emphasis is on the word 'deliver', on the schedule for delivering projects. In the absence of efficiency gains the number of public projects, in the long term, cannot be higher with PPPs than without, given the same financial resources; but in the short term it can be higher by transferring costs to future generations. From a Nordhausian viewpoint, PPPs adjust very well to the political cycle because they allow for a short-term increase in the delivery of infrastructure and public services, transferring their costs to the following cycle. Myopic voters will not care about the transfer of costs from the current generation to future generations.

Following a Nordhausian approach, we may say that PPPs reinforce the political cycle in the short run, and that this reinforcement will decline in the subsequent cycles, because the PPP whole-life costing approach tends simultaneously to smooth the business cycle and the link between the political cycle and the business cycle. If public projects delivered as PPPs present positive net benefits (as we should expect from a public project selected by politicians acting on behalf of the public), the transfer of costs into the future would not be a real problem, because in that future, when taxpayers start paying for the projects, they will also benefit from them, and benefits will be higher than costs.

A public-choice problem

In the public-choice context described above, the real problem is the lack of accountability induced by PPPs. In a framework of short-term budgetary analysis, year by year, incumbent politicians must obtain from Parliament authorization for spending up to a certain amount on a set of projects. But PPPs do not generate public expenditure in the first years (because typically payments start only after the completion of the infrastructure, several years after the go-ahead decision, and several years after contract close).

So, in countries lacking effective multi-annual budgetary appropriations, lacking a strong control of large public projects by the Treasury and Parliament (or some other entities responsible for public expenditure health), and lacking an effective specific (and strict) framework for the appraisal of PPP projects, politicians may launch infrastructure and public service projects with no parliamentary scrutiny (and so with no scrutiny by the media and the voters/taxpayers). Even worse: not subject to constraints, and not subject to project competition, politicians may reduce their concerns with project assessment and assume that more important than selecting the best projects is delivering the maximum number of projects.

Bureaucrats – called to present projects, and to help select and procure them – perceiving the lack of political accountability, and aware that private partners will deliver the projects (not the bureaucrats), also reduce their worries and accept to continue with incompletely researched projects. In the end, the public administration starts procuring badly prepared projects, without knowing if they deliver positive net (economic or social) benefits.

However, those incompletely researched projects need to be converted into PPP projects. That is the role of external consultants, hired in order to prepare procurement in the shortest amount of time. Effective competition is not the highest priority in this context. The lack of PPP expertise in the public administration tends to transfer project leadership from bureaucrats to external consultants, in a clear conflict of interest, as the main consulting firms work also for the private entities that will bid for those PPP contracts, albeit in different moments or for different projects.

Private firms are then invited to deliver public projects, sometimes presenting doubtful public interest. But, having a client willing to pay (in the future, but credibly) for those projects, they do not miss the opportunity. If forced to accept too many risks, they simply increase the risk premium accordingly. They try to contain risks and exploit errors and omissions in tender documents for later use in shifting risks back to the public sector. Public procurement, in practice led by external consultants not keen to expose their own failures in preparing the tender documents, is focused on rapid contract close, not on competition or efficiency, and so avoids cost-assessment or risk-assessment activities.

After contract close, private providers will be in charge of delivering infrastructure and services. And some public entity will be formally responsible for managing the contract. When problems surface, there will always be external consultants willing to help public authorities. Projects are implemented, but not in a cost-efficient way.

In the context described above, even if no agent behaves in an illegal way, the public interest suffers. Politicians obtain what they want (more public projects), entrepreneurs and external consultants are the main beneficiaries, bureaucrats are saddled with problems for their remaining working life, and citizens/taxpayers (the current ones and, most of all, the future ones) get non-optimized infrastructures and public services and harder expenditure constraints in the future, given the need to pay PPP concessionaires for a long period.

By substituting private finance for public debt, governments may possibly be improving the maintenance of infrastructure or the management of public services, but are also – in this public-choice context – substituting non-transparent project selection for open appropriation and budgeting of projects. In the end, the quality of public projects and the mix of public services may be affected.

A more complex context

If we make a small change to the above public-choice context, we can obtain more disturbing results: just consider, for each type of player, a sub-type consisting of corrupt agents, those willing to pay or receive in order to change public decisions on behalf of some private interest. As Stiglitz (2002, p. 58) says that corrupt decision-makers 'have realized that privatization meant that they no longer needed to be limited to annual profit skimming [and that] by selling a government enterprise at below market price, they could get a significant chunk of the asset value for themselves, rather than leaving it for subsequent office holders', we may say that inefficient PPP procurement (and inefficient contract management) may simply be a way for corrupt decision-makers to get a large chunk of future government revenue. There will be concerted action by some private firms, politicians and bureaucrats, aiming at creating contractual inefficiencies or contract-management inefficiencies that allow for rent collection later in time. As a matter of fact, they do not need to affect procurement; they need only to induce chance (certain types of change, politically induced, or politically managed) or to degrade contract management – so they can extract rents from PPP projects that were more efficiently managed in the past by corrupting the institutional framework for managing contracts and change.

Sources of risk in infrastructure projects

Uncertainty affects infrastructure projects in many ways. There is uncertainty regarding the current conditions for project development (cost, geology, environmental impact, range of possible technical solutions) and uncertainty regarding the future (concerning the national and international business environment, demographics, technology, politics etc.). And there is uncertainty related to informational asymmetry between the players: uncertainty, at the procurement phase and at each moment of contract life, regarding the efficiency of the other player (a hidden characteristic, related to the possibility of getting the least possible cost and maximal benefits from the project); and uncertainty regarding the effort delivered by the players (a hidden action). The hidden characteristic creates concerns regarding adverse selection during the tender; the hidden action creates concerns regarding moral hazard and strategic behaviour by players.

In uncertainty regarding the future environment, we should include the public partner's uncertainty regarding its own ability to manage the PPP contract and to regulate its environment in order to maximize social welfare.

Adverse selection
The uncertainty regarding project costs is typically solved through the use of competitive tender; the public authority may (and should) compute a public sector comparator (PSC) during project assessment and selection, and use it as an upper bound on contracting costs. Tender competitiveness depends critically on the likelihood of opportunistic contract renegotiation: if bidders have an expectation of renegotiating the contract (during the final stages of tender or after contract close) in order to increase prices or soften its requirements, the public authority may have an inefficient bidder winning the contract through the presentation of prices below its costs.

Consider several firms bidding for a project. Each firm's bid should be based on its best estimate for the (net) cost of the project (and on the competitors' costs), plus a risk premium reflecting the possible changes in the project environment. Subject to competitive pressure, we should expect the winner to be the most efficient firm. But two types of competitors may present an advantage in the tender:

- bidders that are not good at evaluating costs and risks – the 'fools'; and
- bidders that assign a low probability of occurrence to costly scenarios, because they are willing to influence public policy in order to protect themselves from those scenarios – and among them we single out the corrupt agents, those that, by experience and by lack of integrity, know that they can influence public decision beyond legal boundaries.

Those two types of bidders (the fools and the corrupt) may benefit from an advantage during tender, because they can compensate for production inefficiency with lower risk, and so present bids lower than efficient firms' bids.

Moral hazard

The uncertainty regarding the effort delivered by the private partner is unavoidable, as the project will be implemented by that partner and the public authority will be forced to stay away from project management in order to avoid being accused of disturbing project performance. So the public authority will rely mainly on incentive mechanisms in the framework of a principal–agent relationship. Those mechanisms, including the rewards and penalties schemes, should align the private partner's interest with the public interest. For instance, reward rules should always be perceived as incentive schemes, aimed at influencing behaviour, and not just at paying services. Penalties (addressing mainly the deviations from the intended outcome, and not simply deviations from formal non-compliance) should also be perceived as incentive schemes; in many cases this implies non-proportionality, and sometimes prohibitive penalties should be applied.

Contractual clauses are important, but also the contract-management institutional design, which is supposed to enforce those clauses and prevent pernicious strategic behaviour by private partners.

Optimal mechanism design

Both adverse selection and moral hazard can be mitigated through the design of an incentive mechanism that includes the PPP contract and an institutional framework that provides efficiency in project selection, procurement and contract management. This should also be subject to a general requirement of accountability (and so involving not only bureaucrats but also politicians, not only government but also Parliament, the media and the public). In this framework, bidders and private partners will create their expectations on usual uncertainty factors but also on future contract management and change management. Figure 12.1 presents the global mechanism for PPP efficiency as a mechanism much larger than the simple tender mechanism. During procurement and during the life of the contract, efficiency will depend critically on the expectations regarding possible changes and the ability of both partners to manage the partnership in the context of change.

There is always a significant degree of subjectivity in risk assessment, even when a party has relevant empirical or technological information. The public authority faces informational problems that prevent the assignment of probabilities in frequency or propensity terms – it has scarce information, but mainly it suffers from an optimism bias that induces it to consider probability distributions that (first-order) stochastically dominate (in the Hirschleifer and Riley, 1992 sense) the real distribution, leading to underestimated costs and overestimated revenues. Therefore

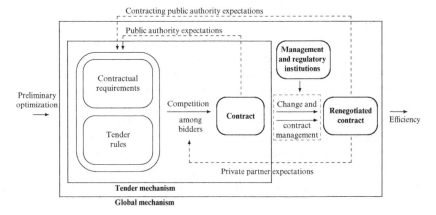

Figure 12.1   Global mechanisms influencing PPP efficiency

inviting private bidders to bid for a long-term project, if expectations are correct and bidders are locked into a credible contractual relationship, delivers a supposedly non-biased estimate.

The degree of confidence in that estimate depends on the expected credibility of commitments by both parties. The private party's commitment relies on the significant amount of private capital (provided by them and by their financing entities) at stake in the project. Due diligence by financing entities has a special role here because that capital is hostage capital.

The commitment of the public authority depends on the institutional mechanisms that are implemented, for example, contract manager teams and contract-management rules, PPP knowledge centres, accountability mechanisms, finance ministry overseeing, access to information by Parliament and media.

Decision-making is usually not based directly on expected utility, but on risk-capping and mainly on bounding the downside of risk. Contract design aims at creating incentives, but also at eliminating or bounding public sector risks, or at least extreme risks.

Some deficiencies of traditional risk analysis
Our view on uncertainty is strongly based on independent events. Since the first scientific studies on probability by Girolamo Cardano (the first to use binomial coefficients and combinatorial calculus to compute probabilities) and Abraham de Moivre (the first to obtain the now-called Gauss curve as the limit for a sequence of binomial coefficients), independent and non-truncated density functions were used for risk analysis. The central-limit theorem – stating that an infinite sum of independent and

identical distributed random variables (even non-symmetrical variables) has a Gaussian distribution – reinforced the biased perception that, even in the context of strong cost-containment efforts, aggregate risks may be treated as symmetrical and non-truncated.

In the PPP case, the usual assumptions of risk symmetry or Gaussian distribution (bell-shaped) fail. First, they fail because design, construction and maintenance risks are inherently asymmetrical and strongly correlated, as they depend on the efficiency of the PPP concessionaire and its contractor; second, because firms benefit from limited liability; third, because the public authority bears *force majeure* risks, not the private partners; and last, but not least, because the public sector is politically responsible for the provision of public infrastructure and public services, and so major risks disturbing the public service turn out to be political risks that governments must face (and not business risks that the private operator must face).

So the usual risk simulations not only disregard project characteristics, but also typically fail to consider possible perverse strategic behaviour by private partners. Therefore, even using the same risk matrix, public and private partners have inherently different risk expectations. The public sector may have a naïve view of risk, whereas private, profit-motivated risk perception will be more realistic. Different risk expectations create – through adverse selection and moral hazard – new risks for public authorities. Gigerenzer (2002) addresses similar risk perception problems in other contexts; the author's experience, in many developed and developing countries, shows that these problems are pervasive in infrastructure procurement and deserve research.

Risk, uncertainty and subjectivity
Almost one century ago, the influential Chicago economist Frank Knight (1921) distinguished between risk and uncertainty: 'risk' was randomness that we may quantify in an objective way, i.e. based on objective probabilities (such as those obtained from empirical frequencies), whereas 'uncertainty' would correspond to subjective probabilities. The Knightian distinction between uncertainty and risk lost relevance after the Second World War, being replaced by a formal definition of risk based on subjective probability. In their survey on uncertainty and information, Hirschleifer and Riley (1992, p. 9) assume that 'each person is able to represent his beliefs as to the likelihood of the different states of the world (for example, as to whether Nature will choose rain or shine) by a "subjective" probability distribution'. In economics, and especially in microeconomics, uncertainty problems are usually modelled on the basis of a set of actions that agents may choose from, a set of states that nature may select, an

outcome function measuring the consequences of actions and states, a probability function, and a utility function evaluating the different possible outcomes. The probability function (or probability density function, in other cases) is implicitly or explicitly subjective, but always quantified. According to Hirschleifer and Riley (1992, p. 7):

> The approach here does not allow for the psychological sensations of vagueness or confusion that people often suffer in facing situations with uncertain (risky) outcomes. In our model the individual is neither vague nor confused. While recognizing that his knowledge is imperfect, so that he cannot be sure which state of the world will occur, he nevertheless can assign exact numerical probabilities representing his degree of belief as to the likelihood of each possible state. Our excuse for not picturing vagueness or confusion is that we are trying to model economics, not psychology . . . The ultimate justification . . . for theories of decision under uncertainty, is the ability of such models to help us understand and predict behavior.

In the infrastructure context, we associate risk with a probability distribution on an event, typically obtained from the empirical evidence, but including also the evaluation, by each agent, of its own ability to influence adverse events, and its expectations on the characteristics and behaviour of the other players (the other bidders, and the public authority). So risk will be the equilibrium probability distribution resulting from the equilibrium of the game between the several private players (bidders) and the contracting public authority. When there is a policy change, or a change in contract-management capacity, or the expectation of a policy change or a capacity change, there will be a change in the equilibrium risk profile. When some entity assumes a risk, it is assuming the consequences of that probability distribution as perceived by that entity.

Expected utility and idiosyncrasy
Decision-making under uncertainty is usually modelled on the basis of expected utility. In the PPP world, all agents act according to expected utility, but simultaneously try to protect themselves against extreme events and against strategic moves, so they try to affect the probability of occurrence of some events.

Frank Knight presented a concept that is relevant for us today: the agent's trust in his probability estimates, i.e. 'his estimate of the chance that his estimates are correct'. Consider a risky situation A, and an agent that, based on empirical frequencies, assigns a probability 0.5 to each possible event (Yes or No). And consider a risky situation B, similar to A, but where the agent has no empirical evidence, albeit assigning equal probability to the events, Yes and No (i.e. 0.5 to each one). Naturally, the agent's trust in his estimates regarding A is higher than trust regarding estimates on *B*, regardless of probabilities being the same. (Due to this difference, the agent would be less willing to bet on *B* estimates than on *A*.) This concept is similar to the Daniel Ellsberg (2001) paradox illustrating the distinction between the expected value of a draw and the probability of obtaining a specific result in a single draw. In the infrastructure case, even having a large volume of empirical data on infrastructure costs or on the costs of a specific contractor, each project is a specific project, presenting its own idiosyncrasies. The private partner (the special purpose vehicle created for the project) will implement a single project, not a sequence of projects. So the expected value presents a lower relevance, the occurrence of extreme events being much more important.

Optimism bias
The evidence proves that public authorities are not good at assessing infrastructure risks, albeit there is a high degree of awareness regarding infrastructure risks (see Treasury, 2003a, 2003b). According to Flyvbjerg et al. (2004, p. 16), 'Cost escalation has not decreased over the past 70 years. No learning seems to take place.' Psychologists present four major sources of uncertainty: ignorance of risk, miscommunication of risk, clouded thinking and the illusion of certainty (see Gigerenzer, 2002). In the present case, there is certainly no ignorance of risk, and miscommunication is not the main problem. The illusion of certainty, inducing experts to focus on a few usual states of nature, is certainly relevant, but Flyvbjerg (2003) argues that the main reason for risk mismanagement in public infrastructures is the willingness of several agents to bias costs and revenues. Flyvbjerg et al. (2004) develop the following argument: for large infrastructure projects, politicians (and their consultants) prefer to bias downward the expected costs, and to bias revenue upwards, in order to maximize the probability of obtaining approval for their projects. Flyvbjerg (2003) presents additional reasons for this bias: (a) lack of involvement by the public and most stakeholders, combined with lobbying by contractors and financing institutions; (b) unclear identification of public-interest goals to be satisfied by public projects; and (c) unclear role of government (conflicts of interest between public authorities as infrastructure managers and public authorities as guardians of the public interest). Akerlof and Dickens (1982) note that this *ex ante* behaviour may be reinforced later: racetrack bettors place much higher odds on their horse after they have made the bet than beforehand. Governments refer now to the optimism bias and to the need to correct it. But we can still observe the usual cognitive dissonance: politicians always base their arguments on the success cases, systematically avoiding learning from failure cases; the focus is always on effectiveness, not on efficiency.

PPP contracts as risk transfer and as risk creation
In the evolution from the project-finance context (between private partners) to the public–private partnership context, two important differences have been disregarded:

- one partner is a public entity, an entity with a large ability to absorb risk – almost infinite, in the case of the state – and endowed with low incentives for efficient risk management;
- the partnership ultimate goal is the delivery of public services (or is somehow related to the provision of public services).

These two characteristics may jeopardize the optimal allocation of risks in PPP and induce contracting public authorities to implement suboptimal contractual schemes. Suboptimal contracts allow private partners to shift risks back to public partners, and allow current public decision-makers to transfer costs and risks into the future, for future generations to pay. But the design of efficient PPP contracts and efficient PPP institutional mechanisms implies addressing these two characteristics.

PPP and public service
By their own nature, PPPs deal with the provision of public service, or infrastructures essential to the provision of public service. Those services are politically sensitive: any risk disturbing provision will be a political risk. So, even when formally transferred to the private partner, the risk of service disruption or quality degradation is always a public partner risk – a political risk, but also a budgetary risk. As Weizsäcker et al. (2005, p. 356) say: 'The transfer of risks is often illusory. Politically, governments cannot afford to allow companies supplying essential public services to collapse. In many cases, there are irresistible pressures to bail out private providers, even when their problems are self-inflicted.'

The solution to this 'public service' problem, in general, is not to avoid PPPs, but to create incentive mechanisms that minimize the probability of disruption or significant disturbance to the service, and that allow the public authority to act preventively and correctively. And step-in rights should be assigned to the financing entities, therefore providing credibility to the contractual risk transfer.

Specific problems in the public–private relationship
Any long-term contract creates the possibility of differences arising, over time, between the interests of the parties and the contract provisions. As a matter of fact, in the long run many changes will happen in the commercial and technological environment, demographic, social and economic

characteristics will change, and some public policies will change. And so the parties may want to change some contract clauses. Those changes (a contract renegotiation) typically require a bilateral agreement.

Two problems (linked to the bargaining asymmetry between partners) affect the long-term PPP relationship:

- the bargaining weakness of the public sector regarding the private sector; and
- the possibility of unilateral change (with compensation) by the public authority.

The bargaining weakness of the public sector results from the public-service characteristic we referred to before, from informational asymmetries, from difficulties in the decision process, and from some institutional rigidity. Informational asymmetry may be mitigated by better information collection and processing, but never eliminated, because private partners are managing the services and so benefit from privileged information. Decisional difficulties may also be mitigated through a better coordination of the several public interests involved, but the private partners – with a special purpose vehicle (SPV) driven by a single interest, profit, will always have a decisional advantage.

The special role of the state and its public commitment to pursue the public interest tend to induce a rigid approach to negotiation: the public negotiator cannot deviate from stated public interests and cannot easily commit to a new proposal. That rigidity may be partially overcome through recourse to a negotiator with some degree of independence, avoiding the public assumption of bargaining commitments. However, it is not possible to create commitment ability such as the one private entities can deliver, and some rigidity will always come from extra-negotiation political compromise.

The possibility of a public sector unilateral change of contractual requirements is something we need to prescribe contractually, but at the same time should be expected to be an extreme and low-probability event.

Contractual partition of risks

An efficient PPP contract will not transfer as much risk as possible from the public sector to the private partner, but only those risks that the private partner is better able to manage than the public authority. Excessive risk transfer will imply paying an excessive risk premium to the private partner, and may even translate into the failure of the private operator, creating political and budgetary risks.

Public managers tend to avoid risks that affect the delivery of public service and to accept financial costs and risks that reduce delivery risks and will only affect future budgets. However, given the relative risk aversion – lower for the public authority – the optimal PPP contract should only transfer to the private partner enough risk to induce the adequate incentives for performance and efficiency. Risk transfer is mainly an incentive device, aimed at creating incentives for efficient project management by the private operator.

So an efficient PPP contract will not operate a full transfer, to the private partner, of all the risks that the private partner is more able to manage than the public sector. The public partner will share responsibility for extreme risk situations.

Public sector budgetary risks in PPP projects
In this section, building on Monteiro (2008), we shall focus on public sector risks arising from PPP projects – they are budgetary risks, or political risks that ultimately translate into budgetary risks. PPP budgetary risks have two main sources: the characteristics of public service that weaken the position of the public sector as a partner; and the perverse incentives that arise from using long-term contracts in a short- or medium-term budgetary framework.

The first source of budgetary risk is inherently unavoidable, but should be subject to specific risk management procedures.

The second source may be controlled, requiring a specific framework for PPP project appraisal and a specific budgetary procedure or a full long-term budgetary appropriation scheme.

Fiscal risks arising from the characteristics of public service
The usual risk analysis for PPP projects uses a methodology developed for project finance, striving for the careful allocation of risks between partners. Having been developed in the private sector, this methodology disregards the high ability of government to assume and accept risk, and also the special nature of public service. The basic characteristics of public service require public authorities to keep the public service running once it starts operating, giving rise to an inherent asymmetry in the PPP – the public sector will always try to avoid service disruptions, while the private partner may regard disruptions as a means of strengthening its bargaining position. This relative asymmetry will naturally depend on the kind of public service, the degree of government commitment to the provision of the service, and the ability of the government to negotiate and use pre-emptive strategic moves.

This is compounded by possible deficiencies of public sector procurement and contractual management:

- Private players are usually better prepared than government departments to negotiate, manage and renegotiate PPP contracts because they are focused from the very beginning on project output and outcomes, while government departments are usually still trying to move away from the traditional focus on the production of services (concerned with inputs and processes) to the PPP focus on the real results of the projects (output quantity and quality).
- Public procurement rules requiring transparency and fairness force public sector entities to operate under a strict procurement framework, while private players benefit from broader room for manoeuvre. Recent legal developments aimed at reinforcing transparency and fairness create additional constraints on already complex procurement processes. For instance, the contracting authority through the call for tender commits itself to a certain scheme, which by law may not be subject to significant changes during the tender process – implying the need to prevent possible strategic moves by bidders exploiting loopholes in the call for tender, or informational asymmetries. In fact, the complexity of PPP procurement (with its negotiation phase) demands a greater effort in the preparation of tender documents and the strategic management of the procurement process to cope with new but essential procurement regulations.

These last factors may be compensated or corrected by appropriate measures, but the nature of public service must be faced up to and incorporated within any efficient and sustainable approach to PPP development. This calls for a more strategic view on risk management, based on game-theoretical insights and a better understanding of the workings of government.

Fiscal risks arising from the lack of a long-term budgetary framework
PPP contracts typically present a profile of payments from the public sector to the private partner that is not well accounted for by the mechanisms of short-term budgetary appropriation. Contractual clauses generally provide for payments to start only after the completion of infrastructure construction or provision of other long-term assets, so payments will typically be zero for the first four years, and then the payments profile will be smoothed for the whole life of the project. Consequently, the main decisions on the project – to go on with it, to call for tender, or to close the contract – will be made between six and four years before starting the payments, implying that no payment will be made by the incumbent government during that period. So in the absence of a specific budgetary procedure for PPPs or of a full long-term budgetary process, PPP projects

are typically not subject to appropriation, and public decision-makers will thus tend to regard them as zero-cost, jeopardizing the efficient selection of projects. Only a few countries (e.g. the Netherlands) require full appropriation of the net present value of PPP payments, in order for the budget to be neutral regarding the decision to procure a project under traditional or PPP schemes.

Without effective appropriation, some non-priority projects could be selected because – as all projects are perceived as zero-cost projects – the selection will tend to be made on the basis of benefits, not on a cost–benefit basis. Even worse, governments may be induced to approve projects that on a cost–benefit basis would never be accepted.

The usual appropriation mechanisms designed to cope with current expenditure and traditional procurement of capital projects no longer apply. In the absence of a specific framework for PPP assessment, line ministers cannot be made accountable for long-term projects that generate a long-term flow of payments starting only outside the scope of the current legislature and government. Moreover, as project payments will typically burden ministers not responsible for the project's approval, these ministers may be perceived as sharing in the responsibility, thereby creating pressure to put those PPP projects outside the line ministries' budget commitments. This may be the case if PPP projects' payments are never included in the budget for the first few years – and perhaps the typical case. This is because initial payments will be zero (or even negative, for example, through initial disbursements from the private partner to the public partners, as payment for transferred assets or goodwill), and long-term payments will not be included in short- or medium-term budget documents.

Budgetary risks, in practice
The analysis of budgetary risks arising from PPP projects has not been central in the international PPP debate. The risk analysis is typically the one developed in project finance, addressing risks in private projects (see European Commission, 2003; Yescombe, 2007; Akintoye et al., 2003). Some critical research was published (e.g. the works of Allyson Pollock, Jean Shaoul and their research partners – see Pollock et al., 2002; Pollock, 2004, Shaoul et al., 2006, 2008; Hellowell and Pollock, 2009), but much of it suffered from assumed lack of reliable data and/or from ideological bias. It is usual to compare real PPP projects with conceptually biased virtual projects (the 'all efficient' public sector project or the 'all inefficient' public sector project) instead of building a realistic counterfactual.

The cumulative PPP experience in several countries points towards the need for better assessment of budgetary/fiscal risks during the life of the contracts, and to changes in the budgetary frameworks in order to address

PPP projects. The IMF recently delivered several reports and country studies focusing on PPP fiscal risks (see IMF, 2004a, 2004b, 2005a, 2005b; Schwartz et al. 2008; Irwin, 2007).

Risk classification may differ, but the underlying risks are typically the same. The most important are the construction risk (including site-related risks, licensing, delays and cost overruns), licensing risks, demand risks and the maintenance risk. *Force majeure* risks have a specific regime. The contractual allocation of risk is typically translated into a table, the so-called 'risk matrix', where each specific risk is addressed in detail, registering its nature, its impact and probability of occurrence, the contractual allocation, and risk mitigation by subcontracting or by insurance.

In this section, we shall focus on risks that need a more careful scrutiny when we consider strategic behaviour by private partners. These risks should be carefully evaluated during the preparation of the PPP scheme and tender documents, during bid evaluation, and throughout the life of the contract.

Project error risk
Design errors or misspecifications made by the public partner may lead to a low-quality project or to cost overruns (to be transferred to the government). The main cause for cost overruns in traditional procurement comes from 'project errors', such as design errors in the architectural and engineering plans presented by the public party to the private party for inclusion in the contract. If and when the private partner is asked to correct these errors by the public partner, compensation claims arise from the former, directed to the latter.

In principle, PPPs are supposed to transfer design risk to the private partner, as they are required to provide certain (infrastructure) services for a prescribed period through the provision of appropriate infrastructure. This way, they are allowed (and induced) to do a whole-life costing of the project, obtaining the efficiency savings that will pay for the added financing costs and the operator profits. In practice, these efficiency savings may not occur. Allocating responsibility for project design to the private partner is also a tool for reducing the propensity of government to ask unilaterally for changes in the project, before or during construction, or during the operational phase.

Construction risks
The risks related to the construction and completion of the infrastructure relate to site acquisition and access, to the obtaining of permits and licences, risks relating to the contractor, construction cost overrun, delay in completion, inadequate performance on completion and third-party

risks. Those risks are the ones most easily transferred to the private sector; however, in the event that licensing risks occur, some construction risk may be transferred back to the public authority.

Licensing risk

This is the risk of delayed or overly restricted issuance of permits or licences. If not addressed before tender call, licensing risks (including environmental licences and local authority licences) may substantially increase the overall cost of a PPP project. Transferring licensing risk to the private partners is costly, as bidders put a high premium on this risk. Retaining this risk in the public sector, as typically occurs, has two main consequences: (i) the government has to pay for unforeseen project changes required in the licensing process; and (ii) private partners (by default not subject to competitive pressure) are able to obtain economic rents from these changes.

Licensing risks mostly come into play when certain environmental standards need to be respected, but are not properly accounted for before the tender, and when local authorities are interested parties in the development of a PPP, or at least are allowed to benefit from the project (e.g. through the associated construction of city infrastructure to compensate for the 'impact on the community'). In these cases, their commitment to the project should be secured before tender – otherwise, they will enjoy some veto power during tender or even after contract close, generating additional project costs, most likely paid by the public partner.

For example, highway projects may experience cost overruns and delays owing to changing environmental regulations; light rail projects may suffer the consequences of veto power by local authorities, eager to collect their share of benefits.

Demand risk

When the public authority contractually transfers to the private partner the risk that the demand for a service does not match the levels planned, projected or assumed, some demand risks may still affect the fiscal position of government. Transferring demand risk smoothes government revenue and may present efficiency properties (e.g. the acceptance of highway demand risk by a private partner may signal that the private sector is assigning high probability to high demand, and so the project is a welfare-enhancing project). For low-demand risks, the usefulness of risk transfer is low as government will pay a risk premium for a risk it may easily accept. For high-demand risks, there are several risks kept on the public side. One of them is, of course, the risk that a very low actual demand leads the private partner to fail, transferring back the full project into government hands.

But the two main risks relate to contractual protection and to strategic risk-devolution moves. In order for the private partner to accept demand risks, the public authority usually protects the private partner from opportunistic public sector action, such as the construction of an alternative road or bridge that diverts traffic – this protection creates constraints on public policies and they may not be sustainable in the long term, forcing compensation or renegotiation of the contract. However, if demand is low and the consequences are significant, the private partner may be induced to engage in strategic moves (lobbying, influencing policy, or corrupting officials) in order to get contractual changes that alleviate the impact of low demand. (If we search for renegotiated contracts, we may easily perceive that many renegotiations initiated by government have in fact solved a few private–partner problems.) Also when a government signs contracts requiring payments between public and private parties depending on demand, there is an explicit budgetary risk, as final payments may actually be quite different from projected ones.

Renegotiation risk
This is the risk of accepting back some costs and risks (owing to information and bargaining asymmetries) whenever the government needs to engage in renegotiation with the private partner. In principle, renegotiations can be a useful instrument to address any contract shortcoming. In practice, their high incidence (and cost for the government) suggests opportunistic behaviour of concessionaires. In order to avoid this, contracts should prescribe rules for renegotiation in the event that unforeseen situations arise.

Although in certain circumstances the public partner is able to keep some bargaining power – for example, cases in which the private partners need to care about a good reputation, or show the ability of the private sector to deliver high quality at low cost through PPP projects – the private partner is generally in a stronger position whenever the government feels the need to renegotiate a contract.

Bankruptcy risk
The concessionaire may go bankrupt, forcing government to call immediately for a new tender or assume operations of the PPP. In the event of a bankruptcy threat, the private partner presents a (paradoxically) higher bargaining power if it creates conditions for contract renegotiation, financial rebalancing or regulatory change. Because the public partner will always care about the continuity of undisturbed public service, the contract (and the contract-management institutions) needs to provide a clear mechanism for the swift transfer of the PPP to another private partner.

Giving financing entities step-in rights reduces this risk but does not replace a careful design of contract-management rules and the building up of contract-management capacity.

In long-term contracts for the provision of public services, bankruptcy will induce a government to take *ad hoc* measures that are typically costly if provisions for the continuous delivery of service are not prescribed into the contract. Unwilling to see a company go bankrupt, in case of problems a government may have to permit an unscheduled price increase for the services or inject taxpayers' money into the company. In other words, customers and taxpayers may end up bearing more risk than would appear from the regulations governing the private infrastructure project.

Effective PPP concessionaires sometimes threaten to fail and so induce public authorities to protect them, by way of contract renegotiation, compensation, or simply by 'buying back contract years' (see, e.g. the Connex rail case, NAO, 2005).

Operating risks
We consider here the general operating risks, including maintenance and operating cost overruns, risk of performance degradation and availability risk. These risks are typically supposed to have been transferred to the private partner. Technology risk may be effectively transferred to a private partner in a road project, but hardly in a project subject to rapid technological change (such as IT projects); for the latter projects, whenever a contracting public authority tries to transfer technological risks to private partners, it will face significant moves (by lobbies or simply by mass movements promoted by the private partners) aimed at inducing unilateral changes to the project and so allowing for the technological improvements to be paid by the public partner as part of a contractual change (besides paying higher contract costs for the supposed risk transfer). So, better than simply checking for contractual risk allocation, we need to address the degree of change and the real ability of private partners to accept and manage those risks.

Risk management in PPP projects
If risks are not clearly allocated to the private partner, it could realize that it is more profitable to try to shift risks to the public sector than to manage those risks. This way, the focus of the private partner could be risk devolution, and not the provision of quality services to government/end-users.

During tender, as well as during the life of the contract, the profit-seeking nature of the private partner will induce him to transfer back some risks to the public partner, formally, during procurement, or, effectively, during contract life. This may also jeopardize the efficiency of PPPs.

PPPs and credible cost and revenue estimates
Because PPPs transfer risks to the private sector, efficient and competitive procurement processes force bidders to undertake credible due diligence, preventing the usual strategic moves by public sponsors. The evidence (see Flyvbjerg, 2003) shows that public sector project teams tend to underestimate costs and overestimate revenues; we easily realize that sponsoring ministers will welcome the bias, as it increases the publicly perceived benefits accruing from the project, and also increases the probability of having the project approved by the government; initial budgetary commitment to the project, and high public interest in the project, help later to obtain additional public funding for the project when cost overruns (or revenue shortfalls) happen. Using PPPs, the business case for an infrastructure project is delivered in a credible way (because it will be subject to market testing). Projects initially perceived as low-cost, high-revenue are reviewed and adjusted, leading to the cancellation of negative-utility projects and to the redesign of low-utility ones. Real case studies here include the UK tram projects, the Coimbra tram system, the new Lisbon airport, the Dublin metro, and the Paddington health campus. Value for money audit reports, published by national courts of auditors, such as the National Audit Office (www.nao.org.uk), Tribunal de Contas (www.tcontas.pt), or the Algemene Rekenkamer (www.rekenkamer.nl) are a good source of information).

Identifying and managing risks
Risk identification, risk assessment and risk allocation are basic activities in the process of designing a partnership scheme and its draft contract, as well as in the process of negotiating the contract during tender. This requires an *ex ante* process including:

identification ➤ assessment ➤ allocation

After contract close, the contract manager should review carefully the risk allocation, using a similar process:

identification ➤ assessment ➤ mitigation ➤ monitoring

which will include, in some rare cases, the (re)allocation of new or changed risks:

identification ➤ assessment ➤ (re)allocation ➤ mitigation ➤ monitoring

Identification and assessment

Risk identification comes from two complementary sources: the careful study of the PPP contract, its prescriptions and omissions; and the study of the business model and the (legal, technological, commercial, demographic and political) environment in which it will be applied. Additionally, knowledge regarding experience on other projects (at home or abroad), in the same activity or in different ones, is surely useful for risk identification. Risk classification may follow different standards, based on the time schedule (planning, construction, operational phases) or on either institutional aspects (entities involved), or process aspects.

Ideally, risks should be quantified (probability of occurrence, and impact) in order to facilitate prioritization of mitigation and monitoring activities; alternatively, risks should be classified according to their probable impact (not only financial, but also operational and political) and their probability of occurrence.

If not quantifiable, the impact may be classified as: (a) critical, (b) high, (c) medium, or (d) low. A critical risk is one that jeopardizes the development of the project according to the established contract – a risk that creates financial collapse of the private partner, or such financial stress that induces degradation of operational conditions, or a politically unsustainable situation. The probability of occurrence may be roughly measured using historical data, or estimated from experts' reports, or the average opinion of an assessment panel.

For some risks, it is useful to assess occurrence according to the time frame – some risks are not likely in the initial years, but only later; other risks are most likely during construction or the start of operations; yet others will surface only in the terminal years of a contract. Some risks present a very low probability of occurrence in any given year, but there is a high probability that they will occur at least once during the life of the contract.

Risk mitigation

There are four main strategies for risk mitigation: risk elimination, risk reduction, risk transference and risk retention. Some risks may be eliminated simply by changing the project or changing the contractual scheme. Lack of rigorous scrutiny of public projects may invite contracting agencies to keep (or create) risks that normally they would not accept – for example, locations presenting high geological risk, or shadow-toll payments for roads with high demand risk – in the false hope that private partners could manage those risks or deliver technical solutions that eliminate risks. Sometimes changing the contractual scheme reduces risks for both parties – for instance, shadow-toll contracts create a demand risk for the private partner and a political/budgetary risk for the public partner (the contractual protection of PPP operator revenue may be politically unsustainable in the long term and so create a need to renegotiate and compensate the operator) and so (if tolling is not acceptable on political or technical grounds) present fewer benefits than availability-payment contracts. Risk reduction is based on uncertainty reduction, on the reduction of the spread of results, or on the reduction of its impact.

Risk transfer is the basis for PPP efficiency, and so the allocation of risks is a major task in preparing a PPP project. At contract close, the risk matrix is determined. However, change is pervasive and the effective risks will change during the life of the contract. Strategic contract management allows the public authority to keep critical risks in the hands of the private partner, and to influence allocation of newly created risks.

Risk assessment during project preparation
The complexity of the PPP problem prevents the public sector from applying expected-utility maximization directly. Most large risks are addressed through sub-mechanisms that create contractual constraints and incentives for private partners, in order to prevent certain events or actions, or bound some public sector risks. Those incentives, being contractually prescribed, are typically designed by the contracting public authority on the basis of a risk-assessment procedure. If this assessment fails to perceive all the political and budgetary risks, we may face not only suboptimal draft contracts and suboptimal procurement rules, but also an inefficient selection of projects.

It is very important to distinguish between project-design risks – the risks that are specific to the infrastructure being considered – and project-scheme risks – the risks that depend on the kind of contract being proposed. Whereas construction risk is a project-design risk (whatever the PPP scheme, the project will face construction risk), demand risk is a project-scheme risk (under a shadow-toll regime there will be demand risk, but under an availability regime there will be no demand risk for the project). Consider now an accommodation project: if some non-infrastructural services (e.g. catering) are included in the scheme, services' demand risk will affect the contract; if those services are to be provided by a third party, there will be no demand risk, but the scheme will now be affected by interface risks.

Risk assessment during procurement
Because PPP procurement aims at allowing for innovation as a source of efficiency savings and quality improvement, there is some room for bidders to influence effective risk allocation – through contractual clauses

added to the draft contract, or through the specific proposal for the design of the project.

For instance, a proposal may present significant savings for the public authority in a certain policy scenario, but high costs in alternative scenarios – so proposals during tender may influence policy design, and then the mere existence of a PPP contract may foster or delay policy changes.

Risk management during the life of the contract

Public authorities cannot ignore risk management after contract close. First, because some risks are kept in public hands; second, because the defence of public interest implies checking if the public partner is really managing the risks they are supposed to manage; third, because under some conditions, private sector risks may be transferred back to the public sector, by action or omission of the latter; and fourth, because new risks will be created or identified during contract life. During contract life, private partners may engage in strategic moves aiming at converting negative events into opportunities for obtaining compensation, or in plain rent-seeking activities – it is critical for the public authority to prevent those moves and react to them effectively. Risk management is an integral component of effective contract management.

Contractual risk partition and risk devolution

If risks are not clearly allocated in the draft contract (included in the Invitation to Tender), bidders will do their best to reallocate risks in the final contract. Unclear allocation of risks may also prevent effective competition and transparency during the tender.

After contract close, risk allocation is written down in the contract, so it is supposed to be established for the whole life of the contract. However, risk devolution, from the private to public partner, is always possible if there is no proper contract management by the public authority, namely if the contract manager is not permanently concerned with risk management and with the prevention of strategic moves by the private partner.

After signing a PPP contract, the private partner will have plenty of opportunities to transfer risks to the public sector, due to: (a) technological, commercial, or demographic change; (b) political change; (c) *force majeure* events; and (d) some other unforeseen events (e.g. archaeological discoveries).

Improper contract management (by the public authority in charge of the contract) creates excellent opportunities for the private partner to transfer risks back to the public sector, shifting costs to the public sector, or simply by not keeping up to the prescribed quality of service. Beside the usual contract-management goals, in the PPP case there is the long-term partnership characteristic that requires a mix of cooperation and scepticism. The three goals for PPP contract management are:

- *Contract enforcement*: enforce the contract in order to achieve its objectives: (a) manage information interchange; (b) supervise asset and staff transfer; (c) supervise the construction phase; (d) supervise the operational phase; (e) measure production and performance; (f) manage changes and conflicts; and (g) prepare/manage termination.
- *Partnering/cooperation*: facilitate cooperation between public and private partners: (a) improve relations between private and public partners; (b) improve interfaces with other public entities: communication, licensing, regulation, feedback; and (c) improve interfaces with end-users, taxpayers and media.
- *Strategic contract management*: manage public sector risks, preventing strategic behaviour that may damage public interest: (a) identify, monitor and mitigate all risks potentially affecting the contracting authority and the public sector, for the full life of the contract; and (b) be aware of possible strategic behaviour (by private partners or other stakeholders) that may affect the service or the public interest.

These three goals require a mix of abilities. Contract enforcement requires careful planning and fast response, and it 'goes by the book', i.e. according to the contract. Partnering is based on a cooperative approach, while strategic contract management requires a (game-theoretical) non-cooperative reasoning and a sceptical approach. In a certain sense, partnering activities aim also at balancing this scepticism with improved cooperation.

Underperformance by the private provider (low production or overproduction, low quality etc.), if undetected, leads to the payment of services not really provided, and affects users. Private partners may also engage in perverse behaviour such as cream-skimming, demand fostering, or client rebuffing. As well, they may create *de facto* situations that, mixed with lobbying and other rent-seeking activities, can effectively change the *ex ante* risk-partition rules, devolving back some risks.

Public sector capacity and public interest
Evidence tells us that PPP operators tend to hire former members of government and top civil servants. (The Prison Service in the UK and the Portuguese road agency unwillingly provided staff for private firms; and in the boards of some major European PPP operators we find former senior

and junior ministers.) This way those operators increase their technical capacity, and also acquire expertise in the process of political decisions. On the other hand, the public sector loses capacity, and not only because of transfers to the private sector. PPPs change the relationship between bureaucrats and politicians, giving politicians a false feeling that they can manage public services through contractual agreements with private players, with no role for bureaucrats. Because PPPs blur the borderline between the public and private sectors, we perceive a stronger need to reinforce mechanisms for the identification of the public interest.

Conclusion

The conventional PPP risk analysis is typically based on a few assumptions that do not agree with reality. We need to develop a non-naïve approach to PPP, recognizing that change is pervasive, and that private partners will naturally engage in strategic behaviour aimed at influencing change on their behalf. A better perception of real PPP risks will induce a better public–private relationship.

Typically, PPP projects provide effectiveness through rapid delivery of infrastructure. But we must say that efficiency is not always assured. Because of poor project preparation, because of poor contract management, or simply because of unmanaged changes in public policy, PPPs may turn out as inefficient projects. Regardless of their effectiveness and of the public perception, projects such as the Skye bridge, the Vasco da Gama bridge, the STEPS contract, the SCUT shadow-toll contracts, the HSL–Zuid high-speed rail, the Rostok and Lübeck tunnels, all lack some efficiency characteristics (for their case studies, check published reports by national courts of auditors).

Are PPPs fiscally sustainable? PPP projects raise concerns regarding their global affordability. In countries with extended recourse to PPPs (for example, the UK and Portugal), they create concerns, among parliamentarians and fiscal experts, that they may be used as a way of transferring costs from current to future generations, inducing fiscal unsustainability. On the other hand, if properly handled, PPPs create nice tools for credible whole-life costing of public projects.

As we said before, PPPs may significantly reduce project risks for the public sector. But, if the appraisal framework is not appropriate, PPPs may bias the selection of public projects, inducing the government to procure low-value projects, and endangering overall fiscal discipline.

So PPP risk management, being long-term contract-management, requires building an effective institutional framework aimed at keeping the balance of risks as it was contractually prescribed. This implies building stronger institutions for efficiency assessment and accountability.

This includes analytical departments, internal auditing, courts of auditors, contract-management teams, parliament specialized committees, and information to the media. And it implies using game-theoretical reasoning for risk assessment and risk management.

Recall Buchanan's (1989, p.18) allegation, allegedly based on Wicksell (1896), that:

> To improve politics, it is necessary to improve or reform the rules, the framework within which the game of politics is played. There is no suggestion that improvement lies in the selection of morally superior agents who will use their powers in some 'public interest'. A game is described by its rules, and a better game is produced only by changing the rules.

The rules needed for effective PPP risk management by public authorities imply creating internal capacity for PPP assessment (knowledge centres, or PPP units, plus well-staffed, trained and motivated procurement and contract-management teams) and external pressure for guaranteeing efficiency and affordability (specific budgetary rules and information-disclosure procedures).

References

4ps (2007), *A Guide to Contract Management for PFI and PPP Projects*, London: Public Private Partnership Programme.

Akerlof, George A. and William T. Dickens (1982), 'The economic consequences of cognitive dissonance', *The American Economic Review*, **72** (3); reprinted in George A. Akerlof et al. (2005), *Explorations in Pragmatic Economics*, Oxford, UK: Oxford University Press, pp. 178–93.

Akintoye, Akintola, Matthias Beck and Cliff Hardcastle (2003), *Public–Private Partnerships: Managing Risks and Opportunities*, Oxford: Blackwell Science.

Buchanan, James M. (1989), *Essays on the Political Economy*, Honolulu, HI: University of Hawaii Press.

Confederation of British Industry (CBI) (2006), *Realising Best Practice on Procurement and Contract Management*, November.

Ellsberg, Daniel (2001), *Risk, Ambiguity and Decision*, with an introduction by Isaac Levi, New York: Garland Publishing.

European Commission (2003), *Guidelines for Successful Public–Private Partnerships*, coordinated by Roberto Ridolfi, Directorate-General for Regional Policy.

Flyvbjerg, Bent (2003), *Megaprojects and Risk: An Anatomy of Ambition*, Cambridge, UK: Cambridge University Press.

Flyvbjerg, Bent, Mette K. Skamris Holm and Søren L. Buhl (2004), 'What causes cost overrun in transport infrastructure projects?', *Transport Reviews*, **24** (1), 3–18.

Gigerenzer, Gerd (2002), *Reckoning with Risk: Learning to Live with Uncertainty* (first published as *Calculated Risk*), London: Penguin Books.

Hellowell, Mark and Allyson M. Pollock (2009), 'The private financing of NHS hospitals: politics, policy and practice', *Economic Affairs*, **29** (1), 13–19.

Hirschleifer, Jack and John G. Riley (1992), *The Analytics of Uncertainty and Information*, Cambridge, UK: Cambridge University Press.

IMF, International Monetary Fund (2004a), *Public Private Partnerships*, Washington, DC: IMF, Fiscal Affairs Department, March.

IMF, International Monetary Fund (2004b), *Public Investment and Fiscal Policy*, Washington, DC: IMF, Fiscal Affairs Department, March.

IMF, International Monetary Fund (2005a), *Government Guarantees and Fiscal Risk*, Washington, DC: IMF, Fiscal Affairs Department, April.

IMF, International Monetary Fund (2005b), *Public Investment and Fiscal Policy: Lessons from the Pilot Country Studies*, Washington, DC: IMF, Fiscal Affairs Department, April.

Irwin, Timothy C. (2007), 'Government guarantees: allocating and valuing risk in privately financed infrastructure projects', Washington DC: World Bank.

Knight, Frank (1921), *Risk, Uncertainty and Profit*, Boston, MA: Houghton Mifflin.

Monteiro, Rui Sousa (2008), 'PPPs and fiscal risks: experience of Portugal', in G. Schwartz, A. Corbacho and K. Funke (eds), *Public Investment and Public–Private Partnerships: Addressing Infrastructure Challenges and Managing Fiscal Risks*, New York: Palgrave Macmillan and International Monetary Fund.

National Audit Office (2005), *The South Eastern Passenger Rail Franchise*, Report 457 2005–2006, London: National Audit Office.

Nordhaus, William (1975), 'The political business cycle', *Review of Economic Studies*, **42** (April), 169–90.

Partnerships Victoria (2001), *Risk Allocation and Contractual Issues*, June.

Pollock, Allyson M. (2004), *NHS plc: The Privatisation of our Health Care*, London: Verso.

Pollock, Allyson M., Jean Shaoul and Neal Vickers (2002), 'Private finance and "value for money" in NHS hospitals: a policy in search of a rationale?', *British Medical Journal*, **324** (18), 1205–9.

Schwartz, Gerd, Ana Corbacho and Katja Funke (eds) (2008), *Public Investment and Public–Private Partnerships: Addressing Infrastructure Challenges and Managing Fiscal Risks*, New York: Palgrave Macmillan and International Monetary Fund.

Shaoul, Jean, Anne Stafford and Pam Stapleton (2006), 'Highway robbery? A financial evaluation of design build finance and operate in UK roads', *Transport Reviews*, **26** (3), 257–74.

Shaoul, Jean, Anne Stafford and Pam Stapleton (2008), 'The cost of using private finance to build, finance and operate hospitals', *Public Money & Management*, **28**, 101–8.

Stiglitz, Joseph E. (2002), *Globalization and its Discontents*, New York and London: W.W. Norton and Penguin.

Treasury (2003a), *The Green Book: Appraisal and Evaluation in Central Government*, London, available at: www.hm-treasury.gov.uk/d/green_book_complete.pdf.

Treasury (2003b), *Supplementary Green Book Guidance: Optimism Bias*, London, available at: www.hm-treasury.gov.uk/d/5(3).pdf.

Treasury (2006a), *PFI: Strengthening Long Term Partnerships*, March.

Treasury (2006b), *Operational Taskforce Note 1: Benchmarking and Market Testing Guidance*, October.

Treasury (2007), *Operational Taskforce Note 2: Project Transition Guidance*, March.

Weizsäcker, Ernst Ulrich, Oran R. Young and Matthias Finger (2005), *Limits to Privatization: How to Avoid Too Much of a Good Thing*, a report to the Club of Rome, London: Earthscan.

Wicksell, K. (1896), *Finanztheoretische Untersuchungen*, Jena: Gustav Fischer.

Yescombe, E.R. (2007), *Public–Private Partnerships: Principles of Policy and Finance*, Burlington, MA: Elsevier.

13 Governing partnerships
Chris Skelcher

The significance of PPP governance

PPPs are a subset of the tools of government – institutional arrangements through which public policy is mediated. Their status as instruments of the public interest, yet bodies that actively engage private actors, means that questions of governance are particularly important. The design of appropriate governance mechanisms provides a way in which that public interest can be protected despite the delegation of authority to business concerns. It creates constraints on the agency of private actors, reducing possibilities for self-interested behaviour at the state's expense. And in contradistinction to the first point, governance structures act as a constraint on the state, enabling private actors to realize the innovative potential that PPPs are intended to promote by virtue of not being part of the state's bureaucracy. In other words, they promote opportunities for self-governance of public activity by private actors at arm's length to the state (Baker et al., 2009).

The tension between these two purposes of PPP governance is evident in the policy and practice of PPPs, although the weight given to one or the other is influenced by the ideological stance of the observer. Those seeing PPPs from a statist position will emphasize the need to ensure that governance protects the public interest, and thus favour rather more in the way of rules and safeguards than observers who regard PPPs as a way through which risk can be transferred, innovation released and public benefit enhanced. Every PPP failure brings a call for reform in the regulatory framework; but whether this should be enhanced or reduced regulation is a matter of ideological predisposition.

It is also important to contextualize the debate about PPPs and their governance. Some countries, such as the UK, have developed considerable experience with the use of PPPs, a development facilitated by some three decades of neoliberal political consensus and a well-established set of norms regarding property rights and legal compliance. Asian countries have social and cultural norms that differ from those in Europe and the USA, and PPP governance therefore is somewhat different (Common, 2000). And within Europe itself, there are significant differences in national contexts that need to be taken into account. For example, Hofmeister and Borchert (2004) argue that Switzerland's culture of consensual decision-making and incremental change, combined with recent significant business failures in that nation, have increased scepticism towards public-management reforms based on business models.

Governance, then, is inimical to the debate about PPPs. Governance is a widely used and seldom defined term. In the context of this chapter it refers to the rules that prescribe who should be accountable for the conduct of a PPP, and in what way that conduct should be exercised, for example through consultation with interested parties, transparency in decision-making and so on. These rules may be defined *a priori* by government, an international regulatory agency, or some other legitimate actor. They can also emerge more informally as the day-to-day practices of actors involved with the PPP become institutionalized. The result is a situation where publicly legitimated rules sit alongside those that are determined privately (Mathur and Skelcher, 2007). This chapter explores four facets of PPP governance: legal, regulatory, democratic and corporate governance. The emphasis is on publicly legitimated forms of governance; the implication of emergent private rule-making requires a fuller treatment than is possible here (see, e.g. Weimar, 2006). The chapter concludes with a discussion of the future governance of PPPs.

Legal governance
PPPs can take a number of legal forms. Each has implications for the allocation of roles and responsibilities between the parties to the PPP, the PPP entity itself, and the state and citizens more widely. The exact form of legal governance will depend on the legislative framework and constitutional norms of individual nations and their relevant jurisdictions. However, a number of overall types can be identified (see Table 13.1).

Public corporations are a longstanding instrument for state enterprises, regulatory bodies, and arm's-length service delivery (Wettenhall, 1998). In a PPP context, public corporations can provide a legal structure that retains a strong connection to the state and thus in theory, but not inevitably, to public interest concerns.

Companies offer the same benefits as public corporations in terms of enabling the PPP to be composed of a single, independently constituted legal entity for a PPP. But unlike public corporations, which have a statutory origin, companies operate under a regime of commercial law. Their establishment thus depends on registration with the relevant regulators. Some companies are limited by shares. For example, some of the PPPs undertaking the improvement of the London Underground are companies whose shares are owned either by a consortium of construction firms or accessed through the market by investors. In this way, the PPP can attract outside investment by selling equity stakes in the company. The benefits of this arrangement have to be considered alongside the disadvantage, which

Table 13.1   Structures for legal governance of PPPs

Legal form	Description	Primary accountability
Public corporation	Statutory body created through legislation and with defined duties and powers. This creates a public entity that incorporates the various parties in a PPP. May be employed in place of incorporation as a company	To government
Company limited by shares	A body incorporated as a company limited by shares. Members of the company will be the parties in the partnership. Shares may be owned by the parties, or may be traded in the open market, thus diluting control. However government may hold a 51% stake or a 'golden share' in order to retain the final say in the public interest	To the members, shareholders, and others as required by the legislation governing companies
Company limited by guarantee	As above, except there are no shareholders. Members of the company agree to pay a nominal amount against any debts of the company in event that it ceases trading	To the members, and others as required by the legislation governing companies
Memorandum of understanding or unincorporated association	A non-corporate entity, in which the partners agree to work together for the objectives, and in the ways, set out in a non-legally binding memorandum of understanding. Because it is not a corporate entity, the PPP cannot enter into contracts or hold funds. These functions are normally undertaken on behalf of the PPP by one of the partners' organizations	To the members

Source: Adapted from Sullivan and Skelcher (2002).

is that the ownership of the PPP can change over time and its value can vary in light of stock market conditions. An alternative arrangement is for the company to be limited by guarantee (the term used may vary depending on the company law of different nations), in which case the members of the company agree to pay a nominal amount to any debtors should the company cease trading. This approach maintains ownership in the hands of members, but restricts the company's ability to access external financing by selling equity.

Rather than constituting a separate corporate entity, contracts are widely used as a form of legal governance for PPPs. The contract sets out the obligations of the two or more parties involved in the PPP, including what is to be delivered or achieved, the payment schedule, discretion on the agent, and the principal's rights of oversight. Private Finance Initiative (PFI) PPPs frequently utilize contracts as the form of legal governance. Other than very simple contracts, specification can never be complete, and this opens the way for opportunism by the agent and the possibility of legal disputes regarding the exact meaning of terms.

A form of PPP often used for community-based partnerships is the memorandum of understanding (MoU) or unincorporated association. This is a non-corporate entity created on the basis of an agreement between the individual member bodies, and setting out the purpose of the partnership and how it will be governed. MoU PPPs do not have a separate legal identity and thus cannot enter into contracts, employ staff, or own or control assets. These functions, if necessary, are normally undertaken by one of the member organizations (often a statutory body) on behalf of the partnership. This form of legal governance offers the most flexibility and fewest constraints on its members. It can be created, adapted and closed as the members desire. The agency role performed by the organization nominated to manage contracts and assets means that the PPP can effectively spend resources and undertake activities with a financial dimension, but without the formality or constraints of a company or public corporation. The disadvantage is that the voluntary agreement that created the PPP may not be sustainable over time, and thus this arrangement is not suitable for typical large PPP infrastructure projects.

Some countries have common ownership forms of legal governance, for example cooperatives and mutual societies, in other words non-state public-interest companies. The advantage of this form is that it relaxes some of the legal requirements that apply to normal profit-seeking companies, because it is recognized that a public-interest company is working for the wider public benefit, not for a narrow private interest. This can help to overcome some of the constraints on directors in companies, who typically are required by company legislation to put the interests of the company first. This can cause problems where the directors are representatives of participating organizations, and thus may not be able adequately to reflect their interests.

Corrigan et al. (2001) argue that the use of such public-interest forms of

Table 13.2   Indicative relationships between legal forms and PPP types

PPP type	Indicative legal form	Rationale
Institutional cooperation for joint production and risk-sharing	Public corporation	Maintains state involvement in management of production and risk
Long-term infrastructure contracts	Company or contract	Enables partners to manage finances and contracts. Company enables opportunities to seek additional financing through sale of equity stakes
Public policy networks	Memorandum of understanding	Offers flexibility for looser network arrangements
Civil society and community development	Memorandum of understanding or public interest company	Offers flexibility for variety of civil-society organizations; or legal structure in which public interest is basis of governance rules
Urban renewal and downtown economic development	Company	Enables partners to undertake range of activities associated with renewal, including infrastructure works, marketing, start-up financing

legal governance enables greater opportunity to innovate, and yet remain accountable to and work in the interest of the wider community. This is a model that might have advantages for partnerships that wish to incorporate so that they are able to employ staff, enter into contracts and act on their own behalf, yet where accountability to the community is particularly important and the idea of a company limited by guarantee does not seem appropriate.

The decision on the legal form to utilize will be influenced by two factors. The first factor is the type of PPP, discussed by Hodge et al. (Chapter 1 in this volume). Each type of PPP is better suited to one of the forms of legal governance discussed above. Thus long-term infrastructure contracts would normally be best suited to a company form of legal governance, while in institutional cooperation for joint production a public corporation model could provide the necessary framework. Although there are no hard-and-fast rules about which legal form fits best which type of PPP, there are clearly some general indications (see Table 13.2).

Second, the choice of legal form reflects the extent to which the constituent parties agree to integrate their activities into a separate entity. PPPs can be loose associations in which partners maximize their autonomy consistent with undertaking some collective activity, or agree to combine their resources into a new entity of which they are members but not necessarily in a controlling position. This is the classic joint venture, a new body established by a set of organizations on the basis that its independence will generate benefits for them. Over time, partners' attitudes to integration or autonomy will change. And so it is important to understand the temporal aspects of partnership formation and incorporation. It may take a period of operation as a MoU PPP before the partners will be willing to move to greater integration as a company.

Regulatory governance

Regulatory governance concerns the system of rules that connect the PPP to the public client. It covers the legal and contractual obligations on parties, the procedures through which they are enforced, and the softer norms that operate around these. It is what Koch and Buser (2006, p. 551) term 'metagovernance': 'various types of soft law, incentives, guidelines, brokering activities and legal mechanisms'. Because government is the guarantor of last resort for a project, market incentives on the PPP and its commercial partners are reduced. Thus there is a corresponding need for effective regulatory oversight to ensure that the public's policy and fiscal interests are served. Problems of governmental capacity are even more pronounced in developing and transitional states. A case study of China's urban water sector shows that the fragmentation and diversity of the regulatory systems inhibits the effective involvement of foreign direct investment in PPPs to improve water management (Zhong et al., 2008).

At the most fundamental level, the public client will be subject to legal requirements concerning the process to be followed and criteria to be applied in the procurement of private actors to participate in a PPP. The scope, detail and complexity of these legal rules will vary from country to country. In the EU, for example, there is a set of procurement regulations that apply to all member states (Maslyukivska and Sohail, 2007). This compares with, for example, China, where the public-law framework is more limited due to the tradition of state ownership of production and absence until recently of significant private actors in a market context. Here, the legal framework was inadequate to enable effective separation of public and private assets, and only recently has legislation to protect private assets been introduced into the legal code (Adams et al., 2006).

The rationale for such overarching legal frameworks is to provide transparency for the process of determining the selection of the private actor to participate in a PPP, and the way in which public and private resources will be applied to the PPP. This creates, at least in theory, a level playing field for potential investors, as well as prescribing mechanisms for the resolution of any disputes and agreement of contract variations. Given the scale of infrastructure PPPs, such frameworks should reduce the risk of corruption and opportunism. They should also ensure that the public interest is protected, for example by requiring security bonds to be issued against financial default or non-performance by the private actor (Deng et al., 2003). However, Bloomfield (2006) points out that in the US case, if not elsewhere, the unique structure of PPPs combined with an environment in which deregulation is the norm leads to a situation in which there may be special waivers of standard procurement procedures.

There has been considerable discussion in the literature about the value or otherwise of legal as opposed to quasi-legal and relational contracting (Sullivan and Skelcher, 2002). PPPs require some form of legal contract because they involve public resources. However, the question is whether the interaction between the parties should be regulated as a matter of legal obligations, and thus tested through the courts, or by way of quasi-legal arbitration mechanisms or through softer forms of regulation. The solutions to these problems are inevitably contingent. Societal norms and the underlying attitudes towards the way in which business should be conducted will be important determinants. The impartiality of the courts may or may not be assured. And the imperatives for project delivery may also be important considerations, with speed of delivery leading to a more pragmatic approach to contract relations on the part of public actors.

Arbitration mechanisms provide a reasonable middle way between legalistic and informal modes of regulatory governance, provided the social infrastructure can offer a reasonable guarantee of impartiality. They offer the parties an opportunity to put their cases before a knowledgeable but independent arbitrator or arbitration panel, who may be able to identify and broker solutions not previously considered by the parties. In Europe and some other parts of the world it is now common practice for construction contracts to include provision for arbitration before any legal dispute resolution. Professional associations may offer their own arbitration service, enabling a process of peer judgement to be applied.

Relational contracting occurs where the parties engage in dialogue about issues arising from the interpretation of contracts, unforeseen events, changes in operating conditions, or external contingencies that affect implementation of the PPP. This is often mistakenly presented as a softer form of regulatory governance, but can be quite hard edged. Private actors can deploy negotiating and commercial relationships skills for which public actors are unprepared, including the practice of offloading less profitable parts of the operation to third parties over whom there is less control and attempting to renegotiate aspects of the contract as it is being implemented.

The unfortunate conflation of relational contracting with the idea of 'trust' adds to the problems public actors can face, since it creates the impression that all that is required is good interpersonal relations. Rather, trust should be considered as a measure of predictability of behaviour. The behaviour could be virtuous or wicked from a public-interest perspective, and thus trust is a normatively neutral concept rather than one associated with positive virtues. Predictability would be a better concept to use, in the sense that it avoids the normative baggage of 'trust'. Thus a public client might well predict on the basis of past experience that a given private actor would behave opportunistically. In this sense, a healthy dose of *mis*trust would be beneficial for the public interest!

Governments can assist public actors with minimizing problems of regulatory governance, and avoid legal dispute resolution, by generating and transferring knowledge from PPP experience. Research on the German case shows that PPP task forces and knowledge centres can improve procurement processes and enhance value for money (Fischer et al., 2006). In the Netherlands, the PPP Competence Centre provides a similar role, and there are equivalent bodies in a number of other countries. Bodies such as Partnerships Victoria, a division of the Victorian State government in Australia, take this approach one step further by providing a single gateway for potential PPP projects, bringing together both expertise in developing and managing PPPs with public-interest considerations.

Democratic governance
PPPs raise important issues of democratic governance due to the changed nature of the state when it transfers public responsibilities in whole or in part to third parties, or engages in cooperative activities with third parties. Ranson and Stewart (1994, p. 94) argue that 'organisations in the public domain are required to account for their actions in the public arena of discourse and there has to be a means by which they are held to account by the public on whose behalf they act'. But forms of third-party government like PPPs muddy the waters of accountability. They introduce the problem of the 'democratic deficit', which refers to the shortfall in the accountability arrangements of a non-elected public body with reference to those applying in the elected sector. This is not just a matter of whether electoral arrangements do or do not exist, but also refers to the other systems that support democratic accountability, including access to information and codes regulating standards of conduct (Sands, 2006).

PPPs embody two potentially competing institutional logics – the logic of democratic accountability in a public arena and the logic of commercial competitiveness in a private setting. Thus, for democrats, PPPs are too private and lack the transparency normally associated with governmental activity. That transparency covers input, throughput and output stages in the policy process. In contrast, the prevailing logic in business is to see accountability at the output/outcome stage – in terms of sales to customers and profit to owners. This is the pre-corporate social responsibility (CSR) market logic, in which why and how a good or service is designed and produced is immaterial to the customer; what matters is whether it does what the customer expects, or can be persuaded to expect. CSR is changing the orientation of business to give greater attention to input and throughput considerations (e.g. the sourcing of products from renewal stock and the ethics of employment conditions in a global market). But CSR remains a matter of debate in the face of a deeply embedded institutional logic of competitiveness in which global production obviates a level ethical playing field for the foreseeable future.

This raises the empirical and normative question of what the level and form of constitutional oversight of PPPs is, and what it should be (Bovaird, 2004; Skelcher, 2005). Currently, oversight other than of outputs is limited. There are plenty of reports by government audit agencies on the results of using PPP mechanisms, and some interim analysis, for example of the application of the public sector comparator (PSC) in particular cases (e.g. from the UK's National Audit Office). These are sometimes considered by relevant committees of state and national legislatures, or by ministers. But public oversight and debate about individual PPPs as they develop is much more limited.

This is not just a matter of commercial confidentiality. Pro-PPP governments benefit from this opacity given the sometimes very marginal decisions made in PSC analysis, and the opportunities to massage the assumptions fed into the process (National Audit Office, 2001). More fundamentally, the problem of classification comes into play. PPPs are a form of quasi-governmental body, yet like other quangos they emerge through pragmatic and *ad hoc* processes and in a multiplicity of forms (Guttman, 2003). They are frequently a function of executive rather than legislative decision, and thus comprise a judgement about technically appropriate means rather than public policy ends. The creation of effective constitutional oversight requires as a first step the clear demarcation of this class of organizations.

Corporate governance

Corporate governance concerns 'the procedures associated with the decision-making, performance and control of organisations, with providing structures to give overall direction to the organisation and to satisfy reasonable expectations of accountability to those outside it' (Hodges et al., 1996, p. 7). Its focus is on the organization's board, the roles of chief executive, the chair of the board, directors and senior management in the context of structures and systems for strategy, financial and risk management. Essentially, corporate governance concerns itself with ensuring that the enterprise is managed in a manner that does not put the future of the business and investors' funds at undue risk.

We know very little about the corporate governance of PPPs. This is an issue where few researchers have ventured. In part this may be due to problems of access into an arena where commercial and political sensitivities are pronounced. But it may also be that the academic debate has concentrated on the theoretical, financial and substantive pros and cons of PPPs at the expense of empirical examination of their internal workings. Some literature is now beginning to appear. Johnston and Gudergan (2007) use the case of Sydney's Cross City Tunnel to show how the different incentives operating on public and private partners threatened the viability of the PPP company and ultimately caused its collapse. Rubin and Stankiewicz (2001) provide a detailed analysis of the Los Angeles Community Development Bank, an innovative PPP for economic revitalization. However, we still lack a sufficient number of detailed studies of the day-to-day corporate governance of PPPs.

The two studies cited above both reveal that the structural tensions built into a PPP, by virtue of operating in both public and business environments, have a significant impact on the viability of the two examples. This suggests that there is a particular challenge for the development of systems of corporate governance for PPPs. The PPP cannot be regarded as a unitary organization with a singular institutional logic. Rather, it is a multi-organization encompassing several institutional logics. It is also an open system, where the external environment can have a significant and immediate impact – for example, a change in government policy. The approach to corporate governance may therefore need to be more flexible and adaptive than is conventionally the case, mediated through broker or boundary-spanning roles that facilitate early warning of changes in the environment and the opportunity for dialogue and negotiation at an early stage (Baker, 2008).

PPP governance: key imperatives and conditions
The legal, regulatory, democratic and corporate governance of PPPs are all concerned with managing the risks inherent in third-party government (Salamon, 1981). These risks are well understood at a theoretical level in the institutional economics framework, with its concern for the

analysis of principal–agent relations under different governance regimes. However, scholars need to explore other areas of theory that have the potential to offer new insights into the governance of PPPs. For example, political science has a conceptual language to describe the accountability, transparency and public-interest issues involved with PPPs, but the theoretical formulations relevant to third-party governance are less well developed. Equally, methods of analysis are still relatively simplistic due to the domination of approaches oriented to elected bodies (Mathur and Skelcher, 2007). Thus the prescriptions generated by this discipline are not so well advanced. Newer areas of theory, for example complexity science, can make a contribution to understanding the structure and evolution of PPPs under different and changing environmental conditions, for example through the use of concepts such as 'fitness landscape' (Klijn, 2008). In essence, my argument is that scholars need to expand from the tried and tested areas of theory and search out literatures that can generate new understandings of PPPs, and in the process inform public debate, policy and practice.

The significance of national contextual factors, discussed earlier in this chapter, means that generic prescriptions for PPP governance need to be expressed at a relatively broad level. Smith et al. (2006) offer a set of such generic prescriptions based on their study of partnerships in the UK, which is adapted here:

1. *Deliberative governance design*: the process of governance design should be deliberative, engaging those groups and agencies relevant to the partnership's policy goals in exploring and determining the governance form.
2. *Proportionality*: the governance systems should be proportional to the responsibilities and risks of the partnership. Some PPPs spend considerable amounts of money and have a major impact on the community; others have few resources and are essentially about facilitating cooperative effort.
3. *Balancing performance with conformance*: PPPs are created to deliver projects. This performance imperative needs to be balanced against conformance with regulatory conditions.
4. *Facilitating new legal forms*: the limitations of public company forms are well known. The debate on 'public-interest companies' and cooperative legal entities offers an important way forward.
5. *Mechanisms for public accountability*: there should be a regular and stable process whereby the intentions, decisions and actions of a PPP can be exposed to the scrutiny of the public. Accountability should not rest purely on the output side of the policy process.

This discussion of the various aspects of PPP governance brings us back to the constituting conditions for public action. These require government that works in the wider public interest, follows proper standards of conduct, is transparent in its decision-making, and is accountable to citizens. It is clear to see how this might operate in an elected body or executive agency, but it becomes more complex for a PPP because of the different legal forms that it could take, the tendency to weaker standards of corporate governance, and the principal–agent problems in effective regulation. And underlying these differences is the fundamental tension with which we started the chapter – that between tighter governance to protect the public interest on the one hand, and on the other the case for weaker governance to enable risk-taking and innovation, and incentivized private actor participation in the provision of public services and infrastructure.

In conclusion, the key task in developing the governance of PPPs is less to do with their financial probity, and more with aligning their mode of operating to the fundamental democratic values of the wider public service. The flexibility in legal and corporate governance available to PPPs offers the opportunity for interesting and creative ways of addressing this imperative. Thus far, the governance of PPPs has predominantly been used to remove them from public scrutiny and informed debate, justified on the grounds of commercial confidentiality or managerial discretion. But, as I argued at the start of this chapter, PPPs are inherently instruments of public action. The challenge for normative theory and institutional design is to ensure that the public purpose of PPPs is properly expressed in the form of governance and its constitutive rules, and is subjugated neither to an ideology of commercialization nor an alternative form of governance arising from the formalized practices of the private actors involved in managing a PPP.

References

Adams, J., A. Young and W. Zhihong (2006), 'Public–private partnerships in China: system, constraint and future prospects', *International Journal of Public Sector Management*, **19** (4), 384–96.

Baker, K. (2008), *Strategic Service Partnerships and Boundary-spanning Behaviour: A Study of Multiple, Cascading Policy Windows*, Doctoral thesis, Birmingham: University of Birmingham.

Baker, K., J. Justice and C. Skelcher (2009), 'The institutional design of self-governance: insights from public–private partnerships', in E. Sørenson and P. Triantafillou (eds), *The Politics of Self-Governance*, Farnham, UK: Ashgate, pp. 77–94.

Bloomfield, P. (2006), 'The challenging business of long term public–private partnerships: reflections on local experience', *Public Administration Review*, **66** (3), 400–11.

Bovaird, T. (2004), 'Public–private partnerships: from contested concepts to prevalent practice', *International Review of Administrative Sciences*, **70** (2), 199–215.

Common, R. (2000), 'The East Asia region: do public–private partnerships make sense?', in S. Osborne (ed.), *Public–Private Partnerships: Theory and Practice in International Perspective*, London: Routledge, pp. 134–49.

Corrigan, P., J. Steele and G. Parston (2001), *The Case for the Public Interest Company: A New Form of Enterprise for Public Service Delivery*, London: Public Management Foundation.

Deng, X., Q. Tian, S. Ding and B. Boase (2003), 'Transparency in the procurement of public works', *Public Money and Management*, **23** (3), 155–62.

Fischer, K., A. Jungbecker and H.W. Alfen (2006), 'The emergence of PPP Task Forces and their influence on project delivery in Germany', *International Journal of Project Management*, **24**, 539–47.

Guttman, D. (2003), 'Contracting United States government work: organisational and constitutional models', *Public Organization Review*, **3** (3), 301–16.

Hodges, R., M. Wright and K. Keasey (1996), 'Corporate governance in the public services: issues and concepts', *Public Money and Management*, **16** (2), 7–13.

Hofmeister, A. and H. Borchert (2004), 'Public–private partnerships in Switzerland: crossing the bridge with the aid of a new governance approach', *International Review of Administrative Studies*, **70** (2), 217–32.

Johnston, J. and S.P. Gudergan (2007), 'Governance of public–private partnerships: lessons learnt from an Australian case?', *International Review of Administrative Sciences*, **73** (4), 569–82.

Klijn, E-H. (2008), 'Complexity theory and public administration: what's new?', *Public Management Review*, **10** (3), 299–317.

Koch, C. and M. Buser (2006), 'Emerging metagovernance as an institutional framework for public private partnership networks in Denmark', *International Journal of Project Management*, **24**, 548–56.

Maslyukivska, O. and M. Sohail (2007), 'European infrastructure procurement through PPP', *Institute of Civil Engineers' Management, Procurement and Law*, **160**, 159–67.

Mathur, N. and C. Skelcher (2007), 'Evaluating democratic performance: methodologies for assessing the relationship between network governance and citizens', *Public Administration Review*, **67** (2), 228–37.

National Audit Office (2001), *The Channel Tunnel Rail Link*, HC 302, Session 2000–2001, London: The Stationery Office.

Ranson, S. and J. Stewart (1994), *Management for the Public Domain: Enabling a Learning Society*, New York: St Martin's Press.

Rubin, J.S. and G. Stankiewicz (2001), 'The Los Angeles Community Development Bank: the possible pitfalls of public–private partnerships', *Journal of Urban Affairs*, **23** (2), 133–53.

Sands, V. (2006), 'The right to know and obligation to provide: public private partnerships, public knowledge, public accountability, public disenfranchisement and prison cases', *University of New South Wales Law Journal*, **29** (3), 334–41.

Salamon, Lester M. (1981), 'Rethinking public management: third-party government and the changing forms of government action', *Public Policy*, **29** (3), 255–75.

Skelcher, C. (2005), 'Public–private partnerships and hybridity', in E. Ferlie, L.J. Lynn Jr and C. Pollitt (eds), *The Oxford Handbook of Public Management*, Oxford: Oxford University Press, pp. 347–70.

Smith, M., N. Mathur and C. Skelcher (2006), 'Corporate governance in a collaborative environment: what happens when government, business and civil society work together?', *Corporate Governance: An International Review*, **14** (3), 159–71.

Sullivan, H. and C. Skelcher (2002), *Working Across Boundaries: Collaboration in Public Services*, Basingstoke: Palgrave Macmillan.

Weimar, D.L. (2006), 'The puzzle of private rulemaking: expertise, flexibility and blame avoidance in US regulation', *Public Administration Review*, **66** (4), 569–82.

Wettenhall, R. (1998), 'The rising popularity of the government-owned company in Australia: problems and issues', *Public Administration and Development*, **18** (3), 243–55.

Zhong, L., A.P.J. Mol and T. Fu (2008), 'Public–private partnerships in China's urban water sector', *Environmental Management*, **41**, 863–77.

PART III

EMPIRICAL EXPERIENCE IN PUBLIC–PRIVATE PARTNERSHIPS

PART II

14 The UK's Private Finance Initiative: history, evaluation, prospects
Mark Hellowell

Introduction

The Private Finance Initiative (PFI), under which groups of private companies finance the design, building and maintenance of new economic and social infrastructure, is the dominant method of large-scale public investment in the UK. As of April 2009, contracts for 641 PFI projects had been signed between public authorities and private sector consortia, with a nominal capital value[1] to the public sector of £63.8 billion (HM Treasury, 2009a). Privately financed projects have been commissioned by every department of state and operate in most areas of public service, with transport, healthcare, defence, education and waste management among the most important sectors. This chapter provides an account of the PFI's political and economic origins, a description of the policy's size, scope and significance within overall public capital investment, a review of the evidence on the PFI's cost-efficiency (or 'value for money'), and an analysis of the policy's medium-term prospects.

Politico-economic origins – from New Right to Third Way?

The PFI was introduced by John Major's Conservative government in the autumn budget statement of 1992. This began a five-year process of legal and bureaucratic reforms intended to promote the use, by the public sector, of the design, build, finance, operate (DBFO) model for the delivery of capital investment projects. Underpinning the government's move was a mix of philosophical, financial and political considerations that combined to make PFI an attractive policy. Philosophically, it suited the party's neoliberal agenda, providing a means of growing the private sector's role in parts of the public sector where outright privatization was regarded as unachievable (Hellowell, 2003).

Financially, the PFI allowed public capital spending to bypass the public sector borrowing requirement (PSBR), and thereby provide the impression of prudent fiscal management, an important matter in the wake of the Maastricht Treaty of 1992. Politically, it meant that the voters could be provided with new roads, prisons and hospitals today without the related investment having an immediate budgetary impact. Public sector net investment was projected by the Conservatives to fall from 1.6 per cent of GDP to 0.75 per cent of GDP by 2001 (Clark et al., 2001). In effect, the PFI was designed as a substitute for orthodox capital expenditure, releasing money in the short term for recurrent expenditure.

After some initial hostility while in opposition, the Labour Party embraced the concept of private finance in 1994, under the leadership of John Smith – before the formal arrival of New Labour under Tony Blair. That year, three senior Labour spokesmen – Gordon Brown (subsequently chancellor and later prime minister), Robin Cook and John Prescott – published 'Financing infrastructure investment: promoting a partnership between public and private finance' (Brown et al., 1994), which outlined Labour's distinctive approach to the PFI. From an ideological perspective, the paper had a distinctly Keynesian flavour, linking the use of private finance with job creation. In media briefings accompanying the launch of the paper, John Prescott claimed that 'private finance will help put people back to work' (*The Observer*, 1994, p. 1).

From a financial point of view, there was a clear focus on the ability of PFI to facilitate additional (rather than substitutional) public investment, by virtue of its ability to hide expenditure from calculations of the UK's national debt. The paper suggests that the Conservative government's decision to use private finance for public service projects only where it could deliver savings over conventional procurement was no more than 'an excuse for refusal', since public finance would always provide a lower cost (*The Observer*, 1994, p. 14). It proposed that the key test should, instead, be between the cost of private finance and the overall welfare cost (in terms of social, environmental and economic losses) of not undertaking the project.

'Financing infrastructure investment' was also a highly political document – in two respects. Undoubtedly, the document was an attempt to 'steal a march on the Conservatives', as Gordon Brown put it in briefings with the press, by suggesting a major expansion of one of the government's flagship policies (*The Observer*, 1994, p. 1). More significantly, however, the paper was a seminal moment in Labour's attempt to develop a new relationship with private industry, and in particular those elements that, historically, had been hostile to Labour – notably, the financial institutions of the City of London and their advisers.

In the critique of Conservative policy, the document makes extensive use of the private sector's own reports. It quotes the management consultancy Ernst & Young and the Royal Bank of Scotland in criticizing the government's unwillingness to intervene in PFI to ensure its implementation (the Conservatives had preferred a 'hands-off' approach, consistent with their view that investment decisions ought to be made by the market and not by government). Shortly after the report's launch, Labour leader

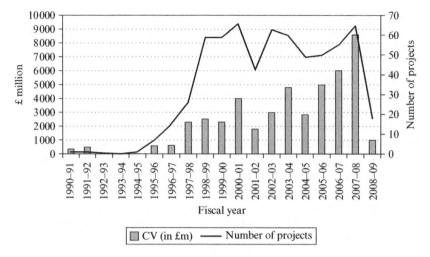

Note: To better reflect the growth trend of the 'mainstream' PFI programme, the three London Underground PPP contracts (with an overall capital value £17.6 billion) are omitted from the graph.

Source: HM Treasury (2009b).

Figure 14.1 Signed PFI projects (n = 638) and their capital value (in £m) per fiscal year (1990/91–2008/09)

John Smith joined key banking figures and the Conservative Treasury's head of private finance, Alistair Morton, for a conference on PFI at Mansion House in the City of London. This was billed by *The Times* as 'proving the [Labour] party's allegiance to British industry and commerce' (Leathley, 1994).

In his 1995 budget the Conservative chancellor, Kenneth Clarke, responded to the Labour Party challenge and the views of UK industry with a much more interventionist approach to the PFI. He announced a relaunch of the PFI with a £9.4 billion list of 'priority' projects – a tacit admission, perhaps, that the PFI could not progress in the absence of government stewardship. As Figure 14.1 shows, this period was the key breaking point in the PFI's development. Before this, it was a high-profile but dysfunctional policy idea; after this, it became an effective financing mechanism. Just three large contracts – all toll roads – were signed between April 1990 and April 1995. Between April 1995 and Labour's election in May 1997, 24 major deals were signed, with a combined capital value of some £1.25 billion.

In the first few years of the Labour government, the pace of contract closures rapidly increased, with 28 schemes with a combined capital value of £2.3 billion reaching contract close in 1997–98 and 59 schemes, with a value of £2.4 billion, being signed in 1998–99.

The PFI under the Labour government

For the incoming Labour government of Tony Blair, who had led the party from July 1994 and rebranded it 'New' Labour, PFI was held to provide a number of financial and political benefits. On the economic front, PFI had the crucial advantage that borrowing undertaken through it did not score against the main calculations of national debt. So long as schemes were recorded as off balance sheet, borrowing through PFI was invisible to the fiscal measure used to determine convergence with the Maastricht criteria. In addition, regardless of balance-sheet treatment, borrowing through PFI did not (and still does not) score against public sector net debt (PSND).[2]

In this way, PFI offered Labour the same advantage as it had offered the Conservatives, in providing a superficial relaxation of the UK government's borrowing constraint (superficial since, as Heald and Geaughan, 1997, note, the effect of using the PFI is to alter the timing of the debt principal and interest payments associated with the borrowing, not their magnitude).

However, for Labour, this fiscal advantage probably had even greater salience. In particular, there was a strong incentive to minimize PSND, as this was the aggregate against which the government's 'sustainable investment rule' was based. This rule, which stipulated that the PSND should not exceed 40 per cent of GDP, was a key measure of New Labour's competence and control over the public finances (Gosling, 2003). The party's use of PFI also provided a bridge between it and parts of the business community, in particular the City of London. Under the Conservatives, there had already been a significant injection of private sector personnel into the central government bureaucracy in order to deal with the implementational challenges of the PFI. Under Labour, this process was enhanced.

Initially, a PFI Treasury Taskforce was established, with a policy arm staffed by civil servants and a projects arm staffed by private sector practitioners. This latter component of the taskforce was in 1999 reconstituted as a limited company, Partnerships UK (PUK) and, in the following year, 51 per cent of the firm was sold to a selection of private companies – all of them large players in the PFI programme – for £45 million. Thus PUK became a joint venture whose majority owners were financiers and active players in the PFI industry (see Table 14.1 for current shareholders). Its staff, including chief executive James Stewart, a former head of project finance at equity group Newport Capital, were drawn from financial

Table 14.1   Current private sector shareholders (and shareholding) of Partnerships, UK

Shareholders	Share (%)
The Bank of Scotland	8.8
The Prudential Assurance Company	8.8
Santander	6.7
Sun Life Assurance Society	6.7
The British Land Company	2.2
Barclays	6.1
The Royal Bank of Scotland	6.1
Serco	3.3
Global Solutions Limited	2.2
Total	51

institutions and management consultancies. While, in theory, PUK's role was in implementation, as opposed to policy, in practice, the line between these elements has become blurred over time.

PUK derives much of its income from fees, paid by public authorities and the Treasury for the delivery of projects. But the firm also writes the government-wide *Standard PFI Contracts*, manages taskforces on refinancing and post-contractual issues, and provides staff on secondment to assist in setting up new initiatives and agencies. Agencies owned by PUK designed, developed and manage the Local Improvement Finance Trust (LIFT) programme – under which public–private joint ventures deliver new primary healthcare facilities – and the Building Schools for the Future programme, which channels several billion pounds a year into England's secondary education estate, mostly through PFI contracts.

PUK has, in other words, became an extremely important part of the policy-making nexus in Whitehall under New Labour. The Treasury's private finance unit, which has 44 per cent of PUK shares, is also largely staffed by private sector individuals, and has been led by a succession of prominent private sector individuals on secondment, namely Geoffrey Spence from Deutsche Bank (now head of global infrastructure at HSBC), and two senior managers from PricewaterhouseCoopers, Richard Abadie and the current (2010) incumbent Charles Lloyd.

The influx of private sector individuals into the core of Labour's PFI policy-making network undoubtedly transformed the party's relations with certain parts of private industry.[3] The Treasury in particular, under Chancellor of the Exchequer Gordon Brown, regarded the promotion of PFI across the UK public sector and internationally as a means of cementing relations with the City of London. In a speech to the Confederation of British Industry in May 2003, Gordon Brown stated that the government would use its influence to expand PFI in the EU, as part of a broader push to open up the markets of the continent (Brown, 2003). PUK provided support for PPP programmes being designed by governments around the world, including those of the Czech Republic, Mexico and South Africa. The technical procedures and guidance for public authorities in these countries are strongly based on those of the UK, facilitating market entry by UK banks and other businesses.

PFI and New Labour's 'Third Way'

It has been claimed that PFI is 'the cornerstone of the government's modernizing agenda for key public services' (Shaoul et al., 2007, p. 480). Indeed, many of the policy's characteristics are underpinned by the prescriptions of new public management (NPM), such as the contracting out of services, the use of performance indicators and the creation of economic incentives – elements that underpin many other examples of public sector reforms undertaken by New Labour (Broadbent and Laughlin, 2005). But PFI is also something of an anomaly. Perhaps the seminal document in describing the 'Third-Way' approach to public service reform, *Reforming our Public Services: Principles into Practice* (Office of Public Service Reform (OPSR), 2002), prescribes a more orthodox NPM approach, with the role of government reduced to standards-setting and contract-writing; with delivery of services undertaken by a diverse array of providers operating in a market defined by consumer choice.

Since 2003, a number of policies and programmes have been established on this model, key examples being Foundation Hospitals (quasi-independent NHS organizations with the power to raise finance directly), Independent Sector Treatment Centres (ISTCs) (private clinics operating in competition with local NHS units for the delivery of elective healthcare); and the Academies programme in secondary education (privately sponsored schools operating free from local authority control). The PFI is clearly distinct from this broader marketization and choice agenda – the structure involves, for example, no direct interface between the private provider and the ultimate consumer.

Indeed, from 2005, ministers and officials regularly briefed against the PFI, which some began to see as a barrier to more wide-ranging private sector involvement. In June 2005, Julian Le Grand, adviser to Tony Blair and a longstanding advocate for the introduction of markets and choice in public services delivery, told journalists that PFI had proved an 'expensive waste' (Davoudi and Timmins, 2005). The following month, Bob Ricketts, an official in charge of the health department's ISTC programme, argued

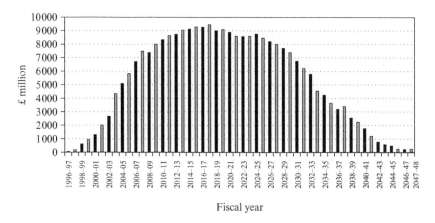

Fiscal year

Source: HM Treasury (2009b).

Figure 14.2   Unitary charge payments for fiscal years 1996/97–2047/48 (in £m)

that PFI for hospitals had produced unnecessary 'white elephants', as opposed to flexible healthcare. The NHS needed 'a fundamental rethink about how much [it] invest[s] in capital, rather than human resources', he reportedly said (Timmins, 2005).

On taking office in May 1997, Labour rebranded PFI as a 'public private partnership' – and it was under this 'third way' title that the policy was exported around the world. But to see PFI as a core component of Third-Way ideology is probably a misinterpretation. The use of PFI did help New Labour to build a relationship with the City of London. It did help the chancellor, Gordon Brown, to cement this relationship through the policy's promotion internationally. But it is likely that Labour's consistent (and continuing) support for PFI is, in large part, due to its ability to deliver investment today without that investment affecting today's public finance statistics. This is an advantage that has appealed to Conservative and Labour governments alike, just as it has proved irresistible to governments around the world.

The PFI programme: size, scope and significance
As of April 2009, contracts for 641 PFI projects had been signed between public authorities and private sector consortia, with a total nominal cost to the public sector of some £273.8 billion over the full length of these contracts (see Figure 14.2). The annual cash cost of PFI contracts signed as of April 2009 will reach a peak of £9.5 billion in the fiscal year 2017–18, and

Table 14.2   Number and capital value of projects signed by UK government departments

Government department	Capital value (£m)	Number of projects
Cabinet Office	342.00	2
Crown Prosecution Service	19.80	1
Department for Business, Enterprise and Regulation	38.33	2
Department for Children, Schools and Families	5284.42	124
Department for Communities and Local Government	1979.65	60
Department for Culture, Media and Sport	238.41	14
Department for Environment, Food and Rural Affairs	1974.09	21
Department for Innovation, Universities and Skills	22.00	1
Department for Transport	22747.25	50
Department for Work and Pensions	1138.31	4
Department of Health	10898.39	102
Foreign and Commonwealth Office	91.00	2
HM Revenue and Customs	840.00	8
HM Treasury	141.00	1
Home Office	799.53	25
Ministry of Defence	8725.33	49
Ministry of Justice	696.60	26
Northern Ireland Executive	1360.62	33
Scottish Government	5926.12	92
Welsh Assembly Government	541.81	24
Total	63804.65	641

tail off thereafter. However, these figures will of course increase as more contracts are signed.

By capital value, the transport sector has been by far the largest recipient of PFI contracts in the UK, with some £22.7 billion of investment so far committed (see Table 14.2). However, £16 billion of this relates to the three PPP contracts for the London Underground metro system which, when combined, probably constitutes the largest PPP infrastructure scheme in the world. Much of the remaining £5 billion is accounted for by investment in large strategic infrastructure such as motorways, in addition to a smaller programme of light rail schemes.

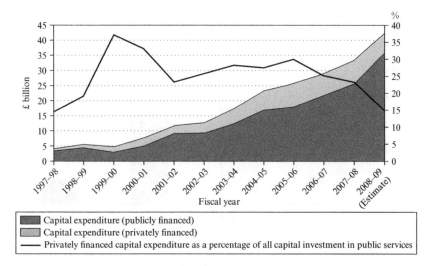

Source: HM Treasury (1997–2009).

Figure 14.3   Total capital investment in the UK public sector (1997–2009)

Defence has also been an important sector, with PFI projects in operation in all three armed services (the Royal Air Force, the Royal Navy and the Army). The UK government has utilized PFI to deliver a diverse array of defence equipment, training services and accommodation, including a £430 million refurbishment of the Ministry of Defence Headquarters in London, the design, development and management of a £2.7 billion airborne refuelling aircraft and the launch of a £1.08 billion 'Skynet' military satellite system. However, private finance has not to date been used for front-line equipment and services (largely due to opposition to this from the armed forces themselves), which limits the potential scale of this programme.

Since 1997, private financing has constituted between 15 per cent and 37 per cent of annual capital expenditure in the UK's public sector (see Figure 14.3). However, this understates the prevalence of PFI in certain parts of the public sector. In healthcare and education, for example, it has been the overwhelmingly dominant form of procurement for new infrastructure. Contracts for 127 hospital projects were signed between May 1997 and May 2009, and of these some 97 came through PFI. Private finance accounts for around 90 per cent of the £11.64 billion committed under the programme (Department of Health, 2009). While it is likely that the hospital-building programme is now drawing to a close, with just one project (a £475 million scheme for the North Bristol hospital) in

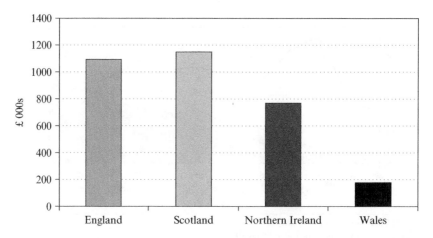

Sources: HM Treasury (2009b) and Office for National Statistics (2007).

Figure 14.4   Capital value of signed PFI schemes per capita, by country

procurement, increased private financing in sectors such as waste management and social housing are expected to offset this (HM Treasury, 2009d).

The use of private finance by the devolved administrations (the Scottish government, the Northern Ireland executive and the Welsh Assembly government) has varied significantly. Until 2007, the Scottish government was the world's most enthusiastic consumer of PFI projects, with higher per capita expenditure through PFI than any other country (see Figure 14.4). This has changed since May 2007, when the Scottish Nationalist Party took power from the previous Labour–Liberal Democrat administration. The SNP came to power with a manifesto commitment to abolish the PFI and replace it with a 'Scottish Futures Trust', which would fund projects through 'bonds and other appropriate commercial financial instruments at rates which will be cheaper than PFI' (Scottish National Party, 2007, p. 9).

However, once in power, the SNP downgraded the role of the Futures Trust from a financing mechanism to that of a simple advisory organization (Scottish Government, 2008), which will deliver programmes of conventional and privately financed contracts. Between May 2007 and April 2009, nine schemes with a combined capital value of £1.06 billion have been signed, although the scale of PFI in Scotland has reduced since the SNP took power: there are just nine private financed schemes in development in Scotland (Hellowell and Pollock, 2009).

In contrast, the devolved administrations of Northern Ireland and

Wales have used PFI to a relatively minor extent in the past and are now planning significant expansion. As of April 2009, there were 33 signed PFI contracts in Northern Ireland, with a combined capital value of £1.36 billion. The relatively small number of PFI contracts in Northern Ireland is a reflection of political instability in the years since the Good Friday Agreement, and is despite an impressive level of political support for the policy among domestic political parties and the London-based Northern Ireland Office. With devolution restored in 2006, followed by three years of relative stability, the PFI programme is expected to grow. As of April 2009, there were 12 contracts in procurement and it is projected that this will increase the capital value of PFI projects to some £3.22 billion by the final quarter of 2011–12 (Northern Ireland Executive, 2008).

In Wales, the relative absence of significant PFI investment (just 24 schemes have been signed as of April 2009, with a combined capital value of £541.8 million) is the result of a conscious attempt by the devolved Labour-led administration to establish 'clear red water' between it and the New Labour administration in Westminster, signifying a more traditional socialist or social democratic approach to public policy, and, in particular, a rejection of private sector involvement in public services (Reynolds, 2008). However, in the absence of significant capital funding from the London government, the result of the Welsh approach has been a lower rate of capital expenditure than in any other part of the UK. In an apparent U-turn, the assembly government has now said that it will consider adopting a PFI programme in all sectors with the exception of healthcare, and it intends to reopen the PPP unit that was closed down in 2004 (Davies, 2008).

Evaluation

As noted by the World Bank (2007), lower public debt associated with the use of private finance is an artefact of governments' standards for financial reporting. In a standard PFI contract, payments do not depend on the government's subsequent demand for the services: so long as the private partner has properly constructed and maintained the facilities, the government must pay. While the government's obligations to make these payments may not entail an accounting liability, they do entail an economic liability: all the debt will be repaid by the public sector along with interest and returns for promoters. The primary economic impact of the switch from public to private finance is to alter the timing of payments, not their magnitude, which will be greater unless PFI can provide greater cost-efficiency – that is, provide a given outcome at a lower cost than the available alternatives.

The cost-efficiency of PFI relative to other forms of procurement and financing is therefore the central evaluative question facing this policy. While there is a substantial literature on the operation of PFI in the UK, in terms of both parliamentary audit and conventional academic research, this work has not yet provided a conclusive answer to the cost-efficiency question. This section provides a detailed description of the PFI model and a plausible framework for evaluation. Findings from the available empirical literature are evaluated according to this framework, and some tentative conclusions are drawn.

The PFI model in detail

The scope of services involved in the operational component of a PFI varies between different sectors and projects. While in a typical prison PFI the private sector consortium delivers all 'core' services, including prison management and the employment of security staff, in other sectors the role of the private sector is restricted to facilities management and the delivery of certain 'ancillary' functions. For example, in a typical PFI hospital, the private sector will maintain the building and manage the catering, cleaning, portering and laundry services, but clinical care remains the responsibility of the public healthcare authority.

In return for the capital investment committed by the private sector, along with its management of the construction process, maintenance and services, the public authority pays to the private sector an annual unitary charge, which is in large part fixed so long as performance is satisfactory. This model results in the transfer to the consortium of project-specific risks, such as those associated with design, construction and life-cycle operation, and certain market risks, such as the risk of unexpected inflation or economic recession.

A PFI consortium will generally involve a mixture of 'operational' investors such as construction companies and facilities management firms, and 'financial' investors such as equity institutions and the investment arms of major banks. On signing the contract for the project, the consortium will form a 'special purpose vehicle' (SPV)[4] – a legal entity established with the specific purpose of delivering the project in accordance with the agreed contract. Execution of the contracted activity requires the involvement of a number of parties. The SPV will enter into subcontracts with one or more organizations (usually the operational investors mentioned above) to deliver the project. The SPV also raises 'pure' equity and subordinated debt (loans) from its member companies; and senior debt from banks and/or the financial markets. Senior debt, which has the first call on project resources in the event of a reduction in cash flow or contract termination, typically provides around 90 per cent of the finance required to complete the capital investment of the project, with the higher-risk forms of risk finance – subordinated debt and equity – providing 9 per cent and 1 per cent respectively.

The price offered by the private sector will comprise a number of known input costs, such as transaction costs, and a larger number of projected costs, such as those relating to capital expenditure and operating expenses; and projections of the cash flows to the project investors – from which the internal rate of return (IRR) on all the various sources of private capital employed can be calculated.[5] For the DBFO model to deliver greater cost-efficiency than the alternatives (for example, design–build–operate contracting), the presence of the 'F' component must result in greater cost-efficiency – either on its own account through lower finance costs, or through its ability to improve the efficiency with which the operational components of the project are delivered. In evaluating PFI's cost-efficiency, it is therefore useful to separate out the financial and operational elements of the model.

The relative cost of public and private finance
The relative cost of public and private finance is an issue that has long exercised financial economists. It is clear that government gilts will typically provide the lowest yield in the market, and is therefore in cash terms the cheapest available source of money for governments. However, in the 'perfect capital markets' (PCM) view, this apparent advantage is the result of certain costs being hidden. Klein (1997), for example, states that public borrowing appears cheaper than private only because the government is able to coerce future taxpayers into meeting the cost of downside risks should they materialize. The view that there is no economic benefit to public finance has been held by the UK Treasury since the introduction of PFI. For example, in a 2003 policy document, it argues that

> A great part of the difference between the cost of public and private finance is caused by a different approach to evaluating risk. Typically, the private sector takes account of risk by discounting future cash flow at a higher rate. A risk premium is therefore made explicit in the private sector cost of capital, and the level of return on capital is *competitively determined according to the risks assessed in the project* . . . (Klein, 1997, p. 41; emphasis added)

The PCM argument is that, so long as there is competition between suppliers, a near-enough PCM will ensure that the finance cost implied by the terms of the PFI deal necessarily represents the true cost of the risks involved in the project. As mentioned above, if public finance is available at a lower cost, this is not economically beneficial; rather, it is simply that the risk associated with the project has been transferred to current and future taxpayers, who will have to meet the expense of any downside risks that materialize.[6]

To understand this point it is necessary to explore the means by which private financiers are assumed, in the PCM approach, to value their investments. Textbook corporate finance theory dictates that project-specific or 'idiosyncratic' risks, such as the possibility of delays, or difficulties in construction and/or operation, should not be reflected in the cost of finance for two reasons. First, as noted above, these risks are reflected in the 'expected costs' of investment and operation, which are adjusted to take account of the potential for underperformance in construction or service delivery (Brealey et al., 2008). What is left over in terms of free cash flow to the project investors is therefore a risk-adjusted cash flow.

In addition, while there is a possibility that actual operational costs will be different to those projected, the risk of such variability can be 'pooled' and 'spread' across a diversified portfolio, such that overall portfolio returns are unaffected. Discount rates should, therefore, take account only of 'systematic risks' – that is, those that cannot be diversified away by virtue of their correlation with the market so that all investments are exposed.

The capital asset pricing model (CAPM) of Sharpe (1964) and Lintner (1965) formalizes this idea, and is much the most common model used by investors to calculate their cost of capital (Brealey et al., 2008). It is based on the insight that the appropriate discount rate for valuing projected returns is a function of the time preference rate (reflected in the risk-free rate) plus a premium for systematic risk. Specifically, it states that the cost of capital is derived by adding to the risk-free rate of return the 'beta' of the investment – or the covariance of the projected return on the investment with the return on the market as a whole – multiplied by the 'market risk premium' (i.e. the risk in the market as a whole).

The hypothesis of the PCM approach is that the rate of return on private finance will approximate this discount rate, given adequate competition between suppliers. The rate of return on a competently managed investment will not be lower than the discount rate because this would result in a negative net present value (NPV). But neither will the rate of return be much higher than the discount rate since, in a functioning competitive market, rival investors should be available to provide the public authority with a lower price.

The cost of borrowing from the private sector in UK PFI contracts is not generally identifiable from information in the public domain and, as a result, the literature on this topic is extremely limited. In 2000, a study commissioned by the Treasury examined a sample of PFI schemes from across the sectors, and stated that the cost of private finance was '1–3 percentage points higher than public sector borrowing as measured by current gilt rates' (Arthur Andersen and Enterprise LSE, 2000, p. 4).

This range has since been used by the Treasury as evidence that the interest rate differential between public and private finance is not significant (HM Treasury, 2000). However, this statement, contained in the executive summary of the report, is inconsistent with the document's main text, which states that the 1–3 per cent range applies only to the senior debt finance costs on 'most schemes' in the sample, and not the overall financing cost. The main text acknowledges that 'higher returns will be demanded for junior [subordinated] debt and equity finance' (ibid., p. 9).

Another consultancy-led study, commissioned by the Office of Government Commerce and carried out by PricewaterhouseCoopers and the LSE economist Julian Franks (2002), provides an evaluation of the overall projected post-tax rates of return on 64 PFI projects by comparing returns with project-specific cost of capital benchmarks. To provide these benchmarks, a risk-adjusted cost of equity was calculated via the CAPM, with a risk premium calculated from a beta of UK water and gas utility companies and a market risk premium of 5 per cent, along with the actual cost of debt for each project.

The PwC–Franks report found an 'excess cost' on private finance of some 2.4 per cent. From a policy perspective, this finding is undoubtedly very significant. The crux of the argument about whether private finance costs more than public finance for public capital investment rests on whether the undoubtedly higher rate of interest paid to private investors accurately reflects the costs of the risks that they bear. If private finance costs 2.4 per cent more than public finance, even after accounting for the risk that investors bear, then the value-for-money case for PFI is weaker than has been claimed by the UK Treasury (and many economists).

For PFI to be more cost-efficient than other procurement forms, this additional cost of private finance must be offset by its ability to increase the cost-efficiency with which the other components of the PFI model are delivered. It is to these elements of the structure – the design and build, maintenance and support services – that this chapter now turns.

Design, construction and whole-life costing
The bundling of the construction and operation components of infrastructure contracts is sensible in cases where the desired outcomes can be adequately specified and monitored. Where a single private sector entity undertakes both the construction of a building and its subsequent long-term operation, it has an incentive to make investments in the construction phase in order to reduce maintenance costs in the operation phase and thereby enhance overall cost-efficiency. In other words, bundling of phases encourages up-front investment that will contribute to cost reduction

over the asset's life cycle and, assuming competitive contracting, this will reduce the overall cost to the public sector. In contrast, if two separate firms undertake the construction and operation phases, such investments will not be made in the construction phase, and the overall cost may be higher.

Expanding the scope of this bundle to include finance theoretically sharpens this incentive since the value of the project to the SPV membership is determined by the expected performance of the project over its whole life. As HM Treasury (2003, p. 35) states:

> This incentive to create a public asset with long-term value enables construction contractors to take a long-term interest in the project, even after they have completed their construction task. This also enables the various contractors to the PFI project and investors to work together with a common interest in creating an optimum, whole-of-life, cost-effective project and provides the right incentives to seek the best performance in the form of the performance regime set out in the PFI contract and actively remedy deficiencies.

The empirical evidence on this issue is limited, but the work that has been done does not support the prediction that higher investments will be made to curtail long-term costs. The National Audit Office (NAO), the UK's supreme public sector audit institution,[7] commissioned the Building Research Establishment (BRE) to analyse the build quality of eight PFI hospitals and eight comparator hospitals that were publicly procured (NAO, 2007a). These 16 hospitals were assessed against a set of design quality indicators, including the quality of external materials, internal fabric and finishes, fitness for function and flexibility for layout change and extension. Score against indicators were given with a range of 0 (very poor) to 5 (outstanding), with 4 and 5 judged by BRE as 'best practice' and 3 as 'good practice'.

The BRE judged that, on all counts, there were 'no meaningful differences' between PFI build quality and that at non-PFI comparator hospitals. On average, scores for whole-life costing were 0.69 higher in the publicly financed schemes, with an average of 3.3, versus 2.6 for the PFI schemes. This result was reached despite the fact that the average age of the publicly financed comparator hospitals was around 20 years older than that of the PFI sample.

By far the most sophisticated examination of the relative cost of construction under private finance and public finance arrangements is Blanc-Brude et al. (2006). This study uses a multiple regression analysis to test the hypothesis that privately financed contracts will exhibit higher *ex ante* construction costs than traditional procurements, and employs a database of 227 road projects (including 65 DBFOs) financed by the European

Investment Bank (EIB) between 1990 and 2005. The study estimates that, on average, the *ex ante* construction cost of a DBFO road was 24 per cent higher than a traditional procurement, all else being equal. Superficially, this finding might be taken as evidence that the 'bundling' hypothesis is correct – that additional investments are made to reduce overall project costs.

However, as Blanc-Brude et al. note, the 24 per cent figure is consistent with estimates of 'optimism bias' in projections of construction costs in traditional procurement – i.e. the difference between projected and outturn costs in public procurement. For example, Flyvbjerg et al. (2002) found average cost escalation during construction of 28 per cent overall and 22 per cent for the EU roads sector. For large projects (greater than €150 million) across different sectors, Mott MacDonald (2002) identified an average cost escalation from contract award of 21 per cent.

Blanc-Brude et al. (2006, p.30) state:

> the close correspondence between the (average) optimism bias in traditional public procurement and the (median) increase in *ex ante* costs in [DBFOs] suggests that the public sector is paying more for a [DBFO] road *ex ante* primarily to avoid time- and cost-overruns; that is, the largest part of the estimated difference represents the cost of passing on the construction risk to the private sector partner.

This finding is significant for the cost-efficiency of the DBFO model. It suggests that additional investments are not made by private investors in order to lower operational costs (a finding consistent with the NAO evidence presented above), and that the *ex post* build costs of a DBFO project and a traditionally procured public project are very similar.

The apparent conflict between the predictions of the economic literature and the empirical reality in this context may be explained once the impact of senior debt on contractual performance is considered. Providers of senior debt exert a powerful influence on the contractual structure of a PFI scheme, carrying out due diligence services (eliminating optimism bias from the SPV's projections), and allocating risk to the party best able to manage it so as to ensure that the project will generate sufficient cash flow for the debt to be repaid. Given that on a UK PFI scheme an SPV will generate cash flow only after it is complete and successfully in operation, senior debt providers in particular are likely to favour conservative, as opposed to innovative, design and construction solutions, even where these solutions fail to maximize cost-efficiency in the operational period. To this extent, the involvement of private finance may in fact weaken incentives for whole-life cost solutions over those in place in a publicly financed design, build and operate scheme.

*Table 14.3   Comparison of services provided by PFI and non-PFI
hospitals*

	Security	Linen and laundry	Portering	Cleaning
Cost of PFI vs non-PFI provision	Higher	Higher	Lower	Higher
Quality of PFI vs non-PFI provision	Higher	Ranking dependent on measure	Lower	Lower

The cost and quality of services

Evidence on the cost-efficiency of support services is limited. However, in the healthcare sector, data on the cost of quality of non-clinical services have been collected by the NHS Healthcare Commission. In 2005, it made available the results of a one-off review of facilities management costs and quality across all NHS Trusts across England and Wales. These results allow for a comparison between 12 operational PFI and 141 non-PFI hospitals in terms of the following support services: security; linen and laundry; portering services; and cleaning. These data are summarized in Table 14.3, and show that, with the exception of portering, services provided under PFI were more costly than in the comparator hospitals. Only in the case of security was this increase in cost accompanied by an increase in quality.

Unfortunately, the Healthcare Commission data do not allow for a cost and quality comparison of maintenance services – one very crucial component of the PFI structure in the hospital sector, where contracts are largely based on availability payments.

However, the NAO (2007b) report on operational performance contains the results of interviews with managers at 19 NHS Trusts with operational PFI hospitals on the quality of maintenance. It found that half the Trusts considered availability deduction schedules to be inadequate to ensure that PFI contractors return unavailable areas to use as soon as possible, providing strong evidence of insufficient risk transfer. A particular problem was recorded in respect of reactive (as opposed to planned) maintenance, where only a third of managers recorded performance as good, with a further third describing performance as 'adequate' and a third as either 'poor' or 'very poor'. Against this, 14 of the 19 hospital managements in the PFI hospitals considered that the maintenance of buildings had improved when compared to their recent experiences in conventionally funded hospitals.

Possible source of inefficiency

Because of the financial complexity and long-term nature of PFIs, transaction costs – such as those associated with tendering, bidding and writing contracts – are high relative to other forms of procurement. The process of negotiating contracts is especially costly (for both the public and private sector parties) because of the high cost of legal, financial and technical advisory services. Dudkin and Välilä (2005) found that, for a sample of 25 hospital PFI procurements in the UK, *ex ante* transaction costs for the public sector and the winning bidder were some 8 per cent of the total investment cost (split evenly between the public sector and the winning bidder). Of course, the public sector procurer ultimately bears both sets of transaction costs – its own, and the private sector's, through higher contract prices.

The expense of the PFI process also has an indirect impact on cost-efficiency by providing a significant barrier to entry for potential bidders, preventing firms from bidding and undermining competition in procurement. The National Audit Office (2007b) found that PFI hospitals and schools projects attracted a lower number of bidders than other forms of procurement, and that competition had declined over time. In a sample of 46 contracts signed between April 2004 and May 2006, one-third attracted only two bidders at the point when they were requested to submit detailed bids. The NAO stated that 'it was rare for procuring authorities to choose to eliminate weaker bids as the choice was out of their hands' (NAO, 2007b, p. 12).

Established firms are also likely to have an absolute cost advantage over potential market entrants since senior debt rates are known to be unfavourable for firms with limited PFI experience (Standard and Poor's, 2004). The absence of competition in procurement clearly presents risks that private sector bidders will be facilitated in seeking excess returns.

The procurement process is an additional source of potential inefficiency. Because bidding consortia need to secure loans from banks before contracts are signed, bidders are not required to create fully worked-up bids during the competitive phase of procurement. Instead, there is a period of exclusive negotiation following selection of a preferred bidder – a period that is typically very extensive. The UK's National Audit Office (2007b) found, in a sample of 20 hospital procurements, that the average procurement time was 38 months, almost half of which time was taken up by the preferred bidder stage. It was common for major changes to be made to projects during this period, including increases to prices.

Most public authorities in the NAO's survey also identified the preferred bidder stage as the point at which advisory costs begin to escalate. During this phase, both public and private parties are making significant investments that are specific to the transaction. Given the scale of these investments, we might view this stage of procurement as a 'bilateral monopoly', in which the power of the monopoly seller is balanced by the monopsony power of the buyer such that a mutually advantageous contract can be developed (Williamson, 1985). However, as Lonsdale (2005) has argued, the private sector is in an advantageous bargaining position during the preferred bidder stage. The NAO (2007b) has noted that, once chosen as a preferred bidder, private consortia know that they are 'virtually guaranteed' the contract (ibid., p. 21). Indeed, a succession of NAO investigations (e.g. NAO, 1999, 2002, 2007a) provide strong evidence that bidders have been able to exploit this, by passing risk back to the public sector while increasing prices during this stage.

Summary
While a comprehensive evaluation of the cost-efficiency of the PFI model is inherently complex, it becomes somewhat more manageable once the different components of the DBFO bundle are considered separately. Because of the size of its sample, the PwC–Franks analysis can be regarded as strong evidence that private finance has proved more expensive than public finance, even after an objective appraisal of the cost of risks transferred. The cost and quality of privately financed construction appear to be about the same as those of conventional procurement, while the cost and quality of operational delivery in DBFO (including the quality and cost of support services) show no consistent advance on past experience. The evidence is not conclusive and is frequently sector-specific, but the case for PFI's cost-efficiency is clearly not proven, and there is a need for more research.

The impact of the financial crisis
The global financial crisis has led to a significant increase in the cost of private finance – in particular the senior debt component. Commercial bond finance – hitherto the cheapest form of senior debt for PFI projects – has been unavailable since mid-2008, when many of the big US 'monoline' insurers such as Ambac and MBIA lost their 'triple-A' credit rating in the midst of the 'subprime' mortgage crisis. These institutions had played a key role in the provision of senior debt for large projects, by guaranteeing ('wrapping') repayments to bondholders in return for a fee and thereby reducing overall financing costs. The withdrawal of the monolines' ability to provide a triple-A guarantee has removed commercial bond financing as a low-cost option for the foreseeable future.

At the same time, banking sector liquidity has reduced dramatically as the financial crisis has developed. There has been a strong trend away from the traditional 'lead arranger' model where one bank manages a

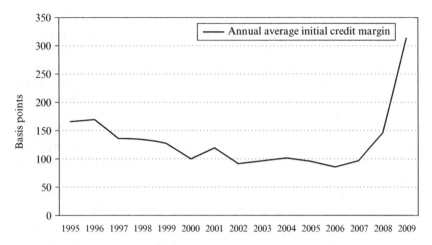

Source: ThomsonOneBanker (2009).

Figure 14.5 Annual average initial credit margin on PFI projects 1995–2009 (n = 198)

transaction, underwrites the whole debt and then syndicates part of the debt to other banks to reduce their exposure to project risk. Many banks now refuse to accept syndicated debt due to a widespread breakdown of confidence and trust between institutions.

Where transactions can be done, there is a trend towards 'club' deals, in which banks group together to fund the deal, and spread the debt between them (typically in packages of between £25 million to £50 million each). For example, on the recent £187 million Kirkaldy hospital project, a club of four funding banks (Helaba, Lloyds Banking Group, NAB and SMBC) was established, each contributing £42.5 million to the senior debt requirement. The involvement of a large number of lead banks for each PFI project is naturally a source of high transaction costs (which are ultimately borne by the public sector in the form of higher annual charges). Perhaps more importantly, the clubbing together of banks in this manner results in a significant erosion – or perhaps a complete elimination – of competition between senior debt providers.

The impact of this has been stark. Between June 2000 and June 2008, the average initial 'credit margin' (the initial premium that banks charge borrowers above their own cost of raising capital, typically based on the London Inter-Bank Overnight Rate, or LIBOR) was less than 1 per cent for PFI projects. As shown in Figure 14.5, this increased to 180 basis points or 1.8 per cent by the end of 2008, and 312 basis points (3.12 per cent) by the end of the first quarter of 2009 (ThomsonOneBanker, 2009). Theoretically, a bank's credit margin on an investment is determined by the level of default risk (i.e. the risk of at least one missed payment of capital and interest) associated with the project. It is likely that senior lenders regard the level of default risk as somewhat higher during the current recession (the risk of contractor liquidation, for example, may be regarded as higher in conditions of serious economic downturn). However, the size of the increase in margins over the 12 months to April 2009 indicates that senior debt finance provided in this period contains a substantial premium that is unrelated to default risk, and is associated with credit constraints and the oligopolistic nature of the senior debt market.

In this period, other changes in the financing landscape combined to reduce significantly the economic attractiveness of the PFI model to the public sector. A review of the financing terms in post-July 2008 transactions, recorded in the database Project Finance International, shows a significant hardening of the terms on which banks were willing to lend (Project Finance International, 2009). Post-July 2008, banks typically required an increase in the amount of cash that is generated by the project to meet senior debt interest and principal repayment (i.e. the amount of cash flow projected to be available after the payment of operational costs).

They also commonly demanded a longer 'tail' – a period at the end of a contract during which no senior debt payments are scheduled to be made, such that all cash flow in the project after meeting operational costs is available to remunerate the SPV. The purpose of both these requirements is to ensure that projects generate substantial surplus cash flow, which helps to 'derisk' the project from the banks' perspective. But the effect is to increase, on average, the return to SPV investors – and thereby significantly reduce value for money for the public authorities involved.

In addition to the hardening of senior debt financing terms on transactions that have occurred, since mid-2008 many schemes have been delayed as a result of the lack of available credit (Hellowell, 2009). Responding to this in March 2009, the UK Treasury announced the establishment of a new private limited company, the Treasury Infrastructure Finance Unit (TIFU), which will be wholly owned by the government but will provide senior debt to projects on 'commercial terms' (HM Treasury, 2009b). The Treasury has confirmed that the government's all-in margin 'will reflect that of the other commercial lenders in the banking group' (HM Treasury, 2009, personal communication). The intention is that the Treasury intervention will be short-term, and TIFU will withdraw from the market when the opportunity for SPVs to refinance their loans emerges. In effect, what is being proposed is that the government will lend to public authorities on a basis of commercial interest rates that contain a substantial premium in excess of the level of risk being borne.

Conclusion

Public sector net debt is due to reach 76.2 per cent of GDP in 2013–14, from 43 per cent in 2008–09 (HM Treasury, 2009c). In this context, the government has confirmed that public sector capital spending will be reduced significantly over the coming years, from more than £37 billion in 2008–09 to £22 billion in 2013–14.

With the national debt rising and the rate of capital funding diminishing, the fiscal advantage of private finance is, from a political perspective, probably more attractive than ever to the government; and ministers confirmed in the annual budget statement of April 2009 that its 'strong commitment' to private finance will continue (HM Treasury, 2009c). There are currently 117 PFI projects in procurement, with a combined capital cost of £12.4 billion. Contracts for £4.4 billion of PFI projects are to be signed in 2009–10, with a further £3.54 billion signed in 2010–11 (HM Treasury, 2009c). After a great deal of uncertainty and speculation about the future of PFI between mid-2008 and early 2009, the medium-term prospects for the model now look very positive.

However, as current expenditure is predicted to fall in real terms over the coming years, the costs of contemporary PFI projects will clearly be a major call on public sector budgets. The extent to which the public sector is getting value for money for these schemes is therefore an issue of the first importance. The balance of the existing empirical evidence available suggests very strongly that private finance in the UK has contained, on average, an excess cost to the public sector – a premium that does not appear to be related to the risks borne by investors. This premium increased significantly in the wake of the financial crisis, particularly in respect of the senior debt component. As credit conditions ease, senior practitioners expect that senior debt interest rates will moderate somewhat, although not to the level that was normal before the financial crisis (Leftly, 2008).

Even before the financial crisis, however, the evidence suggests that PFI has not provided clear advantages in terms of more efficient construction, maintenance or support services. To date, the advantage of private finance in improving the delivery of public infrastructure projects (which could, theoretically, offset the higher cost of finance), has not been demonstrated – indeed, the available evidence, which should not be regarded as conclusive, suggests that, overall, PFI is associated with higher cost delivery. In this context, there is a clear imperative for more research on the economic credentials of private financing within the public sector.

Notes

1. The capital value of a project is a government estimate of what the scheme would have cost had the finance for their delivery been provided by the public sector under traditional procurement. The measure has only a loose association with the (much larger) amount of capital investment actually delivered by the private sector.
2. In April 2009, the UK government moved from Generally Accepted Accounting Practice (GAAP) to International Financial Reporting Standards (IFRS). The result has been that the vast majority of PFI assets have moved on to the balance sheets of the public authorities where previously the vast majority were off balance sheet. However, for central government, the level of capital expenditure will continue to be measured according to the European System of Accounts, which is based on a different theoretical framework to that of IFRS. The effect is that the vast majority of PFI investment will continue to remain invisible to public sector net debt (PSND).
3. In contrast, the embrace of PFI also had the effect of alienating the trade unions and a considerable section of the academic community, both of which were, from an early stage of the PFI's development, hostile to the policy. Along with the public sector union Unison, academics such as Jean Shaoul of the University of Manchester, and Allyson Pollock at the University of Edinburgh, have maintained a prolonged counter-argument regarding the costs of PFI and its detrimental effects on the service capacity of the public sector (see, e.g., Pollock, 2000; Pollock et al., 2002; Gaffney et al., 1999). As Greenaway et al. (2004) have noted, the Labour government has reacted to this criticism by ignoring it.
4. The SPV structure is used in PFI projects to ensure that lending to the project is 'non-recourse', providing comfort to investors. SPV members have limited liability, so that if the project goes wrong and payments are reduced, the parent company itself need not be affected. This structure also benefits senior debt providers, since the project is to a large degree insulated from a potential bankruptcy of any of the SPV shareholders.
5. Mathematically speaking, the IRR is the discount rate that brings to zero the NPV of a stream of cash flows. The two most important measures of return are the IRR on blended equity (based on the cash available to remunerate the SPV) and the IRR on the project (based on the cash flow available to meet capital and interest payments on subordinate and senior debt, and the remuneration of equity).
6. Critics of this position, such as Michael Spackman, the former head of public expenditure economics at the Treasury, argue that this view is misguided since risk is not constant between the sectors (Spackman, 2002). Following the work of Arrow and Lind (1970), Spackman suggests that the cost of risk to the government is lower than for the private sector because it can spread risk across a population of several million individuals. Spackman notes that, in order to provide a benchmark cost of finance for the purposes of comparing against the rate of return to private investors, a risk premium of less than 1 per cent should be added to the gilt rate.
7. The NAO has had a significant impact on the development of PFI policy in the UK. At the time of writing, the NAO has produced 65 reports on PFI, and a large number of policy changes have been enacted in response. The NAO's report on the 'windfall' gains that SPVs have generated through refinancing their loans (NAO, 2000) led to Treasury guidance in 2001 requiring such gains to be shared with the public sector on a 50–50 basis.

References

Arrow, K. and R. Lind (1970), 'Uncertainty and the evaluation of public investment decisions', *American Economic Review*, June, **60**, 364–780.

Arthur Andersen and Enterprise LSE (2000), *Value for Money Drivers in the Private Finance Initiative*, London: HM Treasury.

Blanc-Brude, F., H. Goldsmith and T. Välilä (2006), *Ex Ante Construction Cost in the European Road Sector: A Comparison of Public–Private Partnerships and Traditional Public Procurement*, EIB Economic and Financial Report 2006/01, Luxembourg: EIB.

Brealey, R., S. Myers and F. Allen (2008), *Principles of Corporate Finance*, 9th edn, New York: McGraw-Hill.

Broadbent, J. and R. Laughlin (2005), 'The role of PFI in the UK government's modernisation agenda', *Financial Accountability and Management*, **21** (1), 75–97.

Brown, G. (2003), Speech given to the annual dinner of the Confederation of British Industry, europa.eu.int/constitution.

Brown, G., R. Cook and J. Prescott (1994), 'Financing infrastructure investment: promoting a partnership between public and private finance', London: The Labour Party.

Clark, T., M. Elsby and S. Love (2001), 'Twenty-five years of falling investment? Trends in capital spending on public services', London: The Institute for Fiscal Studies.

Davies, A. (2008), 'Written response from the Minister for Finance and Public Service Delivery', available at: www.assemblywales.org, November.

Davoudi, S. and N. Timmins (2005), 'Critics say NHS mega-hospitals show need for different initiative', *The Financial Times*, p. 3, available at: www.ft.com, 1 July.

Department of Health (2009), 'Prioritised Capital Schemes approved to go ahead since May 1997 (England)', available at: www.dh.gov.uk.

Dudkin, G. and T. Välilä (2005), 'Transaction costs in public–private partnerships: a first look at the evidence', *EIB Economic and Financial Report 2005/03*, Luxemburg: EIB.

Flyvbjerg, B., M.S. Holm and S.L. Buhl (2002), 'Underestimating costs in public works projects: error or lie?', *Journal of the American Planning Association*, **68** (3), 279–95.

Gaffney, D., A.M. Pollock, D. Price and J. Shaoul (1999), 'The politics of the Private Finance Initiative and the new NHS', *British Medical Journal*, **319**, 249–53.

Gosling, T. (2003), *3 Steps Forward, 2 Steps Back: Reforming PPP Policy*, London: IPPR.

Greenaway, J., B. Salter and S. Hart (2004), 'The evolution of a "meta-policy": the case of the Private Finance Initiative and the health sector', *The British Journal of Politics and International Relations*, **6** (4), 507–26.

Heald, D. and N. Geaughan (1997), 'Accounting for the Private Finance Initiative', *Public Money and Management*, **17** (3), 11–16.

Healthcare Commission (2005), 'Acute hospital portfolio reviews', unpublished.

Hellowell, M. (2003), 'The PFI pioneer: Sir Malcolm Rifkind', *Public Private Finance*, London: Centaur Media PLC, 10 December.

Hellowell, M. (2009), 'Loss of initiative', *The Guardian*, 4 February, available at: www.guardian.co.uk/society.

Hellowell, M. and A. Pollock (2009), 'Non-profit distribution: the Scottish approach to private finance in public services', *Social Policy* and *Society*, **8** (3), 405–14.

HM Treasury (1997–2009), *Budget Reports*, London: The Stationery Office.

HM Treasury (2000), *Public–Private Partnerships – The Government's Approach*, London: The Stationery Office, April.

HM Treasury (2003), *PFI: Meeting the Investment Challenge*, London: The Stationery Office.

HM Treasury (2009a), *SoPC Addendum April 2009 – Amended Refinancing Provision*, London: The Stationery Office, available at: www.hm-treasury.gov.uk.

HM Treasury (2009b), 'PFI Signed Projects List', available at: www.hm-treasury.gov.uk/documents/public_private_partnerships/ppp_pfi_stats.cfm HM Treasury 2009b – TIFU letter.

HM Treasury (2009c), 'Safeguarding government investment', press release, London: The Stationery Office, available at: www.hm-treasury.gov.uk.

HM Treasury (2009d), *Budget Report 2009*, London: The Stationery Office, available at: www.hm-treasury.gov.uk, 09/06/2009.

Klein, M. (1997), 'The risk premium for evaluating public projects', *Oxford Review of Economic Policy*, **13** (4), 29–42.

Leathley, A. (1994), 'Smith out to steal a march on the Tories', *The Times*, 21 February, p. 3.

Leftly, M. (2008), 'There was a time when you couldn't talk about nuclear power at dinner parties: an interview with Tim Stone', *The Independent*, London, 2 November.

Lintner, J. (1965), 'The valuation of risk assets and the selection of risky investments in stock portfolios and capital budgets', *Review of Economics and Statistics*, **47**, 226–37.

Lonsdale, C. (2005), 'Risk transfer and the UK Private Finance Initiative: a theoretical analysis', *Policy and Politics*, **2**, 231–49.

Mott MacDonald (2002), *Review of Large Public Procurement in the UK*, Croydon: Mott MacDonald.

National Audit Office (1999), *The PFI Contract for the new Dartford and Gravesham Hospital*, London: The Stationery Office.

National Audit Office (2000), *The Refinancing of the Fazakerley Prison PFI Contract*, London: The Stationery Office.

National Audit Office (2002), *The PFI Contract for the Redevelopment of West Middlesex University Hospital*, London: The Stationery Office.

National Audit Office (2007a), 'Improving the PFI tendering process', London: The Stationery Office, available at: www.nao.org.uk/publications.

National Audit Office (2007b), 'The operational record of the first wave of PFI hospitals', unpublished, pp. 8–29.

Northern Ireland Executive (2008), 'Budget 2008–2011', available at: www.pfbudgetni.gov.uk.

The Observer (1994), 'Labour's private cash bombshell', 20 February, p. 1.

Office for National Statistics (2007), 'Population estimates for UK, England and Wales, Scotland and Northern Ireland – current datasets', available at: www.statistics.gov.uk/.

Office of Public Service Reform (OPSR) (2002), *Reforming our Public Services: Principles into Practice*, London: The Stationery Office.

Pollock, A.M. (2000), 'PFI is bad for your health', *Public Finance*, October, 30–31.

Pollock, A.M., J. Shaoul and N. Vickers (2002), 'Private finance and "value for money" in NHS hospitals: policy in search of a rationale', *British Medical Journal*, **324** (7347), 1205–9.

PricewaterhouseCoopers and J. Franks (2002), *Study into Rates of Return Bid on PFI Projects*, The Office of Government Commerce, London: The Stationery Office.

Project Finance International (2009), 'NHS Fife PFI hospital closes', available at: www.pfie.com (subscription only), 20 May.

Reynolds, D. (2008), 'New Labour, education and Wales: the devolution decade', *Oxford Review of Education*, **34** (6), 753–65.

Scottish Government (2008), 'Taking forward the Scottish Futures Trust', available at: www.scotland.gov.uk/Publications/2008/05/19155435/12.

Scottish National Party (2007), *Manifesto 2007*, Edinburgh: SNP.

Shaoul, J., A. Stafford and P. Stapleton (2007), 'Partnerships and the role of financial advisors: private control over public policy?', *The Policy Press*, **35** (3), 479–95.

Sharpe, W.F. (1964), 'Capital asset prices: a theory of market equilibrium under conditions of risk', *Journal of Finance*, **19**, 425–42.

Spackman, M. (2002), 'Public–private partnerships: lessons from the British approach', *Economic Systems*, **26** (3), 283–301.

Standard and Poor's (2004), 'PFI projects reshape the credit profile of Europe's construction companies', *Infrastructure Finance*, February.

ThomsonOneBanker (2009), 'Project finance listings', available at: OneBanker.com.

Timmins, T. (2005), 'Doubts on funding NHS monuments', *The Financial Times*, 10 June, p. 3.

Williamson, O. (1985), *The Economic Institutions of Capitalism*, New York: The Free Press.

World Bank (2007), 'Public private partnerships in the new EU member states: managing fiscal risks', Washington: World Bank.

15 Empirical PPP experiences in Europe: national variations of a global concept

Gerhard Hammerschmid and Tamyko Ysa

Global diffusion of an Anglo-Saxon concept

The idea of public–private partnership (PPP) as a model for public procurement and financing public investments arrived on a wave of public management modernization issues in the early 1990s in Europe and was first implemented on a broader basis in the UK under the Private Finance Initiative (PFI). A European Investment Bank (2007) report clearly shows that the UK is still a forerunner in terms of both number of PPP projects and volume. Out of a cumulative value of €194.7 billion that has been signed up until the end of 2006, the UK accounts for 57.7 per cent. However, it is also clear that the UK market is maturing (e.g. Ysa, 2007), whereas the rest of the European PPP market is growing.

International organizations such as the World Bank, the OECD and the International Monetary Fund, together with multinational professional companies (e.g. PwC, 2005; Deloitte, 2006a, 2006b; DLA Piper, 2007; Ernst & Young, 2008), played an important role in the international diffusion of PPPs both as promoters and as knowledge carriers. Within Europe especially, the European Commission has given a strong impetus in a similar form when launching a Green Paper on PPPs in 2004 (European Commission, 2004).

PPPs have raised high expectations among scholars, governments and practitioners in Europe alike. They are seen as 'a new generation of management reforms' (Pollitt, 2003, p. 53) and have found their way into many government programmes throughout Europe. The German federal government programme from 1999, '*Moderner Staat – Moderne Verwaltung*', for example, claims that partnerships will help to stimulate public administration, de-bureaucratization and modernization. Ham and Koppenjan (2002, p. 594) refer to partnerships as 'one of the most important challenges facing organizations in the public and private domain in the first decade of the new millennium'. The attractiveness of PPPs is mostly argued with regard to contributing to wider societal goals such as competitiveness, economic development and innovation.

As has been described by Wettenhall (2003), the currently dominating notion of PPP both in the literature and among regulating bodies is thoroughly Anglo-Saxon, putting more continental European or Scandinavian corporatist public–private arrangements in the rear. Thus contractually formalized cooperation tends to dominate current PPP debates in Europe. This comes in various forms of build, operate, transfer (BOT) models along with principles of competition, transparency and equality of treatment and experiences from the UK (HM Treasury, 2006; see also Chapter 14 in this volume).

We might begin by understanding PPP as both a management or governance concept and a currently powerful label signalling modernity and progress. This, in turn, raises the question of how this concept, with its specific Anglo-Saxon moulding, has spread within other European countries with their distinctive state traditions. As all organizational practices are influenced by socially construed, regulative, normative or cognitive rule sets that have path-dependent histories (e.g. Scott, 2001), institutional embeddedness of concepts such as PPPs should attract scholarly attention with the need for country-specific observations. Despite European integration and global trends, national institutional contexts as well as state and administrative traditions of individual states can be expected to have a strong influence on how global trends are interpreted, translated and transformed during their diffusion into national structures (Czarniawska, 2002).

More and more studies challenge the notion of homogeneity and convergence (e.g. Pollitt, 2001; Pollitt and Bouckaert, 2004; Christensen and Lægreid, 2007), particularly for the European public management context (e.g. Page, 2003; Olsen, 2006; Gualmini, 2008; Meyer and Hammerschmid, 2010) and draw attention to a variety of contextual factors that structure the way in which countries organize their administrations. Recently even the OECD – in the past one of the grand observers of 'universal trends' of public administration modernization and itself a driver of homogenization – has become more cautious and has stressed diversity and the relevance of context (OECD, 2005).

This chapter aims to provide a structured overview of the spread of PPPs in several countries of Central, Eastern and Southern Europe (for the UK and Scandinavia, see separate chapters). This follows earlier research (Albareda et al., 2007; Meyer and Hammerschmid, 2010) that indicated considerable institutional differences between these three country clusters. We shall thereby focus on the long-term infrastructure contracts (LTIC) form of PPPs as outlined by Hodge et al. in the introductory chapter of this volume and for pragmatic reasons have decided to focus on a sample of European countries within these three country clusters. For Central Europe we focus on Austria, Belgium, France, Germany, the Netherlands and Switzerland. Within the Eastern European states, the Czech Republic,

Hungary, Poland and Romania promise to be instructive and, for the Southern European countries, Italy, Portugal and Spain were included for this chapter.

Beyond a pure mapping of single-country developments, we aim to look for similarities and dissimilarities of PPP implementation throughout Europe. The analysis of national experiences is structured alongside several points of comparison. After outlining the important role of the EC in promoting the development of PPPs and shaping discussions at an EU-wide level, we analyse the institutional–legal framework that PPPs meet in the various European countries. Besides specific PPP regulation we are interested in the establishment of special taskforces and government initiatives to foster PPP. The section covers PPP practice, whereby we map the implementation dynamics of PPPs in various European countries with regard to policy fields and sectors, government levels as well as types of existing PPP projects. The final section provides some first insights into recent research and evaluations on PPPs to learn about the main challenges that confront PPPs within Europe.

Although we are impaired by rather limited comparative data, we show that all three of the above-mentioned institutional factors (i.e. the legislative framework, establishment of taskforces and government initiatives) indicate an increasing relevance and adoption of PPPs in Europe, but at quite different speeds. And in spite of the observed heterogeneity among the various European countries, we try to capture some commonalities such as a rather reluctant implementation, a stronger focus on institutional instead of contractual forms of PPPs, or a much higher relevance of legal questions and constraints that differentiate European experiences from the Anglo-Saxon world.

The EC Green Paper as the cornerstone of the European discussion

Basically the use of PPPs remains the responsibility of the EU member states. None the less, the EU has shown strong interest in promoting the idea in general as well as regulating its application (Werner, 2008). In 2003 the European Commission drafted a first document entitled *Guidelines for Successful Public–Private Partnerships* (European Commission, 2003), which included examples of good practices. In 2004 the Commission then presented a Green Paper with the aim of launching a greater debate about the use and potential of PPPs and eventually necessary amendments of EU legislation (European Commission, 2004). Its main focus lay on the question of how the rules and principles derived from Community law on public contracts and concessions were to be applied when a private partner was being selected, and in the context of different types of PPP, how they applied throughout the subsequent duration of the contract.

Following the EU Green Paper (European Commission, 2004, p. 4), partnerships have to be understood as a 'forms of cooperation between public authorities and the world of business which aim to ensure the funding, construction, renovation, management or maintenance of an infrastructure or the provision of a service'. The European Commission distinguished PPPs of a purely contractual nature (e.g. concessive models and various forms of build, operate, transfer – BOT) and PPPs of an institutional nature in the form of a distinct mixed entity ('institutionalized partnership'). The specific agreements tend to differ considerably in their allocation of risks and responsibilities, in the ownership of the assets and their duration.

The consultation process on this Green Paper resulted in the finding that a special EU regulation was necessary only in specific areas such as concessions or new tendering procedures such as a competitive dialogue (COM(2005)0569). The Commission also communicated policy options to 'ensure effective competition for PPPs without unduly limiting the flexibility needed to design innovative and often complex projects'. An EU Parliament 'Resolution on public–private partnerships and Community law on public procurement and concessions' similarly opposed the creation of a separate legal regime for PPPs but recognized the need for legislative initiatives in the areas of concessions and tendering procedures (2006/204(INI)). In 2008 the Commission adopted an 'Interpretative Communication on the application of community law on public procurement and concessions to institutionalised public-private partnerships' (European Commission, 2008), entailing further legal amendments on national level. Beyond political promotion and triggering legal amendments within the member states, the EU also played an important role in promoting PPPs over its bodies such as directorates-general and especially the European Investment Bank (EIB). The EIB plays a major role in financing the development of infrastructure in particular with regard to Trans-European Networks (EIB, 2004, 2007). For this reason, the EIB is mobilizing resources and promoting PPPs through both advice and loans (as early as 2003, the EIB had already signed loans for PPP projects amounting to a total value of €14.7 billion (Thomson, 2005)). A considerable motivation for the popularity of PPPs in Europe also came from the euro convergence criteria (Maastricht criteria) setting up binding limitations for annual national budget deficit (below 3 per cent of GDP) and national public debt (below 60 per cent of GDP) and triggering member states' efforts to find alternative arrangements to finance public infrastructure investments.

Such developments at EU level faced considerable scepticism from academia, public-law experts and public administration in several EU countries. This scepticism is articulated, for example, in critical contributions to the EU Green Paper consultation process. Among public management academia in Germany, PPP was seen as 'a profound problem' making way for a 'minimal state reduced to sovereign tasks' (Eichhorn, 2004, pp. 6–7). In addition, common references are made to a longstanding and successful tradition of public–public or public–private cooperation at local government level in the form of municipal enterprises in many countries. This form of institutionalized partnership with often in-house contracts is regarded as being threatened by the current EU initiatives focusing on more competitive and less cooperative arrangements.

The institutional framework for PPPs in European countries
The resonance and adoption of PPPs is strongly influenced by the institutional frameworks existing in the various countries. In this chapter, we shall concentrate on three specific aspects: the establishment of PPP taskforces; PPP legislation; and specific government initiatives to foster PPPs. These factors can be expected to have a considerable effect on the diffusion and implementation of PPPs in a country. Research in the social sciences suggests that the existence of such an institutional framework offers options and incentives for the actors but does not force them to act in a certain manner (Scharpf, 1997; Campbell, 2004; Christensen and Lægreid, 2007). It can therefore be regarded as both an indicator of political attitude towards PPP and the reform dynamics on a national level.

PPP taskforces
A first important component of the institutional framework is taskforces, formed as specific bodies to coordinate, consult, collect and stimulate the establishment of PPPs. Some are even mandated to evaluate current practices and make suggestions for legal amendments. In all countries covered in this chapter, such bodies have been established, albeit in quite different forms, at different levels of government, and at different times. The first one was established in the Netherlands in 1999 (the Kenniscentrum PPS). Isomorphism seems to play a role in this dynamic: the creation of the mixed-ownership 'Partnerschaften Deutschland AG' body in Germany in 2008 explicitly referred to the 'British Partnerships UK plc' as a role model.

The most common model has been the establishment of a taskforce as a specialized unit within a ministry, mostly the one with the responsibility for traffic and infrastructure, finance or economics (see Table 15.1). This can be observed in the Czech Republic, France, Germany, Hungary, Italy, the Netherlands, Poland or Portugal. In some cases such as the Czech Republic, this was an explicit reaction to failures in early PPP projects. It has also been a common phenomenon that several PPP taskforces exist in

Table 15.1   Taskforce models for PPP developed in Europe

Taskforce models	Countries
Specialized public unit	Belgium, the Czech Republic, France, Germany (initially), Hungary, Italy, the Netherlands, Poland, Portugal, Spain
Intersectoral taskforce	Germany (after some years), Switzerland, the UK
Private sector-initiative taskforce	Austria

Source: Authors' own.

parallel, indicating an increasing degree of specialization. Different ministerial taskforces can be established for different policy fields, as well, such
as occurred in France. In the case of Portugal, too, a general taskforce
within the Treasury is complemented by a sector-specialized taskforce for
health and a further agency focusing on project finance issues, similar to
the Italian 'Cassa Depositi e Prestiti'.

A second reason for multiple taskforces is related to different government
levels. Often parallel to a national taskforce, similar arrangements can exist
on the regional or state level, as is the case in Belgium, Germany, Italy or
Spain. In Spain, no taskforce has been established at the national level due
to a rather high degree of regional autonomy and considerable transfer of
responsibilities towards the regional level. Madrid, Catalonia and Murcia
indeed have all created such taskforces at regional level. Such decentralized
forms unavoidably thwart coordination and competency bundling, but
also allow room for context-specific adoptions and innovation.

Another type of PPP taskforce observable in Europe is the intersectoral
agency. Launched jointly by government and business, such agencies themselves constitute a form of PPP and fit well to the traditional corporatist
arrangements in many European countries. The Swiss case is an interesting
example, where all three government levels in cooperation with companies and universities established a joint taskforce. Germany, on the other
hand, started with a typically ministry-based PPP taskforce which evolved
towards a mixed-ownership agency after several years. PPP infrastructure
projects constitute a promising business area for the finance sector, consultants and professional service firms (PwC, 2005; Freshfield Bruckhaus
Deringer, 2005; Deloitte 2006a, 2006b; DLA Piper, 2007; Button, 2008;
Ernst & Young, 2008), universities and different industries, all of whom
play an important promoter role in many European countries. A third and
quite rare model with considerably less legitimacy and influence is a purely
non-state taskforce based on companies or academies such as in Austria,

where government at all three state levels stood back rather than establishing any form of institutional arrangement on their own.

PPP regulation

A second important institutional factor is appropriate PPP legislation. Legislation clarifying legal uncertainties as well as adjusting existing public procurement and investment regulation and models has played a crucial role in triggering PPPs in Europe, and all European countries have made legal amendments, albeit to varying degrees. It is evident, for example, that the legalistic *Rechtsstaat* tradition of many European states – contrary to the Anglo-Saxon law tradition – led to a strong focus on legal aspects and uncertainties that are considered one of the major PPP obstacles. Many of these amendments were caused by EU directions that had to be implemented by member and candidate states, and in most Eastern European countries the EC accession process was a key driver of PPP reforms (Ernst & Young, 2008).

Several countries passed legal amendments for specific policy areas to allow the use of PPP arrangements. As early as the mid-1990s, Austria, Germany, Italy, Poland and Romania had established the legal framework to allow private finance for motorways. Some years later – between 2002 and 2007 – Germany and other countries, such as the Czech Republic, France, Poland and Portugal, took the further step of passing specific PPP legislation in face of mounting problems. Spain (with its recent Contract Law for the Public Sector, L30/2007) for the first time introduced a specific contract called 'collaboration between the public and private sector', which shelters the notion of partnership and multiple complex contracts in one arrangement, although concessions for transport and motorways have been used for decades. A high complexity of different laws for different sectors, contract types and government levels along EU-driven amendments often resulted in confusion and the need for further legal amendments. Other countries, such as Austria, Bulgaria, Hungary, the Netherlands and Switzerland, however, saw no such need for a specific PPP law, as they regarded the flexibility of existing public procurement and finance rules as sufficient.

Partnership arrangements for public investments also have a quite different history in the various European countries. For example, Southern European countries such as Portugal and Spain enjoy a long history and, through this experience, have adjusted laws concerning concession models, for instance. Interesting differences can also be observed with regard to the content of PPP legislation. Portugal, for example, not only approved a PPP law in 2003 but even implemented the duty of all public bodies to carry out a value for money (VfM) and sustainability test. In most other EU countries legal amendments focused on public tendering and contracting rules. The legal changes with regard to standardization and regulation aimed to reduce both insecurity and necessary resources for such processes to allow a wider range of PPP applications. However, there is also the danger of PPP regulation that is too rigid or too complex. For example, since the legal amendment in Spain in 2007, for more than one year not a single project could be implemented under the newly created collaborative contract regime. The competitive dialogue was considered the main difficulty, with which neither the civil servants nor the companies felt at ease. Furthermore, the legislation itself determined that this contract could only be implemented after proof that none of the other already existing contract types offered a better fit to the needs. A specific challenge of such PPP legislation has also been the need to integrate quite different legal areas such as public sector and private contract law, budgetary laws, regulations regarding public financing, administrative law and tax law.

Government initiatives
Government reform initiatives are also expected to have a considerable impact on the adoption of PPPs, as has been the case for the UK Private Finance Initiative (see Chapter 14 in this volume). Screening our country sample, we can discern two kinds of political initiatives. First, a majority of governments regard PPP as a promising solution to cope with increasing demands to finance public infrastructure in various policy fields. This is, for example, demonstrated by the Bulgarian National Healthcare Plan, the German state modernization programme mentioned in the introduction, the Italian Economic and Financial White Paper, the Polish Housing Programme, the Portuguese Infrastructure Programme, the Spanish Transport and Infrastructure Plan, and the Romanian Strategy to Modernize Public Administration.

Also, most initiatives at the regional or local level show a similar positive reception of PPPs, for example the City of Milan Plan for City Reorganization or the Madrid Regional Government Hospitals Project (€800 million for seven new hospitals – infrastructure only – combining the PFI model and a concession contract). For these large-scale investment programmes, PPPs are constitutive and a central marketing argument. Eastern and Southern European countries especially use PPP as a model to finance their huge needs in infrastructure, which are seen as basic conditions for economic development, with quite different starting points. Whereas in Italy, Portugal and Spain PPPs are not regarded as something new and enjoy quite a high amount of political support due to the need for competitive public infrastructure,[1] in Eastern European countries PPP initiatives face much higher political risk due to their transition time legacy.

A second somewhat different kind of political initiative, however, has occurred in continental European countries such as Belgium (Flanders), France, Germany and the Netherlands, with less urgent demands for public infrastructure investments (or alternative funding to develop them). For these countries, PPPs have not only been a model to finance public investments but in a broader form have also been seen as a general driver for public sector modernization. The Netherlands and Flanders published a government programme on PPPs as early as 1999. The German federal government programme in 1999 and the Austrian federal government programme in 2000 are clear examples for this. However, in most cases these two kinds of motives are difficult to separate and often become blended.

Figure 15.1 summarizes the institutional environments for PPPs with regard to taskforces, legislation and government initiatives in the relevant European countries. Such comparisons and classifications always have to be taken with caution due to data limitations and ongoing change. None the less, the rather high degree of taskforces, legislation and reform initiatives is a clear indicator of the political will to foster PPPs in most European countries. In this vein, Belgium (Flanders), the Czech Republic, France, Germany, Italy, Poland and Portugal all show a rather high degree of political will to improve the institutional framework for the implementation of PPPs, while countries such as Austria, Bulgaria, Romania and Switzerland are clearly lagging behind. All countries in our sample experimented in the period 1999 to 2007 with different parts of the institutional framework, and it is obvious that these developments are not yet complete and are under the steady influence of external issues. Irrespective of national variations, the overall development of institutional frameworks indicates an increasing dynamic towards PPP arrangements in Europe, albeit in a more reluctant way than in most Anglo-Saxon countries due to legal difficulties, the ideological link to plead for a strong defence of the welfare state, and clear differences between single countries.

We also have to be aware that the institutional framework encompassing taskforces, legislation and political initiatives covers only some of the several factors affecting the diffusion and implementation dynamics for PPPs at the national level. Other relevant factors such as financial pressures, administrative cultures, earlier experiences or the local political situation will also have a considerable impact, but could not be covered in this chapter.

Mapping implementation of PPPs in Europe
The LTIC-type of PPPs derived its origin in Europe in the UK at the beginning of the 1990s, when they reached an impressive share of public investments of about 10 to 15 per cent (see Chapter 14 in this volume). HM

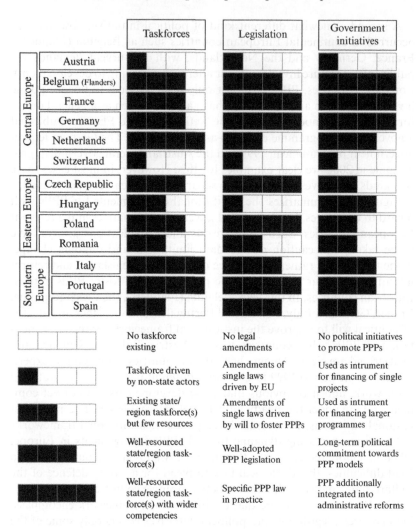

Source: Authors' own (based on information in Button, 2008).

Figure 15.1   Institutional environment for PPPs in Europe

Treasury (2006) details UK information on number of projects, volume, share of public investments as well as financial performance. With regard to most other European countries, reliable data – especially in a comparative form – are not available, leading to a rather vague and sketchy picture of the current PPP landscape in Europe (Button, 2008; OECD, 2008). This is especially due to different contract typologies. It is still difficult to decide, for instance, if some specific contracts should be classified as PPP or not, and administrative-law traditions differ among countries. It is a Sisyphean task to assess the practical implementation of PPPs over such a large spectrum of different countries, and for our analysis, we often have to refer to government or professional organization reports.

Looking at continental European countries, we see considerable differences in implementing LTICs even within clusters of similar countries. Both Switzerland and Austria feature a very low number of PPP projects (Bolz, 2002; BMF, 2008) with some larger-scale projects tendered in the last few years and a general preference towards institutionalized forms of PPPs. On the other hand, in other Central European countries such as Belgium, France, Germany and the Netherlands, we find a large variety of initiated and even signed PPP projects. Aside from all the differences, there seems to be a common preference for using such arrangements to procure transport, health and education infrastructure. With regard to government level, a clear picture is again difficult to discern due to quite different national arrangements of allocating tasks to the various governmental levels. In France and the Netherlands, national government is strongly involved in the health sector and public housing, while in Germany, these sectors are the responsibility of the *Länder* and the municipalities. As a broad observation, we can note that the national level in Central European countries is mostly engaged in rather big transport infrastructure projects, although the number of completed projects is relatively modest to date. Austria, Belgium, Germany, France and the Netherlands have signed some large-scale railway or motorway projects in recent years. In 2007 France entered into concession agreements for 35 projects in the areas of transport, schools and health (Ernst & Young, 2008).

Below the national level the situation is rather difficult to map. In Germany the *Länder* level is less active in PPP, albeit with considerable variations. North Rhine–Westphalia can be described as a front-runner, with early attempts and a clear policy and legislation. Also school infrastructure – being part of local government – has become a major area for PPP arrangements in Germany throughout the last decade (DIfU, 2005). It is therefore not surprising that the majority of German PPP projects can be found at the local government level, mainly in the subgroup of larger cities. In France, the regional level is traditionally quite weak, unlike the case of Belgium, where Flanders has become the key promoter of PPPs. Flanders has 46 PPP projects with a value of €4.7 billion mostly in transportation and education (Van Garsse, 2006; Vandermeeren, 2009). Although the Belgium federal government, Wallonia and Brussels have all taken steps to investigate PPPs, there have not been any concrete investment plans up until now in these areas (DLA Piper, 2007).

Overall, then, one can come to only rough estimates with regard to the distribution of PPP projects in continental European states. In spite of a rising interest, contractual cooperation for infrastructure projects in various forms of build, operate, transfer (BOT) or build, own, operate, transfer (BOOT) models are a relatively novel form of organizational practice and practical implementation still seems to be comparatively sparse (Bastin, 2003; DiGaetano and Strom, 2003; BMWA, 2004; BMF, 2008; Button, 2008). The gap between rhetoric and practice seems to be substantial. The experiences in the Netherlands illustrate clear differences between political desideratum and practical implementation (Teisman and Klijn, 2002; Klijn et al., 2007; Edelenbos and Klijn, 2009). Although PPPs have quite early on become an important instrument in government policy, the initial interest in the 1990s after two road tunnel projects and two railway projects waned. Projects were too expensive, or did not attract financial private investment. Initial expectations were reduced and only relatively few projects – mostly for infrastructure projects and in area development – were completed. Research indicates that 'whilst the contractual form of PPP dominates the policy discussion, it is the partnership form (often in a rather loosely coupled organizational form) that has so far been dominant in practice' (Klijn et al., 2007, p. 79), an observation that can be made for many continental European, but also Scandinavian, countries and somehow explains the strong EU Commission focus on institutionalized forms of partnerships.

For the Eastern European country cluster, practical implementation also seems to have been quite hesitant, although interest of national governments is quite high due to a strong need for infrastructure investments and limited financial capabilities. As pointed out in the previous section, PPPs mostly serve as an instrument for procuring and financing public infrastructure investments in these countries, and implementation is considerably driven by international fund-providing organizations such as the World Bank or the EIB. Motorways financed through concession models are at the heart of PPP implementation in these countries. But airports, railways, utilities and higher education buildings have been implemented or are at least in the planning stage (e.g. DLA Piper, 2007; Button, 2008). With regard to policy fields, a very broad spectrum of applications can be observed and the number of projects varies considerably between the single countries. At the national level, Bulgarian projects have not passed the planning stage yet, while Hungary and Poland have already tendered several motorway projects. Overall, therefore, the situation appears similar to the continental European experience, with the number of signed and finished projects being rather small. Hungary can be called a precursor with a rather large number of projects at planning stage (DLA

Piper, 2007; Button, 2008). Unfortunately, almost no reliable comparative information is available for PPP implementation at sub-national and local government level. Also, larger projects are planned only for capital cities, where it is unclear whether the impetus came from the city itself or from the national level.

In contrast, the Southern European sample of Italy, Portugal and Spain shows large-scale implementation of PPP models and more resilient data. PPPs are regarded by quite different actors as a useful tool that is able to fill the infrastructural gap cumulated during the last decades, especially in key sectors such as transportation. According to the Italian PPP taskforce, Italy counts about 1500 planned PPP projects alone for the period 2000 to 2003, with most of them in the field of transportation infrastructure (De Pierris and Foschi, 2008; Milotti and Patumi, 2008). Taking into account that not all planned projects are realized, it is still an impressive number, which demonstrates the broad acceptance and use across different administrative levels and sectors. On the other hand, these PPP projects are mostly quite small ones at the local government level. Higher public attention was raised by large-scale projects such as the Messina bridge, a new metro line in Rome or several highways (Freshfield Bruckhaus Deringer, 2005). The high number of PPPs is also quite equally distributed across the Italian regions. The diffusion of PPPs in Spain has to be seen in context of administrative competencies and structures that became highly regionalized throughout the last few decades (Torres and Pina, 2001). So the potential use of PPP on the national level is limited to supra-regional projects or particular sectors, like railways where the national state still has its infrastructure responsibilities. At the regional level, for instance, the Autonomous Community of Madrid used the PPP model to build seven hospitals facilities based on a 30-year concession (Rodríguez, 2006) and in Catalonia, from 2003 until 2008, roads, the City of Justice, prisons, police stations, courts, tram lines and a new tube line have been developed as partnership arrangements with a total value of about €7.1 billion (Abelaira, 2009). More recently, the Spanish government also launched a policy initiative to expand wind-power energy, almost entirely financed through PPP arrangements (Dinica, 2008). In 2007, about 30 projects across all sectors were at the planning stage, indicating the ongoing attractiveness of this model in Spain (DLA Piper, 2007). For Portugal also, a rather high implementation of PPP projects can be observed for the last decade. PPPs were mostly implemented in the transport sector (Button, 2008), with main projects including motorways, a new airport in Lisbon, ports and high-speed railways, but also quite a large hospital programme.

An overall assessment of these developments in Europe can only be made with considerable caution. We can detect a much higher openness towards PPPs and implementation dynamic in the Southern European states compared to Central and Eastern Europe. Regarding policy fields, we can also observe a frequent adoption in the wide field of transport infrastructure (roads, bridges, tunnels, rail), and especially motorways. The reason for this focus seems to lie in its estimated impact for economic growth, which in most cases is at the heart of political motivation to promote PPPs, as well as in the fact that road tolling allows a quite straightforward and established way of user charging. The second most important area of application, albeit with a large distance, is health infrastructure (hospitals) and education (schools), where especially regional and municipal authorities have initiated and implemented quite a large number of projects. Other significant sectors include water and waste management, defence, sports and leisure facilities, government buildings and prisons (DLA Piper, 2007; Button, 2008).

Current challenges of PPPs in a European context

More recent experience in Europe to establish PPPs as a model for public procurement and public infrastructure investment clearly indicates that such projects are faced with many challenges. Against the background of the rather short history of PPPs in most European countries and the low number of implemented projects, we should not be surprised at the rather limited evidence on outcomes, efficiency or performance of such arrangements. In addition, there is no monitoring of PPP activities at European level (EIB, 2007), with data mostly collected by organizations with vested interests. There are several challenges worthy of note here.

Existing taskforces are often not adequately equipped or mandated to provide systematic evaluation of existing experiences. An exemplary positive example is the Czech PPP centre, with an explicit focus on evaluation and research. In Hungary, the strong political belief in the importance of PPP for economic development also favours evaluation. In Western Europe such evaluations are more common and can be found in Belgium, France, Germany and the Netherlands. In Italy, a special body promoted by the Ministry of Economics and Finance collects data of all PPP projects and publishes a yearly report. There is no information available on the outcomes, but a quite clear impression of volume, policy fields and levels is none the less given. In Portugal, the taskforce within the Treasury also aims to serve as an evaluation unit. Overall, we can conclude that the PPP evaluation capacity is not well developed in most European countries.

For nearly all of the countries covered in this chapter, reliable empirical evidence especially with regard to long-term outcomes is still missing. Evaluations and research mostly come in the form of single-project assessments, recommendations for legal adjustments or hands-on practitioner guidelines. What can be more easily assessed is the success or failure of single projects. Indeed, the assessment of earlier pilot projects often had an important impact on the further development dynamics in various countries. In Austria and the Czech Republic, for example, the failure of highly visible pilot projects affected both public attitude and political will in a quite negative way, leading almost to a halt of any further activities. The opposite happened in France, where, after the governmental change in 2002, the political climate switched to a pro-PPP position although there had been quite negative experiences with early attempts in the 1980s.

Germany is faced with a high number of PPP projects, but it is difficult to estimate their efficiency (DIfU, 2005). In Eastern European countries, concession models to finance motorways were one of the earliest and most common forms of implementing PPPs. Importantly, their performance can hardly be called successful in the eyes of private investors. Due to mis-estimation of the future traffic volume, investors suffered substantial losses both in the Czech Republic and Hungary (Kierzenkowski, 2008). In Hungary, the Czech Republic and Romania, motorway PPPs had to be cancelled for such reasons. Despite such setbacks, however, the PPP idea stayed alive in these countries.

In Southern European countries the higher spread of and political support for PPPs indicate a more successful implementation path. However, in Portugal, similar to Italy and Spain, several failures of PPP projects can be observed. Many of the concession-based motorways in the 1990s, for example, failed for reasons quite contrary to the Eastern European experiences (Castelos and Melo, 2008). The shadow-toll concept without direct user tolls resulted in a higher user rate than expected. Government then had to discharge higher concessions to the private investor. This motorway programme contained seven concessions with a value of about €3.4 billion. To date this was the biggest PPP programme in terms of investment value. The final costs for the public sector doubled and had a crucial impact on the government budget. A second source of difficulty was the insufficient implementation of environmental standards (Monteiro, 2005). However, all these defects could be overcome and none of the projects had to be cancelled. At the same time, large projects such as the Vasco da Gama bridge, with an investment value of €1 billion stayed on the agenda.[2]

Overall, we can observe both successes and failures in implementing large-scale PPP infrastructure projects in Europe. As a consequence, most countries put considerable efforts into the development of more standardized PPP models to reduce transaction costs and project risks. We have to understand PPPs as a different model compared to traditional ways of procurement or investments, and as such, it naturally causes considerable challenges for both government and private actors. The question of cooperation and interaction between actors from different domains with different and sometimes even opposing motives, goals, interests, values and traditions is of high relevance (e.g. Klijn and Teisman, 2003). 'Boundary-spanning' (Noble and Jones, 2006) can indeed be regarded as the main managerial challenge for PPPs, especially in many European countries often characterized by a rather pronounced demarcation between the sectors.

All countries covered in this chapter were active in adjusting their institutional framework in terms of setting up taskforces, and regarding legislative amendments. Taskforces can help to solve the lack of competence and experience in dealing with PPP, although such taskforces were not always able to fulfil these ambitious needs. Coordination of taskforces across different government levels or different ministries is one further challenge in states with a more devolved state structure, as in the federal countries Austria, Germany, Spain or Switzerland. Eastern European countries, on the other hand, seem to suffer from a lack of state and administrative capacity and quality to tackle PPPs successfully. As long as the counterpart on the public side lacks necessary competencies and resources, PPP solutions can hardly develop or can even lead to fiscal damage (Budina et al., 2007).

Compared to Anglo-Saxon countries, the amendment of legislation to support PPPs has proven to be far more complex and demanding in most European countries. Nevertheless this is a crucial point for the use of PPPs. Existing laws of procurement or budget are sometimes opposed to PPPs. The consequences of legal uncertainties are even more crucial due to the long-term duration, high volume and importance of delivered services and goods for public life of many PPP arrangements. So it was a logical step for most of the countries to adjust their legal framework, although few did this in a holistic form and passed a specific PPP law.

A common finding seems to have been that a high degree of trust and confidence between partners is essential for long-term relational contracts (Budäus and Grüb, 2008). A lack of trust easily leads to tensions and eventually to the collapse of a PPP project, as has been the case in several Eastern European projects but also some large-scale projects in Austria and Germany. Especially for Eastern European countries, the effect of a loss in confidence by private partners can be quite harmful due to the extensive need for investment. Political stability has been a further important factor, and regular political changes in many Eastern European countries are a clear inhibiting factor (Brenck et al., 2005). In Hungary, a renationalization focus in the election campaign in 1998 led to the cancellation of two motorway pilots and a government change in 1998 in Poland had similar consequences. Unstable political climates bear substantial risks for private investors and lead to policy inconsistency. Especially in Eastern Europe, these new arrangements also make considerable room for corruption due to institutional deficiencies, substantial transparency deficits or a generally low level of media pressure (European Commission, 2006).

Conclusions

Overall, the picture emerging from this analysis of PPPs in Central, Eastern and Southern European countries is still rather vague and more one of heterogeneity than of a common European path. None the less, some lessons can be drawn. Internationally PPPs started in the transport sector as a model of financing motorways or railways (OECD, 2008, p. 28), and this can also be observed for most European countries. Transportation is still the largest part of the European PPP market, with investments for bridges, tunnels, roads and rail amounting to about 82 per cent of the total European PPP market in 2006 (DLA Piper, 2007). Following initial experiences in this policy field, PPPs found their way into sectors such as school and health infrastructure and services, as well as waste and water management, government buildings and prisons (EIB, 2004; Button, 2008). Essentially, there is no limit to the sectors where a PPP may be applied and the observed countries show a great variety of applications.

With regard to country-specific development paths, the current analysis looking at both institutional frameworks and practical implication confirms earlier analyses indicating quite different development stages in Europe (CBI, 2007; Button, 2008). Whereas the Southern European country cluster as well as various continental European countries such as France and Germany feature a much higher overall dynamic, most other countries can be regarded as in an early developmental stage. A lower pressure for public infrastructure investment, along with a less critical budget situation and a specific state tradition with a rather strong demarcation of public and private sectors, has resulted in a more hesitant approach in many continental European countries. An interesting case here is Switzerland, where low budget pressures as well as a lack of incentives and institutional frameworks stood against a wider diffusion of PPPs (Lienhard, 2006). Political will has also been a more important factor in Central Europe than in the Eastern European sample, where external demands of international organizations as well as institutional deficiencies seem to have played a stronger role. For the Southern European country cluster, a much higher political will was also observed due to a longer tradition of similar arrangements and more urgent infrastructure demands.

Moreover, financial constraints were strong drivers in both Southern and Eastern European countries. Often PPP serves as a compromise used when EU funds or EIB loans are limited. This is unsurprising. Also unsurprising was the central role of the ministries of finance, traffic or infrastructure. Infrastructure demands were also relevant in nearly all European countries, with the Maastricht criteria contributing to the attractiveness of PPPs, albeit to a varying degree. Especially for countries such as Germany, the Netherlands and Belgium (Flanders), the desire to enhance the efficiency of large-scale projects and to push forward public administration modernization were also central additional motives to foster PPPs.

In most continental, Eastern and Southern European countries, observers are confronted with insufficient and contradictory empirical data about the use of PPPs with regard to project numbers, volume, policy fields and administrative levels. This is especially the case in relation to the outcomes of such projects. A quite flexible use of the notion of PPPs, the lack of common criteria for them, a field very much in flux and a myriad of projects at various government levels, many of which exist below the radar of international research, hamper a thorough assessment of European-wide implementation. What can be stated is that PPPs will not replace traditional procurement and investment on a large scale. Such arrangements will remain of limited macroeconomic relevance, even in sectors like transport, schools or health where they are most common (EIB, 2007, p. 22).

None the less, based on an examination of the recently adopted institutional frameworks in countries like Belgium, the Czech Republic, France, Germany, Hungary and the Netherlands, but also taking into consideration the ongoing commitment of the EU Commission to promote the use of PPPs,[3] a boost in projects can be expected within the upcoming years (only toned down but not stopped by the current financial and economic crisis). In Southern Europe the number of projects is already quite high and will probably stay at this level. Experiences gained from pilots in combination with rising financial demands will foster political support and implementation of the already large project pipeline in many countries. Efficiency, performance indicators and outcomes of such projects remain difficult to assess, with examples of both failed and successful PPPs in most European countries. Without doubt there is a continuous and increasing demand for further research and evaluation of the practical implications of PPPs. However, the basic question whether it is a practicable tool or just a theoretical phenomenon (Teisman and Klijn, 2002) already seems to have been answered for all three European country clusters analysed in this chapter.

To conclude, the further use of PPPs in Europe will require focus, confidence and prudence. Partnerships should be used only when they add value and provide value for money. As already noted in the EC Green

Paper (2004, p. 4), 'experience shows that, for each project, it is necessary to assess whether the partnership option offers real value added compared with other options' and, because managing a partnership is more complex, it requires different skills and implies considerable risks. Such arrangements should not be adopted only as a means to find solutions to financial limits because, if the partnership fails, the party affected the most is not the private sector but the public sector and the users. As such, ultimate accountability, no matter how well distributed the risk, will fall on the public player and, in particular, on the politicians, as some experiences in Europe have clearly shown.

Notes

1. Note that the high degree of political support in these countries has not exempted PPPs of criticism from trade unions that fear that private sector involvement will have negative impact on the number of jobs and employment conditions, as advanced by Hackett (2007).
2. Some other examples of failed projects include the Italian Messina bridge and a nationwide water canal in Spain that never reached a stage beyond planning. These were caused by a mixture of technical reasons, overall complexity, issues of efficiency and finally shortages in finance.
3. In a communication published in November 2009, EC President José Manuel Barroso called on European public authorities to 'make more and better use of PPPs' and emphasized the Commission's will to give a fresh impetus to PPPs in line with the European Economic Recovery Plan.

References

Abelaira, A. (2009), 'La col laboració públic-privada en l'àmbit de la Generalitat de Catalunya' [Public–private collaboration at the Regional Government of Catalonia], Presentation, Barcelona.

Albareda, L., J.M. Lozano and T. Ysa (2007), 'Public policies on corporate social responsibility: the role of governments in Europe', *Journal of Business Ethics,* **74,** 391–407.

Bastin, J. (2003), 'Public–private partnerships: a review of international and Austrian experience', in T. Eilmansberger et al. (eds), *Public Private Partnership*, Vienna: Linde Verlag, pp. 1–26.

BMF (Austrian Federal Ministry of Finance) (2008), *Ergebnisbericht über die PPP-Projekte der Bundesministerien sowie der ausgegliederten Bundesgesellschaften* (Report on PPP projects of federal ministries and federal corporatizations), Vienna: BMF.

BMWA (Bundesministerium für Wirtschaft und Arbeit) (ed.) (2004), *Public Private Partnership International. Ein Unternehmerleitfaden für PPP-Engagements im Ausland*, Berlin.

Bolz, U. (ed.) (2002), *Public Private Partnership in der Schweiz, Grundlagenstudie – Ergebnis einer gemeinsamen Initiative von Wirtschaft und Verwaltung*, Zürich/Basel/Genf: Schulthess Verlag.

Brenck, A., T. Beckers, M. Heinrich and C. von Hirschhausen (2005), 'PPP in new EU member countries of Central and Eastern Europe: an economic analysis with case studies from the highway sector', *EIB Papers,* **10** (2), 82–112.

Budäus, D. and B. Grüb (2008), 'Public private partnership: zum aktuellen Entwicklungs – und Diskussionsstand', in H. Bauer, C. Büchner and F. Brosius-Gersdorf (eds), *Verwaltungskooperation*, Potsdam: KWI Schriften, pp. 33–50.

Budina, N., B. Polackova and T. Irwin (2007), *Public Private Partnerships in the new EU member states*, World Bank Working Paper No. 114, Washington.

Button, M. (ed.) (2008), *A Practical Guide to PPP in Europe*, London: City & Financial Publishing.

Campbell, J.L. (2004), *Institutional Change and Globalization*, Princeton, NJ: Princeton University Press.

Castelos, M. and P. Melo (2008), 'Portugal', in M. Button (ed.), *A Practical Guide to PPP in Europe*, London: City & Financial Publishing, pp. 342–59.

CBI (2007), *The World of Public Private Partnerships*, London.

Christensen, T. and P. Lægreid (eds) (2007), *Transcending New Public Management. The Transformation of Public Sector Reforms*, Aldershot: Ashgate.

Czarniawska, B. (2002), *A Tale of Three Cities. Or the Glocalization of City Management*, Oxford: Oxford University Press.

De Pierris, L. and M. Foschi (2008), 'Italian PPPs: an update', in *Infrastructure Journal*, available at: www.utfp.it/docs/articoli/IJ_Italian_Final.pdf (accessed July 2008).

Deloitte (2006a), *Building Flexibility – New Delivery Models for Public Infrastructure Projects*, London.

Deloitte (2006b), *Closing the Infrastructure Gap: The Role of Public–Private Partnerships*, London.

DIfU (Deutsches Institut für Urbanistik) (ed.) (2005), *Public Private Partnership Projekte. Eine aktuelle Bestandsaufnahme in Bund, Ländern und Kommunen*, Berlin.

DiGaetano, A. and E. Strom (2003), 'Comparative urban governance. An integrated approach', *Urban Affairs Review*, **38** (3), 356–95.

Dinica, V. (2008), 'Initiating a sustained diffusion of wind power: the role of PPP in Spain', *Energy Policy*, **36** (9), 3562–71.

DLA Piper (2007), *European PPP Report 2007*, London.

Edelenbos, J. and E.-H. Klijn (2009), 'Project versus process management in public–private partnership: relation between management style and outcomes', *International Public Management Journal*, **12** (3), 310–31.

Eichhorn, P. (2004), 'Public private partnership: ein profundes Problem', in Gesellschaft für öffentliche Wirtschaft (ed.), *Public Private Partnership: Formen – Risiken – Chancen*, Berlin, pp. 6–8.

Ernst & Young (2008), *Bridging the Gap: Investing in European Infrastructure 2008*, London.

European Commission (2003), *Guidelines for Successful Public–Private Partnerships*, Brussels.

European Commission (2004), *Green Paper on Public–Private Partnerships and Community Law on Public Contracts and Concessions* [COM(2004)0327 final], Brussels.

European Commission (2006), *Monitoring Report on the State of Preparedness for EU Membership of Bulgaria and România*, Brussels.

European Commission (2008), *Commission Interpretative Communication on the Application of Community Law on Public Procurement and Concessions to Institutionalised Public–Private Partnerships (IPPP)*, [C(2007)6661], Brussels.

European Investment Bank (2004), *The EIB's Role in Public–Private Partnerships*, Luxembourg.

European Investment Bank (2007), *Public–Private Partnerships in Europe: An Update*, Luxembourg.

Freshfield Bruckhaus Deringer (2005), *PPP in Europe: An Overview*, London.

Gualmini, E. (2008), 'Restructuring Weberian bureaucracy: comparing managerial reforms in Europe and the United States', *Public Administration*, **86** (1), 75–94.

Hackett, P. (2007), *Public and Private: Partners in the Public Interest*, The Smith Institute.

Ham, H. and J. Koppenjan (2002), 'Building public–private partnerships. Assessing and managing risks in port development', *Public Management Review*, **4** (1), 593–616.

HM Treasury (2006), *Strengthening Long Term Partnerships*, London.

Kierzenkowski, R. (2008), 'The challenge of rapidly improving transport infrastructure in Poland', Economics Department Working Papers, No. 640, Paris: OECD.

Klijn, E.-H. and G. Teisman (2003), 'Institutional and strategic barriers to public–private partnership: an analysis of Dutch cases', *Public Money & Management*, July, 137–46.

Klijn, E.-H., J. Edelembos and M. Hughes (2007), 'Public–private partnership: a two-headed reform. A comparison of PPP in England and the Netherlands', in C. Pollitt, S. van Thiel and V. Homburg (eds), *New Public Management in Europe: Adaptation and Alternatives*, Basingstoke: Palgrave Macmillan, pp. 71–89.

Lienhard, A. (2006), 'PPP in Switzerland: experiences, risks, potentials', *Public Administration Review*, **4**, 547–63.

Meyer, Renate E. and Gerhard Hammerschmid (2010), 'The degree of decentralization and individual decision making in central government human resource management: a European comparative perspective', *Public Administration*, **2** (88), 455–78.

Milotti, A. and N. Patumi (2008), 'Il finanziamento delle infrastrutture di trasporto' [Financing transport infrastructures], Rome: Egea.

Monteiro, R.S. (2005), 'Public–private partnerships: some lessons from Portugal', *EIB Papers*, **10** (2), 72–81.

Noble, G. and R. Jones (2006), 'The role of boundary-spanning managers in the establishment of public–private partnerships', *Public Administration*, **94** (4), 891–917.

OECD (2005), *Modernising Government*, Paris.

OECD (2008), *PPP: In Pursuit of Risk Sharing and Value for Money*, Paris.

Olsen, J.P. (2006), 'Maybe it is time to rediscover bureaucracy', *Journal of Public Administration Research and Theory*, **16** (1), 1–24.

Page, E.C. (2003), 'Europeanization and the persistence of administrative systems', in J. Hayward and A. Menon (eds), *Governing Europe*, Oxford: Oxford University Press, pp. 162–7.

Pollitt, C. (2001), 'Convergence. The useful myth?', *Public Administration*, **79** (4), 933–47.

Pollitt, C. (2003), *The Essential Public Manager*, Maidenhead, UK: Open University Press.

Pollitt, C. and G. Bouckaert (2004), *Public Management Reform. A Comparative Analysis*, 2nd edn, Oxford: Oxford University Press.

PwC (2005), *Delivering the PPP Promise: A Review of PPP Issues and Activity*, London.

Rodríguez, N. (2006), 'Perspectivas de la colaboración público-privada en la Comunidad de Madrid' [Perspectives on public–private collaborations in Madrid], *Presupuesto y Gasto Público*, **45** (4), 153–66.

Scharpf, F. (1997), *Games Real Actors Play: Actor-Centered Institutionalism in Policy Research*, Oxford: Oxford University Press.

Scott, W.R. (2001), *Institutions and Organizations*, 2nd edn, Thousand Oaks, CA: Sage.

Teisman, G. and E.-H. Klijn (2002), 'Partnership arrangements: governmental rhetoric of governance scheme?', *Public Administration Review*, **62** (2), 197–205.

Thomson, C. (2005), 'Private–public partnerships: prerequisites for prime performance', *EIB Papers*, **10** (2), 113–35.

Torres, L. and V. Pina (2001), 'PPP and private finance initiative in the EU and Spanish local governments', *The European Accounting Review*, **19** (3), 601–19.

Van Garsse, S. (2006), *PPS en Participatieve PPS op Vlaams niveau* [PPP on the level of Flanders], Flemish Knowledge Centre PPP.

Vandermeeren, F. (2009), *Public Private Partnerships in Flanders*, mimeo.

Werner, M. (2008), 'European Union', in M. Button (ed.), *A Practical Guide to PPP in Europe*, London: City & Financial Publishing, pp. 13–28.

Wettenhall, R. (2003), 'The rhetoric and reality of public–private partnership', *Public Organization Review*, **3** (1), 77–107.

Ysa, T. (2007), 'Governance forms in urban public–private partnerships', *International Public Management Journal*, **10** (1), 35–7.

16 P3s in North America: renting the money (in Canada), selling the roads (in the USA)

Anthony E. Boardman and Aidan R. Vining

Introduction

This chapter focuses on the experience with public–private partnerships in the USA and Canada (hereafter, North America) since 2000. (For information about the experience in North America before 2000, see Boardman et al., 2005; Vining et al., 2005; Vining and Boardman, 2008a.) In the USA, public–private partnerships are generally referred to as PPPs, while in Canada they are generally referred to as P3s. Here, we adopt the P3 abbreviation.

Different authors have defined P3s in different ways. In this chapter, we use a relatively narrow definition that focuses on PFI-type P3s, that is, infrastructure projects where the private sector engages in a significant part of the finance (F), design (D), build (B), operate (O) and maintain (M) activities and where ownership is either immediately or ultimately transferred (T) to the public sector: effectively long-term FDBOMT contracts for the provision of public infrastructure. However, to fit within our definition of a P3, the private sector partner does not have to comprehensively engage in the finance, design, build, operate *and* maintenance activities in order to be thought of as a P3 – just most of them.

The beginning of the twenty-first century has seen the emergence of a number of developments that will determine the future role of P3s in North America. A dominant trend in the early part of the decade (2002–07) was the emergence of governmental institutional structures for the development and management of P3s. Across North America, governments at both the national and sub-national levels (states in the USA or provinces in Canada) established a variety of P3 agencies. The essential *raison d'être* of these agencies was the promotion and development of P3s. And indeed, partly as a result of these institutions, P3s have proliferated since 2000.

However, in the latter part of the decade, between late 2007 and early 2010, the dominant trend has been a reduction in private sector sources of capital for infrastructure stemming from the global financial meltdown, and an increase in the cost of capital from remaining lenders. Foreign (non-North American) banks, who were major sources of long-term financing for Canadian P3s, have reduced their long-term credit facilities. The Macquarie Group (and the Royal Bank of Scotland), a major P3 financier, has undergone major restructuring. Other commercial and investment banks have failed, resulting in consolidation. The remaining banks have increased both their capital reserves and the rates they charge borrowers. Other sources of private financing (e.g. insurance companies, public sector pension funds or the bond market) will almost certainly require relatively higher returns to invest in P3s than in the past. As a result, the viability of P3s as a major delivery mechanism has been thrown into some doubt in North America, just as the governmental institutional structures to promote P3s have been put in place.

There has been a third important change, especially in Canada. In the 1990s, some P3s assumed revenue risk (or 'use risk') (Vining and Boardman, 2008a). Indeed, this was one of the most important rationales for P3s. However, few private sector firms in North America have shown themselves to be actually willing to accept much (or any) revenue risk. How, then, do current P3s differ from traditional contracts? We believe there are two key elements. The first element is that P3 contracts pertain to fairly complex bundles of FDBOMT activities. From the government's perspective and from a social welfare perspective, it is not clear whether this bundling is more or less efficient than a larger number of (smaller) unbundled contracts. Partly as a result of this bundling, P3s are basically a complex form of contracting out. The second key element is the financing burden and timeframe. In effect, most P3s transfer the cost of infrastructure from current taxpayers to some mix of future users, future taxpayers and future governments. In traditional contracts, there might be deferral of some payments, but most payments are made up front and during the design and construction phases. While it is generally no longer possible to place P3 financing 'off budget' because financial controllership organizations (e.g., in the Canadian context, auditor generals) have flagged this practice and made it less feasible, it remains politically appealing to shift the payment burden to the future: 'Issuing debt is one means of realizing current preferences, while shifting some of the costs forward in time' (Clinger et al., 2008, p. 168). Thus, a key *raison d'être* of P3s is becoming 'rent the money'.

This chapter has two parts, one on P3s in Canada and one on P3s in the USA. It is necessary to treat them separately because the experiences have been quite different. We begin with a discussion of the Canadian experience because there has been much more P3 activity in Canada than in the USA. For each country, we list and briefly discuss recent P3 projects. We then describe government-linked P3 agencies that have been created to manage and often to promote P3s. Subsequently, we describe some major private sector (although often non-profit) P3 agencies. Each section concludes with a brief review of the evidence on the performance of P3s in each country and contains some thoughts about P3s in the future.

P3s in Canada

P3s took off in Canada in the 1990s. The best-known early P3s were Highway 407 (1999), the Confederation Bridge (1997) and the Pearson Airport in Toronto (1996) (Boardman et al., 2005; Vining et al., 2005). This section focuses on developments since 2000.

Table 16.1 summarizes the picture in Canada for P3s where project construction began in 2000 or subsequently. It demonstrates that many Canadian governments have embraced the use of P3s. The main use of P3s since 2000 has been for the construction or expansion of hospitals or healthcare facilities, or for new roads. However, the P3 format has also been utilized for bridges, water treatment facilities, light rapid transit, schools, court buildings and a data centre. As shown in the table, the provinces have engaged in more P3 activity than has the federal government. British Columbia (BC), Alberta, Ontario and Quebec have been the most active provinces, while other provinces and territories have only engaged in a few P3s.

Table 16.1 provides the name of the public and private 'partners', the start year for construction, the length of the operating period, the (estimated) present value of the cost of the contract, the type of P3 (i.e. the nature of the contract), the current stage of the project (as of about June 2009) and whether the private sector took on any revenue risk. Several of the private sector companies mentioned in the table have participated in a number of different P3s. For example, PCL Construction is involved in six of the P3s listed, Johnson Controls in four P3s, and ABN Amro is partially financing three of the P3s, suggesting that some companies specialize in P3 projects. The cost of the P3s shown ranges from $27 million for the Britannia Mine Water Treatment Plant to $1.9 billion for the Canada Line (previously known as the RAV Line). Most of the P3s are finance, design, build, operate and maintain contracts. However, in some P3s the private sector does not operate the facility and in some P3s in Ontario the private sector is not responsible for maintenance. Out of the total, only two P3s in Quebec commit the private sector partner to any revenue risk.

Unlike in the USA, in Canada there are no P3 road 'concessions' on existing roads or highways. In 2003, the BC government did announce that it was planning to sell the Coquihalla highway to a private sector concessionaire, but this proposal was eventually abandoned due to political pressure from businesses and voters in the interior of the province. Indeed, in 2008 the government reversed gear and scrapped tolls on this highway completely. Although this appears to have been driven by political

Table 16.1 Canadian P3s since 2000

Project	Public partner	Private partner	Start year	Operating period	Present value	Type of P3	Project stage	Revenue risk
British Columbia								
Abbotsford Regional Hospital and Cancer Center – BC	Ministry of Health; Fraser Health Authority; Provincial Health Services Authority; BC Cancer Agency; Fraser Valley Regional Hospital District; Partnerships BC	Access Health Abbotsford; Design: Musson Cattell Mackey/ Silver Thomas Hanley; Construction: PCL Constructors Westcoast; Finance: ABN Amro; Facilities maintenance and operation: Johnson Controls International and Sodexho	2004	30 years	$424 m	FDBOM	Operational	No
Sierra Yoyo Desan Resource Road	Ministry of Energy and Mines; Partnerships BC	Ledcor Group; McElhanney Consulting Services; Buckland & Taylor; Trow Associates; Triton Environmental Consultants	2004	16 years	$40 m	FDBOM	Operational	No
Gordon and Leslie Diamond Health Care Center	Ministry of Health; Vancouver Coastal Health Authority; University of British Columbia Faculty of Medicine; Partnerships BC	Access Health Vancouver; Design: IBI/HPA; Construction: PCL Constructors Westcoast; Finance: ABN AMRO; Facilities maintenance and operation: BLJC	2004	30 years	$95 m	FDBOM	Operational	No

357

Table 16.1 (continued)

Project	Public partner	Private partner	Start year	Operating period	Present value	Type of P3	Project stage	Revenue risk
Kicking Horse Canyon Phase Two	TransLink (Greater Vancouver Transportation Authority); Partnerships BC	Trans-Park Highway Group: Bilfinger Berger BOT Inc.; Flatiron Constructors Canada; Parsons Overseas Company of Canada; HMC Services Inc.	2005	25 years	$163 m	FDBOM	Construction	No
Sea-to-Sky Highway Improvements Project	Ministry of Transportation; Partnerships BC	S2S Transportation Group; Macquarie North America Limited; Peter Kiewit Sons Co.; JJM Construction Limited; Hatch Mott MacDonald; Miller Paving; Capilano Highway Services	2005	25 years	$600 m	FDBOM	Construction	No
William R. Bennett Bridge	Ministry of Transportation; The British Columbia Transport Finance Authority; Partnerships BC	Okanagan Lake Concession Limited Partner: SNC-Lavalin Constructors; Vancouver Pile Driving Ltd.; Sun Life Assurance; Ontario Teacher's Pension Plan Board	2005	30 years	$144 m	FDBOM	Operational	No

358

Project	Public partners	Private partners	Year	Term	Value	Model	Status	User fee
Britannia Mine Water Treatment Plant – BC	Ministry of Agriculture and Lands; Ministry of Environment; Partnerships BC	EPCOR Water services Inc.; Lockerbie Stanley Inc.; Stantec Consulting Ltd; BioteQ Environmental Technologies Inc.	2005	21 years	$27.2 m	FDBOM	Operational	No
Canada Line	Government of Canada; Ministry of Transportation, Province of British Columbia; Greater Vancouver Transportation Authority; City of Vancouver; Vancouver International Airport Authority; Partnerships BC	InTransitBC (a company owned by): SNC-Lavalin Inc.; B.C. Investment Management Corporation; Caisse de dépôt et placement du Québec	2005	35 years	$1.9 bn	FDBOM	Construction	10% of ridership revenue
Golden Ears Bridge	TransLink (Greater Vancouver Transportation Authority); Partnerships BC	Golden Crossing General Partnership: (Golden Crossing Constructors Joint Venture (GCCJV))	2006	35.5 years	$808 m	FDBOM	Operational	No

Table 16.1 (continued)

Project	Public partner	Private partner	Start year	Operating period	Present value	Type of P3	Project stage	Revenue risk
Vancouver Island Health Authority (VIHA) Residential Care and Assisted Living Capacity Initiative	Ministry of Health; Vancouver Island Health Authority; Partnerships BC	The Ahmon Group; Baptist Housing Society of BC; Capital Region Housing Corporation and Beckley Farm Lodge Society; Good Samaritan Canada; Jones Development Corporation and inSite; New Horizons Care Corporation; Retirement Concepts; Sooke Elderly Citizens' Housing Society	2006	20 years	$210 m	FDBOM	Operational	No
Royal Jubilee Hospital Patient Care Centre Project	Vancouver Island Health Authority; Partnerships BC	ISL Health; Health Care Projects Ltd; Acciona/Lark; Cannon Design; Angus Consulting Management Western Limited; DEPFA Bank plc; Dexia Crédit Loca	2008	30 years	$282.5 m	FDBM	Construction	No
Surrey Outpatient Hospital	Fraser Health Authority; Partnerships BC	BC Healthcare Solutions: Bouygues Batiment International; HSBC Infrastructure Fund Management Ltd; Ecovert FM Ltd; Kasian	2008	30 years	$239 m	FDBM	Construction	No

Project	Authority/Sponsor	Consortium	Year	Duration	Cost	Type	Status	
Kelowna and Vernon Hospitals Project	Interior Health Authority; Partnerships BC	Architecture Interior Design and Planning Ltd; Bird Construction; Helios Group; DEPFA Bank plc Infusion Health	2008	30 years	$432.9 m	FDBOM	Construction	No
Alberta Anthony Henday South East	Government of Alberta; Government of Canada	Access Roads Edmonton; Marshall Macklin Monaghan; Stantec Consulting Ltd; ERES Geotechnical; Golder Associates Ltd; Earth Tech Canada Inc.; Bel MK Engineering Ltd; PCL–Construction Management; PCL-Maxam, a Joint Venture; Lafarge Canada Inc.; Sureway Construction Ltd.; ABN AMRO Bank N.V.; Transportation Systems Management Inc.	2005	30 years	$493 m	FDBOM	Operational	No

Table 16.1 (continued)

Project	Public partner	Private partner	Start year	Operating period	Present value	Type of P3	Project stage	Revenue risk
Calgary Ring Road (Northeast)	Government of Alberta; Alberta Infrastructure	Stony Trail Group: Flatiron Construction Corp.; EarthTech; Carmacks Enterprises; Bilfinger Berger BOT; Parsons; Graham	2007	30 years	$650 m	FDBOM	Construction	No
Alberta Schools	Government of Alberta; Alberta Infrastructure	BBPP Alberta Schools Limited: Babcock & Brown Public Partnerships Ltd.; Graham Design Builders; Bird Design-Build Limited; Barr Ryder Architects & Interior Designers; Maintenance and Renewal – Honeywell	2008	32 years	$624 m	FDBM	Construction	No
North Edmonton Ring Road	Government of Alberta	Nothwest Connect	2008	30 years	$1.42 bn	FDBOM	Construction	No
Ontario								
William Osler Health Centre	Government of Ontario	The Healthcare Infrastructure Company of Canada: Ellis Don; Carillion Canada; Borealis Infrastructure Management	2004	25 years	$550 m	FDBOM	Operational	No

362

Project	Authority	Consortium	Year	Duration	Value	Model	Status	
Royal Ottawa Hospital	Government of Ontario	The Healthcare Infrastructure Company of Canada: Ellis Don; Carillion Canada; Borealis Infrastructure Management	2004	20 years	$256 m	FDBOM	Operational	No
Durham Consolidated Courthouse	Ministry of the Attorney General; Ontario Infrastructure Project Coordination	Access Justice Durham: Babcock & Brown Infrastructure Group; PCL Constructors Canada Inc.; Johnson Controls LP; WZMH Architects	2004	30 years	$377 m	FDBO	Construction	No
Sault Area Hospital	Ministry of Health and Long Term Care; Infrastructure Ontario	Hospital Infrastructure Partners Inc.: Carillion; EllisDon; LPF Infrastructure Fund (the Labourers' Pension Fund of Central and Eastern Canada); CITI Financial Canada	2007	30 years	$898 m	FDBO	Construction	No
North Bay Regional Health Centre	Ontario Infrastructure Project Coordination; North Bay Regional Health	Plenary Health team: Plenary Group; Deutsche Bank AG; PCL Constructors Canada; Johnson Controls	2007	30 years	$551 m	FDBO	Construction	No

363

Table 16.1 (continued)

Project	Public partner	Private partner	Start year	Operating period	Present value	Type of P3	Project stage	Revenue risk
Guelph New Data Center	Ontario Infrastructure Project Coordination; Minister of Government and Consumer Services	The Plenary Properties: Plenary Group; Deutsche Bank; PCL Constructors; Modern Niagara; Plan Group; Adamson Associates; Smith and Anderson and Johnson Controls	2008	30 years	$637 m	FDBO	Construction	No
Woodstock General Hospital	Ministry of Health and Long Term Care; Infrastructure Ontario	Integrated Team Solutions: EllisDon, LPF Infrastructure Fund, Honeywell, CIT, Sunlife Assurance Company, Great West Life and Industrial Alliance.	2008	30 years	$685 m	FBM	Construction	No
Quebec								
Completion of Autoroute 25	Ministère des Transports du Québec	Concession A25 Consortium: Macquarie Group; Kiewit-Parsons; GENIVAR; Ciment St-Laurent; Miller Paving; TransCore	2007	31 years	$207 m	FDBOM	Construction	Shared (established thresholds)

								Shared (established thresholds)
Completion of Autoroute 30	Ministère des Transports du Québec; Government of Canada	Nouvelle Autoroute 30, S.E.N.C.: Acciona Concessions Canada Inc.; Iridium Concessions Canada Inc.; Acciona Infrastructures Canada Inc.; Dragados Canada Inc.; S.I.C.E.; Arup Canada Inc.; Construction DJL Inc.; Verreault Inc.	2008	35 years	$1.5 bn–$1.9 bn	FDBOMT	Construction	
Highway Service Areas	Ministère des Transports du Québec	Immostar Inc.	2008	30 years	$30 m	FDBM	Construction	No
New Brunswick								
Moncton Water Treatment Facility	City of Moncton	USF Canada Inc.	2005	20 years	$85 m	FDBOM	Operational	No
New Brunswick Trans-Canada Highway Project	New Brunswick Department of Transportation	Brun-Way Group	2004	30 years	$543.8 m	FDBOM	Operational	No
Northwest Territories								
Aurora College Family Student Housing	NWT Provincial Government	Aurora Building Developers	2000	20 years	$4.7 m	FDBOM	Operational	Unknown

Table 16.1 (continued)

Project	Public partner	Private partner	Start year	Operating period	Present value	Type of P3	Project stage	Revenue risk
Deh Cho Bridge Construction	NWT Provincial Government	Deh Cho Bridge Corporation Ltd.	2007	38 years	$165 m plus annual operating costs of $600 K	FDBOM	Construction	No

considerations, it probably increased allocative efficiency (Boardman et al., 1994).

Canadian government P3 agencies
The proliferation of P3s in Canada is at least partially attributable to the establishment of the federal and provincial agencies that promote them. This section briefly describes these agencies, explains why they were set up, what their mandates are and how they operate. We begin with the federal agencies and then move roughly from west to east to north.

Federal agencies: Building Canada and PPP Canada
In the 2007 budget, the Canadian government established the $33 billion Building Canada Plan (BCP) to modernize public infrastructure.[1] The Infrastructure Framework Agreement outlines how the BCP will operate in each province and establishes a joint governance framework between the federal and provincial governments.[2] All provinces and territories had signed up to the BCP by the end of 2008. Under it, the parties agreed that 'P3s can further the public interest by providing access to private sector financing, innovation and expertise and by ensuring a suitable allocation of risk between the private and public sectors'.[3]

As part of the BCP, the federal government allocated $1.25 billion to the Public–Private Partnerships Fund. In late 2008, it established PPP Canada Inc. as a federal crown corporation to manage and invest this Fund's budget. PPP Canada's mandate is to 'work with the public and the private sectors towards encouraging the further development of Canada's P3 market'.[4] The Fund is explicitly designed to encourage the use of P3s for infrastructure: the federal government requires 'all Eligible Recipients seeking funding under the Major Infrastructure Component, for which the Federal Government's contribution would equal or exceed $50 million, must demonstrate, to the satisfaction of the Minister, that the option of undertaking the project as a P3 has been fully considered'.[5]

British Columbia: Partnerships BC and the capital asset management framework
In May 2002, the BC government announced a capital asset management framework (CAMF) to guide capital planning in the province. This framework included guidelines for managing capital assets (Province of British Columbia, 2002). While the use of a P3 is not explicitly required for new capital assets, it is encouraged. The guidelines claim that 'a defining feature of P3s is the opportunity they provide to share or transfer risks' (ibid., pp. 15, 33). Concurrently, Partnerships BC (PBC) was created to support the government's plan to deliver more infrastructure projects (Partnerships

British Columbia, 2003). PBC is an entity of the province, governed by an independent board of directors, that reports to the provincial minister of finance. It is comprised of former managers of both private and public corporations, from various functional backgrounds.

The CAMF establishes guidelines for all provincial public sector agencies (e.g. ministries, health authorities, school districts and crown corporations) for the management of all public capital assets, regardless of their dollar value or how they are financed.[6] Agencies are assigned a threshold above which any new project must be reviewed against the CAMF. Each ministry determines who will perform the review, which can be conducted by internal or external auditors, ministry staff or external agencies.[7] Specific standards of compliance are set through Treasury Board decision letters or letters of expectations for individual agencies.[8]

PBC's involvement in the P3 evaluation and execution process might include some or all of the following: (1) business case analysis to determine the best model for delivering a project; (2) management of the competitive selection process, including writing and issuing requests for qualifications and requests for proposals, facilitation of fair evaluation of proposals, and final negotiations to reach a contract that meets the project objectives and delivers value; (3) project and contract management throughout the life of the project.[9]

In principle, P3 projects were traditionally procured by selecting the lowest bidder or consortia that presented the greatest benefit to the public. However, starting with the Sea-to-Sky Highway Improvement Project, the procurement process shifted to an 'annual affordability ceiling' (AAC).[10] In this process, the government sets a maximum payment ceiling. Bidders must meet certain minimal contractual obligations and then specify the 'additional benefits' that they can achieve within the fixed price. The additional benefits in the Sea-to-Sky Highway, for example, included safety and environmental enhancements.[11] During the request for proposals (RFP) evaluation process, PBC divides the AAC review into three distinct stages: mandatory submission requirements; baseline improvements; and scored evaluation. This process is meant to determine and score the benefits created above the project's baseline requirements.

By 2008, PBC has overseen nearly $9 billion worth of infrastructure projects, utilizing $5 billion of private sector capital. PBC and other BC government agencies have undertaken the largest number of completed and ongoing public infrastructure projects of any jurisdiction in North America. PBC also provides consulting services regarding the delivery of P3s in other jurisdictions.[12] However, the process has been controversial, with critics claiming that the cost of private capital has been high and that only minimal risk, at best, has been transferred in the P3 approach.

Alberta: Alberta Infrastructure and Alberta Transportation

In 2003, the Province of Alberta created an 'alternative project delivery mechanism' team to analyse and make recommendations on alternative project delivery mechanisms for the province. The team considered a number of mechanisms, including P3s, outsourcing, reengineering, part-nering and privatization, and was also asked to develop a design, build, finance, operate P3 model.[13] It developed what has been called a 'made in Alberta model' for P3 project delivery. Alberta Infrastructure and Alberta Transportation manage P3 projects for the government of Alberta.

In transportation, P3 projects have the following characteristics: DBFO contracts with two payment streams, one (fixed) for capital repayment, and one (index-linked) for operation, maintenance and rehabilitation; 30-year term; predetermined performance specifications; payments linked to performance rather than utilization; development control by the ministry; procurement by an open (i.e. non-limited) request for qualifications (RFQ), followed by a request for proposals (RFP) from a short-list of three candidates; significant honorarium for losing RFP short-listed bidders; RFP requires all proponents to satisfy all technical, commercial and legal requirements before submitting price (payment stream); project awarded to contractor with lowest net present value (NPV) payment stream. The NPV is calculated using a discount rate based on the borrowing rate of the province.

Alberta signed the Building Canada framework agreement in April 2008. Between 2007/8 and 2013/14, the projected funding available under the BCF in Alberta will be $840.73 million, subject to parliamentary appropriations.[14] Some municipalities are also implementing P3s. In September 2008, for example, the City of Calgary approved a set of guiding principles for P3 delivery.[15] In December 2008, it released a framework to guide managers in developing P3 projects from initial conception through completion (City of Calgary, 2008).

Saskatchewan: Investment Saskatchewan and Saskatchewan P3
Secretariat

As Table 16.1 indicates, Saskatchewan has not developed many P3s, although this appears to be changing. Initially, P3s were administered by Saskatchewan Inc. (IS), a crown corporation with a mandate to enhance economic growth and diversification through the provision of investment capital and financing.[16] While it is not specifically a P3 agency, the President's Office & General Counsel had responsibility for P3 initiatives. In January 2009, the government announced the establishment of the Saskatchewan P3 Secretariat to procure P3s in the province (Wood, 2009). Any infrastructure project with a cost in excess of $25 million must be screened by the Secretariat for consideration as a P3 (CUPE Research, 2009).

Ontario: Infrastructure Ontario

Infrastructure Ontario (IO) describes itself as 'an arm's length Crown corporation dedicated to the renewal of the province's hospitals, courthouses, roads, bridges, water systems and other public assets'.[17] For projects in the range of $50 million to $300 million or more, IO is mandated to set project criteria, bring together public and private sector organizations, conduct a procurement process to select a private sector consortia and ensure the public interest is upheld throughout the life of the project.[18] IO also provides Ontario municipalities and universities with access to loans to build and renew local public infrastructure.[19]

Québec: L'Agence des partenariats public-privé du Québec (PPP Québec)

L'Agence des partenariats public-privé du Québec (PPP Québec) was created in 2005 pursuant to Bill 61 as a mandatary agency of the state to advise the provincial government on any P3 matter.[20] It is administered by a board of directors composed of the CEO and eight other members appointed by the government, four of whom are from public bodies and four are from the private sector. Under Quebec's Public–Private Partnership Framework Policy, government decision-makers are required to identify potential P3 project candidates and must refer all major projects to PPP Québec.[21] Such projects generally must improve service delivery to the population, involve significant provincial financial commitments, be technically complex and high-risk, have a potential for creativity and innovation that could take advantage of the know-how of the private sector, and reflect an existing, competitive market.[22] The criteria for determining which projects have good P3 potential include confirmed, justified need; emphasis on results (public bodies must look at a range of possible solutions and give precedence to user needs), affordability (determine each project's overall costs), value for money (VfM); fair, transparent process, public service quality and continuity, accountability, protection of public interest, and fair treatment of public sector employees.[23] The Quebec government does not necessarily expect the private sector 'partner' to provide financing, although we do not know of a P3 where they do not.

The approval process follows a standard, comprehensive method with most of the analysis conducted by the public body seeking approval for a project. It includes a VfM assessment in which comparison between P3 provision and the public sector comparator (PSC) is presented in both quantitative and qualitative terms. Public bodies must consult PPP

Québec for guidance in this comparison, which is based on the method-ology set out in the business case guide of the Framework Policy.[24] If a potential project is 'green lighted', it moves to the procurement stage, where the public body draws up a P3 contract and specifies risk-sharing and the performance criteria linked to payment.[25] For projects reaching this stage, PPP Québec works with the public body responsible for the project to promote competition and to ensure fairness and transparency.[26] It also provides support throughout the contract management process and helps to obtain ministerial and government approval.

In line with its mandate under Bill 61, PPP Québec does not cur-rently work with municipalities as it is set up to handle larger projects. Unsolicited proposals from the private sector may be submitted to the most appropriate public body, which must then follow the P3 approval process and respect the confidential nature of the unsolicited proposal.[27]

Nova Scotia: Partnerships BC (PBC) consults
Nova Scotia is currently using PBC as a consultant for potential P3 projects. In April 2008, Nova Scotia signed a one-year memorandum of understanding with PBC to complete an evaluation of ten potential P3 projects. These projects include a hospital replacement or upgrade in Halifax and work on the Trans-Canada Highway.[28]

New Brunswick
New Brunswick has only entered into a few P3s. The province has a P3 policy, but does not have a dedicated P3 agency. According to the Government of New Brunswick (2000), a P3 may be pursued only after alternative delivery mechanisms have undergone careful evaluation and a P3 is demonstrated to offer the best solution. This source lays out the ground rules for evaluating P3 provision.

Prince Edward Island (PEI): Framework Agreement
PEI does not have a dedicated P3 agency, but in 2008 it signed a $270 million agreement with the Government of Canada under the Building Canada programme. As with all provinces that have signed the agreement, PEI infrastructure initiatives in eligible categories will also have the oppor-tunity to utilize funds from the Public–Private Partnership Fund.[29]

Manitoba; Yukon Territories; Northwest Territories and Nunavut
These regions do not have dedicated P3 agencies. However, all of them have signed the Building Canada Framework Agreement. Thus far, we can only find that the Northwest Territories has engaged in a P3.

Canadian private sector P3 proponent institutions

The Canadian Council for Public–Private Partnerships was established in 1993 as a member-sponsored organization with representatives from the public and private sectors. The organization's mandate is to promote the use of P3s at all levels of Canadian government. It conducts and publishes research, facilitates forums for discussion and sponsors an annual conference on topics related to P3s.[30]

Evaluation of P3s in Canada and a glimpse into the future

In spite of the establishment of numerous government institutions to promote P3s and the existence of many P3s, independent studies of Canadian P3s are rare. Canadian governments do not appear to have been interested in systematically and rigorously investigating either their own, or other governments', experience with P3s. Vining and Boardman (2008a) provide the most extensive recent review of the Canadian evidence based on ten P3 case studies. They argue that the appropriate criterion for evaluating the use and value of P3s is whether they have lower total social costs, which includes transaction costs as well as production costs, than alternative delivery mechanisms. They then assess the transaction costs in the case studies and reach a conclusion about whether each P3 was successful or not. Their overall assessment of the performance of P3s in Canada is mixed. For example, they conclude that Highway 407 in Ontario was not a successful P3. There are two main reasons. First, the provincial government tried to transfer too much risk to the private sector. This included financing risks, construction risks, operating risks and revenue risks. Eventually, however, few of these risks were transferred and the construction phase became a develop, design, build fixed-price contract. Second, the P3 raised tolls repeatedly and were then sued by the government, which resulted in large transaction costs as well as a failed lawsuit. A number of other P3 projects failed due largely to poor government contract management skills. Potentially, though, over time one might expect the P3 process to lead to an improvement in government contract management skills. The process is more open to multiple bidders and governments are pushed to pay more attention to performance measures: outcomes, outputs and quality. However, governments could probably have achieved these benefits in another way at much lower costs.

The Canada Line (CL) in Vancouver, a more recent P3, illustrates some of the advantages and disadvantages of the P3 format. The almost \$2 billion CL has attracted considerable opposition and controversy. The final price proposed by the P3 consortium was lower than the cost of the PSC largely because it came up with a more innovative design that was less costly to build. The route of the CL runs from the Vancouver Airport in Richmond (and the centre of Richmond), down Cambie Street, through downtown Vancouver to the waterfront.[31] In the major retail part of Cambie Street, construction consisted of cut-and-cover – the street was dug up, the line was installed and then covered over. Obviously, many adjacent businesses suffered considerably during the construction period. In other words, the project created significant negative externalities – a significant social cost that is not reflected in the budget. (The negative externalities of the PSC would not have been so high as it called for more tunnelling.)

Cambie Street merchants have now successfully sued the project for damages.[32] If, in contrast, the government had conducted the project, then there would not have been any lawsuit because individuals (including corporations) cannot sue the government. In this respect, a P3 is more risky for government than government provision.

Not surprisingly, Canadian unions oppose the use of P3s, most prominently the Canadian Union of Public Employees (CUPE). Following the Saskatchewan government's recent statement that it was establishing the Saskatchewan P3 Secretariat, CUPE launched a campaign against P3s labelled 'Pay more, get less'. They argue that P3s are 'a horrendous waste of money'.[33]

In addition to Vining and Boardman, a few other analyses of P3s are now appearing (Murray, 2006; Parks and Terhart, 2009). Since the payment period in P3s can be over very long time periods (often 30 years or more), a key issue in the evaluation of P3s is the choice of the discount rate. As the government spreads out its payment stream in a P3 (and shifts more payments to the future), using a higher discount rate lowers the present value of the cost of a P3 and increases its desirability. Parks and Terhart (2009) conclude that Partnerships BC has used an inflated discount rate, thereby overestimating the benefits of P3s relative to the PSCs.[34] This problem has also been noted elsewhere, for example in the Australian states of Victoria (Hodge, 2004) and New South Wales (GAO, 2008).

Despite these limitations, most Canadian governments still appear to be supportive of the P3 approach. Table 16.2 lists proposed Canadian P3s as of July 2009. The projects are very similar in nature to those shown in Table 16.1. Some proposed P3s are quite substantial projects, with one projected to cost more than $2 billion.

Since July 2009, however, there have been some substantial changes in Quebec. Following various criticisms of PPP Québec, the Quebec government introduced and passed Bill 65, an Act that renamed PPP Québec as Infrastructure Quebec and changed its mandate.[35] In November 2009, the auditor-general of Quebec presented the conclusions of his watch over P3 projects to modernize Montreal's University Health Centres (UHC): Centre hospitalier de l'Université de Montreal (CHUM), Centre de

Table 16.2 Proposed P3s in Canada

Project	Public partner	Private partner	Start year	Operating period	Present value	Type of P3	Project stage	Revenue risk
Federal								
Communications Security Establishment Headquarters	Government of Canada	Unknown	2011 expected	30 years	$880 m (est.)	FDBM	Advance notice to vendors	TBD
British Columbia								
BC Cancer Agency's Centre for the North Project	Provincial Health Services Authority (PHSA); BC Cancer Agency (BCCA); Partnerships BC	Unknown	Jan 2009 expected	30 years	TBD	FDBM	Procurement (RFP)	No
Fort St John Hospital and Residential Care Project	Northern Health; Partnerships BC	Unknown	Jan 2009 expected	30 years	$268 m (est.)	FDBOM	Procurement (RFP)	No
Prince George Gateway Residential Care Facility	Ministry of Health Services, Northern Health	Westen Industrial Contracting Ltd	2009	Unknown	$42m	Unknown	Procurement (RFP)	No
South Fraser Perimeter Road	Ministry of Transportation and Infrastructure; Province of BC; Partnerships BC	Unknown	Late 2009	24 years	TBD	FDBOM	Procurement (RFP)	No

Project	Sponsor							
Surrey Memorial Hospital Redevelopment and Expansion: Critical Care Tower	Ministry of Health Services, Fraser Health	Unknown	2010	Unknown	$500 m–$600 m (est.)	FDBOM	Procurement	Unknown
Alberta								
Saline Creek Plateau Public–Private Partnership Project	Government of Alberta; Oil Sands Sustainable Development Secretariat; Regional Municipality of Wood Buffalo	Unknown	TBD	TBD	TBD	TBD	Procurement (RFEI)	TBD
Manitoba								
Disraeli Bridge	City of Winnipeg	Unknown	2009 (expected)	30 year (expected)	$125 m –$165 m (expected)	FDBM	Procurement (RFP)	No

375

Table 16.2 (continued)

Project	Public partner	Private partner	Start year	Operating period	Present value	Type of P3	Project stage	Revenue risk
Ontario								
Niagra Health System	Ministry of Health and Long Term Care; Infrastructure Ontario	Plenary Health includes: Plenary Group; PCL Constructors; Bregman + Hamann Architects; Silver Thomas International Architects; Johnson Controls; Deutsche Bank	2009 (expected)	30 years	TBD	FDBO	Signing	No
Infrastructure Ontario's Nuclear Procurement Project	Ontario Power Generation; Ministry of Energy; Ministry of Finance; Infrastructure Ontario	Bruce Power	2009 (expected)	TBD	TBD	FDBOM	Procurement (RFP)	TBD
Ontario Highway Service Centres	Ontario Ministry of Transportation; Infrastructure Ontario	Unknown	2009 (expected)	TBD	TBD	FDBOM	Procurement (RFP)	No

Toronto South Detention Center	Ministry of Community Safety and Correctional Services; Infrastructure Ontario	Unknown	2009 (expected)	TBD	TBD	FDBM	Procurement (RFP)	TBD
Waterloo Region Consolidated Courthouse	Ministry of the Attorney General; Ontario Infrastructure Project Coordination	Unknown	2009 (expected)	TBD	TBD	FDBM	Procurement (RFQ)	No
Bridgepoint Health	Ministry of Health and Long Term Care; Infrastructure Ontario	Unknown	2009 Expected	TBD	TBD	FDBM	Procurement (RFP)	No
Women's College Hospital	Ministry of Health and Long Term Care; Infrastructure Ontario	Unknown	TBD	TBD	TBD	FDBM	Procurement (RFP)	No
Centre for Addiction and Mental Health (CAMH) – Phase One	Ministry of Health and Long Term Care; Infrastructure Ontario	Unknown	TBD	TBD	TBD	FDBO	Procurement (RFQ)	No

Table 16.2 (continued)

Project	Public partner	Private partner	Start year	Operating period	Present value	Type of P3	Project stage	Revenue risk
Quebec								
McGill University Health Centre	Centre hospitalier de l'Université de Montréal (CHUM)	Groupe immobilier Santé McGill or Partenariat CUSM	2009	35 years	$2.2 bn	FDBOM	Procurement (RFP)	No
Residential and long-term care centre	The Social Services and Health Department	Groupe Savoie	2009	25 years	$200 m	FDBOM	Construction	No
New Acoustic Concert Hall of Montreal	Ministry of Finance; Ministry of Government Services; Ministry responsible for government administration; Chair of the Conseil du Trésor; Minister of Culture, Communications and the Status of Women	GROUPE IMMOBILIER OVATION: SNC-Lavalin Inc.; Busac Inc.; Diamond and Schmitt Architects Inc.; Aedifica Inc.; Groupe Aecon ltée; Solotech Inc.; Gala Systems Inc	2009 Expected	30 years	$259 m	FDBOM	Signing	No
Modernization of Quebec City's Hôtel-Dieu hospital	Unknown	Unknown	TBD	TBD	$535 m	TBD	Procurement (RFEI)	No

378

reserche du Centre hospitalier de l'Université de Montreal (CHCHUM) and the McGill University Health Centre (MUHC).[36] This report found many problems associated with the VfM assessment conducted by PPP Québec. These include failure to consider reasonable alternative provisioning mechanisms (in addition to conventional public sector provision and P3), unreasonable assumptions for the PSC regarding asset maintenance and renewal costs and deficit, failure to justify the selection of a higher discount rate (8 per cent) than that used in other P3 projects (6.5 per cent), absence of proper sensitivity analysis, and failure to consider factors that could not be quantified. The auditor general also identified improper decision-making processes, including the absence of a critical, expert and independent assessment of the quality of the analysis in the value for money study conducted by PPP Québec.

Despite PPP Québec's unconvincing VfM study and improper decision-making processes, the Quebec government confirmed (in November) that the projects to modernize Montreal's UHC would be via a P3. However, this P3 has encountered financing problems. In December 2009, the government announced that it will provide over 45 per cent of the costs of these projects (Aubin, 2009) which will amount to about $1 billion.

Since the global financial meltdown, a number of P3s that would have been included in Table 16.2 have either been cancelled or have reverted to more traditional government procurement. In BC, the most notable example has been the Port Mann bridge: a ten-lane bridge and highway improvement project. Initially, the private sector partners in the P3 assumed both cost risk and revenue risk. However, in early 2009, the private sector partners could not comply with this agreement owing to the inability of Macquarie Bank to secure financing. Now the project is planned to go ahead with a fixed-price, design–build contract of $2.46 billion financed by the province.[37] Other P3s that have been cancelled or converted to traditional contracts include the Alberta Schools Project 2, which will now also go ahead as a design–build contract, and Quebec's Turcot Interchange.

The future of P3s in Canada appears to depend to a considerable degree on two uncertain factors. First, the extent to which left-of-centre (New Democratic Party – NDP), centre (Liberal), or right-of-centre (Conservative), governments hold power. This left–right distinction might not be useful in many parliamentary systems for understanding the evolution of P3s, but it is useful in the Canadian context. Canadian political culture, at both the federal and provincial levels, has maintained a tripartite party system where left-of-centre parties on the political spectrum have little incentive or opportunity to espouse 'third-way' policies. Specifically, the left-of-centre NDP has long criticized P3s, claiming that they are more costly than traditional procurement or, even, government provision. The BC NDP has indicated that it would repeal the Significant Projects Streamlining Act in BC and the requirement that all projects over $50 million be P3s (BCNDP Platform, 2009, p. 11). However, the NDP did not get elected to office in 2009.

The second factor is the uncertain state of global financial capital markets. However this unfolds, it is likely that traditional private large-scale capital will be scarcer and more expensive than it was over the previous decade. At the margin, this could herald a return to public sector financing of major infrastructure projects. Alternatively, we could see the emergence of a new 'we have the project/you have the money' partnership form, where the capital is provided by public sector or private sector pension funds (Robson, 2007), which we call P4s. The supply is there (pension money looking for relatively long-term and relatively safe investments in infrastructure) and the demand is there (governments looking for external sources of funding for capital-intensive infrastructure projects). Previously, there was relatively abundant private sector capital and P3 promotional institutions did not have the incentive to seek non-private sector capital. It is not clear whether they now have the desire or the entrepreneurial skills to design and implement P4s.

Regardless, a number of factors suggest that the P3 glory days with substantial private financing (with governments 'renting the money') are unlikely to return. First, the spreads between the costs of capital for the private sector and for the public sector have widened considerably, and this is unlikely to change for the foreseeable future. Second, the price of debt is likely to be higher. Debt holders are increasingly realizing that their interests are not completely aligned with equity participants. This problem is exacerbated when leverage is high. As Blanc-Brude and Strange (2007, p. 94) summarize it:

> PF [P3] deals have highly leveraged, limited- or non-recourse capital structures that aim to shield equity investors from most of the financing risk and significantly decrease the cost of finance for the project. But if much of the appeal of project finance derives from its ability to minimize funding costs by achieving high leverage, such high leverage is also its main point of vulnerability . . . PF structures can be endangered by overly ambitious borrowing programs that eliminate room to manoeuvre around other problems or structural deficiencies.

As a result, there is more likelihood that equity investors will walk away from high-leverage projects. Third, governments have to face the reality that they have not been able to transfer some of the risks that they hoped to transfer when they initially engaged in P3s. This is especially the case with use risk (i.e. demand risk/revenue risk) (Vining and Boardman, 2008a), but it applies to other types of risk as well. Indeed, P3s appear to have generally been low-risk for the private sector equity investors (Blanc-Brude and Strange, 2007, p. 95). Fourth, interest groups in Canada that oppose P3s have coalesced, organized and responded more forcefully over time. Initially, during the expansionary boom many governments essentially engaged in P3s 'under the radar'. The case for P3 projects was made in the technical language of 'value for money' and 'public sector comparators'. Opponents of P3s were generally ineffective at understanding or refuting these technical rationales. Governments that used P3s were also generally able to defend them on the basis of 'on time and on budget'. Opponents are now becoming more effective at pointing out the weaknesses of these arguments as rationales for P3s (see, e.g., Grey and Cusatis, 2008). Fifth, there is something of a ticking political and economic time bomb. Thus far, neither the public nor future governments have had to really face the financial costs of P3s. This will perhaps be most acute in the healthcare area. Many recent and in-progress P3s are expanding hospital facilities. Consequently, public healthcare authorities face substantial, long-term, ongoing liabilities. These authorities also face severe financial pressures due to an ageing population and shortages of nurses and other healthcare professionals. Currently, healthcare accounts for by far the largest component of provincial budgets. The financing system might not be sustainable, even without the burden of paying for these P3s.

In our opinion, it is quite likely that there will be relatively more public sector financing of infrastructure in Canada. There are two main reasons for this. First, private sector capital has in some cases become unavailable or excessively expensive. Second, it does not make sense for governments to rent or borrow expensive capital from the private sector when they can borrow the equivalent amounts at considerably lower cost. None the less, it is not clear what the provision mechanism will be and whether the government will capture the benefits. Perhaps governments will do more traditional procurement. Perhaps they can form P4 partnerships with public sector pension fund capital, possibly including banks and insurance companies. Contract management skills in government have improved. Perhaps they no longer need to use the P3 delivery mechanism.

P3s in the USA
In the USA, the term 'public–private partnership' is generally interpreted more broadly than in Canada and perhaps more broadly than in any other country. In US parlance, a P3 includes almost any project that jointly involves the public and private sectors. The first private turnpike in the USA, chartered in 1792, would certainly fall within this broad definition

of a P3. Similarly, the widespread provision of municipal services by franchise contracts during the 1800s would also fall within this broad definition of P3s. More recently, inner-city urban renewal projects have also been described as P3s. These 'major redevelopment projects (were) privately controlled and often publicly subsidized' (Keating et al., 1995, p. 332). The US General Accounting Office (GAO) even considered conventional contracting out of government services and outright privatization as falling under the P3 umbrella (GAO, 1999). In March 2009, the US Treasury set up the Public–Private Partnership Investment Program to use $75 to $100 billion of Troubled Asset Relief Program (TARP) capital and capital from private investors to buy 'legacy assets', including real-estate loans made by banks.[38] Perhaps most controversially, many well-known US companies could now be considered P3s because they are partially owned by the government. This would include GM (about 60 per cent owned by the US government, and 12.5 per cent owned by the Canadian government (Raum, 2009)), and Citigroup (about 34 per cent owned by the US government as of June 2009) (*New York Times*, 2009). However, for the purposes of this chapter we restrict discussion of US P3s to FDBOMT-type infrastructure P3s.

Table 16.3 lists chronologically those P3s in the USA that began construction in 2000 or subsequently. Obviously, the USA has not adopted P3s to the same extent as has Canada. The main use of P3s during this period in the USA has been for roads/highways, especially at the state level, and to some extent for water treatment/desalination plants, especially at the municipal level. Indeed, many P3s have been initiated by municipal governments. Overall, relatively few state agencies have been involved in P3s. The most active states are California, Virginia, Florida, Massachusetts, Texas and Washington.

Table 16.3 shows comparable information to that shown in Table 16.1: the names of the public and private 'partners', the start year, the length of the operating period, the estimated present value of the cost of the contract, the type of P3 (i.e. the nature of the contract), the current stage of the project and whether the private sector assumed revenue risk. Unlike in Canada, there have been quite a few P3s where the private sector did not provide financing. Furthermore, even where the private sector has provided some financing, it is not necessarily complete financing. For example, in the I-495 Capital Beltway HOT Lanes project, the private equity partner provided financing for only $349 million of the $1.93 billion total.[39]

One noteworthy difference between the USA and Canada is that road concession agreements have been more common in the USA. For a description see, for example, Pagdadis et al. (2008). Two of the most

Table 16.3   US P3s since 2000

Project	Public partner	Private partner	Start year	Operating period	Present value	Type of P3	Project stage	Revenue risk
Massachusetts Route 3 North Project	Commonwealth of Massachusetts	Route 3 North Transportation Improvements Association	2000	30 years	$385 m	FDBOM	Operational	No
El Paso County Water Treatment Services	El Paso County Water Authority	ECO Resources, Inc.	2000	20 years	$6.7 m	FDBOM	Operational	No
Route 3 North (Boston)	Massachusetts Highway Department and the Massachusetts Executive Office of Transportation	Modern Continental	2000	30 years	$385.1 m	FDBOM	Operational	The developer may pursue surface, sub-surface, and air rights development to generate non-project revenues. The developer may pursue development rights, receiving 40 % of ancillary development revenues under the negotiated Development Agreement
Water Treatment Facility (Tampa)	Tampa Bay Water	Veolia Water North America	2000	15 years (with option for 5 more)	$144 m	DBOM	Operational	No

383

Table 16.3 (continued)

Project	Public partner	Private partner	Start year	Operating period	Present value	Type of P3	Project stage	Revenue risk
Lacklands Air Force Base Housing (TX)	US Air Force	Landmark Organization Incorporated	2001	50 years	$42.6 m	DBOM	Operational	No
Cedar River Water Treatment Plant (Seattle)	City of Seattle	CH2M Hill	2002	25 years	$113 m	DBOM	Operational	No
Southwest Water Treatment Plant (San Juan Capistrano, CA)	Capistrano Valley Water District	ECO Resources	2003	20 years	$25 m	DBOM	Operational	No
Lake Pleasant Water Treatment Plant (AZ)	City of Phoenix	American Water	2003	15 years	$336 m	DBOM	Operational	No
South Bay Expressway (SR 125) (San Diego County)	State of California	California Transportation Ventures, Inc., a wholly owned subsidiary of Macquarie Infrastructure Group	2003	35 years	$635 m $138 m for connector and interchange	FDBOM	Operational	State of California allows developer to set market rate tolls. Franchise allows a maximum 18.5% return on total investment with additional allowed incentive return for action to increase average vehicle occupancy on the toll road

Project	Authority	Contractor	Year	Term	Value	Model	Status	Tolling/Revenue
District Energy Systems (Nashville)	City of Nashville	Constellation Energy Projects & Services Group, Inc. (CEPS)	2003	15 years	$46 m	DBOM	Operational	No
Chicago Skyway	Illinois Toll Highway Authority	Skyway Concession Company (Cintra Concesiones de Infraestructuras de Transporte S.A. and Macquarie Infrastructure Group)	2004	99 years	$1.83 bn	FBOM	Operational	Yes – toll and concession revenue
Indiana Toll Road	Indiana Finance Authority	ITR Concession Company LLC: Cintra; Macquarie Infrastructure Group	2006	75 years	$3.8 bn	FBOM	Operational	Limited tolling authority (Evansville-to-Martinsville leg)
Taunton River Desalination Plant	Massachusetts Municipal Authority	InimaUSA Corp. for Aquaria Water	2006	20 years	$60 m	DBOM	Operational	No
I-495 Capital Beltway HOT (High Occupancy Toll) Lanes (Virginia)	Virginia Department of Transportation	Fluor-Transurban	2008	80 years	$1.9 bn	FDBOM	Construction	Tolls based on demand (congestion pricing). Revenue above agreed benchmarks will be shared with the Commonwealth

Table 16.3 (continued)

Project	Public partner	Private partner	Start year	Operating period	Present value	Type of P3	Project stage	Revenue risk
Bridge Improvement Project	Missouri Department of Transportation	KTU Constructors	2008	25 years	$600 m – $800 m	Changed from FDBOM to DB	Construction	N/A
Port of Miami Tunnel	Florida Department of Transportation	Miami Access Tunnel	2008	31 years	$914 m	FDBOM	Contract Awarded	No
Interstate 595 Express	Florida Department of Transportation	ACS Infrastructure Development	2008	35 years	$1.79 bn	FDBOM	Awarded	No
Santa Paula Water Recycling Facility	City of Santa Paula	Santa Paula Water, LLC	2008	30 years	$60 m	FDBOM	Construction	No
Carlsbad Desalination Project	City of Carlsbad	Poseidon Resources Corporation	2008	30 years with two additional 30 year terms	$300 m	DBOM	Construction	No
Oregon Solar Highway	Oregan Department of Transportation	Solarway	2008	20 years	$1.3 m	FDBOM	Construction	Partner will construct, own, operate and maintain the solar systems, selling all electricity generated by the systems to ODOT under a Solar Power Purchase Agreement, for a term from six to 20 years, or longer

Huntington Beach Water Desalination Facility	City of Huntington Beach	Poseidon Resources Corporation	2009 (Expected)	30 years	$250 m	DBOM	Awarded	No
Lakeland Electrical	Florida Municipal Power Agency	SunEdison	2009 (Expected)	20 years	Undisclosed	FDBOM	Awarded	Unknown
State Highway 130 (Texas)	Texas Department of Transportation	SH 130 Concession Company, LLC (Lone Star Infrastructure)	2008	50 years	$1.3 bn	FDBOM	Construction	A share of the toll revenue over the next 50 years, beginning with the first dollar earned on the toll road. The state's share of toll revenue over the next 50 years is estimated to be $1.6 bn
Trans Texas Corridor-I35	Texas Transportation Commission	Cintra	2009	50 years	$7.2 bn	FDBOM	Design	Collect tolls and pay back a specified amount to the state

prominent road concession agreements are the Chicago Skyway and the Indiana Toll Road. When an existing road or highway is leased out for a specified period to a private operator, it is not clear whether it makes sense to think of it as a P3 or as a form of privatization. Either way, there is greater willingness in the USA, compared to Canada, to toll roads and to have the private sector collect the tolls, possibly in the belief that this is more acceptable to toll-payers. However, the normative economic rationale for engaging in concession-type P3s is different, and almost certainly weaker, than the normative argument for P3s that generate incremental infrastructure. As concessions are by definition largely financing arrangements (the road already exists), their consequences are mostly distributional (i.e. involve transfers), rather than generating real economic costs or benefits.

Table 16.4 shows proposed P3s in the USA. Most of them are transportation projects.

US government or quasi-government P3 agencies

As of July 2009, 23 states and one US territory had passed legislation giving private sector entities the legal authority to participate in transportation infrastructure projects.[40] In most states, the authority to develop toll roads is limited to special public authorities. New enabling legislation would be needed to expand and transfer these powers. Many US states have historically had legislation in place that inhibited the use of P3s. These ranged from requirements for low-bid awards on construction contracts to prohibitions against design/build or the outsourcing of state agency functions. In addition, there were prohibitions against tolling or commingling public and private funds.[41] The US Department of Transportation website contains a list of the key elements of state P3 enabling legislation for highway projects and identifies those states that have passed each provision.[42] For example, in Alaska, Arizona, California, Indiana, Missouri, North Carolina and Tennessee, P3 projects are limited to 'pilot' or 'demonstration' projects (although this restriction has now been lifted in California).

US Department of Transportation, Federal Highway Administration
The Federal Highway Administration (FHWA) is the agency of the US Department of Transportation (DOT), which implements federal highway programmes in partnership with state and local agencies.[43] It has encouraged the use of P3s through an array of financing mechanisms and initiatives. The most important programmes are:

- SEP-15 is 'a new experimental process for FHWA to identify, for trial evaluation, new P3 approaches to project delivery'.[44] Several

Table 16.4 Proposed P3s in the USA

Project	Public partner	Private partner	Start year	Operating period	Present value	Type of P3	Project stage	Revenue risk
Knik Arm Bridge (Alaska)	Alaska Department of Transportation & Public Facilities	TBD	2009 (Expected)	up to 55 years	$500 m – $600 m	FDBOM	Environmental Impact Studies	No
First Coast Outer Beltway	Florida Department of Transportation	Unknown	2009 (Expected)	35–75 years	$1.8 bn	FDBOM	Procurement (RFQ)	TBD
Jackson Airport Parkway Project	Mississippi Department of Transportation	Unknown	2009 (Expected)	50 years	$400 m	FDBOM	Procurement (RFP)	TBD
Pennsylvania Turnpike (I-95)	Pennsylvania Turnpike Commission	Unknown	TBD	TBD	$650 m	FDBOM	Concept	TBD
Southport Marine Terminal	Commonwealth of Pennsylvania	Unknown	2009 (Expected)	25–40 years	$200 m – 400 m	FDBOM	Procurement (RFP)	TBD
Production of Mo-99	Idaho State University	Positron Systems	TBD	TBD	TBD	Unknown	Letter of Intent	TBD

of the P3s shown in Tables 16.3 and 16.4 were developed under this programme.

- Private Activity Bonds (PAB) provide private developers and operators with access to tax-exempt interest bonds, which lowers the cost of capital significantly. As of the end of 2008, the US DOT had approved a total of $4.9 billion in PAB allocations between eight projects (with almost half of the money allocated to I-595 in Florida).[45] However, the only project for which bonds had actually been issued was for the I-495 Capital Beltway HOT Lanes project.
- The Transportation Infrastructure Finance and Innovation Act (TIFIA) established a federal credit programme for eligible transportation projects of national or regional significance. Under it, DOT may provide three forms of credit assistance – secured (direct) loans, loan guarantees and standby lines of credit.[46]

The I-495 Capital Beltway HOT Lanes project was largely financed as a mix of private activity bonds ($586 million) and TIFIA loan financing ($585 million). In addition, the state contributed $409 million.[47]

National Conference on State Legislatures

The National Conference of State Legislatures (NCSL) is a bipartisan organization that serves the legislators and staffs of all 50 states and territories. NCSL provides research and technical assistance on pressing state issues.[48] In December 2008, it announced the 'Partners Project on Public–Private Partnerships' to develop expertise and offer educational sessions on various aspects of P3s, including evaluation and implementation.[49] It focuses on roadways, but might also incorporate linked water-based systems or intermodal installations.

California: 'performance-based infrastructure'

In January 2006, Governor Schwarzenegger launched his Strategic Growth Plan designed to invest several billion dollars into infrastructure over the following years.[50] In November 2006, voters approved $42 billion for the plan. In 2007, $7.7 billion in lease-revenue bond authority was authorized for prisons and jails and for medical services within the correctional system. In 2008, the governor instituted a 'performance-based infrastructure' (PBI) initiative, which is essentially a P3 initiative.[51] He also proposed the establishment of PBI California 'to help determine which projects can benefit from PBI, represent the state in negotiations with PBI participants, ensure transparency, and monitor performance' (ceNews Staff, 2008). PBI California is explicitly modelled on Partnerships BC. In 2009, Governor Schwarzenegger approved a bill that allowed regional transportation agencies and Caltrans to enter into P3s, removing the previous constraints on the use of P3s.[52] All of these developments suggest that California is gearing up for much greater use of P3s. Unless the global financial meltdown or the state's own large budget deficits restricts its access to capital, California is likely to be the US laboratory for large-scale institutionalized P3s.

Oregon Innovative Partnerships Program

The Oregon Innovative Partnerships Program (OIPP) was passed by the Oregon Legislature in 2003. The purpose of OIPP is to develop transportation projects for solicitation of private sector proposals for partnership and to respond to proposals initiated by private firms and units of government. OIPP evaluates proposals, both solicited and unsolicited, and selects those proposals that it considers offers the best value for the state.[53]

US private sector P3 proponent institutions

The National Council for Public–Private Partnerships

The National Council for Public–Private Partnerships is a non-profit organization, created in 1985. Its mission is 'to advocate and facilitate the formation of public–private partnerships at the federal, state and local levels, where appropriate, and to raise the awareness of governments and businesses of the means by which their cooperation can cost effectively provide the public with quality goods, services and facilities'.[54] Not surprisingly, it is an unabashed proponent of P3s.

The Privatization Center

The Privatization Center is part of the Reason Foundation, a libertarian think tank. It has conducted research and analysis, performed case studies and provided advice on various aspects of privatization, contracting out and P3s.[55] It produces an annual privatization report. The Center specializes in government services, health services, social services, public safety, as well as infrastructure, airports, electric power, highways, transit, and water/wastewater facilities.

Washington Policy Center

The Washington Policy Center (WPC) is a non-profit organization with a mission to promote free-market solutions through research and education.[56] It is much smaller than the Reason Foundation and acts as a vehicle for the promotion of P3s in Washington State; see, for example, Ennis (2007).

Evaluation of P3s in the USA and thoughts about the future
If one takes a narrow PFI-type definition of the meaning of a P3, the US experience with them has been limited. How well have these P3s performed? While arm's-length empirical evidence on the performance of P3s is quite extensive in some countries, it is still quite limited in the USA. Vining et al. (2005) reviewed three early P3s: the Dulles Greenway in Virginia, State Route 91 in Orange County and the Tampa Bay Seawater Desalination Plant in Florida. They also reviewed the evidence concerning P3s in the US prison system. They conclude that '(t)he evidence suggests that (the) potential benefits are often overwhelmed by contracting costs and opportunism. The reality that "there are no free lunches" applies to P3s as much as it does to anything else' (ibid., p. 215). Vining and Boardman (2008a) describe in detail the opportunistic behaviour of both the private sector and governments that raise transaction costs.

In 2008, the US General Accountability Office (GAO, previously the General Accounting Office), issued a major analysis and assessment of highway P3s. Along the lines of Vining et al.'s (2005) conclusion that 'there are no free lunches', the GAO emphasized 'there is no free money'. In aggregate, the GAO's assessment of P3s was cautious and essentially non-committal on their potential value: 'In some instances, the potential benefits of highway public–private partnerships may outweigh the potential costs and trade-offs . . . in other instances, the potential costs and trade-offs may outweigh the potential benefits, and the public interest may not be well served by using such an arrangement' (GAO, 2008, p. 38). At the same time, the GAO (ibid., p. 9) noted that 'while direct federal involvement has been limited to date in the highway public–private partnerships we reviewed, the administration and the DOT have actively promoted highway public–private partnerships through policies and practices, including the development of experimental programs that waive certain federal regulations and encourage private investment'. Finally, it is worth noting the GAO, although not directly criticizing concession-style P3s, has called for the use of a national 'public-interest test' for evaluating the use of P3s. This could be interpreted as a call for a social cost–benefit test (see Boardman and Vining, Chapter 8 in this volume).

As mentioned above, US governments have not adopted P3s for infrastructure projects to the same extent as have their Canadian counterparts. Apart from the federal government, California, and a few other states, much of the activity has been limited to concession-type agreements. This is surprising given that: (1) US governments have generally been more private sector friendly than Canadian governments; (2) there are several influential market-oriented think tanks that have advocated P3s; (3) much of the national infrastructure is frequently described as 'crumbling'

(Pagdadis et al., 2008); (4) many states have huge funding shortfalls; (5) some states and some branches of the federal government are willing to provide significant assistance in financing; and (6) P3s offer the promise of new infrastructure without the burden all falling on current taxpayers. In spite of the GAO's major note of caution, we would expect more pressure to adopt P3s.

Conclusion
It should be clear that the experience with P3s is different in Canada and the USA, with many more PFI-type P3s in Canada than in the USA. One important commonality is that governments in both countries have been promoting the use of P3s and have set up P3 agencies (often at the state level in the USA or at the provincial level in Canada). These agencies often serve two, three or sometimes four major purposes: (a) to analyse the desirability of any project (although this is often made on political grounds); (b) to decide which alternative provisioning mode to employ (e.g. a P3 or PSC); (c) to administer the contract process; and (d) to evaluate the overall success of the project. Vining and Boardman suggested that these purposes should be assigned to four separate agencies. They argue:

> These separations may seem like bureaucratization gone mad, but otherwise any monolithic P3 agency will turn into an agency that sees its main job as boosting P3s. Although it may be inevitable that the administering agency turns into a political poodle, it needs to be flanked by junkyard dogs. Although the skills involved in agencies (b) and (d) are similar and potentially combinable, a combination would create incentive problems: Agencies almost never like to criticize their own earlier decisions. (2008b, p. 157)

The recent problems in Quebec are indicative of the problems of not having separate agencies. P3 agencies have been P3 proponents and have conducted VfM analyses that were biased in favour of P3s. The use of an inappropriately high discount rate is quite common in Canada (see Boardman and Vining, Chapter 8 in this volume). Unfortunately, neither Canada nor the USA appear to be interested in systematically and rigorously investigating their own *ex post* experiences with P3s. Evidence that P3s meet the public interest is scarce. In practice it can only be done by agencies with the power to access the relevant information, such as the attorney general in Canada or the GAO in the USA, and such agencies focus on fiscal costs, not social costs.

In Canada one of the most important earlier motives for P3s was to shift risk to the private sector. However, the private sector has never liked to assume risk and will only do so if the price is sufficiently high. Vining and Boardman (2008a) found that the private sector would usually take on cost risk but not revenue (use) risk. Furthermore, it has recently emerged that the government's (or P3 agency's) risk of being sued increases with a P3, as evidenced by the success of the Cambie Street merchants with respect to the Canada Line. Given that risk transfer is much lower than originally expected, and there are other contractual arrangements that could achieve this transfer without resorting to a P3, it appears that leading up to 2008, the prime motive for P3s in Canada was the ability to 'rent the money' – that is to provide public infrastructure for current voters while shifting payment to future generations (and future voters). However, since the 2008–09 financial crisis, private sector financing has dried up or become more expensive. The Quebec hospital project and the Port Mann bridge project demonstrate increasing dependence on public sector financing. Thus the main positive rationale for P3s (renting the money) disappears. Governments and their P3 agencies should and probably will cut back on the use of P3s. The mandates of the recently created federal and provincial P3 agencies should no longer promote P3s *per se*. Rather, they should operate in the public interest. They should seriously consider traditional government provision and other reasonable alternatives, and select the best alternatives. Furthermore, such evaluations should be open to independent scrutiny. P3 projects should be evaluated *ex ante* and *ex post* by independent experts.

In the USA the situation is different. In the transportation area, new P3 toll roads and selling P3 concessions on existing roads have a positive impact on short-run government cash flow. For this and other reasons, we expect there will be more of them. However, as the GAO has pointed out, there are advantages and disadvantages to P3s and there is a need for independent analyses of P3s that consider the public interest.

Acknowledgements
Michelle Barnes and Joel Jaffe provided excellent research assistance. We would also like to thank Tom Ross and the UBC P3 project for financial assistance.

Notes
1. See *Building Canada – Modern Infrastructure for a Strong Canada*, available at: www.buildingcanada-chantierscanada.gc.ca/plandocs/booklet-livret/booklet-livret-eng.html (accessed 30 July 2009).
2. See, for example, *Canada-Alberta: Infrastructure Framework Agreement*, available at www.buildingcanada-chantierscanada.gc.ca/plandocs/agreements-ententes/ifa-eci-ab-eng.html (accessed 30 July 2009).
3. Ibid., Section 3.3.7, p. 7 (accessed 30 July 2009).
4. Source: www.appointments-nominations.gc.ca/prflOrg.asp?OrgID=PPPC&type-typ=&lang=eng (accessed 30 July 2009).
5. *Canada-Alberta: Infrastructure Framework Agreement*, Section 3.3.7, p. 7.

6. Specific principles include: spending on capital assets must be managed within fiscal limits; capital asset management decisions must be supported by rigorous business case analysis; costs and risks (such as legal, environmental, health and safety, construction) must be identified, analysed and managed throughout an asset's life cycle, which includes planning, acquisition, use, maintenance and disposal or renewal; risks must be allocated to those parties best able to manage them at the least cost while serving the public interest. Those parties might be in the public, private or non-profit sector – or a combination of the three. While the underlying principles of the CAMF guidelines apply to P3s, the VfM process and fairness auditor's report are the mechanisms by which P3s are judged for their compliance to the principles.

7. Ministry of Finance (2007), Capital Procurement Checklist Overview, 4, www.fin. gov.bc.ca/tbs/NEW%20-20MERGED%20Capital%20procurement%20checklist%20 FINAL_%202007_12_11.pdf.

8. Province of British Columbia (2002), 'Capital Asset Management Framework', 2, May, available at: www.fin.gov.bc.ca/tbs/camf_overview.pdf.

9. Partnerships BC, FAQ, available at: www.partnershipsbc.ca/files/faqs.html.

10. The AAC is also used in the UK; see HM Treasury (2000).

11. See www.partnershipsbc.ca/pdf/SeatoSkyFinal.pdf.

12. *Project Finance Magazine* (2008), 'Wide open', Canadian Infrastructure Report 2008, available at: www.projectfinancemagazine.com/default.asp?Page=20&PUB=157&ISS =24984&SID=711190

13. Alberta Transportation (2004), 'Alberta's experience with public private partnerships presentation to Financing Road System Investment Committee of the World Road Association', 5, available at: www.cnc-piarc-aipcr.ca/lib/Tech_Committee_C1.2/albertappp.pdf.

14. Infrastructure Canada (2008), 'Infrastructure Framework Agreement A: Canada – Alberta', available at: www.buildingcanada-chantierscanada.gc.ca/plandocs/agree ments-ententes/ifa-eci-ab-eng.html.

15. The City of Calgary, Finance and Supply (2008), 'Council Policy for Public–Private Partnerships, Report to S.P.C. on Finance and Corporate Services', available at: publicaccess.calgary.ca/lldm01/livelink.exe?func=ccpa.general&msgID=LKqerrqrgC&msg Action=Download (accessed 29 July 2009).

16. Investment Saskatchewan (2006), 'Investment Saskatchewan', available at: www. investsask.com/.

17. Infrastructure Ontario, Infrastructure Ontario, About Us, available at: www.infrastructureontario.ca/en/about/index.asp.

18. Infrastructure Ontario, 'How Infrastructure Ontario Supports Infrastructure Development', available at: www.infrastructureontario.ca/en/about/develop.asp.

19. Ibid.

20. See Partenariats public-privé Québec, 'L'Agence des partenariats public-privé du Québec: About Us', available at: www.ppp.gouv.qc.ca/index.asp?page=home_ en&lang=en (accessed 30 July 2009).

21. That is, those with a capital cost of $40 million or more. The Framework Policy applies to the following public bodies: government departments and agencies; cegeps; school boards; universities; public health and social services establishments and regional health and social services boards; municipal agencies for projects funded primarily by the government or its agencies.

22. Government of Québec (2004), Public Private Partnership Framework Policy, 1

23. Ibid., 2.

24. Ibid., 5.

25. Ibid., 6.

26. Ibid., 5.

27. Ibid.

28. W. Elliot (2008), 'Union Dues: CUPE says P3 sucks', *Nova Scotia Business Journal*, available at: www.novascotiabusinessjournal.com/index.cfm?sid=126678&sc=107, April.

29. Infrastructure Canada (2008), 'Canada and Prince Edward Island sign $270-million Infrastructure Agreement', available at: www.buildingcanada-chantierscanada.gc.ca/media/news-nouvelles/regions/pe/20080521summerside-eng.html.
30. The Canadian Council for Public Private Partnerships, 'About Us', available at: www.pppcouncil.ca/aboutus.asp.
31. See www.canadaline.ca/aboutOverview.asp (accessed 30 July 2009).
32. See www.vancouversun.com/news/Cambie+Street+merchant+wins+damages+Canada+Line+construction/1635935/story.html (accessed 30 July 2009).
33. See cupe.ca/public-private-partnerships/CUPE-launches-P3-ad (accessed 30 July 2009).
34. For a full discussion of the appropriate discount rate to use to evaluate P3s see Boardman and Vining, Chapter 8 in this volume.
35. See Bill 65: An Act respecting Infrastructure Quebec, available at: www2.publications-duquebec.gouv.qc.ca/dynamicSearch/telecharge.php?type=5&file=2009C53A.PDF (accessed 21 December 2009).
36. See Press release no. 5, 18 November 2009, available at: www.vgq.gouv.qc.ca/en/salle-de-presse/Communiques/index.aspx (accessed 21 December 2009).
37. See www.th.gov.bc.ca/gateway/PMH1/contrctr_select.htm and Gilbert (2009).
38. See tg-65, US Treasury, available at: ustreas.gov/press/releases/tg65.htm (accessed 21 December 2009).
39. See www.fhwa.dot.gov/ppp/case_studies_i495_capital.htm (accessed 30 July 2009).
40. US Department of Transportation, Federal Highway Administration, Public Private Partnerships, available at: www.fhwa.dot.gov/ppp/tools_state_legis_statues.htm (accessed 30 July 2009).
41. US Department of Transportation. Federal Highway Administration, FAQs, available at: www.fhwa.dot.gov/PPP/faqs.htm.
42. US Department of Transportation, Federal Highway Administration, 'State PPP Enabling Statutes Key Elements of State PPP Enabling Legislation for Highway Projects', available at: www.fhwa.dot.gov/PPP/tools_state_key_elements.htm.
43. Ibid.
44. www.fhwa.dot.gov/PPP/tools_sep15.htm.
45. www.fhwa.dot.gov/PPP/tools_pabs.htm (accessed 30 July 2009).
46. US Department of Transportation, 'The Transportation Infrastructure Finance and Innovation Act', Transportation Infrastructure Finance, tifia.fhwa.dot.gov/ (accessed 30 July 2009).
47. See www.fhwa.dot.gov/ppp/case_studies_i495_capital.htm (accessed 30 July 2009).
48. The National Conference of State Legislatures, available at: www.ncsl.org/AboutUs/tabid/305/Default.aspx (accessed 30 July 2009).
49. www.ncsl.org/default.aspx?tabid=17528 (accessed 30 July 2009).
50. gov.ca.gov/pdf/gov/CSGP.pdf (accessed 30 July 2009).
51. See gov.ca.gov/issue/performance-based-infrastructure/ (accessed 30 July 2009).
52. www.dot.ca.gov/hq/innovfinance/Public-Private%20Partnerships/PPP_main.html (accessed 30 July 2009).
53. Office of Innovative Partnerships and Alternative Funding, Innovative Partnerships Program, available at: www.oregon.gov/ODOT/HWY/OIPP/innovative.shtml
54. www.ncppp.org/aboutus/index.shtml (accessed 30 July 2009).
55. www.privatization.org/about.html, (accessed 30 July 2009).
56. www.washingtonpolicy.org/aboutus/missionstatement.html (accessed 30 July 2009).

References

Aubin, Henry (2009), 'This delay is OK: new setback in hospital construction could turn out to be a good thing', *The Gazette*, 15 December, A 21.
BCNDP Platform (2009), *Take Back Your BC*, available at: www.bcndp.ca/files/u108/BCNDP09_Platform_2009-_Final-April9_last3.pdf (accessed 30 July 2009).

Blanc-Brude, Frederic and Roger Strange (2007), 'How banks price loans to public–private partnerships: evidence from the European markets', *Journal of Applied Corporate Finance*, **19** (4), 94–105.

Boardman, Anthony E., Wendy L. Mallery and Aidan R. Vining (1994), 'Learning from ex ante/ex post cost–benefit analysis comparisons: the Coquihalla Highway example', *Socio-Economic Planning Sciences*, **28** (2), 69–84.

Boardman, Anthony E., Finn Poschmann and Aidan R. Vining (2005), 'North American infrastructure P3s: examples and lessons learned', in Graeme Hodge and Carsten Greve (eds), *The Challenge of Public-Private Partnerships: Learning from International Experience*, Cheltenham, UK and Northampton, MA, USA: Edward Elgar, pp. 162–89.

ceNews Staff (2008), 'Schwarzenegger proposes public–private partnerships for California infrastructure improvements', *ceNEWS.com*, 29 January, available at: www.cenews.com/article.asp?id=2620 (accessed 30 July 2009).

City of Calgary (2008), Public–Private Partnerships Council Policy Framework, Finance and Supply.

Clinger, James C., Richard C. Feiock, Barbara Coyle McCabe and Hyung-Jun Park (2008), 'Turnover, transaction costs, and time horizons', *American Review of Public Administration*, **38** (2), 167–79.

CUPE Research (2009), The Saskatchewan P3 Secretariat, March, available at cupe.ca/updir/Fact_Sheet__The_Saskatchewan_P3_Secretariat_-4.pdf, accessed 30 July 2009.

Ennis, Michael (2007), 'The case for public/private partnerships in transportation planning: building transportation projects in Washington State', available at: www.washington-policy.org/Centers/transportation/legislativememo/07_ennis_publicprivate.html (accessed 30 July 2009).

General Accounting Office (GAO) (1999), 'Privatization: lessons learned by state and local governments', GAO/GGD-97-48, report to the Chairman, House Republican Task Force on Privatization.

General Accountability Office (GAO) (2008), 'Highway public–private partnerships: more rigorous up-front analysis could better secure potential benefits and protect the public interest', GAO-08-44, Washington, DC: GAO, February.

Gilbert, Richard (2009), 'Port Mann P3 deal falls through as province turns to design–build contract', *Canadian Journal of Commerce*, 4 March, available at: www.journalofcommerce.com/article/id32884 (accessed 30 July 2009).

Government of New Brunswick (2000), *Public Private Partnerships*, available at: www.gnb.ca/0158/reports/protocol/protocol.htm (accessed 30 July 2009).

Grey, Gary J. and Patrick J. Cusatis (2008), *An Analysis of the Proposed Lease and Reinvestment Program for the Pennsylvania Turnpike*, study commissioned by the Democratic Caucus, Pennsylvania House of Representatives, June, available at: www.pahouse.com/docs/16-Final_Copy_June_Turnpike_Report.doc (accessed 17 December 2009).

Hodge, Graeme (2004), 'Governing with accountability: has Parliament abdicated in the age of public–private partnerships?', paper presented to the National Conference of Parliamentary Environment and Public Works Committees, Canberra, Australia, 11–14 July.

HM Treasury (2000), *Public Private Partnerships: The Government's Approach*. London: The Stationery Office, available at: www.hm-treasury.gov.uk/d/80.pdf (accessed 30 July 2009).

Keating, W. Dennis, Norman Krumholz and John Metzger (1995), 'Populist public–private partnerships', in William Dennis Keating, Norman Krumholz and David C. Perry (eds), *Cleveland: A Metropolitan Reader*, Kent, OH: Kent State University Press, pp. 332–50.

Murray, Stuart (2006), *Value for Money? Cautionary Lessons about P3s from British Columbia*, Vancouver, BC: Canadian Centre for Policy Alternatives, June, available at: www.policyalternatives.ca/documents/BC_Office_Pubs/bc_2006/P3_value_for_money.pdf (accessed 30 July 2009).

New York Times (2009), 'Citi sets plan to convert $58 billion in stock', *New York Times*, 10 June, available at: dealbook.blogs.nytimes.com/2009/06/10/citi-sets-plan-to-convert-58-billion-in-stock (accessed 30 July 2009).

Pagdadis, Sotris A., Stephen M. Sorett, Frank M. Rapoport, Courtney J. Edmonds, Scott G. Rafshoon and Marcia L. Hale (2008), 'A road map to success for public–private partnerships of public infrastructure initiatives', *Journal of Private Equity*, Spring, 8–18.

Parks, Ronald and Rosanne Terhart (2009), *Evaluation of Public Private Partnerships: Costing and Evaluation Methodology*, Vancouver, BC: Blair, Mackay and Mynett Valuations Inc.

Partnerships British Columbia (2003), *Service Plan 2003/04 – 2004/05*, available at: www.bcbudget.gov.bc.ca/2003/sp/crowncorps/pbc.pdf (accessed 30 July 2009).

Province of British Columbia (2002), *Capital Asset Management Framework Guidelines*, May, available at: www.fin.gov.bc.ca/tbs/camf_guidelines.pdf (accessed 30 July 2009).

Raum, Tom (2009), 'Obama: nationalization of GM to be short-term', *ABC News*, 1 June, available at: abcnews.go.com/Politics/wireStory?id=7726160 (accessed 30 July 2009).

Robson, William B. (2007), 'Found money: matching Canadians' saving with their infrastructure needs', C.D. Howe Institute, e-brief, 8 March.

Vining, Aidan R. and Anthony E. Boardman (2008a), 'Public–private partnerships in Canada: theory and evidence', *Canadian Public Administration*, **51** (1), 9–44.

Vining, Aidan R. and Anthony E. Boardman (2008b), 'Public–private partnerships: eight rules for governments', *Public Works Management and Policy*, **13** (2), 149–61.

Vining, Aidan R., Anthony E. Boardman and Finn Poschmann (2005), 'Public–private partnerships in the U.S. and Canada: "There are no free lunches"', *Journal of Comparative Policy Analysis*, **7** (3), 199–220.

Wood, James (2009), 'Gov't explores public–private partnerships: new secretariat to evaluate proposals', *Saskatoon Star Phoenix*, 2 January.

17 The Australian PPP experience: observations and reflections
Graeme A. Hodge and Colin F. Duffield

Australia has, over the past four decades, been a keen reformer of public sector activities. The introduction of public–private partnerships (PPPs) as an alternative infrastructure delivery method has been no exception, and long-term infrastructure arrangements between governments and private businesses have become increasingly popular. Today's PPPs operate with sophisticated and far-reaching contracts, and promise better efficiency and strengthened monitoring and accountability as well as a host of other benefits. In the midst of an increasing amount of international evidence now available on the extent to which these promises are being met, debate remains both loud and determined. Some interpret the introduction of this reform as a sensible evolutionary step in the professional delivery of large infrastructure projects. PPP to these people is simply a sophisticated way to deliver modern professionalized public sector services. Others, though, see the infrastructure PPP movement as a triumph of the interests of bankers and professional consultants over the interests of citizens, whose needs should be represented through the parliament.

This chapter looks at some of the recent Australian experience of PPPs. It discusses first the national historical context and notes that the desire for government to marry up its own capacities with the private sector is in fact not new. This has been achieved over the past two centuries through a variety of public–private mix arrangements at federal and state level. Second, we review the more recent foundations upon which Australian governments have then built reforms in public sector services, including PPP policies and the disciplines behind these policy ideas. A particular interest is the more aggressive policy leadership of the state of Victoria. The chapter then examines three specific case studies with the aim of illustrating the range of PPPs undertaken to date as well as some of the factors critical to success or failure. Finally, the chapter briefly comments on the performance outcomes published for PPP initiatives thus far and the lessons learned from experience. Overall, then, we focus particularly on the historical and cultural foundations upon which the Australian PPP phenomenon has been built, its style thus far and the policy lessons learned to date, rather than on technical project delivery processes.

Historical context

Australia comprises six states and two territories, and with a land mass of almost the same size as the USA, has a population of around 21.2 million people. It enjoys a national political system based on the values of the UK's Westminster tradition but with a federal system of government. In this, the federal government shares power with several state and territory governments. Different Australian governments have through the 1990s adopted quite different stances on PPPs. States such as Victoria have led the charge with an aggressive approach to PPP, whilst other states such as Queensland have been slower to implement PPP ideas. Interestingly, too, until recently, the federal government has remained almost entirely sceptical, despite its pro-market and pro-privatization orientation throughout the past two decades. In recent times, there appears in particular to have been a degree of alignment between the views of the states and those of the federal government towards the PPP model for infrastructure.

Australia's past has seen a wide range of ownership and regulatory structures. Like New Zealand and other South Pacific nations, Australia has enjoyed a large state-owned enterprise (SOE) sector, not through any particular ideological bent for state socialism, but as a pragmatic response to the failure of early market attempts at essential service provision, and the need to meet high community expectations for the provision of comprehensive and effective infrastructure for energy, transport, finance and insurance, and telecommunications. Indeed, the evolution of a widespread public enterprise sector was overseen largely by conservative political parties in the main (Wettenhall, 1983) under the general ethos of stimulating economic development.[1] In essence, it was a method of combining the capacity and long-term vision of the public sector with the commercial service and efficient production orientation of the private sector in pursuing the community's developmental goals. It was, as Wettenhall (2003) suggests, an early way of the public and private sectors working together in 'public–private mix'. The notion of 'public–private mix' became well established and was widely accepted as a successful way of delivering economic development and public infrastructure. This was particularly the case after the Second World War, when public enterprise was, for three decades, assumed to be a useful employment policy tool for governments. There was more to success than just marrying the two sectors together, however. Often supported by charismatic managerial leaders such as Sir John Monash,[2] Australian SOEs were frequently innovative and creative, and were assisted by the adoption of the independent statutory corporation model in preference to more traditional public-service-oriented models of State Department, Board or Trust.[3] Not surprisingly, Australia, like its neighbours, saw its public enterprise become a large and well-oiled machine. Over the century, Australian public enterprises also demonstrated progressively more independence and commercial viability, and delivered significant improvements in productivity and financial viability at the same time as being highly regarded by citizens.

Having said this, Australia's history also saw loud debates throughout the twentieth century on the benefits and costs of using private contractors for public works and services in comparison to a public labour force. Today's sensitivity to the public–private divide is therefore not a new phenomenon,[4] and modern-day debates in many ways simply see us further down the path of this 'well-rehearsed argument' around the effectiveness, efficiency and probity of these two types of service production systems (McIntosh et al., 1997). By the mid-1980s to 1990s, though, Australia was increasingly turning to market solutions and private ownership ideas. Likewise, our New Zealand neighbours were also turning to ideas of fundamental economic reform through privatization and the greater use of markets for traditional government activities.

Foundations of the Australian PPP movement
Looking back, both the drive for PPPs and the professional capacity to support their evolution came from two quite different sources: the practices of our project engineers and infrastructure construction managers; and the changing culture of Australia's political economy. Both sides contributed much to the ascension of the partnership era.

First, Australia enjoyed throughout the twentieth century a high degree of professionalism and pragmatism in its project management and engineering sectors. Many icons were constructed through the cooperative employment of both sectors. The Sydney Harbour Bridge, for example, employed the public sector (up until the bridge approaches) and the private sector for the steel 'coat-hanger' from which the bridge received its nickname. Likewise, the huge Snowy Mountains hydro-electric infrastructure scheme was also an iconic development in which there had been no hesitation to employ private contractors to undertake the massive works (Wettenhall, 2005). The provision of electricity structures to carry power around the State of Victoria was another cooperative effort, with major private companies largely undertaking the work, but under the guidance and supervision of the SECV.[5] In roads, too, the healthy mix of public and private involvement continued, with private contractors being commonly employed in addition to public works employees so that a healthy scepticism remained through not fully allowing one sector or other to monopolize works provision.

Infrastructure provision as a sector, however, was continually evolving. And while infrastructure projects themselves were often seen as worthy, and the use of the private sector contractors to deliver infrastructure projects was unquestionably successful, the methods adopted to deliver the projects came increasingly under scrutiny. In particular, the trend towards more litigious approaches and the presence of multiple legal challenges for major projects led to the need to rethink how major infrastructure projects were provided. This rethink was brought to a head by a joint working party of the National Public Works Conference and National Building and Construction Council in their report titled *No Dispute* (NPWC/NBCC, 1990). A strong view developed that it was possible to better manage construction risks and provide efficiencies for project management and delivery processes by alternative means to traditional construction contracts through improved allocation of risk. This questioning set the field for an alternative solution, which came by way of an unsolicited scheme to solve part of the transport problems of Sydney. This scheme resulted in the first BOOT (build, own, operate, transfer)-style project to construct and operate the Sydney Harbour Tunnel (begun in 1988) (Tiong, 1990). The expertise to deliver a BOOT project relied heavily on the concession discussions and experience in the UK, which was formalized as PFI (Private Finance Initiative) in 1992.

The second basis for the drive and capacity underpinning Australia's PPPs came from the changing culture within Australia's national political economy. A stream of different policy ideas and practices, in retrospect, provided the major underpinnings of the evolving PPP movement over time.

To begin with, Australia's public sector had progressively come to regard the use of contracts and the employment of private sector firms to build infrastructure as a sensible professional practice. This history of using private contractors for the delivery of government services of many types indeed became a natural precursor to the outsourcing movement that swept through the public administration in the 1980s and 1990s. Encouraged to 'steer rather than row',[6] the country saw the progressive opening up of government services to competitive tendering and policies encouraging outsourcing of government services. High-profile aggressive examples of outsourcing initiatives at the state and local government levels included the Kennett Government's Compulsory Competitive Tendering policy in Victoria, requiring 50 per cent of all local government services expenditure to be competitively tendered.[7] And at the federal level, both the Whole of Government IT Outsourcing Initiative, promising to reduce IT expenditures by AUS$1 billion,[8] and the Department of Defence's Commercial Support Program initiative were prominent. Importantly, competitive tendering and outsourcing policy reforms encouraged a real increase in the capacity of public servants across both federal and state governments to specify services required up front, to conduct rigorous competitive tenders and to then become proficient contract administrators over the life of the contract. This cultural change and the upskilling required in this were both natural forerunners to the subsequent move to PPP.

Australia and New Zealand were also both willing privatizers throughout the 1980s and 1990s. Both were ranked in the top three of the OECD scale of size of proceeds from sell-offs during the 1990s compared to gross national product (GNP). A huge range of business types was divested, mostly through trade sales.[9] Various political justifications were adopted, and proceeds were generally used to reduce public sector debt levels.[10] Of the Australian states, Victoria was again the most aggressive privatizer by far. These divestitures occurred in tandem with the introduction of independent regulators for all utility sectors. Whilst a range of evaluations of these reforms have been completed, in areas such as electricity supply, evaluations were more buoyant and were judged as most successful (Hodge et al., 2004).

Another crucial aspect of Australia's political economy leading up to the PPP era was a series of economic policy reforms under the title of 'national competition policy'. Through the auspices of the COAG (Council of Australian Governments), all Australian governments signed a National Competition Policy Agreement in 1995[11] aiming to increase the competitiveness of government businesses so that all providers – whether public or private – operated under conditions of 'competitive neutrality' within a market for services. This was achieved by removing unnecessary restrictions to competition and placed SOEs on the same financial footing as private sector businesses. It was a significant Federal Labor government initiative.[12] The Australian Competition and Consumer Commission (ACCC) now comprehensively enforces legislation guarding against anti-competitive and unfair market practices, product safety/liability and third-party access to facilities of national significance. National markets in essential services such as electricity and gas have since been established with strong and highly professional regulators.

Within the public administration, as well, there was a changing culture emphasizing performance measurement, and a range of new management ideas and practices under the 'new public management' (NPM) rubric. Building on the early ideas of the performance measurement movement from the time of Frederick Taylor's influential observations on the nature of production work efficiency, public sector reformers saw numerous performance-oriented advances occurring through notions such as zero-based budgeting, programme budgeting, programme priority and planning, performance indicators and performance budgeting, to name a few. Over time, informal performance measurement systems and service agreements inside public organizations gradually gave way to formally specified contracts, many of which were then let to competition. This gradual contractualization of public sector services, moves towards performance payment-based systems for contracted staff and formal contracts for the provision of infrastructure through the specification of nominated 'output' services simply constituted another step along this long line. Furthermore, added to these dynamics was a range of managerial thrusts in service delivery and in performance management of staff. Each subsequent performance reform wave sought to promote greater specification, greater measurement and greater control over the production agent. The common underlying ethos among these advances held that careful and formal specification through contracts promoted better performance and was preferable to traditional work arrangements. Importantly, too, the trend to better measure and better manage also occurred across a wide range of service types, from traditional simple services such as cleaning and maintenance, through services such as policy advice to the provision of complex and large infrastructure.

However we define NPM, the aims of the PPP philosophy seemed to fit the NPM ethos like a glove. PPP became a textbook example of the NPM ideal and, indeed, even moved one step beyond it. Instead of building (or purchasing) a public asset, a new approach emphasizing deliverables and performance was being pursued. The government did not even have to see itself as buying an asset, but as buying services at agreed quality, quantity, costs and time lines, with reduced payments if these were not delivered. The PPP approach therefore became a leading-edge NPM instrument. To reformers, it clearly assigned responsibility for project delivery, adopted explicit performance measures through performance contracts with strong economic incentives and emphasized the achievement of results. Symbolically, it also adopted private sector management styles and promised economy.

Overall, then, PPP was therefore viewed as a leading-edge, sophisticated and professional approach to project delivery not only by the project engineers and construction sector, but by reformist public administrators[13] as well. Building on decades of public sector reforms, it came to symbolize a 'post-NPM' or perhaps 'third-way' approach to modern government. And as with earlier privatization policy learning, Australia also adopted the PPP policy platform after learning from the worst of the UK's initial teething problems. Looking back, then, today's PPP era might be viewed as a logical and evolutionary policy stepping stone for governments. Being an initiative concerning the private sector and involving major public works, though, it was inevitably also controversial.

PPP experience

The more recent predecessors of the PPP movement came out of early moves by the states to get around public finance restrictions on borrowing funds for important capital projects. In Victoria, for instance, the late 1980s and early 1990s saw governments seeking to establish arrangements for much-needed infrastructure and 'to achieve off-balance sheet financing which would not be caught by the global limits set by the Australian Loan Council' (PAEC, 2006, p. 50). These moves paralleled the practices also occurring in the UK and in parts of the private sector around this time,[14] all with the dubious aim of taking transactions off balance sheet. Not surprisingly, many of these arrangements were deemed both artificial and inefficient, and some of them 'were later unwound at high costs to the taxpayer' (PAEC, 2006, p. 15). This was also the case in other states, such as New South Wales.

A characteristic of these early projects, in addition to encouraging the involvement of the private sector in public infrastructure projects, was maximizing the degree to which risk could be removed from government and placed with the private sector. This was an early lesson, in that, as the PAEC (2006, p. 18) explained, 'early projects involved the provision of guarantees and indemnities by government to the private sector, which had the substantive effect of reverting major financing risks back to the state'. PPP policy philosophy then evolved towards one of 'optimal risk allocation' – where it sought to 'minimise both project costs and risks by allocating risks to the party in the best position to control them' (PAEC, 2006, p. 18).

The transition towards formal adoption of the PFI movement as Australia's own PPP policy seems to have come from an admiration of the UK Blair project and a desire by our own 'New Labour' governments to copy their electoral and policy success. Close-hand advice from increasingly powerful advisers in Victoria such as management consulting companies and merchant banks may also have helped here, along with support from Treasury bureaucrats whose policy priority under the previous political regime had been to privatize the state. By the start of the new century, Australia's PPP movement had gained considerable strength, and had become a 'dominant slogan in turn-of-the-century discourse about government and governance', as Wettenhall (2003, p. 80) put it, with an agenda characterized by 'a strong belief in its inherent policy worth'.[15]

PPP policy platforms

Australia's leading state on infrastructure PPPs has been Victoria. Following the theme introduced earlier, that of policy evolution or learning, it is instructive to look briefly at its journey. The early definition for a PPP adopted by Victoria was that it was simply 'a contract for a private party to deliver public infrastructure-based services' (DTF, 2001, p. 4). Whilst this definition explicitly did 'not cover outsourcing or other service delivery arrangements where no capital investment is required', it was certainly simpler than the common ground between academics, who usually defined PPP as a situation where a government has a business relationship, it is long term, with risks and returns being shared, and private business becomes involved in financing, designing, constructing, owning or operating public facilities or services. The state of New South Wales has also been active in its use of PPPs, with the overall number of projects delivered being similar to that of Victoria. Early PPPs were managed in Victoria under the *Infrastructure Investment Guidelines* and *Policy* (IIPV; Department of Treasury, 1991, 1994). Similarly, in NSW these early projects were undertaken by guidelines for private sector participation in the provision of public infrastructure (NSW DSD, 1990; NSW Government, 1995; NSW DPWS, 1998).

Importantly, Victoria has never had a specific legislative platform as the framework for selecting, developing, managing, financing and reporting PPP projects. These areas are addressed through government policy (PAEC, 2006).[16] The Victorian government released its refined PPP policy, *Partnerships Victoria*, and with supporting guidance material, in 2000. Subsequently updated and expanded, it comprised some 16 separate documents before becoming the basis for the national PPP policy framework. These documents included a series of policy statements, guidelines, technical notes and advisory notes, as shown in Table 17.1.

These supporting materials are technically comprehensive and clearly impressive, totalling some 1208 pages of guidance.[17] As can be seen from the dates of the various documents, they have also been developed in response to reviews and in the light of new information, experience and policy learning. Other Australian jurisdictions have also developed PPP policies in the past several years, mostly modelled on the Victorian developments.

Subsequently, the Partnerships Victoria policy and guidelines, as the leading jurisdiction, were essentially adopted for the country as a whole (as well as internationally),[18] with the release of the 'National PPP Policy and Guidelines' in 2008. At the federal level, the 'National PPP Policy Framework' now provides a common strategic direction for all states, and achieves a greater degree of consistency than was previously the case. It requires jurisdictions to 'apply the National PPP Guidelines to the procurement of PPP projects', which it defines as being where both 'the private sector provides public infrastructure and any related services', and where 'there is private investment or financing'.[19] Symbolically, it commits the Council of Australian Governments (COAG) to 'considering

Table 17.1   Partnerships Victoria supporting guidance material

Title	Pages	Year published	Comment
Policy			
1 Overview	28	2000	
2 Partnerships Victoria Policy	16	2000	Outlines the scope, objectives and principles of Partnerships Victoria. Addresses at a high level issues such as core services, public interest, risk allocation and VfM
3 Contract Management Policy	6	2003	Outlines the components of the Contract Management Framework and sets out the accountabilities and responsibilities for contract management in Partnerships Victoria projects
4 NMU Water Authority Approval Process for Partnerships Victoria Projects	12	2001	Outlines the streamlined process for a Non-Metropolitan Urban Water Authority when pursuing water and wastewater projects under the Partnerships Victoria policy
5 Public Disclosure Policy	12	2007	Outlines public disclosure requirements for Partnerships Victoria projects
Guidelines			
6 Practitioners' Guide	164	2001	Addresses the what, why and how questions in relation to Partnerships Victoria projects and sets out the approach to key commercial issues (e.g. payment structures and bid evaluation) and public process issues (e.g. public interest test, probity and disclosure)
7 Risk Allocation and Contractual Issues	206	2001	Outlines the background methodology for risk allocation, describes major types of project risks and contractual issues, and sets out the government-preferred approach for each. See also the Updated Standard Commercial Principles published in 2008
8 Contract Management Guide	184	2003	Provides guidance on contract management issues throughout the life cyle of a Partnerships Victoria project

Table 17.1   (continued)

Title	Pages	Year published	Comment
9 Updated Standard Commercial Principles	179	2008	Details the current considered position of the state in relation to Partnerships Victoria risk allocation
Technical Notes			
10 Public Sector Comparator	112	2001	Provides detailed guidance on the construction and application of the public sector comparator (PSC), essentially the government's financial benchmark for the project. See also Supplementary Note below
11 Public Sector Comparator Supplementary Technical Note	140	2003	Builds on the initial PSC Technical Note released in 2001. Provides additional practical guidance in the form of 'lessons learnt' and a detailed hypothetical worked example on constructing a PSC
12 Use of Discount Rates in the Partnerships Victoria Process	59	2003	Provides specific guidance on calculating and using discount rates in undertaking discount cash flow analysis for the purposes of constructing a PSC and evaluating bids
Advisory Notes			
13 Determining the Inflation Rate	13	2005	Recommends that the inflation rate used in Partnerships Victoria project financial modelling will continue to be sourced from the State Budget papers
14 Managing Interest Rate Risk	21	2005	Outlines for practitioners the principles of managing interest rate risk up until financial close for a project
15 Disclosure and Management of Conflict of Interest for Advisors	27	2005	Provides guiding principles and tools for practitioners to manage diverse conflicts of interest that may emerge in engaging advisers for Partnerships Victoria projects
16 Interactive Tender Process	29	2005	Provides an overview of recent experience with the interactive tender process used in some Partnerships Victoria projects

infrastructure delivery options that make the best use of the resources', including PPP, which it sees as 'a proven infrastructure procurement method'. Crucially, it requires that all states evaluate the potential use of PPP as a procurement method for relevant public infrastructure projects when seeking government approval. It emphasizes that 'value for money [will be] the driver for adopting the PPP approach, rather than capital scarcity or the balance sheet treatment', and aims to 'encourage private sector investment in public infrastructure and related services where [VfM] can be clearly demonstrated'. The national policy applies to projects with a capital value over AUS$50 million, and also notes the importance of transparency and disclosure, stating that 'the use of PPPs should not diminish the availability of information on the use of government resources to Parliaments, taxpayers and other stakeholders'. Furthermore, it notes specifically that 'under current accounting standards, the majority of PPP projects will be recorded on the Government's balance sheet'.

Having said all this, there is also a degree of ambiguity apparent in the policy statement, with one of the benefits of the framework being seen as 'a stronger pipeline of PPP projects', along with 'minimis[ed] transaction costs, [and] removal of disincentives to participation', rather than the provision of a neutral evaluation tool. In a further ambiguity it states that all investment evaluation decisions 'will consider the potential impact on public interest matters such as privacy, accountability, health and safety, consumer rights, public access and equity', but that 'each jurisdiction will have its own methods for considering public interest matters'. This seems to leave open the use of political decision-making in these cases. It also acknowledges the role of Infrastructure Australia in publishing this policy, but says little else about the role and influence of the new Commonwealth entity 'Infrastructure Australia'.[20]

Overall, then, this new national policy acknowledges the potential role of PPP in infrastructure delivery, but apart from mandating its assessment as an option, it seems a little more subdued and measured than the policies of its forerunner, the state government of Victoria. Of course, given the complexity and debates surrounding PPP evaluation methods determining a public sector comparator (PSC) and the initiation in most states of central PPP units, time will tell whether this national policy has performed as a step in the right direction for Australia's infrastructure needs, or has become a Trojan horse and a licence for international capital markets to increase the supply of private finance for political ends.

Across Australia, there are currently 49 PPP projects under way, with an aggregate value of some AUS$32.3 billion, based on the information provided by all governments at state, territory and federal levels. These are summarized in Table 17.2. This table shows the Victorian jurisdiction

Table 17.2   Number of PPP projects in Australia

State	Number	Value (AUS$ billion)	Average (AUS$ billion per project)
Victoria	19	9.7	0.51
Western Australia	1	0.1	0.13
South Australia	3	1.9	0.63
Northern Territory	1	1.0	1.00
Queensland	6	9.1	1.52
New South Wales	16	10.0	0.63
Tasmania	1	0.1	0.09
Commonwealth	2	0.4	0.21
Total	49	32.3	

Source: State government websites as at November 2009.

continuing to lead the way if we judge by the number of projects under way (i.e. 19 of the 49 projects, or 39 per cent). Interestingly, though, New South Wales now occupies top billing on the basis of project funds committed.[21]

PPP projects include some massive infrastructure such as Queensland's North–South bypass tunnel and its Airport Link (with each project at around some AUS$3 billion), Victoria's desalination plant (at AUS$3.5 billion) and its Eastlink toll road (at AUS$2.5 billion), and the Western Sydney Orbital road (Westlink M7) in New South Wales (at AUS$1.86 billion). Interestingly though, the largest PPP project listed currently is the 'Replacement of RailCorporation's Electric Passenger Rollingstock' (at some AUS$3.65 billion).

A diversity of projects across sectors is also evident. Examples here include:

- Health infrastructure (with seven hospital PPPs around the country ranging in size from the AUS$1.7 billion 'New Royal Adelaide Hospital' in South Australia and the AUS$1.1 billion 'Royal North Shore Hospital' redevelopment in Sydney, to Victoria's 'Casey Community Hospital' at AUS$120 million)
- Education infrastructure (with six education PPPs ranging from the large 'South East Queensland Schools' PPP (at AUS$1.1 billion), down to the 'New Schools' PPP in New South Wales (at AUS$235 million) or the 'Education Works – New Schools' PPP in South Australia (at AUS$134 million))
- Justice infrastructure (with six PPPs ranging from the New South

Wales 'Long Bay Prison' project (at AUS$303 million) and Victoria's 'Correctional Facilities' (at AUS$275 million) to projects such as Western Australia's 'CBD Courts Complex' (at AUS$128 million) or 'Regional Police Stations and Courts' in South Australia (at AUS$40 million))

• Roads infrastructure (with 11 projects ranging from the large projects noted previously, the AUS$1 billion 'Darwin Waterfront Project' port in Northern Territory, and the AUS$700 million 'Cross City Tunnel' in New South Wales, down to the 'Chatswood Transport Interchange' (at AUS$81 million))

• Water infrastructure, with four projects in Victoria ranging from their huge desalination plant down to the 'Wodonga Wastewater Treatment Plant' (at AUS$32 million).

Comprehensive information on these projects is still being collected for analysis, but these examples do give a sense of the variety of PPPs in Australia in terms of size, sector and jurisdictional styles. They also give a sense that whilst transport infrastructure continues to be the biggest con-tributor by sector (at AUS$10.3 billion or 32.6 per cent of the total), it is by no means the dominant type of facility. Interestingly, as well, they point to the Commonwealth's surprisingly modest contribution to Australian PPP activity thus far (at AUS$413 million, or just 1.3 per cent).

So, what can be learned from Australia's PPP projects? We now focus on three case studies from Victoria to illustrate some recent PPP experience.

Three Australian infrastructure case studies
The construction of Melbourne's CityLink transport project, the County Court facility and the Southern Cross Railway Station redevelopment all provide relevant recent examples of major PPPs. Whilst not strictly repre-sentative of the wide variety of PPP applications now under way across all jurisdictions, these three projects nevertheless each illustrate some of the important policy lessons to date and offer an opportunity for reflection. These three case studies are also interesting as they transcend Victoria's earlier IIPV policy (Department of Treasury, 1994) for CityLink, a hybrid IIPV and Partnerships Victoria approach for the County Court and the Partnerships Victoria Policy for the Southern Cross Railway Station.

Melbourne CityLink
Melbourne's CityLink road infrastructure project is regarded as part of Australia's PPP folklore and an important early demonstration of recent PPP project delivery philosophy. Although it now looks dated, it none the less stands tall as a case study given the riskiness of the undertaking

in both technological and political terms, the innovations demonstrated in the project arena and the speed at which it was delivered. In its day, it provided an important building block for improving PPP governance arrangements, and it still presents broader lessons for governments in all jurisdictions.

The CityLink road infrastructure project was a massive BOOT[22] undertaking. One of Australia's largest recent public infrastructure projects, it became a symbol of the former Kennett government's approach to public infrastructure. The CityLink project linked up three major freeways in Melbourne – the South Eastern, West Gate and Tullamarine Freeways through the construction of 22 km of road, tunnel and bridge works.[23] The project involved the construction, operation and maintenance of several sections of roadway, including new and upgraded roads, some elevated, and 6 km of tunnels through difficult silt conditions as well as other works.

Following an Environmental Effects Statement in 1994 and the subsequent public inquiry, a brief was issued calling for parties to register their interest in completing the project. Two consortia were chosen for further development of ideas for the links, and following a second project brief specifying requirements in 1995, the Transurban CityLink Ltd consortium was nominated as the preferred bidder.[24] The estimated cost of the whole CityLink project was approximately AUS$2.1 billion, including AUS$1.8 billion financed by the consortium and AUS$346 million of associated works and other costs financed by the state. Opened over the period 2000/2001, the consortium has leased land from the state to operate a public toll-way for 34 years,[25] with ownership reverting to the state at no cost and in a fully maintained condition.[26] The predicted benefit–cost ratio for these works was 2.0, with a net present value of AUS$1.3 billion according to economic studies.[27] The Melbourne CityLink also indicated that initial investors should expect to receive a real rate of return of 17.5 per cent after tax for the life of the project, according to Walker and Walker (2000, p. 208). To govern the project, specific enabling legislation (the Melbourne CityLink Act 1995), was established, along with a statutory authority (the Melbourne CityLink Authority) as the state's contract manager (Russell et al., 2000).[28]

Political and policy observations
This project crossed the lives of two governments, and both sides of politics agreed to the need for this infrastructure. Indeed, after having previously identified this need, the former Kirner Labor government moved the project forward to the stage of bidding documentation. The new Kennett Liberal government then reviewed this documentation and renegotiated the deal. This paved the way for the PPP mechanism.

But several factors then made this project a divisive political hotbed. Forecasts of net project benefits varied wildly, and were initially inaccessible to the public. The Victorian Freedom of Information Act did not apply to this 'special project'.[29] Accusations were made that favourable treatment was given to the consortium[30] and that misleading environmental impact emission information on tunnel air quality was provided by the consortium to the MCLA.[31] Also, amidst water shortages for citizens, Melbourne's drinking water was for some time being pumped into the tunnel surrounds to ameliorate a lowered groundwater table and structural problems with the tunnel.[32]

After cracks began to appear in the tunnel walls (not acknowledged by CityLink until 17 months later in *The Age* (Davidson, 2001a)), the tunnel needed to be redesigned in 1998. Further engineering problems also delayed the tunnel opening (Das, 2001; Davidson, 2001b). State-of-the-art electronic technology was tested, almost on the run.[33] Additionally, direct tolling (rather than a shadow toll paid by government based on traffic volumes) probably diverted between 15 and 37 per cent of traffic off the link and into adjacent side streets (Russell et al., 2000). A constant stream of legal controversies in the CityLink project between members of the consortium alleged various contract breaches for cost overruns, construction delays and faulty design.[34] Even the government itself was accused of delays and breaches of contract, and it alleged negligence by the builders and designers. These issues, along with the Kennett government's use of a 'crash-through' political culture legitimized through the legal powers of the project,[35] provided a colourful cocktail of politics and power to deliver this PPP.

Evaluating the CityLink PPP

Substantial risks were indeed transferred to the private sector in this project. Private contractors, for instance, bore almost all of the construction risks, along with most of the design, construction, operating, financing and market risks based on the contract.[36] Also, the majority of the legal conflicts were between private parties, with few involving the government directly – despite the good newspaper copy.[37] Overall, then, we might conclude that most of these commercial risks were indeed borne by the private sector investors and that they deserved to earn a margin.[38]

The larger concern regarding project risks seems not to come from the commercial or technical sides, which were mainly well managed, but from the perspective of political governance. Several shortcomings were evident in governance. No publicly available economic or financial evaluation had been undertaken before this project was begun, and no comparison occurred between undertaking this task in the public or private sectors

(Victorian Auditor General, 1996). This partnership deal was essentially a two-way affair rather than including citizens' interests directly. The state's enabling legislation even provided scope to override any potential delays from the normal complications of due process (Russell et al., 2000). There was no separate provision for the protection of consumers, and little apparent concern that the concession period might in the end be as high as 54 years in an effort to achieve profitability for the consortium. Magnifying long-term governance policy concerns, the former state treasurer, an ardent supporter of privatization policies and PPPs, took on a top job with Macquarie Bank in its Infrastructure Investment Group, to lead future PPP efforts.

There has been disappointingly little debate on whether the CityLink achievements were worth the price paid. Dufty (1999), for one, argues that investors' interests were protected over citizens' interests, with high returns to private investors being achieved by minimizing risks through concession deed arrangements. The financial arrangement for the annual concession fee payable to the state for this monopoly facility was also far from clear, despite assurances to the contrary. A review by a team of lawyers of metres of legal documents found that payment by the contractor to the state for this monopoly facility could, at the contractor's choice, vary by a factor of four depending on timing options and only if both a reasonable rate of return had been earned by the private investors and if sufficient cash flow were available. In other words, it was not at all clear, even when the contract documentation had been analysed, what the 'deal' was that the state had committed itself to.[39] Citizens of Victoria paid a price in terms of lack of clarity here as well as a financial price. Considerable uncertainty existed until recently, when the deal was reappraised by the State's Auditor General.[40] Clearly, the state should in future avoid, where possible, contractual obligations that affect its discretion for up to 54 years, and regulatory powers should be established for such projects through the state's independent regulatory authorities such as the Essential Services Commission.[41] Critics also stressed that future projects should be subject to stronger parliamentary and public scrutiny before implementation.

Victorian County Court facility
The Victorian County Court was hailed early on as one of the most effective case studies of the PPP model and of the potential of the state government's 'Partnerships Victoria' policy. It was, as Fitzgerald (2004, p. 7) put it, 'a case study of the timeliness of delivery and the quality of finish that can be obtained from a PPP'. An integrated complex in the heart of Melbourne's legal precinct, it is a landmark building combining

modern court design principles with state-of-the-art technology such as video-conferencing and remote-witness facilities. Australia's largest court complex, it was billed as the first major social infrastructure project under the Partnerships Victoria policy of the Bracks/Brumby Labour governments. The Victorian County Court is the state's busiest trial court, and handles most criminal trials with a significant workload of civil cases. It has 54 courtrooms, including an additional eight courtrooms commissioned in 2008, a jury pool area that can accommodate up to 400 people, and attractive public spaces.

The provision of this new County Court aimed at reducing waiting times for court appearances, providing better security, reducing court costs and improving facilities for jurors, victims, and the public as well as the legal community. All court services integral to the administration of justice remain in government control (in accordance with Partnerships Victoria policy that core services should be provided directly by government). Several government agencies who are stakeholders in courtroom work and reporting are part of this partnership group.

The contract with the Liberty Group (now owned by Challenger Financial Services Group) was to design, build, finance and provide building management services, security and information technology systems. This company was granted a 99-year lease over the crown land on which the court is situated, for a peppercorn rent. Interestingly, the contract term was 20 years, but unusually, the court building remains the property of the Liberty Group at the end of the contract period.

So how might we evaluate this project, and how did it perform in the interests of citizens? The project was certainly completed in under two years following the finalization of the contract, and both the quality of the building and the high level of services provided into the facility have, in the words of Fitzgerald (2004, p. 7), been 'commended by the judiciary, the legal profession and by the public'. Clearly, the new public infrastructure was appreciated by the direct users. The project today continues to meet the demand for court facilities and, under the contract, the consortium provides a maintained court building, building management services, security and information technology systems.

The project demonstrated the innovation that a PPP can bring to manage long-term demand. The Liberty Group took a calculated risk that the state would require increasing courtroom services over time. To accommodate this, their bid included the construction (but not fit-out) of two building floors for later expansion, at no cost to the taxpayer until (and if) the additional courtrooms were required. The additional eight courtrooms were commissioned in 2008 in what appears to be a win–win outcome, with government making a substantial saving over building a new court complex and the Liberty Group enhancing its return on investment through the provision of increased services.

In terms of broad financial numbers, it had an NPV (as at October 2000) of AUS$195 million, whilst over the 20-year contract life, the state will pay an estimated AUS$519 million. So, how have subsequent reviews assessed this project? The major review of Fitzgerald (2004) noted that the Auditor General had provided an opinion that the consortium did in fact bear substantial risks associated with the construction, financing and operation of the court facility. As well as this observation, however, his review also noted the absence of any real-life benchmarks as the foundation for cost comparisons, compared to the more nebulous and potentially manipulatable PSC framework. This was implicitly viewed as disappointing, given the recent construction of another court facility nearby. Also, Fitzgerald questioned the degree to which any demand risks existed in reality, given that government had signed up, and was highly unlikely to be unable to pay its agreed contractual obligations.

A later review conducted by a parliamentary committee in Victoria added some crucial detail to these earlier concerns, and considerably strengthened the tenor of the policy lessons. There were six lessons here.

First, whilst the sales pitch of PPPs had been all about 'purchasing services' rather than talking of building assets, the Parliamentary Committee judged that this was a mistake. Given that the public was paying for both the infrastructure and associated services, the ownership of the asset should not have remained with the private company. The Committee found that

> A build own operate model was applied to the . . . Melbourne County Court and was based on a concept contained in the *Partnerships Victoria* policy, whereby the government only needs to purchase services from the private sector and not the infrastructure, despite having paid for the building under the leasing arrangements with the developer . . . The Committee considers policies that treat multi-million dollar purpose built government funded assets as disposable early in their life span need to be revisited by the government. (PAEC, 2006, p. 184)

Second, whilst the transfer of risks clearly does matter in financial calculations, these risks had also been overplayed in the PPP policy sales pitch here, and some were simply not transferred as calculations assumed. In other words:

> The Committee observed from its review of certain PPP projects that despite paying large premiums for the assumption of risks by private sector consortia, it has been common practice for certain risks to revert back to government without any adjustment . . . (PAEC, 2006, p. 21)

Third and fourth, an accusation had for some time been around that government had, through PSC calculations, been adopting a discount rate that was excessively high. This practice favoured the private finance option. Also, a further concern was that risks transferred were being given excessive weight (and financial value) in these calculations. In this respect, the Committee again judged both concerns as well founded. It even found the private financial partners coming out and advising that 'for existing PV projects, like the County Court project . . . it is unlikely they will ever need a public bailout'. In their words:

> In July 2003, the government subsequently acknowledged that with accommodation projects, such as the County Court . . . there is a low market risk and the discount rate should have been 5 per cent as compared with the 8.65 per cent discount rate. (PAEC, 2006, p. 60)

Moreover, a fifth lesson from the Committee was that the practice of independent project review would have assisted in minimizing any future systemic wastage of taxpayers' funds. Here, it was noted that

> The Committee seeks to demonstrate the importance of having ongoing, independent, post project reviews publicly reported to highlight any advantages and deficiencies in contractual arrangements. Benefits can be noted and deficiencies highlighted then systematically addressed in further projects. (PAEC, 2006, p. 60)

Lesson six concerned the lack of real risk-bearing by project financiers, and the speed at which profitable returns were being generated for them, but at taxpayers' expense. Rather than risks being borne over the long term of the assets and associated services, it was reported that

> The Committee understands that for two of the major Victorian projects (County Court and the Spencer Street Station redevelopment) the sponsor (ABN Amro) sold its majority interest at a profit within 18 months of signing the deal. In relation to the redevelopment of Spencer Street Station this represented a profit of $50 million. Lessons learnt from this resulted in the next public private partnerships project, EastLink, having refinancing built into the contract. (PAEC, 2006, p. 141)

Overall, then, it is apparent that, on the one hand, the PPP project had certainly been well designed and had been delivered on time and on budget. The operation of the facility has also provided a service standard higher than the adjacent publicly run courts in the precinct. The arrangements adopted, however, had rewarded project financiers handsomely for these services. It could also be argued that the project was subject to excessive policy salesmanship and optimism from PPP advocates. These lessons were another valuable step in the Australian PPP story.

Southern Cross Station

Southern Cross Station (formerly the Spencer Street Station) was in need of redevelopment. Badly requiring renewal, it is now a gateway to Melbourne and the regions, and features an iconic world-class design. It also links the emerging Docklands precinct with Melbourne's central business district. The station project is managed on behalf of the Victorian government by the Southern Cross Station Authority in partnership with the Civic Nexus Consortium.

The PPP project included two components. First was the transport interchange redevelopment (for which the government entered into a long-term service contract with Civic Nexus). Second, a commercial redevelopment was undertaken that included a retail precinct, car parking and offices. One of the challenging and interesting aspects of this PPP was the need for the station to remain operational throughout the upgrade. This proved to be a major task for the successful consortium to manage, and included not only an interface with the state but also an interface with the many private businesses and franchisees who have the responsibility for operating metropolitan and regional passenger and freight rail services.

An amount of AUS$309 million (NPV as at June 2002) was the net cost to government for this PPP and was a key part of broader policy goals to revitalize Victoria's rail network and services. The Southern Cross Station Authority was created by the Victorian government in 2000 to manage the 25-hectare redevelopment site and manage the facility for 30 years. Executed in July 2002 after a two-step tendering process involving an 'Expression of Interest' followed by a formal request for a proposal by short-listed proponents, the contract was let with Civic Nexus to design, build, finance and maintain the transport interchange. It was completed in 2006, one year late.

A most significant event for construction was the announcement to the Stock Exchange that the project was one year late and over budget, requiring a further $110 million. The reason for this was that the complex roof structure proved more difficult to complete than initially expected, with limited access during the night time and the need for favourable weather.[42]

In 2007, the station was awarded the Royal Institute of British Architects (RIBA) Lubetkin Prize for the most outstanding building outside the EU, and the RIBA International Award. The Station has also collected some Australian awards for construction achievement.

What might we make of this PPP in terms of evaluation? There are four points here. The 'world-class' and 'iconic' design aside, this was a high-profile construction task attracting an eager media coverage. To begin with, there was first some disquiet about the various figures that were floating around as to the real cost of the project. These varied from the government's figure of AUS$309 million (for NPV) to other figures as high as 'just over one billion dollars' (for the total nominal contractual payments excluding inflation effects), and even up to the Fitzgerald (2004) figure of AUS$1762 million (which he carefully referenced to the *State Financial Report*, 2002–03) and which covered the government's actual projected contractual payments over the 30-year contract life including adjustments for forecast inflation. Such large differences between the up-front (NPV) figure, and the actual nominal payouts (either with zero allowance for inflation or else including an inflation allowance) might be clear to a 'time-value-of-money'-savvy financial analyst, but such differences were certainly not clear to the public. Part of the complexity of establishing the real cost lies in the mix of costs for the public infrastructure railway station versus the overall construction cost for the precinct, which includes costs for the private development. There is every chance that the state may have received a discount on the reported cost of the station in the bid to enhance the likelihood of making a successful bid. Here, PPP financial sophistication led to uncertainty as to the veracity of the official project analyses. Again, the government went on the front foot and countered with media examples, including the state premier talking about taking out a housing loan, which we all pay off over decades.

Second, after the project announced delays and budget problems, media interest was heightened with some high-profile calls from the contractor for the state government to join in the spirit of what was meant to be a 'partnership' and help resolve the obvious construction issues. The contractor, in other words, used the partnership language and attempted to play the political game to his advantage. To the credit of the state government, however, it consistently argued that the risks of the project were both known up front and taken on by the contractor. So, under the legal contract, he was not due for payment before completion of the job. The government, in other words, successfully resisted any temptation to buy its way out of the negative media spotlight at the expense of citizens. As a result of this, the third-party builder incurred a substantial loss. This event proved to be a win for both the PPP policy stance and for professionalism in project delivery ideals.

Third, and in line with the earlier observation regarding the complexity and length of the CityLink contracts, the Parliamentary Committee that later reviewed Victoria's PPP projects commented explicitly that these deals ought to be more accessible to citizens. It noted:

> Many PPP contracts are complex and lengthy (for example the Southern Cross Station contract is 620 pages). A succinct summary should be made publicly available. A project summary would also enhance public understanding of PPPs.

Fourth, there was a degree of discomfort in the estimates of the state over the value of rights compared to the offer made by the contractor and the consequent effect on the decision to proceed with a PPP in preference to traditional project delivery. The Committee noted that the PSC was some AUS$17.2 million less than the winning bid, but that the rights value ascribed to the PPP was AUS$26.1 million more than the value ascribed under the PSC – thus tipping the balance in the favour of the PPP option. The Parliamentary Committee did not go so far as to make accusations of error or even misleading conduct, but simply stated that 'more attention and expertise' was required and that a policy ought to be developed in this direction.[43]

Overall, then, a world-class infrastructure facility had been achieved by marrying together political leadership and innovative project delivery mechanisms. And whilst the policy implementation task was again largely successful, several more timely lessons for the state were also apparent.

Reflections on Australia's PPP performance and lessons

Looking then at our learning over the past two decades of partnerships (including the most recent but narrower version of Partnerships Victoria under the Bracks/Brumby governments), what may we conclude? We have come a long way, and there are many lessons to learn. Interestingly, we suspect that both sides have come closer together in what they know, and both have learned from each other. Lessons have arrived from both the international experience as well as the local Australian case studies.

Internationally, much has been written on PPPs, although this has often amounted, as we said in Chapter 5, to little more than blatant policy salesmanship and stinging critical rhetoric. International studies show widely varying results, with some studies claiming high VfM compared to traditional infrastructure delivery approaches and others claiming just the opposite. On the matters of governance, too, findings have likewise been mixed. Hodge and Greve (2009b), for instance, argued that all three new aspects of PPPs (the preference for private finance; the complexity of bundled contracts; and the altered governance and accountability assumptions) seemed to experience governance shortfalls, at least under the early PPP policies. The habit of some governments to hide behind contract complexity, the lack of clarity around deals from the perspective of citizens, conflicts of interest being badly handled and the lack of democratic project oversight all exemplified such concerns. And in the background was the risk of new powerful lobby groups representing infrastructure suppliers and bankers moving quietly in alongside elected governments.

To be fair, there has been an appreciable effort in more recent PPP policy platforms to counter some of the early concerns. The current PV/

Infrastructure Australia policy is a good example here. This national policy specifically includes a public interest test (adopted from the Victorian guidelines) in order to address some of the earlier governance issues. But to the degree that trenchant criticism of the PPP model continues in Australia,[44] ongoing governance shortfalls threaten to reduce the potential legitimacy of PPPs and provide sobering observations even after almost two decades.

But a little reflection also reveals that both sides may have stories to tell here – with both sides having in fact moved closer together. How could this be? Our observation is that, on the one hand, PPP advocates have needed to change, adjust, reshape, evaluate and acknowledge some serious deficiencies and weaknesses in their models and practices. In other words, policy learning occurred. But on the other hand, critics, too, have needed to acknowledge that PPPs have strengths, and that they seem to be able to quickly deliver to political actors things that previous techniques were not able to achieve. In terms of the Australian (and particularly the Victorian) experience, we might list a few of these strengths and weaknesses.

In terms of weaknesses identified and acknowledged over the past two decades we could mention:

(a)   Discount rates in the PSC calculation have been too high (favouring PPP options).
(b)   PSC calculations have been manipulated (and treated as unduly robust).[45]
(c)   The size and value of risks have been based on guesstimates and assumptions rather than any degree of science, with dubious risk calculations resulting.[46]
(d)   Either side of the partnership can take advantage of the other if negotiations are poor.[47]
(e)   Deal complexity has too often been used as a figleaf for governments to shelter behind instead of explaining and summarizing the deal to citizens.
(f)   Financial gains made in the event of refinancing were spectacular in the early UK deals, but they may now be shared with the public sector.
(g)   Long-term equity is required to keep the banks focused on the long-term responsibilities of PPP deals.

In each of these areas, there have been improvements to practice. For example, brief summaries are now available to citizens for deals made, some PSC discount rate calculations have been lowered and gains made when refinancing are now shared with the public sector.

In terms of PPP strengths, we should also acknowledge that:

(a) PPPs do provide governments with a mega-credit card, and that given our domestic use of such credit instruments, they can have advantages when properly monitored and managed.

(b) Collaboration from both sectors can lead to new and innovative solutions to major infrastructure problems, and collaboration of some type or other is probably inevitable in determining new and innovative approaches to infrastructure delivery.

(c) As a governance tool, bundling of multiple contracts through PPPs can raise the profile of an issue (which might otherwise get buried in public or political debate) and encourage policy support for much-needed infrastructure.[48]

(d) The requirement for sophisticated business cases may have had flow-on effects across both government and businesses, leading to more rational resource allocation in the context of infrastructure decision-making.

(e) Given the language-games possible when interpreting PPPs, there is plenty of space for governments to reshape partnership policies over time, and to alter existing assumptions concerning what is and what is not a partnership. This leaves the political process with much room to manoeuvre on PPPs in the world ahead. In other words, PPPs may well continue to grow in some form or other and continue as a 'potentially promising institutional transplant', as de Jong (2008, p. 315) termed them.

Having said all this, there are of course also some issues on which we seem to have a long way to go in our policy learning, and which will inevitably remain concerns for PPPs. These include issues such as transparency and disclosure, including excessive use of 'commercial-in-confidence' claims, and the nasty risk of governments protecting their own interests above those of the public. Second, questions of conflicts of interest continue. Such conflicts occur at the level of consultants, who are often conflicted, for ministers, who may one minute be political leaders and the next minute merchant bankers, and for government itself.[49] Third is the question of sufficient competition, given that in many cases, only two or three bidders may tender for large PPP tasks. The last issue here concerns the need for independent evaluations of PPP policy success.[50] Perhaps, because this last set of issues essentially challenges power itself, they may remain eternally tricky. But it is remarkable that in Victoria, after almost two decades of PPP experience, the Parliamentary Committee could publish its report, stating baldly that the Committee cannot conclusively state whether the PPP policy is delivering value for money over the life of the projects, compared with traditional procurement methods used by government. (PAEC, 2006, p. 20)

Conclusions

This chapter presented a range of PPP experiences from Australia. With a largely pragmatic approach to government and business relations in the past, Australia has had a strong history of building a productive marriage between its own government capacities with those of the private sector through a variety of public–private mix arrangements. It is concluded that the desire for such business–government relations is not new, but that it has generally been unacknowledged during the more recent evolution towards a narrower perspective of PPPs. There is, though, a wide range of modern-day PPPs completed or currently under way and the policy support being enjoyed by this technique is unlikely to disappear. The PPP philosophy essentially offers governments another means to 'buy now, pay later' (or a new mega-credit card) for high-priority infrastructure, and in doing so, raise the profile of priority infrastructure to the top of the public agenda for support.

Learning from both the international evidence to date, and from the experience of Victoria, Australia, however, shows that outcomes for PPPs to date have been mixed, with many lessons relevant to both achieving better VfM and stronger governance. Importantly, both the critics and the advocates of PPPs have probably been moving closer together over the past two decades. Both sides now should acknowledge that the PPP as a model has strengths and weaknesses. Both sides, too, need to admit that with almost two decades of experience, the PPP model has grown and matured into a sophisticated policy platform. To the degree that it has indeed evolved from an immature idea into a more sophisticated policy implementation technique, we need also to recognize that PPPs have been a moving target for evaluators. One implication here is that shortfalls found and criticisms made of earlier forms of PPP may not now be applicable. And the continued criticism of PPP based on old assessments may also be quite unfair. Another implication may equally be that some of the early claims of advocates may well have been overblown. And similarly, repeating early optimistic claims should be seen as little more than lazy advertising.

Either way, governments still clearly need to approach future PPP deals in terms of the old adage, *caveat emptor*. And in light of growing citizen expectations, a better balance of governmental energies devoted to policy evaluation and stewardship, as distinct from policy advocacy, is always a long-term nirvana for which we should all strive.

Notes

1. The reliance on government as the 'economic developer' has been a common theme in OECD countries (Hodge, 2007).
2. Sir John Monash oversaw the creation of a vertically integrated coal mining and electricity generation and distribution system across Victoria.
3. See Russell (1990) and Wettenhall (1965).
4. The Royal Commission of 1896 into competitive contracting and tendering is an early example of such tensions.
5. The State Electricity Commission of Victoria (SECV).
6. See Osborne and Gaebler (1992), who made famous the preceeding work of Savas.
7. Under this policy, targets were set at 20 per cent, 30 per cent and 50 per cent of local government services to be subject to competitive tender by mid-1995, 1996 and 1997 respectively. Over half of all Victorian local government operating expenditure is spent on services now provided by external contractors.
8. The analysis of Hodge and Rouse (2006) suggested that the financial effectiveness of this reform was minimal.
9. Australia, for example, received revenues amounting to some AUS\$96.6 billion from these sales. Revenues were roughly equally spread between federal- and state-level governments, and covered traditional utility services such as electricity and gas, as well as transport, communications and financial services. Telstra (AUS\$30.33 billion) and the Commonwealth Bank (at AUS\$8.16 billion) were the two most important sales, along with the sale of Victoria's assets in the electricity (AUS\$22.55 billion) and gas (AUS\$6.28 billion) sectors.
10. Having said this, we ought to note that large slices of SOE sectors still nonetheless remain in public hands in most Australian states. For instance, whilst electricity provision in Victoria is now effectively entirely privately based, New South Wales continued to provide electricity through a wholly government-owned electricity sector. Likewise, whilst public transport in Victoria now operates largely under a series of private franchises, most public transport across other states has remained essentially in public hands until the recent events discussed later in this article.
11. This followed the recommendations of the Hilmer report (Hilmer et al., 1993).
12. A notable sweetener encouraging states to review legislation for anti-competitive clauses was the fact that in return for such progressive reviews and the opening up of areas of government service provision to competition, a series of 'competition payments' was made by the federal government.
13. This is not to say that the recommendations of the global consultants, along with the national habit of copying ideas from our third-way cousins in the UK had no influence. These influences were both considerable. But the consultants acted more as the foot-soldiers of political leaders in policy battles rather than the generals presiding over policy processes. See Hodge and Bowman (2006) on this point.
14. The now globally infamous practices of the Enron corporation in the USA were one of the highest-profile examples here.
15. The appearance of a new, warmer, partnership rhetoric was almost a welcome relief to the abrasive ethos of competition. The PPP policy label was also certainly preferable to the less attractive 'private'- and 'finance'-dominated UK phraseology, albeit with 'little precision as to how the term is used' (Wettenhall, 2003).
16. There is, none the less, for some projects, new or amending legislation to reflect their specific characteristics from time to time, but this is a project-by-project matter, not a system-wide intervention.
17. These follow in the footsteps of the Victorian government's earlier overly voluminous guidelines for outsourcing, but thankfully represent a marked improvement. Of course, we all trust that guidelines exist to provide rational guidance enabling greater-value and higher-quality services to be achieved for taxpayer funds. These early Victorian *Guidelines* (DTF, 1996), however, amounted to some 612 pages and detailed around 470 steps in the outsourcing decisions of government. Although entirely comprehensive

these *Guidelines* were probably produced for the political purpose of silencing outsourcing critics at the time, and as an attempt to bolster the legitimacy of the government's pro-outsourcing decisions already made.

18. The Victorian *Guidelines* have been influential in the development of practices in jurisdictions as wide afield as South Africa, Canada, Ireland, Hong Kong and South Korea, for example.

19. Interestingly, it sees PPPs as 'distinct from early contractor involvement, alliancing, managing contractor, traditional procurement (design & construct) and other procurement methods', guidance for which is 'covered by other government guidelines'.

20. Infrastructure Australia is a new Commonwealth government entity formed (under the Infrastructure Australia 2008 Act) and charged with a range of responsibilities, including: advising on matters relating to infrastructure in terms of national needs and priorities, policy, pricing and regulatory issues; efficiency options and reforms; and mechanisms for financing investment in infrastructure. It may also conduct audits, develop 'Infrastructure Priority Lists'; evaluate investment proposals; and promote investment in infrastructure. Infrastructure Australia consists of 12 people appointed by the Minister. It comprises five people from the consulting, banking or construction industries, five career bureaucrats, an academic and a member of an industry superannuation funds group. (Infrastructure Australia should not be confused with 'Infrastructure Partnerships Australia' (IPA), which is the chief lobby group for Australia's infrastructure industry, and advertises itself as 'the nation's peak infrastructure forum'. IPA is chaired by Hon. Mark Birrell, who is one of the appointed industry members to Infrastructure Australia.)

21. The funding levels listed in Table 17.2 have been estimated on the basis of project PV at the time of commitment, but the precision of these estimates is uncertain, as differing definitions of PV appear to have been adopted by different governments. States also appear to have adopted different starting points for this listing of current PPP projects.

22. This project outline is based on Hodge (2002).

23. This description draws on the previous work of Hepburn et al. (1997).

24. Transurban CityLink Ltd is a joint venture between Transfield Pty Ltd and Obayashi Corporation.

25. This project life had stretched out to 37.75 years by the time of the review by Russell et al. in 2000.

26. See Victorian Auditor General (1996).

27. See Allen Consulting Group, John Cox and Centre for Policy Studies (1996).

28. Also, an Office of Independent Reviewer was established to approve the technical adequacy of the project throughout the design and construction phases.

29. See Walker and Walker (2000, p. 216).

30. For example, land valued at AUS$80 million was rented for the concession period for a paltry AUS$100 per annum, according to Costa (1997).

31. See Holmes (2000).

32. See Das (2001).

33. The experience of Melbourne's abysmal 'Met Ticket' automated ticketing system debacle in the background did not help here, with public transport ticketing being regarded widely as a mess after a decade of ticket machine problems and constant criticism.

34. See Hodge and Bowman (2004) for details of these controversies.

35. The often-cited example here was the use of the state's infringement notice system of debt collection.

36. From a technical point of view the CityLink project was indeed a very challenging one, requiring a large technical advance in the tolling technology, real construction risks in tunnelling through soft Yarra River river silt and considerable risks in environment issues concerning air quality and the height of the water table around the river. The private sector took on these risks fully and in accordance with the signed contracts.

37. In reality, notwithstanding the colourful political symbolism of legal actions against

government, the one-off AUS$10 million settlement in relation to alleged project delays and the ongoing AUS$37 million claim against government for constructing a new public road nearby were small relative to the size of project achievements. Government litigation nevertheless raised serious questions of accountability and good governance in terms of publicly funding both PPP projects and legal defences in contractual suits. In this regard, the AUS$10 million 'taxpayer saving' settlement to the project consortium and the ongoing AUS$37 million compensation claim for reduced earnings both appeared to tarnish the project's early political success (Hodge and Bowman, 2004).

38. A more conservative conclusion might also be that in recognition of the early stage in the life of the project, the jury is essentially still out at present.

39. As documented in Hodge (2002), this information was 'not readily ascertainable from the Concession Deed in the Schedule to the *Melbourne City Link Act 1995*', but Russell et al. report that 'the stipulation that the fee can be paid in Concession Notes appears in a separate agreement, the Master Security Deed' . . . and . . . 'in Exhibit W inserted by the First Amending Deed clause 3.1 (b)'.

40. See Victorian Auditor General (2007).

41. See Russell et al. (2000) and Hodge (2002). The first claim is opposed by policy proponents, who see PPPs as providing governments with 'strategic flexibility'.

42. See Duffield and Regan (2004).

43. Explicity, it was stated that 'The Committee observed from a financial analysis undertaken in 2001 of the Southern Cross Station project that the preferred developer was willing to pay the state $68.6 million for the commercial rights to the interchange facility and adjoining properties. Under the public sector comparator, these rights were estimated under a traditional process to be worth $39.9 million, a variance of $28.7 million or 72 per cent less than the Civic Nexus offer. Civic Nexus eventually paid $66 million for the rights, a factor that substantially influenced its winning bid, as the tender for the interchange facility and rail modifications was $313.9 million, substantially more than the PSC of $296.7 million . . . The Committee makes the further observation that more attention and expertise should be directed towards identifying and valuing commercial rights in any future projects. The Committee acknowledges the complexity of this issue, but considers a policy should be developed on the exploitation of commercial rights. Such a policy should form part of the *Standard Commercial Principles*, issued by *Partnerships Victoria* in June 2005.'

44. See, for example, Davidson (2008a, 2008b), who argues that PPPs in Victoria amount to 'financial turpitude on a scale hard to imagine'. He suggests that the state will be paying AUS$675 million each year for a desalination plant that would have cost AUS$425 million as a publicly funded project.

45. Initially identified through early UK Public Accounts Committee work, clear examples of PSC manipulation are detailed in Shaoul (2005).

46. Little wonder, then, that the Victorian Public Accounts and Estimates Committee in its 2006 report stated that 'the Committee has reservations about the reliability of the public sector comparator because of its theoretical approach to estimating and comparing costs, particularly in relation to the valuation of risks'.

47. Examples here include Sydney's Cross City Tunnel, where the NSW government blamed the private sector in the Parliament, cowardly avoiding any accountability for their significant part in that PPP project failure. On the other hand, in the Victorian County Court case, the private sector made a substantial financial gain through the deal, but at the cost of taxpayers, who had placed excessive faith in the competence of government negotiators.

48. The classic example could be new prisons. In Victoria, the application of PPP to this domain delivered new prisons quickly and effectively in the 1990s. In an environment essentially dominated by traditional and powerful unions of prison warders, it not only led to new prisons, but also to a newer, more professional prison culture.

49. We appear to be slow to acknowledge that governments act, when it comes to PPPs, with many conflicts – in the roles of policy advocate, economic developer, steward for

public funds, elected representative for decision-making, regulator over the contract life, competitive builder of infrastructure, infrastructure funder using public taxes, commercial signatory to the contract and planner.

50. When independent reviews occur, they can be worth their weight in gold. The PAEC (2006, p. 20) review, for example, was fearless in stating that 'although Victoria is promoted as being at the forefront of using the PPP model in Australia, the Committee found that certain overseas jurisdictions – notably the United Kingdom and British Columbia – had taken steps to address many of the criticisms about the public sector comparator, high discount rates, and the premiums paid for the transfers of risk to the private sector that are used in PPP arrangements'.

References

Allen Consulting Group, John Cox and Centre for Policy Studies (1996), *The Economic Impact of Melbourne City Link Transurban Project*, Consultancy report to the Melbourne City Link Authority, April, Melbourne.

Costa, G. (1997), 'A case study on competition and private infrastructure: the Melbourne CityLink Project', *AQ*, **69** (2), 39–49.

Das, S. (2001), 'Tunnel expert urged delay: the man who oversaw CityLink was worried about the water tables', *The Age*, 7 February, 1.

Davidson, K. (2001a), 'The tunnel of error: the warnings were ignored, whatever investors may lose is dwarfed by the public loss of liveability', *The Age*, 22 February, 17.

Davidson, K. (2001b), 'A failed experiment', *The Age*, 13 December.

Davidson, K. (2008a), 'We're dudded on water but no one rebels', *The Age*, 21 December.

Davidson, K. (2008b), 'Desal plant figures don't hold water', *The Age*, 7 December.

De Jong, W.M. (2008), 'Drawing institutional lessons across countries on making transport infrastructure policy', in Hugo Priemus, Bent Flyvbjerg and Bert van Wee (eds), *Decision-Making on Mega-Projects*, Cheltenham, UK and Northampton, MA, USA: Edward Elgar, pp. 304–26.

Department of Treasury (1991), *Infrastructure Investment Guidelines for Victoria*, Infrastructure Investment Review Group, Victoria: Department of the Treasury.

Department of Treasury (1994), *Infrastructure Investment Policy for Victoria*, Project Finance and Evaluation, Victoria: Department of the Treasury.

Department of Treasury and Finance (DTF) (1996), *Outsourcing and Contract Management Guidelines*, February, Melbourne: Outsourcing and Contract Management Unit.

Department of Treasury and Finance (DTF) (2001), *Partnerships Victoria: Practitioners Guide*, March, Melbourne.

Duffield, C.F. and M. Regan (2004), 'Public private partnership arrangement for the Spencer Street Station upgrade in Victoria, Australia', *Journal of Financial Management of Property and Construction*, **9** (23), 163–77.

Dufty, G. (1999), *CityLink 2000 to 2030: A Hard Road for Victorians*, A Report into the Impacts of the CityLink Tollway on Low-Income Victorians, Melbourne: Victorian Council of Social Services.

Fitzgerald, P. (2004), *Review of Partnerships Victoria Provided Infrastructure, final report to the Treasurer*, January, Melbourne: Growth Solutions Group.

Hepburn, G., M. Pucar, C. Sayers and D. Sheilds (1997), *Private Investment in Urban Roads*, Staff Research Paper, Industry Commission (Australia).

Hilmer, F., M. Rayner and G. Taperell (1993), *National Competition Policy, Report to the Independent Committee of Inquiry into Competition Policy in Australia* (The Hilmer Report), Canberra: AGPS.

Hodge, G.A. (2002), 'Who steers the state when governments sign public–private partnerships?', *The Journal of Contemporary Issues in Business and Government*, **8** (1), 5–18.

Hodge, G. (2007), 'The regulation of public services in OECD countries: an overview of water, waste management and public transport', discussion paper for OECD Group on Regulatory Policy, Paris, 53pp.

Hodge, G.A. and D.M. Bowman (2004), 'PPP contractual issues – big promises and unfinished business', in A. Ghobadian, N. O'Regan, D. Gallear and H. Viney (eds), *Public–Private Partnerships: Policy and Experience*, Basingstoke: Palgrave Macmillan, pp. 201–18.

Hodge, G.A. and D.M. Bowman (2006), 'The consultocracy: the business of reforming government', in Graeme Hodge (ed.), *Privatisation and Market Development: Global Movements in Public Policy Ideas*, Cheltenham, UK and Northampton, MA, USA: Edward Elgar, pp. 97–126.

Hodge, G.A. and A. Rouse (2006), 'Outsourcing government information technology services: an Australian case study', in G. Boyne, K. Meier, L. O'Toole and R. Walker (eds), *Determinants of Organisational Performance*, Cambridge: Cambridge University Press, pp. 212–32.

Hodge, G.A. and C. Greve (2009a), 'PPPs: the passage of time permits a sober reflection', *Economic Affairs*, **29** (1), 33–9.

Hodge, G.A. and C. Greve (2009b), 'Public–private partnership: some international reflections', paper delivered in Tokyo, 6 November, unpublished.

Hodge, G.A., V. Sands, D. Hayward and D. Scott (eds) (2004), *Power Progress: An Audit of Australia's Electricity Reform Experiment*, Melbourne: Australian Scholarly Publishing.

Holmes, D. (2000), 'The electronic superhighway: Melbourne's CityLink Project', *Urban Policy and Research*, **18** (1), 65–76.

McIntosh, K., J. Shauness and R. Wettenhall (1997), *Contracting Out in Australia: An Indicative History*, University of Canberra: Centre for Research in Public Sector Management.

National Public Works Conference and National Building and Construction Council (NPWC/NBCC) (1990), *No Dispute: Strategies for Improvement in the Australian Building and Construction Industry,* National Public Works Conference, Canberra.

NSW Department of Public Works & Services (NSW DPWS) (1998), *Infrastructure Partnerships Implementation Guidelines* (V2), Sydney.

NSW Department of State Development (NSW DSD) (1990), *Guidelines for Private Sector Participation in Infrastructure Provision*, NSW Department of State Development.

NSW Government (1995), *Guidelines for Private Sector Participation in the Provision of Public Infrastructure*, NSW Government.

Osborne, D. and T. Gaebler (1992), *Reinventing Government: How the Entrepreneurial Spirit is Transforming the Public Sector*, Reading, MA: Addison-Wesely.

Public Accounts and Estimates Committee (PAEC) (2006), Public Accounts and Estimates Committee, *Seventy First Report to the Parliament*, Report on Private Investment in Public Infrastructure, Melbourne, October.

Russell, E.W. (1990), 'Builders of Public Enterprise in Victoria', an address to the Royal Historical Society of Victoria, 23 October, Melbourne.

Russell, E.W., E. Waterman and N. Seddon (2000), *Audit Review of Government Contracts: Contracting, Privatisation, Probity and Disclosure in Victoria 1992–1999: An Independent Report to Government*, vol. 3, Melbourne: State Government of Victoria.

Shaoul, J. (2005), 'The private finance initiative or the public funding of private profit', in Graeme Hodge and Carsten Greve (eds), *The Challenge of Public–Private Partnerships: Learning from International Experience*, Cheltenham, UK and Northampton, MA, USA: Edward Elgar, pp. 190–206.

Tiong, R.L.K. (1990), 'Comparative study of BOT projects', *Journal of Management in Engineering*, **6** (1), 107–22.

Victorian Auditor General (1996), *Report on Ministerial Portfolios*, Melbourne, May.

Victorian Auditor General (2007), *Funding and Delivery of Two Freeway Upgrade Projects*, Melbourne, December.

Walker, B. and Walker, B.C. (2000), *Privatisation: Sell Off or Sell Out? The Australian Experience*, Sydney: ABC Books.

Wettenhall, R. (1965), 'Public ownership in Australia', *Political Quarterly*, **36** (4), 426–40; see also in R. Wettenhall (1987), *Public Enterprises and National Development: Selected Essays*, RAIPA (ACT Division) Monograph.

Wettenhall, R. (1983), 'Privatisation: a shifting frontier between private and public sectors', *Current Affairs Bulletin*, **69** (6), 114–22.
Wettenhall, R. (2003), 'The rhetoric and reality of public–private partnerships', *Public Organisation Review: A Global Journal*, **3**, 77–107.
Wettenhall, R. (2005), 'The public–private interface: surveying the history', in Graeme Hodge and Carsten Greve (eds), *The Challenge of Public–Private partnerships: Learning from International Experience*, Cheltenham, UK and Northampton, MA, USA: Edward Elgar, pp. 22–43.

Appendix   PPP projects in Australia (at 2009)

Project name	Start year	Duration	Type of PPP						Size (NPV AUS$ m)	Public partner	Private partner
			Design	Build	Finance	Operate	Maintain	Other			
Victoria											
Biosciences Research Centre	2009	3 years – expected completion in 2012	Y	Y	Y		Y		288	Department of Primary Industries in conjunction with La Trobe University	Plenary Research Consortium
Ballarat North Water Reclamation Project	2006	15 years post-commissioning	Y			Y			50	Department of Sustainability and Environment	United Water International Pty Ltd
Barwon Water Biosolids Management Project	2007	3 years – expected completion early 2010	Y		Y	Y			78	Department of Sustainability and Environment	Plenary Environment consortium
Campaspe Water Reclamation Scheme	2002	25 years post-construction – opened May 2005	Y		Y	Y	Y		40	Coliban Water Authority	Earth Tech Pty Ltd
Casey Community Hospital	2002	25 years post-construction – opened 2004	Y		Y			Facility services	120	Department of Human Services	Progress Health Consortium
County Court	2000	20 years post-construction – opened 2002	Y		Y			Building management services	195	Department of Justice	Liberty Group Pty Ltd

Project	Year	Contract term					Service	Value ($m)	Department	Private partner
Victorian Desalination Plant	2009	30 years post-construction – expected 2011	Y	Y	Y	Y		5720 (net present cost)	Department of Sustainability and Environment	Aquasure
EastLink	2004	39 year concession post-construction – opened 2008	Y	Y	Y	Y	Toll – user-pays system	2500	Department of Transport	ConnectEast
Emergency Alerting System	2004	7 years (plus option for 2-year extension)	Y	Y	Y		Support services	100	Department of Justice	VEC Network Pty Ltd
Melbourne Convention Centre	2004	25 year concession – opened in 2009	Y	Y	Y			367	Department of Industry, Innovation and Regional Development	Multiplex/Plenary Consortium
Metropolitan Mobile Radio	2004	7 years (plus option for 2-year extension)	Y	Y	Y		Support services	120	Department of Justice	Motorola Australia Pty Ltd
Mobile Data Network	2003	5 years (plus option for 2 × 2-year extensions)	Y	Y	Y		Support services	140	Department of Justice	Motorola Australia Pty Ltd
PV in Schools Project	2008	25 years	Y	Y	Y			255	Department of Education and Early Childhood Development	Axiom Education Victoria Consortium

Appendix (continued)

Project name	Start year	Duration	Design	Build	Finance	Operate	Maintain	Other	Size (NPV AUS$ m)	Public partner	Private partner
					Type of PPP						
Royal Melbourne Showgrounds	2005	25 years	Y	Y	Y		Y		108	Department of Primary Industries	PPP Solutions
Southern Cross Station	2002	30 years after construction	Y	Y	Y		Y		309	Department of Infrastructure	Civic Nexus Consortium
New Royal Children's Hospital	2007	25 years post-construction – expected to open 2011	Y	Y	Y		Y		946	Department of Human Services	Children's Health Partnerships Consortium
New Royal Women's Hospital	2005	25 years post-construction – opened 2008	Y	Y	Y			Supporting infrastructure services	364	Department of Human Services	Royal Women's Health Partnership
Victorian Correctional Facility	2004	25 years post-construction – opened 2006	Y	Y	Y			Facility management services	275	Department of Justice	Victorian Correctional Infrastructure Partnerships Pty Ltd
Wodonga Wastewater Treatment Plant	2001	10 years (option for 2 × 5-year extensions)	Y	Y		Y			32	North East Region Water Authority	EGL Water Operations Pty Ltd (formerly PURAC Pty Ltd)

Western Australia										
CBD Courts Complex	2004	24 years (WA Govt will buy back)	Y	Y			Y	195	Department of Justice	Western Liberty Group
South Australia										
Regional police stations and courts	2005	25 years			Accommodation, utilities, and facilities management		Y	40	South Australia Police and Courts Administration Authority	Plenary Justice Pty Ltd
Education works – new schools	2009	Unknown	Y	Y		Y	Y	134	Department of Education and Children's Services	Pinnacle Education Consortium
New Royal Adelaide Hospital	2009	Expected completion 2016	Y	Y		Y	Y	1700	Department of Health	SA Health Partnerships Pty Ltd or Torrens Health Partnership (still up for tender)

Appendix (continued)

| Project name | Start year | Duration | Type of PPP | | | | | | Size (NPV AUS$ m) | Public partner | Private partner |
			Design	Build	Finance	Operate	Maintain	Other			
Northern Territory											
Darwin Waterfront Precinct and Darwin Convention Centre	2006	Due for completion 2020	Y	Y	Y	Y	Y	Repairs, commissions	1000	Darwin Waterfront Corporation	ABN Amro, Sitzler Pty Ltd, Sitzler Laing O'Rourke joint venture, Toga Group, Macmahon, and Ogdan IFC
New South Wales											
Royal North Shore Hospital Development	2008	Due for overall completion 2014	Y	Y	Y				1116	Department of Health	Infrashore Partnership
Rosehill Camellia Recycled Water project	2008	20 years	Y	Y	Y	Y	Y		60	Sydney Water Corporation	AquaNet Sydney Pty Ltd, Veolia Water Australia Pty Ltd and SPI Rosehill Network Pty Ltd

Project	Year	Duration				Service category	Value ($m)	Government agency	Private partner
Bathurst, Orange and Associated Health Service	2007	28 years	Y	Y	Y	Facilities management	531	NSW Health	Pinnacle Healthcare
Bonnyrigg Living Communities Project (Social Housing PPP)	2007	30 years	Y	Y	Y	Management services	368	Department of Housing	Bonnyrigg Partnerships
Replacement of RailCorp's electric passenger rollingstock	2006	37 years	Y		Y		3650	RailCorp NSW	Reliance Rail Consortium
Police Property Portfolio	2006	Unknown					Unknown	Ministry for Police	United Group Services Pty Ltd
Long Bay Prison and Forensic Hospitals	2006	28 years	Y	Y	Y		303	NSW Health, Corrections Health Service, Dept of Corrective Services	PPP Solutions Consortium
NSW New Schools Project II	2005	30 years	Y	Y	Y	Other selected services	235	Department of Education and Training	Axiom Education NSW No. 2
Newcastle Mater Hospital Re-Development	2005	28 years	Y	Y	Y	Other selected services	389	NSW Health, Hunter Area Health Service	Novacare Consortium

Appendix (continued)

Project name	Start year	Duration	Type of PPP							Size (NPV AUS$ m)	Public partner	Private partner
			Design	Build	Finance	Operate	Maintain	Other				
Newcastle Community Health Centre	2005	20 years (option for 2 × 5 years extensions)	Y	Y	Y			Y	Unknown	Hunter Area Health Service, NSW Health	Austcorp
Chatswood Transport Interchange	2005	Unknown	Y	Y					81	RailCorp NSW	CRI Australia Pty Ltd
New Schools Project I	2002	30 years	Y	Y	Y				142	Department of Education and Training	Axiom Education NSW No. 1
Cross City Tunnel	2002	34 years	Y	Y	Y	Y	Y		700	Roads and Traffic Authority	CrossCity Motorway Consortium
Westlink M7	2002	35 years	Y	Y	Y	Y	Y		1540	Roads and Traffic Authority	Westlink Motorway Consortium
Eastern Creek Alternative Waste Technology Facility	2002	25 years	Y	Y	Y	Y			70	Waste Recycling and Processing Corporation	Global Renewables Eastern Creek Pty Ltd
Lane Cove Tunnel	2003	35 years	Y	Y	Y	Y	Y		193	Roads and Traffic Authority	Lane Cove Tunnel Consortium

436

	Year	Contract/Status					Notes	$m	Agency	Consortium
Queensland										
SEQ Schools Project	2009	30 years post-construction	Y	Y		Y		1100	Department of Education and Training	Aspire School Consortium
Airport Link	2007	45 years	Y	Y	Y	Y	Commissioning period of 45 years	3000	Department of Infrastructure	Bris Connections Operations Pty Ltd
Northern Busway	2007	45 years	Y	Y	Y	Y	Commissioning period of 45 years	728	Department of Infrastructure	Bris Connections Operations Pty Ltd
Airport Roundabout Upgrade	2007	Expected completion 2012	Y	Y		Y		327	Department of Infrastructure	Bris Connections Operations Pty Ltd
North South Bypass (Clem7)	2006	45 years (concession period)	Y	Y		Y	Concession for tolling for 45 years	3000	Brisbane City Council	RiverCity Motorway
Southbank Education and Training Precinct	2005	30 years (concession period)	Y	Y		Y	Management services provided also	550	Department of Education	Axiom Education Consortium
Tasmania										
Risdon Prison Redevelopment	2001	Completed 2006	Y					90	Department of Justice	John Holland and Fairbrother Pty Ltd

Appendix (continued)

Project name	Start year	Duration	Type of PPP						Size (NPV AUS$ m)	Public partner	Private partner
			Design	Build	Finance	Operate	Maintain	Other			
Commonwealth											
Project Single Leap	2006	30 years	Y	Y	Y	Y	Y		113 + 60 for each year of construction	Corporate Services and Infrastructure Group's (CSIG) Strategic Infrastructure Projects Branch	Plenary Living
Defence Headquarters Joint Operation Command Facility	2006	30 years	Y	Y	Y	Y	Y	Infrastructure and other ancillary services	300	Department of Defence	Praeco Pty Ltd

438

18 Public–private partnerships: the Scandinavian experience
Carsten Greve and Ulrika Mörth

Introduction

What have been the experiences with public–private partnerships (PPPs) in Scandinavia in recent years? Are PPPs an old or a new phenomenon? What explains the apparent lack of interest in infrastructure PPPs and the comparatively low number of PPP projects in Scandinavia?

This chapter examines the Scandinavian countries' experiences with PPPs. Scandinavia comprises Denmark, Sweden and Norway. We examine four areas in particular: (1) the broader framework of public–private cooperation; (2) government policy towards PPPs; (3) overview of the empirical PPP infrastructure projects; and (4) evaluation of the developments.

One of the main themes and questions in this handbook is whether PPPs are a new or an old phenomenon. The Scandinavian cases suggests that the label of 'PPP' is new, but that the phenomenon of governments working with the private sector to build and develop infrastructure has deep historical roots in the Scandinavian corporatist tradition. This is especially true for the local urban communities (Pierre, 1997). It could also be argued that the corporatist tradition, with close collaboration between the public and the private spheres, does not square at all with the Anglo-Saxon version of public–private collaboration. Superficially, they are both about close collaborative arrangements between public and private actors, but the corporatist model is rather hierarchical and informal, whereas PPPs are formal contracting arrangements between two equal partners. In addition, there are ideological and democratic differences between a more pluralist model of public–private collaboration and the corporatist tradition. They entail different models of the relationship between the state and society. The corporatist tradition is very much linked to the idea of a strong public sector and to participatory democracy. The ideological underpinnings of PPPs are linked to the ideas of new public management (NPM) and how the public sector (often perceived as the state) is overburdened. Partnerships can therefore reduce the state and allow a more market-oriented management style make the government more efficient (Mörth, 2008). The democratic ideal is close to the classic analysis of Schumpeter (1942). So the Scandinavian countries' experience with PPPs is an interesting mix of two different styles

439

of public and private collaborations – corporativism and PPPs – and a mix of two democratic ideals – participatory and party competition.

PPPs in Denmark

In examining the Danish experience with PPP policy, we shall look at the policy or institutional change process concerning PPPs in Denmark over a decade, including the key projects and the activities of the actors.

At a general level, Denmark is often thought of as a consensus-oriented society that emphasizes bargaining, networking and cooperation between actors, especially at the labour market. Denmark's economy has been called neo-corporatist and termed 'the negotiated economy', underlining the close cooperation between the public sector and the private sector (Campbell et al., 2006).

The modern-day version of a PFI-type PPP policy was first introduced in the late 1990s, when the Danish Social Democratic government began to pay attention to the PPP policy currents that were under way in the UK and other places. The Danish Ministry of Finance had traditionally been the key player in the public management policy-making process, and in 1999 the Ministry dedicated a chapter in its annual budget report to PPPs (Ministry of Finance, Denmark, 1999). The Danish government seemed interested in the new policy, but was still reluctant to take any big steps to launching PPP policy.

When a new Liberal–Conservative government was elected in 2001, it was expected that PPPs would gain a more prominent place on the policy agenda. At this time, the policy had been popular with UK governments since the early 1990s. Tony Blair's New Labour government, which the new Danish prime minister, Mr Anders Fogh Rasmussen, tried to learn from in policy-making terms, continued to endorse PPPs. A change in policy-making did not happen. Instead the government carried on the NPM-inspired modernization policies of previous governments, but with more emphasis on the market-type mechanisms of contracting out and consumer choice.

The Danish government's PPP policy for the rest of the decade can be summarized as follows: the Danish government showed little enthusiasm at first, produced a policy paper 'Action plan for public–private partnerships' in the middle of the decade (in 2004), endorsed only a couple of serious PPP projects, delegated the initiative for policy proposals to a smaller government agency, the National Agency for Enterprise and Construction, and then basically kept a low profile for the rest of the decade. By the end of the decade, the policy returned from a narrower PPP infrastructure understanding to a broader, but uncommitted policy agenda of 'public–private cooperation' ('offentlig–privat samspil').

In 2004, an 'Action Plan for PPPs' was published (Ministry of Economics and Business Affairs, Denmark, 2004). The government had sat on its hands for the first two years of its existence, and finally came up with a policy document. But the policy document mainly consisted of a bundle of proposals and initiatives that had no coherence. The policy responsibility was shared between the Danish Ministry of Finance and the Danish Ministry of Economics and Business Affairs, and other ministries. The government declined to make a restrictive PPP definition, and started to distinguish between a partnership and the broader term of partnering. The former term, partnership, or PPP, was reserved for the more formal arrangements of design, build, finance, own, operate and transfer that reminded one of the UK Private Finance Initiative projects.

The responsibility for the policy, which had been firmly placed in the Danish Ministry of Finance, was less easily placed when the government changed. A new Ministry of Economics and Business Affairs, a merger of the former Economics Department and the Ministry of Business and Commerce, was given some responsibility. The Danish Ministry of Transport also had an interest in PPP policy. But nobody seemed to take the initiative, and a civil service committee was formed, consisting of employees from the three ministries. The Ministry of Business Affairs delegated the day-to-day responsibility to the National Agency for Enterprise and Construction. The Agency was more engaged with providing the tools for PPPs and less with overall policy-making. It embarked on creating networks between relevant public sector organizations and private companies. However, it began to invite private sector organizations to meetings, and took initiatives to a so-called PPP network that included researchers and other public sector bodies, including those local governments that were interested in PPPs. A Danish version of the 'public sector comparator' (PSC) was developed. A standardized 'boiler-plate' PPP contract was developed. And a report on the economic prospects of the Danish PPP market was issued, which estimated the value for the PPP market for 2005–10 to be in the region of DKK22–27 billion (roughly €4 billion) (KPMG, 2005). In a building legislation piece, however, a PPP circular was proposed and accepted that required all construction projects by central government organizations to consider the PPP's solution.

In the transport sector, a report was produced by the Danish Ministry of Transport that examined various economic and financial models for financing and building a new bridge between Denmark and Germany in the Fehmern Belt. The PPP option was considered, but was found unacceptable. The report instead endorsed the well-established Danish model of establishing a state-owned company, a solution that had been used in the construction of both the Great Belt Bridge and the Oresund Bridge.

In the second half of the decade, the Ministry of Transport was supervising the government's 'Infrastructure Commission'. The report from the Infrastructure Commission also produced a section on PPPs in its final report (Infrastructure Commission, Denmark, 2008).

A number of cases at the local level had made local governments suspicious of the PPP concept. A regional hospital in the county of Frederiksborg tried for some time to establish a PPP for a hospital with the private company, ISS. Not enough bidders came forward when the hospital was put up for sale. Farum local government began to experiment with sale-and-leaseback arrangements and mechanisms for involving private finance in public infrastructure. Farum local government already had a track record of introducing contracting out and was considered the premier contracting local government of the day. Farum began by selling its water provision part to a private company and lease it back again. In the late 1990s, the Farum local government started a process that would build a new sports indoor venue and rebuild its outdoor football stadium by bringing in private sector organizers and financing partners. The project went ahead and attracted a lot of media interest, but also a fair share of criticism. In the summer of 1998, the Minister of the Interior had been forced to issue an administrative order that ensured that any private finance received in public infrastructure projects had to be deposited so that it did not leave a local government with a huge cash influx. Later in the 2000s, a scandal about mismanagement emerged in Farum that eventually led to imprisonment of the former mayor.

The government was re-elected in March 2005 and again in 2008. It was expected that there would be a boost for the PPP policy. But still nothing happened. The government seemed to be content to wait for the result of the national 'pilot project' of the National Archive, which was still in its pre-deal phase at the time, the transport projects (a motorway), and the local government initiative with the new primary school building. No policy review was announced. A policy review was finally announced in 2007. No such review has yet surfaced. In 2009, the government made preparations to formulate a policy, including hosting an experts' seminar at the beginning of 2009 and a workshop in October 2009. The final policy review was promised to be ready 'by the end of 2009'.

Private sector policy
The private sector has been actively trying to push for a more coherent and consistent PPP policy. Private firms have produced pamphlets and reports endorsing PPPs. An early example was the ISS report, 'New goals, new partnerships', which was interesting as ISS had been a controversial part in contracting out in Danish local governments during the 1990s. ISS

saw PPPs as opposed to traditional contracting-out policy. In September 2006, a pension fund, ATP, met the government with a proposal for financing a renovation of the Danish rail tracks as a PPP project. The Ministry of Transport agreed to stay in touch with ATP on the prospect of using the PPP model for the renovation of the railway tracks. The minister of transport promised ATP that a report would be ready for 'the summer of 2007'. In a later statement, in November 2006, another member of the government and deputy prime minister, Bendt Bendtsen, said that he could not envisage a private pension fund paying for Danish rail tracks renewal.

The EU released its conclusions about the public consultation on PPPs in late 2005 (McCreevy, 2005), but did not introduce new rules concerning member states' use of them. The European Commission (2004, p. 3) had published a Green Paper on PPPs. The Commission stated:

> The term public–private partnership is not defined at community level. In general, the term refers to forms of cooperation between public authorities and the world of business which aim to ensure the funding, construction, renovation, management or maintenance of an infrastructure or the provision of the service.

Each government, including the Danish government, had a chance to relate to the Green Paper. In late 2005, the European Commission presented its report on the public consultation on the Green Paper on PPPs. The report endorsed PPPs, but only to a certain extent, and only as long as they do not conflict with the basic competition rules that apply in EU law.

The OECD (2005) issued a report on modernization of the public sector and did endorse PPPs, but not enthusiastically. It continued the same argument in its later report (OECD, 2008), and warned that PPPs would not solve all public finance problems and should be used with caution. A high-level meeting was held at the OECD concerning PPPs in 2006. There was evidence from Canada, Australia and other countries. No Danes participated.

The next sub-section will briefly describe the limited number of PPP infrastructures in Denmark and focus on the two 'showcase examples' in central government and local government: the National Archive project and the project concerning a new primary school in Trehøje, Jutland.

The National Archive project

A new national archive building in Copenhagen had been discussed for a long time, but without being connected to the PPP idea. The government quite abruptly decided that the project should be its pilot project for PPPs.

At the central government level this was the Palace and Properties Agency in Denmark, responsible for the National Archive project. The responsible ministries were the Ministry of Economics and Business Affairs, and the Ministry of Culture. The project itself was a design, finance, build, own, operate, transfer project. The private partner would design the project in cooperation with public sector specifications. The private sector would finance the project, build the archive, operate the archive and, after a 30-year period, transfer the project to the state. The project was first announced in 2004 and a decision was to be reached originally in 2005. KPMG issued a report for the Ministry of Finance on the prospects of the National Archive being a PPP. The report did not fully endorse a PPP solution, and warned against the 'special character' of an archive project, and the lack of a project stream (not many other national archives are likely to be built in Denmark in the foreseeable future!). A project unit was established within the Palace and Properties Agency. The final tendering material was issued in 2006. The consortia project bidders were announced in August 2006. The selection of the bidders was announced in 2007. The new National Archive building was ready in 2009.

The school project
In 2004, a reform-minded local government in Trehøje, Jutland announced that its new primary school would be built as a PPP. A representative of the Trehøje local government had attended one of the network meetings in the National Agency for Enterprise and Construction and was made aware that the agency had some funds available for starting up new PPP projects. The reform-minded local government grabbed the idea immediately, and started the process of seeking private partners to design, build, finance, own and operate the school building before transferring it after a 30-year period. The interest in the Trehøje project was huge. The local government boasted a '10 per cent savings' on the project. The National Agency for Enterprise and Construction supported the project from the beginning and funded consulting services to investigate the possibility for a PPP project. Together with consultants, public managers from the Trehøje local government arranged a study trip to the UK to hear about PPPs there. The interest from private consortia in the project was enormous. Twelve consortia initially bid for the contract. Five of these consortia were then invited to prepare detailed bids. The winning bid came from a consortium of a German bank, a Danish construction company and a Danish facility management company in 2005. People from the National Archive project have been in close contact with the Trehøje local government, and even sat in during some of the negotiations with the bidders! Trehøje was granted an exemption from the tax rules by the Ministry of the Interior

because the tax rules were not clear. The Ministry of the Interior agreed to underwrite any risk that the local government might face in the project that was connected to the uncertainties connected to the tax rules. The new school was ready by the end of 2006. Today the school operates under the new merged local government of Herning.

Other PPP projects

Other PPP projects include a motorway project in Southern Jutland, an indoor music arena in Odense and another primary school in Langeland. In January 2006 the Road Directorate in central government took over responsibility for a motorway project that the Southern Jutland county government had planned since 2003. The project was worth DKK1.1 billion and consisted of building, operating and transferring a motorway. The country government was about to be closed down as part of the Structural Reform in Denmark and the new regional government of Southern Denmark did not want to have responsbility for the project. In August 2006, Odense local government received bids for a new concert hall worth DKK90 million to be built as a PPP. Unfortunately, not enough qualified companies responded to the call, and there were some errors in the tender material. The school in Langeland was a project much like the primary school in Trehøje, where efforts of many actors went into making the PPP a showcase to inspire other projects.

Evaluation

The Danish public policy towards PPPs can be characterized as follows. The Danish government has made an effort to keep a relatively low profile on PPPs. The government has not issued any major, coherent policy initiatives, has supported few policy developments, has been passive on or absent from the international scene, has had only a few showcase projects, and has not created a viable market for PPPs. Importantly,the Danish Ministry of Finance did not fully embrace the PPP policy. It was not convinced of the financial benefit of the policy. Seen in hindsight and after the financial crisis, of course, this might have been a wise decision.

PPPs in Sweden

Involving private companies, business interest organizations and trade unions in public policy- and decision-making processes is at the very core of corporatist tradition in Austria, Germany and Sweden. Historically it can be explained by the non-feudal structure in these countries (Katzenstein, 1985). A common and often-used definition of corporatism is that it is 'a system of interest representation in which the constituent units are organized into a limited number of singular, compulsory, non-competitive, hierarchically ordered and functionally differentiated categories, recognized or licensed (if not created) by the state, and granted a deliberate representational monopoly within their respective categories in exchange for observing certain controls on their selection of leaders and articulation of demands and supports' (Schmitter, 1974, p. 94). This definition entails a hierarchical relationship between the state and society. The state grants the societal actors permission to participate in various public policy processes in return for societal stability and by giving the political decisions societal legitimacy.

In Swedish politics, 'the Swedish model', Harpsund democracy or the spirit of Saltsjöbaden, represents a corporatist tradition where representatives of the Labour movement as well as trade and industry have agreed on the economic policies for the country. The Swedish state has allowed certain organized groups to participate in the official decision-making process. This model has, according to Peter Katzenstein, proved to be a successful way for small states to deal with the global economy (1985). However, in recent years, Swedish corporatism has been pronounced all but dead (Rothstein and Bergström, 1999). This is true for so-called public administration corporatism as well as for labour market corporatism (Forsberg, 2000). One clear sign of this de-corporatization is that the interest organizations no longer have any formal representation in the central administration authorities (SOU, 2000). Pia Forsberg says the following regarding the changes in 'the Swedish model': 'The specific combination of labour market relations and social political measures that have developed over more than four decades, known as "the Swedish model", have fundamentally changed during the 1980s and the 1990s' (Forsberg, 2000, p. 123).

There are also people who claim that elements of corporatism still exist within the Swedish system but that these manifest themselves in a more indirect way, as opposed to representation at the central administration authorities (Hermansson et al., 1999). In addition to this, major interest groups are still a part of various public bodies (ibid.). One key issue is therefore whether or not new ways of institutionalizing the relationship between private and public actors have developed. An official report states that de-corporatization paves the way for relationships between different organizations and the state that are more informal and less hierarchical. 'In other words, actors seek new methods for influencing the political decision-making. The decision-making becomes less formal, the competition for attention from politicians increases . . . In such a society, lobbying becomes . . . increasingly more important in the political decision-making process' (SOU, 2000, pp. 89–90). This development is especially noticeable within the EU. However, it is important to point out that the EU is a complex organization where lobbying as well as more corporatist structures coexist.

In the political science literature, there are two ideal types of interest representation, corporatism and pluralism. One important difference between the two is that in the corporatist system, industry and other interest organizations participate within the frames of a state-centric, hierarchical political system. The pluralistic system operates in a more society-based political system. This is where we will find phenomena such as lobbying in the form of non-institutionalized participation in decision-making processes. That means temporary rather than long-lasting relationships.

The big question is how partnerships are to be understood. Partnerships can be seen as a sort of new corporatism in the sense that they are a close and organized collaboration between the public and the private sphere. Partnerships can also be interpreted as a result of pluralism since they take place in a more society-oriented steering and decision-making process. However, as in the corporatist system, a partnership is an institutionalized form of collaboration, if by institution we mean a long-lasting form of collaboration. Another feature distinguishing corporatism from pluralism is who the dominating actor in the decision-making process is and who the key player is in terms of setting the rules for participation. The corporatist tradition expects the public sphere to define the rules, whereas the pluralistic tradition considers independent lobbyists as the key players. PPPs are ideally more focused on the participants developing rules for the partnership together. Whether or not this works in practice is an empirical question. As a result, there is a point to be made that the intertwining of the two spheres is not something new but rather that the structure for the intertwining is new. The emphasis of the partnerships on all participants being equal partners would consequently be an outcome of such a new structure regarding the relationship between the private and the public sphere. The partnership would therefore be characterized as dominated by 'governance' rather than 'government'. In the Anglo-Saxon literature a distinction is made between a hierarchical system of command and control and a more vertical and network-oriented counterpart. This means that corporatist state centrism, which among other things was built on the state interest of creating legitimacy and getting support for reforms as well as getting different interest groups to consider the public good, has changed fundamentally (cf. Forsberg, 2000; Rothstein and Bergström, 1999). Instead, it deals with political processes with several legitimate wielders of power and interest from both the private and the public sphere.

Indeed, PPPs are often linked to NPM. Partnerships are part of a broad shift in the workings of government and the search for new forms of governance in which the government is the enabler and coordinator rather than the direct provider of services. A management culture has emerged that focuses on customers, 'accountability for results, investigation of a wide variety of alternative service delivery mechanisms, and competition between public and private bodies for contracts to deliver services, consistent with cost recovery and achievement of value for money' (Grimsey and Lewis, 2004, p. 52). One important device for political control is therefore contracting. The idea of contracting out public services is not something new. 'Government has always employed contracting out as a tool for arranging certain simple services such as catering or cleaning' (Lane, 2000, p. 7). What is new with the NPM is that governments are contracting out in more areas, such as education and healthcare and that the NPM 'also deals with *contracting in . . .*' (Lane, 2000, p. 7, emphasis in original). This means that governments manage the public sector by means of various types of contracts that are regulated by private law instead of by public law mechanisms. Contracting is more important than the traditional tools of government, such as law, regulations and budgets. 'Contracting involves bargaining and reciprocity, whereas authority is based upon domination' (ibid., p. 193). NPM 'changes the coordination mechanism in public resource allocation from authority or command to contracting or exchange' (ibid., p. 195). Indeed, the main goal is to raise efficiency in the provision of goods and services, and this is done by using various private sector mechanisms: 'privatisation, incorporation of public services, the introduction of internal markets, the employment of the purchaser-provider separation, contracting out, the use of massive contracting, bench-marking . . .' (ibid., p. 60).

The NPM reform is global but has had different effects and interpretations in different countries. Pollitt and Bouckaert (2004) argue that Sweden belongs to the group of 'modernizers', which means that the country believes in a large role for the state but is also active in making fundamental changes in the public sector. There has been a lot of deregulations and opening up for competition in formerly monopolistic sectors, such as: electricity, postal services, telecommunications, domestic air traffic, rail and taxi services (Swedish Agency for Public Management, 2005). It is, however, difficult to establish whether these deregulations have increased the number of PPPs in Sweden. According to the available statistics, and specifically those provided by the European Investment Bank, there are very few PPPs in Sweden (EIB, 2006).

It is quite clear, however, that the Swedish state is both contracting in and contracting out, and that steering through contracting is increasingly important. Indeed, the Swedish government has a rather market-friendly policy towards increased participation of business actors in the public sector, but the very label 'partnership' is seldom used in the political rhetoric. The Swedish label for public and private projects is 'samverkan'. It is a difficult concept to translate but it is close to the concepts of collaboration or cooperation.

The reasons for the low number of PPPs can therefore be explained by the Swedish reluctance to use the label 'partnerships' when public and private actors build bridges or roads. The prestigious project of building the Arlanda Express (the train from the Arlanda airport to Stockholm city) was presented as a joint project between public and private actors and not as a PPP (interview with Lars Rekke). It certainly looked like a PPP in the sense that it was a formal contract between the actors and there was a shared risk-taking between the actors. Another case in point is the bridge between Sweden and Denmark – 'Öresundsbron'. It was a big project between business actors and the Swedish/Denmark governments, but it was not presented as a PPP, although it was a contracting relationship with the expectation of mutual benefits of the involved partners. The public actors needed private risk capital and the private actors got a promise of a potential profit.

This reluctance to present public and private collaborations can certainly be derived from the corporatist tradition in Swedish politics. Since Swedish EU membership in 1995, the label 'PPP' is increasingly used by Swedish politicians and agencies. The recent years of EU reforms – Better Regulation, the Growth Initiative and the Lisbon Process – have entailed an increased emphasis on performance in European public policy. One important means of achieving a more efficient public policy is PPPs (Mörth, 2008). This development is also evident in Sweden.

In a Swedish public study on regional growth in 2006, the very title of the study is *Swedish Partnerships. An Overview* (SOU, 2006). The choice of title is motivated by the authors by the fact that the term partnership is 'imported from the EU' (ibid., pp. 4 and 23). The report further states that Swedish partnerships is an umbrella concept for many types of public and private collaborations, and that these are especially the result of the EU's policy on structural funds and other regional growth policy instruments. The number of regional PPPs in Sweden is not specified, but the overall estimation is that there are more than a hundred, depending on how they are defined (SOU, 2006).

In sum, PPPs are a well-established phenomenon in Sweden if defined as close collaborations between public and private actors. The very label is new in Swedish politics, but it is more than a new label. PPPs are part of the trend towards NPM, a reform heavily approved by the former Social Democratic Government (2002–06) and the current right-wing government (2006–). EU membership and the recent years of the reform agenda in the EU have increased the number of PPPs in Sweden and 'normalized' the use of the label 'partnership' in Swedish politics.

PPPs in Norway

PPPs for infrastructure projects have not played a central role in policy developments in Norway. Norway is famous for its many resources, and is one of the strongest economies in the world. In particular, it has enjoyed a stream of financial benefits from North Sea oil production and it has not had any economic or financial need to adopt a comprehensive PPP policy.

PPPs have been introduced in Norway, though, and the spotlight has mainly been on the transport sector. Early in the 2000s, the Norwegian Ministry of Transport took an interest in the new PPP policy and the first project was the E39-highway project (Norwegian Public Roads Administration, 2001). In 2001, the Norwegian parliament approved three PPP pilot projects for building new highways: the 'E39 Lyngdal-Flekkefjord' highway, the E18 Grimstad-Kristianssand, and the E39 Klett Bårdshaug. The first project for a highway was proposed in 2001, signed in 2003 and completed in 2006. The Norwegian Public Roads Administration (2008) has been responsible for overseeing the projects. There was, however, no overall policy on PPPs in Norway in the 1990s (Semlitsch, 2009).

The Norwegian PPP model works as follows: the planning and the assessment of the project is the responsibility of the Norwegian Public Roads Administration. The design, construction, building, financing and operating the road is the responsibility of the PPP company to which the contract for the E39 project was awarded. The project for the E18 project was awarded to Angder OPS Vegselskap AS, owned by Bilfinger Berger BOT, E-Pihl and Sons and Sundt AS.

Discussion

At least two questions need to be addressed regarding the Scandinavian countries. What does this development towards more of a contracting relationship between public and private actors mean from a democratic perspective? Why did the Scandinavian countries not follow the international trend of establishing PPPs?

On democracy

It could be argued that there has been a shift from participatory democracy towards the partnership model, with more focus on efficiency and output legitimacy. Partnering would thus be legitimate through efficiency rather than through fulfilling the demand of participatory democracy. In the Swedish analysis of the increase in the number of partnerships, there is an emphasis on what is lost from a democratic point of view. An official report on democracy declares:

> The execution of the political decisions in the EU is at large carried out through the establishment of partnership with official bodies at a national as well as regional and local levels but also with representatives of specific industries, companies and interest organizations. These bodies rarely meet the demands of democracy regarding decision-making, transparency, participation, influence and accountability. (SOU, 2000, p. 124)

Steering through contracts has more to do with law and less to do with politics. In a dispute or if there are problems between the public and the private actors, it becomes a question of accountability from a legal point of view rather than a democratic one. There are also partnerships evolving more slowly that are characterized by informal relationships. Looking at it from a private actor's point of view, this does not have to be a problem as long as there is a possibility to explain and defend them before shareholders and other stakeholders. To the private sector, a partnership appears as a flexible way to meet the demands of the public while avoiding direct regulations. However, for the public sphere, the problems are greater. Jon Pierre expresses the fundamental conflict of interest between the private and the public in the following way:

> Public actors and institutions – whether elected representatives, bureaucrats or public organizations – have other motives compared to profit driven organizations or interest groups within urban communities. No matter how closely connected the political institutions and leaders might be with the private companies, they still have a formal political obligation in trying to consider the interest of other groups within the political realm of the urban communities. (Pierre, 1997, p. 114)

The public actors have to take the public interest into account, whereas the private actors each have their own interest to focus on. On the other hand, Pierre continues, the industry actors have an interest in being considered as legitimate actors in the political process rather than simply following their own needs.

> The closer the relationship between the private companies and the public institutions and the more they are connected to the decision-making process in the urban community, the more important it is for their presence to be considered to be legitimate and in the interest of others rather than simply the private companies. (Ibid., pp. 114–15)

Cooperation and co-dependency between the public and the private sphere can from a democratic point of view be described as a dilemma, at least from a public perspective; the public sphere needs closer collaborations with the private sphere – steering through horizontal networks, while the public sphere traditionally follows a hierarchical chain of command and control (Mörth and Sahlin-Andersson, 2006). A clear separation of power and responsibility between the public and the private sphere is desirable from a democratic perspective, however problematic from an efficiency point of view. The distinction between the public and the private sphere is important in order to maintain the democratic legitimacy of the public sphere but, at the same time, the distinction makes it difficult to uphold an efficient decision-making process as well as an efficient crisis management. A clear line between the two spheres could also reduce the possibilities for society to provide its citizens with important collective products and services. The dilemma between the capacity to act and efficiency and democratic legitimacy is rarely given much attention in official documents regarding the need for cooperation between the public sector and industry. These emphasize instead the importance of collaboration between the two spheres without discussing the tension that exists between efficiency and democracy (see, e.g. *Regeringsproposition* 2001/02, p. 158).

Why did PPPs for infrastructure projects not catch on in Scandinavia? The experience with PPPs in Scandinavia with a limited number of long-term infrastructure projects can be explained by what follows. First, there was already a tradition of public–private cooperation, mainly rooted in the corporatist tradition. Governments and other organizations have not seen PPPs as bringing substantial new ideas. Public organizations and private organizations have always cooperated. Consequently, there is less of a tradition to privatize. It is possible to see the Scandinavian countries in a path-dependency perspective (Pierson, 2004), where countries stay on paths of close cooperation once chosen. Consequently, there has been less need to bring the public sector and the private sector closer to each other. Second, there was a lack of sufficient financial pressure on the Scandinavian welfare states in the 2000s for them to pursue a PPP policy for purely financial reasons. Simply put, the Scandinavian governments were to a certain extent able to raise finance to pay for infrastructure projects without resorting to the PPP model, and have not been forced to cooperate with the private sector the way the UK did. The Ministry of Finance in Denmark opposed a more active and coherent PPP strategy (Helby Petersen, 2007). This is a political-economy argument: there was less need for private finance in the Scandinavian countries. This might be changing in the years to come, but in the period of the 2000s, when many other countries were relying on private finance in infrastructure projects, the Scandinavian governments did not experience the same need. Third, PPPs have not been seen as a politically important enough springboard to use by governments in public management reform policy. PPPs have been seen as a 'low-politics' area that has been kept out of the government's main priorities. This is a political-science argument, saying that PPP has not been important on any electoral platform. Going for a PPP model and making critique of the welfare state was not politically wise in the 2000s for most of the Scandinavian governments. No particular electoral success was guaranteed by endorsing a PPP model, so the Scandinavian governments chose to downplay its importance in the overall political strategy.

Conclusions

PPPs appear from many aspects as a new label for an old phenomenon in the Scandinavian context. The label PPP is important and reflects both the symbolic and the actual shift in power between public and private actors. From a symbolic standpoint, PPPs appear as an attractive way of collaborating for both the private and the public sphere. Coercion and hierarchy have been replaced with voluntary and horizontal relationships. Who opposes voluntariness? The name PPP also reflects real changes in power. The public can no longer dominate corporatist relationships (if this was ever done). The corporatist relationships were built on an ideal principal–agent relationship and within a hierarchical system of control. Private–public partnerships are more likely to take place in a network-oriented system of control. However, the democratic legitimacy and the possibilities for accountability are still based on representative democracy. This poses a dilemma for the public sphere since it needs a close collaboration with the private sphere – steering through horizontal network relationships – while the public sphere traditionally follows a hierarchical chain of command and control. A clear division of power and accountability between the public and the private sphere is desirable from a democratic point of view but problematic in terms of efficiency. The border between the private and the public is important in order to maintain the democratic legitimacy of the public sphere while it makes an efficient decision-making process as well as an efficient crisis management more difficult. A clear line between the two spheres could also reduce the possibilities for society to provide its citizens with important collective products and services.

PPPs as infrastructure projects did not have the same appeal in Scandinavia as they did in other parts of the world. The Scandinavian experience can show only a limited number of infrastructure PPP projects, mainly in the transport (roads) and education sector (primary schools). The reason for the lack of enthusiasm for PPPs in Scandinavia may be found in a combination of at least three factors: historical development of the Scandinavian welfare states, economics, and politics. The history of the Scandinavian welfare states has been a history of blending public priorities with private priorities mainly though corporatist arrangements. Therefore PPPs as such were not seen as something new. The Scandinavian economies all did comparatively well during the last decade, and the state often had ways to finance infrastructure projects themselves. Consequently, there has been less need for private finance and therefore for PPPs. Finally, politics also played a part. PPPs were not needed for macroeconomic reasons and they were not associated with electoral success, so governments in Scandinavia mostly steered clear of promoting PPP policies. The advent of the financial crisis in 2008–09 was seen as confirmation by Scandinavian governments that they were right in not jumping on the PPP bandwagon.

References

Campbell, John, John Hall and Ove K. Pedersen (eds) (2006), *National Identity and Varieties of Capitalism: The Danish Experience*, Montreal and Copenhagen: McGill Press and DJOF Publishing.

European Commission (2004), Green Paper on Public–Private Partnerships and Community Law on Public Contracts and Concessions. COM/2004/327/Final. Brussels: European Commission.

European Investment Bank (EIB) (2006), *Operations Evaluations – Overview*, Luxemborg: EIB.

Forsberg, Pia (2000), 'Nya former för institutionaliserat samarbete mellan stat, arbete och kapital?', in Anders Neergaard and Ylva Stubbergaard (eds), *Politiskt inflytande*, Lund: Studentlitteratur, pp. 100–125.

Grimsey, Darrin and Mervyn K. Lewis (2004), *Public Private Partnerships: The Worldwide Revolution in Infrastructure Provision and Project Finance*, Cheltenham, UK and Northampton, MA, USA: Edward Elgar.

Helby Petersen, Ole (2007), 'Hvorfor så få offentlig-private partnerskaber i Danmark? Et ministerielt spil om indflydelse, interesser og positioner', *Økonomi & Politik*, **82** (1).

Hermansson, Jörgen, Anna Lund, Torsten Svensson and PerOla Öberg (1999), *Avkorporativisering och lobbyism*, Stockholm: SOU, 121.

Infrastructure Commission, Denmark (2008), *The Danish Transport Infrastructure 2030. Summary in English*, Copenhagen: Danish Ministry of Transport.

Katzenstein, Peter (1985), *Small States and World Markets – Industrial Policy in Europe*, Ithaca, NY: Cornell University Press.

KPMG (2005), *OPP-markedet i Danmark* [The PPP Market in Denmark], Copenhagen: KPMG.

Lane, Jan-Erik (2000), *New Public Management*, London: Routledge.

McCreevy, Charles (2005), Speech by Charles McCreevy, European Commissioner for Internal Markets and Services, 17 November.

Ministry of Economics and Business Affairs, Denmark (2004), *Handlingsplan for offentlig–privat partnerskaber* [Action Plan for Public–Private Partnerships], Copenhagen: Ministry of Economics and Business Affairs.

Ministry of Finance, Denmark (1999), *Budget redegørelse '99* [Budget report 1999], Copenhagen: Schultz.

Mörth, Ulrika (2008), *European Public–Private Collaboration. A Choice Between Efficiency and Democratic Accountability?*, Cheltenham, UK and Northampton, MA, USA: Edward Elgar.

Mörth, Ulrika (2009), 'The market turn in EU governance – the emergence of public–private collaboration', *Governance*, **22** (1), 99–120.

Mörth, Ulrika and Kerstin Sahlin-Andersson (eds) (2006), *Privatoffentliga partnerskap*, Stockholm: SNS Förlag.

Norwegian Public Roads Administration (2001), PPP Project. E39 Klett-Baardshaug, Information memorandum, Oslo: Norwegian Public Roads Administration.

Norwegian Public Roads Administration (2008), 'PPP-projects in Norway', National Public Roads Administration, available online at www.vegvesen.no.

OECD (2005), *Modernising Government. The Way Forward*, Paris: OECD.

OECD (2008), *Public–Private Partnerships. In Search of Value for Money and Risk Sharing*, Paris: OECD.

Pierre, Jon (ed.) (1997), *Partnerships in Urban Governance – European and American Experience*, London: Macmillan.

Pierson, Paul (2004), *Politics in Time*, Princeton, NJ: Princeton University Press.

Pollitt, Christopher and Geert Bouckaert (2004), *Public Management Reform. A Comparative Analysis*, 2nd edn, Oxford: Oxford University Press.

Regeringsproposition 2001/02:158 (Law in the Swedish Riksdag/Parliament).

Rekke, Lars, Director General of the Swedish Civil Aviation Authority, interviewed in October 2006.

Rothstein, Bo and Jonas Bergström (1999), *Korporativismens fall och den svenska modellens kris*, Stockholm: SNS Förlag.

Schmitter, Philippe (1974), 'Modes of interest. Intermediation and models of societal change in Western Europe', in Philippe Schmitter and Gerhard Lehmbruch (eds), *Trends Towards Corporatist Intermediation*, London: Sage, pp. 124–37.

Schumpeter, Joseph (1942), *Capitalism, Socialism and Democracy*, New York: Harper & Brothers.

Semlitsch, Kjersti (2009), 'Public–private partnerships. Norwegian challenges', presentation by Senior Audit Advisor, Office of the Auditor General Norway, Powerpoint Presentation (accessed 21 December 2009).

SOU (2000), *En uthållig demokrati! Politik för folkstyrelse på 2000-talet*, Stockholm: SOU.

SOU (2006), *Svenska Partnerskap. En översikt*, Stockholm: SOU.

Swedish Agency for Public Management (2005), *Competition at the Public/Private Interface*, Stockholm: Swedish Agency for Public Management.

19 Empirical evidence of infrastructure public–private partnerships: lessons from the World Bank experience

Paul Noumba-Um

Introduction

Governments worldwide have expressed strong interest in public–private partnerships (PPPs)[1] to finance the development of infrastructure systems or facilities crucial for their economic growth and development. While this surge of interest in PPPs is recent, private sector participation in the delivery of key infrastructure facilities and services is not a contemporary innovation. Indeed, public authorities envisaged very early on asking private parties to carry out public services activities on their behalf and under their control. In France, as early as the sixteenth century, the government signed its first concession with Adam de Craponne for the construction of a canal in 1554.[2] In 1568, the City of London accepted to concession its water supply to private companies. The eighteenth and nineteenth centuries also witnessed the multiplication of public–private partnership schemes regarding the development of key infrastructure facilities such as bridges and canals in Europe and elsewhere.

Although the current enthusiasm for PPPs is real, it raises new challenges to development institutions such as the World Bank. PPPs are complex and costly to implement, and may not be affordable to many governments struggling with other pressing social needs in the developing world. The World Bank and other international financial institutions (IFIs) therefore face a 'PPP paradox' in the sense that they need to strike a sensible balance between forceful advocacy for PPPs and effective management of client countries' expectations of what can be achieved through PPPs. The reality of fiscal space limits the ability of many governments to increase budgetary allocations to infrastructure projects. Likewise, although this is often overlooked, fiscal space also limits the ability of governments to service long-term payment commitments that can result from PPP agreements. In fiscal terms it means that PPP contracts with long-term payment commitments from governments are not much different from public debts that governments contract to fund their activities or finance infrastructure projects. PPP payment commitments and public debt repayments are fiscally equivalent, though with one important caveat that relates to the fact that PPPs payments are made if agreed services have been successfully delivered. This urges a conservative use of PPPs.

This chapter reviews the experience of the World Bank in promoting private sector participation in the delivery of infrastructure in its client countries. It argues that PPPs are not a panacea for infrastructure development. PPPs represent a procurement tool that client governments can use to finance the development of strategic infrastructure projects that would not otherwise be developed due to fiscal space[3] constraints or other important deficiencies hampering public sector effectiveness in the developing world. The remainder of the chapter is organized in three sections. The first section sets the floor for our discussion by reviewing the magnitude of infrastructure challenges that currently prevail in developing countries, and discusses how these challenges can be addressed. The second section reviews decades of World Bank involvement in financing infrastructure investments in developing countries, and highlights successive shifts that have characterized its policies in this area. The third section discusses pragmatic PPP approaches currently being advocated by the World Bank Group, and highlights the variety of instruments made available to support client governments' efforts to develop successful PPP programmes. A conclusion is derived in the form of the way forward to reflect on new challenges posed by the current global crisis.

The magnitude of infrastructure investment needs in developing countries
The catalytic role of infrastructure in growth, social inclusiveness and poverty reduction is widely recognized. Access to basic infrastructure services such as water, sanitation, electricity, transport and telecommunications is critical in creating new economic opportunities and lifting millions of people out of the poverty trap. According to World Bank poverty counts, more than 1 billion people live on less than US$1.25 per day.[4] These people also need access to clean water, adequate sanitation, energy, transport, information and communication services. Ensuring that affordable and quality infrastructure services are made available to them is crucial for them to be empowered to build productive lives, support their families and contribute to growth and wealth accumulation. Wagstaff and Cleason (2004) estimate that 600000 women die every year due to childbirth complications that could have been prevented if all-weather roads were available everywhere to ease their timely access to childbirth-related care. In an impact evaluation study of the water sector privatization in Argentina, Galiani et al. (2005) show that child mortality dropped by 5–7 per cent more in areas with private water providers. Their study also finds that increased access to the water and sanitation network, as well as improvements in service quality and costs incurred by consumers, had a

direct and positive impact on health outcomes among age groups most vulnerable to waterborne diseases.

The World Bank (2008) estimates that there are approximately 884 million people without access to safe drinking water, 2.5 billion without adequate sanitation, 1.6 billion without access to electricity and more than 1 billion people without access to telephone services. Access gaps remain large across regions, and in particular in Sub-Saharan Africa (SSA) and South Asia (SA). Despite progress made during the past decade, development opportunities remain severely hindered in many parts of the developing world. In SSA, one-quarter of the population has access to the electricity network, whereas reliability of supply hampers firms' competitiveness across countries. If access to safe water appears to be at acceptable levels, regional averages hide wide disparities between regions and in particular between rural and urban areas. Inadequacy of sanitation systems represents major health and environmental hazards in SSA and SA, with respectively 43 per cent and 23 per cent of the population having access to such systems. In contrast, the telecommunications sector has witnessed impressive developments during the current decade thanks primarily to technology evolution and the implementation of market liberalization policies in market segments where competition was feasible. In less than two decades, access to mobile telephony has increased from almost 0 per cent in the early 1990s to 15 per cent in 2006 in SSA.

Overall, the infrastructure access gap in the developing world is much harder to address due to the solvency gap of its population (see Table 19.1). It is well known that the sustainability of infrastructure investments requires the implementation of effective cost recovery mechanisms (tariffs or taxpayers' contributions) that enable appropriate maintenance, renewal and expansion of infrastructure stock. If the government or private investors finance the construction of infrastructure projects, it is after all consumers and taxpayers who ultimately have to cover the costs. To highlight the tricky situation facing developing countries, let's assume that each poor household in a given country allocates on average 15 per cent of its US$2 per person's income per day for the consumption of infrastructure services (water, electricity and energy, transportation, telephone). This gives a potential cash flow stream of about US$0.30 per person per day, compared with the average infrastructure investment needs of US$0.45 per person per day.[5] This shows an average investment gap of approximately US$0.15 per person per day that can only be covered by additional transfers from local or international taxpayers. Bridging this service delivery gap[6] is consequently the key determining factor for the sustainable development of infrastructure in low-income countries. If the services could be paid for by the general population at a tariff set at full

Table 19.1   Infrastructure access indicators

		EAP	ECA	LAC	MENA	SA	SSA
Population (in millions)[1]		1,899	459	555	310	1,492	770
Living population with less than $1 per day (in million)[2]		169	4.4	47	4.4	446	298
Urban population (%)[3]		42	64	78	57	29	36
Urban population in 2030 (%)[3]		70	63	92	61	40	52
Access to electricity (%)[4]		89	99	90	78	52	26
Access to water	Urban	93	95	94	95	94	83
supply (%)[5]	Rural	67	82	66	77	80	44
Access to sanitation	Urban	73	91	86	93	67	73
(%)[5]	Rural	35	81	52	70	22	43
Access to telephone	Fixed	23	25	18	17	3	1
per 100 population[6]	Mobile	35	63	55	36	15	14
Access to rural transport[7]		90	82	59	59	57	34

Notes: EAP: East Asia and Pacific; ECA: Europe and Central Asia; LAC: Latin America and the Caribbean; MENA: Middle East and North Africa; SA: South Asia; SSA: Sub-Saharan Africa.
[1]   World Bank Development Database, 2006.
[2]   World Bank Development Economics Data Group (DEC), October 2007 – data from 2004.
[3]   World Bank Development Database, 2006.
[4]   International Energy Agency (IEA), 2005. EAP data include China, while MENA does not include Northern African States.
[5]   Joint Monitoring Program Database (wssinfo.org). 2004 data.
[6]   World Development Indicators, 2006.
[7]   Rural Access Index (RAI) estimates the proportion of rural population, which has access to an all-weather road, based on household survey data: 2002–04.

cost recovery level, then the infrastructure financing gap would not be so acute. This solvency gap limits the extent to which governments in developing countries can rely on PPPs to overcome the infrastructure coverage and access gap they face.

Therefore one key question for policy-makers is how much investment they need to allocate in infrastructure in order to sustainably bridge the current access gap. To respond to this question, Fay and Yepes (2003) and Yepes (2008)[7] have assessed the level of infrastructure stock that is required, either as consumption goods or as input into the production function, to sustain economic growth in a given country at a specified level. The results of their study indicate that the developing world will require annual investments of about $1.1 trillion (6.6 per cent of GDP) through to 2015 to satisfy demand for infrastructure services by residential and business consumers, assuming current GDP growth and demographic trends (Table 19.2). Of this amount, about 40 per cent will be required for capital expansion of infrastructure and 60 per cent for maintenance of both current and future infrastructure.

Table 19.2 also shows that investment needs will represent as a share of GDP: 12.5 per cent in low-income countries, 8.2 per cent in lower-middle-income countries and 2.3 per cent in upper-middle-income countries. The distribution across sectors shows that the highest investment needs are in energy (46 per cent) and transport (35 per cent). The share of water is esti-mated at 9.8 per cent in developing countries, although regional averages vary significantly.

Table 19.2   Annual investment needs, 2008–15 (in 2005 US$ millions)

	Sector				Total
	Transport	Telecoms	Electricity	W&S+WW	
Region					
EAP	121 496	29 009	226 119	33 321	409 945
ECA	88 744	15 284	72 034	7 287	183 349
LAC	50 591	20 523	66 858	11 950	149 923
MENA	25 220	8 068	38 387	6 861	78 535
SA	73 351	23 508	79 348	31 155	207 361
SSA	28 924	10 138	26 386	19 082	84 530
Income group					
LIC	107 871	33 811	104 638	53 003	299 323
LMIC	221 234	60 225	339 875	50 001	671 335
UMIC	59 223	12 494	64 618	6 652	142 986
Investment type					
Maintenance	309 558	57 876	248 967	55 771	672 172
Capital	78 769	48 653	260 164	53 884	441 471
Total	388 327	106 530	509 131	109 656	1 113 644
Percentage of total	34.9	9.6	45.7	9.8	100.0

Notes: EAP: East Asia and Pacific; ECA: Europe and Central Asia; LAC: Latin America and the Caribbean; MENA: Middle East and North Africa; SA: South Asia; SSA: Sub-Saharan Africa; LIC: low income countries; LMIC: low middle income countries; UMIC: upper middle income countries; W&S+WW: water supply+waste water.

Source: Yepes (2008).

To gauge the magnitude of the infrastructure investment gap, it is necessary to compare Yepes's (2008) estimates against actual investment levels observed in developing countries. Figure 19.1 indicates that, on average, developing countries have allocated during the past years (1995–2005) approximately half of what they should have invested in infrastructure in order to sustain their economic growth prospects at current levels. Bearing in mind the limitations surrounding all these estimates, the second question facing policy-makers and development institutions is how to effectively bridge the resulting investment gaps. Clearly there is no miracle solution. There are only three main sources of financing of infrastructure investments. Infrastructure investments can be financed either by the public sector[8] or by private investors through equity and debt financing; or by donors' grants in the case of low-income countries. These three sources of financing are not, however, of equal importance. During the past two decades, public financing has represented between 70 per cent and 80 per cent of the infrastructure investments, while private financing has reached its peak between 15 per cent and 20 per cent of the total financing mobilized (see Figure 19.1). Grants from donors to low income countries (LIC), though in the decline, have represented between 5 per cent and 10 per cent of the financing mobilized for infrastructure. An important conclusion to be drawn from these facts is that public financing for infrastructure will remain as the main source of financing in future. In considering PPP

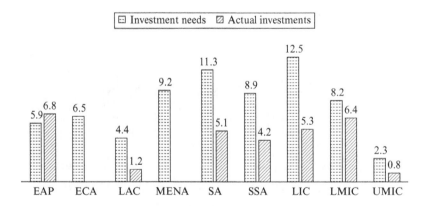

Notes: EAP: East Asia and Pacific; ECA: Europe and Central Asia; LAC: Latin America and the Caribbean; MENA: Middle East and North Africa; SA: South Asia; SSA: Sub-Saharan Africa; LIC: low income countries; LMIC: low middle income countries; UMIC: upper middle income countries.

Source: Yepes (2008).

Figure 19.1 Infrastructure investment needs versus actual investments (US$)

options, governments should also improve, in parallel, the quality of public spending on infrastructure.

World Bank infrastructure development policies and PPPs[9]

The World Bank, also known as the International Bank for Reconstruction and Development (IBRD), was created after the Second World War at the Bretton Woods conference. Its mandate then was to financially support the reconstruction of Western Europe, and primarily the reconstruction of its infrastructure destroyed by the war. From 1946 to approximately 1987, World Bank loans in infrastructure projects represented between 50 per cent and 60 per cent of its total lending. Infrastructure loans reached US$8.5 billion in 1987. By 1998, World Bank lending in infrastructure went down to represent only 40 per cent of its total lending, and by 2003 infrastructure lending was just approximately 30 per cent. What happened?

Among the main infrastructure sectors, the decline was most pronounced in the energy sector, reflecting the particularly high expectation about private participation in this sector. Transportation was the least affected, although the decline in this sector was also substantial. At the regional level, World Bank lending went down to about one-half of the 1970 levels in East Asia and the Pacific (EAP), Europe and Central Asia (ECA), and Latin America and the Caribbean (LAC). This sharp decline

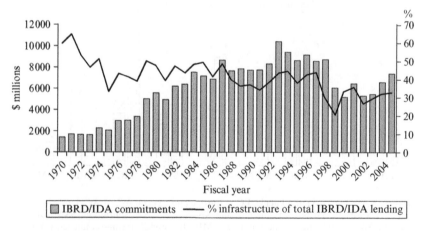

Note: Includes guarantees.

Source: World Bank (2006).

Figure 19.2   IBRD/IDA infrastructure lending, 1970–2005

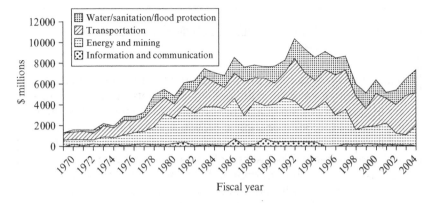

Note: Includes guarantees.

Source: World Bank (2006).

Figure 19.3 Infrastructure lending by sectors

in World Bank lending was observed primarily in regions that were able to attract the bulk of private infrastructure investments in the developing world. In contrast, SSA and SA, regions that were less successful in attracting private financing, experienced a small increase in infrastructure lending by the World Bank.

The World Bank policy and approach regarding infrastructure, from its inception, was about offering public financing to infrastructure projects sponsored by state-owned enterprises. Starting in the 1980s, there was growing disillusion with public sector delivery of infrastructure services. In a number of developing countries, the large infrastructure investments did not translate into sustained service improvements. The cost of failure, in foregone growth and poverty reduction, were increasingly seen as being unacceptably high. State-owned enterprises proved largely inefficient as they were plagued with many problems, including political interferences, patronage, below-cost tariffs and overstaffing. By the mid-1990s, the Bank became reluctant to lend to governments to finance bricks-and-mortar infrastructure projects, and opted increasingly for pro-market-based solutions wherever possible (see Box 19.1).[10]

The general view in the Bank reflected the Washington Consensus policies that assumed that the rapid growth witnessed in private sector investment in infrastructure would continue and even amplify, provided host countries were effective in creating and maintaining policy and regulatory environments conducive to private investments. During these years, the Bank issued a series of operational policies[11] that stated that it would focus

BOX 19.1   WORLD DEVELOPMENT REPORT –
            1994

Major investments have been made in infrastructure stocks, but
in too many developing countries, these assets are not generating the quantity or the quality of services demanded. The costs of
this waste in forgone economic growth and loss of opportunities
for poverty reduction and environmental improvement are high
and unacceptable. The causes of past poor performance and the
source of improved performance lie in the incentives facing providers. To ensure efficient, responsive delivery of infrastructure
services, incentives need to be changed through the application
of three instruments: commercial management; competition; and
stakeholder involvement.

its development efforts on infrastructure sectors to assisting client governments to establish an enabling environment for private sector participation. The Bank progressively shifted away from financing state-owned
enterprises or utilities, and started forcefully advocating for increased
private sector participation in infrastructure. The 1980s and 1990s also
saw growing concerns with the environmental and social impacts of infrastructure projects, including those financed by the Bank. In response, the
World Bank tightened its safeguards policies.

The early 2000s were a period of disappointment with private participation in infrastructure in the developing world. Private investment flows,
after a rapid growth in the mid-1990s, started to decline in the late 1990s.
Soon it became clear that, with the exception of the telecommunications
sector, the aim of replacing wasteful public infrastructure providers by
efficient private companies would not be realized in the near future in most
developing countries. The effects of the East Asia financial crisis; difficulties with independent power producers in Indonesia, Pakistan and elsewhere; stalled water privatizations in Bolivia, Argentina, the Philippines
and Tanzania; distressed toll-roads projects in Latin America (primarily
in Mexico); and Argentina's economic crisis negatively affected financiers'
risk perceptions. Private infrastructure investment in developing countries
dropped to a seven-year low in 2003.

Though almost forgotten today, the shift in World Bank policy in
infrastructure was conceptualized with the publication of the *World
Development Report* (*WDR*) in 1994.[12] *WDR 1994* explored the links
between infrastructure and development, and reviewed ways in which

developing countries could improve both the stock and the quality of infrastructure services. To reverse the poor performance cycle of state-owned infrastructure service providers, *WDR 1994* advocated a different approach for infrastructure development in developing countries. It recommended new ways to meet infrastructure needs with an efficient, user-responsive, environmentally friendly and more resourceful use of both the public and the private sectors' resources and skills. The report emphasized that increasing infrastructure spending was not a sufficient condition for improving the development outcomes expected from better and more infrastructure use by the society and the economy. Low operational efficiency of utilities or inadequate maintenance and lack of attention to the needs of customers play a crucial role in hampering the development impact of infrastructure investments. Therefore institutional reform was considered a desirable centrepiece of the World Bank approach as it facilitated the establishment of the right incentives and accountability framework to ensure efficient delivery of infrastructure services.

Interestingly, the *WDR 1994* advocated explicitly for the multiplication of public–private partnerships (PPPs). Surprisingly, the public component of such partnerships was limited to policy and institutional reform support. The report did not envisage a situation whereby the public sector would channel capital contribution to a PPP project. The belief was that private capital would flow into infrastructure sectors provided the right policy and institutional environment were in place. By the early 2000s, infrastructure investment in many developing countries had declined below the levels of ten years earlier. In most developing countries, large and growing infrastructure gaps accumulated. By 2003, there was a sense that the decline in World Bank financing in infrastructure had exacerbated the overall reduction of infrastructure investments, in particular by indirectly signalling to the international development community and to client countries that infrastructure sectors were no longer a major development priority.

Persistent requests from client governments (Figure 19.4) and growing difficulties encountered in the mobilization of private capital for infrastructure projects led to a reconsideration of the Bank's position regarding its role in financing infrastructure. In 2003, the World Bank adopted the Infrastructure Action Plan (IAP). The IAP committed the World Bank to scale up financial and analytical support to client countries for the delivery of basic infrastructure services through a balanced and pragmatic approach. At the end of the IAP implementation in 2007, the World Bank was successful in increasing its financing in infrastructure from US$22.3 billion over the preceding four time periods to US$32.8 billion.[13]

The IAP was succeeded in 2008 by the Sustainable Infrastructure Action Plan (SIAP). The SIAP is an umbrella framework that brings together the

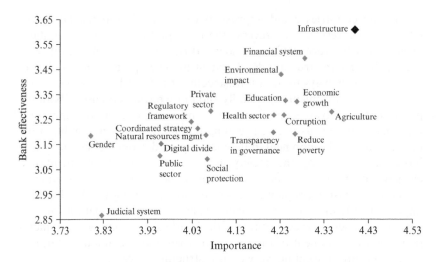

Note: Based on survey responses from more than 6000 key opinion-makers in 35 countries.

Source: External Affairs, World Bank, *Client Survey 2004 Review.*

Figure 19.4   World Bank interventions, effectiveness and importance

lessons of the World Bank Group (WBG)[14] infrastructure experiences. Its objectives are to: (i) support governments to respond to and mitigate the impact of climate change; (ii) crowd in private sector by expanding PPPs and strengthening the capacity of public agencies to perform as reliable and effective partners in PPPs; and (iii) address spatial disparities in infrastructure that hamper development effectiveness. The SIAP commits to mobilize between US$59 and 72 billion for infrastructure investments over the period 2009–11. This amount will leverage between US$45 and 109 billion from the private sector and contributions of overseas development agencies.

World Bank approach and experience in PPPs
An important lesson emerging from the World Bank experience is that neither the public nor the private sector alone can meet the access, quality, financing and policy infrastructure gaps. During the past decades, the World Bank has learnt that public financing was the main source of financing for infrastructure development across countries, and will continue to play a pivotal role in future. The Bank has also learnt that even though public financing was the centrepiece of infrastructure financing, it was important to recover costs to ensure the renewal, expansion and

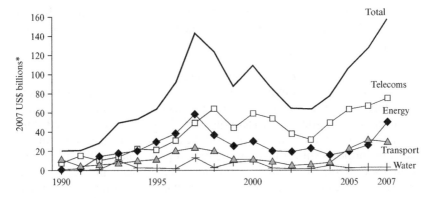

Note: * Adjusted by the 2007 US CPL

Source: PPI Database (2009).

Figure 19.5   Private investments commitments to infrastructure projects, 1990–2007

maintenance of the stock of infrastructure capital in countries. Recovering costs entails the implementation of appropriate pricing mechanisms to be supplemented by effective social protection measures. While the determination of tariffs could be delegated to autonomous regulators, the decision on tariffs levels and structure was in most countries kept under the control of ministerial authorities. Therefore, based on social and political considerations, governments can decide to fix the tariffs below the cost of their efficient supply, but when tariffs are set below costs, governments should put in place appropriate mechanisms to subsidize service providers. During the past decade, the Bank also embraced subsidies as a legitimate public policy tool, in particular to promote the delivery of infrastructure services to poor communities. Ensuring that the poor benefit from equitable access to infrastructure services has important positive externalities, and the lack of subsidies would simply delay access to these services due to affordability issues. More importantly, the Bank concluded that such subsidies should be targeted to consumers who need them most.

During the IAP period, the World Bank shifted its focus from privatization (sale of assets) to a flexible range of PPPs. This shift also signalled the important role that governments have to play besides devising appropriate policies for the development of strategic infrastructure projects. As shown in Figure 19.5, private investments to infrastructure grew steadily to reach US$140 billion in 1997, and then declined until 2003. The decline cycle was reversed in 2004. Unfortunately, throughout the decline phase of private investments, countercyclical investments that could have been mobilized from the World Bank or other development agencies fell short of filling the gap.[15]

What was learnt from these developments in sectors

During the 1990s, telecommunications and energy were the leading sectors regarding growth in private investment. This expansion in private sector participation was spurred by technological change that has reduced sunk costs, thus lowering barriers to entry and exit. Investments in telecommunications projects with private participation grew continually in 1990–98 from about US$7 to 35 billion. Cumulative investments in telecommunication amounted to 43 per cent of flows to all infrastructure sectors in that period. Investments in energy projects with private participation, which were only about US$2 billion in 1990, peaked at about US$46 billion in 1997 before declining sharply to US$27 billion in 1998. The energy sector claimed about 36 per cent of cumulative investments in 1990–98. In transport and water, technological change was less pronounced and lagged behind energy and telecommunications. The two sectors nevertheless represented altogether approximately 21 per cent of cumulative private investments in infrastructure.

In electricity, establishing a competitive market proved to be an overambitious goal for most developing countries. One of the barriers to achieving sustainable competition in generation, besides competitive access to primary energy resources and market size, was the financially distressed distribution companies that could not afford the costs of PPAs[16] because of below-cost retail tariffs and the uncertainty prevailing over their automatic tariff adjustment mechanism to reflect changes affecting the wholesale market. In telecommunications, the World Bank experience across regions, countries and income levels shows that strong competition has driven growth in this sector.

In transport, public investment for roads remained the global norm. Well-planned road investments generally generate high social returns (World Bank, 2006). Thus major highway projects, bridges, tunnels and multi-year maintenance contracts were procured using PPPs in some countries. In railway infrastructure, most of the increase in private participation was in freight rail. The main reasons are that freight transportation is less politically controversial, and more capable of achieving independent financial viability than passenger rail transportation. In airport infrastructure, private involvement has been prominent for decades, but limited to larger airports able to fairly secure revenue streams.

In water and sanitation, the Bank learned the importance of addressing critical political economy issues associated with tariff and sector reforms.

In particular, it learned how to integrate social protection measures in infrastructure reform packages as a means to minimize the social impact of institutional changes and tariff reforms. At present, the majority of the world's water distribution and sanitation networks are publicly owned and operated. This will continue to be the case for many years to come.

Lessons drawn for the development of successful PPP programmes
PPPs face a wide variety of obstacles in developing countries. These range from a weak policy and regulatory environment; lack of a pipeline of viable and bankable projects; and weak capacity of public institutions to process PPPs to underdeveloped domestic financial and capital markets. In general, establishing a robust PPP policy and legal framework has proven to be challenging in most countries as it entails in-depth institutional reform in the way government operates and performs. In many countries in the developing world, there remains a gap between written policies and enacted legislations, and their implementation or enforcement on the ground.

Likewise, the development of pipelines of PPP projects has remained a far-reaching goal in many of the Bank's client countries. Preparing a realistic pipeline of PPP projects has been more challenging than originally expected. The factors for this are multiple and often contradictory. In one client country, the pipeline of PPP projects consisted primarily of projects for which line ministries had problems in mobilizing public financing, whereas commercially viable projects were retained to be implemented as public investment. In another client country, though committed to its PPP programme, the government took four years to put together a realistic pipeline of PPP projects. Having such a pipeline has proven to be an important driver for PPPs' success, as investors could anticipate a flow of transactions over a given period of time. PPPs are costly and time-consuming procurement processes. Therefore most investors look at the prospects of development of future PPP transactions in a given country before deciding to commit their resources to that country. Another issue that has been characteristic of PPPs in the Bank's client countries relates to over-optimistic expectations from governments. First, in many cases, governments failed to understand that not all of their infrastructure projects should be undertaken as PPP projects. Second, when they understood that basic principle, in many cases client governments failed to put in place appropriate mechanisms to screen and identify projects that are the most appropriate to be implemented as PPP projects. Third, in many cases, unfortunately, governments failed to ensure consistency between their capital development programmes in infrastructure and the pipeline of PPP projects. Finally, and more importantly, governments failed to appropriate adequate budgetary resources to cover the cost of preparation of PPP projects[17] and often imposed unrealistic schedules on project teams.[18]

Another critical issue has been the weak capacity of public institutions to deal with PPP specificities. PPP projects focus on output and not on input specifications, as opposed to traditional public procurement. But devising output specifications for PPP projects can be a complex process, in particular in such sectors as health and education where PPPs are used for facilities development and management. For client countries, the definition of output specifications requires the development of a new set of skills that are not usually available in house when the PPP programme is initiated. In one country where the government decided to launch an ambitious PPP programme, the decision was made to start the programme with a PPP project for the design, construction and facility management of hundreds of schools. Though plagued by other institutional and design issues, this project quickly foundered on the definition of output specifications. Evolving from an input-based model to an output-based model, where the emphasis is on performance-based contracts, proved across countries to be a major challenge for newly established PPP units.

A Standard & Poor's global survey found that 88 per cent of PPP projects are delivered on time and at cost, whereas only 30 per cent of traditionally procured projects achieve the same performance.[19] However, as discussed in previous sections, PPPs do not come without costs. While they can be a means of changing for ever the way governments can deliver public services, PPPs are by their nature and structure complex instruments requiring a thorough reflection on how they should be used to deliver the best outcomes. Ensuring value for money in the delivery of infrastructure PPPs is in fact about strengthening the public sector ability to become more effective in delivering services to citizens and businesses. To draw the best from the use of such instruments, developing a visionary approach that outlines the objectives of the programme, its scope and how it will be implemented is crucial. From this broad assessment of PPP policy, institutional and regulatory issues will unfold the key strategic directions necessary to guide the detailed elaboration of the programme. In many countries, however, this conceptual stage was often oversimplified, thereby leading to disappointment. The key, as it results from international experience, is for governments to prepare a vision for their PPP programme, and mobilize their institutions for its implementation in a timely and coordinated way.

Establishing a PPP unit to coordinate the implementation of the PPP programme comes out as a necessary but not a sufficient condition for success. PPP units can perform different mandates (Public–Private Infrastructure Advisory Facility (PPIAF), 2006), but PPP units are only justified in a given country if a sizeable pipeline of potential PPP transactions is likely to materialize in the medium term. When this is not possible, it makes more sense to strengthen the capacity of existing institutions than to establish a PPP unit from scratch. But PPP units can serve other important functions, such as reviewing and ensuring that candidate projects comply with regulatory requirements at all stages of their preparation. This is an important role as it ensures a consistent enforcement of the PPP regulations across sectors and projects. Another important function that PPP units perform is the management and the valuation of fiscal risks associated with PPP projects. Governments do indeed appear to play a dual role in processing PPP projects.[20] As a grantor, the government or public entity signs the PPP agreement and commits in certain cases to long-term payments to the private party against the successful delivery of agreed services. The other important function that governments perform relates to promoting the development of private investments in the economy, and in particular in infrastructure. In the latter case, most governments offer a variety of incentives, including tax holidays, guarantees, in-kind contributions or capital subsidy to attract foreign or domestic investments. For a prudential fiduciary management of PPP fiscal implications, the PPP unit can play an important role in valuing and managing fiscal risks associated with PPPs.

Finally, in many developing countries, capital and financial markets remain at infant development stage. With the exception of a handful of countries (Chile, India, South Africa etc.), the lack of depth and breadth of capital and financial markets in developing countries limits their ability to meet the long-term equity and debt financing needs of infrastructure PPP projects. The Bank learned that in these countries, although domestic banks have plenty of liquidity, they are often ill equipped to appraise complex PPP projects and price accordingly the risks that are associated with them. Cross-border debt has therefore become, until the 2008–09 global financial crisis, the main source of financing for infrastructure PPP projects undertaken in the developing world. With the financial crisis, liquidity has dried up and the cost of lending has escalated, thus negatively affecting many PPP projects. Therefore there is no better substitute for foreign exchange risk mitigation than matching the currency of revenue generation with the currency of the debt payment services. In most countries, infrastructure PPP projects with some few exceptions (air transport services, ports) generate local currency revenues whereas they need to service a debt that is usually denominated in foreign currency. This creates an asset–liability mismatch that could be relieved if the local debt market were developed. This asset–liability mismatch also generates a whole set of additional risks that are difficult to allocate between project sponsors, government and end users.

To match assets and liabilities when the PPP financing is in foreign currency ultimately entails the mobilization of additional support from the government through guarantees, whereas domestic institutional investors (pension funds, insurance companies, life annuities etc.) have a natural demand for long-term local currency debt instruments to match their liabilities. It is in the government's best interest to stimulate, via adequate securities regulations, the development of local capital markets as a source of long-term local currency funding for needed infrastructure PPP projects.

How the World Bank Group supports PPPs in practice

The World Bank Group, through its different affiliates' institutions, can mobilize a wide spectrum of lending and non-lending instruments in support of PPP initiatives launched by client governments. On the public sector side, IBRD/IDA (International Development Association) combines lending and non-lending products that client governments can use to support the implementation of their PPP programmes. As part of its policy and regulatory advisory services, IBRD/IDA provides technical assistance programmes to set up PPP frameworks and to develop institutional capacity for PPPs. For instance, the World Bank is currently advising the municipality of St Petersburg in Russia on the implementation of a US$5 billion PPP programme including the development of an airport, a ring road and a light-rail system. Similar supports are also provided in Egypt, Syria, Kuwait, Nigeria, India, Mongolia, Indonesia, Peru, Kazakhstan, Jordan and Pakistan, among others. IBRD/IDA also extends direct financing support to PPP projects as part of host governments' capital contribution commitment. The construction of a 40-km toll road has been made possible in Senegal thanks to a US$105 million World Bank loan to the government of Senegal that will be used to cover part of the costs related to the project implementation. In numerous cases, IBRD/IDA guarantee products have been crucial in enhancing the creditworthiness of Independent Power Producer (IPP) projects in SSA (Azito in Côte d'Ivoire, Bujagali Dam in Uganda, coal-power plant in construction in Bostwana etc.), in the Middle East and North Africa (Amman East power plant in Jordan, Jorf Lasfar power plant in Morocco) and in East Asia (Nam Theun dam in Laos).

On their part, IFC (International Finance Corporation) and MIGA (Multinational Investment Guarantee Agency) focus on extending World Bank Group support to the private sector parties involved in a partnership with the government. MIGA provided up to US$1 billion of guarantee exposures in 2007. MIGA guarantees cover for political risk (expropriation, transfer restriction, breach of contract, war and civil unrest) to which private investors are exposed in the developing world. IFC, which is the private sector arm of the World Bank Group, provides transaction advisory services for PPPs and extends financing to project sponsors through direct lending (A loan) or syndication (B loans). In 2007, IFC lent about US$3.7 billion to infrastructure PPP projects in the developing world.

To address PPP market supply-side weaknesses, the World Bank Group has initiated a series of new interventions in a sample of target countries that aim to explore the feasibility of establishing dedicated new institutions that catalyse the development of the PPPs. For instance, in many emerging economies, developing a robust pipeline of viable PPP projects is often a challenge. Whilst governments may underspend on the identification, preparation and procurement of publicly procured infrastructure projects, cutting corners on the preparation of PPP projects will be more costly. The cost of poor due diligence or preparation of PPP projects will be reflected in the bids submitted by the private sector and will lead to costly PPP contracts for the government. To mitigate the risks of poor preparation of PPP projects by client governments, the Bank recommends the establishment of dedicated projects development funds (PDF) that can make resources available on a grant basis to:

- ensure that line ministries or agencies undertake good due diligence while designing or structuring PPP transactions; and
- enable line ministries or agencies to mobilize needed technical assistance from professionals to prepare and implement PPP projcts.

For PPPs that are economically justified but not commercially remunerative, governments can consider the establishment of a dedicated fund that could provide capital subsidy needed to make them commercially viable (see Box 19.2). A 'viability gap fund' can be a useful instrument to make PPP projects affordable. Such funds or similar have been established in India, Brazil and South Korea, with the most successful examples provided by rural telecommunications funds (Chile, Peru, Colombia etc.) or rural electrification funds (REA in the USA, Sri Lanka etc.). Box 19.3 discusses examples of viability gap funds established in India and South Korea.

Despite the large amount of liquidity that has characterized the banking sector in most developing countries during the past decade, most infrastructure projects have been primarily financed through cross-border debt. Borrowing in local currency has proven to be more difficult due to lack of long-term liquidity in local currency and the weak capacity of commercial banks to appraise and price the risks associated with infrastructure PPP projects. The lack of long-term debt finance is a particularly acute problem that requires intervention by governments. In Egypt, local banks have participated in the financing of infrastructure PPPs when there has been

---

BOX 19.2   INDIA INFRASTRUCTURE PROJECT DEVELOPMENT FUND

While the Indian economy is now recording a growth rate of 8% per year, it is estimated that US$488 billion would be required for investment in the infrastructure sectors. A significant share of this is expected from the private sector through PPPs. Considering that the quality of advisory services is critical to procuring affordable, value for money PPPs, the Government of India has created the '*India Infrastructure Project Development Fund*' – as a revolving fund which will be replenished by the reimbursement of investments through success fees earned from successfully bid projects. The project development fund will cover up to a maximum of 75% of project development expenditures incurred by State and respective agencies in preparing and processing PPP projects. The fund will be seeded by contributions by the government of India and multilateral institutions. It will operate under specific funding and reporting requirements.

Source: Ministry of Finance, Government of India, *Scheme and Guidelines for the India Infrastructure Project Development Fund.*

---

leadership by international financiers and ironclad guarantees. Although the Egyptian banking market is highly liquid, it has been unable to offer long-term debt with tenure beyond five to seven years, and with floating interest rates thereafter. In such circumstances, the World Bank has come to the conclusion that government intervention was justified to catalyse the development of the domestic capital market through the establishment of a dedicated non-bank financial institution (NBFI) that can progressively crowd in commercial banks in the financing of infrastructure PPP projects. The proposed NBFI should be established and managed as a private and commercially oriented financial institution. It will include commercial banks and multilaterals among its shareholders, and will raise capital by issuing bonds in the domestic capital market and by borrowing from IFIs (Delmon, 2009). It will then lend these resources to PPP projects granted and demonstrating creditworthiness.

The way forward
Future prospects for PPPs are, however, hard to predict. The global financial crisis that started in 2008 has severely curtailed the ability of

---

BOX 19.3   EXAMPLES OF INFRASTRUCTURE VIABILITY GAP FUNDS

India – The Viability Gap Funding Scheme provides financial support in the form of grants, one-time or deferred, to infrastructure projects undertaken through PPPs with a view to making them commercially viable. The Indian Viability Gap Fund is administered by the Ministry of Finance. To be eligible for the Fund, PPP projects must meet the following criteria: (i) the project should be implemented by a private sector company to be selected under a transparent competitive bidding process; (ii) the criterion for bidding should be the amount of viability gap funding required by the private operator to implement the project; (iii) the project should provide service against payment of a predetermined tariff or user charge; (iv) total viability gap funding cannot exceed 20 per cent of the total project cost; (v) the viability gap funding is transferred in the form of a grant at the construction stage.

South Korea – For infrastructure facilities that are deemed to be of high priority in the mid- to long-term investment plan of the government, subsidy or long-term loan can be granted for purposes such as land compensation cost or construction cost within the boundaries of the planned budget. The competent authority calculates the standard user fee assuming that no financial support is provided (calculated user fee) and a fair user fee taking into account the financial support; the government fills the gap.

---

private investors to participate in PPP tenders. In mid-2009, a few PPPs projects were still reaching financial closure, though with higher interest rates. The number of PPP projects that reached financial closure was 23 per cent lower than at the same time the previous year. The financial crisis has affected all the main participants in PPP projects. Equity investors are facing difficulties in sourcing their equity investment, and the funding that they use to develop projects has become costly or even scarce. Lenders have incurred massive losses due to the financial crisis, and the ensuing credit crunch has deprived them of the abundant liquidity that was previously available. As *Project Finance International* reports: 'banks for the most part are choosing smaller commitments and limiting lending to key clients, demanding higher spreads and fees for shorter tenors'.[21] Construction companies have seen their stock valuation wiped out, and are finding it harder to access capital. Governments on their side have witnessed a decline in fiscal proceeds due to sluggish economic activity, and face harder fiscal constraints that prevent them from extending more support to PPPs. Finally, rising unemployment due to the crisis is translating into demand contraction, thereby making infrastructure PPPs more vulnerable to demand and market risks.

The question this new development poses is how to reshape or recraft the infrastructure PPP agenda in the developing world with embryonic capital markets. In general terms, and as part of a short-term adjustment action, governments can restructure or redesign or delay some of their PPP projects that are at early stage of development. As part of a medium-term action plan, governments have to take advantage of the current adverse time to refine their policy and regulatory framework regulating PPPs. More importantly, they should take advantage of the current market downturn to further develop their PPP market supply-side institutions so to be able to reap the benefits when the market recovers.

Previous crises have taught us that public spending in infrastructure is one of the expenditure categories that is most severely cut by governments under financial stress. In Latin America, 50 per cent of the fiscal adjustment in the 1990s was borne by cuts in infrastructure public spending. Calderon and Serven (2008) estimate that as a result of cuts in public infrastructure investment, the region lost between 1 per cent and 3 per cent in economic growth. Likewise, countries in South East Asia also drastically cut their public spending in infrastructure in the aftermath of the 1998 financial crisis. Indonesia's total investment in infrastructure dropped from 7 per cent of GDP in 1995–97 to 2 per cent in 2000, while private sector investment fell from 2.5 per cent to 0.09 per cent during the same period.

To avoid a repeat of an already-known scenario, the World Bank has proposed a countercyclical programme – INFRA (Infrastructure Recovery and Assets) – that aims to preserve the quality of existing stock of infrastructure in client countries by making needed financial resources available to governments so that they ensure appropriate maintenance or continue to upgrade their infrastructure systems.

Notes

1. PPPs are defined as a long-term contract between a public sector party and a private sector party for the design, construction, financing and operation of a public infrastructure by the private sector party, against which the private sector party will be entitled to collect payments for the use of the facility from the users, the public sector party or a combination of both, and with the infrastructure facility remaining or reverting to the public sector party at the end of the PPP contract.
2. Severine Dinghem (2005), *Les Échos de la Banque Mondiale*, No. 3, December, pp. 6–10.
3. Heller (2005) defines fiscal space as room in a government's budget that allows it to

provide resources for a desired purpose without jeopardizing the sustainability of its financial position or the stability of the economy.

4. In 2005, the regional distribution of poverty was as follows: (i) 16.8 per cent in East Asia and Pacific; (ii) 3.8 per cent in Eastern Europe and Central Asia; (iii) 8.2 per cent in Latin America and the Caribbean; (iv) 3.6 per cent in the Middle East and North Africa; (v) 40.3 per cent in South Asia and (vi) 50.9 per cent in Sub-Saharan Africa.

5. This figure is derived from Yepes (2008).

6. The service delivery gap reflects the difference between cost recovery and affordability (or willingness to pay).

7. Yepes (2008) updates the results of Fay and Yepes (2003). These two papers estimate the level of investment in infrastructure that is needed for a country to sustain a given level of growth.

8. Directly through tax proceeds and indirectly through tariffs.

9. When Paul Wolfowitz became President of the World Bank in June 2005, he requested that a review be undertaken on the experience of the Bank in assisting client countries to develop their infrastructure. This review led to the publication of a book in 2006 entitled *Infrastructure at the Crossroads: Lessons from 20 Years of World Bank Experience* (World Bank, 2006). This section builds from this important assessment and explains how the successive shifts in its infrastructure development policies have impacted PPPs development in developing countries.

10. This shift in policy is reflective of the Washington Consensus or neoliberal stabilization policies adopted by IFIs in the early 1990s. The consensus consisted of a combination of policies promoting (i) trade and financial liberalization, (ii) deregulation of the economy, (iii) privatization and (iv) fiscal restraint or responsibility.

11. See the operational policies issued for telecommunications and energy in 1993.

12. World Bank (1994).

13. Infrastructure lending reached US$13 billion in 2007 against US$5.7 billion in 2000.

14. The World Bank Group includes the following institutions: International Bank for Reconstruction and Development (IBRD), International Development Association (IDA), International Finance Corporation (IFC), MIGA (Multilateral Investment Guarantee Agency), International Centre for Settlement of Investment Disputes (ICSID).

15. For instance, World Bank lending dropped from US$10.6 billion in 1993 to US$5.4 billion in 2003.

16. 'PPAs' stands for 'power purchase agreements'.

17. A survey of the UK National Audit Office (NAO) (2007) shows that the cost of preparing PPP projects can reach up to 2.6 per cent of the capital costs of the projects considered.

18. In the UK, recent empirical evidence shows that schools projects take on average 25 months from pre-qualification to financial close, against an average duration of 38 months for hospital projects. Additionally, the average time between selection of the preferred bidder and financial close is estimated at around 15 months.

19. Standard & Poor's 'Public-Private Partnerships – Global Credit Survey' (2005).

20. More precisely, governments have seven or perhaps more roles: policy advocate, economic developer, steward for public funds, elected representative for decision-making, regulator over the contract life, commercial signatory to the contract and planner.

21. Deirdre Fretz, 'Banks vs bonds', in *Project Finance International*, 410, 3 June 2009.

References

Calderon, Cesar and Luis Serven (2008), 'The effects of infrastructure development on growth and income distribution', unpublished manuscript, World Bank.

Delmon, J. (2009), 'Private sector investment in infrastructure: project finance', *PPP Projects and Risk*, 2nd edn, PPIAF, The Netherlands: Wolters Kluwer.

Fay, M. and T. Yepes (2003), 'Investing in infrastructure: what is needed from 2000–2010', World Bank, Policy Research Working Paper, 3102.

Galiani, S., P. Gertler and E. Schorgrodsky (2005), 'Water for life: the impact of the privatization of water services on child mortality', *Journal of Political Economy*, **113** (1), 83–120.

Heller, Peter (2005), 'Understanding fiscal space', IMF Policy Discussion Policy Paper, PDP/05/4, 19 pages.

Public–Private Infrastructure Advisory Facility (PPIAF) (2006), 'Assessment of the Impact of the crisis on new PPI projects – Update 3'.

UK National Audit Office (NAO) (2007), 'Improving the PPP tendering process', report by the Comptroller and Auditor General, March, 37 pages.

Wagstaff, A. and M. Cleason (2004), *The Millennium Development Goals for Health: Rising to the Challenges*, Washington, DC: World Bank.

World Bank (1994), *World Development Report: Infrastructure for Development*, New York: Oxford University Press.

World Bank (2006), *Infrastructure at the Crossroads: Lessons from 20 Years of World Bank Experience*, Washington, DC: World Bank.

World Bank (2008), 'Sustainable Infrastructure Action Plan FY 2009–11', mimeo, Washington, DC: World Bank.

Yepes, T. (2008), 'New estimates of infrastructure expenditure requirements', Washington, DC: World Bank.

20 Public–private partnerships: the United Nations experience

Benedicte Bull

The UN's interest in forming partnerships with the private sector started in the 1990s and was strengthened during the first years of the new millennium. This signified both a new practice and a new ideological approach to the relationship between public authority and the private sector in the UN system. The public–private partnership (PPP) approach of the UN invoked severe criticism from scholars as well as NGOs (non-governmental organizations) for jeopardizing the legitimacy of the UN (Martens, 2007; Zammit, 2003). The weight of this argument depends in part on how we define legitimacy (Bull, 2010). However, it also depends on the exact roles that the private actors play in the PPPs and the impact the PPPs have had on the UN organizations.

This chapter discusses the forms of PPPs that the UN has entered into and how they distribute roles and responsibilities between public and private actors. It shows that the term PPP covers a great variety of arrangements in the UN system, but in general they involve relatively little transfer of responsibility towards private businesses: business contributes with technology and know-how, but generally with relatively little in terms of investments or direct financial contributions, and business is generally reluctant to deviate from its regular strategies in order to accommodate the goals of the UN organizations.

However, the move towards PPPs has involved significant contributions from foundations often closely related to private business, and the involvement of these foundations has been an important factor behind the rising trend of PPPs. The financial constraints experienced by these foundations from 2007 may make them less influential actors than they were previously. Thus, although private companies may be increasingly interested in entering into PPPs with the UN, we may expect PPPs to be a less significant aspect of the UN's mode of operation in the future.

The chapter proceeds as follows. First, a brief historical introduction to the rise of PPPs in the UN system is given. This will be followed by a discussion of different kinds of PPPs, distinguishing them along various different dimensions, but focusing mainly on the distribution of roles and responsibilities. The third section discusses the impact of PPPs in the UN organizations. The fourth section discusses the possible future of PPPs in the context of increased financial constraints.

For the purpose of this chapter, PPPs are defined as 'voluntary and collaborative relationships between various parties, both State and non-State, in which all participants agree to work together to achieve a common purpose or undertake a specific task and to share risks and responsibilities, resources and benefits' (UN General Assembly, 2005, p. 4).

The rise of PPPs in the UN system

PPP is one of several concepts – including, among others, 'multi-stakeholder initiatives' and 'policy networks' – aiming to describe new forms of multi-actor collaboration at the global level. Several of these include the UN organizations as partners.

The background for the UN's search for partnerships is a combination of financial constraints and ideological shifts, both related to a change in the global political economic system. With some notable variations, many UN organizations have experienced significant financial constraints from the 1980s. Over the course of the 1990s, the private flows to developing countries (foreign direct investment, portfolio investment and debt repayment) came to outstrip the public flows by far, although the situation differed across continents. In terms of public flows, the share of official development assistance passing through the multilateral organizations diminished compared to bilateral flows, and it was the UN that was hardest hit. Yet a parallel and often overlooked phenomenon was the rise in the endowments and annual giving of private foundations. Between 1975 and 2003 the total giving by US foundations increased from US$6 billion to US$32 billion, and although international giving was a relatively small proportion of this, it increased at the same rate (Foundation Centre, 2009a).[1] Thus, many UN organizations found themselves in a position of severe financial constraint in a context of relative private sector affluence.

Yet, although often cynically interpreted as a sign of the UN's financial constraints, the rise of PPPs in the UN system is a part of a more systemic shift and cannot be understood without also taking into account a fundamental change in the ideas about the role of the private sector in development. The UN organizations were founded in the context of what Ruggie (1982) has termed 'embedded liberalism': a liberal international infrastructure of global economic management, predicated on the domestic interventions for social protection by the modern capitalist state. In this system, the UN organizations played a double role: they embodied the rules that facilitated the expansion of the existing order, but they were also the site of struggle between conservative and transformative forces aimed at reaching new compromises to protect vulnerable sectors at the international level (Cox, 1983, 1992). Several UN organizations came to be associated with this latter role and until the 1990s there had emerged a general understanding that the UN was anti-business (Tesner and Kell, 2000). One important process that contributed to this image was the (ultimately unsuccessful) attempt to develop binding codes of conduct for multinational enterprises under the UN Conference on Trade and Development (UNCTAD), and the work done by the UN Center for Transnational Corporations (UNCTC).

Beginning in the 1980s, the removal of many interventions for social protection at national level, combined with the deepening of the liberal framework at the global level, led to the concept of the 'embedded liberalism compromise' and to the conclusion that this had broken down (see, e.g., Ruggie 1997). At the same time, initiatives to formally regulate capitalism at the international level were weakened partly due to the increase in the size, reach and political and economic clout of large corporations, which reduced the ability of states and international organizations to impose regulations (Harrod, 2006). PPPs were proposed in this context as an alternative to regulation and direct interventions as a means to make corporations pull in the same direction as states and multilateral organizations (Ruggie, 2004).

The closing down of the UNCTC in 1993 is often viewed as a symbol of the weakening of the multilateral system *vis-à-vis* the private sector (Hummel, 2005).[2] However, the major turning point came with the appointment of Kofi Annan as Secretary-General in 1997. He had a business background himself, and he introduced entirely new ideas about the UN's relation to the private sector. On 1 February 1997, four weeks after assuming office, he addressed the World Economic Forum in Davos, Switzerland, and declared that there was now 'a new universal understanding that market forces are essential for sustainable development' (Tesner and Kell, 2000, p. 32). The same year, the UN received the historic gift by Time Warner Vice-Chairman Ted Turner, which led to the establishment of the UN Foundation (UNF), and later its operational arm, the UN Fund for International Partnerships (UNFIP).[3] This also prompted the creation of the UN Office for Partnerships to advise the UN and possible partners on the opportunities for partnerships.[4]

The next major milestone in the evolution of the UN–business relationship was the speech given by Kofi Annan to the World Economic Forum in January 1999, where the idea of a 'global compact of shared values and principles' was launched. In this speech Annan outlined nine principles, based on a series of UN conventions, that should serve as a frame of reference to stimulate best practices among transnational companies and to bring about convergence around universally shared values.[5] Due to the overwhelming response to the initiative, six months later the UN Global Compact was established directly under the Secretary-General, aimed at making businesses voluntarily adhere to the core principles (Gjølberg, 2003).[6]

Later the same year, Kofi Annan issued his report for the millennium session of the General Assembly. In the report, called '*We the Peoples': The Role of the United Nations in the 21st Century* (Annan, 2000), Annan stressed several times that the challenges faced by the UN could not be tackled without close cooperation with the private sector. In the Millennium Declaration that resulted, one of the millennium goals (goal 9) was dedicated explicitly to 'develop a global partnership for development', meaning, among other things, partnerships with the private sector.

On 17 July 2000, the Secretary-General issued the UN Guidelines for Cooperation with the Business Community.[7] This was the result not only of increasing support for the idea of PPPs, but also increasing concern about the various risks it involved for the UN. Over the course of the following five years, the General Assembly issued three resolutions concerning partnerships with the private sector. Later in 2000, the General Assembly issued a resolution in which it supported the idea of PPPs, at the same time as it requested the Secretary-General to submit a report on the views by all the member states on this matter to the 56th session of the General Assembly (A/Res/55/215, A/RES/56/76, A/RES/68/129). These resolutions express increasing support for partnerships and encouragement of their development, but also raise certain concerns regarding their compatibility with UN integrity, their management, and issues of transparency and accountability. Also, at various World Summits, a change towards a focus on partnerships was noticeable. The first important steps were taken at the UN Conference on Environment and Development (UNCED, the Earth Summit) in Rio de Janeiro in 1992, when the Conference's Secretary-General Maurice Strong invited the newly formed World Business Council for Sustainable Development (WBCSD) to write the recommendations on industry and sustainable development. According to Richter (2002), these replaced the recommendations made by the UN Centre for Transnational Corporations (UNCTC).

This trend was strengthened during a series of subsequent summits. The report from the International Conference of Financing for Development in Monterrey, Mexico, in 2002, stressed that greater cooperation between the public and the private sector was crucial for overcoming the shortcomings of development finance. Resulting from that, the UN Economic and Social Council (ECOSOC) launched the Financing for Development Initiative (FfDI) jointly with the World Economic Forum (Witte and Reinicke, 2005). Yet the great breakthrough for the idea came at the World Summit on Sustainable Development in Johannesburg, South

Africa in September 2002, which resulted in the launch of more than 200 partnerships. As argued by Zadek (2004, p. 3), 'Just as Rio was as much about legitimizing the role of NGOs in global governance as it was about the environment, Johannesburg was about the legitimacy of the role of business in development.'

However, the increasingly favourable attitude towards collaboration with the private sector was not uniform across different UN institutions. The inclination to seek partnerships with the private sector depended on organizational culture as well as on formal structure. The pioneer among the organizations was the UN International Children's Fund (UNICEF), which from an early point has sought business funding and collaboration. The International Labor Organization (ILO) was created as a tripartite organization with representatives of governments, employers and labour. This structure hindered the ILO from officially forming partnerships with individual businesses until 2008, when the governing body adopted a resolution that provided the platform for the formation of partnerships (ILO, 2008). In some cases it has been the leadership of a general director with an inclination towards collaboration with business that has contributed to a change of strategy. This was the case when Gro Harlem Brundtland became General Director of the World Health Organization (WHO) in 1999. Brundtland, who had been a key person behind the Rio Summit as the leader of the World Commission on Sustainable Development, was also a promoter of partnerships in the WHO. In other cases the shift of strategy related more to a change of the political constituency. An example of this was the UN Educational, Scientific and Cultural Organization (UNESCO), which in spite of early efforts to approach business as a partner, did not place major emphasis on this until the USA rejoined the organization in 2003 after almost 20 years of absence.

Yet, in spite of organizational differences, there is no doubt that there has been a general trend towards seeking partnerships with the private sector in the UN from the late 1990s on. By 2005, Broadwater and Kaul (2005) identified 400 partnerships between private actors and the UN organizations. However, the number is clearly much higher. As of December 2007, the UNFIP alone had partially funded 422 partnership projects (UN General Assembly, 2008), and the Commission for Sustainable Development (CSD) had alone registered 345 partnerships as of March 2009. Thus the number is significant, but what exactly do the different partnerships involve? To this we now turn.

Types of partnerships
The term partnership is used in the UN system for a variety of arrangements in which the UN and the private sector play various roles. In some

cases it is difficult to distinguish what a partnership is, and also to draw the line between a UN partnership and an independent partnership institution. For the purpose of this chapter, a UN–PPP is defined as a voluntary and collaborative relationship between the UN, private sector parties and possibly others (governments, NGOs) in which all participants agree to work together to achieve a common purpose or undertake a specific task.

There is a great variety of arrangements that fall into this category. There are many different typologies of partnerships (see, e.g., Tesner and Kell, 2000; UN General Assembly, 2003, 2005; Witte and Reinicke, 2005; Börzel and Risse, 2005). The fourfold typology summarized in Table 20.1 essentially groups partnerships based on their goals, and clarifies the roles and responsibilities for the UN and for the private sector partners.

'Resource mobilization partnerships' seek to mobilize private resources either by direct fundraising, or by promoting and facilitating foreign direct investment (FDI) flows to poorer countries. Multilateral fundraising is an activity that has been going on for many years and, as mentioned above,

Table 20.1   Types of partnership

	Goals	What does the UN contribute?	What does the private sector contribute?	Example
Resource mobilization partnerships	● Fundraising ● Public– private investment	● Expertise ● Image ● Policy networks	● Money ● In-kind donations	IKEA's donations to UNICEF UNDP's growing sustainable business initiative
Advocacy partnerships	● PR campaigns ● Advocacy	● Expertise ● Legitimacy	● Technology ● Access to media	World Heritage Maps UNICEF's early childhood development partnerships
Policy partnerships	● Change of policy ● Development of standards/ norms	● Expertise ● Policy networks	● Access to policy actors	UN partnership to fight human trafficking Global Compact
Operational partnerships	● Long-term procurement ● Product development	● Coordination of resources to create markets ● Policy networks	● Technology ● Production facilities	The Global Alliance for Vaccines and Immunization (GAVI)

UNICEF is the organization with the longest experience and most success in this area. It has a list of 193 corporate partners, each of which has contributed more than US$100 000 to UNICEF. Several of these contribute significantly more. For example, IKEA in 2009 pledged a contribution of US$48 million for UNICEF in India. And although UNICEF's international partners did not contribute more than 3.4 per cent of the international budget in 2007, if one also counts the contributions to the national UNICEF committees that make up approximately one-third of UNICEF's budget, the percentage will be much higher.[8]

The other main kind of resource mobilization partnership is partnerships intended to channel private investments to specific projects. Several multilateral organizations have positioned themselves so as to leverage FDI flows to those countries and regions where the money is needed most. This has been mainly a role for the World Bank and the regional development banks, but the UN organizations are also involved in such partnerships to some extent. The UNDP's Money Matters Institute (in partnership with private banks and financial institutions), and its Growing Sustainable Business initiative, both aim at encouraging FDI in emerging markets. Also the Public–Private Partnerships for the Urban Environment of the UNDP has that as a goal. This seeks to establish joint ventures with private companies in order to solve pressing urban infrastructure problems.

Multilateral agencies are now making a special effort to channel credit to small and medium-sized enterprises (SMEs) in developing countries, whether in response to criticism of partnerships with large TNCs (transnational corporations) or as a matter of good development policy. The UN Industrial Development Organization (UNIDO) is taking a lead role on this front, with its Business Partnership Programme that encourages the integration of SMEs into the so-called 'global value chain'.[9] Deutsche Bank's Microcredit Development Fund, in partnership with United Nations Environment Programme (UNEP), offers loans to local microfinance institutions.[10] The UN Capital Development Fund, in cooperation with the UNDP and partners such as the Ford Foundation, aims to provide micro-finance to poorer countries.[11]

However, fundraising is viewed by many as an 'old-fashioned' form of partnership. Increasingly, the multilateral organizations want not only money from the private sector, but also access to their expertise, management skills and networks. Similarly, many private companies want to participate actively in implementation, not simply donate funds. Resource mobilization is therefore increasingly combined with one or more of the types of partnerships discussed below.

The primary aim of 'advocacy partnerships' is to raise awareness concerning the global issues addressed by the UN, or to add a further issue to the global agenda. These partnerships often seek to combine the expertise of the private sector, the legitimacy of the UN, and the resources of both partners. Advocacy partnerships may take various forms. One example is the partnership between National Geographic, Hewlett Packard and UNESCO to create World Heritage Maps in order to raise awareness of the World Heritage Convention.[12] Another example is UNICEF's Advocacy partnerships for Early Childhood Development, which seeks to bring together different partners to raise awareness of the importance of investing in children's health and education.[13]

'Policy partnerships' typically establish both formal and informal dialogue and knowledge-sharing between the UN and the private sector with the aim of changing the policy of international organizations, governments or corporations. In some instances the partners can be seen as largely promoting the same agenda; in other instances the partnerships are rather attempts to reconcile differences regarding policies. One main function of such partnerships is the development of norms and standards. In these partnerships, UN bodies generally bring with them a degree of authority and expertise to policy debates while providing a 'neutral platform' for convening civil society, government officials and business. An important example of such partnerships is the already mentioned UN Global Compact, created in 1999 aimed at improving the social conduct of companies that joined, but also to make the norms and standards developed by the UN applicable in different business communities.[14] Another example is the UN partnership to end human trafficking, which promotes a change of policy towards zero tolerance of human trafficking among governments as well as a change of approach by the business community.[15]

'Operational partnerships' are often formed in order to compensate for market imperfections, information failures and political hurdles obstructing provision of essential goods and services. These partnerships are in many respects the most demanding; they often involve long-term commitment by both parties, and close collaboration. Collaboration on R&D as well as production of lines of goods in accordance with development goals would fall into this category. Some partnerships within the already mentioned Growing Sustainable Business initiative of the UNDP would fall into this category. Here the UNDP, in partnership with companies, develops products particularly suited to serve the poor. The UNDP contributes in these cases with expertise, and the translation of needs of the poor into viable business opportunities.[16]

Such product development partnerships may be established with large TNCs. An example of that would be the partnerships formed between the WHO and pharmaceutical companies, focused on the development of medicines for typical 'poverty diseases' for which there are few financial incentives. As will be discussed below, this can be both costly and risky for the companies: this is not a one-off donation or engagement in a limited project that can be relegated to the corporate social responsibility (CSR) department. It requires substantial investments, and may thus mean a change of the company's business practices. Thus such partnerships may therefore be a 'litmus test' for the power of PPPs to alter business's actions in accordance with the goals of the UN.

Product development partnerships may also be formed with small companies. An example of this is the partnership between the International Fund for Agricultural Development (IFAD) and various small producers in Uganda to develop production of palm oil identified as a viable product for Ugandan business.[17]

However, UN–PPPs not only differ regarding their goals and purpose. They also differ regarding their relationship to the UN organizations. Partnerships may be closely related to the UN and included in its organizational structure, or they may be formed as independent institutions but with UN participation. At the one end of the scale we have partnerships that form a part of UN organizations, as for example the multifaceted partnership between IKEA and UNICEF that has lasted since 2001 and that spans most of the categories of partnerships listed above. In the middle there are organizations like the Global Fund to Fight Aids, Tuberculosis and Malaria, which is a partnership organization created on the initiative of UN representatives and working in close collaboration with the UN, but as an independent institution. At the other extreme we find partnerships in which UN leaders have been instrumental in the process of establishment, but where the UN plays no major role in the continuation. The Alliance for a Green Revolution in Africa (AGRA) is one such case; it was initiated by then Secretary-General of the UN, Kofi Annan, in 2004, but lives on as an organization aiming to forge partnerships to ensure increased food production in Africa, supported by private foundations but independent of the UN.

One may also distinguish between direct partnerships and what may be called meta-partnerships. The different UN organizations have entered into various large alliances with foundations, companies, NGOs and donor governments that are set up partly to foster further partnerships. AGRA, mentioned above, and the UNF are examples of that. The UNF has been an important mover behind the formation of further partnerships. It boasts a list of some 123 partnerships, with a great variety of partners ranging from other UN organizations and large foundations to small companies. Thus some of the most significant movers of partnerships are in themselves partnerships.

The impact of PPPs on the UN system

Partnerships with the UN have been immersed in a discourse of superlatives about best practices, synergy effects and win–win situations. Indeed, many of the definitions used to describe the phenomenon are characterized by being 'up-beat' and normatively loaded, as for example the following definition of PPPs as 'a mutually beneficial agreement between one or more UN bodies and one or more corporate partners to work towards common objectives based on the comparative advantage of each, with a clear understanding of respective responsibilities and the expectation of due credit for every contribution' (Tesner and Kell, 2000, p. 72).

But what have really been the consequences of the PPPs for the UN organizations? What are the roles and responsibilities of the private companies and foundations in the PPPs? There are many ways to approach this question. The first is to look at burden-sharing in terms of costs. To what extent has the private sector alleviated the financial constraints faced by the UN? There exist no global numbers, but examples from individual UN organizations show that with the mentioned exception of UNICEF, the private sector in total contributes less than 1 per cent of the budget of UN organizations.

However, in order to evaluate this matter, it is important to distinguish between the private sector as individual companies and the private sector as private foundations. As opposed to what is the case in, for example, infrastructure partnerships with individual governments, private companies have generally been insignificant financial contributors to the UN–PPPs. There are some exceptions. For example, the Global Fund has received US$127 million from (Product) RED, which is a group of companies whose products take on the Product (RED) mark and donate a share of their profits to Global Fund-financed programmes in Africa. It has also received a donation of US$30 million from one single company – Chevron Corporation. However, by 2008, private companies had contributed only 1.16 per cent of the total funds to the Global Fund.[18] The Global Alliance for Vaccines and Immunization (GAVI) gets the lion's share of its funding from donor governments and the Bill and Melinda Gates Foundations. A category of 'other private donors' has contributed 0.43 per cent to the total budget, and in this category there may be companies, although there may also be other private foundations.[19] Regarding the more than 300 so-called Type II multiple stakeholder partnerships that have registered under the UN Commission for Sustainable Development (UNCSD), business is in fact a part in less than 20 per cent of total partnerships, and business contributions account for less than 1 per cent of total funding (Hale and Mauzerall, 2004). Thus, although no overall numbers exist, one may conclude that private companies do not constitute a substantial source of funding for the UN or for UN–PPPs.

Looking at private foundation funding, the picture changes in some cases. Several partnerships are based on large-scale foundation donations. One example is the GAVI that was created with a US$750 million donation from the Bill and Melinda Gates Foundation in 2000 and that has contributed US$1.51 billion directly to GAVI over 15 years, in addition to US$50 million to financial mechanisms administered by it. It is thereby the largest single donor to GAVI, and accounts for about 28 per cent of its total funding. The Global Fund has also received significant donations (US$450 000 so far) from the Bill and Melinda Gates Foundation, but the total funding from the private sector is in fact not more than 5.4 per cent of the total.

Governments are thus still the major funder of the UN and of individual PPPs. It is difficult to arrive at an overall figure of how much of the UN's money is set off for PPPs. The WHO's biannual budget of US$4227 million for 2008–09 does include US$695 million dollars set off for partnerships. This amounts to approximately 16 per cent of the budget. Yet, whether these are additional funds received from different partners or what the WHO sets aside from regular funds for this purpose is unclear.

However, money is not all that the private sector contributes. A main aim of partnerships is to make business and the UN pull in the same direction: to encourage them to work towards similar goals. If, for example, a chocolate company, as a result of being part of a UN-initiated partnership, improves its production chain management so as to ensure that no child labour is used at the cocoa plants and that the adult workers get improved conditions and are able to send their children to school, the partnership has contributed to reaching a goal of the UN system, but it would of course not show up in any budget. Similarly, if a pharmaceutical company improves the cold-chain management technology and thus allows for vaccines to reach children in remote tropical areas, they do contribute to a key health goal, but it would – again – not show up in any budget.

However, in many cases it is also difficult to distinguish between cases where business really contributes to the goals of the UN and where it simply seizes new business opportunities. The fact that many initiatives involve significant public funding and funding from private foundations does of course also mean that there are contracts to compete for on regular business terms and that collaborating with the UN does not necessarily mean that business takes on responsibilities that move beyond what it regularly takes on in doing business.

In order to evaluate this question, one has to examine in some detail the single partnership. One interesting case is GAVI, mentioned above, which is a multi-purpose partnership including aspects of resource mobilization, advocacy, policy work and product development. Private companies do not contribute much in terms of financing, but they are present at the board and are key partners in the work to ensure supply of vaccines as well as development of new and improved vaccines suited to developing-country needs. The main goal of GAVI is to increase the vaccination level of a handful of new vaccines in developing countries. It does so mainly by reimbursing governments for each individual child vaccinated, but also by providing some support for necessary vaccine infrastructure. However, in addition, GAVI was created with the mandate of contributing to the development of new and improved vaccines better suited to the needs for developing countries. This is clearly a more demanding task than collaborating on supply for pharmaceutical companies. While collaboration on procurement is basically a convenient way of getting an overview on future markets, development of new or improved vaccines demands significant investments. GAVI has attempted to implement various mechanisms in order to give companies incentives to invest, but with limited success (Chee et al., 2008). The most recent of these, the Advance Market Commitment (AMC), was created in 2007 and is administered by GAVI. Under the AMC, companies that are interested may enter into a contract with the AMC board and when the vaccine is ready for the market it will be guaranteed a subsidy that makes up for the low purchasing power in the intended markets. The first pilot AMC is for a pneumococcal vaccine for which a subsidy of US$3 billion is promised. However, the pilot is for the improvement of an existing vaccine on which the two companies that got the contract (Wyeth and GlaxoSmithKline) already make good money, and the companies therefore take on a very moderate risk. GAVI has also put an extraordinarily generous price on the vaccine. Whereas internationally renowned experts have estimated the price to be between US$1 and US$2, GAVI pays the companies US$5. Thus, according to the critics, the pilot is not really an AMC but rather a huge subsidy of 'big pharma' (Light, 2007; Farlow et al., 2005).

The UN organizations are of course acutely aware that they do not always have the same goals as private companies, and that in order to evaluate the benefits of PPPs it is necessary to conduct a detailed analysis of goals and goal compatibility. This is a part of the most recent tool for assessing sustainability and impact of PPPs developed by the UNDP, the Global Compact, the UNITAR (UN Institute for Training and Research) and the United Nations Office for Partnerships. This will enable UN officials to evaluate up front the potential benefits and risks of entering into PPPs with different companies (UN Global Compact, 2007).

At the more fundamental level, the rise of PPPs in the UN system raises questions about the direction in which it will move the entire multilateral apparatus. The private sector turn of the UN organizations is not limited to the formation of PPPs. The search for PPPs is a part of a change in the UN system that also has included an adaptation of the structure and culture of the organizations to the private sector mode of operation. Moreover, the attention dedicated to the search for partnerships has shifted the emphasis both between sectors and between departments, and in some cases gave new direction to strategies. An example of that is the impact of the partnership formed between UNESCO and Microsoft in 2004 (UNESCO, 2005), which not only meant a shift from its long-standing strategy to support free and open source software (FOSS), but also made ICT a privileged item on the educational agenda in spite of its relatively modest part in UNESCO's own strategic plan for the period (UNESCO, 2002; Bull and McNeill, 2007, ch. 6). There are several other examples of PPPs moving the UN system towards the private sector agenda while also preventing the UN from challenging the very principles of the market-oriented global economic system. Thus we have previously used the label 'market multilateralism' to describe a system that is distinguished by the involvement of public as well as private actors, processes of rapprochement between different actors, but also the adherence to basic market principles (Bull and McNeill, 2007; Bull, 2010).

The future of partnerships
It was argued in the introduction that the emphasis on partnerships was partly the result of a changing global political–economic context that disfavoured direct governmental control of TNCs and favoured the increased role of private investors and donors. From the last half of the first decade of the new millennium this context started to change. The question is how this will influence the desire and feasibility of future UN–PPPs. This will depend, first, on the future availability of funding for this kind of activity and, second, on possible shifts in the ideas about the roles of the state and the private sector in development.

There are several factors of importance here, and they point, to some extent, in different directions. General PPPs between governments and companies are likely to be struck hard by the financial constraints experienced by private companies. However, since, as shown above, private company funding is not very significant in UN–PPPs, this is likely to have less effect on the PPPs discussed in this chapter. What will be more significant for the future of the UN–PPPs is the related financial constraints experienced by private foundations. The US Foundation Center reported in the beginning of 2009 that international spending by US foundations was up from US$5 billion in 2007 to US$5.4 billion in 2008 (Foundation

Center, 2009a). However, at the end of the year the same centre reported that 2009 had seen a 10 per cent decline in foundation giving and that the trend was likely to continue (Foundation Center, 2009b). About half of the increase taking place in US foundation giving since 2000 is due mainly to one single foundation: the Bill and Melinda Gates Foundation. This foundation continued to increase its spending in 2008 in spite of the fact that its endowment was down about 20 per cent that year. But it signalled that it would not be able to continue to increase its spending. Other foundation endowments are down even more. Thus there is little doubt that foundation spending will be less generous in the future. European foundations have so far been less significant sources of funding for the UN than the US foundations. However, they are also significant potential contributors (EFC, 2005). A survey conducted by the European Foundation Centre in 2008 about the impact of the financial crisis on their giving showed similar patterns as in the USA. A majority of the foundations answered that they would still be able to meet all grant-making programme commitments in 2009, but two-thirds said they were considering significant changes in their investment strategy and asset allocation in the future (EFC, 2009).

There are also changes at the ideological level that may affect the drive towards UN–PPPs. Arguably, the policies that have been launched to confront the global financial crisis imply recognition of the regulatory role of the state and reduced belief in the market and the private sector's ability to provide the solutions by itself. On the other hand, the public reaction to the financial crisis involves several new PPPs. Thus the current shifts do not necessarily mean that there will be a move away from PPPs. Perhaps the most likely outcome is a continuation of the formation of PPPs but a shift in emphasis and ideology away from one that has attempted to mimic the private sector way of operating, and idealize markets and the benefits emerging from relying on them, towards a more realistic view of distribution of roles and responsibilities.

Conclusion

The formation of PPPs became an important mode of operation in the UN system from the 1990s on. This signified not only a new way of organizing projects but indeed a new approach to the private sector in the UN system, although several individual organizations also had close relations with business before this general drive.

Although the financial motives of the UN are most often quoted as a driving force behind this strategy, the financial contributions of business to the partnerships have indeed been miniscule. Private foundations have had a somewhat more important role as donors but, including their contributions, the public sector remains the overwhelmingly most important donor to the UN system.

However, that does not mean that the UN–PPPs have been of no significance. This chapter has outlined the different roles and responsibilities the private sector has taken on in partnership with the UN. These range from being policy advocates to providers of technical know-how. However, in general, the PPPs have operated within a global liberal order and they have not attempted to challenge the fundamental principles of that order or the companies' prime concern, which is to make profit. Thus the kind of multilateralism that has emerged from the UN–PPPs may be characterized as a 'market multilateralism'.

What then may happen when the basic principles of the system are in the process of change, which is what may be the outcome of the financial crisis of 2008–09? This chapter has argued that whereas the financial constraints experienced particularly by foundations may be of high significance, PPPs have gained such an important position within the UN that they are likely to continue, but in a different form, which places more emphasis on the role of the states and of international organizations in which they are members. What we may see is thus a continuation of PPPs with the UN but a normalization that means that they will be shielded from the highly vocal criticism that they have so far been subject to, but also will face the same kind of financial, organizational and political constraints that most UN operations must deal with (Bull and McNeill, 2010).

Notes

1. See Bull and McNeill (2007, ch. 3) for an elaboration of the financial background for the rise of PPPs in the multilateral system.
2. It was not officially closed down, but transferred to UNCTAD.
3. UNFIP funds partnerships and projects implemented by UN organizations. By 2005, it had supported 324 projects in four priority areas: women and population; environment; children's health; and peace security and human rights. It has also funded several partnerships, among them the Global Reporting Initiative, which is a tool for encouraging businesses to publish reports on their environmental and social impact.
4. For more information, see www.un.org/partnerships/.
5. Later a tenth principle on corruption was added.
6. The Global Compact was initially run by a small secretariat depending for its existence on support from governments and non-profit organizations. The loose governance structure was intended to maintain its flexibility and independence from the UN system and businesses. In September 2005, a new governance structure was adopted that added a triannual Leaders' Summit, a Board, Local Networks, and annual Local Networks Forum, but the emphasis is still on a non-bureaucratic and network-based organizational structure.
7. For more information, see www.un.org/partners/business/otherpages/guide.htm.
8. For more information, see www.unicef.org.
9. For more information, see www.unido.org/doc/4364.
10. For more information, see www.cib.db.com/community/htm/db_microcredit_dev_fund.html.

11. For more information, see www.uncdf.org/english/.
12. For more information, see whc.unesco.org/en/events/302.
13. For more information, see www.unicef.org/earlychildhood/index_40753.html.
14. For more information, see www.unglobalcompact.org/.
15. For more information, see www.ungift.org/ungift/en/about/index.html.
16. For more information, see www.undp.org/partners/business/gsb/.
17. For more information, see www.ruralpovertyportal.org/web/guest/country/voice/tags/uganda/oil.
18. For more information, see www.theglobalfund.org/en/mobilization/?lang=en.
19. For more information, see www.gavialliance.org/support/donors/index.php.

References

Annan, K. (2000), *'We the Peoples': The Role of the United Nations in the 21st Century*, New York: United Nations.

Börzel, Tanja and Thomas Risse (2005), 'Public–private partnerships: effective and legitimate tools of transnational governance?', in E. Grande and L.W. Pauly (eds), *Complex Sovereignty: Reconstituting Political Authority in the Twenty-first Century*, Toronto: University of Toronto Press, pp. 195–216.

Broadwater, Ian and Inge Kaul (2005), 'Global public–private partnerships: the current landscape', available at: www.thenewpublicfinance.org/background/current_landscape. pdf (accessed 25 March 2009).

Bull, Benedicte (2010), 'Rethinking multilateralism: global governance and public–private partnerships with the UN', in Morten Ougaard and Anna Leander (eds), *Business and Global Governance,* Warwick studies in Globalisation, London and New York: Routledge, pp. 179–99.

Bull, Benedicte and Desmond McNeill (2007), *Development Issues in Global Governance: Public–Private Partnerships and Market Multilateralism*, London and New York: Routledge.

Bull, Benedicte and Desmond McNeill (2010), 'From business unusual to business as usual: the future legitimacy of public–private partnerships with multilateral organizations', in Magdalena Bexell and Ulrika Mörth (eds), *Democracy and Public–Private Partnerships in Global Governance*, Basingstoke: Palgrave Macmillan, pp. 103–21.

Chee, Grace, Vivikka Molldrem, Natasha His and Slavea Chankova (2008), 'Evaluation of the GAVI Phase 1 Performance (2000–2005)', prepared for the GAVI alliance, Cambridge, MA, Lexington, MA and Hadley, MA, Bethesda, MD, Chicago, IL: Abt. Associates Inc.

Cox, Robert.W. (1983), 'Gramsci, hegemony, and international relations: an essay in method', reprinted in R.W Cox and T.J. Sinclair (eds), *Approaches to World Order*, Cambridge: Cambridge University, 1996, pp. 124–43.

Cox, Robert W. (1987), *Production, Power and World Order. Social Forces in the Making of History*, New York: Columbia University Press.

Cox, R. (1992), 'Multilateralism and world order', reprinted in R.W. Cox with T.J. Sinclair (1996), *Approaches to World Order*, Cambridge: Cambridge University Press.

EFC (2005), 'Foundation facts and figures', Brussels: The European Foundation Centre, available at: www.efc.be/projects/eu/research/FactsFigs.htm (accessed 25 March 2009).

EFC (2009), 'EFC survey: how are members responding to the economic downturn?', available at www.efc.be/projects/crisis/default.htm (accessed 25 March 2009).

Farlow, Andrew, Donald Light, Richard Mahoney and Roy Widdus (2005), 'Concerns regarding the Center for Global Development Report "Making Markets for Vaccines"', Submission to Commission on Intellectual Property Rights, Innovation and Public Health, WHO, 29 April.

Foundation Center (2009a), 'International grantmaking IV: an update on U.S. Foundation trends', available at: foundationcenter.org/gainknowledge/research/internationaltrends. html (accessed 25 March 2009).

Foundation Center (2009b), 'Foundation's year-end outlook for giving and the sector', available at: foundationcenter.org/gainknowledge/research/pdf/researchadvisory_econo my_200911.pdf;jsessionid=DPNHBMZV55ONFLAQBQ4CGW15AAAACI2F (accessed 30 November 2009).

Gjølberg, M. (2003), 'The United Nations Global Compact: i hvilken grad bidrar Global Compact, via næringslivet, til FNs mål om bærekraftig utvikling?', Prosus Rapport 6/03, Oslo: Prosus/Senter for Utvikling og Miljø.

Hale, T. and D.L. Mauzerall (2004), 'Thinking globally, acting locally: can the Johannesburg Partnerships coordinate action on sustainable development', *Journal of Environment and Development*, **13** (3), 20–39.

Harrod, J. (2006), 'The Century of the Corporation', in C. May (ed.), *Global Corporate Power*, International Political Economy Yearbook, Vol. 15, Boulder, CO and London: Lynne Rienner Publishers, pp. 23–46.

Hummel, H. (2005), 'The United Nations and transnational corporations', paper for the conference 'Global Governance and the Power of Business', 8–10 December 2005, Wittenberg, Germany.

ILO (2008), 'Public–private partnerships', GB 301/TC/1.

Light, Donald (2007), 'Is G8 putting profits before the world's poorest children?', *The Lancet*, **370**, 297–8.

Martens, Jens (2007), 'Multistakeholder Partnerships – future models of multilateralism? Dialogue on globalization', Occasional Papers, No. 29/ January, Berlin: Friedrich Ebert Stiftung.

Richter, Judith (2002), 'Codes in context: TNC regulation in an era of dialogues and partnerships', *The Corner House Briefing* 26, available at: cornerhouse.icaap.org.

Ruggie, John G. (1982), 'International regime, transactions, and change: embedded liberalism in the postwar economic order', *International Organization*, **36**, 379–415.

Ruggie, John G. (1997), 'Globalization and the embedded liberalism compromise: the end of an era?', Max Planck Institute for the Study of Societies, Working Paper 97/1, January, available at: www.mpi-fg-koeln.mpg.de/pu/workpap/wp97-1/wp97-1.html (accessed 25 March 2009).

Ruggie, John G. (2004), 'Reconstituting the global public domain – issues, actors, and practices', *European Journal of International Relations*, **10** (4), 499–531.

Tesner, S. and G. Kell (2000), *The United Nations and Business: A Partnership Recovered*, New York: St Martin's Press.

UN General Assembly (2003), 'Enhanced cooperation between the United Nations and all relevant partners, in particular the private sector', Report of the Secretary-General, A/58/227, United Nations General Assembly.

UN General Assembly (2005), 'Enhanced cooperation between the United Nations and all relevant partners, in particular the private sector', Report of the Secretary-General, A/60/214, United Nations General Assembly.

UN General Assembly (2008), 'United Nations Office for Partnerships', Report of the Secretary General. A/63/2/57, United Nations General Assembly.

UN Global Compact (2007), 'Enhancing partnership value: a tool for assessing sustainability and impact', UN Global Compact, United Nations Office for Partnerships, UNITAR, UNDP, available at: www.globalcompactsummit.org/docs/UNGC07-EnhancingPartnershipValue.pdf (accessed 24 March 2009).

UNESCO (2002), 'Medium-term strategy 2002–2007', 31C/4, UNESCO.

UNESCO (2005), 'UNESCO's position on free and open source software (FOSS)', Briefing Notes & Frequently Asked Questions, The CI Sector, UNESCO, April.

Witte, J.M. and W. Reinicke (2005), 'Business unusual: facilitating United Nations report through partnerships', report commissioned by the United Nations.

Zadek, S. (2004), 'Civil partnerships, governance and the United Nations', background paper for the Secretary General's Panel of Eminent Persons on Civil Society and UN Relationships, available at: www.un.org/partners/business/otherpages/guide.htm.

Zammit, A. (2003), *Development at Risk: Rethinking UN–Business Partnerships*, Geneva: South Centre and UNRISD.

PART IV

CRUCIAL ISSUES FOR THE FUTURE

21 The global public–private partnership industry
Carsten Greve

Introduction

How does the corporate world influence the development of public–private partnerships (PPPs)? The advent of PPPs has been accompanied by a flock of corporate organizations that play a role in assisting PPP deals to be formulated, entered and implemented. The corporate organizations include banks, consultancy companies, construction/infrastructure companies and law firms. The literature on PPPs is full of evidence about how governments act to promote PPPs, but little is actually known about the role of corporate organizations in the development of PPPs. Hodge and Bowman (2006) made a contribution a few years ago when they discussed the emerging 'consultocracy' that was related to the rise of the privatization policy development. For Hodge and Bowman, the consultocracy meant that 'the business of reforming government itself needs to be recognized by governments worldwide as having produced a new, powerful professional interest group' (ibid., p. 121). Because the literature is relatively sparse on the influence of private sector companies on global PPP policy development, this chapter takes a first look at the way corporate organizations have been related to the PPP movement. The aim of the chapter is to present an explorative perspective on the role of the 'PPP industry' and to point to questions for further research. The most appropriate point of departure of this chapter is deemed to be a political-economy perspective that examines the relationship between business and politics, often in a historical context.

The main argument of the chapter is that there are signs of an emergent 'PPP industry', and that this PPP industry is closely tied to countries that have gained previous experience with the privatization of public enterprises and therefore were ready to make PPPs the next obvious move. The consequence of this development is that such a PPP industry is likely to flourish in those countries that pursue PPP policy. The remaining question that the chapter will pose, but is not able to answer, is 'what is really the relationship between business and government empirically in relation to PPP policy?' Is it true that the industry has only been serving the political masters in government in assisting with formulating and implementing

PPP policy, or could it be that the industry itself has been a driver behind the reforms, influencing governments and, later on, international organizations to adopt PPP policies?

The chapter is structured as follows. The next section briefly elaborates the theoretical concept of path dependency. The third section focuses on painting a picture of the emerging PPP industry and explores the link with the privatization experience from previous decades. The fourth section discusses the findings and examines the relationship between the PPP industry and government, and the policy paths chosen. The fifth and final section summarizes the main points in a conclusion.

Theoretical perspective on path dependency

Because little work has been done in the area of the PPP industry, one way to start the investigation could be to examine another and more recent part of 'the privatization family' (Hodge, 2006), the privatization of public enterprises that began in the 1980s and continued over the following decades (Parker, 2006). Privatization as a term is normally attributed to Drucker in the late 1960s, and the early advocacy work done by commentators such as Savas (see Savas, 2000 for a condensation of his approach) in the 1970s, who looked at privatization from a more ideological perspective. Privatization as a policy practice is usually associated with the coming of the Thatcher government in the UK. The story of the UK privatization programme has been highlighted in many research publications, and a recent authoritative account can be found in Parker (2009). Other countries, such as Australia and New Zealand, followed suit and have also practised privatization policies in recent decades. The worldwide interest in privatization practices has been well documented in the literature (Hodge, 2000). Like the new public management (NPM) reforms more generally, there seem to be a number of core countries that have gone furthest with privatization and NPM as policies for shaping the relationship between the public sector and the private sector. Barzelay (2001) identified a core number of 'NPM benchmark countries' in his work on a comparative perspective on public management reform developments.

The way that countries follow certain policy paths and not others has been addressed in that part of the literature on political economy dealing with institutional change and development (see Streeck and Thelen, 2005 for an overview). This literature argues that once a specific policy course of action is chosen, institutions will be directed towards that 'path' and other alternatives will be excluded or not prioritized in the same way as the preferred policy. Using inspiration from economics, Pierson (2004) has talked about the 'increasing returns' that come from adopting a specific policy path. A contemporary example from consumer behaviour would be an iPod on which to store and share music and videos. Since more and more people began using an iPod, the device quickly became the preferred brand for mp3 players, leaving others behind. More and more services and advantages came with more people using the same kind of mp3 player. So even if there were to be a superior mp3 player later on in terms of technological specificities, it would have a hard time being chosen by the buying public because they had already invested time, money and prestige in the iPod model. This chapter will use the historical institutional perspective of 'path dependency' (Pierson, 2004) to explore how the PPP industry may have emerged in certain countries that were presented as 'advanced PPP countries'.

Historical institutional theory is concerned with understanding historical political processes, and how institutional change and stability occur (Steinmo et al., 1992). One of the key concepts has been 'path dependency', which can be explained as follows: once a course is set, development will take place along a designated path for a considerable period of time. Direction changes take place during critical junctures, which then sets off another path. Historical institutionalists begin with the premise that change takes place in 'crucial founding moments of institutional formation that send countries along broadly different developmental paths' (Thelen, 1999, p. 387). Orren and Skowronek (1994, p. 312, quoted in Thelen, 1999) observe how historical institutionalism 'brings questions of timing and temporality in politics to the center of the analysis of how institutions matter'. Institutions evolve and respond to activities in their environment, but they are formed in this development by trajectories from the earlier activities. Pierson (2004, p. 21) refers to path dependency as 'social processes that exhibit positive feedback and thus generate branching patterns of historical development'. According to Levi (1997, quoted in Pierson, 2004, p. 20), path dependency means 'that once a country or region has started down a track, the costs of reversals are very high. There will be other choice points, but the entrenchment of certain institutional arrangements obstructs an early reversal of the initial choice'. Levi prefers a 'branch' metaphor instead of the path or the track (which explains Pierson's use of the word 'branching' in the quote from p. 21 above). An important part of the argument concerns sequencing. The order in which changes occur can be crucial. The aim is to be able to point to 'under what circumstances are occurrences like X more or less likely' (Pierson, 2004, p. 58). Pierson continues: 'Given a particular set of institutional rules, steps in a sequence of choices become *irreversible*. The rules dictate that alternatives rejected in early rounds are dropped from the range of possible later options . . .' (ibid., p. 64). In later passages in the book, Pierson is, interestingly, less categorical about change. He states:

Over time, 'roads not chosen' may become increasingly distant, increasingly unreachable alternatives. Relatively modest perturbations of early stages may have large influences on these processes. In many cases, the significance of early events or processes in the sequence may be amplified, while that of later events or processes is dampened. Thus, *when* a particular event or process occurs in a sequence will make a big difference. (ibid., p. 64)

And later again: 'The sequence in which alternatives present themselves may be crucial to the eventual outcome, but that outcome may be far different from the initial result or trajectory that emerges at a critical juncture' (ibid., p. 69). For the purposes of this chapter, the concept of path dependency can help us when discussing the different paths that countries have taken towards PPP policy experience, and how that path may have connections to the development of a PPP industry.

A PPP industry?
Is there a PPP industry? Hodge and Bowman (2006) talked about a 'consultocracy' surrounding privatization policy practices in recent decades. They discussed and documented how privatization has spawned groups of consultants that worked for the privatization option. In one sentence characterizing their perspective, Hodge and Bowman (ibid., p. 97) stressed how '[t]he business sector is now a trusted adviser, an essential human resource and even a strong reform ally in governing today'.

In this chapter a different term – 'the PPP industry' – is used to discuss much the same issues, just with a focus on PPP policy development. The term 'consultocracy' depicts a situation where consultants rule. It is perhaps still too early in the literature on PPPs to determine the absolute influence of consultants, and they are also seen in this chapter as a part of an attempt to build a wider PPP industry.

If there is a distinct PPP industry, then which actors are engaged in it? At least four main categories of corporate actors appear to be involved. A first task is to find out what tasks are carried out by the industry. Their main tasks can be characterized the following way (the list is not complete):

1. Advising on defining project need and viability
2. Advising key parties to the contract
3. Formulating contracts
4. Providing and managing finances
5. Market analysis
6. Implementing (constructing and delivering) PPP projects
7. Monitoring compliance activities

A list of the main types of actors engaged in these activities would include consultancy companies, banks, construction/infrastructure companies and legal firms.

What does the industry look like? There is no overall database to draw data from regarding the PPP industry. We shall therefore have to make do with more piecemeal indicators. A report issued by a UK organization, Partnerships UK (2007), provides information on the UK market. The most important consultancy companies in that report were PwC, Deloitte, Grant Thornton, KPMG and Ernst & Young. The biggest contractors for designing and building infrastructure projects in the UK were Skanska, Balfour Beatty, Mitie, AMEC and Interserve. The Swedish-based, but globally operating, company Skanska was among the leading PPP providers in the UK around 2005. Skanska had a portfolio of over £3 billion in the areas of healthcare, custodial, education, transportation and defence services. Skanska had developed 'in house teams responsible for the development of design, construction, operation and hard facilities services' (Skanska, 2008). Among the many projects Skanska had conducted was, for example, a secondary-school project in the London borough of Bexley. Skanska designed, constructed and financed two major secondary schools for the borough in a deal worth £36 million. One of the new schools could hold 2100 pupils and included the development of new sports facilities and a new centre for computing and information technology. In Derby, Skanska remodelled and developed the existing Derby City General Hospital for the Southern Derbyshire Acute Hospitals NHS Trust (Skanska, 2008). Serco is another example of an influential company in the UK market. Serco describe how they 'design, deliver and manage change in markets as diverse as defence, transport, civil government, science and the private sector' and how the diverse portfolio 'exposes us to more opportunities for growth, protects us against downturns in individual markets and enables us to share experience and best practice between sectors' (Serco, 2010). According the UK-based PPP Forum (www.pppforum.com), it counted among its membership 28 corporate members, 28 financial institutions and 35 professional organizations. The corporate organizations included the following: Balfour Beatty Capital, Interserve, ISS Mediclean, Serco, Siemens, Skanska, United Medical and the Wates Group. The banks included organizations such as AIB, Bank of Ireland, HSBC Specialists, Lloyds TSB, Macquarie, Nationwide, Nord LB, Royal Bank of Scotland and UBS Investment Bank. The consultancy companies included organizations such as Deloitte, Ernest & Young, Grant Thornton, McGrigors, Norton Rose and PwC.

Looking at PPPs on a more global scale, several characteristics can be seen (Deloitte, 2006). Globally, there are different needs that a market for

PPPs can address. These needs are often referred to as an 'infrastructure investment gap'. In Canada, for example, there was a need for US$66 billion to be invested in urban roads and bridges over a ten-year period; in Europe, the energy sector requires US$1.2 trillion during the next 20 years; in Australia, the infrastructure deficit was estimated to be US$19 billion; in the USA the investment need for infrastructure was believed to be US$1.6 trillion over five years (corresponding to Italy's GDP); and in East Asia the need for infrastructure investment was thought to be US$165 billion per year (Deloitte, 2006, p. 3, Figure 1). Deloitte distinguished between three types of 'market maturity' in its report. The dimensions were the sophistication of the market and the activity of the market. The most mature markets were characterized by the following factors:

> refine new innovative models; more creative, flexible approaches applied to role of public and private sector; use of more sophisticated risk models; greater focus on total lifecycle of project; sophisticated infrastructure market with pension funds and private equity funds; public sector learns from private partner methods as competition changes the way government operations function; underutilized assets leveraged into financial assets; organizational & skill set changes in government implemented to support greater role of PPPs. (ibid., p. 6)

Countries characterized as being at 'stage three', the highest form, were only the UK and Australia (with Ireland waiting to join them), while the middle group included countries such as the Netherlands, Spain, France, Italy, Canada, Germany and the USA. Countries still at stage one included Belgium, South Africa, Denmark, Poland, Russia and India (ibid., p. 6, Figure 2). For a PPP market to function, 'there should be an appropriate number of projects coming into the market at the right pace to ensure that constructors and facility management firms have the capacity and financial ability to keep pace with the potential projects' (ibid., p. 12). One of the key challenges for countries that embark on a PPP policy course is that there is not usually a sufficient number of projects to sustain a healthy market. The following areas were all reported by Deloitte as being active markets: transport, water/wastewater and waste, education, housing and urban regeneration, hospitals, defence, prisons (ibid., p. 20). Take the transport sector as a case in point. Despite our desire for 'healthy and competitive markets', it is usually the case that 'only a small group of companies may have the financial capability to deliver cost-effective PPP projects. The range of complex financial arrangements required for transport PPPs and the relative lack of expertise in such matters also narrow the scope of potential partners' (ibid., p. 21). In the UK, the organization Partnerships UK (www.partnershipsuk.org.uk) listed the following areas as 'business sectors' in relation to PPPs: commercialization, defence, education, environment and waste, health, housing, information technology and change, international, justice and custodial, local authorities, operational task force, property and regeneration, standardization and market support, transport and ventures.

Bovaird (2006, p. 85) has pointed to the fact that PPP procurement is different from contracting out. The policy of the Private Finance Initiative (PFI) leads to bigger players becoming relevant in the marketplace. Other researchers may see the development differently and claim that it does not matter whether the phenomenon is contracting out or PPPs; the issue is still going to be about the influence exercised by market players over government organizations and ultimately over the public at large.

Discussion: the PPP industry and path dependency
This section focuses on the relationship between the experiences of different countries with PPPs and the emerging PPP industry. It will also follow the line of reasoning drawn from the path-dependency literature. Using this philosophy, certain countries have had experience with market-based governance for a relatively long period of time, and in the case of privatization reforms, at least since the 1980s. These countries include the benchmark NPM countries that Barzelay (2001) identified. The countries include the UK and Australia. New Zealand was strongly linked with NPM and privatization, but PPPs did not catch on in the same way in New Zealand as might have been expected. There is no obvious reason why New Zealand chose not to continue with the privatization policy except for the country's recent reconsideration of its radical NPM reforms in the 1980s and 1990s. But in both the UK and Australia, the interest in PPPs became quite evident in the 1990s, as documented elsewhere in this handbook. The UK is internationally recognized as being the leader of a certain infrastructure type of PPP through the PFI scheme. By 2010, there had been some 693 PPP projects signed in the UK since 1992, amounting to £63 billion according to the website 'PPP Forum' (www.pppforum. com), which documents UK developments. Over 540 of these PPP projects were operational. Australia – as has been well documented by Hodge and others – took its cue from the UK and pursued a policy of PPPs from the late 1990s. In both of these countries, an industry related to PPPs has sprung up. These companies include banks (Macquarie Bank and Royal Bank of Scotland, for example) and some of the other companies related to the UK experience mentioned above. The big consultancy firms have also been key players in supporting PPP as a policy idea and later supporting it by advising governments on PPPs and helping in the implementation of PPPs. Internationally we have seen that other countries look to the

UK and Australia and other leading PPP countries for advice on how to proceed: they look to the government, but also to the companies that have expertise with PPPs.

Internationally, we also see the extensive use of the global consultancy companies. Deloitte, KPMG and others do worldwide reviews of policies, legal frameworks and practices with PPPs that rival anything that any government has so far been able to come up with. Hodge and Bowman (2006, pp. 100–101) noted the highly visible role of 'the big four' consultant companies: Deloitte, Ernst & Young, KPMG and PwC. Their size, too, has also been noted earlier in this handbook: almost half a million employees spread across more than 140 countries, with revenues in 2009/10 estimated at around US$192 billion (Chapter 5). As seen earlier, these companies were also in the top consultancy companies advising on PPP projects in the UK in the mid-2000s. Many of these firms have their origin in UK accountancy firms, but are under US ownership today (Hodge and Bowman, 2006, p. 101). For sheer expertise on the development of the legal frameworks concerning PPPs and the actual practice on the ground in leading countries, the global consultancy firms, given their superior knowledge of how PPPs are progressing, have few rivals.

What is the implication of this development for the future of PPPs? A correlation between the growth of a PPP industry and the PPP projects in progress in a country means that some countries are more likely to continue with PPP and other market-based governance mechanisms than countries with little PPP experience, with few companies interested in the subject and with lack of experience of how to structure and procure a PPP project. It means that we should expect to see the so-called 'leading' countries continue with PPPs or indeed other types of market-based governance mechanisms for delivering public infrastructure projects (all other things being equal), and that other countries – with less experience – will be unlikely to follow suit. In a path-dependency framework, the notion that all countries will at some point adopt a PPP policy for their infrastructure projects is not realistic. In the terms used by Deloitte, many countries in the current 'stage one' of developing PPPs are unlikely to progress to 'stage two', and even less likely ever to reach a 'stage three' where both the market for PPPs is 'highly sophisticated' and the activities with PPP projects are at the 'high' end of the scale. We should also expect a division between countries, with some countries reporting high activity, but perhaps a majority of countries reporting very little activity at all.

This is a challenging conclusion. What does it mean for the PPP industry? The PPP industry can be expected to grow further if more PPP projects are supported by governments in the leading countries. It could even be envisaged that some companies – or sub-industries – will try to join forces in new types of company. After all, many of the PPP contracts expect consortia or alliances to form a group that can then bid for a PPP contract. Maybe some of the companies will find it worthwhile to pursue further cooperation if they have been cooperating on a number of PPP projects. Clearly, there is a need for empirical data on how companies act together in the different consortia and their membership of different alliances. In the privatization era, it was not uncommon to see the same banks or financial advisers being chosen again for the different privatization projects that were pursued. In Denmark, for example, Danske Bank has been the chief choice of a bank almost every time the Danish government has sought advice on privatizing public enterprises.

A number of issues could be raised in order to further explore the PPP industry–government relationship. The PPP industry may have already become a viable 'export industry' for the countries in question, and thus the relevant governments could be interested in protecting them. For the UK, their privatization experience, and now maybe the PPP story, may have been consolidating the City of London as one of the world's leading financial centres. The PPP industry's interest-group or lobbying role could also be elaborated upon in further research. In other words, how much influence do such companies have over policy? Hodge and Bowman noted the complexity of the issue when they looked specifically at privatization and the growing role of consultants:

> Of course, there is also no doubt that consultants lobby for change. Self-interest drives this, and whether they were able to get a share of the 100 billion USD per year enterprise sales market revenues throughout the 1990s, a slice of the accompanying outsourcing trend, or else a slice of the more recent public–private partnership market, the motivating principle of self-interest still holds. However, as willing foot-soldiers of political change rather than its masters. Claims that the consultocracy sells the reform agenda to a simple-minded government are too simplistic in most jurisdictions. But the related charge that the consulting business needs to be seen as a new advocacy group in its own right is legitimate. (Hodge and Bowman, 2006, p. 111)

The point made in the quote above is vivid. There is a strong hypothesis that needs to be tested further: that the consultants – and other companies in the PPP industry – are asserting some kind of influence on policy and practice with PPPs. The relationship, however, is probably more complex when more closely examined, and there is not convincing evidence at the moment to suggest anything definitive about the degree of the influence that the PPP industry holds. Perhaps the point to be made here is a warning about making claims that are 'too simplistic', so clearly more research and evidence about the relationship between the PPP industry and government is needed. A further issue for future exploration is the observation that in much of the literature so far, the story of PPPs has essentially been told from the government's point of view. Learning has been from the perspective of a government entering or considering entering into a PPP deal with the private sector. As a consequence, a logical further point to be made by this chapter is to assert that scholars should equally be looking into the private sector side of the story as well, and be ready to examine that sector's motivation in more depth.

Conclusion

This chapter has explored the question of an emerging PPP industry. Three main points have been emphasized. First, there are signs of an emerging PPP industry understood as companies that are involved with – and stand to gain in some way from – the development of a PPP policy and PPP projects pursued by governments around the world. Second, following the ideas of the theoretical literature on path dependency in historical institutionalism from political science and political economy, countries that have previous experience with privatization and other market-based governance mechanisms are also those countries that seem most associated with PPPs. The UK and Australia appear to be leading the way among a focused number of countries. The emergent PPP industry seems related to these countries, although a number of companies are increasingly global in character and cannot be said to 'belong' to any one country in particular. Third, there is a need for more empirical data on exactly how many of these companies are associated with PPPs and what their relationships are to governments and international organizations. If some of the considerations in this chapter can be of inspiration, future research should not only look at PPPs from the government's perspective, but also try to tackle the issue of why and how companies in the private sector – in the PPP industry – are themselves involved in developing PPPs.

References

Barzelay, Michael (2001), *The New Public Management*, Berkeley, CA: University of California Press.
Bovaird, Tony (2006), 'Developing new forms of partnerships with the "market" in public procurement services', *Public Administration*, **84** (1), 81–102.
Deloitte (2006), *Closing the Infrastructure Gap. The Role of Public–Private Partnerships*, Washington, DC: Deloitte.
Hodge, Graeme (2000), *Privatization*, Boulder, CO: Westview Press.
Hodge, Graeme (ed.) (2006), *Privatization and Market Development. Global Movements in Public Policy Ideas*, Cheltenham, UK and Northampton, MA, USA: Edward Elgar.
Hodge, Graeme and Diana Bowman (2006), 'The "consultocracy": the business of reforming government', in Graeme Hodge (ed.), *Privatization and Market Development. Global Movements in Public Policy Ideas*, Cheltenham, UK and Northampton, MA, USA: Edward Elgar, pp. 97–126.
Levi, Margaret (1997), 'A model, a method, a map: rational choice in comparative and

historical analysis', in Mark I. Lichbach and Alan S. Zuckerman (eds), *Comparative Politics*, Cambridge: Cambridge University Press, pp. 19–41.

Orren, Karen and Stephen Skowronek (1994), 'Beyond iconography of orders: notes for a "new institutionalism"' in Lawrence Dodd and Calvin Jillson (eds), *The Dynamics of American Politics*, Boulder, CO: Westview Press, pp. 311–30.

Parker, David (2006), 'Enterprise sales: Thatcher leads the charge', in Graeme Hodge (ed.), *Privatization and Market Development. Global Movements in Public Policy Ideas*, Cheltenham, UK and Northampton, MA, USA: Edward Elgar, pp. 9–35.

Parker, David (2009), *The Official History of Privatization, Volume 1: The Formative Years 1970–1987*, London: Routledge.

Partnerships UK (2007), *PFI: The State of the Market*, London: Partnerships UK.

Pierson, Paul (2004), *Politics in Time*, Princeton, NJ: Princeton University Press.

Savas, E.S. (2000), *Privatization and Public–Private Partnerships*, Chatham, NJ: Chatham House.

Skanska (2008), 'Skanska is a leading PFI/PPP Service provider in the UK', www.skanska.co.uk (accessed 25 February 2008).

Steinmo, Sven, Katheleen Thelen and Frank Longstreth (eds) (1992), *Structuring Politics*, Cambridge: Cambridge University Press.

Streeck, Wolfgang and Kathleen Thelen (eds) (2005), *Beyond Continuity. Institutional Change in Advanced Political Economies*, Oxford: Oxford University Press.

Thelen, Kathleen (1999), 'Historical institutionalism in comparative politics', *Annual Review of Political Science*, **2**, 369–404.

Websites

Partnerships UK, www.partnerships.org.uk.
PPP Forum, www.pppforum.com.
Serco (2010), www.serco.com, 4 June 2010.

22 Towards a process perspective on public–private partnerships
Guðrið Weihe

Introduction

This chapter departs from the observation that public–private partnerships (PPP) have hit the public management agenda globally, that it is widely spread, and that massive public as well as private resources are devoted to the implementation of PPPs. This necessitates and justifies research that addresses how this policy tool functions in practice. Regardless of whatever pros and cons may be associated with PPPs, it is important to understand economic as well as social aspects of cooperation. The latter line of research is, however, currently missing in the PPP literature. Limited scholarly attention has been devoted to the 'ongoing managerial life of a PPP' and to the cooperative practice at the micro-level of cooperation (Noble and Jones, 2006). Processes for the ongoing management of PPP are still developing (Clifton and Duffield, 2006, p. 573), and there is limited 'navigational help' available for PPP managers who are now experiencing difficulties with managing PPP projects *ex post* implementation (Reeve and Hatter, 2004, p. 7). This chapter argues for a shift in focus away from the dominating structural and technical perspectives towards a process perspective on PPPs. In this perspective, the patterns of interaction and cooperative practices in implemented projects become the centrepiece of attention. The chapter draws upon related research on another type of partnerships (private–private partnerships/alliances), which suggests that what happens after contracts are signed can have significant performance implications.

A few years ago Steve Kelman proclaimed that 'Public management needs help!' (Kelman, 2005). The key message was that mainstream organization theory can help enrich our understanding of the public sector problems we are studying. Kelman pointed out that although much of the pioneering work in organization theory was written about public organizations, attention to public organizations has withered in recent decades (ibid.). Correspondingly, it is argued here that strategic alliance research can help enrich our understanding of PPPs. The common denominator for the two research fields is that they are both occupied with analysing cooperation across organizational boundaries. Similarly, in both cases a key object of study is dyadic inter-organizational relationships.[1] One field studies private–private cooperation (alliances) and the other public–private cooperation (PPPs). Although both fields are studying the same object, i.e., inter-organizational cooperation, little or no cross-disciplinary communication has yet taken place. This is regrettable because, as already noted above, there is a specific demand for guidelines and instruction on how to handle the managerial challenges that PPP projects pose once they have hit the implementation stage. Moreover, recent PPP research indicates that non-structural and non-technical aspects of cooperation can have performance implications (see Edelenbos et al., 2007; and Weihe, 2008b). While there is currently a lack of guidelines in the PPP literature, the strategic alliance literature contains useful knowledge about managerial aspects of cooperation and other non-formal facets influencing partnership performance.

The aim of this chapter is twofold: first, to demonstrate that alliance research can enrich our understanding of behavioural and operational aspects of PPPs, and that it is an obvious area where public and business management scholars can join forces. The second aim is to draw attention to non-contractual aspects of cooperation that are emphasized by some alliance scholars but have until recently been neglected in the PPP literature.

A tentative overview of the PPP literature
The PPP literature has been dominated by an institutional- and organizational-level focus, to the detriment of a micro-level focus on the role of individual actors (Noble and Jones, 2006, p. 891). Research efforts have moreover primarily addressed material and economic concerns (Ghobadian et al., 2004, p. 289), and focus has for the most part been directed at the front end of the partnership process: for instance at how contracts are designed, and at how risk is allocated between the involved parties (Reeve and Hatter, 2004, p. 5). What happens after contract signature has received limited attention; that is, as already noted above, operational processes at the micro-level have been more or less black-boxed. Formal and structural aspects of cooperation, such as designing the contract, financial issues, insurance issues, accounting issues, allocating risk as well as political issues, have been dealt with at some length (e.g. Coghill and Woodward, 2005; Corner, 2005; Evans and Bowman, 2005). Additionally, substantial work has by now been done to explore the conceptual boundaries of the PPP concept (e.g. Hodge and Greve, 2007; Van der Wel, 2004; Weihe, 2008a; Wettenhall, 2006). The same applies to work on the performance of PPP projects (e.g. Hodge and Greve, 2007), and PPP research on policy related issues such as cross-country comparative

Table 22.1   Alliances and PPPs: an overview

Formal structures	Public–private partnerships	Alliances (private–private partnerships)
Joint organizational expression	Cooperation that involves joint organizational expression, e.g. a partnership board or forum Public–private limited companies (e.g. the LIFT programme in the UK)	Joint ventures, different types of equity arrangements involving a joint institutional expression (a new entity is formed between two companies)
Contractual link	PFI, BOOT, DBO, different types of service contracts (e.g. LTICs)	Buyer–seller agreements, other contractual relationships between private firms (e.g. supplier–automaker exchange relationships)

studies of PPP policy development (e.g. Greve and Hodge, 2007). Some work has moreover been conducted on PPPs from a democratic account-ability perspective, where questions concerning transparency and account-ability have been addressed (e.g. Shaoul et al., 2007). However, as already suggested above, little attention has been directed at PPP governance proc-esses (including operational processes and behavioural aspects of coop-eration). Some exceptions are Edelenbos et al. (2007),[2] Noble and Jones (2006), Reeves (2006), Reeve and Hatter (2004) and Weihe (2008b).[3]

PPPs and alliances: conceptual similarities and differences
A PPP is commonly defined as 'cooperation of some durability between public and private actors in which they jointly develop products and serv-ices and share risks, costs and resources which are connected with these products' (van Ham and Koppenjan, 2001, p. 598). Alliances, meanwhile, have been defined as 'voluntary arrangements between firms involving exchange, sharing, or co-development of products, technologies, or serv-ices. They can occur as a result of a wide range of motives and goals, take a variety of forms, and occur across vertical and horizontal boundaries' (Gulati, 1998, p. 293). Both alliances and PPPs can thus materialize in a variety of institutional forms of co-production, and cover a parallel scope of formal arrangements (see Table 22.1). To use the terminology of the introductory chapter of this handbook, both terms cover a number of dif-ferent 'families'. Or, to put it more bluntly, just as the PPP term has been argued to be nebulous (Weihe, 2005, 2008a), so too can the alliance term

be argued to be tenuous. The features of cooperation and the degree of formal integration between the involved organizations – in PPPs as well as in alliances – can vary significantly. In some contexts, however, the alliance term appears to have a more restricted meaning (for an example, see Davies, 2008). It is thus important to emphasize here that in the context of this chapter, the focus is on how the term is used in the management literature on strategic alliances. A specific legal understanding or usage of the term is not used here.[4]

When looking at the PPP literature and the strategic alliance literature, two general categories of PPPs and alliances can be identified (see Table 22.1). First, both terms are used to describe inter-organizational relationships based on joint ownership/joint organizational structure; for instance, a joint venture in the case of alliances, and a public–private limited company in the case of PPPs (for some examples of this definition of PPP see Bergström, 2007, p. 2; Van der Wel, 2004). The point to stress here is that the alliance and the PPP term are used to describe cooperation that has reached some sort of joint organizational expression. Cooperative endeavours based on this type of formal structure are positioned at the high end of the integration continuum. Some PPP scholars suggest that 'real' partnerships involve this type of organizational arrangements (Wettenhall, 2006, appendix 1), and that the contractual PPP is merely a 'revamped form of tendering' (Klijn and Teisman, 2005, p. 103). In relation to the alliance term, the concept initially referred mainly to joint ventures. However, as indicated in Table 22.1, the alliance term today also includes a range of non-equity arrangements, for instance buyer–seller agreements (Casson and Mol, 2006, p. 23).

The second general category is the contractual link. In relation to the PPP literature, the most familiar example of the contractual link type of PPP would be some version of the UK-based Private Finance Initiative (PFI) projects. These have been defined as 'partnerships between the public and the private sectors for the financing, design, construction, operation and maintenance, and/or provision of assets or infrastructure and associated services, which have traditionally been provided by the public sector' (Evans and Bowman, 2005, p. 62). It is increasingly in this particular context that the PPP label is being used (ibid.). However, some PPP scholars complain that this version of PPP is far too limiting (Wettenhall, 2005, p. 22) as it excludes all other cooperative arrangements than those that involve some combination of infrastructure and associated service delivery. Similarly the alliance term also includes a broad range of types of contracts that fall 'between the extremes of discrete, short-term contracts and the complete merger of two or more organizations' (Contractor and Lorange, 2002, p. 4).[5]

The first point to stress here is that both concepts are open-ended and have been assigned a variety of meanings in their respective literatures. The second point is that both terms cover a similar range of formal structural arrangements. The key difference is that they do so in different contexts. In the case of alliances, research is mainly confined to private sector cooperation between firms. In the PPP context, one of the firms is replaced by a public sector actor.

Reasons for caution
In the context of public and private sector cooperation, there are of course reasons to be cautious when utilizing research findings from a research field (i.e. strategic alliance studies) that deals exclusively with cooperation between private firms. It could be argued that the differences between public and private organizations are so great and the logics of cooperation so different that it makes little sense to transfer knowledge between these two research fields. As Allison (1992) noted, public and private organizations are perhaps 'fundamentally alike in all unimportant aspects'. There may be several reasons for this. First, an alliance between two private firms is situated in a competitive setting; the involved firms are cooperating with a potential competitor. In a PPP, the competitive element is not present to the same extent. This might lead to differences in behaviour. Second, a PPP is situated in a political context while an alliance is not – at least not directly. Third, public sector goals may be viewed as more complex and diverse than private sector goals. Public goals are supposedly more vague and intangible than private organizational goals, and public sector goals can also be in conflict (Rainey et al., 1976, p. 237); there can for instance be conflicting goals between effective and efficient cooperation on the one hand, and following the standard and rule-bound procedures of public administration on the other. Fourth, the public bureaucracy was 'never designed to maximize on efficiency, flexibility and customer friendliness but rather to ensure a uniform and unbiased implementation of the law' (Peters and Pierre, 2003, p. 6). Unlike business organizations, public organizations have a constitutional foundation, and therefore the objective of public organizations is not primarily the attainment of gain but the furtherance of the welfare of the society (Lynn, 2003, pp. 16–17). The two sectors have inherently different foundations on which they build their legitimacy. In the private sector, legitimacy comes from legal and profitable behaviour, while in the public sector legitimacy comes from much broader values such as transparency, accountability, just behaviour and representativeness. A fifth difference may be that public sector managers enjoy less autonomy than their private sector counterparts; they may be less flexible because of a greater use of formal

regulations and more levels of review in the public sector (Rainey et al., 1976).

Scholars are increasingly proposing, however, that the differences between public and private organizations may not be so far-reaching after all. While early research was mostly preoccupied with stressing the differences, it appears that later contributions focus more on similarities between public and private organizations (e.g. Rainey and Bozeman, 2000). Correspondingly, (business) scholars now suggest that the standard perception that private organizations are driven exclusively by a profit and market-share motive is far too limited. Private sector organizations, so the argument goes, are becoming more political (e.g. Frankel, 2004), and therefore the traditional definitions of private organizations are no longer sufficient. In a similar vein, the recent decades of worldwide new public management (NPM) related reforms of public administrations suggests that public organizations are perhaps becoming more business-like (e.g. Hood, 1991). These developments suggest that perhaps many of the differences between what is purely private and what is purely public are becoming more blurred. To paraphrase Bozeman (1987), perhaps the public–private dichotomy is more imagined than real. This view is corroborated by the proposition that many of the 'widely held a priori assumptions' about public organizations – i.e. untested assertions and foregone conclusions about the differences between public and private organizations – are not always supported by empirical research (Rainey and Bozeman, 2000). As public and private organizations grow more alike, the relevancy of the lesson drawing between research on public organizations and research on private organizations may be increasing.

Identifying some promising learning potentials

Keeping in mind the above reasons for caution, let us now return to the issue of how strategic alliance research can be useful *vis-à-vis* PPP research. There are in particular two areas in which this sister discipline may prove to be valuable: (a) research that analyses informal aspects of cooperation; and (b) research on cooperative processes. First, alliance scholars have accumulated a significant stock of knowledge about the importance of a broad range of informal (behavioural) factors in alliance relationships. Aspects of cooperation such as relational quality and trust between the partnering organizations have been studied in depth and are suggested to have significant performance implications (e.g. Dyer and Singh, 2004). Second, alliance scholars have identified partnership processes as being important performance antecedents too (Ariño and de la Torre, 1998; Doz, 1996; Ring and Van de Ven, 1994). The key message in this latter line of research is that inter-organizational relationships cannot *a priori* be designed to function in certain ways; rather, they can be viewed as 'socially contrived mechanisms' that are constantly 'shaped and restructured' by the involved actors (Ring and Van de Ven, 1994, p. 96). In this perspective, simple neoclassical accounts of economic action are not sufficient to explain partnership behaviour but need to be supplemented by analyses of social structures and social interaction (Granovetter, 1985).

In the following, the segments of alliance research will be briefly described. The intention is not to provide a general review of the alliance literature (for that, see Auster, 1994). Instead, the efforts here are concentrated on outlining some of the key findings from alliance research relating to the importance of informal factors and partnership processes.

Strategic alliance research: cooperative processes and behavioural factors
Strategic alliance research can generally be classified into two main tendencies (Aulakh and Madhok, 2002, p. 26). First, there is the strand of research preoccupied with the motives underlying alliance formation. This line of research tries to explain why firms form alliances (e.g. Kogut, 1988). The second strand is concerned with how to manage alliances. It can be divided into two sub-categories: research that focuses on formal aspects of the relationship such as the choice of formal governance structures; and research that focuses on informal governance mechanisms (e.g. Ring and Van de Ven, 1994). Among other things, the first sub-category focuses on ownership structure and a variety of contractual mechanisms, while the second sub-category is more concerned with relationship processes (Aulakh and Madhok, 2002, p. 26). Within this sub-category, scholars have argued that the pattern of interaction can be more important for efficiency than structural properties (ibid., p. 27, originally Granovetter, 1985). It is the latter sub-category of alliance research that will be addressed here. Two key points can be extracted from this line of research:

1. The way partnerships evolve over time can have significant implications for partnership performance, and
2. Behavioural aspects of cooperation can have significant performance implications.

First, alliance scholars have demonstrated that the way cooperation evolves over time affects performance. Some suggest that the operational phase can ultimately determine the success or failure of cooperation (Thallman and Phene, 2006, p. 140). Others similarly suggest that partnerships 'fail for reasons other than the soundness of the business plan or the ability to execute according to that plan' (Spekman et al., 2000, p. 33; see also Ireland et al., 2002; Kanter, 2002; Ring and Van de Ven, 1994; Doz,

1996; Ariño and de la Torre, 1998). In this view, the degree to which value is created in partnerships is contingent upon a number of operational and behavioural factors. Success is not exclusively reliant on formal structures, or what happens before the signing of the contracts. Others have similarly recognized alliance management as a source of competitive advantage (Ireland et al., 2002; Kanter, 2002), and that 'managing the alliance relationship over time is usually more important than crafting the initial formal design' (Doz and Hamel, 1998, p. xv).[6] In a process perspective, alliances can thus be viewed as evolutionary processes rather than a set of fixed formal structures (Ariño and de la Torre, 1998; Doz, 1996; Ring and Van de Ven, 1994). They evolve continuously in their possibilities, and grow or fail just like relationships between people (Kanter, 2002). A key point in this approach is that the way cooperation evolves is not exclusively determined by formal arrangements but instead relationships and psychological contracts supplement formal role relationships and increasingly substitute for legal contracts (Ring and Ven de Ven, 1994, p. 91). Therefore, in this perspective, it is important to look at the continuous cooperative processes and not to confine research to the front end of the process (i.e. at pre-contract-signature issues). Instead more attention should be directed towards how partnership plans are implemented, negotiated and continually assessed and reassessed by the involved actors. Such processes can determine whether or not partnerships evolve into vicious or virtuous cycles of cooperation.

Second, alliance studies suggest that behavioural aspects of cooperation are important performance antecedents. There is an extensive amount of research that analyses how trust influences partnership performance. By and large this research suggests that trust lowers transaction costs, increases information-sharing, facilitates dispute resolution, reduces the amount of formal contracts, increases learning and reduces harmful conflict (Das and Teng, 1998, p. 494; Dyer and Chu, 2003; Luo 2002; Rousseau et al., 1998, p. 394). As an example, one study of buyer–supplier relationships found that the least trusted company had procurement (transaction) costs that were five times higher than the other comparable companies in the study (Dyer and Chu, 2003). Research on trust and alliances is closely related to research that deals with the importance of 'relational quality' in strategic alliances. Relational quality can be defined as 'the extent to which the partners feel comfortable and are willing to rely on trust in dealing with one another' (Ariño et al., 2001, p. 111). Relational quality is a broader concept than trust as it also involves other aspects of cooperation such as the degree of compatibility of corporate cultures, compatibility of decision-making styles, degree of convergence of world-views and other organizational characteristics. Relational quality can also be understood as the state of trust and confidence between the cooperating parties (Büchel and Killing, 2002). Although relational quality is somewhat elusive, alliance scholars seem to view it as an important concept. Generally, greater relational quality is believed to enhance alliance performance. For instance, one empirical study suggests that efforts at maintaining relational quality after the contract has been signed – in addition to initial relational quality – are positively related to performance (Büchel and Killing, 2002, p. 751). The argument is that the relationship itself can be viewed as a resource for value creation and realization, and therefore it is important for organizations to recognize beforehand the need to invest in the ongoing collaborative relationship in order to attain such synergies (Madhok and Tallman, 1998, pp. 326–7). In addition to research on trust and relational quality, there is a growing number of alliance studies that address what sort of collaborative capabilities make an organization successful at cooperating with other organizations (e.g. Schreiner et al., 2005; Heimeriks, 2004; Duysters and Heimeriks, 2002): that is, what types of collaborative competences enhance a firm's alliance performance. As noted by Heimeriks (2004), studies have shown that the failure rate of alliances is very high (often failure rates in the range of 30–70 per cent are reported in the literature), and moreover it has been reported that some firms consistently derive more value from their collaborative arrangements compared to other firms. This has sparked off research that tries to identify the competences that enhance alliance performance. This line of research is typically captured under such terms as 'collaborative capability' (Schreiner et al., 2005), 'alliance competences' (Spekman et al., 2000), 'alliance capabilities' (Heimeriks, 2004), 'relational capabilities' (Dyer and Singh, 2004), 'relational assets' (Dunning, 2002) and 'collaborative know-how' (Simonin, 2002). The underlying assumption of the capability research is that collaborative capabilities enhance alliance performance. Scholars generally distinguish between two groups of factors: structural and behavioural factors (Duysters and Heimeriks, 2002, pp. 2–3). The former group refers to tangible capability factors such as the presence of alliance functions, tools and other resources that aid organizations in managing their alliances (ibid.). The latter group of capability factors focuses on intangible aspects of cooperation such as trust and relationship quality. Different authors stress different sorts of collaborative capabilities as being important for performance. Not only are structural factors such as alliance tools important, but behavioural factors such as an organization's ability to conduct 'meaningful social exchange' with other organizations (Schreiner et al., 2005, p. 9) and its 'willingness and ability' to partner (Dyer and Singh, 2004, pp. 366–7) are discovered to be important for performance too. In this latter line of research, having the right technical skills does not automatically make organizations successful in their partnership activities. Rather, alliances are viewed as 'living systems that evolve progressively in their possibilities'; beside the immediate reasons for collaborating, the relationship itself offers unforeseen opportunities (Kanter, 2002, p. 100) as it can be viewed as a rent-generating source in itself (Dyer and Singh, 2004).

Issues for future research

Overall, the knowledge of operational and relational aspects of cooperation, which has been accumulated throughout the past few decades within the alliance field, suggests that it would be expedient to direct more attention towards the collaborative processes of PPP.

One first step in this direction could be to map empirically what actually goes on within the black box of PPP cooperation. How does interaction take place in practice once PPPs hit the implementation stage? What are the resources required? Who are the key actors? What is the pattern and frequency of interaction? What is the content of interaction? What is the quality of interaction? How are different types of monitoring regimes executed in practice? How do the involved actors deal with change over time? How are disputes resolved? What types of professional competences and skills are required by the partnership manager? And how does all this influence overall PPP performance? Analysing PPP processes can potentially improve our knowledge of what the drivers of collaborative advantage are and enhance our understanding of the mechanisms that determine partnership performance. The research agenda proposed here departs significantly from earlier proposed research agendas, which have primarily encouraged research on a range of technical, policy and performance related aspects of cooperation (see Broadbent and Laughlin, 1999). The approach recommended here calls for qualitative research that can address concepts such as processes, social dynamics, trust, goodwill and other intangible aspects of cooperation.

Focusing more on collaborative processes and the implementation stage of PPPs becomes only the more important when considering soft or new-style collaborative PPPs in which the partnering relationship is given greater importance compared to the traditional infrastructure PPP.

The alliance literature has some immediate value for PPP managers. First of all, it directs attention towards the notion that aspects beyond the immediate contract can be significant for overall performance. Second, it suggests that it may be useful to consider how relationship processes can be managed over time. Moreover, the findings propose that more resources should be devoted to the management of the PPP contract over the full lifetime of the project (and not only the formative phase of structuring the deal and signing the contract). Not enough thought has been devoted to this in the past – neither in PPP policy practice nor in the PPP literature. Taking into consideration that value for money is a key rationale for implementing PPPs, an effective cooperative relationship throughout the whole project life cycle becomes all the more relevant. More effective cooperation, and ultimately better performance, can be realized by focusing more explicitly on *ex post* contract signature aspects of cooperation. After all, well-managed trust-based partnership projects where processes are deliberately structured have proven to be cost-efficient. The ever-increasing international dissemination of PPP as a policy tool only emphasizes further the importance of a more comprehensive approach to PPP – that is, a policy approach that takes into account not only the formative and technical aspects of cooperation, but also recognizes the importance of the ongoing processes and the relational dimension of cooperation.

Conclusion
Public services are today increasingly being delivered in some sort of partnership between public and private organizations. This stresses the importance of bringing about sophisticated analyses of public–private cooperation that can feed back into policy decision-making processes and PPP practice. This chapter calls our attention towards the importance of directing more intellectual firepower at aspects of cooperation that go beyond structural and technical aspects. Alliance research on private–private business relations suggests that operational processes and managing the relationship over time influences partnership performance. Therefore, although careful consideration must always be given to the public–private distinction, alliance research is promising in assisting us in our efforts to fill some of the current gaps in the PPP literature. Alliance research can in particular enrich our understanding of the dynamic and evolutionary nature of cooperation and how non-contractual aspects can influence partnership performance. Moreover, alliance research can be used to fill the current knowledge gap that practitioners are experiencing when managing PPPs. By utilizing the knowledge accumulated in the alliance field, the potential of PPP research to relieve the distress that PPP managers are experiencing may be improved.

In conclusion, the aim here is not to suggest that formal structures are unimportant for cooperation, and that it does not matter how contracts are drawn up. A sound formal foundation is a prerequisite for successful cooperation. Rather, the claim here is that formal structures do not exclusively determine the success or failure of cooperation, and that therefore it would be expedient to concentrate more on cooperative practices. The pattern of interaction can be equally important for efficiency as structural properties (Aulakh and Madhok, 2002, p. 27, originally Granovetter, 1985). To paraphrase Granovetter (1985), both under-socialized and over-socialized approaches should be avoided.

Notes

1. The focus here on the dyadic inter-organizational relationship is the reason why other related disciplines such as network research, which studies multi-organizational relations (e.g. Agranoff and McGuire, 2001), and governance research, which is more inclined towards the changing institutional set-up of society rather than features and mechanisms relating to the nature of bilateral organizational relationships (Kooiman, 2003; Lynn et al., 2001), are not included here. Similarly, research on collaboration addresses collaboration as a phenomenon and not dyadic inter-organizational relationships (e.g. Sullivan and Skelcher, 2002; Wood and Gray, 1991); and the same goes for the theory of collaborative advantage that explores in a generic manner the factors contributing to collaborative advantage (see Huxham and Vangen, 2005). Therefore, in the context of this chapter, these related research disciplines will not be addressed. What we are interested in demonstrating here is exclusively how strategic alliance research on dyadic inter-organizational relationships contains valuable lessons for PPP research and practice. However, it should be mentioned that there are branches of alliance research with other perspectives than the inter-organizational one. For instance, there is an intra-organizational perspective, and also a social network perspective in the alliance literature (see, e.g. Heimeriks, 2004; Gulati, 1998).
2. Edelenbos et al. have conducted a couple of quantitative surveys measuring how behavioural factors such as trust influence partnership performance. In their most recent survey (2007) the general conclusion is that trust is an important factor in long-term public and private relationships.
3. In policy practice, a similar bias in focus can be identified. In the UK, attention was only recently directed at the operational phase of cooperation in policy practice. This is reflected in the establishment of an operational task force by the HM Treasury in 2006. Moreover, some recent official reports have addressed issues related to the ongoing PPP relationship (e.g. HM Treasury, 2006; Partnerships UK, 2006). Because of the initial bias towards focusing on the front end of the PPP process, PPP practitioners now experience difficulties with managing operational PPP projects. Some managers evoke analogies of 'spinning compasses', 'lights going on and off', 'intermittent engine function' and 'radio silence' when describing their experiences with managing PPPs (Reeve and Hatter, 2004, p. 7).
4. Davies (2008, p. 2) specifically contrasts 'alliance contracts' with other forms of procurement. He stresses that the alliance contract to a far greater extent than other arrangements (such as joint ventures, strategic alliances and partnerships) emphasizes 'teaming' and is built on an explicit 'no-disputes', 'no-liability' framework.
5. There could be argued to be even a third category of cooperation which is less formalized than the two other categories, i.e. a category where cooperation is not based on formalized agreements (contracts). In the PPP literature, a number of scholars use the PPP label to cover non-contractual policy relationships, and other non-formalized and non-time-delimited relationships between private and public actors (e.g. Rosenau, 2000). Likewise, alliance scholars also address non-institutional relationships between firms: e.g. research that adopts a social network perspective on alliances (Gulati, 1998).
6. Correspondingly, a study conducted by management consulting firm McKinsey has shown that 50 per cent of alliances fail because of governing and operating processes (Bamford and Ernst, 2003, p. 323).

References

Agranoff, R.I. and M. McGuire (2001), 'Big questions in public network management research', *Journal of Public Administration Research and Theory*, **11** (3), 295–396.

Allison, Graham T. (1992), 'Public and private management. Are they fundamentally alike in all unimportant aspects?', in Jay Shafritz and Albert Hyde (eds), *Classics of Public Administration*, Belmont, CA: Wadsworth, pp. 457–75.

Ariño, Africa and José de la Torre (1998), 'Learning from failure: towards an evolutionary model of collaborative ventures', *Organization Science*, **9** (3), 306–25.

Ariño, Africa, José de la Torre and Peter Smith Ring (2001), 'Relational quality: managing trust in corporate alliances', *California Management Review*, **44** (1), 109–31.

Aulakh, Preet S. and Anoop Madhok (2002), 'Cooperation and performance in international alliances: the critical role of flexibility', in Farok J. Contractor and Peter Lorange (eds), *Cooperative Strategies and Alliances*, Oxford: Elsevier, pp. 25–48.

Auster, Ellen R. (1994), 'Macro and strategic perspectives on interorganizational linkages: a comparative analysis and review with suggestions for reorientation', *Advances in Strategic Management*, **10** (Part B), 3–40.

Bamford, James D. and David Ernst (2003), 'Growth of alliance capabilities', in James D. Bamford, Benjamin Gomes-Casseres and Michael Robinson (eds), *Mastering Alliance Strategy: A Comprehensive Guide to Design, Management, and Organization*, Chichester: John Wiley & Sons, pp. 321–33.

Bergström, Maria (2007), 'A PPP analysis from a community law perspective: some preliminary notes', paper presented at a Nordic PPP workshop at Stockholm University, Sweden.

Bozeman, Barry (1987), *All Organizations are Public: Bridging Public and Private Organizational Theories*, San Francisco, CA: Jossey-Bass.

Broadbent, Jane and Richard Laughlin (1999), 'The private finance initiative: clarification of a future research agenda', *Financial Accountability and Management*, **15** (2), 95–114.

Büchel, Bettina and Peter Killing (2002), 'Interfirm cooperation throughout the joint venture life cycle: impact on joint venture performance', in Farok J. Contractor and Peter Lorange (eds), *Cooperative Strategies and Alliances*, Oxford: Elsevier, pp. 751–71.

Casson, Mark and Michael J. Mol (2006), 'Strategic alliances. A survey of issues from an entrepreneurial perspective', in Oded Shenkar and Jeffrey Reuer (eds), *Handbook of Strategic Alliances*, Thousand Oaks, CA: Sage, pp. 17–37.

Clifton, Chris and Colin F. Duffield (2006), 'Improved PFI/PPP service outcomes through the integration of alliance principles', *International Journal of Project Management*, **24**, 573–86.

Coghill, Ken and Dennis Woodward (2005), 'Political issues of public–private partnership', in G. Hodge and C. Greve (eds), *The Challenge of Public–Private Partnerships. Learning from International Experience*, Cheltenham, UK and Northampton, MA, USA: Edward Elgar, pp. 81–94.

Contractor, Farok and Peter Lorange (eds) (2002), *Cooperative Strategies and Alliances*, Oxford: Elsevier.

Corner, David (2005), 'The United Kingdom private finance initiative: the challenge of allocating risk', in G. Hodge and C. Greve (eds), *The Challenge of Public–Private Partnerships. Learning from International Experience*, Cheltenham, UK and Northampton, MA, USA: Edward Elgar, pp. 44–61.

Das, T.K. and Bing-Sheng Teng (1998), 'Between trust and control: developing confidence in partner cooperation in alliances', *The Academy of Management Review*, **23** (3), 491–512.

Davies, John Paul (2008), 'Alliance contracts and public sector governance', PhD thesis, Australia: Griffith Law School, Griffith University.

Doz, Yves L. (1996), 'The evolution of cooperation in strategic alliances: initial conditions or learning processes?', *Strategic Management Journal*, **17**, 55–83.

Doz, Yves L. and Gary Hamel (1998), *Alliance Advantage. The Art of Creating Value through Partnering*, Boston, MA: Harvard Business School Press.

Dunning, John H. (2002), 'Relational assets, networks and international business activity', in Farok J. Contractor and Peter Lorange (eds), *Cooperative Strategies and Alliances*, Oxford: Elsevier, pp. 569–93.

Duysters, G. and K. Heimeriks (2002), 'The influence of alliance capabilities on alliance performance: an empirical investigation', working paper, The Netherlands: Eindhoven Centre for Innovation Studies, Department of Technology Management, Technische Universiteit Eindhoven.

Dyer, Jeffrey H. and Wujin Chu (2003), 'The role of trustworthiness in reducing transaction costs and improving performance: empirical evidence from the United States, Japan, and Korea', *Organization Science*, **14** (1), 57–68.

Dyer, J.H. and H. Singh (2004 [1998]), 'The relational view: cooperative strategy and sources of interorganizational competitive advantage', in Jeffrey J. Reuer (ed.), *Strategic Alliances: Theory and Evidence*, Oxford: Oxford University Press, pp. 349–77.

Edelenbos, Jurian, Erik-Hans Klijn and Bram Steijn (2007), 'The role of trust in public private partnerships: does trust matter?', *Tidsskriftet Politik*, **3** (10), 63–82.

Evans, Joanne and Diana Bowman (2005), 'Getting the contract right', in G. Hodge and C. Greve (eds), *The Challenge of Public–Private Partnerships. Learning from International Experience*, Cheltenham, UK, and Northampton, MA, USA: Edward Elgar, pp. 62–80.

Frankel, Christian (2004), *Virksomhedens politisering*, Copenhagen, Denmark: Forlaget Samfundslitteratur.

Ghobadian, Abby, David Gallear, Howard Viney and Nicholas O'Regan (2004), 'Future of the public–private partnership', in Abby Ghobadian, David Gallear, Nicholas O'Regan and Howard Viney (eds), *Public–Private Partnerships. Policy and Experience*, Basingstoke: Palgrave Macmillan, pp. 271–302.

Granovetter, Mark (1985), 'Economic action and social structure: the problem of embeddedness', *The American Journal of Sociology*, **91** (3), 481–510.

Greve, Carsten and Graeme Hodge (2007), 'Public–private partnerships: a comparative perspective on Victoria and Denmark', in T. Christensen and P. Lægreid (eds), *Transcending New Public Management*, Aldershot, UK: Ashgate Publishing, pp. 179–202.

Gulati, R. (1998), 'Alliances and networks', *Strategic Management Journal*, Special Issue **19** (4), 293–318.

Heimeriks, Koen H. (2004), 'Developing alliance capabilities', PhD dissertation, Technische Universiteit Eindhoven.

HM Treasury (2006), *PFI: Strengthening Long Term Partnerships*, London: HM Treasury.

Hodge, Graeme and Carsten Greve (2007), 'Public–private partnerships: an international performance review', *Public Administration Review*, **67** (3), 545–58.

Hood, C. (1991), 'A public management for all seasons?', *Public Administration*, **69**, 3–19.

Huxham, Chris and Siv Vangen (2005), *Managing to Collaborate: The Theory and Practice of Collaborative Advantage*, London: Routledge.

Ireland, R. Duane, Michael A. Hitt and Deepa Vaidyanath (2002), 'Alliance management as a source of competitive advantage', *Journal of Management*, **28** (3), 413–46.

Kanter, Rosabeth Moss (2002), 'Collaborative advantage: the art of alliances', *Harvard Business Review on Strategic Alliances*, Boston, MA: Harvard Business School Press, pp. 97–128.

Kelman, Steve (2005), 'Public management needs help!', *Academy of Management Journal*, **48** (6), 967–9.

Klijn, Erik-Hans and Geert R. Teisman (2005), 'Public–private partnerships as the management of co-production: strategic and institutional obstacles in a difficult marriage', in Graeme Hodge and Carsten Greve (eds), *The Challenge of Public–Private Partnerships. Learning from International Experience*, Cheltenham, UK and Northampton, MA, USA: Edward Elgar, pp. 95–116.

Kooiman, Jan (2003), *Governing and Governance*, London: Sage.

Kogut, B. (1988), 'Joint ventures: theoretical and empirical perspectives', *Strategic Management Journal*, **9** (4), 319–32.

Luo, Yadong (2002), 'Building trust in cross-cultural collaborations: toward a contingency perspective', *Journal of Management*, **28** (5), 669–94.

Lynn, Laurence E. Jr (2003), 'Public management', in G.B. Peters and J. Pierre (eds), *Handbook of Public Administration*, London: Sage, pp. 95–116.
Lynn, Laurence E. Jr, Carolyn J. Heinrich and Carolyn J. Hill (2001), *Improving Governance. A New Logic for Empirical Research*, Washington, DC: Georgetown University Press.
Madhok, Anoop and Stephen B. Tallman (1998), 'Resources, transactions and rents: managing value through interfirm collaborative relationships', *Organization Science*, **9** (3), 326–39.
Noble, Gary and Robert Jones (2006), 'The role of boundary-spanning managers in the establishment of public–private partnerships', *Public Administration*, **84** (4), 891–917.
Partnerships UK (2006), *Report on Operational PFI Projects*, undertaken on behalf of HM Treasury in 2005.
Peters, B. Guy and Jon Pierre (2003), 'Introduction: the role of public administration in governing', in G.B. Peters and J. Pierre (eds), *Handbook of Public Administration*, London: Sage, pp. 1–10.
Rainey, Hal G. and Barry Bozeman (2000), 'Comparing public and private organizations: empirical research and the power of the a priori', *Journal of Public Administration Research and Theory*, **10** (2), 447–69.
Rainey, Hal G., Robert W. Backoff and Charles H. Levine (1976), 'Comparing public and private organizations', *Public Administration Review*, **36** (2), 233–44.
Reeve, Stephen and Warren Hatter (2004), *Beyond Contract: What Makes a PPP Successful?*, London: New Local Government Network.
Reeves, Eoin (2006), 'The practice of contracting in public private partnerships: transaction costs and relational contracting in the Irish school sector', paper presented at the Tenth International Research Symposium on Public Management, 10–12 April, Glasgow, Scotland.
Ring, Peter Smith and Andrew H. Van de Ven (1994), Developmental processes of cooperative interorganizational relationships, *Academy of Management Review*, **19** (1), 90–118.
Rosenau, Pauline (ed.) (2000), *Public–Private Policy Partnerships*, Cambridge, MA: The MIT Press.
Rousseau, Denise M., Sim B. Sitkin, Ronald S. Burt and Colin Camerer (1998), 'Introduction to special topic forum: not so different after all: a cross-discipline view of trust', *Academy of Management Review*, **23** (3), 393–404.
Schreiner, Melanie, Daniel Corsten and Prashant Kale (2005), 'Collaborative capability of the firm and its impact on interfirm-relationship outcomes', paper presented at International Center for Strategic Management and Globalization, Copenhagen Business School, Denmark.
Shaoul, J., Anne Stafford and Pam Stapleton (2007), 'Private finance: public infrastructure without accountability? The case of privately financed roads in the UK', *Tidsskriftet Politik*, **3** (10), 28–37.
Simonin, Bernhard L. (2002), 'The nature of collaborative know-how', in Farok J. Contractor and Peter Lorange (eds), *Cooperative Strategies and Alliances*, Oxford: Elsevier, pp. 237–63.
Spekman, Robert E., Lynn A. Isabella and Thomas C. MacAvoy (2000), *Alliance Competence: Maximizing the Value of your Partnerships*, New York: John Wiley & Sons, pp. 237–63.
Sullivan, Helen and Chris Skelcher (2002), *Working across Boundaries: Collaboration in Public Services*, Gordonsville, VA: Palgrave Macmillan.
Thallman, Stephen and Anupama Phene (2006), 'Structuring and restructuring alliances: a theory-based process model', in Oded Shenkar and Jeffrey J. Reuer (eds), *Handbook of Strategic Alliances*, Thousand Oaks, CA: Sage, pp. 133–47.
Van der Wel, Paul (2004), 'Privatisation by stealth: the global use and abuse of the term "public–private partnership",' Working Paper Series no. 394, The Hague, The Netherlands: Institute of Social Studies.
van Ham, Hans and Joop Koppenjan (2001), 'Building public–private partnerships: assessing and managing risk in port development', *Public Management Review*, **3** (4), 593–616.
Weihe, Guðrið (2005), 'Public–private partnerships: addressing a nebulous concept', working

paper, International Center for Business and Politics, Copenhagen Business School, available at: ir.lib.cbs.dk/paper/ISBN/8791690161.

Weihe, Guðrið (2008a), 'Ordering disorder: on the perplexities of the public–private partnership literature', *Australian Journal of Public Administration*, **67** (4), 430–42.

Weihe, Guðrið (2008b), *Public–Private Partnerships: Meaning and Practice*, PhD Series, Copenhagen: Copenhagen Business School.

Wettenhall, Roger (2005), 'The public–private interface: surveying the history', in Graeme Hodge and Carsten Greve (eds), *The Challenge of Public–Private Partnerships. Learning from International Experience*, Cheltenham, UK and Northampton, MA, USA: Edward Elgar Publishing, pp. 22–43.

Wettenhall, Roger (2006), 'Public–private mixes and partnerships: some Australian case studies', paper presented at EROPA Seminar, Bandar Seri Begawan, Brunei Darussalam.

Wood, Donna J. and Barbara Gray (1991), 'Toward a comprehensive theory of collaboration', *The Journal of Applied Behavioural Science*, **27** (2), 139–62.

23 PPPs in developed and developing economies: what lessons can be learned?
David Parker and Catarina Figueira

It is now generally acknowledged that a prerequisite for economic growth is the provision of efficient, reliable and affordable infrastructure services, such as water, electricity, roads, hospitals, schools, airports, ports and public transport. The question is, are they better privately or publicly supplied? The history of state provision reveals many examples of service failure and huge cost overruns, which led to the programmes of privatization and market liberalization from the 1980s. But in many cases governments have proved unwilling to give up control of infrastructure services because of their strategic importance to the economy and because of obvious direct effects on social welfare. This has meant that the services have not been privatized in the usual way through share flotations, sales to other companies or management and employee buyouts. This is complete privatization. Rather, the approach has been to retain a high degree of public funding and public control but to attract private capital because of perceived management and risk-taking benefits.

There has therefore been a growing trend towards publicly funded but privately supplied infrastructure services, in the form of public–private partnerships (PPP). In the UK this development is commonly referred to as 'the Private Finance Initiative' (PFI). PPP is the label used to cover a range of different types of partnerships with the private sector, of which PFI is a type formulated in the UK; HM Treasury (2008). For most purposes the two terms can be used interchangeably, and this is the case in this chapter. A number of other industrialized economies have also been active in promoting PPP schemes, such as the Netherlands, and the practice has spread to lower-income developing economies.[1] In developing countries PPPs have taken forms such as 'build, operate, transfer' schemes and leasing and concession agreements. In these countries the priority is to raise investment, reduce the backlog of poor facilities and improve the environment for sustained economic development.

In one sense the public sector procuring services from the private sector is not new. No government department produces its own stationery or computers, and construction projects have normally been undertaken by private sector firms. What was new from the 1980s was the greater reliance on the private sector for activities previously undertaken in house, such as the operation of information technology systems and the management of building schemes. Under PPP/PFI the public sector enters into long-term contractual arrangements, which involve private sector companies designing, building, financing and in many cases operating infrastructure assets.[2] This chapter assesses PPPs in the context of both developed and developing countries. In terms of developed countries, the lessons are illustrated from the experience in the UK. This is in part because the authors are most familiar with the UK's experience, but also because the UK has led in terms of the value and scope of PPPs in Europe.

PPPs in the UK

In the UK, the government has stated clearly that when deciding on whether to use the private sector or provide a service in house, the decision will be based on 'a rigorous assessment of value for money with no bias in favour of any particular procurement route' (HM Treasury, 2003, p. 1). Value for money (VfM) is the basis on which the public sector is expected to decide whether to produce internally or procure externally. Central to the interpretation of VfM is the concept of shifting risk. In essence, PPP/PFI is intended to shift risk from the public sector, and hence taxpayers, on to the private sector, and hence company shareholders. In return for taking risk, the private sector is rewarded by the opportunity to profit from its superior project management skills.[3]

The origins of what became the PFI programme of the 1990s, in the UK, goes back to the early 1980s. At the time there was an expectation that the introduction of private capital into the financing of public sector projects and service delivery would help reduce public borrowing. This was the time of privatization and 'Thatcherism', when the tide of public policy was strongly with private over public investment. It was also felt that the private sector would be able to input management skills missing within government. In response, the treatment of private capital for public projects was reviewed by the Treasury. This led to certain 'rules' or criteria that departments were expected to take account of when deciding whether to use private capital to fund public projects. The rules were formulated by Sir William Ryrie, a senior Treasury official, and were released in 1981 by Leon Brittan, the then Chief Secretary of the Treasury. Brittan summed up the central message of the rules as follows: 'funds for investment should be taken under conditions of fair competition with the private sector, that is, that the latter should not obtain a normal equity profit without accepting a normal equity risk'.[4]

In broad terms, the expectation was that the benefits from using the private sector should be set against the differential cost of financing in the private sector compared with the public sector. But because of the low risk of default, governments can generally borrow at a lower cost than private sector firms.[5] This meant that, in effect, the 'Ryrie rules' required that in the UK the net yield of a PPP project should be greater than if it were publicly financed by at least enough to cover the increased cost of raising risk capital from the financial markets. In other words, the gains would have to more than offset the additional cost of raising finance from the private sector, compared to gilts sales, if the proposal were to be approved. As one commentator concluded: 'They [the Ryrie rules] became a standing joke. Ryrie drew them so tightly as to make them inoperable. Not a pound of private/public investment was allowed through under the "Ryrie rules"' (Jenkins, 1995, p.28). This may be an extreme judgement, but what is certainly clear is that the 'rules' severely constrained the uptake of PPPs in the 1980s and for some time afterwards (HM Treasury, undated).

During the 1980s there were a number of unsuccessful attempts to navigate around the Ryrie rules, and this left the private sector in the UK doubtful as to whether the government was committed to the use of private finance for public sector projects. For example, the first major infrastructure project to be seriously considered for private financing was a proposed new road in the Midlands,[6] with revenue to the contractor to be based upon a 'phantom toll' over a 25-year concession period. The 'phantom toll' would be set on the basis of the number of vehicles using the new road, involving a measurement of traffic volume by the Department of Transport. However, the Treasury rejected the proposal on economic grounds. The main stumbling block was the Ryrie rules.

However, in March 1986 the proposal for a new privately financed Dartford River Crossing was successful. The project involved building a new bridge across the Thames at Dartford and the purchase of two existing tunnels there, at a price equal to the outstanding debt relating to their original construction. In September 1986, following a tender and negotiations, a consortium led by Trafalgar House won the contract. The consortium would be responsible for building and operating the new bridge, and operating and maintaining the two tunnels during the concession period, of up to 20 years. Tolls would be levied by the consortium to finance the scheme, which was expected to cost in the region of £170 million. At the end of the concession period or when all of the debt from the new bridge and tunnels had been repaid, whichever was the earlier, the bridge and tunnels would be transferred to government ownership free of charge. Should the venture fail at any time, the bridge and tunnels would revert immediately to government ownership.

The Dartford River Crossing concession was important in the evolution of what became known as PFI because it was the first major infrastructure development in the UK to be financed by the private sector since 1945. A new company, the Dartford River Crossing Company, was formed, with a nominal equity of £1000. The main financing for the project came from 20-year subordinated loan stock, 16-year loan stock and £85 million as a term loan from banks. The banks also committed to further loans of up to £20 million to cover any cost overruns. The contractor that built the bridge took the risk that it might cost much more to build than expected, and operating and financial risks were effectively borne by the debt holders. As risk had been transferred to the private sector, the scheme was deemed to fulfil the Ryrie rules (de Pelet, 1988). The Dartford scheme demonstrated that, with careful navigation, the Ryrie rules were not the formidable barrier to private financing of public infrastructure that many had assumed.

Following agreement on this concession, the government encouraged the private sector to take the initiative and bring forward other infrastructure schemes for consideration. As a result, private finance was attracted into a number of major infrastructure projects, including the Channel Tunnel and the other transport projects mentioned earlier. From the early 1990s a full-blown PPP policy developed in the UK, aimed at increasing investment in the country's infrastructure without calling on large amounts of additional public sector funding. Governments were able to continue to reduce public borrowing as a percentage of GDP while at the same time improving infrastructure services.

PPPs appeared to offer a 'win–win' of better infrastructure with the cost taken 'off balance sheet' as far as the public sector accounts were concerned. In 2003/04 in the UK, PPP/PFI schemes accounted for 39 per cent of capital spending by government departments, although this fell to 11 per cent in 2005/06. By January 2008 there were over 500 operational PPP/PFI projects with a total capital value of around £44 billion and a further number in the pipeline. In the UK the largest sector by value for PPP/PFI has been transport due to large schemes such as the Second Severn Crossing, the Docklands Light Railway extension, the Heathrow–London rail link, the Channel Tunnel Link and the M6 relief road around Birmingham, followed by health and defence. Currently the government is using the private sector to help turn around the decaying stock of hospitals and schools.

Emerging difficulties

A National Audit Office report in 2001 revealed that some 73 per cent of traditionally procured central government construction projects in the UK had come in over budget. Therefore, in the UK there was considerable scope to improve the procurement of public infrastructure through

PPP/PFI deals. But this does not mean that the expectation has necessarily been fulfilled.

Under traditional government procurement, typically the public sector designs the project and the private sector builds to this design, using either cost-plus contracts (with their well-known moral hazard problems) or fixed-price contracts (which the private sector dislikes, understandably, given unpredictable inflation). By contrast, under PPP/PFI, typically the public sector sets the goals of the project (e.g. in terms of the general specification of a new bridge, tunnel or hospital), but allows the private sector to come forward with differing ways of achieving the specification. Also, very often the private sector becomes responsible not only for constructing, but also for managing and running the facility for a specified number of years, and therefore the 'whole-life costs' of the project are internalized. For example, if the private contractor skimps on the initial build, the higher costs of maintenance and repair will fall on its budget later. More traditional public sector procurement was prone to incentives to minimize construction costs with limited attention paid to later maintenance and repair ('whole-life') costs.

In the UK, the standard approach to arranging PPP/PFI contracts is for the relevant public body (government department, NHS etc.) to announce the proposed scheme and advertise for bids. The bidders are then short-listed based on ability to deliver and price tendered. A 'preferred bidder' is then chosen, but generally some months may pass during which this bidder seeks the remaining information it needs to finalize the bid. This introduces an immediate difficulty. The final contract price can vary from the amount initially bid, and often does so. The public body has the opportunity to reject the final bid and go back out to contract, although if it does so, many months will have been lost. This introduces an element of moral hazard into the tendering process, in the sense that the preferred bidder can factor into its calculations the likelihood that the public body will challenge the new price and reopen the bidding. Given that the delay caused by re-bidding adds to costs within government and may mean that the project has to be withdrawn if in the meantime public sector budgets have been tightened, it can mean that departments are reluctant to reopen the bidding.

The argument for PPP/PFI is that by using the private sector, taxpayers benefit from the project management skills of private sector firms and civil servants can concentrate on doing what they do best – running their departments. But PPP/PFI schemes often have lives of 20 to 30 years or more. Typically annual price increases are built in to reflect inflation, with other price changes negotiated periodically during the life of the contract, to reflect changing circumstances and specifications and costs not reflected in the national inflation rate. Nevertheless, it is inevitable, given the long life of the projects, that changes will be needed not just to prices but to the other terms of provision of services and assets. In turn this puts a considerable emphasis on the need to develop appropriate procurement skills within the public sector. Arguably these skills are still very underdeveloped. Not only does this affect the results of PPPs from the perspective of taxpayers; it also leads to complaints from bidding companies of protracted and difficult negotiations. In 2000 Partnerships UK (PUK) was set up to replace a Treasury Taskforce established by the Labour government in 1997, with the objective of reinvigorating the PFI programme. Its objective was to improve PPP/PFI procurement processes within government.[7] But difficulties remain. For example, an estimated £180 million was paid by public authorities to PFI contractors to undertake contract changes in 2006.

There are other possible problems associated with the use of PPP/ PFIs. The first is that they can be adopted, as in the case of the 2005–10 Labour government, as a 'second-best' substitute for full privatization or more public funding. Whether building and running schools and hospitals through PPP/PFI is a long-term solution to a failing public sector education and NHS is highly debatable. Ricketts (2009, p. 11) concludes that public sector provision is 'capable of obscuring the exercise of political and other special interests, and is unlikely to reflect purely commercial considerations. The nature of the inefficiencies induced through state action mutate as organizational structures change.' If he is right, then the solution lies not in PPP/PFI but in the far greater distancing of politicians from economic decision-making.

What is clear is that PPP/PFI may be storing up huge costs for future generations and meanwhile distorting resource allocation.[8] For example, recent years have seen the government in the UK desperately attempting to improve services in the NHS with huge extra funding injected and 'partnerships' arranged with the private sector (Table 23.1). But the results have been disappointing. Hellowell and Pollock (2009) chronicle a litany of PPP/PFI failures and a desperately worrying future financial burden for unsuspecting taxpayers. It is far from clear that the result is a better health service – although the result may cheer up HM Treasury ministers by pushing costs forward into future years or taking them 'off balance sheet'.

In 2005, just under a half of PFI projects were estimated to be off the government's balance sheet and therefore did not count as public sector debt in national accounts. The government's ability to post PFIs 'off balance sheet' has been curtailed, however, following criticism.[9] In turn, there is a suggestion that this has led to reduced interest in arranging PFI deals within government, including HM Treasury.

*Table 23.1   Numbers and capital values of PFI projects signed per year
(full calendar years)*

Year	Number of schemes	Total capital value (£ m)	Average capital value (£ m)
1997	3	206	68.67
1998	7	580	82.86
1999	10	618	61.8
2000	11	635	57.72
2001	7	339	48.43
2002	10	580	58
2003	8	1 012	126.5
2004	17	1 665	97.94
2005	5	716	143.2
2006	6	2 098	349.67
2007	11	1 661	151.54
Total/average	95	10 110	106.42

Source: HM Treasury (2008), 'PFI Signed Projects List', available online at www.hm-treasury.gov.uk/documents/public_private_partnerships/ppp_pfi_stats.cfm; Hellowell and Pollock (2009), p. 14.

Another problem lies in the true long-term costs of PPP/PFI deals being highly uncertain. It has been suggested that in the UK the expense may exceed the costs that would have been incurred under more traditional government procurement methods. It is difficult to be sure because of the complexity of valuing future PPP/PFI costs and the counterfactual of direct public provision. For example, there is the uncertainty of contract defaults: if a private sector company begins to lose money on a PPP/PFI contract and the government refuses to renegotiate the price, then it is possible that the private sector will withdraw, leaving the taxpayer to pick up the pieces. As typically consortia of firms bid for PPP/PFI contracts, bringing together the necessary skills, the PPP/PFI contract is normally with a 'special purpose vehicle' or company set up to build and manage the project. It is this company that is put into receivership. The collapse of Metronet in July 2007, a consortium operating part of the London Underground, after severe cost overruns, is a case in point. Metronet ran out of cash to undertake its commitments, and after a request for additional payments was rejected, it went into administration (Office of the PPP Arbiter, 2007). With no likelihood of a replacement private sector contractor taking over the contract, the functions were returned to the public sector in the form of Transport for London. Nor is this an isolated incident: in 2004 the construction company Jarvis was brought to its knees by a PFI contract signed four years earlier to refurbish eight schools in the North West of England. Jarvis made the mistake of quoting too low for what was, in effect, a fixed-price contract with no clear avenue to renegotiate the price.[10]

In any contracting there are problems of adverse selection and moral hazard arising from information asymmetries. Transaction costs apply in any form of contracting between principals and agents that involves 'incomplete contracts' – and long-term PPP/PFI contracts are inherently incomplete. The transaction costs arise from the costs of negotiating, monitoring and enforcing the contracts. Ideally, if the contract is a true 'partnership', then the transaction costs should be reduced because 'opportunistic behaviour' is curtailed by mutual trust. The public and private sectors work harmoniously together on a project, adapting and compromising as they go on. In the Netherlands this true partnership form of PPP appears to have made some headway. But in the UK trust too often remains lacking and too often 'partnerships' quickly fall apart in a manner similar to the failure of traditional principal–agent contracts. A number of PPP/PFI schemes have collapsed after recriminations more reminiscent of a battlefield.[11]

In so far as there are grounds for mistrust at the outset of the contracting, the contract tends to be quite tightly specified, leaving limited scope for adaptation later. On the one hand, government justifies the case for detailed contract specification to protect the Exchequer from later demands from the contractor for more financing and to protect against shoddy work. The private sector may also favour tight contracts if it is suspicious of future behaviour by government. On the other hand, this tells against adopting true 'partnership' agreements, in which incomplete contracts are inherent. The third difficulty with PPP/PFI, therefore, lies in the legacy of distrust that exists between the public and private sectors in the UK; this is notwithstanding occasional HM Treasury guidance to government department in an effort to improve the arrangements (HM Treasury, 2006a).

Such difficulties are not assisted, of course, by the tendency of politicians to change 'the rules'. For example, the Labour government, under pressure from trade unions, decided that contractors should operate specified employment practices more similar to those in the public sector, which in turn reduced the scope for cost savings to contractors. This sort of problem is not limited to the UK. The World Bank has discovered a high incidence of contract renegotiation for PPP-type contracts with the private sector in low- and middle-income economies. The transportation and water sectors are especially prone to recontracting, with rates of 55 per cent and 75 per cent, respectively, in Latin America and the Caribbean. Moreover, much of the renegotiating occurs quite quickly: the time between the start of operations and renegotiation averaged a mere two years (Guasch, 2004). A number of low- and middle-income economies suffer from a degree of political turbulence that tells against even short-term arrangements with the private sector, as discussed in more detail below. In the UK contractors complain about the costs of bidding, changes to bid specifications and delays in decision-making by government departments. The government has responded by changes aimed at reducing the cost of bids to companies.

Fourth, in deciding on whether to procure through PPP/PFI, public sector bodies in the UK are expected to test the cost against other forms of delivery, such as retaining the activity in the public sector. This should occur at the initial stage of deciding on the bids and periodically during the life of the PPP/PFI, where the contract involves the longer-term provision of services. The tests are usually expected to take place at five- to seven-year intervals. Value testing may involve comparing the incumbent's provision with comparable services ('benchmarking'), or may even involve inviting other suppliers to compete for the work in open competition ('market testing'). However, in the health sector at least, for example, the record of VfM testing is far from satisfactory. In October 2006 HM Treasury issued new guidance to departments in an endeavour to improve practices (HM Treasury, 2006b).

Clearly the programme of PPP/PFI in the UK has faced emerging difficulties. Nevertheless, the March 2008 budget confirmed the government's continuing support for PPP/PFI to deliver a range of public services (HM Treasury, 2008). There is no outward suggestion of any lessening of support for this method of procurement in the Cabinet or HM Treasury, although there is some concern, privately expressed, about both VfM and the long-term cost to taxpayers.[12] Elsewhere in government, however, worries are more openly voiced about the quality and cost of some PPP/PFI schemes, in terms of both delivering good public services and VfM. Such views surface from time to time in reports from the National Audit Office, the body mandated on behalf of Parliament to assess government spending in terms of VfM. A recent NAO report revealed that of the 600 PFI projects already let, around 500 were now at the operational phase. On VfM testing, after investigating admittedly a small number of the projects, the NAO disclosed that 'in some of these initial cases the value testing had demonstrated value for money was being achieved, but in other cases the outcome was uncertain' (NAO, 2007a, p. 4).

Two particular difficulties were identified in the NAO report. The first was a lack of adequate benchmarking data to assess VfM, and the second was the time taken to undertake value testing, typically nine to 25 months. The result was a recommendation from the NAO that government departments should ensure that their PFI project teams were familiar with and adopted HM Treasury guidance on benchmarking and market testing. However, past experience of civil servants receiving new guidelines suggests that this is no guarantee of improved performance across government. Also, deficiencies have been identified by the NAO in the tendering for contracts phase (NAO, 2007b) and concerns voiced about the degree of true competition and benchmarking that enters into the negotiation and renegotiation of PPP/PFI contracts (NAO, 2008). While the empirical evidence on the performance of PPP/PFIs is still insufficient to draw firm conclusions from, there is no real suggestion that they have led to an obvious step change in the quality and cost of infrastructure investments in the UK.

The experiences of the UK in operating PPP/PFIs to date (around two decades) may not be entirely representative of other developed countries. For instance, as already mentioned, the Netherlands appears to have had more success in building true 'partnerships' in provision based more on trust than arm's-length contracting. At the same time, it is difficult to believe that many of the difficulties experienced in the UK are not experienced elsewhere in the developed world. We now turn to looking at the experiences of PPPs in lower-income economies.

PPPs in developing countries
Since the mid-1980s, PPPs have been an important feature of growth in FDI in lower-income economies. This type of partnership has been mainly geared towards the development of infrastructure in these countries. As described by the World Bank (2009, p. 1), PPPs are

> the preferred financing scheme for infrastructure projects . . . [used by] governments . . . mainly to achieve Value for Money (VfM) and to deliver better quality of services for the same amount spent by the public sector. A second reason . . . is the desire to provide increased infrastructure provision and services within imposed budgetary constraints by utilising private sources of finance via off balance sheet structures, and to accelerate delivery of projects which might otherwise have to be delayed.

By the mid-1990s, private sector participation in infrastructure projects in developing countries had reached US$128 billion and it still continues to increase (see Figures 23.1 and 23.2), although the number of these projects decreased (for a few years) at the end of the 1990s primarily as a result of the Asian financial crisis.[13] The World Bank's Private Participation in Infrastructure (PPI) database shows that in the 1990s,

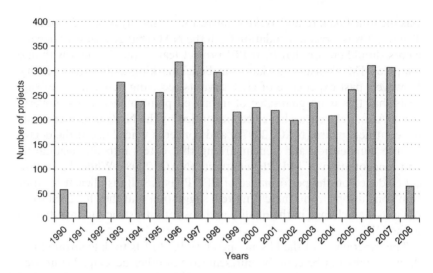

Source: Adapted from World Bank and PPIAF, PPI Project Database.

Figure 23.1   *Private participation in infrastructure (number of projects),*
1990–2008

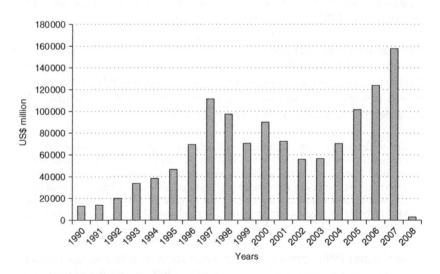

Source: As for Figure 23.1.

Figure 23.2   *Private participation in infrastructure (US$ million),*
1990–2008

132 low- and middle-income countries engaged in private participation in infrastructure, primarily in the transport, energy, telecommunications and water sectors.

In terms of the location of PPPs around the world, all regions have been benefiting from this type of initiative, although Latin America has been particularly successful throughout the period considered, together with South Asia (mainly in the last few years), as can be seen in Figure 23.3.

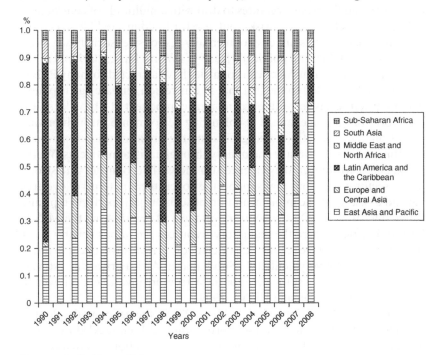

Source: As for Figure 23.1.

Figure 23.3 Distribution of private participation in infrastructure by world region, 1990–2008

However, not all initiatives have been successful in terms of the investments made and the outcomes that have been achieved (see, e.g. Sirtaine et al., 2005). Some of the problems that have emerged are certainly similar in nature to those in the developed countries, and are mainly related to the lack of support from government authorities, lack of transparency or indeed corruption (as discussed extensively by Klitgaard, 1998) and/ or lack of competitiveness in the procurement of infrastructure and in the implementation of the necessary work. In addition, weak levels of coordination among government departments in ensuring that the project is implemented effectively also contribute to the failure of some of these partnerships.

Therefore the existence of a solid regulatory environment is of vital importance for these projects to be carried out effectively. Because public governance is weak, and because there is limited private sector involvement in many developing countries, there is a 'need not only for innovative regulatory and financial structures to deal with a multitude of contractual, political, market, and credit risks, but also for building credible structures to ensure that projects are environmentally responsive, socially sensitive, economically viable, and politically feasible' (World Bank, 2009, p. 1). The main reason why Latin American countries have attracted so many PPIs is most probably related to the fact that in this region, private participation in infrastructure has constituted an integral component of a broader sectoral reform programme, aimed at enhancing performance through private operation and competition and generating the financial resources needed to improve service coverage and quality through tariff adjustments (World Bank, 2003). Moreover, the evidence also shows that countries with strong public sector institutions that support the government in terms of overseeing and assisting in the implementation of such projects perform typically better than the rest. On the contrary, in most of South Asia, the Middle East and Africa, where the regulatory resources are in particularly short supply and governance regimes are often poor, private investment in infrastructure has been very limited. In Sub-Saharan Africa private investment has been negligible – yet the need for infrastructure investment is nowhere more pressing (Jackson and Hlahla, 1999).

Since the 1980s, as claimed by Sobhan (2005), the deficit in developing countries in terms of infrastructure provision had been tackled by donor bodies at least partially through promoting privatization and market liberalization policies.[14] However, since the 1990s, there has been growing evidence that privatization has failed to bring about the benefits promised.[15] As a result, donor support has been redirected towards regulatory reform, in accordance with one of the main pillars of the Post Washington Consensus on economic development (Onis and Sentes, 2005).

Donor agencies have since been heavily involved in the design and implementation of regulatory improvements – in fact, this type of involvement accounts for over a quarter of their total development assistance. However, this initiative seems to centre on improving the regulatory climate for private investment and is often not sufficient to address poverty issues. On the contrary, there are fears that some of the actions taken may contribute to policy reversals in developing countries that undermine the reforms intended to raise economic growth, so that the potential 'long-run' benefits of the Post

Washington Consensus become irrelevant. Admittedly, the World Bank has not ignored this issue and it has developed the tool of 'output-based aid' (OBA), where subsidies are given to private companies only when expansion of service targets has been met or previously designated needy sections of society have had their needs supplied. Other recommended schemes for encouraging the expansion of services into poorer and rural areas are to build in such requirements to concession contracts, backed by financial penalties for non-compliance (Hussain and Hanjra, 2004). Or companies might competitively bid for infrastructure concessions, where the winner requires the smallest government subsidy to provide basic services in targeted areas. However, while all of these initiatives are to be welcomed, in the absence of a much better understanding of how regulation is actually impacting on poverty, the threat of policy failure remains.

As a response to these threats, donor agencies are increasingly shifting their support towards facilitating the creation of PPPs in developing countries (often *à la* the USA or Europe). This is particularly the case for a number of infrastructure industries, including telecommunications and energy. For example, in the Philippines, approximately 20 regulatory agencies have been set up in the last few years, some of which were possible only due to the support provided by donor agencies (Cariño, 2005).

So what makes for a good PPP in developing economies? There are a number of factors that contribute to the success of such projects; these are discussed in the next section.

What makes for a good PPP in developing economies?

PPPs are often large projects involving several parties, some private and other(s) governmental, and, as such, tend to be quite complex in terms of the set-up and its implementation. Moreover, there are aspects to these projects that are specific to the industry they focus on, the country where they take place and ultimately the particular type of infrastructure they aim at creating or improving. Nevertheless, there are also a number of parameters (of a general nature) that are central to project success and need to be taken into account when considering a PPP in a developing country. These parameters include institutional and financial support, adequate project preparation, which should meet the necessary formal requirements in order to ensure approval from the relevant authorities, management of fiscal risk (Dachs, 2008) and interaction between the public and private entities and the civil society (Franceys and Weitz, 2003).

In order to improve the success rate of PPPs, robust legislation/ regulations need to be in place. This helps in reducing the risk associated with the project and provides clear guidelines in terms of the approach taken by the private sector towards the implementation and completion of the project. An international law firm, Gide Loyrette Nouel (2008), highlighted some impediments to the implementation of PPP projects in Russia, due to inadequacies in the legal framework. These relate mainly to drawbacks of the legislation on concession agreements and the risk of requalification of civil law PPP agreements into concessions. However, they also noted that there is increasing political support for PPP projects in Russia and steps are being taken to minimize the above impediments.

In terms of institutional support, we have seen that PPPs have worked best in countries that have formal advisory institutions that provide assistance to government. These include projects in South Africa, where a PPP unit has been established, in South Korea, which holds a public and private infrastructure investment management centre, as well as in the Philippines and India, where similar agencies have been formed, both at the central level and, in the case of India, also at the regional level.

Another central element to the success of PPPs has been the existence of close links between such programmes and the government's fiscal support. This kind of explicit support, although subject to variations among countries, often takes the form of capital grants, funds and/or service payments. For instance, in India, a viability gap fund has been created where approved projects may receive grants of up to 20 per cent of the total amount of the project. This is supplemented by an equal amount provided by the state authority. Moreover, an infrastructure fund is also available, in order to provide additional support to the private sector (Ramchand, 2008). Other government-led initiatives have also been taking place in India, particularly since 2001, with a view to laying the foundations for additional funding and investment, mainly in the sectors of roads and ports, energy and telecommunications, as discussed by Sarangi (2002).

Also central to the success of PPP projects is adequate project preparation and approval. These are related to the existence of formal and clear requirements in terms of project feasibility and bidding procedures. It has been observed that where projects have been successful, these procedures have been taken into account in order for the projects to be considered for financial support. These procedures include the incorporation of competitive bidding into the process and formal approval by the relevant authority, often the Ministry of Finance (UNECE, 2004). In countries where assistance agencies had their effectiveness diminished (e.g. in the Philippines), this seems to have been the result of lack of formal budget support and procedures concerning approval.

Finally, as claimed by Franceys and Weitz (2003) in their study of PPPs, which involved the provision of water and sanitation services in urban areas in Asia, it is also important that public and private entities involved in a PPP establish links with the relevant community to investigate the potential social benefits and costs to the people being served (see also Osumanu, 2008, who discusses a PPP in Ghana). It is sometimes the case that some of the outputs created as a result of PPPs do not reach the poor in lower-income economies, which was the aim in the first place.

The importance of PPPs in rural development
According to Harris (2003), empirical evidence has highlighted some benefits of PPPs to developing economies mainly where the commercial risk is moved to the private sector. Moreover, research has also shown that significant welfare gains, considerable improvement in social indicators and expansion of services in some of these economies have benefited the poor and are the result of PPPs.[16] These have primarily been taking place in urban areas – projects of this kind are still uncommon in rural areas, and yet such areas are in dire need of help (Inforesources, 2005). The livelihood of many people in developing areas still depends on agriculture, farming and forestry. Therefore there are great opportunities for PPP initiatives in rural regions, as they can potentially contribute to the opening of agricultural markets across regions and across lower-income economies. Inforesources (2005) highlights three cases of PPP success in rural Ghana, Vietnam and Honduras.

The Oda-Kotoamso Community Agroforestry Project in Ghana was intended to deal with the problem of forestry slash-and-burn methods to clear areas for cultivation. Constraints on licence rights, poor soil productivity, together with population growth, proved that livelihood in this area was unsustainable. As part of a PPP project, farmers were encouraged to concentrate on ecological farming and cultivation of trees, through financial incentives and training. Moreover, new sources of income in the area were identified, such as apiculture, snail farming, pisciculture and wood carving, and efforts were made to market these new products and provide infrastructure facilities for the population in this area to gain access to markets and processing industries.

Another example of success of a PPP took place over a number of years (2001–04) in Vietnam and was directed at restoring a sustainable basis for coffee production in Quang Tri Province, by concentrating on improving the quality of coffee as a response to worldwide overproduction, together with the improvement of general infrastructures in the area.

Finally, in Honduras, the potential for small enterprises in rural areas to market their products had scarcely been exploited. However, two Swiss companies became involved in a PPP – 'The Melon Export Project' – aimed at strengthening the service sector for agricultural businesses. This was achieved by orienting production towards market needs and developing new products that display profitability potential, improving processing of products, marketing, promoting further entrepreneurial activity and providing accessibility to new markets (which include exports). The overall results of the partnership between these two companies and the Honduran Ministry of Agriculture proved to be a success: productivity increased and producers became more confident in running their small agricultural businesses, and were able to exploit new opportunities which had not been identified before (Inforesources, 2005).

However, the above three examples of successful partnerships do not signify that collaborations between governments and the private sector are not without serious challenges. There remain a number of questions that need to be answered. The most important element of such collaborations however is the (in)ability to establish the balance between private companies that invest in projects with profits in mind, while the public sector often seeks to support exactly those areas that at least in the short run, seem to deliver less profitability. Experience so far with PPPs in developing countries demonstrates that there are no clear recipes for success; however, the experience from previous projects can help derive some important lessons to avoid failure in the future. These are discussed in the next section.

Key lessons to prevent failures

This section concentrates on highlighting the key lessons that should be learned from past PPP projects in developing countries, in order to avoid future failures and ensure that the proposed new projects are effective in achieving what they propose. These lessons relate to five main points, described below.

1. *Planning* Planning is central to such projects and, more often than not, projects fail because they are supported by inadequate feasibility studies, which include weak capacity by public authorities to fulfil their contribution to funds, and distorted risk-sharing.
2. *Solid revenue and cost estimations* Related to planning is the importance of a detailed financial and economic analysis of the project, backed by solid forecasting projections. This element of a PPP is central in ensuring not only that the project is attractive to private companies but also that, if they are to be involved, these investors are ultimately able to service the debt. In Hungary, for instance, a PPP was created to construct a motorway (contract no. TREN/05/FP6TR/ S07.41077/513499). As a result of inadequate traffic volume forecasting (which turned out to be much lower than anticipated), the private investor was unable to service the debt and the government ended up covering the high costs.

3. *Compliance with contractual agreement* PPP projects' profitability and their success in the long term is heavily dependent on the government's adherence to contractual agreements (Franceys and Weitz, 2003). If this does not happen, then the whole project may be compromised and, as a result, costs may spiral out of control, as was observed with the PPP project on Don Muang Tollway in Thailand in 1996 (Cuttaree, 2008).

4. *Strong institutional arrangements* These relate to the control that the government has over the project. It should be ensured that there is adequate coordination between the state authorities and the private party, that technical support is provided where required and that there are regular checks on progress. To achieve this, government staff need to be trained and have the relevant experience to ensure that the project meets the requirements set at the beginning throughout the different stages. This contributes to the avoidance of two very common problems in PPPs: delays in the completion of the project, and costs that are sometimes well above what was estimated at the start.

5. *Value of competitive procurement* Competitive bidding should be regarded as key in any PPP project. This is important, not only to guarantee transparency throughout the process, but it also contributes towards obtaining better deals among private investors. Evidence has shown that where uncompetitive procurement takes place, the private investor tends to take advantage of its position in the process by means of increasing costs unnecessarily, delaying the completion of the project substantially and often not taking responsibility for the risk associated with the project. This often creates an additional burden to the government and is pivotal in the failure of some PPPs, as was observed with the Bulgaria Motorway Project in 2006 (Cuttaree, 2008).

Conclusions

Despite shortcomings in the track record of PPP/PFIs in the UK, discussed earlier, and the experiences in developing economies, it does seem that PPP/PFIs are now a firm part of the institutional framework of government in both higher-income and lower-income countries. Nor is this likely to change. With governments in the developed world now cash-strapped, following the recent international financial crisis, it seems more than ever likely that they will resort to more and larger public–private deals in the future. Equally, there appears to be no appetite to reverse the growing reliance in developing countries on private sector investment in infrastructure assets.

However, it is also clear that to date the experience of PPP/PFI has been far from completely happy. There needs to be more effort to build true 'partnerships', allowing for the collaborative evolution of arrangements over time between government and suppliers as circumstances change, in place of distrust and complete reliance on contracts. There also needs to be more research into the actual operation of PPP/PFIs, in both developed and developing economies, to identify the circumstances when they are most likely to produce net benefits over traditional government procurement. This will necessitate much clearer whole-life accounting for PPP/PFI deals and VfM evaluation.

Finally, governments in both the developed and developing world need to protect taxpayers from the consequences of the private sector walking away from PPP/PFIs when things turn sour. The private sector cannot reasonably expect that obtaining PPP/PFI contracts is a certain bet.

However, given the current economic climate and the UN Millennium Development Goals, which highlight clearly the need to reduce world poverty, PPPs represent an attractive model towards achieving at least some of the UN objectives. Increasing cooperation between government and private investors provides additional resources that are of vital importance to governments with limited financial capability to implement certain projects by themselves. This is particularly the case with infrastructure projects, but also encompasses other, often community-based, projects. Through PPPs, governments can make use of the know-how provided by private companies, which may contribute to increased efficiency, project sustainability and, through these companies, forging contacts that allow them to break into new markets.

At the same time, and particularly in developing economies, large companies are increasingly interested in having a better understanding of local markets and respective culture and legislation in order to increase their footprint in these economies, which often display great potential as new sources of revenue generation. Moreover, by being involved in such initiatives, foreign companies can also contribute to the restoration of public trust in private investors, who are often viewed with suspicion and can, therefore, improve the receptiveness of local communities to new lucrative entrepreneurial initiatives.

In conclusion, PPPs are very attractive to governments of developing economies, particularly at a time when these economies face multiple simultaneous challenges to develop capacity across different areas. Although there are no simple recipes for success, it is certainly the case that these partnerships need to be underpinned by strengthened professional as well as organizational capacities. In addition, it is important that the 'rule of law' is reinforced to enhance trust in the governmental authorities.

Notes

1. For studies of the experiences with PPP internationally see Osborne (2000), Grimsey and Lewis (2004) and Hodge and Greve (2005).
2. See HM Treasury (2003).
3. This section draws heavily on Parker (2009).
4. Cited in de Pelet (1988).
5. However, the fact that the government finances a project does not necessarily reduce risk. The risk of project failure in the public sector is ultimately borne by taxpayers. Therefore the lower cost of raising finance in the public sector results from the compulsory imposition of risk on the rest of us. Nevertheless, it is a fact that, using conventional accounting, government raises money more cheaply than private sector companies.
6. A large but not quite central region in England, with the main city being Birmingham.
7. PUK manages the Treasury Operational Taskforce overseeing PFI. Private finance units exist in major government departments.
8. For a study leading to similar conclusions see Shaoul et al. (2008).
9. See, e.g. 'Critics say NHS mega-hospitals show need for a different initiative', *Financial Times*, 1 July 2005, p. 3; 'PFIs stay the course despite chequered history', *Financial Times*, 26 June 2007, p. 3.
10. 'PFI may be complex but bankruptcy is simple', *Daily Telegraph*, business section, 31 July 2004, p. 29.
11. The difficulty inherent in incomplete contracts is amusingly illustrated by one NHS PFI for running services in a hospital. The contract specified that the private operator would provide toast for patients' breakfasts, but no one thought to include marmalade. Later the NHS trust agreed to pay extra for the marmalade and for litter clearance, which it had also neglected to specify in the original contract (Clark, 2005).
12. According to the NAO (2008), future payments across all PFI projects up to 2031–32 will amount to £91 billion at current prices.
13. The data for 2008 are not complete. They include statistics only for the water sector.
14. There are opposing views on the benefits of donor support. For instance, Padmanabhan (2001) considers that this type of support tends to fail due to the incompatibility between market forces and the objectives that generally underpin local projects.
15. See, e.g., Estimo (2007) on this point.
16. In terms of benefits associated with PPPs, Shirley (2002) discusses welfare gains, Galiani et al. (2005) focus on improvements in child mortality and Estache et al. (2000) and Ros (1999) investigate expansion in services.

References

Cariño, L.V. (2005), 'Regulatory governance in the Philippines: lessons for policy and institutional reform', mimeo, National College of Public Administration and Governance, University of the Philippines.

Clark, R. (2005), 'The worst of both worlds', *The Spectator*, 4 June, pp. 20–21.

Cuttaree, V. (2008), 'Successes and failures of PPP projects', The World Bank, Europe and Central Asia Region, Warsaw.

Dachs, W. (2008), 'PPP models from around the world', in *PPP in Vietnam Workshop Proceedings*, Hanoi., pp. 1–16.

de Pelet, P. (1988), 'Private finance and management of infrastructure', in E. Butler (ed.), *The Mechanics of Privatization*, London: Adam Smith Institute, pp. 59–66.

Estache, A., A. Gomez-Lobo and D. Leipziger (2000), 'Utility privatization and the needs of the poor in Latin America: have we learned enough to get it right?', Policy Research Working Paper 2407, Washington, DC: World Bank.

Estimo, R.F. (2007), 'The curse of the MWSS water utility privatization in the Philippines', Kyoto: Maynilad Water Supervisors' Association.

Franceys, R. and A. Weitz (2003), 'Public–private community partnerships in infrastructure for the poor', *Journal of International Development*, 15, 1083–98.

Galiani, S., P. Gertler and E. Schargrodsky (2005), 'Water for life: the impact of the privatization of water services on child mortality', *Journal of Political Economy*, **113** (1), 83–120.
Gide Loyrette Nouel (2008), 'Implementing PPP projects in Russia', *Russia & CIS Airfinance Conference Proceedings*, Moscow (June).
Grimsey, D. and M.K. Lewis (2004), *Public–Private Partnerships: The Worldwide Revolution in Infrastructure Provision and Project Finance*, Cheltenham, UK and Northampton, MA, USA: Edward Elgar.
Guasch, J.L. (2004), *Granting and Renegotiating Infrastructure Concessions: Doing it Right*, Washington, DC: World Bank.
Harris, C. (2003). 'Private participation in infrastructure in developing countries: trends, impacts, and policy lessons', World Bank Working Paper No. 5, Washington, DC.
Hellowell. M. and A.M. Pollock (2009), 'The private financing of NHS hospitals: politics, policy and practice', *Economic Affairs*, **29** (1), 13–19.
Hodge, G. and C. Greve (eds) (2005), *The Challenge of Public–Private Partnerships: Learning from International Experience*, Cheltenham, UK and Northampton, MA, USA: Edward Elgar.
HM Treasury (2003), *PFI: Meeting the Investment Challenge*, London: Stationery Office.
HM Treasury (2006a), *PFI: Strengthening Long-term Partnerships*, London: Stationery Office.
HM Treasury (2006b), *Benchmarking and Market Testing Guidance*, London: Stationery Office.
HM Treasury (2008), *Infrastructure Procurement: Delivering Long-term Value*, London: Stationery Office.
HM Treasury (undated), 'Public expenditure control: the sale of assets and other financial transactions', HM Treasury Paper, in E(DL) Part 11.
Hussain, I. and M.A. Hanjra (2004), 'Irrigation and poverty alleviation: review of the empirical evidence', *Irrigation and Drainage*, **53**, 1–15.
Inforesources (2005), 'Rural development through public–private partnerships?', *Focus*, 1/05.
Jackson, B.M. and M. Hlahla (1999), 'South Africa's infrastructure service delivery needs: the role and challenges for public–private partnerships', *Development Southern Africa*, **16** (4), 551–63.
Jenkins, S. (1995), *Accountable to None: The Tory Nationalisation of Britain*, London: Hamish Hamilton.
Klitgaard, R. (1998), 'International co-operation against corruption', in *Fighting Corruption Worldwide. Finance and Development*, **35** (1), Washington, DC: World Bank.
NAO (2007a), *Benchmarking and Market Testing the Ongoing Services Component of PFI projects*, London: Stationery Office.
NAO (2007b), *Improving the PFI Tendering Process*, London: Stationery Office.
NAO (2008), *Making Changes in Operational PFI Projects*, London: Stationery Office.
Office of the PPP Arbiter (2007), Press Notice 03/07, 16 July.
Onis, Z. and F. Sentes (2005), 'Rethinking the Post Washington Consensus', *Development and Change*, **36** (2), 263–90.
Osborne, S.P. (2000), *Public–Private Partnerships: Theory and Practice in International Perspective*, London: Routledge.
Padmanabhan, K. (2001), 'Poverty, microcredit, and Mahatma Gandhi: lessons for donors', *The International Social Science Journal*, **53** (169), 489–98.
Parker, D. (2009), 'PPP/PFI – solution or problem?', *Economic Affairs*, **29** (1), 2–5.
Ramchand, K. (2008), 'PPP – an Indian experience', in *PPP in Vietnam Workshop Proceedings*, Hanoi.
Ricketts, M. (2009), 'The use of contract by government and its agents', *Economic Affairs*, **29** (1), 7–12.
Ros, A. (1999), 'Does ownership or competition matter? The effects of tele-communication reform on network expansion and efficiency', *Journal of Regulatory Economics*, **15**, 65–92.

Sarangi, D. (2002), *Infrastructure Development: A Public–Private Partnership in India*, New York: UNESCO.

Shaoul, J., A. Stafford and P. Stapleton (2008), 'The cost of using private finance to build, finance and operate hospitals', *Public Money & Management*, **28** (2), 101–8.

Shirley, M.M. (2002), *Thirsting for Efficiency: The Economics and Politics of Urban Water System Reform*, Washington, DC: World Bank.

Sirtaine, S., M.E. Pinglo, J.L. Guasch and V. Foster (2005), 'How profitable are private infrastructure concessions in Latin America? Empirical evidence and regulatory implications', *The Quarterly Review of Economics and Finance*, **45**, 380–402.

Sobhan, R. (2005), 'Increasing aid for poverty reduction: rethinking the policy agenda', *IDS Bulletin*, **36** (3), 61–70.

UNECE (2004), 'Building public–private partnerships for infrastructure development', *United Nations Economic Commission for Europe Weekly*, 84 (6–10 September).

World Bank (2003), *Private Participation in Infrastructure: Trends in Developing Countries in 1990–2001*, Washington, DC: World Bank.

World Bank (2009), 'About public–private partnership in infrastructure', available at: web.worldbank.org / WBSITE / EXTERNAL / WBI / WBIPROGRAMS / PPPILP / 0,,content MDK:20271509~menuPK:461109~pagePK:64156158~piPK:64152884~theSitePK:461102,00.html.

24 A review of transport public–private partnerships in the UK
Jean Shaoul

Introduction

This chapter has two interrelated objectives: first, to review the experience of transport PPPs, including roads, bridges, rail and air traffic control, in the UK; and second, to present the financial evidence about the actual costs of different types of transport PPPs. Such a review and analysis would inform the international policy debate about the use of private finance and its broader implications for accountability. This is particularly important given the absence of *ex post facto* financial evaluation of the policy or scrutiny of the cost of current, renegotiated or terminated projects by the official watchdogs (Pollock and Price, 2008).

The focus is on transport because, while PPPs now encompass most sectors and services and all types of public bodies, national, local and non-departmental, the transport sector is by far the largest internationally. The UK, as one of the foremost exponents of the policy, illustrates the varied forms and outcomes of transport PPPs in developed countries. Since the engineering standards for transport projects are by and large universal at least in developed countries, unlike public services such as health and education, where the requirements are more likely to be tailored to local social and institutional needs and constraints, any assessment of the experience is likely to have more general applicability.

Transport projects in the UK have typically taken one of a number of forms. First, a contractual-type arrangement: the public sector pays for the use of the asset and its dependent services under terms set out in a contract, which may contain incentives for good and/or penalties for poor performance. Such contracts are usually designated as Private Finance Initiative (PFI) projects or design, build, finance, operate (DBFO) projects in the transport sector. Examples in the UK transport sector include the main trunk roads, where the public agency commissions the private sector to enhance, operate and maintain roads, paying for them on the basis of usage under a system known as shadow tolls. Second, a free-standing project or concession: the private sector designs, builds, finances and operates a road, but typically a bridge or a crossing, and charges the users directly (toll charge), as for example a number of estuarial crossings and the M6 toll-road. Third, an alternative free-standing project or concession: there is both public and user funding for either the construction and/or the service element. One example is the Skye Bridge, originally a free-standing project, where the Scottish Office paid some of the construction costs and later the Scottish Executive subsidized the tolls before ultimately terminating the contract. Another is the London Underground PPP, a contractual arrangement, where the public authority, London Underground, pays the private sector partner, but receives a grant from central government, in effect a subsidy to the private sector, and charges passengers. Fourth, a joint venture (joint ownership) arrangement: the partnership may charge either the public sector as in health and education, or the users (National Air Traffic Services).

But partnership arrangements have become ever more complex and include a proliferating number of hybrids and pre-existing formats. For example, the UK government now calls the fragmented and privatized railways, various parts of which receive extensive capital grants, operating subsidies and debt guarantees, a public–private partnership (DfT, 2004). It should be noted that not only has there been a proliferation of partnership structures; the terminology is also used interchangeably – for example PFI is used to denote free-standing projects and PPP is used in the case of London Underground to denote a contractual arrangement. Furthermore, as well as the confusion over terminology, there is also confusion over the distinction between funding and financing: although the finance for the capital expenditure comes largely from the private sector, the funding to service the charges may come from either the public sector or users.

PPP projects require a revenue stream to pay the charges, which will be a function of the size of the initial investment (typically large), usage, operating costs (typically relatively low), the cost of finance and the period of the loan. That is, the revenue must enable the PPP to recover its full costs over the life of the project, including the cost of debt and equity, under conditions where the demand is rarely sufficient to recover costs. This is particularly the case in transport, where demand may be high on individual routes but inadequate over the network as a whole, as the railways illustrate. While high-volume routes can be repaid within a relatively short period, political realities may dictate low user charges or tolls spread over a longer period. Should, however, traffic flows be low or lower than predicted, then trains, roads and bridges will operate below capacity, making them difficult to fund, necessitating some combination of higher charges, capital grants and public subsidy. This is one of the reasons why the state provides most infrastructure and public services: they are simply too capital intensive and thus financially risky to be provided commercially on a universal and comprehensive basis.

But there is a further problem. It is more costly for the public sector to use the private sector as financial intermediaries, due to the higher cost of commercial over public debt, the cost of the profit margin of both the private partner and its extensive supply chain, and the not inconsiderable legal and financial advisers' fees to structure and negotiate the deal. In the case of the flagship London Underground PPPs, advisers' fees amounted to a staggering £500 million. Furthermore, private contractors will seek to recover the not inconsiderable cost of unsuccessful bids from future successful contracts, increasing the cost of subsequent PFI deals. The higher cost of capital under private finance is particularly important in the context of roads and bridges, where the capital as opposed to the operating cost is typically high. Nevertheless, as explained in an earlier chapter, the proponents of the policy justify the higher cost of private finance in terms of the value for money (VfM) to be derived from the greater efficiency and innovation of the private sector and the transfer of some of the risks to the private sector.

The international experience has reflected these realities. While the research literature relating to both developing and developed countries has generally been short on detailed financial evidence, it has shown that while many private road concessions and DBFO projects have been successful, where 'success' means commercial viability, a significant number have not. Some have had to be renegotiated on more favourable terms to the private sector or taken over by government when the concessionaires faced inadequate revenues due to users' dislike of tolls and/or higher than expected costs. The broad conclusion is that in order to make such schemes financially viable and attractive to the private sector and users alike, a high degree of political commitment is required. Such political commitment is reflected in various forms of financial support, not all of which are clearly visible to the public, and/or the elimination of competition from roads without charges (see, e.g., Farrell, 1997; Silva, 2000; Freeman, 2004; Ehrhardt and Irwin, 2004; Estache and Serebrisky, 2004; Bel and Fageda, 2005; Boardman et al., 2005). In the context of rail, the capital-intensive nature of the industry has meant that it has proved impossible to run a large network on a commercial basis, irrespective of ownership structure, and without subsidy, capital grants, loan guarantees or debt forgiveness.

The focus in this chapter is on the financial or distributional, as opposed to the broader transport, outcomes. This is because the PPP policy assumes first that the project itself is the best of all the available transport options; and second that the choice of public or private finance will be based upon a financial appraisal methodology that emphasizes risk transfer to the private sector and thus the least cost over the life of the project. That is, the choice is simply between different forms of finance, although clearly the social and economic benefits of the project will differ in terms of consumer surplus to the users and environmental benefits/damages.

The chapter adopts a political-economy or stakeholder perspective and considers the financial costs and rewards to the various stakeholders involved. It uses financial evidence derived from the research literature, official and regulatory reports, statistical sources and the press, although the stakeholders will vary according to the type of arrangement (the taxpayers, users, providers of finance, contractors etc.). As such, therefore, financing transport is also about the politics of and accountability for such projects.

The chapter is organized in several sections. The first section considers the first eight DBFO road contracts paid for via a system of shadow tolls by the Highways Agency and the first and, thus far, only toll motorway concession. The second section examines first the national railways, reviewing the experience of the passenger rail franchises, which are largely but not entirely subsidized concessions with user charges via passenger fares, and second, a metro system, reviewing the experience of the three London Underground PPPs. The third section considers the sale in 2001 of a 51 per cent stake in National Air Traffic Services to the private sector, which the government has designated a PPP. The final section draws out the implications for accountability and choice of financing method.

Road transport

DBFO contracts
Shaoul et al. (2006) examined the first eight of the Highways Agency's 14 contracts to extend and maintain its roads. Their analysis is dependent upon the limited information provided by the private sector partners, not the Highways Agency or its auditors and the public watchdogs.

These eight contracts, operational since 1997, are paid for by the Highways Agency on the basis of traffic volumes or shadow tolls. The evidence relating to one of these roads, and there is no reason to believe that the results are substantially different for the others, suggests that in engineering terms, the road was constructed in accordance with the contractual requirements and its operation and maintenance are broadly satisfactory, although these are considered in isolation from the cost (Shaoul et al., 2007a). Certainly, the Highways Agency views them as a success, although it has published no financial evidence about the operation of the contracts to demonstrate whether they constitute VfM in practice.

The concessionaires are 'special purpose vehicles' (SPVs) or consortia, typically composed of a financial institution and construction and maintenance companies, which raise debt to finance the projects. As shell companies with no employees, the SPVs typically subcontract the work to their sister companies. The Agency pays about £220 million a year for these eight DBFO contracts, indicating a total cost of about £6 billion over the 30-year life of the contracts. With traffic volumes rising, the SPVs are commercially successful companies. Payments in just three years for which information is publicly available were £618 million, more than the £590 million cost of construction.

The annual cost of finance, interest payable and post-tax profits was about two-thirds of the revenues received from the Highways Agency, although in some years this was even higher due to refinancing gains. It illustrates the importance of capital, as opposed to operating costs, in roads. The additional cost of private over public finance was estimated to be more than 20 per cent of revenues a year. This was, however, a conservative estimate, since the parent companies have additional, undisclosed sources of profit via subcontracting the construction, operation, maintenance and financing of the projects to related companies, as well as refinancing gains, making it impossible to establish the total cost of using the private sector as financial intermediaries.

The additional cost of private over public finance raises two issues: the cost of risk transfer and affordability. The higher cost of private finance is justified in terms of risk transfer. But since risk and risk transfer are *ex ante* concepts, it is impossible to quantify the risk *ex post facto* and thus determine whether or not it constitutes VfM. There are several indications that the risk transfer was minimal and/or generously priced.

First, the contracts involved not new roads but road improvements that had already been designed and had gone through all the planning stages, thereby reducing some of the main risks (NAO, 1998; Shaoul et al., 2007a). Second, most of the risk transfer is attributed to the construction phase. This was in some cases at least low since about 40 of the SPVs, across a range of sectors including two of these eight DBFO contracts, refinanced their deals after construction by taking out a larger loan over a longer period, repaying the original debt, leaving a surplus for their parent companies. These refinancing deals, however, create additional risk for the public sector (NAO, 2002a, 2005, 2006). Should the contract be terminated for any reason, the public sector could face higher costs. Furthermore, this increased exposure would occur when the private sector had received most of the benefits and be facing additional costs associated with long-term maintenance, thereby tempting the private sector in adverse circumstances to cut and run, as indeed has been the case with unprofitable rail franchises (see later).

Third, some of the companies took an alternative route, selling their equity in the PPP consortium at a considerable profit on their original stake and at several times the level of annual post-tax profits. This has reflected the high profits from these contracts in the early stage of the projects when profits were not expected to be high and implies that their new owners envisage little risk, with continuing and attractive rates of return on their investment. Fourth, the main cost, as shown earlier, is in fact the cost of finance. Should the SPV be put into administration or terminate its contract with the commissioning agency due to low traffic volumes, then the public sector must continue to honour the financial obligations to the banks. There is therefore little direct risk to the parent companies (whose initial investment was in any event very small) and almost none to the banks, since the state *de facto* guarantees the debt.

The higher cost of private over public finance, equivalent to at least 20 per cent of the companies' receipts from Highways Agency every year, also raises questions about the impact of these schemes on the rest of the Agency's budget. According to a Highways Agency official, the commitments for all its DBFO projects are about £300 million a year, or 20 per cent of its budget, for 8 per cent of its network (Taylor, 2005). He said that the new contract for the M25 would add a further £300 million a year, meaning that 40 per cent of the budget will be committed for a very small proportion of the network. Thus, while these roads will be maintained, there may be little money left over for the rest of the network, which may not be the most rational way of prioritizing road maintenance.

Several interrelated conclusions flow from this analysis. The costs of the DBFO shadow toll road projects are in line with other UK DBFO road projects (Shaoul et al., 2008a) and hospitals (Shaoul et al., 2008b), and both toll and shadow toll roads in Spain (Acerete et al., 2009). The evidence suggests that the Highways Agency has paid a high price for risk transfer and challenges the notion that risk transfer delivers VfM. It also raises questions about affordability and suggests that these contracts must entail cuts elsewhere. This in turn means that, far from providing additionality, the new construction (and maintenance) comes at the expense of other Highways Agency projects.

M6 toll-road

In 1989, the then Conservative government proposed a privately funded and financed venture to build a new road to relieve congestion on the motorways around Birmingham. The concession for the M6 toll road would run for 53 years, expected to be three years of construction and 50 years of operation. After long planning delays, the road opened at the end of 2003, with a construction cost of about £700 million. With its charges unregulated, the road operator originally set its prices to minimize its future maintenance costs by pricing heavy goods vehicles off the road.

Shaoul et al., (2008a) found that, in 2006, revenues, including those from the service station, were £51 million. This was widely acknowledged to be less than expected due to lower-than-forecast traffic volumes, although traffic was rising and had reached 50 000 on an average working day (company's website). Intended to relieve congestion, the new toll road still carries only 20 per cent of the traffic on the existing motorway, despite reducing its charges for heavy goods vehicles from £11 to £7, and has thus failed to achieve its stated *raison d'être*.

The company was financed by debt, which at £819 million was considerably more than the construction cost of the road (about £700 million). The interest payable to service the debt was £45 million, an effective interest rate of 5 per cent. While this is as yet low and only marginally more than the cost of public debt, it may increase, as typically the interest payments are deliberately set low in the early years when revenues may be low. After paying interest, the company made a post-tax loss of £21 million in 2006. Losses have continued and have risen to £28 million in 2008.

With construction complete and evidently having cost less than expected since the debt was larger than the cost of construction, the company refinanced its debt in June 2006, taking on a larger debt that would release about £350 million cash for investments elsewhere. This serves to increase the concessionaire's risk. It also increases the risk to the Highways Agency, which will have to assume responsibility for the road should the concessionaire go under.

Anxious to increase the low traffic volume, the concessionaire came to an agreement with the government to use £110 million of the proceeds to finance the construction of two new road developments that would feed into the M6 toll road, which would not themselves be tolled. This would increase revenues and reduce the burden of interest charges. Although the Highways Agency refused to release both the strategic case and the contract for the developments under a 'Freedom of Information' request for reasons of commercial confidentiality, it did confirm what was implicit in the announcement: the project had been agreed without advertisement or competition and the road had not yet received planning approval.

Irrespective of the fact that the road will be built without cost to the taxpayer as a means of sharing the refinancing gains and there may be no breach of the procurement rules, this means that the road has jumped the capital prioritization queue as a result of an unsolicited proposal. That is, instead of the Highways Agency using its share of the refinancing gain for other projects, it has enabled the construction of a new road to go ahead that may not have been justified on broader economic grounds in order to make the toll road viable, shielded from public visibility and scrutiny under the rubric of 'commercial sensitivity'. Moreover, the route in terms of traffic management makes little sense. In other words, further initiatives have been taken to make a private road viable that may not have been justified on broader economic grounds. Or to put it another way, like the cuckoo, once in the nest, it chases the other birds out.

Rail

Passenger rail franchises
Since privatization in the mid-1990s, the railways have been part-funded by a system of operating subsidies to private sector train operating companies (TOCs), which have a franchise to run designated services for a specified period. The train operators use the subsidies to lease the trains from privately owned rolling-stock companies and access the track from Railtrack, the privately owned infrastructure company, as well as defray their other costs. Railtrack was later replaced by Network Rail, a private not-for-profit network infrastructure company, when Railtrack collapsed in 2001 under a mountain of debt. The costs of leasing the rolling stock, the broad outline of which was set at privatization, and of accessing the track, whose charges were set by the rail regulator to cover the cost of approved investment, maintenance and renewals, are essentially fixed costs for the franchise operators. While some fares are regulated and allowed to rise no more than 1 per cent above inflation, some are unregulated. These two fixed costs, the leasing and track-access charges, the expected level of demand, the fare levels and the cost of running train services determine the level of subsidies required.

The stated purpose of breaking up the integrated industry into numerous private companies linked by contracting relationships was to generate the efficiency and dynamism presumed to be lacking in the publicly owned operator, British Rail (BR) (Department of Transport, 1992). Competition for the franchises to run passenger services, if not competition on the tracks, would ensure efficiency and VfM. The leasing of rolling stock would enable companies to bid for the franchises and permit new entrants to the market. Together, the new structure would generate competition and efficiency bringing benefits to all.

In terms of PPPs, the railways therefore represent a mix of public and private finance *and* funding channelled largely through a system of concessions or franchises, whose service levels, frequencies and routes are set out in their contracts (not publicly available) and monitored by regulation, with inadequate performance against targets subject to penalties.

The first round of franchises, 1995–2004 The right to operate the train services was divided into 25 franchises for which competitive bids were invited between 1994 and 1997. Franchises were generally awarded to the bidders requiring the lowest level of subsidy, with only one awarded without subsidy. Subsidies were more than double that given to BR in the 1980s and the early 1990s before the restructuring of the industry for privatization. Although the intention was that subsidies would decline to £0.9 billion by 2003, that had still not been achieved by 2009. The 25 franchises were awarded to just 11 companies, a number that has since halved as companies have merged, been taken over or left the industry.

The much-vaunted performance targets were no more demanding than those set for BR in the interim regime 1994–96. Thus no improvement was built into the franchise system, belying the government claim that services would improve. Performance indicators of punctuality and reliability are no longer published in a way that permits direct comparisons with standards of performance before privatization. Performance deteriorated, particularly in the period 2000 to 2005, after Railtrack's failure to maintain the track in a safe condition, and subsequent collapse. Although much improved, even in 2009 performance has still not attained BR's level. But even these results would not have been achieved if the train operators had not made extensive use of a loophole in the regulations that allows them to exclude from performance data days when they have serious problems and have to extend the scheduled time. The deterioration in levels of service is widely attributed to the de-manning that took place after privatization and the lack of capacity on parts of the network due to inadequate investment, leading to overcrowding and delays.

By 2006, the combined revenues of the 25 franchises had risen from £4.6 billion in 1997 to £6.2 billion, more than double BR's total revenues in the last year (1993–94) of the *ancien regime* (Shaoul, 2006). This was the result of several factors: fare increases on some routes that were higher than the rate of inflation; increased passenger numbers alongside a general increase in all modes of travel due to the expanding economy and traffic congestion on the roads; 'revenue protection' measures to ensure that passengers paid for their journeys; and the end of the sale of discounted fares on board the trains. But finally, and most importantly, revenues rose because subsidies were considerably higher than in the 1980s and early 1990s: they accounted for £2.1 billion, 71 per cent of total income in 1996, declining to £1.1 billion, 17 per cent in 2006. It should, however, be noted that it is extraordinarily difficult to get clear and consistent information about the payments of subsidies to the train operators (Shaoul, 2006).

However, the increase in revenues notwithstanding, the majority of the franchisees are totally dependent upon subsidies to recover their costs and deliver a profit. Only a handful of the TOCs made a profit. Without subsidies, aggregate losses in 2006 would have been £1.1 billion, a sum equivalent to their subsidies. The TOCs paid out £144 million in dividends to their parent companies in 2006 and £1.5 billion since privatization, due to the extensive system of public subsidies, not superior performance.

Had the 'market' and the franchise agreements operated as intended, many of the TOCs would have gone out of business. While the original franchises were let 'competitively', that is, to the bidder requiring the lowest level of subsidy, the bids turned out to be hopelessly optimistic on the TOCs' part (Transport Select Committee, 2004). With the government refusing to countenance renationalization in any form, termination of the contracts and bringing passenger services back in house was not normally perceived to be an option. The regulator, the short-lived Strategic Rail Authority (SRA), was therefore obliged to step in to 'ensure continuity of train services' and amend the franchise agreements.

First, the SRA increased the subsidies (SRA, 2003). In one of the more egregious examples, Connex South East received £58 million in 2002 due to differences in its cost and revenue assumptions. 'They had got their numbers wrong', as the SRA chair explained to the Transport Select Committee (Transport Select Committee, 2004). In the event, shortly after increasing the subsidy, the SRA terminated the franchise due to the TOC's poor performance. In January 2003, the press reported that more than half the TOCs received emergency bailouts in the preceding two years amid claims that the SRA was imposing 'gagging clauses' on the TOCs to prevent them disclosing information about their bailouts. By way of contrast, the information became publicly available because the stock market requires the disclosure of information that affects corporate profitability.

Second, the SRA converted some of the franchises into management-only contracts, with payment on a 'cost-plus' basis and a higher subsidy for less risk, prior to retendering the franchises. In 2003, 'over one third of the franchises' (SRA, 2003, p. 47) were operated in this way, which the SRA admitted 'had become expensive' (ibid., p. 39).

The second round of franchises While the SRA had renegotiated the first round of franchises at the taxpayers' expense, in 2004 it negotiated a second round that has proved no more successful. The routes were restructured to make them more commercially viable, and the only companies eligible to bid were those in the transport sector, thereby confirming the monopoly position of the existing concessionaires. A few of the lines, such as the East Coast Main Line (ECML), were believed to be sufficiently profitable to enable the franchisees to pay the government an annual premium, and were awarded on that basis. In an effort to ensure the profitability of the franchises and thereby avoid any future contract renegotiation, the government sought to limit the operators' risk by assuming some of its revenue risks, the key risk. New franchises included clauses that would after four years reimburse the operators for 50 per cent of any shortfall in revenue below 98 per cent of the original forecast and 80 per cent of any shortfall in revenue below 96 per cent, and claw back 50 per cent of any increase in revenue above 102 per cent of the original forecast (Transport Select Committee, 2006).

In the event, GNER Ltd, which won a second seven-year contract for the ECML franchise in return for a £1.3 billion premium over the life of the contract, handed back the keys in 2006 when the franchise proved to be less profitable than its own overoptimistic forecasts had suggested. Indeed, simple projections of GNER's cash flow, based on its annual report and accounts, revealed that it could only have been viable if there had been a most unlikely 10 per cent growth in passenger revenue. GNER then ran the franchise for a further year on a management-only and risk-free basis. Yet its projections had evidently satisfied the Department for Transport's financial advisers, since the then Transport Minister brushed off the industry view at the time that GNER had overbid. He said, 'We crawled over the figures over the last few weeks because we wanted to make sure that the bid actually stood up'.[1] But within two years, it had collapsed.

In August 2007, the government awarded the ECML franchise to National Express in return for a more onerous £1.4 billion premium over seven years. But National Express has been no more successful. After paying the government £85 million in 2008, in April 2009 National Express demanded a renegotiation of its franchise. Not only did it demand to be let off the remaining charge, it also demanded that it be paid to keep running the railway on a management-only, risk-free basis. In response, the Department for Transport (DfT) insisted that it could renegotiate the contract and threatened to invoke a 'cross-default' clause that would strip National Express of its other two profitable franchises if it failed to keep up with payments on the ECML. Later, the government terminated the contract to deter other rail operators from seeking to renegotiate their contracts, increase the subsidies or reduce their premia, as passenger numbers, revenues and profits declined due to the global recession that has undermined the optimistic bids underpinning the recent franchise agreements. It has now re-awarded the franchise on a similar basis to yet another company. Its attempt to strip National Express of its other franchises, held by legally separate subsidiaries, looks set to spark a lengthy legal battle over compensation. Its attempt to strip National Express of its other franchises failed as they are held by legally separate susbidiaries, thereby rendering null and void cross-default clauses, while the transaction costs have proved costly for the government.

The passenger rail franchises have proved to be a failure in terms of both performance and cost to users and taxpayers alike, and this is almost universally recognized – apart from the government, its advisers and the train operators, the beneficiaries of the regime. Such outcomes were entirely predictable. The fragmented and private ownership structure imposed on the industry ignores the basic realities of the industry. First, the essential problem of the railways the world over is that as a highly capital-intensive industry it is difficult if not impossible to recover the full cost of running the industry, including the cost of enhancing the infrastructure and rolling stock, from the fare box, which is why, in the postwar period at least, public ownership and investment were necessary. Privatization, which increases the claims of finance, only exacerbates the problem. Second, in the context of the UK, since the railways already had the lowest subsidies in Europe and the highest labour productivity, it was always going to be difficult to cut costs further to provide the necessary headroom for profits without either affecting service quality and safety or increasing subsidies and/or fares (Shaoul, 2004). Taken together, this means that for all the talk of transferring risk to the private sector, the risks that the government always retains are the demand, default, political and reputational risks – and these are the most important ones.

London Underground
The first phase of the London Underground (LU) PPPs, the Labour government's flagship PFI projects, constitutes a quarter of the capital value of all the £64 billion worth of deals signed by April 2009.[2] The government agreed to the deals despite overwhelming popular hostility to the PPP proposals for LU in the wake of the collapse of the privatized rail infrastructure company, Railtrack, and studies showing that it was neither affordable or value for money (Gaffney et al., 2000; Glaister et al., 2000; NAO, 2000; Shaoul, 2002). Under the PPPs, three private sector companies would maintain and refurbish LU's tracks, signals, stations and rolling stock for 30 years in return for an annual charge. LU would continue to operate passenger services, in effect leasing the track and rolling stock from its private sector partners.

The cost of the PPPs proved so expensive that, first, the investment had to be scaled back and the risk of some cost overruns excluded, and second, the government had to provide about £1 billion a year in subsidy to LU, more than five times the existing grant, despite the fact that the government had originally wanted to withdraw all subsidies. Third, Transport for London (TfL), LU's parent body, would guarantee 95 per cent of the contractors' approved debts in order to reduce the cost of borrowing and reassure their financiers, necessarily more expensive than public sector debt, without any corresponding reduction in debt servicing charges. Fourth, the government itself gave an open-ended commitment to the

City and big business. The Department for Transport (DfT) wrote to TfL, saying that should LU find itself in financial difficulties as a result of the PPPs, the Secretary of State for Transport 'regards it as untenable that' he would not consider further financial aid or that 'he would stand by and do nothing in those circumstances'.[3] As will be seen, the contractors and bankers saw this for what it was – a blank cheque – with the taxpayers footing the bill.

By 2006, the additional costs of the contract, financing and profit margins attributable to the companies' subcontractors, costs that would not otherwise have been borne under public procurement, were 15–21 per cent of the annual payments (based on my conservative calculations on data from Metronet's annual report and accounts).

Despite these subventions, within two years, Metronet, which had two of the three £17 billion contracts, was behind with its investment programme and over budget. In July 2007, it went into administration with debts of at least £2 billion after its owners, five international corporations, refused to put in another penny beyond their original commitment under the terms of the contract. Metronet's bankruptcy was precipitated by the refusal of the Rail Arbiter to award more than a fraction of its appeal for increased payments from LU to fund its near £1 billion overspend and a further £1 billion projected overspend by 2010. In a statement the Rail Arbiter issued to the press on 16 July 2007, he said that if Metronet 'had delivered in an efficient and economic way, its costs would have been lower'. It is yet another – very expensive – refutation of the myth, so assiduously promoted by big business, the civil service and the government, to justify privatization and PPPs: that the corporations are more efficient at delivering public services than the public sector. Many senior civil-service personnel are now recruited by, or are on secondment from, or are even paid by the financial services industry (Shaoul et al., 2007b).

With Metronet's debts guaranteed by TfL – and ultimately the government – the taxpayers, workforce and travelling public will bear the cost. The Mayor of London announced that £750 million would be made available to the Administrator to ensure that the trains would keep running. Metronet would continue its work while in administration and its suppliers – Metronet's sister companies – and the workforce would continue to be paid. TfL decided to retain the work in house, which the London Assembly transport committee believes has saved LU some £2 billion through 'the availability of cheaper finance'.[4] But it has had to defer some of the improvements, such as station refurbishment, expected under the PPP.

So, far from the private sector bearing the risk and cost when things go wrong – another fraudulent myth endlessly parroted by government ministers to justify the higher cost of private over public finance – Metronet, like the franchise operator, GNER, simply handed back the keys and left it to the taxpayer to sort out the mess, a travesty of risk transfer. LU was only one of a number of PFI/PPP projects that collapsed and had to be bailed out. Others include the Channel Tunnel Rail Link, National Air Traffic Services, the Royal Armouries Museums, to name but a few. The information technology (IT) PFI projects have proved so disastrous that even the government has abandoned PFI for IT.

With respect to the remaining PPP with Tube Lines, it too became embroiled in a row with LU over the second 7.5-year period, set to run from 2010 to 2017. Tube Lines claimed that the investment, renewal and maintenance programme would cost £7.2 billion. But the independent Rail Arbiter priced the work at between £5.1 billion and £5.5 billion, leaving a gap of about £2 billion,[5] although LU priced the contract at £4.1 billion, leaving an even bigger gap. The then chief executive of LU stated in April 2009 that he believed that it would cost less if the entire £30 billion PPP programme to renovate the tube network was carried out in house instead of being awarded to a PPP. He attributed the difference in cost to the additional cost of private finance. He warned that if the dispute with Tube Lines over the funding gap was not resolved, then that contract too might have to be abandoned. While subsequent negotiations narrowed the gap, in June 2010, the second 7.5-year contract was abandoned, with LU buying out Tube Lines at a cost of £310 million after the company fell seriously behind with its upgrade to the Jubilee Line.

Air traffic control
Britain's air traffic control operater, National Air Traffic Services (NATS), the third-largest air traffic controller (ATC) in the EU, provides take-off and landing services at 14 UK airports, some international services and, most importantly, *en route* air traffic control services for aircraft flying over the UK and its North East Atlantic airspace. About 80 per cent of NATS' revenues are derived from North Atlantic travel. Its services are vital if the airlines are to operate safely and efficiently. But with the UK's air lanes severely congested, the overarching safety requirement may lead to delays that create extra costs for its customers, the airlines, without careful management. Since the mid-1990s, with short-haul European flights set to rise, capacity in the UK and continental Europe has increasingly become a problem. It can only be increased by some combination of rationalization within the airline industry via mergers and takeovers to get better route structures, larger planes, better equipment, increased sectorization and fewer ATCs.

Reconstituted in 1996 by the then Conservative government as a corporation, NATS operated as a subsidiary of the publicly owned Civil Aviation Authority (CAA). In 1998, the incoming Labour government published plans for a partial sale of NATS to a private partner, under its flagship PPP policy, and introduced the necessary enabling legislation in 2000. In March 2001, the government agreed to transfer a 51 per cent stake in NATS to the Airline Group, a consortium of seven airlines, NATS' UK customers, for about £800 million. But in May, the Airline Group told the government that as a result of the decline in the transatlantic traffic and costs that it had overlooked, it could not afford its offer price and a reduction of £45 million was agreed. In July 2001, the government transferred a controlling stake in NATS to the Airline Group for £750 million, with the expectation that its new owners would invest in new equipment to the tune of £1 billion over ten years. The Airline Group financed the deal with £55 million of their own capital as equity and raised the rest as loans that would be repayable by NATS, with the intention of raising the £1 billion investment funding via additional loans, making a total of about £1.6 billion.

Thus NATS would be a PPP or joint venture between the private sector and the Civil Aviation Authority, NATS' former public sector parent. But within three months, in the aftermath of the terrorist bombing of the World Trade Center in September 2001, which halted transatlantic traffic for three days and the subsequent downturn in traffic volume, NATS' bankers became concerned about NATS' ability to service its debts, forcing NATS to ask for government help to stave off bankruptcy. Given the government's international treaty obligations to provide air traffic services and commitment to its flagship policy, it had no option but to provide financial support.

Although NATS and the government attributed the collapse to unforeseeable events, an analysis carried out before financial close (Shaoul, 2003) that had assumed a £350 million purchase price had shown that the project was unviable: it was never going to be affordable, even without the unprecedented downturn in travel after 9/11. The PPP worsened rather than resolved NATS' financial problems. But no risk assessment was carried out even though the government remained a part-owner and as signatory to international conventions guaranteed service delivery (NAO, 2002b). This was despite the fact that the PPP generated *additional* risks as a result of the high level of private sector loans.

Conclusion

This chapter has sought to provide evidence on the experience of some of the UK's transport PPPs and the financial costs of different types of PPPs to inform the international policy debate about the use of private finance and its broader implications for accountability.

The first point is that there is a lack of clear, consistent and understandable reporting by both the public and private sectors, making it difficult to understand where public money is going, how it is being spent, and the extent of future commitments and liabilities. There have been some useful reports by the official watchdogs, which have far greater access to information into individual projects, typically on process-related issues such as *ex ante* VfM decision-making, contract management, tendering, benchmarking and renegotiation. However, there has been a failure to provide an independent *ex post facto* financial analysis of either the policy as a whole or individual PPP projects. In other words, most analyses have focused on the benefits and limitations of projects in isolation from the financing method and costs to the various stakeholders.

Second, while this study has focused on the financial outcomes of transport PPPs, it is quite clear that the rail projects have failed to deliver the physical outputs expected, despite receiving higher funding than was ever available under public ownership. In relation to road projects, there is no evidence to suggest that they are any better or worse than their conventionally procured counterparts. In so far as the roads are better maintained, and this remains to be demonstrated, then this comes at a high cost and at the expense of other roads.

Third, while this survey of transport PPPs is by no means complete, the financial evidence and analysis confirms the international experience outlined in general terms in the literature. The high capital cost of transport projects makes it difficult if not impossible for such projects to be financially viable and thus attractive to the private sector. This is why governments must ensure some combination of capital grants, subsidies, implicit or explicit underwriting of the private sector's debt or the public authority's payments, bundling together of projects to increase their size relative to transaction costs, project and service downsizing, higher charges for the public authority or the users and a reduction in workers' jobs, wages and conditions. Thus the method of financing that lies at the heart of the policy has broader social and economic implications.

Fourth, the evidence has shown that partnerships have entailed a higher cost of finance. This is a universal phenomenon and independent of partnership form, contractual or joint venture. Likewise, success, as reflected in commercial viability, is also independent of partnership form.

The higher cost of finance has several interrelated consequences. It is justified, *ex ante*, in terms of risk transfer to the private sector. It is however very difficult to assess, post-implementation, whether that risk was priced correctly and therefore the project constituted VfM. If the project is successful, then the public agency pays considerably more than under conventional procurement. If, on the other hand, it is unsuccessful, then the risks and costs may be dispersed as the rail franchises, London Underground and NATS PPPs demonstrate. In effect, the risk transfer is not from the state to the private sector, but from the consortium to its subcontractors and their workforce and to the public as taxpayers and users, a travesty of risk transfer. The beneficiaries are the banks and to a lesser extent the consortia and parent companies, who are shielded from public scrutiny. These distributional effects confirm the experience elsewhere and in other sectors such as IT (Edwards and Shaoul, 2003).

Although a project may fail to transfer risk and deliver VfM in the way that the public agency anticipated, the possibility of enforcing the arrangements and/or dissolving the partnership is in practice severely circumscribed for legal, operational and political reasons, with the result that the public authority may find itself locked into a partnership. The *de facto* lack of sanctions strengthens the contractor's already powerful financial and monopolistic position, forcing the public authority to (re)negotiate on the contractor's terms.

At best, partnerships have turned out to be very expensive, with the inevitable consequences for future service provision, taxes and user charges, not just today but for a long time to come. These projects may burden government with hidden subsidies, diversion of income streams and revenue guarantees whose impact on public finance may not become apparent for many years and may all be triggered at the same time, precipitating a major fiscal crisis.

The high failure rate of the rail franchises, together with the failed London Underground and NATS PPPs, raises questions about the public authorities' appraisals of PPP bids. One franchise has now been let three times on essentially the same terms, despite the fact that the previous two failed within a very short time. For all these projects, simple projections based upon the organizations' annual report and accounts and carried out before financial close, showed that these schemes were simply not viable. Nevertheless, the international firms of legal and financial advisers apparently found otherwise. How is this to be explained?

These same advisers have played a key role in devising the policy, the VfM methodology, the implementation process and promoting the policy internationally. They have a commercial interest in the policy as an important new market, acting as advisers to both the public and private sectors and in some contracts as partners or major subcontractors in their own right (Shaoul et al., 2007b). The case of the failed NATS PPP is particularly instructive. The Department of Transport paid its advisers, one of whose tasks it was to evaluate and manage the risks to NATS' business, some £44 million (£17 million more than expected) and 5.5 per cent of the proceeds, among the highest of all the trade sales examined by the National Audit Office (2002b). CSFB, the lead financial adviser, claimed that their prime motivation was to gain valuable experience of PPPs in order to win future contracts in this new and expanding market. Furthermore, under circumstances where the government is actively promoting the involvement of the private sector in running public services via PPPs by refusing to make funding available for capital investment, policy promotion comes into conflict with rigorous project appraisal. It is therefore perhaps not surprising that the advisers failed to evaluate the PPP correctly, and ignored evidence and advice that did not fit with the government and its own agenda: a signed deal.

In short, this analysis has demonstrated that the outcomes do not match the claims. This is because the government's claims about the value of private finance ignored the competing demands of the numerous stakeholders and the characteristic of transport projects: the highly capital-intensive nature of public goods that makes it impossible to make the return on capital that the stock market requires. In such circumstances, it was and is impossible to reconcile all the conflicting claims on the revenues and protect both the taxpayers and users. The government resolved the conflict in the interest of the banks and corporations and sought – via the mantra of risk transfer and VfM – to make the distributional issue invisible.

The lack of public accountability is therefore unsurprising. The inadequate financial reporting of and accountability for PPP projects hides what the government does not wish to reveal. It makes it difficult to draw any lessons from the experience. It also renders an informed public debate impossible, leading to the wrong policy choice. Even more importantly, public discourse itself becomes meaningless. The broader policy implications of these findings are that any rational government and policy-maker committed to the broader public interest would take note of the independent and impartial evidence, abandon the policy and use public finance for public infrastructure.

Notes

1. GNER referred to a statement by Alastair Darling, the then Secretary of State for Transport, in a comment to a debate in the House of Commons, 19 December 2006.
2. HM Treasury (2009), www.hm-treasury.gov.uk/d/pfi_signed_projects_list.xls, (accessed 29 September 2009).
3. Letter dated 30 December 2002, p. 4, from David Rowlands, the Director General of Railways and Aviation, at the Department of Transport, addressed to all the partners, main contractors and financiers of the London Underground PPP. For further information please contact the author.
4. *New Civil Engineer* (2009), 'London Assembly: Government should plug Tube cash shortfalls', www.nce.co.uk/home/transport/london-assembly-government-should-plug-tube-cash-shortfalls/1995470.article, 11 May 2009.

5. Transport for London (2008), 'Transport for London responds to PPP Arbiter's Guidance on Tube Lines second period funding', www.tfl.gov.uk/corporate/media/news-centre/archive/9308.aspx#, 11 May 2009.

References

Acerete, B., J. Shaoul and A. Stafford (2009), 'Taking its toll: the private financing of roads in Spain', *Public Money and Management*, **29** (1), 19–26.

Bel, G. and X. Fageda (2005), 'Is a mixed funding model for the highway network sustainable over time? The Spanish case', in G. Ragazzi and W. Rothengatter (eds), *Procurement and Financing Motorways in Europe*, Research in Transportation Economics Vol. 15, The Netherlands: Elsevier, pp. 187–203.

Boardman, A.E., F. Poschmann and A. Vining (2005), 'North American infrastructure P3s: examples and lessons learned', in G. Hodge and C. Greve (eds), *The Challenge of Public–Private Partnerships: Learning from International Experience*, Cheltenham, UK and Northampton, MA, USA: Edward Elgar, pp. 162–89.

Department of Transport (1992), 'The franchising of passenger rail services', consultation paper, London: Department of Transport.

Department for Transport (2004), *The Future of Rail*, White Paper, CM 6233, London: The Stationery Office.

Edwards, P. and J. Shaoul (2003), 'Partnerships: for better for worse?', *Accounting, Auditing and Accountability Journal*, **16** (3), 397–421.

Ehrhardt, D. and T. Irwin (2004), 'Avoiding customer and taxpayer bailouts in private infrastructure projects: public policy towards leverage, risk allocation and bankruptcy', World Bank Policy Research Working Paper 3274, Washington, DC: The World Bank, Infrastructure Economics and Finance.

Estache, A. and T. Serebrisky (2004), 'Where do we stand on transport infrastructure deregulation and public private partnership?', World Bank Policy Research Working Paper 3356, Washington, DC: The World Bank.

Farrell, S. (1997), *Financing European transport infrastructure: policies and practice in Western Europe*, Basingstoke: Macmillan.

Freeman, P. (2004), 'Evaluating project performance in transport projects in developing countries', presentation to Transport Research Congress, Istanbul, July, Washington, DC: Operations Evaluation Department, World Bank.

Gaffney, D., J. Shaoul and A. Pollock (2000), 'Funding London Underground: financial myths and economic realities', report, London: *Listen to London*.

Glaister, S., R. Scanlon and T. Travers (2000), 'Public private partnerships and investment in transport', Report for the IPPR Commission on Public–Private Partnerships, London.

National Audit Office (1998), *The Private Finance Initiative: The First Four Design, Build, Finance and Operate Roads Contracts*, Report of Comptroller and Auditor General, HC 476, Session 1997–98, London: The Stationery Office.

National Audit Office (2000), *The Financial Analysis for the London Underground Public Private Partnership*, House of Commons Paper 54, Session 2000–01, London: The Stationery Office.

National Audit Office (2002a), *PFI Refinancing Update*, Report of Comptroller and Auditor General, HC 1288, Session 2001–02, London: The Stationery Office.

National Audit Office (2002b), *The Public Private Partnership for National Air Traffic Services Ltd*, Report by the Comptroller and Auditor General, HC 1096, Session 2001–02, London: The Stationery Office.

National Audit Office (2005), *The Refinancing of the Norfolk and Norwich PFI Hospital: How the Deal can be Viewed in the Light of Refinancing*, Report by the Comptroller and Auditor General, HC 78, Session 20005–06, London: The Stationery Office.

National Audit Office (2006), *Update on PFI Debt Refinancing and the PFI Equity Market*, Report by the Comptroller and Auditor General, HC 1040, Session 2006–07, London: The Stationery Office.

Pollock, A. and D. Price (2008), 'Has the NAO audited risk transfer in operational private finance initiative schemes?', *Public Money and Management*, **28** (3), 173–8.

PPP Arbiter (2007), 'Reference for directions from Metronet BCV Ltd', 16 July, London, available at: www.ppparbiter.org.uk/files/uploads/o_direction/20071665446_Final%20draft%directions.pdf.

Shaoul, J. (2002), 'A financial appraisal of London Underground public private partnership', *Public Money and Management*, **22** (2), 53–60.

Shaoul, J. (2003), 'Financial analysis of the National Air Traffic Services public private partnership', *Public Money and Management*, **3** (23), 185–94.

Shaoul, J. (2004), '*Railpolitik*: the financial realities of operating Britain's national railways', *Public Money and Management*, **24** (1), 27–36.

Shaoul, J. (2006), 'The cost of operating Britain's privatised railways', *Public Money and Management*, **26** (3), 151–8.

Shaoul, J., A. Stafford and P. Stapleton (2006), 'Highway robbery? A financial analysis of the design, build, financing and operation (DBFO) in UK roads', *Transport Reviews*, **26** (3), 257–74.

Shaoul, J., A. Stafford and P. Stapleton (2007a), 'Evidence based policies and the meaning of success: the case of a road built under design build finance and operate', *Evidence and Policy*, **3** (2), 159–79.

Shaoul, J., A. Stafford and P. Stapleton (2007b), 'Private control over public policy: financial advisors and the private finance initiative', *Policy and Politics*, **35** (3), 479–96.

Shaoul, J., A. Stafford, P. Stapleton and P. Macdonald (2008a), *Financial Black Holes: Accounting for Privately Financed Roads in the UK*, Edinburgh: ICAS.

Shaoul, J., A. Stafford and P. Stapleton (2008b), 'The cost of using private finance to build, finance and operate the first 12 NHS hospitals in England', *Public Money and Management*, **28** (2), 101–8.

Silva, G.F. (2000), *Toll Roads: Recent Trends in Private Participation*, Private Sector and Infrastructure Network, Note Number 224, Washington, DC: World Bank.

Strategic Rail Authority (2003), *Strategic Plan 2003: Platform for Progress*, London: Strategic Rail Authority.

Taylor, G. (2005), 'Major road works ahead: 10 years of the UK private finance initiative roads program', in Standard and Poor's, *Public Private Partnerships: Global Credit Survey*, London.

Transport Select Committee (2004), *The Future of the Railway*, seventh report of session 2003–04, Vol. 1, HC 145–1, London: The Stationery Office.

Transport Select Committee (2006), *Passenger Rail Franchising*, HC 1354, Fourteenth Report, Session 2005–06, London: The Stationery Office.

25 Reviewing public–private partnership performance in developing economies

Argentino Pessoa

Introduction

This chapter aims to appraise public–private partnership (PPP) perform-ance and to anticipate some of the crucial PPP-related issues in developing economies. This is a very difficult task not only because there are large controversies about what PPPs are – and what PPPs must be – but also because developing economies are a heterogeneous universe without a unique evolution pattern. Although this is not the right place to take in hand either debate about the PPP concept or the determinants behind the current wave of private participation in public services, it is true that the way this wave emerged has conditioned PPP performance. Therefore, in the next section we deal with the sources of the contemporary wave of PPPs in developing economies and with the advantages that they alleg-edly have as instruments that can contribute to more quickly solving the development gap.

However, the required evaluation must be context specific. There is abundant literature about evaluation of PPPs (mainly as value for money – VfM), but this is of little help for our purpose, not only because it refers to developed countries[1] and is not conclusive (Hodge and Greve, 2009), but because our purpose is to evaluate PPPs in the context of developing countries, and these have specific characteristics that can make a signifi-cant difference (Pessoa, 2006). So, in the third section we shall deal with both the universe of developing economies and with the most frequent justification for the reform towards a higher participation of the private sector in providing goods that formerly were considered public: the scar-city of public funds in conjunction with the huge infrastructure gap in developing economies.

As with any other evaluation, the evaluation of PPP performance can be affected by controversy. It therefore must be clear-headed, and a solid ground is needed as a base here. The development gap is also overwhelm-ing, both in infrastructure and in social services such as education and health, so whilst PPPs can theoretically be used in both social services and infrastructure, a logical question is why we might focus our attention on PPPs in terms of infrastructure. There are two reasons: first, because there is some path dependency on this issue – in other words, PPPs have increasingly been considered as exclusively referring to private participation in infrastructure. Second, the scarce data available often refer to PPPs in terms of infrastructure services.[2] This chapter therefore limits its analysis to the private participation in infrastructure, using data of the World Bank databases: the WDI (World Development Indicators) and PPI (Private Participation in Infrastructure) database on PPPs. The data analysis is carried out in the fourth section.

In a PPP, a sustained collaborative effort is assumed in order to attain a common objective. On the other hand, one important indicator of the failure of a PPP is the degree of dissatisfaction of populations covered by such arrangements. Sometimes this disappointment causes the unexpected end of the PPP. However, the cessation of a PPP project before the formal contractual end is usually a result of divergence between partners. These divergences may have originated from a multitude of factors, but they always indicate problems in the design of the contractual arrangement or in its functioning conditions. Whatever the situation, termination before the contractual end is always a factor that increases the costs or reduces the potential benefits of PPPs. The fifth section thus deals with the cancellation of PPP arrangements.

If evaluation is not easy, anticipating future crucial issues is even more demanding because we are facing reforms that correspond to pendulum movements, inserted in dependency relationships. Some conclusions will be drawn in the last section, which can then be used as a basis on which to speculate about the likely continued success of PPPs as well as related issues.

The current wave of PPPs in developing economies

It is well known that since the 1980s the capacity of governments to provide public services on their own in an effective and efficient way has been questioned. This point of view calls attention to both the invariably inadequate government resources and the quality and efficiency of the services they offer (World Bank, 1994, 1995; Ferreira and Khatami, 1996). Additionally, there have been a range of arguments provided by the NPM (new public management) movement suggesting that traditional public services are ineffective in resource allocation and poor in management (see, e.g. Hood, 1991; Boston, 1996; Minogue et al., 1998; Polidano, 1999). These have contributed to much heated discussion. Furthermore, it has been highlighted that the public sector does not need to compete because it is often the only provider of services, and that as a consequence, it lacks incentive to improve quality. As a result of all these ideas, there has been a strong belief that if the services are provided directly by government they will deteriorate over time, unless a reform occurs that will allevi-ate the bureaucratic procedures and give the public sector the capacity to act quickly to adapt to change. By the late 1980s, therefore, private sector financing began to be viewed as a promising avenue to explore with regard to providing public goods, and in the funding of infrastructure development.

This reform began in developed countries, partly owing to internal political beliefs, as in the UK, and partly influenced by the European Commission.[3] It was soon extended to developing economies. To some extent, this occurred through pressure from international organizations that shared the view of the 'Washington Consensus',[4] which included within its ten principles the reorientation of public expenditures and priva-tization (Pessoa, 2004; Rodrik, 2006). Using this rationale, international funding agencies such as the World Bank insisted on the advisability of 'using markets in infrastructure provision' (World Bank, 1994, 1995).

Although these reforms were influenced by the NPM, with approaches such as the outsourcing or subcontracting of functions, competition and charging for services, they were also usually connected with a new role to the official development aid (ODA). This new role had adopted in reaction to the emerging recognition that conventional support to public providers through loans for capital investment had not achieved the desired results in reducing poverty (Pessoa, 2008a). Consequently, these new sets of reforms relied on PPPs as a policy instrument to attain multiple purposes, including adequate infrastructure, improving welfare, enhancing efficiency and so on (United Nations, 2002).

On the other hand, the observation that the developing world needs far more financing for infrastructure than can be provided by domestic public finances alone and through ODA was an important motivation, too (Ferreira and Khatami, 1996; Hammami et al., 2006; ADB, 2009). The cost of maintaining existing infrastructure and undertaking necessary extensions of its coverage is estimated by the OECD (2005) at 7 per cent of developing country GDP, equivalent to about US$600 billion per year.[5] However, public spending on infrastructure in developing countries is now around 3 per cent. Given the scarcity of public funds in most developing countries, the obvious solution put forward was to invite greater private sector participation, enlarging the use of public–private agreements in infrastructure and relying on ODA to enhance the quality of projects, reduce risks and raise profitability.

Such public–private agreements were responsible for US$1255 billion in infrastructure investments between 1990 and 2007 (PPI database). Some of this money obviously came from public finances, with the private sector having nevertheless contributed significantly to infrastructure development over the period – according to the OECD (2005) far in excess of what governments could have financed on their own – and assumed several of the risks (e.g. commercial and currency risk) that would otherwise have occurred in the public sector (OECD, 2005).

Two points bear repeating here. First, the movement towards PPPs in developing economies did not begin as an exclusively endogenous process. It was advised and propelled by international organizations under controversial guidance known as the 'Washington Consensus'. Second, the most-used argument advocating PPPs has been that the developing world needs far more financing for infrastructure than can be provided by domestic public finances. However, it is far from certain whether this should be a driver for PPPs in itself, because, as is recognized by the European Investment Bank (EIB): 'In a PPP, the private-sector Provider needs to be paid – either by end-users through real tolls, or by the public-sector Promoter through shadow tolls, asset availability fees, etc. These payments have to cover the costs of funding the project, plus Operating and Maintenance (O&M) costs' (EIB, 2005, p. 11).

The specificity of developing economies
For practical purposes one can classify economies according to relative GDP per capita. The World Bank, for instance, classifies economies into basically three groups: low-income, middle-income and high-income countries.[6] Henceforth we shall consider developing economies as the set composed of low-income and middle-income economies. As a whole, low-income and middle-income countries produce 26 per cent of world GDP (current US$), but they correspond to 74 per cent of the world's surface and 84 per cent of the world's population (World Bank, 2009a). This has two implications. First, this is a large potential market not only for domestic firms in developing economies, but also for companies worldwide. Second, given the shortage of domestic savings in most developing countries, international financing must be called upon to play a role (Ferreira and Khatami, 1996).

Table 25.1 presents some illustrative figures following the WDI (World Development Indicators), and divides the developing economies into six geographic regions: EAP (East Asia and Pacific), ECA (Europe and Central Asia), LAC (Latin America and the Caribbean), MENA (Middle East and North Africa), SA (South Asia), and SSA (Sub-Saharan Africa). Dividing the developing economies into these six regions suggests major differences among them. Of course regions themselves are not homogeneous: there are important differences between rural and urban areas, and these differences are typically higher than in developed countries. For instance, in SSA, where the rate of population growth is the highest in

Table 25.1   Some regional indicators in developing economies

Region	Surface area (thousand sq. km), 2007	Population (in millions), 2007	Average annual growth of population (as %), 1980–2007	Life expectancy at birth (in years), 2007	Under-5 mortality rate per 1000 2007	Child malnutrition, % under-weight, 2000–07	Prevalence of HIV (as % for ages 15–49), 2007
EAP	16299	1912	1.3	72	27	13	0.2
ECA	23972	446	0.4	70	23	. . .	0.6
LAC	20421	561	1.7	73	26	4	0.5
MENA	8778	313	2.3	70	38	. . .	0.1
SA	5140	1522	1.9	64	78	41	0.3
SSA	24242	800	2.7	51	146	27	5.0

Source: Based on World Bank (2009a).

the world, while population has increased at a 1.9 per cent annual rate in rural regions, it is 4 per cent in urban areas. Another example is equally significant: in 2006, in this region, while 57 per cent of the urban population had access to improved sanitation facilities, such access only existed for 23 per cent of the rural population (World Bank, 2009a). This confirms the above-noted high potential market for infrastructure, and particularly for infrastructure and utilities oriented towards urbanization.

As shown in Table 25.1, given the vast surface area, huge population and, above all, the growth rate of population, developing economies face important needs in terms of provision of infrastructure services. With the exception of ECA, where the demographic transition was completed long ago, the high rates of population growth exert an increasing pressure on the supply of social and infrastructure services, significantly higher than in developed countries. Moreover, the increasing rates of urbanization force the building of new infrastructure.[7] However, Table 25.1 also shows that the need for providing high quality social services, as in health and education is not less urgent than the lack of infrastructure. In particular we could note the level of child malnutrition, the under-5s' mortality rate, the prevalence of HIV and, consequently, life expectancy at birth, all of which show impoverished states in terms of health conditions. This is especially the case in SSA.[8]

Moreover, even in economies that have registered large improvements in health and education, significant gaps remain. The example of South Asia elucidates this point. Extreme poverty declined from 52 per cent in 1990 to 40 per cent in 2005. In spite of this success, the number of poor people increased and the region remains home to the largest number of extremely poor people: nearly 600 million in 2005. The region has made large improvements in education: the primary education completion rate rose from 62 per cent in 1991 to 80 per cent in 2006 and the ratio of girls to boys in secondary education changed from 59 per cent to 84 per cent between 1991 and 2005 (World Bank, 2009b). In spite of these improvements, though, SA has not yet attained universal primary education, a goal that was achieved by high-income countries a long time ago. To the gaps in social services mentioned above, the paucity of infrastructure can be added, as the Asia Development Bank observes, 'globally, 1.1 billion people lack adequate access to clean water, 2.4 billion lack adequate sanitation, 4 billion lack sound wastewater disposal systems, and 2 billion lack electric power' (ADB, 2009, p. 2).

Consequently, the amount of resources needed to undertake the necessary improvements in health, education and infrastructure, and thus overcome the development gap, is extremely high. Given the level of income creation in these countries and the scarcity of public funds, the obvious solution seems to be to invite greater private sector participation, enlarging the use of public–private agreements in social and infrastructure services. Perhaps authorities in developing economies consider that there is a trade-off between providing social services and infrastructure, and that infrastructure has higher linkages with economic development than social services. Whatever the reason, the fact is that the existence of PPPs appears most popular in building, operating and maintaining infrastructure rather than in providing for social services.

PPPs in infrastructure services: the available data

PPPs and infrastructure services
It is well established that there are growing demands for social services and infrastructure in developing economies. Given the recognized constraints on public resources in developing countries, a call for larger private sector involvement in the provision of both services of the social sector (education, healthcare) and of infrastructure and utilities through PPPs seems to be at least part of the solution (Pessoa, 2006, 2008a).

However, the way the private sector has been called upon to participate in reducing the short supply of social services has been very different from that used in infrastructure services. There are two noteworthy differences: in the former, NGOs[9] have had a more important role; in the latter the key intervention is from foreign for-profit companies, and particularly MNCs (multinational companies) coming from OECD countries. But importantly, private participation in infrastructure services has been associated with a higher level of private investment and with more formal arrangements. These in turn have led to a greater availability of empirical data to work with. So, although there is a wide variety of PPPs in developing economies, when one uses the expression PPP what is usually called to mind is the private sector participation in infrastructure services. This is also the reason why this chapter focuses only on infrastructure and utilities arrangements.

While there is an abundant literature about PPP definitions (Bovaird, 2004; Hodge and Greve, 2007), 'few people agree on what a PPP actually is' (Hodge and Greve, 2009, p. 33), partly because there are many uses for the PPP concept. Elsewhere (Pessoa, 2006), we have defined PPP as a sustained collaborative effort between the public sector and the private sector (including not-for-profit organizations) to achieve a common objective while both players pursue their own individual interests. This is a general definition that attempts to include different types of PPP families. However, our purpose in this chapter is primarily focused on policy instruments that broadly coincide with a particular PPP family: the long-term infrastructure contract (LTIC), as named by Hodge and Greve (2007). Thus a PPP is here identified with any sustained arrangement between a public sector party and a private sector party whereby the private sector assumes total or partial responsibility for infrastructure planning, financing, design, construction, operation and maintenance, against the possibility of collecting payments from the users or/and from the public sector party. This may be considered a restrictive definition, because it considers a PPP as an instrument rather than a social phenomenon, but it is sufficiently operative for our purpose: to confront the available data with the alleged goals of governments and international financing organizations that view PPPs as the best way to solve or reduce the development gap.

PPPs in infrastructure and utilities are therefore understood as projects with private sector participation in four areas of economic activity. All four areas exhibit some monopoly or oligopoly characteristics:[10] energy (generation of electricity, transmission and distribution of electricity and natural gas), telecommunications (telephony, both fixed or mobile and domestic or international), transport (airports, railways, toll roads, port infrastructures), and water (generation and distribution of potable water and collection and treatment of sewerage). In these sectors, the number of PPP projects and the total investment commitments to such projects have had an uneven evolution in the last two decades, with periods of expansion and slowdown. This is shown in Figure 25.1.

It is evident that 140 developing countries implemented at least 4111 projects with private participation (hereafter, PPI projects) between 1990 and 2007. These data have been drawn from the Private Participation in Infrastructure Project Database.[11] Overall, these projects have involved

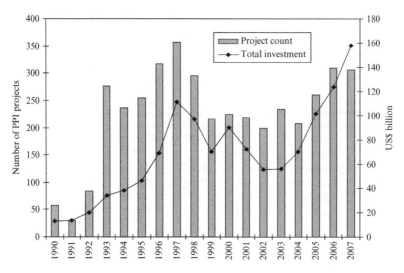

Source: Based on PPI database.

Figure 25.1   Number of projects and investment in PPIs

investment commitments of more than US$1 255 613 million. As Figure 25.1 shows, there is no linear trend either in the number of annual PPI projects or in the associated investment volumes. Why was there a sharp increase in investment until 1997, and a decreasing trend from 1997 to 2002? And were these PPI projects evenly distributed across infrastructure sectors or geographic regions? Has the country's level of development also been a factor here? This assessment of PPI performance in developing economies aims to answer these questions.

Distribution across infrastructure sectors
Looking at the economic activity, it is apparent from Table 25.2 that the bulk of investment was directed to telecommunications, and this accounted for 49 per cent of the cumulative investment in 1990–2007. The highest number of projects, however, came from energy, with particular emphasis on electricity. The technological change inherent in telecommunications has contributed to this leading position, reducing sunk costs and diminishing the barriers to entry. But not exclusively: the big wave of privatization in the sense of asset sales also played a significant role. In fact, there was a significant level of asset sales in Latin America as a consequence of policies following the 'Washington Consensus' and in ECA resulting from the disintegration of the former Soviet Union. Energy, which includes electricity and the distribution of natural gas, also attracted the second-largest share

Table 25.2   PPI by area of economic activity

Primary sector	Subsector	Project counts		Total investment		Investment per project
		Number	%	US$ million	%	US$ million
Energy	Electricity	1 261	30.82	315 132	25.35	250
	Natural gas	328	8.02	55 974	4.50	171
	Total	1 589	38.83	371 106	29.86	234
Telecoms	Telecoms	807	19.72	604 811	48.66	749
Transport	Airports	128	3.13	30 580	2.46	239
	Railway	100	2.44	38 891	3.13	389
	Roads	546	13.34	99 754	8.03	183
	Seaports	325	7.94	41 696	3.35	128
	Total	1 099	26.86	210 921	16.97	192
Water and sewerage	Treatment plant	316	7.72	12 461	1.00	39
	Utility	281	6.87	43 705	3.52	156
	Total	597	14.59	56 166	4.52	94
Total		4 092	100	1 243 004	100	304

Source: Based on PPI database.

of investment, accounting for 30 per cent of the cumulative investment in private infrastructure projects.

In contrast, private participation in the water and sewerage sector has been limited, accounting for 5 per cent of cumulative investments over the same period. The low private involvement in water and sewerage is likely to reflect the 'inherent difficulties' that face reforms in this sector, 'in terms of the technology of water provision and the nature of the product' (Pessoa, 2008a, p. 319). Above all, though, this low involvement is evidence of the scarce private investment in water treatment plants.

This water and sewerage sector investment scarcity has many causes. As Hammami et al. (2006, p. 5) have shown, 'private sector decisions to commit resources are a function of the expected marketability of the goods and services, the technology required, and the degree of "impurity" of the goods or services'. The services supplied by the water and sewerage sector are usually viewed as public goods and this characteristic affects the way consumers react to reforms that increase private participation in the sector. Moreover, reforms that sell assets to the private sector or that require private companies to collect tariffs from consumers are also typically unpopular. So the public-good characteristics of this sector explain the political and social opposition to such reforms, and also at least partly justify the scarce willingness to invest in the water and sewerage sector.

Four other factors also contribute to the low motivation to invest in the water sector:[12]

1. Water supply and sewerage services constitute a natural monopoly and so competition in the sector is limited.
2. The underground assets are difficult to assess, introducing much uncertainty in investment plans.
3. The sector as a whole is plagued with entrenched social and cultural issues (Marin, 2009). These make this sector highly sensitive to social unrest – both in the policy debating sense and also to the extreme stage of threats of riots.
4. The historical level of residential water tariffs, which in most countries do not consider any cost recovery, does not allow the use of PPP modalities that involve assumption of demand risk by the private party, as is recognized by the ADB (2009).

Recognizing the specificities of the water sector, some consider that the main focus of water PPPs should not be about attracting direct private investment, but rather about using private operators to improve service quality and efficiency (Marin, 2009). Although concessions have worked well in a few places, contractual arrangements that combine private operation with public financing of investment appear to be the most sustainable option in many countries (Marin, 2009).

The number of projects in the transport sector (from Table 25.2) represents nearly 27 per cent of total PPI projects, but only 17 per cent of the total investment. Almost one-half of this investment has gone into toll roads, with the rest into railways, seaports and airports. These disparities are probably due to the different expected returns of the activities. For example, highways are usually seen as luxury goods in developing economies, so tolls do not face much opposition. Passenger railways, seaports and airports, however, usually have subsidized tariffs. In the first case this is because transport by rail is traditionally associated with the low cost of labour, and in the other two cases, the functions are deemed to be sovereign responsibilities. This explains why the freight railways sector, a less hot political activity, has attracted more private investment than the passenger railways sector.

PPI types
Table 25.3 illustrates the relative importance of private involvement. It is structured in terms of four main sectors for PPI and also in terms of geographic regions of the developing world. For instance, in the energy sector an investment of US$369 939 million occurred in 1587 PPIs. Greenfield projects represented 61.18 per cent of the total number of projects in this sector and the majority of the investment type (at 55.58 per cent).

Unsurprisingly, greenfield projects, together with divestitures,[13] represented 71.8 per cent of the total number of PPI projects and 86.1 per cent of total investment. On average, while greenfield projects were the most frequent both in number (53 per cent) and in cumulative investment (50 per cent), management and lease contracts were the least widespread in both dimensions (5 per cent and less than 1 per cent, respectively). In developing economies, greenfield projects were the ones facing the lowest opposition and even sometimes enthusiasm on the part of the population because they were new major projects employing a large labour force in the construction phase. Additionally, they were built and operated by the private sector, which took on the commercial risk. They were also projects that national and local governments liked to exhibit as a sign of venture capacity.

On the other hand, management arrangements, which usually had a shorter duration than greenfield projects, were sometimes used in situations of uncertain political environment and limited availability of baseline data. This was the case of the four-year contract of the Gaza Strip in water and sewerage (see Pessoa, 2008a). Lease arrangements were also sometimes used where uncertainty was high and, if successful, as a first step for a concession. This was the case for water supply in Conakry and 16 other towns in Guinea (see Pessoa, 2008a). In both types of these arrangements (management and lease) the public entity remains responsible for investments while the commercial risk is borne by the private sector. The asymmetry of information and consequent difficulty in enforcing any potential gains, however, can be a disincentive that helps to explain the low share of this type of PPI in the total investment.

By sectors, greenfield projects predominated in energy and telecoms while concessions were prevalent in transport, and water and sewerage. Management and lease, clearly in a minority in all sectors, none the less had some importance in water and sewerage, both in number (17 per cent) and in volume of investment (3 per cent). This observation also confirms the point made above about the difficulty in transferring public water and sewerage assets to the private sector. This also explains why concessions were by far the most important form of PPI, not only in transport but also in the water and sewerage sectors, both in number of projects and in cumulative investment.

Table 25.3   Prevalence of PPI types in sectors and regions

Cumulative investment by sector (project counts by sector)	Total, US$ million (project counts)	Concession (%)	Divestiture (%)	Greenfield project (%)	Management and lease contract (%)
Energy	369939	3.73	40.63	55.58	0.06
	(1587)	(6.49)	(30.12)	(61.18)	(2.21)
Telecoms	604811	0.93	46.69	52.38	0.00
	(807)	(1.24)	(25.15)	(72.99)	(0.62)
Transport	210272	51.58	5.85	40.22	2.35
	(1097)	(54.15)	(5.93)	(34.28)	(5.65)
Water and	56166	67.36	12.64	16.76	3.24
sewerage	(597)	(40.37)	(4.36)	(37.86)	(17.42)
Total	1241188	13.35	36.42	49.66	0.56
	(4088)	(23.19)	(18.88)	(52.89)	(5.04)
Cumulative investment by region (project counts by region)					
EAP	276114	16.29	21.10	62.41	0.20
	(1249)	(24.26)	(11.13)	(63.01)	(1.60)
ECA	229631	4.40	47.54	45.52	2.54
	(702)	(6.13)	(48.86)	(37.61)	(7.41)
LAC	474592	17.04	50.57	32.32	0.07
	(1245)	(32.53)	(18.07)	(45.14)	(4.26)
MENA	64558	14.59	22.84	62.32	0.25
	(121)	(14.88)	(7.44)	(62.81)	(14.88)
SA	127577	10.23	11.01	78.75	0.00
	(414)	(26.09)	(4.83)	(66.67)	(2.42)
SSA	68716	10.58	23.07	66.20	0.15
	(357)	(19.89)	(10.08)	(55.18)	(14.85)
Total	1241188	13.35	36.42	49.66	0.56
	(4088)	(23.19)	(18.88)	(52.89)	(5.04)

Note: Figures in parentheses are the corresponding value in project counts.

Source: Based on PPI database.

Among the developing regions, LAC accounted for the great bulk of the cumulative investment in infrastructure. Latin America presented the largest share of concessions, both in number and in total investment. Although divestitures occurred more frequently in ECA, Latin America exhibited the highest volume of money invested. Greenfield projects were preferred in EAP. While contracts of management and lease were evenly distributed by ECA, LAC and SSA, the small cumulative investment in this form of PPI was concentrated in ECA.

Table 25.4 shows the importance of PPIs by sector and region. We can see that concessions correspond to 948 PPI projects with a cumulative investment of US$165 689 million. It is also evident that 8.33 per cent was invested in the energy sector, with this corresponding to 10.86 per cent of total concessions.

By region, policy-makers appear to have shown a preference for greenfield projects, which allow new infrastructure to be built without necessarily having to embark on major structural reforms. Exceptions are found only in Latin America and ECA, where divestitures were more widespread, reflecting major privatization programmes in many countries in these regions. The greatest prevalence of greenfield projects in Asia and of divestitures in the volume of investment in Latin America show that private investment has tended to complement public expenditure in Asia and replace it in Latin America. As a matter of fact, in Latin America private participation in infrastructure was often part of a broader reform programme where divestitures and concessions of existing assets predominated in the cumulative investment in private infrastructure projects.[14] In contrast to Latin America, the Asia region with higher than average economic growth rates has focused on the creation of new assets through greenfield projects. As noted by Ferreira and Khatami (1996, p. 16), the promotion of private infrastructure in Asia was above all seen as a way of 'complementing public sector efforts to keep pace with economic growth'.

Distribution across countries and regions

PPI projects exist in 140 out of 144 economies classified as developing by the World Bank. Notwithstanding this, PPI projects are not evenly distributed across regions and across countries.

Table 25.5 summarizes the volume of investments and the number of projects for the 1990–2007 period. It shows that, while the 50 low-income countries have registered 771 projects, the 53 lower-middle-income economies had more than double this figure with 1691 projects, a number that slightly also exceeded the level of the 37 upper-middle-income countries (1649). Moreover, the dimension of the projects varied with the level of

Table 25.4   Importance of PPIs by sector and region

Cumulative investment by sector (project counts by sector)	Type of PPI (percentage)			
	Concession	Divestiture	Greenfield project	Management and lease contract
Energy	8.33	33.25	33.35	3.24
	(10.86)	(61.92)	(44.91)	(16.99)
Telecom	3.38	62.46	51.40	0.00
	(1.05)	(26.30)	(27.24)	(2.43)
Transport	65.45	2.72	13.72	70.73
	(62.66)	(8.42)	(17.39)	(30.10)
Water and sewerage	22.83	1.57	1.53	26.02
	(25.42)	(3.37)	(10.45)	(50.49)
Total				
(US$ millions)	165.689	452.083	616.423	6.992
(number of PPIs)	(948)	(772)	(2162)	(206)
Cumulative investment by region (project counts by region)				
EAP	27.15	12.89	27.95	7.89
	(31.96)	(18.01)	(36.40)	(9.71)
ECA	6.10	24.15	16.96	83.47
	(4.54)	(44.43)	(12.21)	(25.24)
LAC	48.80	53.09	24.88	4.77
	(42.72)	(29.15)	(25.99)	(25.73)
MENA	˙5.69	3.26	6.53	2.35
	(1.90)	(1.17)	(3.52)	(8.74)
SA	7.88	3.11	16.30	0.02
	(11.39)	(2.59)	(12.77)	(4.85)
SSA	4.39	3.51	7.38	1.50
	(7.49)	(4.66)	(9.11)	(25.73)

Note: Figures in parentheses are the corresponding value in project counts.

Source: Based on PPI database.

development. Table 25.5 shows that higher investments on average were located in upper-middle-income countries.

Although almost all developing countries have used some form of private investment in infrastructures since 1990, private investors have tended to be directed to a small group of developing countries: the ones with relatively large, rich or fast-growing markets. Table 25.6 shows the

Table 25.5   Number of PPI projects and total investment, by income group, 1990–2007

Income group	Region	Project counts		Investment		Investment per project
		Number	%	US$ million	%	US$ million
Low-income		771	18.75	180021	14.44	233.49
	EAP	72	1.75	12115	0.97	168.26
	ECA	21	0.51	1354	0.11	64.47
	LAC	6	0.15	437	0.04	72.79
	MENA	8	0.19	900	0.07	112.46
	SA	390	9.49	124879	10.02	320.20
	SSA	274	6.67	40337	3.24	147.22
Lower-middle-income		1691	41.13	370824	29.75	219.29
	EAP	1084	26.37	215050	17.26	198.39
	ECA	103	2.51	19743	1.58	191.68
	LAC	353	8.59	70166	5.63	198.77
	MENA	98	2.38	60182	4.83	614.10
	SA	24	0.58	2698	0.22	112.41
	SSA	29	0.71	2986	0.24	102.97
Upper-middle income		1649	40.11	695423	55.80	421.72
	EAP	97	2.36	50204	4.03	517.57
	ECA	579	14.08	208534	16.73	360.16
	LAC	895	21.77	406190	32.59	453.84
	MENA	16	0.39	3477	0.28	217.29
	SSA	62	1.51	27019	2.17	435.79
Total		4111	100	1246268	100	303.15

Source: Based on PPI database.

top 12 countries investing in PPI in the 1990–2007 period, by both number of projects and total level of investment. The highest number of PPI projects are shown on the left side and the top 12 destinations for total PPI investment in infrastructures are shown on the right. Several developing countries feature strongly on both lists.

The 12 countries listed on the left side of Table 25.6 represent roughly two-thirds of the total number of projects, and absorb 55 per cent of the investment. To sum up, Latin America accounted for the great bulk of the cumulative investment in infrastructure. Two Latin American countries

Table 25.6   Top 12 of private sector involvement by country, 1990–2007

Ranking by number of PPI projects			Ranking by investment		
Country	Project counts	%	Country	US$ million	%
China	805	19.58	Brazil	196308	15.63
Brazil	328	7.98	China	99953	7.96
Russian Federation	310	7.54	Mexico	86126	6.86
India	306	7.44	Malaysia	50204	4.00
Argentina	193	4.69	Philippines	42243	3.36
Mexico	176	4.28	Indonesia	40676	3.24
Colombia	132	3.21	Turkey	36851	2.93
Chile	107	2.60	Thailand	31954	2.54
Thailand	96	2.34	Poland	31853	2.54
Malaysia	96	2.34	Hungary	27111	2.16
Philippines	88	2.14	Chile	26291	2.09
Indonesia	87	2.12	South Africa	25341	2.02
Top 12	2724	66.26	Top 12	694911	55.34

Source: Based on PPI database.

(Brazil and Mexico) in particular account for more than one-fifth of the total PPP investment in the developing world. However, the countries and regions that have absorbed the greatest bulk of investment are not the ones with the highest need in terms of reducing the development gap.

As Table 25.7 shows, the access to improved water sources is particularly low in SSA. However, this region, together with SA, has profited the least from PPI investment in the water and sewerage sector. As can be seen from Table 25.7, only 0.47 per cent of the total investment in water and sewerage was spent in SSA in the 1990–2007 period. There is also a clear paucity of telecoms in SA and SSA, where land-line and mobile-phone subscribers are at levels of only 26 and 25 per 1000 people respectively. However, of the total investment in telecoms, only 8.2 per cent was applied in SSA and 10.45 per cent in SA. In respect of paved roads, the two regions experiencing the lowest proportions, EAP and SSA, had different performances: while EAP benefited from 35.17 per cent of all road investments going into its roads, SSA only absorbed 1.86 per cent of total PPI road investments.[15] So a first conclusion can be drawn: PPI investment was directed not to countries with the highest need, but to countries and regions that were more attractive to foreign investment.

Table 25.7 *Some key indicators of developing economies*

Region	Development indicators							PPI investments, 1990–2007		
	GNI per capita PPP ($), 2007	FDI, net inflows ($ billions), 2007	Net aid received per capita ($), 2007	Access to improved sanitation facilities (%), 2006	Paved roads (% of total), 2000–06	Phone subscribers (per 1000 people), 2007	Access to improved water source (%), 2006	Roads	Telecoms	Water and sewerage
EAP	4969	175	4.5	66	11.4	67	87	35.17	12.75	49.47
ECA	11262	156	13.0	89	…	121	95	6.32	24.90	7.16
LAC	9678	107	12.2	78	22.0	85	91	46.65	37.07	40.82
MENA	7402	29	56.1	77	81.0	68	89	0.10	6.66	1.62
SA	2532	30	6.8	33	56.9	26	87	9.89	10.45	0.45
SSA	1870	29	44.2	31	11.9	25	58	1.86	8.17	0.47

Sources: Based on World Bank (2009a) and PPI database.

When the third P drops: cancellations and projects under distress

When the third P drops; that is, when the partnership is broken, three factors acquire particular relevance: the increase in transaction costs, the emergence of termination risk and the decrease in PPP trust. All three factors must be considered in evaluating the PPI performance.

One important indicator of the potential failure of a PPP is the degree of dissatisfaction of the population covered by such an arrangement. Sometimes this disappointment causes the unexpected end of the PPI. However, the cessation before the contractual end of the PPI project usually results from divergences between partners in regard to problems in the design of the contractual arrangement or in its functioning conditions. The existence of such problems is likely to increase the transaction costs and, as a consequence, reduce the effectiveness of PPPs over traditional methods of procurement.

One important feature of the PPP philosophy of providing for infrastructure is the correct allocation of risks, which must be identified *ex ante*. The superiority of the PPP method over traditional public provision implies a comparison of risks. But there is a risk in PPP procurement that does not apply to traditional public procurement: the termination risk (EIB, 2005). This risk is borne both by the public partners and the private partners. It is the risk that the PPP arrangement will be terminated early, either through the private partner failing financially, or by the private partner failing to perform technically, for example by not providing the contracted service adequately.[16] This is a risk for the private sector partners as they will almost certainly suffer a material financial loss on termination. However, it is also a risk for the public sector partners: they will still need to arrange for the service to be provided after the termination, based on the project under way. The risk can be partially mitigated by selecting suitable bidders. However, these are long-term contracts and there is a trend for the original technical members of a consortium to be displaced by purely financial investors who may not have the relevant experience and expertise. Public partner failure, on the other hand, may owe to an inappropriate allocation of risk from the beginning. Whatever the situation, termination before the contractual end is always a factor that increases the costs or reduces the potential benefits of PPPs.

Confidence in a PPP policy can also be negatively influenced if partners of the private sector leave infrastructure projects before the contract ends. It can also be reduced when projects face problems that put them under distress. Such problems can affect both the private sector's confidence and the government's self-belief in the robustness and VfM of arrangements. In both cases, uncertainty emerges, and it becomes more difficult to reliably assess the value of PPPs over other alternatives.

The relative number of projects and volume of investment involved in cancellations is an important indicator of the prospects of PPI policy. It is also a crucial indicator of the potential interest of international investors and operators, as recognized by the Asian Development Bank (ADB, 2009). Table 25.8 shows the number and the total investment of projects cancelled[17] and under distress,[18] compared with the total number and investment in PPIs reaching financial closure in developing regions.

According to data presented in Table 25.8, 253 of a total of 4111 projects reported by the PPI database as reaching financial closure in 1990–2007 were cancelled or under distress by 2007. Those accounted for 6.2 per cent of all projects and 7.19 per cent of investment commitments. Significant contributions here were made by EAP (11.1 per cent) and LAC (10.2 per cent) in terms of investment proportions. However, a principal problem has been that in the latest six years, an increasing trend in cancellations has occurred. Indeed, the rate of private sector exit has increased more than twice between 2001 and 2007. Harris et al. (2003) found that for the 1990–2001 period the corresponding figures were only 1.9 per cent of all projects and 3.2 per cent of all investment commitments. This increasing rate of cancellations as time elapses is likely to have negative effects on the popularity of these instruments and shows that a return to the euphoria of the first seven years of the 1990s will be unlikely.

Sometimes difficulties in PPP projects with impacts on the cancellation rate can be the outcome of macroeconomic shocks. Toll road projects in Mexico, water projects in Argentina and power generation projects in Indonesia, all of which suffered from macroeconomic shocks occurring

Table 25.8   Importance of projects cancelled or under distress, 1990–2007

Region	Number of countries with private participation	Projects reaching financial closure		Projects cancelled or under distress	
		Number	Total investment (US$ million)	Number	Total investment (US$ million)
EAP	18	1253	277368	70	30663
ECA	26	703	231331	21	3788
LAC	29	1254	479844	118	48955
MENA	13	122	66858	6	1017
SA	8	414	127577	7	3930
SSA	46	365	72635	31	1890
Total	140	4111	1255613	253	90243

Source: Based on PPI database.

in these countries at different times, contributed significantly to the list of cancelled PPI projects. In fact, the global financial crisis of 2008/9 increased the cost and reduced the availability of project financing. In addition, financial crises have usually led to the renegotiation of many contracts. For instance, it was estimated that the Asian financial crisis a decade earlier led to the renegotiation of 71 per cent of contracts in East Asia (Reside Jr, 2008).

However, often the problems have been endogenous; that is, they resulted from the behaviour of the partners. Examples here might have been the aggressive bidding of the private sector or failures in the design of the policy instruments, including bad project or concession design. Indeed, several cases of early termination can be traced to contracts whose design was not viable or whose bidding process led to unrealistic financial conditions, or both. Cochabamba (Bolivia) was a high-profile case where the contract was awarded following a tender from which all but one consortium had withdrawn. Substantial tariff rises were needed to turn the large investment required from the private operator viable, something that proved socially unsustainable and brought about the rapid failure of the contract (Marin, 2009).[19]

Conclusion

In this chapter we have tried to review PPP performance in developing economies, using data from WDI and the PPI database for the 1990–2007 period. Some points deserve consideration.

First, the current wave of PPPs in developing economies was not determined by an endogenous process. On the contrary, it was due to a coincidence of interests between international organizations that shared the view of the Washington Consensus and a set of countries, notably in LAC,[20] that have considered divestiture the best way to alleviate public deficit constraints (e.g. Argentina, Mexico). This coincidence explains the huge increase both in the number of PPI projects and in the volume of investment from 1990 to 1997 while it highlights, at least partially, the high volume of investment in PPIs in energy and telecommunications, sectors where divestiture was more extensive.

Second, the data reveal a picture of concentration. Two in six regions are responsible for 60 per cent of the total investment in PPI projects: LAC and EAP with 38 per cent and 22 per cent of total investment, respectively. We also observe that within these regions investments are neither evenly distributed across countries nor are the least developed countries those that benefit the most. On the contrary, 12 in a total of 140 developing economies with PPI projects are responsible for the absorption of 55 per cent of the investment in PPPs. These are countries with relatively large, rich or fast-growing markets, characteristics that always attract foreign investment. On the other hand, the poorest economies, notably in SSA, to which the privatization prescription of the Washington Consensus was also blindly applied (Nellis, 2003), went on increasing the development gap.

Third, if, as is frequently advocated by international organizations, the advantage of the PPIs results from the capacity of this type of procurement to reduce the infrastructure gap in developing economies, we can only conclude that the target was not attained. What is apparent is that governments used private sector involvement to provide infrastructure projects as they saw PPPs as a quicker way than other alternatives to get infrastructure in place. But, although PPPs may be attractive to governments, as they allow a reduction – and often a delay – in government expenditures for infrastructure, certain PPP types effectively create (off-budget) future liabilities.

Fourth, there is some disenchantment about the capacity of PPI policy to overcome the existing big gaps between high-income and developing economies. This is evident in the fact that after 1997, the increasing trend of PPI projects both in number and in amount of investment never reached the earlier rate. Furthermore, the yearly amount of investment in PPI projects has never recovered the value achieved in 1997. This disillusionment is also evident in the increasing amount of investment that corresponds to cancelled and under-distress projects.

Fifth, the results of a PPP policy must also be evaluated in a dynamic perspective. A high interconnection between foreign companies and domestic firms has resulted, and this interrelationship has allowed some expansion and upgrading of domestic firms in developing economies. As is shown by Marin (2009), while in 2000 five international water companies accounted for about 80 per cent of the water PPP market in developing countries, by 2007, 28 large private operators from developing countries were in place, each serving a combined population of at least 400 000 people, totalling about 40 per cent of the market.

Sixth, international organizations used to say that PPPs, if well structured, could in reality be the most effective and fastest way of improving utility performance. For instance, the Asian Development Bank has been very explicit in this regard: 'The challenge in introducing PPPs is to make political leaders at all levels understand that PPP, if structured properly, could indeed be the most effective and fastest way of improving utility performance, and the quality and reliability of services provided' (ADB, 2009, p. 33). The continuing advocacy of international organizations may be enough for the stream of PPI projects to go on. However, the appropriate supporting conditions for most of these economies are lacking. As the same organizations recognize, these economies are characterized by a 'lack of institutional capacity, weak governance systems, and unclear or unsuitable rules and regulations, all of which increase transaction costs and risks' (ibid., p. 4).

Therefore a crucial issue for the future is how to provide institutional capacity, how to build strong governance systems and how to increase the rule of law in the majority of developing economies. This is a huge agenda to tackle and probably depends, in turn, on the economic growth of these countries. In the meanwhile, poor people in poorer countries caught in poverty traps need to be served and the rationale underlying the PPI approach cannot give a positive guarantee to these people. Here, the government and the ODA must play a more extensive role than they have played since the emergence of the PPP fashion. The ODA especially cannot be limited to simply enhancing the quality and raising the profitability of PPI projects.

Furthermore, the way international organizations look at development policy is important. The substitution of the Washington Consensus for the recommendations of the Spence Commission (World Bank, 2008) is a first step in the right direction. For the great bulk of developing economies, the means used to provide social and infrastructure services will in future depend on the way governments and multilateral organizations regard development policy. If the rationale of the Spence Commission displaces the assertions of the Washington Consensus and is simultaneously able to avoid both market and institutional fundamentalism, it is likely that new forms of relationship between public and private sectors will emerge. Such new forms may even avoid episodes like Cochabamba and other less visible but abundant episodes in the poor regions of developing economies.

In a developing economy, a PPI is not limited to having one partner of the public sector and another partner of the private sector, but a private sector involving several agents and organizations: one or a consortium of foreign companies linked to domestic firms usually subcontracted, commercial banks and multilateral organizations. Given the lack of institutional capacity, governments need to rely on multilateral organizations for advice and technical assistance, but the organizations that assist governments are the same that provide credit to the companies that build, manage and operate the infrastructure. The way this critical role is played will be fundamental to the credibility of the PPI approach in the future.

Given the huge technological change in the infrastructure sector in the last two decades, developing economies cannot overlook foreign participation in building and managing infrastructure. The critical challenge to a developing economy is how to use such participation to learn and consequently to increase domestic production and management capacity. However, there is a problem: this is easier said than done.

Notes

1. For instance, none of the 25 studies on PPP evaluation reviewed in Hodge and Greve (2009, Table 1) refers to developing economies.
2. In spite of the existence of some studies trying to construct infrastructure databases (Canning, 1998; Estache and Goicoechea, 2005), there is a lack of available and credible data on infrastructures in developing economies. As is recognized by the Spence Commission (World Bank, 2008, p. 139), 'given the importance of infrastructure for long-term growth and inclusiveness, available data are surprisingly hard to obtain'. Although this is true, data on collaboration between the public and the private sector in health and education services are even more difficult to obtain.
3. By the late 1990s, the European Commission had explicitly advocated the use of PPPs to fund Trans-European Network projects. See the communication (COM 97/453) issued by the European Commission, on 10 September 1997 regarding such partnerships. More recently, the European Growth Initiative, approved by the European Council in December 2003, set as one of its objectives to promote the use of PPPs, notably in order to develop growth-related infrastructures.
4. John Williamson coined the name 'Washington Consensus' in 1989. See Williamson (1990).
5. According to a first estimation made by Fay and Yepes (2003, p. 15), 'The infrastructure (except ports, airports and canals) investment needed should amount to about $465 billion per annum or 5.5% of developing countries' GDP over 2005–2010'. In these estimates, resources that might be needed for rehabilitation or for upgrading were not included.
6. In the most recent classification economies are divided according to 2008 GNI per capita using the World Bank Atlas method. The groups are: low-income, $975 or less; lower-middle-income, $976–$3855; upper-middle-income, $3856–$11905; and high-income, $11906 or more.
7. Even if the poorest regions, SA and SSA, remain predominantly rural, rapid urbanization has put significant pressure on urban services and infrastructures.
8. Of course, there are differences among regions. For instance, the access to improved sanitation facilities is in short supply above all in SA and SSA, and the prevalence of HIV is particularly high in SSA. But, even in regions with less unfavourable indicators there is a huge gap to overcome on the road to development.
9. In health, for instance a Swiss NGO, Foundation PH, is dedicated to Partnerships in Health, providing health education and training for the countries of Eastern Europe and Central Asia (see www.partnershipsinhealth.ch). For an overview on PPPs in the education sector, see the examples provided by Pessoa (2008b).
10. More competitive activities, such as airlines and gas production, are not included.
11. This database (hereafter PPI database) collects and disseminates information on infrastructure projects with private participation in low- and middle-income countries. The PPI database is a joint product of the World Bank's Infrastructure Economics and Finance Department and the Public–Private Infrastructure Advisory Facility (PPIAF). The PPI project database collects information from publicly available sources and includes transactions worth $1 million or more or, in water and electricity distribution, transactions that would provide 5000 or more new connections. See ppi.worldbank. org.
12. These factors can also explain why projects in the water and sewerage sector have the highest tendency to cancellation (see Harris and Pratap, 2008).
13. By divestiture we mean that the assets of a public utility are totally or partially sold to the private sector.
14. As Ferreira and Khatami (1996) observe, whilst in Chile the infrastructure services were reformed owing to 'the emerging recognition of private infrastructure advantages', in other Latin American countries like Argentina and Mexico, 'infrastructure privatisation has often been used to generate revenues for government and retire external debt' (pp. 15–16).

15. According to Yepes et al. (2009), Africa has the worst infrastructure endowment of any developing region today, particularly with respect to electrical generating capacity.
16. Most cases of early termination of contracts involved significant disobedience in respect of contractual responsibilities on one or on both sides (Marin, 2009), followed by a degradation of the partners' relationship to the point where ending the partnership was the chosen solution. When PPPs end after having been in place for many years, their anticipated end usually reflects difficulties in adapting the contract over time to changing conditions (Marin, 2009).
17. A project is considered to have been cancelled if, before the end of the contract period, the private company sold or transferred its economic interest in the project to the public sector; the private company physically abandoned the project (such as withdrawing all staff); or the private company ceased operation or closed down construction for 15 per cent or more of the licence or concession period, following the revocation of the licence or repudiation of the contract. See Harris et al. (2003).
18. The PPI database distinguishes between cancellations and distressed projects, defining the latter as projects 'in which the government or the operator has requested contract termination or that are in international arbitration'. For our purposes, however, we consider that both are an indicator of problems in PPI.
19. In this well-documented case, a consortium controlled by US multinational Bechtel signed a 40-year deal to increase water supplies and services to Cochabamba, but six months later, rioting Bolivians chased the company out of the country.
20. According to the World Bank (1995, p. 28), the revenues from divestiture in developing economies, from 1988 to 1993, amount to US$3.2, 17.9, 19.7 and 55.1 billion in Africa, ECA, Asia and Latin America respectively.

References

Asian Development Bank (ADB) (2009), 'ADB assistance for public–private partnerships in infrastructure development. Potential for more success?', Special evaluation study, reference number: SES:OTH2009-31, September, Independent Evaluation Department, Asian Development Bank.

Boston, J. (1996), *Public Management: The New Zealand Model*, Melbourne: Oxford University Press.

Bovaird, T. (2004), 'Public–private partnerships: from contested concepts to prevalent practice', *International Review of Administrative Sciences*, **70** (2), 199–215.

Canning, David (1998), 'A database of world stocks of infrastructure, 1950–1995', *The World Bank Economic Review*, **12** (3), 529–47.

Estache, Antonio and Ana Goicoechea (2005), 'A "research" database on infrastructure economic performance', World Bank Policy Research Working Paper No. 3643, available at: ssrn.com/abstract=757364.

European Investment Bank (EIB) (2005), *Evaluation Report: Evaluation of PPP projects Financed by the EIB*, Operations Evaluation, European Investment Bank, March, available at: www.eib.org/publications/eval/.

Fay, M. and T. Yepes (2003), 'Investing in infrastructure: what is needed from 2000 to 2010', Policy Research Working Paper No. 3102, Washington, DC: World Bank.

Ferreira, David and Kanran Khatami (1996), 'Financing private infrastructure in developing countries', World Bank Discussion Paper No. 343, Washington, DC: World Bank.

Hammami, Mona, Jean-François Ruhashyankiko and Etienne B. Yehoue (2006), 'Determinants of public–private partnerships in infrastructure', IMF working paper, WP/06/99, International Monetary Fund.

Harris, Clive and Kumar V. Pratap (2008), 'What drives private sector exit from infrastructure? An analysis of the cancellation of private infrastructure projects', Washington, DC: World Bank.

Harris, Clive, John Hodges, Michael Schur and Padmesh Shukla (2003), 'Infrastructure projects: A review of canceled private projects', Viewpoint series, no. 252, Private Sector and Infrastructure Network, Washington, DC: World Bank.

Hodge, Graeme A. and Carsten Greve (2007), 'Public–private partnerships: an international performance review', *Public Administration Review*, May/June, 545–58.

Hodge, Graeme A. and Carsten Greve (2009), 'PPPs: the passage of time permits a sober reflection', *Economic Affairs*, March, 33–9.

Hood, C. (1991), 'A public management for all seasons?', *Public Administration*, **69** (1), 3–19.

Marin, Philippe (2009), 'Public–private partnerships for urban water utilities: a review of experiences in developing countries', Trends and Policy Options No. 8, Washington, DC: World Bank.

Minogue, M., C. Polidano and D. Hulme (1998), *Beyond the New Public Management: Changing Ideas and Practice in Governance*, Cheltenham, UK and Northampton, MA, USA: Edward Elgar.

Nellis, John (2003), 'Privatization in Africa: what has happened? What is to be done?', Center for Global Development Working Paper 25, Washington, DC.

OECD (2005), 'Investment for African development: making it happen', Background information in support of Session 5 of the Roundtable: Encouraging Public–Private Partnerships in the Utilities Sector: the role of Development Assistance, 25–27 May 2005, NEPAD/OECD Initiative.

Pessoa, Argentino (2004), 'Institutional innovations, growth performance and policy', ERSA conference papers ersa04p157, European Regional Science Association.

Pessoa, Argentino (2006), 'Public–private sector partnerships in developing countries: prospects and drawbacks', FEP Working Papers 228, Universidade do Porto, Faculdade de Economia do Porto. Also published in Rao and Sisodiya (2009), *Public–Private Partnership Model in India: Concepts, Issues and Outlook*, Hyderabad, India: The ICFAI University Press, pp. 105–32.

Pessoa, Argentino (2008a), 'Public–private partnerships in developing countries: are infrastructures responding to the new ODA strategy?', *Journal of International Development*, **20** (3), 311–25.

Pessoa, Argentino (2008b), 'Educational reforms in developing countries: private involvement and partnership', *The Icfai University Journal of Higher Education*, **III** (3), August 8–37.

Polidano, C. (1999), 'Public management reform in developing countries: issues and outcomes', *Public Management*, **1** (1), 121–32.

PPI database, PPI Project Database World Bank and PPIAF, available at: ppi.worldbank. org (accessed on 13 August 2009).

Reside Jr, R. (2008), *Global Determinants of Stress and Risks in Public-Private Partnerships (PPP) in Infrastructure*, Tokyo: Asian Development Bank Institute.

Rodrik, Dani (2006), 'Goodbye Washington Consensus, hello Washington confusion? A review of the World Bank's economic growth in the 1990s: learning from a decade of reform', *Journal of Economic Literature*, **XLIV** (December), 973–87.

United Nations (2002), *Report of the International Conference on Financing for Development*, Monterrey, Mexico, 18–22 March, New York: United Nations.

Williamson, John (1990), 'What Washington means by policy reform', in J. Williamson (ed.), *Latin American Adjustment: How Much Has Happened?*, Washington, DC: Institute for International Economics, pp. 7–38.

World Bank (1994), *World Development Report: Infrastructure for Development*, New York: Oxford University Press.

World Bank (1995), *Bureaucrats in Business: The Economics and Politics of Government Ownership,* A World Bank Policy Research Report, New York: Oxford University Press.

World Bank (2008), *The Growth Report: Strategies for Sustained Growth and Inclusive Development*, Commission on Growth and Development, Washington, DC: The International Bank for Reconstruction and Development/The World Bank.

World Bank (2009a), *World Development Indicators 2009*, Washington, DC: World Bank.

World Bank (2009b), *World Development Report 2009: Reshaping Economic Geography*, Washington, DC: World Bank.

Yepes, Tito, Justin Pierce and Vivien Foster (2009), 'Making sense of Africa's infrastructure endowment: a benchmarking approach', Policy Research Working Paper 4912, April, The World Bank Africa Region, African Sustainable Development Front Office.

26 Conclusions: public–private partnerships – international experiences and future challenges

Graeme A. Hodge, Carsten Greve and Anthony E. Boardman

Introduction

This international handbook has aimed to make a new contribution to our knowledge of PPPs. As we said at the outset, whether we view PPP as an engineering tool, a governance mechanism or a public policy phenomenon, clearer thinking and wiser learning is warranted. In a publishing exercise of this size, though, there is always a risk that the entire undertaking will be superseded by events, and that whilst each of the chapter authors complete their writing, the questions posed in the initial chapters are rendered irrelevant by a fast-changing world. Despite tumultuous global events, this has not occurred with the PPP phenomenon. Indeed, the importance of this type of partnership has increased rather than decreased in the time since our project was started, as certified also by reports such as OECD (2008).

We began our handbook by suggesting a series of nine crucial research domains for PPP, and it is also clear that they are as cogent now as when first articulated:

1. The merit/worth of LTIC PPPs
2. The circumstances when they may give highest VfM and innovation
3. The circumstances when they may act as a better governance tool
4. How we can better regulate PPPs in the public interest
5. The role and findings of auditors general to date
6. Why their promotion 'succeeds' in some jurisdictions but not in others
7. What is the nature and consequence of the global PPP industry?
8. What is the place of PPPs in the context of development?
9. What is the next chapter for PPPs and the implications?

The astute reader will recognize that there has, throughout the book, been a continuing theme of ambiguity in viewing partnerships. We have offered many alternative perspectives on PPPs – sometimes as simply a project, sometimes more as a governance instrument, and at other times we have purposely seen PPP as a far broader and inherently political phenomenon. Our belief is that this reflects reality. So for this, we do not apologize.

This closing chapter offers an opportunity to build on the central insights and perspectives presented throughout the handbook as well as to reflect on the major themes that have emerged. It broadly follows the four-theme structure taken in the book itself. After some introductory perspectives, we first therefore tackle some of the bigger issues arising from the underpinning intellectual foundations of PPP. Crucial insights from a range of lenses central to each of the professional disciplines involved in PPPs are then outlined. Next, some of the lessons learned from the international empirical experience to date are presented as illustrations of the larger empirical canvas. And issues critical to the future of PPPs are then articulated and discussed before we draw some conclusions.

In pursuing these directions, our aim is to articulate a wide range of frontiers for PPP knowledge today. These will not only help to define what we currently know from both theory and practice, but will, we hope, also provide a foundation for continuing cross-disciplinary enquiries into what is truly a fascinating arena. So, what do we now know about PPPs, and what particular insights have we discovered throughout this work?

A reality check on PPPs
This handbook has provided the field of PPP studies with a much-needed 'reality check'. When PPPs first arrived on the policy scene, they were seen as revolutionary and were presented as:

1. something different from contracting out or privatization;
2. a reform that would unleash synergy activities, from which both the public sector and the private sector would benefit; and
3. a new organizational form that almost defied familiar organizational forms.

A couple of decades later, it is time to expose PPPs to a reality check. No, they are not entirely different from previous forms of market-based governance mechanisms. Competition as an element has not gone away, because many PPP contracts still have to be subject to competitive bidding. This is the case in the EU, for example, which has struggled to find the right legislative words to describe a PPP that would not disturb the established procurement rules for the single European market. No, PPPs do not always lead to synergistic benefits, but can also lead to failures and often demand just as much governance, if not more, to keep them going. As the well-known

American scholar Donald F. Kettl (1993) pointed out almost two decades ago, the strength of governing activities will not diminish when private sector organizations become involved in public infrastructure development. The governing activities themselves will just be of a different kind. Thanks to the empirical evidence presented in this volume, we now have a clearer picture of what results PPPs are capable of yielding, even though there is still some distance to go before we have completely satisfactory empirical data. No, PPPs did not represent entirely new forms of organizing, but have been combining elements from both private sector organizations and more network-like structures. The fact that a PPP deal combines elements of design, finance, build, own, operate, maintain and transfer is evident, but PPPs may also be thought of as a combination of different governing mechanisms, rather than presenting to the world an absolutely new and pure form of organization. Observing how different organizing mechanisms evolve in PPPs can be important, but there is less evidence to suggest that a new and clearly superior organizational form has emerged.

Important as the trend towards PPPs has been in the last decades, it is also important to remember that PPPs did not wipe out public investment, or indeed infrastructure projects handled either by the public sector alone or by the public sector contracting with the private sector in traditional ways. The PPP remains an organizational form that can be seen as an alternative to traditional public infrastructure projects. In the UK, where the trend towards PPPs arguably went furthest, the Treasury department continues to describe the PFI as a 'small, but important part of the Government's strategy to deliver high quality public services' (Treasury website www.h-m.treasury.gov.uk/ppp_index). The reality is that PPPs became a more accepted form of infrastructure project delivery, but not the dominant mode *per se*.

Underpinning intellectual PPP foundations: empirical infrastructure projects and the 'partnership idea'

Many things are now clear. The PPP domain, for example, is huge and covers several families of different meanings. Even for the modern family of long-term infrastructure contracts, we ought to acknowledge multiple levels of meaning. Hodge pointed out nine different interpretation levels (Chapter 5) from PPP as political symbolism to the more pragmatic level of delivering the individual project. And for this project delivery level alone, there are dozens of different types of arrangements (and accompanying acronyms) that can be adopted. Despite all this complexity, it is also apparent that PPPs are as political as they are technical, and to view them as solely a technical engineering project is to attempt to take politics out of an inherently political activity.

Based on the contributions in this volume, it might be useful to distinguish between the empirical long-term infrastructure contracts that we associate with PPPs, and the main focus for the empirical part of this international handbook, and the 'partnership idea' itself, accompanied by the aspirations and many meanings attributed to partnering. We now have more empirical evidence of the experience with PPPs from a number of countries, particularly from those countries with the longest-running activities, such as the UK, Australia, Canada, Ireland and the USA. Yet it seems that even though empirical results are presented and evaluated, and even though some of the empirical results warrant caution towards PPP policy, there is still a yearning for the partnership idea both in theory and among governments and private sector organizations. The 'partnership idea' continues to be a strong ideal for many organizations, and there is an aspiration towards working together. Governments are not likely to give up the idea of partnerships just because results from scholars show that the financial results are not as impressive as first envisaged. Private sector organizations – especially after the financial crisis – do not want to give up partnership ideas that might enable closer cooperation with the government, and may secure new markets for them. Scholars never tire of producing new concepts and theoretical constructs (collaboration, alliances etc.) that try to capture a closer relationship between the public sector and the private sector. And many of the public policy challenges before us (such as global climate change, for example) do urge organizations from across borders to work together in novel ways to achieve common solutions to mutual challenges.

Following from this argument, it will not be likely, or useful for that matter, to declare PPP a concept of the past or a concept that belongs squarely to the 1990s or the 2000s. The 'partnership idea' is highly likely to attract continued attention and to create new efforts in finding ways for the public sector and the private sector to work more closely together in the future. This also means that any attempts to make a clear census or count the number of partnerships that arise are probably in vain. Instead, we should acknowledge that there is likely to be a 'quest' for partnerships in the future, and that these partnership arrangements will take many forms. We can try, as several authors have done in this handbook, to make some sort of classification of them, but there are bound to be new examples that challenge the existing classifications. None the less, what we can do is to carefully evaluate and measure the performance of the long-term infrastructure contract projects that governments around the world have pursued with so much vigour. The PPP policies that many governments pursued, and that many private sector organizations, including consultants, encouraged needs to be exposed to careful empirical examination in the years to come.

Our interest nowadays in PPPs is at a high point, at least from the perspective of public servants and elected ministers. High citizen expectations for effective infrastructure to meet growing demands and buoyant economies as well as policy promises made throughout the political process all contribute here. And yet, none of this suggests that partnership is new. 'Public–private mixing has existed since the beginning of organized government', as Wettenhall points out (in Chapter 2), and whichever partnership theatre we investigated (such as the partnerships of the Achaemenid empire 2500 years ago, privateer shipping, mercenary armies and leased navies, or privately run treasury functions), the strong pedigree of the partnership ideal is clear. Notwithstanding this, there is still little doubt that 'the state must now work with market forces to an extent unthinkable in the earlier period', and with our emphasis now on governance rather than government, the stage has been truly set for us to reorient old debates on 'public versus private' towards more nuanced learning on 'public + private'.

Having said this, we ought to acknowledge that a wealth of intellectual foundations underlies the PPP ideal, as Bovaird argued (in Chapter 3). Also, there is a huge breadth to what we want to achieve through partnership. Our expectations of partnership include matters that are political, economic, financial and cultural, as well as technical. As public policy instruments, they are, as Jeffares et al. (2009, p. 7) so eloquently put it, 'politically loaded' by nature, with the consequence that successful performance itself has a range of meanings. It is little wonder, then, that Hodge was able to present 15 or so objectives of PPPs (in Chapter 5). Given the multiple disciplines with an interest in PPP matters, too, it is little wonder again that cross-disciplinary understanding of PPP and cross-disciplinary evaluations of PPP will guide our path forward. Evidence-based evaluations of PPPs that seek to reach defensible conclusions about cause and effect on partnership performance will need to be far stronger than they have been to date. Importantly, the solid evidence on what might at first appear to be the simple issue of VfM is, for instance, weak at present. Past studies have typically had weak designs and used dirty data, with the consequence that the conclusions reached have had low validity.

To Klijn's mind, there has been much confusion not only around the meaning of PPP, but also around their multiple rationales as well as the best forms of partnership. All this, though, can be reconciled. PPP, to his mind, is a brand for governments. It is a 'hybrid idea' that by definition is ambiguous and aims to evoke images and emotions rather than precision. This brand has power, too, because it enables governments to adopt partnership and PPP in different ways for different purposes. All reforms, though, are imbued with the suggestion of doing things differently and tackling problems together. The 'partnership idea', under this branding rationale, can indeed be a potentially powerful image and metaphor for governments.

Lenses from the professional disciplines

Journeying into the field of professional disciplinary interests provides numerous insights and lessons. This handbook contains contributions from the fields of political science, economics, legal studies, management studies, risk analysis studies and more.

Those from political science, such as Mathew Flinders (Chapter 6), view PPPs as exhibiting a splintered logic. According to this view, 'PPPs are founded on a governing logic that does not sit comfortably with the values and principles on which modern state systems were established during the nineteenth century, and developed during the twentieth century'. Numerous examples exist here, whether it is the logic of the market (which sees citizens treated as consumers), the logic of contestability (where a market contest is conducted for what then becomes a monopoly provider for several decades) or the logic of public expectations (a public that increasingly expects unconstrained choices under constrained tax levels).

One of the interesting aspects of the chapters in this handbook has been the contributions made from the economics perspective. On the one hand, we observe that impressive theoretical pointers and clues already exist for decision-making around PPP. De Bettignies and Ross (Chapter 7), for instance, demonstrate that we have already progressed some distance in terms of the theoretical frameworks and models that can now be applied. Major variables such as the role of perfect information, when to bundle activities and the effects of doing so, which sector to allocate which tasks to, competition, contract length, the effects of externalities and when private finance ought to be applied all come into play here. On the other hand, though, many of these models are more direction pointers and partial clues, and in reality, we have much further to go to calibrate our theoretical ideas with empirical data so that decision-making is clear and evidence-based.

Boardman and Vining (Chapter 8), too, deal with economic matters but are stronger in their assessment. They argue that 'no government has performed normatively appropriate analyses of P3' (as PPPs are called in Canada). They note that 'on-time and on-budget is obviously a weak criterion' and whilst 'VfM is more meaningful', it none the less suffers from several problems and is consequently inadequate. Given the amounts of money currently going into PPPs around the globe, these are serious charges. Boardman and Vining suggest that in choosing between a P3 and the public sector alternative, it would be better for governments to select the alternative with the lowest total social costs (TSC), holding quality constant. This criterion includes not only production costs (which are included in VfM), but also transaction costs and externality costs (which are usually not). Much would be gained in the economic analysis made across governments if they were to adopt the more realistic notion of TSC. The authors then argue that governments ought to seek to improve allocative efficiency and therefore should use cost–benefit analysis to both choose among alternative providers up front and to evaluate PPP effectiveness once delivered. As other critical studies have shown, there is a clear need to examine how governments (and the private sector) make their calculations and financial estimations of PPP deals (Pollock et al., 2007). On the matter of discount rates in economic analyses, they again argue strongly and put it simply, stating that 'many governments and many organizations that perform P3 evaluations use the wrong rate'. After detailed consideration, they propose the most appropriate discount rate for analysis as 3.5 per cent (real). Given these arguments, and acknowledging as well that most evaluations to date have been undertaken by parties whose interests are hugely conflicted (towards the PPP policy solution), governments clearly have a long way to go before claims as to the economic superiority of PPPs are deemed legitimate.

Colin Duffield's chapter (Chapter 9) takes us through a wide range of engineering contract styles from simple public works, through competitive tendering, design and construct, and relationship style contracts in order to outline a range of possible alternatives to PFI-type PPPs. And for the PPP-style contract group alone, he articulates a selection of 20 acronyms to illustrate the breadth of the options. Importantly, too, for each of the various styles of contract, he nominates who does what within the project life cycle (from the project as a concept, to design, to procurement and to construction), and how responsibilities flow through to different task and risk allocations. This approach spells out with clarity whether costs are fixed or actual, and just who makes the decisions on these tasks. The strengths and weaknesses of each group of contract types are also discussed. Crucial to Duffield's chapter is his explanation as to why the earlier culture of contract tendering in Australia needed to be changed, and how the adversarial and dispute-ridden project managers sought to improve delivery. He comments interestingly that attempts at refining contract conditions (which economic theorists would presumably have welcomed as better contract specificity and improved information) made things worse, not better. He particularly highlights, though, the need for improved contract skills in government, the suboptimal performance of PPPs led by financiers, and PPPs' high bidding costs. Importantly, too, he concludes that the choice between procurement strategies is not straightforward, and that whilst PPPs 'are complex and generally require a very large financial transaction, due caution and high levels of expertise' they 'can work well in the right situation'. None the less Duffield cautions about policy exuberance, noting that PPPs 'have strengths and weaknesses', and 'may well apply to only a minority of projects'.

Tvarnø's assessment of legal issues facing PPPs (Chapter 10) reminds us that they can be pivotal to any PPP policy flourishing successfully. Whilst she looks specifically at the challenges facing the EU, the points she makes have far wider implications. She comments that PPPs fall under existing public procurement rules and legislation, and are therefore subject to a regime designed specifically for traditional public contracts. PPPs, though, require a high degree of both negotiation and cooperation in order to achieve the economic benefits promised. Whilst under existing rules, a public authority is allowed to use competitive dialogue in regard to PPPs, this may not be enough. As Tvarnø says, the principles underpinning the present EU, UN and WTO rules 'are to ensure competition, equal treatment and transparency, but not cooperation. Instead there is a general ban on negotiation.' So the degree to which PPP contracts require more cooperative arrangements than usual between public and private parties can itself be a challenge. The roots of this challenge go back to a clash between the general philosophy of private contractual law, which emphasizes the freedom of two parties to do what they wish, and the philosophy of public procurement law, which constrains the freedom of governments to ensure that they behave in a fair, transparent and non-corrupt manner in the public interest. Importantly, there is little recognition of the need for special PPP rules and definitions at present. Tvarnø argues that this is a serious problem, and may be a factor in discouraging PPPs within the EU in practice, as it creates both uncertainty and a high risk of legal claims.

The rhetoric of risk goes hand in hand with every discussion on PPPs. Indeed, many authors regard the transfer of risks from the public to the private sector as a central and defining characteristic of the PPP approach. So it is surprising to read, as Monteiro argues in Chapter 12, that 'the conventional approach to risk in PPPs, borne out of project finance, suffers from some naïvety'. But his idea is powerful. To his mind, the very narrowness of conventional thinking about risk is its downfall. Broadening our traditional risk lens, he uses public-choice ideas to argue that PPPs strengthen the short-run political cycle and enable politicians to deliver more projects in the short term, which is something that they always seek. This is, however, because PPPs transfer costs to future political cycles. He outlines a series of deficiencies in traditional risk analyses, and comments in line with Flyvbjerg's ideas that 'politicians always base their arguments on the success cases, systematically avoiding learning from failure cases'.

Moreover, we seem to focus more on effectiveness than on efficiency. He comments that when PPP projects are undertaken, risk transfers can be illusory, and he worries about the capacity of governments to negotiate and renegotiate PPP contracts with private players who are more deft and able to manoeuvre. Overall, he notes that whilst PPP projects have high public visibility and political style, they seem to 'lack some efficiency' and may well, if not handled properly, be fiscally unsustainable. For Monteiro, improved PPP risk management will require both stronger internal capacity in government as well as stronger 'external pressure for guaranteeing efficiency and affordability'.

Questions of PPP governance are particularly important in that the public interest needs to be protected despite the delegation of authority to private concerns. But at the centre of this governance challenge there is an inherent tension. As Skelcher (Chapter 13) reminds us, tight governance is needed to protect the public interest, but weaker governance is also required to enable risk-taking and innovation, along with incentivized private actor participation. The notion of regulatory governance, which comprises many types of soft law, incentives, guidelines, brokering activities, along with legal mechanisms, such as contract and public procurement laws, is crucial.[1] Together, these mechanisms provide a fair basis for potential investors as well as a framework that should reduce risks of corruption and opportunism. But also, 'PPPs raise important issues of democratic governance', to Skelcher's mind. Whilst 'organizations in the public domain are required to account for their activities in the public arena of discourse', 'forms of third party government like PPPs muddy the waters of accountability', and lead to a 'democratic deficit'. PPPs are, interestingly, much like a form of quasi-governmental body, and they emerge through *ad hoc* processes and in a multiplicity of forms. They are also frequently a function of executive rather than legislative decision. To Skelcher's mind, creating effective constitutional oversight remains a priority challenge for PPPs.

All of these insights from the different academic disciplines are valuable, and they have certainly brought us far in understanding PPPs. But there are also calls for a more multidisciplinary approach, along with a common thread suggesting the need for better oversight capacity to ensure contract integrity and proper evaluation. We shall return to these themes at the end of the chapter.

The international empirical experience

The international experience with PPPs is now empirically rich, although rarely analysed on a rigorous basis.[2] Our empirically oriented handbook chapters skimmed over the experience of only a few dozen jurisdictions, yet both the common themes between these chapters as well as the differences were revealing. The major themes were far-reaching, and whilst we draw here on only our impressions at present, they are none the less noteworthy.

Both the pivotal role played by a country's history and its national administrative culture were central to the PPP story across jurisdictions. This point was made for public management reform by Laurence Lynn Jr (2006) and others, and is also a feature of the literature on 'varieties of capitalism' that distinguishes between 'liberal market economies' and 'coordinated market economies' (Hall and Soskice, 2001). In cases such as the UK, Australia, and to a lesser extent Canada, a history of healthy public and private mixing provided a supportive backdrop to the introduction of the PPP notion alongside NPM, whilst in continental Europe (e.g. Germany) and particularly Scandinavia, with their successful corporatist traditions, PPPs have been greeted as somewhat of an Anglo-Saxon invention (see Chapter 15 by Hammerschmid and Ysa on Europe, and Chapter 18 by Greve and Mörth on Scandinavia). Indeed, in countries such as Sweden, the very label 'PPP' is rarely used and the label 'partnership' has only recently begun to be adopted. A clash of values underneath the PPP idea has also been clear. For example, this clash has been in the form of a public-versus-private battle and has been a long-term tension threatening to undermine the perceived legitimacy of the UN's work, as Benedicte Bull notes (Chapter 20). Also, a broader clash has been evident in terms of the differences between the traditional belief in a strong public sector in charge of a participatory democracy on the one hand as against the more NPM-oriented idea of an overburdened state in the midst of a network that needs markets to rescue it, along with a good dose of efficiency, as Greve points out.

The powerful role of political dynamics has also been evident across the jurisdictions analysed. The attractiveness of PPPs as a 'buy-now, pay-later' arrangement was crystal clear in both the UK and in Canada. So, too, was it clear in the case of the UK and, to an extent, in Australia, that PPPs were supported by both major political parties and served the important function of considerably strengthening the governments' relationships with City financiers. Matthew Flinders (Chapter 6) has suggested that New Labour used PPPs to make assurances to the City of London about their relationship with private businesses. New Labour did not want to see the City as an adversary, and the PFI was a sure and quick way for New Labour to show that the government was not going to be against the private sector. In these jurisdictions, despite some visible failures and policy U-turns, there were clear political attractions for PPP policies to continue. This contrasted with observations in Scandinavia and the USA, where there appear to have been no real political pay-offs for PPPs. Of course initiatives taken by governments, including supportive legislation and regulatory governance arrangements, central PPP units and taskforces, and supporting loan arrangements, have led to greater numbers of partnerships in the field. These were evident in the European institutional analyses by Hammerschmid and Ysa (Chapter 15), as well as the work of Boardman and Vining in their analysis of North American experience (Chapter 16). But even stronger than the need for supportive legislative frameworks was the obvious need for strong and professional capacity inside government to take on these deals. This observation has been made before and has indeed been a continuing concern for some time throughout the recent history of contracting out government services.[3]

A further theme crossing most jurisdictions has been the economic and financial issues dogging PPPs. These have included multiple concerns around VfM calculations, the use of excessively high discount rates (with an additional margin of around 2.4 per cent, according to Hellowell's account of the UK – Chapter 14), unjustified claims of risk transfer, and dubious assertions of greater long-term asset quality. All of these have resulted in a serious questioning (at least in the UK) of not only the claimed general superiority of PPPs but, importantly, of the actual financial sustainability of this policy in the medium to long term. Indeed, the observation made by Greve and Mörth (Chapter 18), if we may reword it slightly, said it all: countries such as Norway and Denmark did not need to take on PPP policies in the first place because they were under little financial or political pressure to spend beyond their means. For example, the Danish Ministry of Finance seems to have actively argued against a prolific PPP policy, and the Danish PPP unit was placed in a smaller government agency far removed from the centre of power. To the degree that PPPs have essentially functioned as a mechanism to provide infrastructure today and put off the costs until tomorrow, we shall be subject to 'the politics of time', as Pierson (2004) noted. He commented that a great deal of contemporary research in political science seems geared to analysing short-term causes and short-term policy consequences. But such a framework is probably inappropriate. By extending our time horizons to analyse longer-term causes of phenomena and longer-term consequences, we may well better understand the phenomenon in the first place and then make better policy decisions for the medium term.

Examining the international experience seems to confirm the core trends noted elsewhere. PPPs were popular in the countries that had most experience with privatization and contracting out, for example the UK and Australia. It seems unlikely that other countries will just follow their example. Some countries are cautious, and international organizations are not necessarily advocating the PPP solution now at all costs. Therefore a significant number of countries in the world, and especially those that enjoy integrated and institutionalized corporatist arrangements, are not likely to display a high activity in PPP use. In the UK in the early 2000s, the think tank the Institute of Public Policy wondered if PPPs were going to be 'the only show in town'. Discussing the international experience with PPPs, we have found that PPPs have certainly entered the vocabulary and toolbox of governments and international organizations, but in many parts of the world they have been only a modest part of the show rather than 'the only show'.

Common issues critical to the future of PPPs
The theoretical themes and the empirical results presented in this international handbook have pointed to a number of issues that need to be addressed in the future. In the wake of the financial crisis, there is a sense that the era of the 'marketization-only' agenda is over, and that governments are once again being pressured into finding a proper role in the economy. Professor Alasdair Roberts (2010) argues in his recent book that 'the logic of discipline' meant that politics and democratic intervention were kept out of more and more decisions during the marketization and privatization era, which he describes as being roughly from the late 1970s to the crash of Lehman Brothers in autumn 2008. Now there is a need for governments to find a new balance as the marketization agenda is reformulated.[4] As US President Obama mentioned, in working towards new regulatory mechanisms, there is now a trend towards making government matter again. This means that PPPs, where both the public sector and the private sector work together in some sort of partnering arrangement, are likely to be a reality for many years to come.[5] As a consequence, there is therefore a need for further examination of the theoretical lenses and the promises of a multidisciplinary approach; a need for more rigorous data collection and analysis; more genuine comparative studies that lead to theory-building; and a closer look at the private sector's view of the development and the political economy surrounding PPPs.

A multidisciplinary approach
As we saw above, different academic disciplines and theoretical lenses have been used to study PPPs. There are new insights from political science and management studies, accounting studies, and very encouraging new work from economics and legal studies. Studies show that careful analysis is needed to get behind the rhetoric, and that there are 'no free lunches' when it comes to PPPs (Vining and Boardman, 2005). However, few of these theoretical approaches seem to address or sometimes even acknowledge

the work from other disciplines. One of the key findings in this handbook is that PPPs are a very complex phenomenon, and that looking at them from a single point of view tells only a small part of the story. Perhaps this is a condition for all knowledge production, but with PPP studies we seem to have reached a point where a multidisciplinary study approach is a prerequisite for presenting a clearer picture of what a PPP is, how it functions and how it performs.

More rigorous analysis
There is a need for more rigorous studies on the performance of PPPs, and more carefully designed analyses. Although this handbook witnesses that progress has been made in economics, for example, there is a clear need to push forward with even more empirical studies of performance, as PPPs are being compared by governments with other alternatives, for example in-house production, contracting out or outright privatization. Indeed, the evaluation task facing us is huge if we want to pursue evidence-based learning. Like the privatization and contracting-out debates that preceded our interest in PPPs, much has been promised. And in parallel with these previous reforms, it is also likely that whilst some achievements will no doubt be delivered, many will not, and the reform will come at a price unless we learn as we proceed. We are babes in the wood here, and many of our views on PPP efficiency at present parallel our views on contracting-out efficiency in the 1970s! We now need, for instance, more sophisticated econometric analyses to help us to discern the importance of the many variables in the mix – but most importantly, controlling for the amount of work done!

More genuine comparative studies of PPP practices that lead to theory-building
Although there have been comparative studies of PPPs (and reviews of international performances), many studies still concern the development of PPPs in a single country. We now need to apply some of the comparative case-study methods in more sophisticated ways. As some of the chapters in this handbook have certified, there are huge variations in how governments around the world promote, decide, implement and evaluate PPPs. From other comparative studies we have a number of categories ('liberal market economies versus coordinated market economies', for example) that can be used as a basis for more intense comparisons. Perhaps PPPs are simply 'an Anglo-Saxon religion', as one Japanese commentator put it to one of the editors. Much of the material is available, so what we need is more carefully designed analyses of comparable countries. These empirical studies could also attempt to formulate theories of factors

that influence the performance of PPPs. While many studies have pointed to the institutional framework, including the legal conditions for PPPs, others (Dutch scholar Erik-Hans Klijn, for example) have mentioned that it is the management of PPPs that is really important regarding their performance (Klijn, 2008; Klijn et al., 2008; Steijn et al., 2008). Governance, too, remains a continuing future challenge. As Skelcher says, whilst there is much opportunity to shape new governance arrangements for PPP, deliberatively designing such arrangements will need to take priority, and mechanisms for public accountability will also need to be explicit. To Skelcher's mind, 'the governance of PPPs has [to date] predominantly been used to remove them from public scrutiny and informed debate, justified on the grounds of commercial confidentiality or managerial discretion'. Given that PPPs are inherently instruments of public action, we need to ensure that 'PPP governance arrangements are properly expressed' and are 'subjugated neither to an ideology of commercialization nor an alternative form of governance arising from the formalized practices of the private actors involved in managing a PPP'. We therefore need further studies, designed to formulate a model of what influences PPP performance in terms of broad questions about the degree to which the public interest is met, as well as narrower issues of project delivery and management.

The other side of the partnership: examining the private sector's role and perspective
It would not be unfair to say that most studies of PPPs presented in the literature so far, and also in this international handbook, have examined PPPs from the government's point of view. Will governments get better performance by using PPPs? What is the proper way for governments to involve the private sector in new infrastructure-building? What about the governance risks and the threat to democratic participation? How are PPPs going to be accountable to the public? All these points are relevant and necessary to investigate, but there seem to be fewer studies that examine the business side of things more closely. This is an important omission. Such studies could be done by analysing how private sector organizations or industries view partnership deals, or studies could be done on profitability from a company's perspective. These would add crucial empirical data to those partnerships that have to date ended up in the media spotlight after a claimed success or visible failure. Another viewpoint might adopt a political-economy perspective and critically examine how a 'PPP industry' occurs. Greve has pointed to some of the issues (in Chapter 21 of this book) where private sector consultants have become an important part in transferring knowledge about PPPs on a global scale. But research could go further than that by examining, for example,

how much the PPP deals mean for specific industries, say the transport industry, and how private organizations organize themselves to become partners for the public sector.

Overall, it is apparent that the future outcome of PPPs will depend on the degree to which we are able to learn from our past. As Wettenhall has pointed out, global market uncertainties and heavy 'rescue' efforts from governments around the globe over the past few years were surely wake-up calls to remind us that both sectors matter. They should also remind us that the best interventions by governments ought to be informed by our past actions, and by the degree to which they led an enhancement of the public interest. This international handbook has charted the rise of the PPP, reviewed the most recent international experiences with PPPs, examined them through a variety of theoretical and professional lenses, explored the various issues and themes that arise as a consequence of PPPs, and pointed to those issues that need further attention. PPPs became part of governments' policy options in many countries around the world during the last few decades, and PPPs can now claim their place as one (but far from the only one) of the key institutional forms used by governments and the private sector to cooperate with each other. Understanding how PPPs work is therefore essential to present a clear picture of organizational responses to the new public policy challenges we face in coming decades. There is still much to learn.

Notes

1. The notion of regulatory governance is part of the broader view nowadays of regulation as a construct and several parallel ideas are apparent here. Governance scholars from law and public policy, for example, now speak of living with a 'regulatory state' (Glaeser and Shleifer, 2003; Moran, 2002; Sunstein, 1990). Those from economics and development speak of 'regulatory governance' (Minogue, 2004), and others from political science talk of 'regulatory capitalism' (Levi-Faur and Jordana, 2005; Braithwaite, 2008). Thus, rather than viewing regulation in the old sense of developing and enforcing rules, or simply about managing risks, these scholars see regulation as crucial to a new order of governance – as about reordering priorities and power. Regulation is now 'a distinctive mode of policy making' or an 'alternative mode of public control', as Majone (1999, p. 1) put it (cited in Minogue, 2002).
2. We might posit a host of reasons for this difference between the appearance of rich empirical PPP studies and the more modest reality of scarce rigorous work. As with all policy debates, we would expect much advertising, advocacy and rhetoric on both sides, and we must also acknowledge the straight technical difficulty of rigorously evaluating PPP. Crucially, though, part of the evaluation difficulty here is in the nature of the beast – most advocating governments, private companies and government PPP units have a preference for less public information rather than transparency and openness. This motivation itself makes serious evaluation difficult, understandably raises the suspicions of many commentators and also undermines the legitimacy of most performance claims made.
3. See, for example, Hodge (2000) on this point.
4. Of course to the degree that we believe PPPs are simply a subset of this marketization

agenda, we could well argue that the modern PPP era itself is also over. This handbook, however, has demonstrated that the PPP ideal is far larger and richer than this marketization agenda, alone, and as such, would imply that PPP as a policy ideal is far from over!

5. Again, the extent to which PPPs remain a high-profile infrastructure policy direction for governments depends on many things. These include the degree to which governments continue to invest in infrastructure, the extent to which they are willing to invest public funds, or alternatively, take on private funding sources, and the presence of competing demands from other high-profile policy areas such as healthcare or climate change, for example.

References

Braithwaite, J. (2008), *Regulatory Capitalism: How it Works, Ideas for Making it Work Better*, Cheltenham, UK and Northampton, MA, USA: Edward Elgar.

Glaeser, E.L. and A. Shleifer (2003), *The Rise of the Regulatory State*, Boston, MA: Harvard University, available at: post.economics.harvard.edu/faculty/shleifer/papers/rise_JEL_JAN_2003.pdf.

Hall, Peter and David Soskice (eds) (2001), *Varieties of Capitalism. The Institutional Foundations of Comparative Advantage*, Oxford: Oxford University Press.

Hodge, G.A. (2000), *Privatization*, Boulder, CO: Westview Press.

Jeffares, Stephen, H. Sullivan and T. Bovaird (2009), 'Beyond the contract: the challenges of evaluating the performance(s) of public–private partnerships', paper for the International Research Society for Public Management conference, Copenhagen, Denmark, 6–8 April.

Kettl, Donald F. (1993), *Sharing Power. Public Governance and Private Markets*, Washington, DC: Brookings Institution.

Klijn, E.H. (2008), *It's the Management, Stupid!: On the Importance of Management in Complex Policy Issues*, The Hague: Klijn, Uitgeverij LEMMA.

Klijn, E.H., J. Edelenbos and B. Steijn (2008), 'Public–private partnerships: organisational form or management activities; the impact of the organisational form and managerial strategies on the outcomes of PPP projects', paper presented at the 12th conference of The International Research Society for Public Management, 26–28 March, Brisbane, Australia.

Levi-Faur, D. and J. Jordana (2005), 'The rise of regulatory capitalism: the global diffusion of a new order', *The ANNALS of the American Academy of Political and Social Sciences*, **598** (1), 12–32.

Lynn, Laurence Jr (2006), *Public Management. Old and New*, London: Routledge.

Majone, G. (1999), 'The regulatory state and its legitimacy problems', *West European Politics*, **22** (1), 1–24.

Minogue, Martin (2002), 'Governance-based analysis of regulation', *Annals of Public and Cooperative Economics*, **73**, 649–66.

Minogue, M. (2004), 'Public management and regulatory governance: problems of policy transfer to developing countries', in Paul Cook, Colin Kirkpatrick, Martin Minogue and David Parker (eds), *Leading Issues in Regulation, Competition and Development*, Cheltenham, UK and Northampton, MA, USA: Edward Elgar, pp. 165–81.

Moran, M. (2002), 'Understanding the regulatory state', *British Journal of Political Science*, **32**, 391–413.

OECD (2008), *Public–Private Partnerships. In Pursuit of Risk Sharing and Value for Money*, Paris: OECD.

Pierson, P. (2004), *Politics in Time: History, Institutions and Social Analysis*, Princeton, NJ: Princeton University Press.

Pollock, A., D. Price and S. Playe (2007), 'An examination of the UK's Treasury's evidence base for cost and time overrun data in UK value-for-money policy and appraisal', *Public Money and Management*, April, 127–33.

Roberts, Alasdair (2010), *The Logic of Discipline. Global Capitalism and the Architecture of Government*, Oxford: Oxford University Press.

Steijn, B., E.H. Klijn and J. Edelenbos (2008), 'The impact of network management in governance networks; exploring the influence of four types of network management strategies on perceived outcomes in governance networks on environmental problems', paper presented at the 12th conference of The International Research Society for Public Management, 26–28 March, Brisbane, Australia.

Sunstein, C. (1990), *After the Rights Revolution: Reconceiving the Regulatory State*, Boston, MA: Harvard University Press.

Vining, A.R. and A.E. Boardman (2005), 'Public–private partnerships in the U.S. and Canada: there are no free lunches', *Journal of Comparative Policy Analysis*, **7** (3), 199–220.

Index

Note: public–private partnership has been abbreviated to PPP throughout the index.

Abadie, R. 311
Abelaira, A. 345
Academies programme 312
accountability 121–2, 123, 266–8
accounting 237–8, 257–8
    charge to the income statement 255–6
    control as the criterion 247–55
        Australia 254–5
        France 255
        GASB, proposed control-based standard 253–4
        IFRIC 12: 247–8, 255
        mirror-image of IFRIC 12, IPSASB version 250–53
        mirror-image of IFRIC 12, UK version 248–50
        South Africa 255
    government financial reporting 241–2, 243, 244, 257
    national accounts 241, 243, 257
    regulation 241–3, 257
    regulation enforcement 244
    risks and rewards as the criterion 244–7
    service concession arrangements 239–41, 251, 255–6
Accounting Standards Board (ASB) 242
    FRS 5A 242, 244, 245, 254, 255
Acerete, B. 553
Adams, J. 297
adverse selection 146, 269, 270, 533
advocacy partnerships 484, 485–6
Africa *see* Middle East and North Africa (MENA); South Africa
AGRA (Alliance for a Green Revolution in Africa) 487
Agranoff, R. 73
air traffic control 561–2
Airline Group 562

Akerlof, G.A. 274
Akintoye, A. 48, 279
Akitoby, B. 238
Alberta 361–2, 369, 375
Alfen, H.W. 189
Allegheny Conference on Community Development (ACCD) 49
Allen Consulting Group 100, 102, 103, 199, 202
Alliance for a Green Revolution in Africa (AGRA) 487
alliances 190–91, 193, 194
    behavioural factors 518–19
    cooperation 516–18
    PPP comparison 512–16
    strengths of 204–6
    see also strategic alliance research
Allison, G.T. 115, 514
allocative efficiency 136, 161
    cost–benefit analysis 170–79
    value for money (VfM) 179–81
Alonso-Conde, A.B. 58
Alter, C. 62
Amalgamated Wireless Australasia Ltd (AWA) 33–4
Anechiarico, F. 122
Anglo-Persian Oil Co. 33, 34
Annan, K. 481, 482, 487
Appleby, J. 125
arbitrage 237–8, 244
arbitration 298, 591
Argentina 457–8, 583, 586
Ariff, M. 33
Ariño, A. 515, 517
Aritua, B. 62
Arrow, K.J. 176
Arrowsmith, S. 217
Arthur Andersen and LSE Enterprise 96, 103
Asian Development Bank 189, 573
Asian financial crisis 587

asset ownership 142–5
  Besley and Ghatak 144–5
  Hart et al. 143–4
  King and Pitchford 144
  Schmidt 143
Aubin, H. 379
Audit Commission 97, 103
Auditor-General of New South Wales
  99
Aulakh, P.S. 516, 521
Auster, E.R. 516
Austin, P. 243
Australia 128, 399–401, 405, 423
  accounting 241, 254–5
  BOOT projects 402, 412
  education infrastructure 410
  health infrastructure 410
  Infrastructure Australia 202, 409,
    425
  infrastructure investment gap 504
  justice infrastructure 410–11,
    414–17
  Melbourne CityLink 58–9, 411–14,
    425–6
  mixed enterprises 33–4
  New South Wales 57, 405, 406,
    434–6
  Northern Territory 434
  Partnerships Victoria 199, 299, 406,
    407–8
  PPP industry 505
  PPP movement, foundations of
    401–4
  PPP policy platforms 405–11
  PPP procurement 208–9
  PPP strengths 422
  PPP weaknesses 421
  PPPs, criticism of 57, 58
  projects at 2009: 409–10, 430–38
  Queensland 437
  roads infrastructure 410, 411–14
  South Australia 433
  Southern Cross Station 418–20
  Sydney, Cross City Tunnel 301
  Tasmania 437
  Victoria 405, 406, 430–32
  Victoria County Court facility
    414–17
  water infrastructure 411
  Western Australia 433

Australian Constructors Association
  (ACA) 201
Austria
  government initiatives 341, 342
  implementation 343
  legislation 339, 342
  project failure 347
  taskforce 338–9, 342
Ayling, J. 29, 30

Bailey, M. 34
Baker, K. 292, 301
Balance-sheet treatment 238, 239, 243,
  244, 246, 256, 310
Ball, R. 58, 102, 103
Bang, H.P. 63
Banks, G. 84
Barlow, J. 227
Bartlett, D.L. 18
Barzelay, M. 500, 505
Bastin, J. 344
Bates Review 199
Bayart, J.-F. 31
Behn, R. 122
Bel, G. 550
Belgium
  evaluation 346
  government initiatives 341, 342
  implementation 343
  legislation 342
  taskforce 338, 342
Bennett, J. 148
Bennett, J.T. 102, 107
Benson, J.K. 75
Bentz, A. 145–6
Berger, R.A. 50
Bergström, J. 446, 447
Bergström, M. 513
Besley, T. 144–5
bidding costs 210
Biersteker, T.J. 27
Bill and Melinda Gates Foundation
  489, 492
Bingham, R.D. 83, 91, 105
Blair, T. 24, 70, 84, 129, 310
Blakely, E. 48–9, 50
Blanc, H. 19
Blanc-Brude, F. 7, 88, 100, 102, 104,
  322, 323, 380, 381
Bloomfield, P. 96, 298

Boardman, A. 88, 99, 101, 103, 104
Bolivia 587, 591
Bolton, P. 150
Bolz, U. 343
Borchert, H. 292
Borys, B. 78
Börzel, T. 484
Boston, J. 569
Bouckaert, G. 334, 448
Bourn, J. 201
Bovaird, T. 26, 300, 505, 574
Bovens, M. 122
Bovis, C.H. 226
Bowman, D. 499, 502, 506, 507, 511, 513
Bozeman, B. 515
brand, PPP as 69–71
Brandon, P. 201
Brazil 231, 473, 583
Brealey, R. 320
Brenck, A. 348
British Columbia 163, 165–7, 170, 357–61, 374–5
British Leyland 32
British Partnerships UK plc 337
British Petroleum (BP) 33, 34
Brittan, L. 527
Broadbent, J. 24, 56, 88, 242, 312, 519
Broadwater, I. 483
Brooks, H. 51
Brown, G. 126, 308, 311, 312, 313
Brundtland, G.H. 483
Buchanan, J.M. 290
Büchel, B. 518
Budäus, D. 348
Budina, N. 348
Building Canada Plan (BCP) 367
Building Research Establishment (BRE) 322
Building Schools for the Future programme 311
Bulgaria 339, 340, 341, 344, 543
Bult-Spiering, M. 120
bundling 263, 321–2, 355
    under complete contracting 145–7
    under incomplete contracting 147–9
    uncertainty and contract flexibility 149
bureaucrats 265, 267
Burnett, M. 217

Burnham, J. 47
Buser, M. 297
Bush, President George W. 10
Button, M. 338, 342, 344, 345, 346, 349

Caiden, N. 28
Calderon, C. 476
California, performance-based infrastructure 390–91
Campbell, G. 6
Campbell, J. 440
Campbell, J.L. 337
Canada 355, 356, 367, 393–4
    Alberta 361–2, 369, 375
    British Columbia 163, 165–7, 170, 357–61, 374–5
    Building Canada Plan (BCP) 367
    Canada Line 372–3
    discount rates 174–7
    evaluation 372–3, 379
    federal agencies 367
    future of PPPs 379–81
    global financial crisis, effects of 379
    government P3 agencies 367–71
    infrastructure investment gap 504
    Kelowna General Hospital 163
    Manitoba 375
    New Brunswick 365, 371
    New Edward Island 371
    Northwest Territories 365–6, 371
    Nova Scotia 371
    Ontario 362–4, 376–7
    Partnerships BC 165–7, 169, 170, 367–8, 371
    PPP Canada Inc. 367
    private sector proponent institutions 372
    projects since 2000: 357–66
    proposed projects 374–8
    Québec 364–5, 370–71, 373, 378–9
    Saskatchewan 369–70
    Sea-to-Sky Highway 166–7, 170, 368
Canadian Council for Public–Private Partnerships 372
capital asset pricing model (CAPM) 320
Cariño, L.V. 539
Carmeli, A. 54
Carter, R. 59
Casson, M. 513

Castelos, M. 347
Channel Tunnel 5
Cheah, C.Y.J. 58
Chee, G. 490
Chen, C. 57
Chevron Corporation 488
Child, J. 55, 59
Chile 583
China 297, 583
Choice Agenda 125
Christensen, T. 54, 334, 337
Chu, W. 517
citizen consumers 125–6
Clark, T. 308
Clarke, K. 309
Cleason, M. 457
Clifton, C. 510
Cline, W.R. 176
Clinger, J.C. 355
Coase, R.H. 140
Coghill, K. 88, 511
collaborative advantage theory 44,
    59–60
collaborative empowerment theory
    44, 45
collaborative processes 519
Collins, H. 226
Colombia 583
commercial confidentiality 108, 122,
    300, 303, 422, 554, 607
commitment problems 152–3
Common, R. 292
Commonwealth Oil Refineries Ltd
    (COR) 33
competition 136, 137, 269
competitive advantage 122
complex adaptive systems theory 44,
    45, 51, 62
complexity in contracting 3, 142, 223,
    339, 419
Concession contracts 190, 264, 539
concession model of public–private
    mix 26
conflict of interest 8, 267
Connex South East 557
conspiracy theories 44, 57
construct only contracts (traditional)
    192, 193, 194
construction management procurement
    strategy 192

consultants 8, 265, 267, 505, 506, 507
contestability 117–20, 128
contract enforcement 288
contract management 210, 212, 287–8
contract renegotiation 269, 282, 533–4
contracting in 448, 449
contracting out 133, 134, 138–42
    ex ante inefficiencies 141–2
    ex post inefficiencies 139–41
    garbage collection VfM evaluation
        102, 107
Contractor, F. 513
contracts 216–17, 225–8
    abbreviations 190
    classic public contracts, alternative
        to 227–8
    clauses in 227
    enforcement of 288
cooperation 288, 513, 514, 520–21
    alliances 515, 516–18
Corner, D. 511
corporate governance 300–301
Corrigan, P. 295
corruption 268, 269
cost–benefit analysis 170–80
    discount rates 174–7
    weighting cash flows to government
        178–9
    weighting investment flows to private
        sector 177–8
Coulson, A. 58
County Court 411, 414–17, 426
Cowie, H. 47
Cox, R. 481
Cresswell, J.W. 82
Crocker, K.J. 140
Crouch, C. 116, 119, 124
culture governance 63
Cusatis, P.J. 381
Cuttaree, V. 543
Czarniawska, B. 334
Czech Republic
    cancellations 347
    evaluation 346
    government initiatives 342
    legislation 339, 342
    taskforce 337, 338, 342

Dachs, W. 539
Dahler-Larson, P. 89, 91, 105–6

Dartford River Crossing 74–5, 528–9
Das, S. 413
Das, T.K. 517
Dasgupta, P. 176
Davidson, K. 413
Davies, A. 317
Davies, E. 33
Davies, J.P. 513
Davies, J.S. 52
Davoudi, S. 312
DBFO model 72, 74–5, 307, 319, 323,
    326, 551–3
de Bettignies, J. 150
de Bruijn, H. 88
de Jong, W.M. 422
de la Torre, J. 515, 517
de Pelet, P. 529
De Pierris, L. 345
definitions of PPPs 4, 5–7, 68
delivery models *see* procurement
    strategies
Delmon, J. 474
Deloitte 102, 503, 504, 506
demand risk 245, 281
democratic governance 299–300
Deng, X. 298
Denhardt, J. 119
Denhardt, R. 119
Denmark 440–45
    evaluation 445
    National Archive project 443–4
    private sector policy 442–3
    privatization 507
    regulation 231
    school project 444–5
Department of Transport 97
design, build, finance, operate (DBFO)
    model 72, 74–5, 307, 319, 323,
    326, 551–3
design and construct procurement
    strategy 192, 204–6
Deutsche Bank 485
developing economies, PPPs 526,
    535–9, 544, 568–71, 587–9
    cancellations 585–7, 591
    distribution across countries and
        regions 580–84
    distribution across sectors 575–7
    failures, prevention of 542–3
    global financial crisis, effects of 471

infrastructure investment needs
    457–62
infrastructure services, data analysis
    573–84
institutional support 540
obstacles to 469–72
PPI types 578–80, 581
private infrastructure investment,
    decline in 464
rural development 541–2
specificity of countries 571–3
success, factors contributing to
    539–41
World Bank infrastructure
    development policies 462–6
World Bank infrastructure lending
    462–3
World Bank support in practice
    472–4
development gap 568, 573, 574, 583,
    588
Dickens, W.T. 274
DiGaetano, A. 344
Dilke, Sir Charles 26
Dinica, V. 345
discount rates 167–9, 174–7, 183
Domberger, A. 102, 107
Donaldson, L. 75
donor agencies 538–9
Doz, Y.L. 227, 515, 516, 517
Dudkin, G. 325
Duffield, C.F. 88, 510
Dufty, G. 414
Dunleavy, P. 117
Dunning, J.H. 518
Dupuy, E.R. 29
Dupuy, T.N. 29
Dussauge, P. 59
Duysters, G. 518
Dyer, J.H. 515, 517, 518, 519
dynamic efficiency 136

early constructor involvement (ECI)
    191
East Asia and Pacific (EAP)
    cancellations and projects under
        distress 586
    development indicators 572, 584
    infrastructure access 459
    infrastructure investment gap 504

infrastructure investment needs 460,
461
PPP types 579, 580, 581
private participation 537
projects and investment 582, 583,
584
World Bank support 462–3, 472
East Coast Main Line (ECML) rail
franchise 557, 558
ECA *see* Europe and Central Asia
(ECA)
Eckel, C. 34
economic development 5, 6, 35, 51, 52,
87, 88, 225, 296, 333, 340, 346,
400, 526, 538, 573
economic theory
asset ownership 142–5
Besley and Ghatak 144–5
Hart et al. 143–4
King and Pitchford 144
Schmidt 143
bundling of PPP tasks
under complete contracting 145–7
under incomplete contracting
147–9
uncertainty and contract flexibility
149
contracting out 138–42
ex ante inefficiencies 141–2
ex post inefficiencies 139–41
privatization of finance function
150–51
Economist, The 24
Edelenbos, J. 344, 511, 512
Edwards, C. 162, 163
Edwards, P. 98, 102, 165, 166, 563
Egan, M. 201, 202
Eggers, W.D. 20
Egypt 473–4
Ehrhardt, D. 550
Eichhorn, P. 337
Eisner, R. 162
Ellsberg, D. 274
Engel, E. 150
English, L. 254
English, L.M. 22, 23
Ennis, M. 391
entrepreneurs 265
Erenburg, S.J. 197
Ernst & Young 8, 503, 506

ESA 95: 243
Estache, A. 550
Europe 349–51
current challenges 346–9
government initiatives 340–41
implementation of PPPs 341–6
infrastructure investment gap 504
regulation 339–40
taskforces 337–9, 342, 348
see also European Union; individual
countries
Europe and Central Asia (ECA) 575
cancellations 586
development indicators 572, 584
infrastructure access 459
infrastructure investment needs 460,
461
PPP types 579, 580, 581
private participation 537
projects and investment 582, 584
World Bank support 462–3
European Investment Bank (EIB) 333,
336, 571
European System of Accounts (ESA)
95: 243
European Union
competitive dialogue 223–4
Green Paper (EC) 219–20, 335–7
institutional public–private
partnerships (IPPPs) 219,
220–22
legal framework 217–22
procurement law 217–18
procurement thresholds 222–4
public procurement law 222
specific PPP rules 229–30
see also Europe
Eurostat 243, 244, 257
evaluation 10–11, 82–3
challenges
evaluand, definition of 85–6
evaluation rigour 90–93
evaluator's role 89–90
multiple discourses and disciplines
88–9
multiple individual studies 93–4
multiple objectives 86–8
cost–benefit analysis 170–80
criteria for 164–70
allocative efficiency 161, 170

on time and on budget 165
total social costs 169–70
value for money (VfM) 165–9,
179–81
evidence 83–5
formative evaluations 105
summative evaluations 105
of value for money (VfM) 94–104
Evans, J. 511, 513
evidence, required for policy-making
83–5
evolutionary theory 44, 45
ex ante inefficiencies 141–2, 150
ex post inefficiencies 139–41, 150
exchange theory 44
Exit, Voice and Loyalty (Hirschman)
121
expected cost 246, 274, 320, 550
export industry 507
externalized rationing 123–4

Fageda, X. 550
Fainstain, S.S. 49, 51, 52
Farazmand, A. 18
Farlow, A. 490
Farrell, S. 550
Farum Scandal 97, 442
Fay, M. 459
FDBOMT projects 354, 355
FDBOOM model 134
Federal Accounting Standards
Advisory Board (FASAB) 242
Felbinger, C.L. 83, 91, 105
Ferreira, D. 569, 570, 571, 580
Financial Accounting Standards Board
(FASB) 241, 242
financial crises 587
see also global financial crisis,
2008–09
financial reporting 241–2, 243, 244,
257
Financial Reporting Advisory Board
(FRAB) 241
financing 134–5, 150–51
'Financing infrastructure investment:
promoting a partnership between
public and private finance' (Brown
et al.) 308
financing gap 459
Fischer, K. 299

Fitzgerald, J.P. 88
Fitzgerald, P. 98, 102, 103, 208, 414,
415, 416, 419
Flexible New Deal programme 56
Flinders, M. 22, 55, 62, 88
Flume, W. 225
Flyvbjerg, B. 263, 274, 284, 323
Fogel, C. 27
Ford Foundation 485
forms of PPPs 73–7
Forsberg, P. 446, 447
Foschi, M. 345
Fosler, R.S. 50
Foundation Hospitals 312
foundations, private 489, 491–2
France 347
accounting 255
evaluation 346
government initiatives 341, 342
government regulation of business
47–8
implementation 343
legislation 339, 342
post-global financial crisis 128
public–private mix, concession
model 26
société économie mixte (SEM) 47
taskforce 337, 338, 342
Franceys, R. 539, 540, 543
Frankel, C. 515
Franks, J. 321
Frederickson, H.G. 73
Freedland, M. 119, 124
Freeman, P. 550
French Utilities 47–8
Friedman, M. 61
Friend, J. 22
Froud, J. 57
FRS 5A 242, 244, 245, 254, 255

GAAP (Generally Accepted
Accounting Practice) 241, 242,
245, 259
Gaebler, T. 61, 71, 117
Gaffney, D. 559
Gage, R.W. 73
Galal, A. 178
Galiani, S. 457
Gallagher, J. 191, 202
Garrette, B. 59

GASB (Government Accounting
    Standards Board) 241–2, 253–4
GAVI (Global Alliance for Vaccines
    and Immunization) 484, 488,
    489–90
Gaza Strip 578
Geaughan, N. 310
Geddes, M. 72
Germany 347, 350
    evaluation 346
    government initiatives 340, 341,
        342
    government regulation of business
        48
    implementation 343
    legislation 339, 342
    taskforce 299, 337, 338, 342
Ghana, rural development project
    541
Ghatak, M. 144–5
Ghobadian, A. 24, 71, 98, 511
Ghuman, B.S. 21
Gigerenzer, G. 272, 274
Giles, C. 237
Gjølberg, M. 482
Glaister, S. 559
Glass, G. 93
Glass, G.V. 94
Glendinning, C. 22
Glennerster, H. 126
Global Alliance for Vaccines and
    Immunization (GAVI) 484, 488,
    489–90
Global Compact 482, 484, 486, 493
global consultancy firms 8, 506
    see also consultants
global economy 27–8
global financial crisis, 2008–09: 35,
    127–8, 129, 474–6, 492
    effect on Canada 379
    effect on developing countries 471
    effect on UK 326–9
Global Fund to Fight Aids,
    Tuberculosis and Malaria 487,
    488, 489
globalization 226
Globerman, S. 169
GNER Ltd 558
Goldsmith, S. 20
Goodman, E. 33

Gosling, T. 310
governance 20, 72–3, 292–3, 301–3
    corporate 300–301
    democratic 299–300
    legal 293–7
    regulatory 297–9
Government Accounting Standards
    Board (GASB) 241–2, 253–4
government financial reporting 241–2,
    243, 244, 257
government goals of PPPs 160–64
Government Procurement Agreement
    (GPA) 224–5
government regulation of business
    46–9
    France, utilities 47–8
    Germany, public ownership of
        private industry 48
    USA, regional and urban
        development 48–9
Granovetter, M. 516, 521
Grant Thornton 503
Green, D. 117
Greve, C. 22, 25, 55, 63, 68, 71, 74, 88,
    97, 102, 126, 197, 420, 511, 512,
    568, 574
Grey, G.J. 381
Grimsey, D. 5, 98, 102, 127, 190, 201,
    206, 208, 448
Groesmeyer, L. 217
Groom, B. 177
Grossman, S.J. 141–2
Growing Sustainable Business initiative
    485, 486
growth coalition theory 45
Grüb, B. 348
Gualmini, E. 334
Guasch, J.L. 534
Guba, E.G. 83
Gudergan, S.P. 301
guidelines 175, 199, 202, 231, 232, 255,
    297, 335, 347, 367, 368, 395, 406,
    407, 421, 424, 425, 474, 482, 511,
    535, 539, 602
*Guidelines for Successful Public–
    Private Partnerships* (European
    Commission) 335
Guinea 578
Gulati, R. 512
Guttman, D. 30, 300

Hage, J. 62
Hale, T. 488
Hall, D. 24
Hall, P. 603
Hall, R.B. 27
Ham, H. 333
Hamel, G. 227, 517
Hammami, M. 570, 576
Hammerschmid, G. 23
Hampson, K. 201
Hanjra, M.A. 539
Hardin, G. 124
Harding, A. 50, 51, 52
Harris, C. 541, 586
Harrod, J. 481
Hart, O. 141–2, 143–4, 147, 150
Hartley, J. 60
Hartley, K. 120
Harvey, D. 52–3, 60
Hatter, W. 510, 511, 512
Hay, C. 117
Head, B. 84
Heald, D. 57, 166, 310
Heimeriks, K. 518
Heinecke, B. 196, 197
Helby Petersen, O. 452
Hellowell, M. 58, 101, 103, 279, 531
Hemming, R. 162
Hepburn, C. 177
Hermansson, J. 446
Hewitt, E. 169
Highways Agency 165, 551, 552, 553
Hills, J. 126
Hirschleifer, J. 270, 272, 273
Hirschman, A. 52
historical institutional theory 45, 501
history of the PPP movement
    government regulation of business
        46–9
    intellectual foundations 44–5
    new public management (NPM)
        54–6
    PFI, public sector accounting
        critique 56–9
    postmodern theory 63
    public governance 60–62
    regional and urban dynamics 49–54
    strategic management approach
        59–60
Hjelmborg, S.E. 217, 226, 228

Hlahla, M. 538
HM Treasury 24, 102
Hodge, G. 22, 55, 63, 68, 71, 74, 126,
    197, 373, 499, 500, 502, 505, 506,
    507, 511, 512, 568, 574
Hodges, R. 242, 301
Hodgson, G. 59
Hofmeister, A. 292
Holland, R.C. 18
Holland, S. 32
Honduras, Melon Export Project
    541–2
Hong Kong 53–4
Hood, C. 71, 117, 119, 123, 252, 515,
    569
Hummel, H. 481
Hungary
    cancellations/losses 347, 348, 542
    evaluation 346
    government initiatives 342
    implementation 344–5
    regulation 339, 342
    taskforce 338, 342
Hunter, J.E. 93
Hussain, I. 539
Huxham, C. 59
hybrid, PPP as
    governance 72–3
    new public management (NPM)
        71–2

I-495 Capital Beltway HOT Lanes 382,
    385, 390
IASB (International Accounting
    Standards Board) 242, 245, 247
    IAS 17: 245, 250, 259
IDA (International Development
    Association) 472
IFC (International Finance
    Corporation) 472–3
IFRIC 12: 247–8, 255
    mirror image of IFRIC 12: 247–8
    IPSASB version 250–53
    UK version 248–50
IFRS (International Financial
    Reporting Standards) 241, 247,
    259
IKEA 485
ILO (International Labor
    Organization) 483

in house procurement strategy 192, 193, 204–6
incomplete contracts 140, 143–5, 533
ideology 303, 313, 492, 607
Independent Sector Treatment Centres (ISTCs) 312
India
  disinvestments 32–3
  private sector involvement 583
  viability gap fund 475, 540
India Infrastructure Project Development Fund 474
Indonesia 476, 583, 586
Inforesources 541
INFRA (Infrastructure Recovery and Assets) 476
Infrastructure Action Plan (IAP) 465
Infrastructure Australia 202, 409, 425
infrastructure investment gap 504
institutional public–private partnerships (IPPPs) 219, 220–22
interest groups 7–8
internalized rationing 123
International Accounting Standards Board (IASB) 242, 245, 247
  IAS 17: 245, 250, 259
International Bank for Reconstruction and Development *see* World Bank
International Development Association (IDA) 472
International Finance Corporation (IFC) 472–3
International Financial Reporting Standards (IFRS) 241, 247, 259
International Labor Organization (ILO) 483
International Monetary Fund (IMF) 27, 238, 241, 242, 257, 280
International Public Sector Accounting Standards Board (IPSASB) 242, 248, 250–53
International Reporting Standards 163
investment gap 458, 461, 504
Iossa, E. 147, 148, 149, 151
Ireland, R.D. 516, 517
IRI shareholding arrangement 32
Irwin, T. 550
Irwin, T.C. 280
ISTCs (Independent Sector Treatment Centres) 312

Italy
  evaluation 346
  government initiatives 340, 342
  implementation 345
  IRI shareholding arrangement 32
  legislation 339, 342
  project failure 347
  taskforce 338, 342

Jackson, B.M. 538
Jackson, G.B. 93–4
Jacobs, B. 49
Jacobs, J. 122
Jarvis 533
Jeffares, S. 89, 598
Jefferies, M.C. 208
Jemison, D. 78
Jenkins, S. 528
Jessop, B. 53
Jezierski, L. 51
Johnston, J. 301
Johnston, M.H. 102, 107
Jones, L.P. 160, 170
Jones, R. 348, 510, 511, 512
Jose, J. 20
Jupe, R. 101, 104

Kanter, R.M. 59, 516, 517, 519
Katzenstein, P. 446
Kaufmann, F.X. 252
Kaul, I. 483
Keating, W.D. 382
Kell, G. 481, 484, 488
Kelman, S. 510
Kelowna General Hospital 163
Kemmet, L. 54
Kenniscentrum PPS 69, 74, 337
Kerr, D. 53
Kettl, D.F. 18, 596
Khadaroo, I. 57
Khatami, K. 569, 570, 571, 580
Kierzenkowski, R. 347
Killing, P. 518
King, S. 144
Kirkaldy hospital project 327
Klein, B. 140
Klein, M. 319
Klijn, E.-H. 22, 55, 96, 302, 344, 348, 350, 513, 607
Klitgaard, R. 537

Knight, F. 272, 273
Koch, C. 297
Kogut, B. 58
Koppell, J. 122
Koppenjan, J. 5, 333, 512
Koppenjan, J.F.M. 8, 22, 73
Kort, M. 74, 76
Kotler, P. 69
Kötz, H. 225
KPMG 503, 506
Krugmann, P. 217
Krumholz, N. 18
Kula, E. 176

labour unions 135
Lægreid, P. 54, 334, 337
Laffin, M. 22
Lane, J.-E. 448
language-games 5, 81, 104, 422
Latham, M. 201, 202
Latin America and the Caribbean
    (LAC)
  cancellations 586
  contract renegotiation 533–4
  development indicators 572, 584
  infrastructure access 459
  infrastructure investment needs 460,
    461, 476
  PPP types 579, 580, 581
  private participation 537, 538
  privatization 575, 580, 590
  projects and investment 582–3, 584
  World Bank support 462–3
Laughlin, R. 24, 242, 312, 519
Le Galès, P. 47
Le Grand, J. 119, 312
lease accounting 245
Leathley, A. 309
Leftly, M. 329
legal governance 293–7
legislation 216–17, 230
  European countries 339–40, 342
  European Union 217–24, 229–30
  legal challenge in regard to PPPs
    228–30
  PPP contract 225–8
  UNCITRAL 1994 Model Law on
    Procurement 225
  WTO, Government Procurement
    Agreement (GPA) 224–5

legitimacy 30, 51, 63, 92, 242, 252, 257,
    338, 421, 425, 446, 447, 451, 452,
    453, 479, 483, 486, 514, 603, 608
Leijten, M. 88
Levi, M. 501
Leviakangas, P. 100, 102
Lewis, M. 98, 102, 127
Lewis, M.K. 190, 201, 206, 208, 448
Lewis, M. 5
Li, B. 48, 209, 210
licensing risk 281
Liddle, J. 22
Lienhard, A. 349
LIFT programme 311
Light, D. 490
Lincoln, Y.S. 83
Lindblom, C.E. 9
Linder, S.H. 22
Lindner, S. 69
Lintner, J. 320
Lipschutz, R.D. 27
Liu, J. 58
Lloyd, C. 311
Local Improvement Finance Trust
    (LIFT) programme 311
local strategic partnerships 61
Lodge, C. 119
Löeffler, E. 60
Logan, J.R. 51, 52
London Underground 293, 549, 550,
    559–61, 564
long-term infrastructure contracts
    (LTICs) 5, 6–7
Lonsdale, C. 326
Lorange, P. 59, 513
Lorrain, D. 47
Los Angeles Community Development
    Bank 301
Loughlin, R. 88
LTICs (long-term infrastructure
    contracts) 5, 6–7
Luo, Y. 517
Lynn, L. Jr 514, 603
Lyon, R.M. 177

M6 toll road 553–5
M25 motorway 553
MacMillan, J. 198
Madhok, A. 516, 518, 521
Maheshwari, S.R. 33

Major, J. 86
Malaysia 583
managerial activity 73, 76
managerial strategies 73, 76, 77
managing contractor procurement
    strategy 191–2, 193, 194, 204–6
Manchester Ship Canal 33
Mandell, M.P. 73
Manitoba 375
Manning, B. 56
Marin, P. 577, 587, 588
marketization 121, 122, 123, 124–5
markets 119, 120–23, 128
Marquand, D. 119
Marston, G. 83, 84
Martens, J. 479
Martimort, D. 146, 147, 148, 149, 151
Marxist theory 45, 52–4
Maslyukivska, O. 297
Masten, S.E. 140
Mathur, N. 63, 293, 302
Mauzerall, D.L. 488
Mawson, J. 47
Mazey, S.P. 237
McAfee, R.P. 198
McCreevy, C. 443
McGuire, M. 73
McIntosh, K. 401
McNeill, D. 491
Meier, K.J. 73
Melbourne CityLink 58–9, 411–14,
    425–6
Mellett, H. 242
Melo, P. 347
memorandum of understanding
    (MoU) 294, 295, 296, 297
mercenaries, use of 29, 31
Merna, T. 197, 213
Metronet 165, 532, 560
Mexico 583, 586
Meyer, R. 23
Meyer, R.E. 334
Microsoft 491
Middle East and North Africa
    (MENA)
    cancellations 586
    development indicators 572, 584
    infrastructure access 459
    infrastructure investment needs 460,
        461

PPP types 579, 581
    private participation 537, 538
    projects and investment 582, 584
    World Bank support 472
MIGA (Multinational Investment
    Guarantee Agency) 472
Milotti, A. 345
Minogue, M. 569
Mitchell-Weaver, C. 56
mixed enterprises 32–5
Model Cities Programme 50
Mol, M.J. 513
Molotch, H.L. 51, 52
Money Matters Institute 485
Montanheiro, L. 23
Monteiro, R.S. 347
Moore, J. 141–2, 150
Moore, M.A. 174, 178
moral hazard 270, 533
Mott MacDonald 97, 103, 323
Mulford, C.L. 75
Murray, S. 373
Muthien, B. 31
Myrdal, G. 52

national accounts 241, 243, 257
National Air Traffic Services (NATS)
    561–2, 564
National Audit Office (NAO) 96, 103,
    242, 322, 534, 535
National Council for Public–Private
    Partnerships 391
National Enterprise Board 32
National Express 558
National Health Service (NHS) 58, 61,
    97, 101, 163, 312, 313, 324, 503,
    530, 531, 545
nationalization 32
Needham, C. 126
Negandhi, A.R. 75
negative externalities 156
Nellis, J. 588
neo-institutional theory 75–6
Netherlands 69, 533
    evaluation 346
    government initiatives 341, 342
    implementation 343, 344
    regulation 339, 342
    regulatory governance 299
    taskforce 337, 338, 342

urban regeneration companies
(URCs) 76
network theory 44
New Brunswick 365, 371
New Edward Island 371
new institutional theory 45
New Labour 24, 60, 70, 310, 312–13,
603
new public management (NPM) 54–6,
71–2, 312, 447–8, 500
New South Wales 57, 405, 406, 434–6
New Zealand 128, 241, 254, 401, 403,
505
Newell, R.G. 177
NHS 312–13, 531
NHS trusts 58, 324, 503, 545
Niederkofler, M. 78
Nielsen, R. 217
Noble, G. 348, 510, 511, 512
Nooteboom, B. 76
Nordhaus, W. 264
North Africa *see* Middle East and
North Africa (MENA)
North America 354–5, 393–4
see also Canada; USA
Northern Ireland 57, 316–17
Northwest Territories 365–6, 371
Norway 450
Nova Scotia 371
NPM *see* new public management
(NPM)

Obama, President 605
objectives of PPPs 86–8
Observer, The 308
Obstfeld, M. 217
OECD 443
official development aid (ODA) 570
Olsen, J.P. 334
'on time and on budget' evaluation
criterion 165
Onis, Z. 538
Ontario 362–4, 376–7
operational partnerships, UN 484,
486–7
optimism bias 270, 274, 323
Oregon Innovative Partnerships
Program (OIPP) 391
Organisation for Economic Co-
operation and Development

(OECD) 14, 62, 95, 241, 257, 333,
334, 343, 349, 403, 424, 443, 570,
571, 573, 594
organization theory 510–11
organizational drift 62
organizational form 73–7
Orren, K. 501
Osborne, D. 61, 71, 117
Osborne, S. 5
Osborne, S.P. 74
O'Toole, L.J. 73
outcomes-oriented commissioning
61–2
outside financing 151
overseas development agencies (ODAs)
466

Pagdadis, S.A. 382, 393
Page, E.C. 334
Parker, D. 4, 76, 120, 500
Parks, R. 373
Parsons, W. 83
partnering contract 227
Partnerschaften Deutschland AG 337
partnership
as brand 69–70
definition of 21–2
partnership contract 227
Partnerships BC 165–7, 169, 170,
367–8, 371
Partnerships UK (PUK) 310–11, 312,
504, 531
Partnerships Victoria 199, 299, 406,
407–8
path dependency 452, 500–502, 505–8,
569
Patumi, N. 345
PBI California 390
Pearce, D. 177
Pech, K. 31
perfect capital markets (PCM) 319–20
Peters, B.G. 514
PFI *see* Private Finance Initiative (PFI)
Phene, A. 516
Philippines 539, 540, 583
Pierre, J. 118, 439, 451–2, 514
Pierson, P. 452, 500, 501–2, 604
Pina, V. 345
Pirotta, G. 28
Pitchford, R. 144

Pizer, W.A. 177
pluralism 447
Poland
    challenges 348–9
    government initiatives 340, 341, 342
    implementation 344
    legislation 339, 342
    private sector involvement 583
    taskforce 338, 342
policing 29–30
Policing Pledge 125
policy network theories 44
policy partnerships, UN 484, 486
Polidano, C. 569
political risk 163–4
politicians 265, 267, 289
Pollitt, C. 70, 72, 333, 334, 448
Pollitt, M. 97, 99, 103
Pollock, A. 97, 100, 102, 103, 316, 342,
    548, 600
Pollock, A.M. 56, 58, 101, 103, 279,
    531
Poot, J. 197
Porter, P.R. 18
Portugal
    evaluation 346
    government initiatives 340, 342
    implementation 345
    legislation 339, 342
    taskforce 338, 342, 346
positive externalities 156
postmodern theory 45, 63
Pouyet, J. 146, 147
Powell, M. 22
Power, M. 118, 246
PPP Canada Inc. 367
PPP Competence Centre 299
PPP definitions 4, 5–7, 68
PPP industry 499, 502–8
PPP movement, history of
    government regulation of business
        46–9
    intellectual foundations 44–5
    new public management (NPM)
        54–6
    PFI, public sector accounting
        critique 56–9
    postmodern theory 63
    public governance 60–62
    regional and urban dynamics 49–54

strategic management approach
        59–60
PPP trust 585
Prescott, J. 308
Price, D. 548
PricewaterhouseCoopers 8, 102, 128,
    246, 321, 503, 506
prime contractor model 56
principal–agent problems 55, 137
principal–agent relation 74–5
principal–agent theory 44, 55
principal–principal relation 74, 75
Private Finance Initiative (PFI) 55, 69,
    318–19
    critique from public sector
        accounting 56–9
    evaluation 317–26
        bundling 321–2
        construction costs 321–3
        inefficiency, possible source of
            325–6
        public and private finance, relative
            cost 319–21
        services, cost and quality 324
        whole-life costing 321–3
    global financial crisis, impact of 326–9
    Marxist view 53
    New Labour 24–5, 310–13
    origins of 23–4, 197, 307–8
private financing 23–4, 150–51
private foundations 489, 491–2
privateer shipping 4–5
private–private partnerships (alliances)
    see alliances
privatization 9–10, 54, 164, 500, 507
Privatization Center 391
procurement law 217–18, 222, 225, 226
procurement strategies 188–93, 204–6
    alliance contracts 190–91, 193, 194,
        204–6
    appropriate choice of 201–2
    conditions suitable for procurement
        208–9, 210, 211
    construct only (traditional) 192, 193,
        194
    construction management 192, 193
    design and construct 192, 193, 204–6
    early constructor involvement (ECI)
        191
    evaluation criteria 202–6

in house 192, 193, 204–6
managing contractor 191–2, 204–6
PPP/PFI 188–90, 193, 204–6, 208–9
and project life cycle 193–4
project management 192, 193
relationship contracts (alliance)
190–91, 193, 194, 204–6
risk and relationships within 193–5
selection, specific factors in 195–201
strengths of 204–6
product development partnerships
486–7
(Product) RED 488
productive efficiency 136
Project Finance International 328, 475
project management procurement
strategy 192, 193
property rights 142
Prosser, T. 32
Przeworski, A. 123
public accounting theory 44
public choice theory 54, 117
public enterprise 19, 32, 34, 37, 400,
401, 499, 500, 507
public expectations 123–6
public interest 12, 22, 47, 54, 81, 87,
137, 201, 203, 206, 211, 220, 221,
228, 232, 233, 264, 267, 270, 274,
276, 284, 287, 288–9, 290, 292,
293, 294, 295, 296, 298, 299, 302,
303, 367, 370, 392, 393, 394, 395,
407, 409, 421, 451, 565, 594, 601,
602, 607, 608
public financing 151
public goods 144–5, 156
public governance 60–62
public procurement law 217–18, 222,
226, 229
public sector accountability 121–2, 123
public sector alternative (PSA) 160
Public Sector Borrowing Requirement
(PSBR) 86, 162, 196, 307
public sector budgetary risks 277–83
bankruptcy risk 282–3
construction risks 280–81
demand risk 281–2
from lack of long-term framework
278–9
licensing risk 280–81
operating risks 283

in practice 279–80
project error risk 280
from public service characteristics
277–8
renegotiation risk 282
public sector comparator (PSC) 57,
103, 160, 269
public sector net debt (PSND) 162,
163, 310, 330
public service ethos 119
public–private mixing 17–21
Public–Private Partnership Investment
Program 382
Public–Private Partnership Programme
(4Ps) 231
Public–Private Partnerships for the
Urban Environment 485
PUK (Partnerships UK) 310–11, 312,
504, 531

quality of services 156, 220, 324, 464,
535
Québec 364–5, 370–71, 373, 378–9
Queensland 437

radical public accounting theory 45
rail PPPs 549, 555–61
London Underground 293, 549, 550,
559–61, 564
passenger rail franchises 555–9
Rainey, H.G. 514, 515
Ramchand, K. 540
Ramsey, F.P. 175, 176
Ransom, S. 299
Raum, T. 382
Rayner, S. 10
Reeve, S. 510, 511, 512
Reeves, E. 512
*Reforming our Public Services:
Principles into Practice* (OPSR)
312
Regan, M. 197, 209
regime theory 44, 45, 49, 51
regional and urban dynamics 49–54
regulatory environment 463, 469, 538
regulatory governance 297–9
Reinicke, W. 482, 484
relational contracting 298–9
relationship contracts (alliance)
190–91, 193, 204–6

renegotiations 269, 282, 533–4
Reside, R. Jr 587
resource dependency theory 44, 45, 75
resource mobilization partnerships,
    UN 484–5
Reynolds, D. 317
Rhodes, R.A.W. 20, 60, 118
Richardson, J. 237
Richter, J. 482
Ricketts, Bob 312–13
Ricketts, M. 531
Riley, J.G. 270, 272, 273
Ring, P.S. 515, 516, 517
risk 263
    contractual partition of 276–7
    public sector budgetary risks 277–83
        bankruptcy risk 282–3
        construction risks 280–81
        demand risk 281–2
        from lack of long-term framework
            278–9
        licensing risk 280–81
        operating risks 283
        in practice 279–80
        project error risk 280
        from public service characteristics
            277–8
        renegotiation risk 282
    retained by public sector 198
risk analysis 246, 263, 271, 277, 279,
    289, 599
risk assessment 262
risk management
    adverse selection 146, 269, 270, 533
    conventional risk management 263–4
    expected utility 273–4
    mechanism design 270–71
    moral hazard 270, 533
    non-naïve approach 283–9
        contractual risk partition 287–8
        cost and revenue estimates 284
        public sector capacity and public
            interest 288–9
        risk assessment during
            procurement 286–7
        risk assessment during project
            preparation 286
        risk devolution 287–8
        risk identification and assessment
            285

risk identification and
    management 284
    risk management during life of
        the contract 287
    risk mitigation 285–6
    optimism bias 274
    public-choice approach 264–8
    risk analysis 263
    subjectivity 272–3
    uncertainty 268–9, 270, 272–3, 274
risk perception 262
risk transfer 56–8, 163, 167, 275–7
    bankruptcy 282–3
    construction 280–81
    demand 281–2
    in different procurement strategies
        195, 196
    licensing 281
    operating 283
    project error 280
    renegotiation 282
    risk retained by public sector 198
Risse, T. 484
road transport 551–5
    Dartford River Crossing 74–5, 528–9
    DBFO contracts 74–5, 551–3
    I-495 Capital Beltway HOT Lanes
        382, 385, 390
    M6 toll road 553–5
    M25 motorway 553
    Sea-to-Sky Highway 166–7, 170, 368
    Skye Bridge 549
Roberts, A. 605
Robinson, G. 197
Robson, W.B. 380
Rodríguez, N. 345
Rodrik, D. 570
Rogers, D.L. 75
Rogers, Lord 72
Rolls-Royce 32
Romania 339, 340, 341, 347
Roos, J. 59
Rose, E. 43, 50
Rosenau, P.V. 62
Ross, T.W. 150
Rothstein, B. 446, 447
Rousseau, D.M. 517
Royal College of Nursing 125
Ruane, S. 24
Rubin, J.S. 301

Rudd, K. 84
Ruggie, J.G. 480, 481
Russell, E.W. 412, 413, 414
Russia 472, 540, 583
Ryrie rules 527, 528, 529

Sahlin-Andersson, K. 452
Salamon, L.M. 20, 301
Samuels, A. 33
Sanchez-Robles, B. 197
Sanderson, I. 83
Sands, V. 299
Sandwell URC 70
Sarangi, D. 540
Saskatchewan 369–70
Savage, J.D. 244
Savas, E.S. 71, 96, 102, 500
Scandinavia 439–40, 450–54
    Denmark 231, 440–45
        evaluation 445
        National Archive project 443–4
        private sector policy 442–3
        privatization 507
        school project 444–5
    Norway 450
    Sweden 445–50
Scharfstein, D. 150
Scharpf, F. 337
Scheuing, E.E. 227
Schmidt, F.L. 93
Schmidt, K.M. 143
Schmitter, P. 446
Schreiner, M. 518
Schröder, G. 129
Schumpeter, J. 439
Schwartz, G. 238, 280
Schwarzenegger, Governor 390
Scotland 316
Scotland, Skye Bridge 549
Scott, C. 27
Scott, W.R. 334
Scottish Futures Trust 316
Scottish National Party (SNP) 316
Sea-to-Sky Highway 166–7, 170, 368
security services 29–31
Semlitsch, K. 450
Senegal 472
Sentes, F. 538
Serco 503
Serebrisky, T. 550

Serven, L. 476
service concessions 239–41, 251,
    255–6
service delivery partnerships 61
service quality 5, 55, 144, 203, 370, 457,
    559, 577
shadow price of capital (SPC) 177–8
Shaffer, M. 166
Shaoul, J. 57, 99, 102, 103, 166, 279,
    312, 512
Sharpe, W.F. 320
Shaw, E. 129
Shearer, D. 31
Shinkfield, A.J. 90, 91
Silva, G.F. 550
Simonin, B.L. 518
Singh, H. 515, 518, 519
Sirtaine, S. 537
Skanska 503
Skelcher, C. 43, 63
Skelcher, C.K. 68
Skillern, M. 22, 23
Skowronek, S. 501
Skye Bridge 549
Smith, J. 308, 309
Smith, M. 302
Smith, N.J. 197, 213
SNA 93: 243
SNP 316
Sobhan, R. 538
social discount rate (SDR) 175–8
Sohail, M. 297
solvency gap 458, 459
Sørensen, E. 73
Soskice, D. 603
South Africa 31, 255, 540, 583
South Asia (SA)
    cancellations 586
    development indicators 572–3, 584
    infrastructure access 459
    infrastructure investment needs 458,
        460, 461
    PPP types 579, 581
    private participation 537, 538
    projects and investment 582, 583,
        584
    World Bank support 463
South Korea 475, 540
Southern Cross Station (Australia) 209,
    418–20, 426

Spackman, M. 330
Spain
  government initiatives 340, 342
  implementation 345
  legislation 339, 342
  post-global financial crisis 128
  taskforce 338, 342
special purpose vehicle (SPV) 189, 190,
    194, 201, 318, 330
Spekman, R.E. 516, 518
Spence, G. 311
Spence Commission 589
SPV *see* special purpose vehicle (SPV)
SSA *see* Sub-Saharan Africa (SSA)
Stadt Halle and RPL Lochau 220,
    232–3
stakeholder theory 45
stakeholders 7–8
Stankiewicz, G. 301
state-owned enterprise (SOE) 160, 400,
    403, 424
Steel, D. 32
Steele, J.B. 18
Steijn, B. 76, 77, 607
Steinicke, M. 217
Steinmo, S. 501
Stern, N. 176
Stewart, J. 299, 310
Stiglitz, J.E. 268
Stoker, G. 60, 125
Stone, C. 51
Strange, R. 380, 381
strategic alliance research 510–11,
    516–20
  behavioural factors 518–19
  cooperative processes 516–18
strategic management approach
    59–60
Strategic Rail Authority (SRA) 557
Streeck, W. 500
Strom, E. 344
Stufflebeam, D.L. 90, 91
Sub-Saharan Africa (SSA) 588
  cancellations 586
  development indicators 571–2, 584
  infrastructure access 459
  infrastructure investment needs 458,
    460, 461
  PPP types 579, 580, 581
  private participation 537, 538

  projects and investment 582, 583,
    584
  World Bank support 463, 472
Suez Canal Co. 33
Sullivan, H. 43, 294, 298
Sum, N.-L. 53
sustainability 60, 62, 187, 209, 210,
    262, 289, 339, 431, 458, 477, 490,
    544, 604
Sustainable Infrastructure Action Plan
    (SIAP) 465–6
Sweden 445–50
Swedish Partnerships: An Overview
    (SOU) 449
Sweet, D.C. 18
Switzerland 338, 339, 342, 343, 349
Sydney, Cross City Tunnel 301
System of National Accounts (SNA)
    93: 243

Tallman, S.B. 518
task allocation 133–6
taskforces 299, 337–9, 342
Tasmania 437
Taylor, G. 553
Taylor, I. 31
Teisman, G. 22, 55, 68, 96, 344, 348,
    350, 513
Teng, B.-S. 517
Terhart, R. 373
Tesner, S. 481, 484, 488
Thailand 543, 583
Thallman, S. 516
Thatcher, M. 32, 33
Thelen, K. 500, 501
Third Way 60, 312–13
Thomson, C. 336
Thynne, I. 21, 27, 33, 54, 61
TIFU (Treasury Infrastructure Finance
    Unit) 328
Tilly, C. 19, 20, 28, 29, 31, 35
Timmins, N. 312, 313
Tiong, R.L.K. 402
toll roads 178–9, 553–5
Torfing, J. 73
Torres, L. 345
total social costs, evaluation criterion
    169–70
traditional procurement 133, 134,
    136–7

tragedy of the commons 124
transaction cost economics 44
transaction costs 169–70, 533
transport PPPs 548–51, 562–5
    air traffic control 561–2
    Dartford River Crossing 74–5, 528–9
    I-495 Capital Beltway HOT Lanes 382, 385, 390
    London Underground 293, 549, 550, 559–61, 564
    M6 toll road 553–5
    M25 motorway 553
    passenger rail franchises 555–9
    rail 555–61
    road transport 551–5
    Sea-to-Sky Highway 166–7, 170, 368
    Skye Bridge 549
Treasury Infrastructure Finance Unit (TIFU) 328
Treasury Taskforce 197, 310
Treasury Technical Note 1 (Revised) (TTN1R) 242, 244, 245–6
Troubled Asset Relief Program (TARP) 382
trust 9, 13, 22, 23, 34, 35, 37, 45, 55, 56, 59, 93, 94, 117, 119, 122, 127, 191, 217, 227, 232, 273, 299, 311, 327, 348, 400, 424, 515, 517, 518, 520, 521, 533, 535, 544
Tube Lines 561
Turkey 583
Turner, Lord 237
Turner, Ted 481
typology of PPPs 74–5

UK 307, 329, 527–35
    capital expenditure 315
    DBFO model 72, 74–5, 307, 319, 551–3
    defence sector 315
    education sector 311, 312, 325
    evaluation 317–26
        bundling 321–2
        construction costs 321–3
        inefficiency, possible source of 325–6
        public and private finance, relative cost 319–21
        services, cost and quality 324
        whole-life costing 321–3

global financial crisis, impact of 326–9
healthcare sector 312, 315–16, 324, 325
mixed enterprises 32, 33
New Labour 310–13
PFI, history of 23–4, 197, 307–13
PFI model 318–19
PPP industry 505, 507
projects, number and size 309, 313–15
taskforce 337, 338
Third Way 60, 312–13
transport sector 314, 548–51, 562–5
    air traffic control 561–2
    DBFO contracts 74–5, 551–3
    London Underground 293, 549, 550, 559–61, 564
    M6 toll road 553–5
    rail 549, 555–61
    road transport 551–5
urban regeneration partnerships 52
UK GAAP (Generally Accepted Accounting Practice) 241, 242, 259
UN Capital Development Fund 485
UN Global Compact 482, 484, 486, 493
UN Millennium Development Goals 544
uncertainty 268–9, 270, 272–3, 274
UNCITRAL 1994 Model Law on Procurement 225
UNCSD (UN Commission for Sustainable Development) 488
UNDP (United Nations Development Program) 484, 485, 486
UNESCO (UN Educational, Scientific and Cultural Organization) 483, 486, 491
UNF (UN Foundation) 481, 487
UNFIP (UN Fund for International Partnerships) 481, 483, 493
UNICEF (UN International Children's Fund) 483, 484, 485, 486
UNIDO (UN Industrial Development Organization) 485
United Nations, PPPs 479, 492–3
    advocacy partnerships 484, 485–6
    future of 491–2
    impact of 488–91

operational partnerships 484, 486–7
partnership types 483–97
policy partnerships 484, 486
product development partnerships
    486–7
resource mobilization partnerships
    484–5
rise of 480–83
Urban Development Action Grant
    (UDAG) 50
urban growth coalition theory 44, 49,
    51–2
urban regeneration partnerships 52–3,
    70, 72, 74, 76
urban regime theory 51, 52
Urban Task Force 72, 74
USA 381–8, 393, 394
    accounting 241–2
    Allegheny Conference on
        Community Development
        (ACCD) 49
    California, performance-based
        infrastructure 390–91
    contracting out, security services 30
    evaluation 392–3
    Federal Highway Administration
        388, 390
    General Accountability Office
        (GAO) 392
    Government Accounting Standards
        Board (GASB) 241–2, 253–4
    government/quasi-government P3
        agencies 388, 390–91
    Housing and Urban Renewal Act
        (1949) 49
    I-495 Capital Beltway HOT Lanes
        382, 385, 390
    infrastructure investment gap 504
    Los Angeles Community
        Development Bank 301
    National Conference on State
        Legislatures 390
    National Council for Public–Private
        Partnerships 391
    Oregon Innovative Partnerships
        Program 391
    PBI California 390
    private sector P3 proponent
        institutions 391
    Privatization Center 391

    projects since 2000: 383–7
    proposed projects 389
    Public–Private Partnership
        Investment Program 382
    regional and urban development
        from 1930s 48–9
    security services 30
    Troubled Asset Relief Program
        (TARP) 382
    urban development from 1960s
        50–52
    Washington Policy Center 391
user-pays 431

Vaidya, K. 76
Välilä, T. 325
value for money (VfM) 199
    critique from public sector
        accounting 56, 57
    evaluation 94–104, 165–9, 179–81
    factors enhancing 209, 210
    National Audit Office assessment
        534–5
    values 33, 58, 82, 85, 89, 90, 92, 95,
        106, 115, 116, 119, 120, 122, 123,
        124, 127, 129, 145, 167, 171, 175,
        176, 303, 348, 400, 481, 514, 532,
        599, 603
Van de Ven, A.H. 515, 516, 517
Van de Walle, S. 85
Van der Wel, P. 511, 513
Van Garsse, S. 343
Van Ham, H. 5, 512
van Leeuwen, H. 197
Van Thanh, N. 33
Van Tiem, P. 33
Vandermeeren, F. 343
venue shopping 237–8
VfM *see* value for money (VfM)
viability gap funds 473, 475, 540
Victoria, Australia 405, 406, 414–17,
    430–32
Vietnam 33, 541
Vincent-Jones, P. 47
Vining, A. 10, 34, 88, 89, 101, 104,
    605

Wagstaff, A. 457
Wales 316, 317
Walker, B. 96, 412

Walker, B.C. 96, 412
Walker, D. 84
Walker, R.G. 254
Washington Consensus 570, 571, 575, 587, 588
Washington Policy Center 391
Watts, R. 83, 84
Wedel, J.R. 30
Weihe, G. 22, 68, 69, 74, 75
Weimer, D.L. 10, 89, 293
Weiss, C.H. 82
Weitz, A. 539, 540, 543
Weizsäcker, E.U. 275
Werner, M. 335
West, K. 47–8
Wettenhall, R. 4, 54, 61, 293, 333, 400, 401, 405, 511, 513
whole of life 195, 199, 200, 203, 204, 207, 209, 259, 322
   whole-of-life cost 203
Wholey, J.S. 90
Wicksell, K. 290
Williams, R. 221
Williamson, O.E. 59, 75, 140, 169, 326
Witte, J.M. 482, 484
Wood, J. 369
Wood, P. 191
Woodward, D. 88, 511

World Bank
   contract renegotiation 533–4
   Infrastructure Action Plan (IAP) 465
   infrastructure development policies 462–6, 535, 538, 570
   infrastructure lending 462–3
   PPP contract definition 189
   PPP experience 466–74
   PPP support in practice 472–4
   Sustainable Infrastructure Action Plan (SIAP) 465–6
World Development Report (1994) 464–5
World Heath Organization (WHO) 483, 489
WTO, Government Procurement Agreement (GPA) 224–5

Yepes, T. 459, 460, 461
Yergin, D. 34
Yescombe, E.R. 279

Zadek, S. 483
Zammit, A. 479
Zarco-Jasso, H. 6
Zhong, L. 297
Zweigert, K. 225